Colli

Collins

English–Hindi Dictionary

हिन्दी – अंग्रेज़ी

HarperCollins Publishers
Westerhill Road
Bishopbriggs
Glasgow
G64 2QT

First Edition 2011

ISBN 978-0-00-738713-7

www.collins.co.uk

A catalogue record for this book is
available from the British Library

Acknowledgements

We would like to thank those authors and publishers who kindly gave permission for copyright material to be used in the Collins Word Web. We would also like to thank Times Newspapers Ltd for providing valuable data.

CONTENTS

Abbreviations	v
English Pronunciation	vi
HINDI-ENGLISH	1–144
ENGLISH-HINDI	145–436

विषय सूची

संक्षिप्तियाँ	v
अंग्रेजी उच्चारण	vi
हिन्दी–अंग्रेजी	1–144
अंग्रेजी–हिन्दी	145–436

Editorial Consultant — सम्पादकीय परामर्शदाता
Shalini Bansal

Translation co-ordination — अनुवाद का समन्वयन
Ajit Shirodkar

Translators — अनुवादक
Sumit Kumar
Amrita Rao

Computing Support — कम्प्यूटिंग सहायता
Thomas Callan

Editors — सम्पादक
Shobha Speer
Gerry Breslin
Freddy Chick
Lucy Cooper
Kerry Ferguson
Paige Weber

Editor-in-Chief — मुख्य सम्पादक
Dr Elaine Higgleton

ABBREVIATIONS संक्षिप्तियाँ

abbreviation	*abbr*	संक्षिप्ति
adjective	*adj*	विशेषण
adverb	*adv*	क्रियाविशेषण
conjunction	*conj*	समुच्चयबोधक शब्द
determiner	*det*	निर्धारक
exclamation	*excl*	विस्मयादिबोधक शब्द
noun	*n*	संज्ञा
noun plural	*npl*	संज्ञा बहुवचन
number	*num*	संख्या
particle	*part*	सामान्य प्रत्यय
preposition	*prep*	पूर्वसर्ग
pronoun	*pron*	सर्वनाम
verb	*v*	क्रिया
intransitive verb	*vi*	अकर्मक क्रिया
transitive verb	*vt*	सकर्मक क्रिया

ENGLISH PRONUNCIATION
अंग्रेजी उच्चारण

The International Phonetic Alphabet is used to show how English words are pronounced in this dictionary.

इंटरनैशनल फोनेटिक एल्फाबेट का प्रयोग करके दिखाया गया है कि इस शब्दकोश में किस प्रकार अंग्रेजी शब्दों का उच्चारण किया जाता है।

Stress स्वराघात

The mark (ˈ) in the phonetics field indicates a primary stress and the mark (ˌ) indicates a secondary stress.

ध्वन्यात्मक क्षेत्र में (ˈ) चिह्न, प्राथमिक स्वराघात का संकेत करता है और (ˌ) चिह्न द्वितीयक स्वराघात का संकेत करता है।

Vowels स्वर

	English Example अंग्रेजी उदाहरण	Explanation स्पष्टीकरण
[ɑː]	*father*	अ/ ा, जिस प्रकार 'कार' शब्द में ा मात्रा का उच्चारण किया जाता है, अतः शब्द को फादर कहते हैं
[ʌ]	*but, come*	'अ' इन शब्दो में पहले अक्षर पर स्वराघात होता है, जैसे कि बतख
[æ]	*man, cat*	'ऐ' कि तरह इसका उच्चारण किया जाता है, जैसे कि सैन्य। यहां प्रथम अक्षर समूह पर स्वराघात होता है।

[ə]	*father, ago*	अ कि तरह इसका उच्चारण किया जाता है, जैसे कि अचार।
[ə]	*bird, heard*	अ इन शब्दों में पहले अक्षर पर स्वराघात होता है, जैसे कि हक
[ε]	*get, bed*	ए/ े, इन शब्दों में े मात्रा के रूप में इसका प्रयोग किया जाता है, जैसे कि मेल या देर
[i]	*it, big*	इ/ि, इन शब्दों में इ या ि मात्रा के रूप में इसका प्रयोग किया जाता है, जैसे कि इत्र अथवा बिस्तर
[i]	*tea, see*	ई/ ी, इन शब्दों में ई या ी मात्रा के रूप में इसका प्रयोग किया जाता है, जैसे कि तीन या सीमा
[ɔ]	*hot, wash*	ऑ/ ॉ, इन शब्दों में ऑ या ॉ मात्रा के रूप में इसका प्रयोग किया जाता है, जैसे कि ऑफिस
[ɔ]	*saw, all*	ऑ/ ॉ, इन शब्दों में ऑ या ॉ मात्रा के रूप में इसका प्रयोग किया जाता है, जैसे कि सॉ या ऑल
[u]	*put, book*	उ/ ु, शब्दों में ु मात्रा के रूप में इसका प्रयोग किया जाता है, जैसे कि पुत्र या बुनियाद
[u]	*too, you*	ू मात्रा के रूप में इसका प्रयोग किया जाता है, जैसे कि टूटा या यूनानी

Diphthongs संयुक्त स्वर

	English Example अंग्रेजी उदाहरण	Explanation स्पष्टीकरण
[ai]	*fly, high*	आ + इ अथवा ा + ि का प्रयोग, जैसे कि फ्लाइ या हाइ
[au]	*how, house*	आ + उ अथवा ा + ु का प्रयोग, जैसे कि हाउ या हाउस
[ɛə]	*there, bear*	ए + अ अथवा े + ा का प्रयोग, जैसे कि देअर या बेअर
[ei]	*day, obey*	ए + े के रूप में प्रयुक्त, जैसे कि डे या ओबे
[iə]	*here, hear*	इ + अ अथवा ि + ा का प्रयोग, जैसे कि हिअर
[əu]	*go, note*	ओ / ो के रूप में प्रयुक्त, जैसे कि गो या नोट
[əi]	*boy, oil*	ऑ + इ अथवा ॉ + इ का प्रयोग, जैसे कि बॉइ या ऑइल
[uə]	*poor, sure*	उ + अ अथवा ु + अ का प्रयोग, जैसे कि पुअर या शुअर

Consonants व्यंजन

	English Example अंग्रेजी उदाहरण	Explanation स्पष्टीकरण
[b]	*big, lobby*	ब के रूप में इस अक्षर का उच्चारण किया जाता है जैसे कि बिल या चाबी, पहले शब्द में पहले अक्षर समूह पर स्वराघात और दूसरे में द्वितीय अक्षर समूह पर स्वराघात
[d]	*mended*	ड जैसे कि मेनडेड, द्वितीय अक्षर समूह पर स्वराघात
[g]	*go, get, big*	ग, विभिन्न मात्राओं के साथ प्रयुक्त, जैसे कि गोत्र, गेहुं या चिराग
[ʤ]	*gin, judge*	ज जैसे कि जिसका या जगह
[ŋ]	*sing*	सिंग, नाक से उच्चारण किया जाता है
[h]	*house, he*	ह, जैसे कि हाथ या ही, पहले अक्षर समूह पर स्वराघात
[j]	*young, yes*	य, जैसे कि यंग या ये, शब्दों के पहले अक्षर समूहों पर स्वराघात
[k]	*come, mock*	क, जैसे कि कलम
[r]	*red, tread*	र, विभिन्न मात्राओं के साथ प्रयुक्त, जैसे कि रेल
[s]	*sand, yes*	स, विभिन्न मात्राओं के साथ प्रयुक्त, जैसे कि सैनिक या बस, पहले शब्द में पहले अक्षर समूह पर स्वराघात और दूसरे में द्वितीय अक्षर समूह पर स्वराघात
[z]	*rose, zebra*	ज़, जैसे कि रोज़ या ज़ेब्रा, पहले शब्द में द्वितीय अक्षर समूह पर स्वराघात और दूसरे में पहले अक्षर समूह पर स्वराघात

Consonants (continued) व्यंजन

	English Example अंग्रेजी उदाहरण	Explanation स्पष्टीकरण
[ʃ]	*she, machine*	श के रूप में इन अक्षरों का उच्चारण किया जाता है, जैसे कि मशीन
[tʃ]	*chin, rich*	च के रूप में इन अक्षरों का उच्चारण किया जाता है, जैसे कि चिन्ह
[v]	*valley*	व के रूप में इस अक्षर का उच्चारण किया जाता है, जैसे कि वैली
[w]	*water, which*	व के रूप में इन अक्षरों का उच्चारण किया जाता है, जैसे कि वॉटर
[ʒ]	*vision*	वि के रूप में इस अक्षर का उच्चारण किया जाता है, जैसे कि विचित्र
[θ]	*think, myth*	थ के रूप में इन अक्षरों का उच्चारण किया जाता है, जैसे कि हाथ
[ð]	*this, the*	द के रूप में इन अक्षरों का उच्चारण किया जाता है, जैसे कि दिवस

हिन्दी – अंग्रेजी

HINDI-ENGLISH

अ

अँगुली *n* finger
अँतड़ी *n* gut
अंक *n* (संख्या) number; (नंबर) point
अंक देना *vt* mark
अंकलजी *n* uncle
अंकुरित फली *npl* beansprouts
अंग *n* organ
अंगड़ाई लेना *vi* stretch
अंगरक्षक *n* bodyguard
अंगूठा *n* thumb
अंगूठी *n* ring
अंगूर *n* grape
अंगूर का बगीचा *n* vineyard
अंगोला *n* Angola
अंगोलियाई *adj* Angolan ▷ *n* Angolan
अंग्रेज़ पुरुष *n* Englishman
अंग्रेज़ महिला *n* Englishwoman
अंग्रेज़ी *adj* English ▷ *n* English
अंडा *n* egg
अंडाकार *adj* oval
अंडाशय *n* ovary
अंडे की जर्दी *n* egg yolk
अंडे की सफेदी *n* egg white
अंडे देना *vt* lay
अंटार्कटिक *n* Antarctic
अंटार्कटिका *n* Antarctica
अंत *n* end
अंतःकरण *n* conscience
अंतःवस्त्र *n* underwear
अंततोगत्वा *adv* ultimately
अंतर *n* margin
अंतर *n* distinction
अंतरंग *adj* intimate
अंतराल/अंतर *n* gap
अंतरिक्ष *n* space
अंतरिक्ष यान *n* spacecraft
अंतरिक्षयात्री *n* astronaut
अंतर्जलीय *adv* underwater
अंतर्ज्ञान *n* intuition
अंतर्राष्ट्रीय *adj* international
अंतिम *adj* last, ultimate
अंतिम चेतावनी *n* ultimatum
अंतिम तिथि *n* deadline
अंतेवासी *n* boarder

अंत्येष्टि *n* funeral
अंत्येष्टि गृह *n* funeral parlour
अंदर *prep* inside
अंदर का *adj* indoor
अंदाज़ लगाना *vt* foresee
अंधकार *n* darkness
अंधविश्वासी *adj* superstitious
अंपायर *n* umpire
अंजीर *n* fig
अंशकालिक *adj* part-time
अंशकालिक रूप से *adv* part-time
अंशतः *adv* half
अकल दाढ़ *n* wisdom tooth
अकुशल *adj* unskilled
अकड़न *n* spasm
अकेला *adj* alone, lonely
अकेलापन *n* loneliness
अकाल *n* famine
अकॉर्डिअन- एक तरह का बाजा *n* accordion
अक्टूबर *n* October
अक्षत/अक्षुण्ण *adj* intact
अक्षम *adj* inefficient
अक्षय/नवीकरणीय *adj* renewable
अक्षर *n* letter
अक्षांश *n* latitude
अक्सर *adj* frequent ▷ *adv* often
अखबारवाला *n* newsagent
अखबार वितरण सेवा *n* paper round
अखरोट *n* walnut
अख़बार *n* paper
अगर *conj* supposing
अगरतला *n* Agartala
अगला *adj* following, next
अगस्त *n* August
अग्निशामक *n* fire extinguisher
अग्र भाग *n* front
अग्रभाग *n* foreground
अग्रसारित करना *vt* forward
अचल *adj* motionless, still
अचानक *adj* sudden
अचेत *adj* unconscious
अच्छा *adj* good
अच्छा आचरण करना *vt* behave
अच्छा सौदा *n* bargain
अच्छी निभना *v* get on
अजमोद (पार्सली) *n* parsley
अजवाइन (ऑरिगानो) *n* oregano

अजवायन *n* thyme
अजनबी *n* stranger
अज़रबैजान *n* Azerbaijan
अज़रबैजानी *adj* Azerbaijani ▷ *n* Azerbaijani
अजायबघर *n* museum
अजीब *adj* funny, weird
अज्ञात *adj* unidentified
अज्ञानता *n* ignorance
अज्ञानी *adj* ignorant
अटका हुआ *adj* stuck
अटलांटिक महासागर *n* Atlantic Ocean
अटारी *n* attic
अटूट *adj* unbreakable
अटैची *n* suitcase
अठारह *num* eighteen
अठारहवां *adj* eighteenth
अड़चन *n* hitch
अड़ियल *adj* stubborn
अडैप्टर *n* adaptor
अणु *n* molecule
अण्डे की ज़रदी *n* yolk
अतएव *conj* therefore
अतर्कसंगत *adj* unreasonable
अति गोपनीय *adj* top-secret
अतिथिगृह *n* guesthouse
अतिरिक्त *adj* additional, extra
अतिरिक्त पुर्जा *n* spare part
अतिरिक्त भुगतान *n* bonus
अतिरिक्त रूप से *adv* extra
अतिरिक्त समय *n* overtime
अतिरिक्त सामान *n* excess baggage
अतिशय *adj* extortionate
अतिशयोक्ति *n* exaggeration
अतीत *n* past
अतीतकालीन *adj* past
अत्यंत *adv* quite
अत्यंत दुःखी *adj* heartbroken
अत्यधिक *adj* excessive ▷ *adv* extremely
अत्यधिक हास्यप्रद *adj* hilarious
अत्यावश्यक *adj* (अवस्था) urgent; (स्थिति) vital
अत्यावश्यकता *n* urgency
अदरक *n* ginger
अदला - बदली करना *v* swap
अदृश्य *adj* invisible
अदृश्य/प्रच्छन्न *adj* hidden
अद्वितीय *adj* unbeatable
अधपका *adj* rare
अधिक *adv* further ▷ *adj* high

अधिक आँकना *vt* overestimate
अधिकतम *adj* most, maximum
अधिकतर *adv* mostly
अधिकता *n* surplus
अधिकृत रास्ता *n* right of way
अधिग्रहण *n* takeover
अधिग्रहण करना *v* take over
अधिभार *n* surcharge
अधिरक्तापीत *n* geranium
अधिवर्ष *n* leap year
अधिशेष/अतिरिक्त *adj* surplus
अधिहृषत/एलर्जिक *adj* allergic
अधिहृषता/एलर्जी *n* allergy
अधीर *adj* impatient
अधैर्य *n* impatience
अध्यापक *n* teacher
अध्यापिका *n* female teacher
अध्यात्मविद्या *n* theology
अध्ययन करना *v* study
अध्याय *n* chapter
अनंत *adj* endless
अनंत काल/अमरत्व *n* eternity
अनंतर/के बाद *prep* past
अनजाने में हुआ *adj* unintentional
अनपढ़ *adj* illiterate
अनपेक्षित *adj* unexpected
अनपेक्षित रूप से *adv* unexpectedly
अनम्य/अड़ियल *adj* inflexible
अनाज *n* cereal, grain
अनाथ *n* orphan
अनार *n* pomegranate
अनावश्यक *adj* unnecessary
अनावृष्टि/सूखा *n* drought
अनिच्छापूर्वक *adv* reluctantly
अनिच्छुक *adj* reluctant
अनियंत्रित *adj* uncontrollable
अनियमित *adj* irregular
अनिर्णीत *adj* undecided
अनिवार्य *adj* compulsory, indispensable
अनिवार्य रूप से *adv* necessarily
अनिश्चय *n* uncertainty
अनिश्चित *adj* uncertain, unsure
अनुकूल बनना *vi* adapt
अनुकूलित *adj* customized

अनुचित *adj* unfair
अनुज्ञा पत्र/परवाना *n* permit
अनुदान *n* grant
अनुदान देना *vt* subsidize
अनुदार/घटिया *adj* mean
अनुपयुक्त *adj* unsuitable
अनुपस्थित *adj* absent
अनुपस्थिति *n* absence
अनुपस्थिति का कारण *n* alibi
अनुपात *n* proportion, ratio
अनुपूरक *n* supplement
अनुबंध *n* contract
अनुबंध/संधि *n* treaty
अनुभव *n* experience
अनुभवहीन *adj* inexperienced
अनुभवी *adj* experienced
अनुभाग *n* section
अनुमति *n* permission
अनुमति देना *vt* allow, let
अनुमान *n* guess
अनुमान लगाना *v* guess
अनुरूप/मुआफ़िक *adj* compatible
अनुवाद *n* translation
अनुवादक *n* translator
अनुवाद करना *vt* translate
अनुशासन *n* discipline
अनुशंसा *n* recommendation
अनुशंसा करना *vt* recommend
अनुशीर्षक *n* caption
अनुसंधान *n* research
अनुसरण करना *v* follow
अनुस्मारक *n* reminder
अनूठा *adj* unique
अनूप झील *n* lagoon
अनैतिक *adj* immoral
अनोखा *adj* exotic
अनौपचारिक *adj* casual, informal
अनौपचारिक रूप से *adv* casually
अन्न/धान्य *n* cereal
अनन्नास *n* pineapple
अन्य *adj* other
अन्यत्र *adv* elsewhere
अन्यथा *adv* otherwise
अन्याय *n* injustice
अण्डा *n* egg
अपच *n* indigestion
अपतृण/जंगली घास *n* weed
अपना/खुद का *adj* own
अपना/मेरा *det* my
अपना (स्त्री) *det* her
अपनी *det* one's
अपने लिए/खुद *pron* oneself

अपमान *n* insult
अपमान करना *vt* insult
अपमानजनक *adj* offensive
अपरंपरागत *adj* unconventional
अपराध *n* (अपराध) crime; (अपराध बोध) guilt
अपराध मानना *vi* own up
अपराधी *n* criminal ▷ *adj* guilty
अपरिचित *adj* unfamiliar
अपरिपक्व *adj* immature
अपरिवर्तित *adj* unchanged
अपरिष्कृत *adj* crude
अपरिहार्य *adj* inevitable, unavoidable
अपर्याप्त *adj* insufficient, scarce
अपवाद *n* exception
अपव्यय करना *vt* squander
अपहरण करना *vt* hijack
अपहरणकर्ता *n* hijacker
अपातकालीन अवतरण *n* emergency landing
अपूर्ण *adj* incomplete
अपूर्वानुमेय *adj* unpredictable
अपेक्षाकृत *adv* comparatively, relatively
अप्रचलित *adj* (पुराना) obsolete, out of date; (कपड़े) unfashionable
अप्रत्यक्ष *adj* indirect
अप्रत्याशित *adj* abrupt, unexpected
अप्रत्याशित रूप से *adv* abruptly, unexpectedly
अप्रवासन *n* immigration
अप्रवासी *n* immigrant
अप्रसन्न *adj* cross, unhappy
अप्रिय *adj* obnoxious, unpleasant
अप्रैल *n* April
अफ़गानिस्तान *n* Afghanistan
अफ़गानिस्तानी *adj* Afghan ▷ *n* Afghan
अफ़वाह *n* rumour
अफ़ीम *n* (फूल) poppy; (नशीला पदार्थ) opium
अफ़्रीका *n* Africa
अफ़्रीकान्स *n* Afrikaans
अफ़्रीकी *adj* African ▷ *n* African
अफ़्रीकेनर *n* Afrikaner
अब *adv* now
अब/इसके बाद *adv* anymore

अबू धाबी - दक्षिणी-पूर्वी अरब का एक अमीरात *n* Abu Dhabi
अभद्र व्यवहार करना *vi* misbehave
अभागा *adj* unlucky
अभिकल्पकार *n* designer
अभिजात्य *adj* sophisticated
अभिनय *n* acting
अभिनय करना *vi* act
अभिनेता *n* actor
अभिनेता समूह *n* cast
अभिनेत्री *n* actress
अभिप्राय रखना/इरादा रखना *vt* mean
अभिमुख होना/सामने होना *vt* face
अभियंता *n* engineer
अभियांत्रिकी *n* engineering
अभियान *n* campaign, expedition
अभियुक्त *n* accused
अभियोग लगाना *v* prosecute
अभिलेख *n* inscription
अभिलेख/सुरक्षित विवरण *n* record
अभिवादन *n* greeting
अभिवादन करना *vt* greet
अभिव्यक्त करना *vt* express
अभिव्यक्ति *n* expression
अभिस्वीकृति *n* acknowledgement
अभी-अभी *adv* just
अभी तक *adv* yet
अभूतपूर्व *adj* unprecedented
अभ्यर्थक *n* receptionist
अभ्यास *n* practise
अभ्यास करना *vt* practise
अमर बेल *n* mistletoe
अमरीका *n* America
अमरीकी *adj* American ▷ *n* American
अमरीकी फ़ुटबॉल *n* American football
अमान्य *adj* void
अमावस्या *n* new moon
अमूर्त *adj* abstract
अमृतसर *n* Amritsar
अम्ल *n* acid
अम्लीय वर्षा *n* acid rain
अयथार्थवादी *adj* unrealistic
अरक्षित *adj* unprotected, unguarded
अरब सागर *n* Arabian Sea
अरबी *adj* Arab, Arabic ▷ *n* Arab, Arabic
अर्जित करना *vt* gain

अरुचिकर *adj* sickening
अरुणाचल प्रदेश *n* Arunachal Pradesh
अरे भाई! *excl* hey!
अर्जेंटीना *n* Argentina
अर्जेंटीनियाई *adj* Argentinian ▷ *n* Argentinian
अर्थ *n* meaning
अर्थ लगाना/विवेचन करना *vt* interpret
अर्थव्यवस्था *n* economy
अर्थशास्त्र *npl* economics
अर्थशास्त्री *n* economist
अर्थात् *abbr* i.e.
अर्द्धकपारी/अर्ध-कपाली *n* migraine
अर्द्धविराम *n* semi-colon
अर्द्धवृत्त *n* semicircle
अर्द्धसत्रीय अवकाश *n* half-term
अर्बुद *n* tumour
अलग *adv* apart
अलग-अलग करना *vt* separate
अलगनी *n* clothes line, washing line
अलग रखना *vt* put aside
अलग होना *vt* part with
अलगाव *n* separation
अलगोज़ा *n* bassoon
अलबेला/बढ़िया *adj* fancy
अलमारी *n* cabinet, cupboard
अलविदा! *excl* goodbye!, cheerio!
अलार्म घड़ी *n* alarm clock
अलाव *n* bonfire
अलोकप्रिय *adj* unpopular
अलौकिक *adj* supernatural
अल्कोहलिक - मादक *adj* alcoholic
अल्ज़ाइमर रोग *n* Alzheimer's disease
अल्जीरिया *n* Algeria
अल्जीरियाई *adj* Algerian ▷ *n* Algerian
अल्पविराम *n* comma
अल्पसंख्यक *n* minority
अल्बानिया *n* Albania
अल्बानियाई *adj* Albanian ▷ *n* Albanian
अल्ट्रासाउंड *n* ultrasound
अल्युमिनियम *n* aluminium
अल्लाह *n* Allah
अल्स्टर *n* Ulster
अवकाश *n* leave, time off
अवकाश केंद्र *n* leisure centre
अवगत *adj* aware
अवज्ञाकारी *adj* rebellious

अवतरण *n* touchdown; (गलियारा) passage
अवधि *n* duration
अवमूल्यन *n* devaluation
अवयस्क *adj* underage
अवरुद्ध *adj* blocked
अवरुद्ध करना *vt* block, obstruct
अवरोध *n* barrier, block, blockage
अवलोकन करना *vt* observe
अवशिष्ट भोजन *npl* leftovers
अवशेष *npl* remains ▷ *n* trace
अवसर *n* occasion, opportunity
अवसाद *n* depression
अवसादकारी *adj* depressing
अवसादरोधी दवा *n* antidepressant
अवस्था/चरण *n* stage
अवाक *adj* speechless
अवांछनीय ई-मेल *n* spam
अवास्तविक *adj* unreal
अविदित *adj* unknown
अविराम *adv* non-stop
अविवादित *adj* undeniable, undisputed
अविवाहित *adj* unmarried ▷ *n* spinster
अविश्वसनीय *adj* unbelievable
अविष्कार *n* invention
आविष्कार करना *vt* invent
अविस्मरणीय *adj* unforgettable
अवैतनिक *adj* unpaid
अवैयक्तिक *adj* impersonal
अव्यवस्था *n* chaos; (अस्तव्यस्त) clutter
अव्यावहारिक *adj* impractical
अशांति *n* turbulence
अशिष्ट *adj* rude
अशिष्ट/घटिया *adj* gross, ill-mannered
अशुद्ध *adj* inaccurate
अशुभ/मनहूस *adj* sinister
असंगत *adj* inconsistent
असंतुलित *adj* unstable
असंतुष्ट *adj* dissatisfied
असंतोषजनक *adj* unsatisfactory
असंबद्ध *adj* irrelevant
असंभव *adj* impossible
असंयमित *adj* outrageous
असंवेदनशील *adj* insensitive
असफल *adj* unsuccessful
असफलता *n* failure
असबाब/सामान *n* luggage

असभ्य *adj* uncivilized
असम *n* Assam
असमर्थ *adj* unable
असम्भाव्य *adj* unlikely
असली *adj* real
असहनीय *adj* unbearable
असहमति *n* disagreement
असहिष्णु *adj* intolerant
असाधारण *adj* exceptional, extraordinary
असाधारण/ध्यानाकर्षक *adj* striking
असामान्य *adj* abnormal, unusual
असामी *n* client
असुरक्षित *adj* insecure
असुविधा *n* inconvenience
असुविधाजनक *adj* inconvenient
असूचीबद्ध *adj* unlisted
असैनिक *adj* civilian ▷ *n* civilian
अस्तर *n* lining
अस्तव्यस्त *adj* chaotic, messy
अस्तित्व होना *vi* exist
अस्थायी *adj* temporary
अस्थायी पता *n* temporary address
अस्थायी कर्मचारी *n* temp
अस्थायी शिक्षक/वैकल्पिक शिक्षक *n* supply teacher
अस्थिर *adj* unsteady
अस्थिरता *n* instability
अस्पताल *n* hospital, infirmary
अस्पताल का कमरा *n* ward
अस्पष्ट *adj* unclear, vague
अस्पष्ट बात/गप *n* waffle
अस्पष्ट/गिचपिच *adj* illegible
अस्वस्थ *adj* unfit, unwell
अस्वास्थ्यकर *adj* unhealthy
अस्वीकार्य *adj* unacceptable
अस्वीकृत करना *v* turn down
अस्सी *num* eighty
अहाता *n* yard

आ

आँख *n* eye
आँखें तरेरना *vi* glare
आँत *npl* bowels
आँधी *n* gale
आंकड़ा *npl* data

आंख की पुतली *n* iris, pupil
आंख मारना *vi* wink
आंखों देखा विवरण *n* commentary
आंग्लदेशीय *adj* British ▷ *npl* British
आंत का फोड़ा *n* appendicitis
आंतरिक *adj* inner, internal
आंतरिक भाग *n* interior
आंध्र प्रदेश *n* Andhra Pradesh
आंधी *n* storm
आंशकावान *adj* apprehensive
आंशिक *adj* partial
आंशिक रूप से *adv* partly
आंसू *n* tear
आंसू गैस *n* tear gas
आइज़ोवल *n* Aizwal
आइसक्रीम *n* ice cream
आइसलैंड *n* Iceland
आइस हॉकी *n* ice hockey
आई पॉड *n* iPod®
आकर्षक *adj* attractive, glamorous
आकर्षक व सजीला *adj* cool
आकर्षण *n* attraction
आकर्षित करना *vt* attract
आकलन *n* estimate
आकलन करना *vt* estimate
आकस्मिक भय *n* alarm
आक्रमण करना *v* invade
आकार *n* shape
आकार/माप *n* size
आखिरकार *adv* (अंतिम) lastly; (अंततः) eventually
आखिर में *adv* last
आखिरी से पहले *adj* penultimate
आगंतुक *n* visitor
आगंतुक सूचना केंद्र *n* visitor centre
आग *n* fire
आगज़नी *n* arson
आगबबूला/क्रुद्ध *adj* furious
आगमन *n* arrival
आगामी *adj* coming, future
आगे *adv* forward
आगे का *adj* further
आगे की शिक्षा *n* further education
आगे झुकना *vi* bend down, bend over
आगे बढ़ना *vi* advance; go ahead
आगे लाना *vt* bring forward
आगे होना *n* lead

आग्रह *n* appeal
आग्रह करना *vi* appeal
आग्रह करना/ज़ोर डालना *vt* insist
आच्छादित/घटाटोप *adj* overcast
आज *adv* today
आजकल *adv* nowadays
आज रात को *adv* tonight
आज़माना *vt* try
आज़ाद *adj* free
आज़ाद करना *vt* free
आज़ादी *n* freedom, liberation
आजीविका *n* career, living
आज्ञा *n* order
आज्ञाकारी *adj* obedient
आज्ञा देना *vt* order
आज्ञा पालन *v* obey
आटा *n* flour
आठ *num* eight
आठवां *adj* eighth ▷ *n* eighth
आड़ू *n* peach
आणविक *adj* nuclear
आतंकवाद *n* terrorism
आतंकवादी *n* terrorist
आतंकवादी हमला *n* terrorist attack
आतंकित करना *vt* terrify
आत्मकथा *n* autobiography
आत्म - केंद्रित *adj* self-centred
आत्मघाती हमलावर *n* suicide bomber
आत्म - नियंत्रण *n* self-control
आत्मनिर्भर *adj* self-contained
आत्मरक्षा *n* self-defence
आत्मविश्वास *n* confidence
आत्मविश्वासी *adj* confident
आत्मसंतुष्ट *adj* smug
आत्मसमर्पण करना *vi* surrender
आत्महत्या *n* suicide
आत्मा *n* soul
आदत *n* habit
आदर *n* respect
आदर करना *vt* respect
आदरणीय *adj* respectable
आदर्श *adj* model
आदर्शतः *adv* ideally
आदान - प्रदान करना *vt* exchange
आदिम *adj* primitive
आदिवर्णिक शब्द *n* acronym

आदी *adj* addicted
आदेश *n* command
आद्यक्षर लिखना/नाम का पहला अक्षर लिखना *vt* initial
आद्याक्षर *npl* initials
आद्योपांत/संपूर्ण *adj* thorough
आधा *adj* half ▷ *n* half
आधा-आधा *adj* fifty-fifty
आधा किलो *n* half kilo
आधा घंटा *n* half-hour
आधार *n* basis
आधारित *adj* based
आधारित होना *vt* ground
आधिकारिक *adj* official
आधी कीमत *adj* half-price
आधी कीमत पर *adv* half-price
आधुनिक *adj* modern
आधुनिक भाषाएँ *npl* modern languages
आधुनिक सुविधाएँ *npl* modern facilities
आधुनिकीकरण *vt* modernize
आध्यात्मिक *adj* spiritual
आनंद *n* joy, pleasure
आनंद उठाना *vt* enjoy
आनंददायक *adj* enjoyable
आनंदित *adj* delighted
आनंदोत्सव *n* carnival
आंटी *n* aunty
आना *vi* come (in) ▷ *v* turn up
आनुपातिक *adj* proportional
आनुवंशिक *adj* genetic
आनुवंशिक रूप से संशोधित *adj* genetically-modified, GM
आनुवंशिकी *n* genetics
आने देना *vt* let in
आने वाला कल *adv* tomorrow
आपत्ति *n* (आपद) catastrophe; (एतराज) objection
आपराधिक *adj* criminal
आपातकाल *n* emergency
आपातकालीन निकास *n* emergency exit
आपूर्ति *n* supply
आपूर्ति करना *vt* supply
आपूर्तिकर्ता *n* supplier
आभासी वास्तविकता *n* virtual reality
आभूषण *n* ornament
आभूषण/गहना *n* jewel
आम *n* mango ▷ *adj* usual
आमंत्रण *n* invitation
आमंत्रित करना *vt* invite

आम चुनाव *n* general election
आम तौर पर *adv* generally
आमतौर पर *adv* usually
आमदनी *npl* (परोपकारी संस्था) proceeds ▷ *n* (आय) income
आमने-सामने *adv* opposite
आमाशय *n* stomach
आय *npl* takings ▷ *n* income
आयकर *n* income tax
आयकर विवरणी *n* tax return
आयत *n* rectangle
आयताकार *adj* rectangular
आयरलैंड *n* Ireland
आयरलैंड से संबद्ध *adj* Irish
आया *n* babysitter, nanny
आयात *n* import
आयाम *n* dimension
आयु सीमा *n* age limit
आयोजित करना *vt* mount, organize
आरंभ *n* outset, start
आरंभ में *adv* initially
आरंभिक *adj* initial
आरक्षित करना *vt* reserve
आरपार *prep* through
आराम करना *vi* unwind
आरामकुर्सी *n* easy chair
आरामदायक *adj* cosy, comfortable
आरामदेह *adj* comfortable, relaxing
आरी *n* saw
आरोप *n* accusation, allegation
आरोप लगाना *vt* accuse, pick on
आरोहण *n* climbing
आरोही *n* climber
आर्कटिक क्षेत्र *n* Arctic
आर्कटिक महासागर *n* Arctic Ocean
आर्कटिक वृत्त *n* Arctic Circle
आर्थिक *adj* economic
आर्मेनिया *n* Armenia
आर्मेनियाई *adj* Armenian ▷ *n* Armenian
आलसी *adj* lazy
आलपिन *n* safety pin
आलिंगन *n* cuddle, hug
आलिंगन करना *vt* hug
आलू *n* potato
आलू का भरता *npl* mashed potatoes
आलूबुखारा *n* plum

आलोचना *n* criticism
आलोचना करना *vt* criticize
आल्प्स - दक्षिण मध्य यूरोप की एक पर्वत श्रृंखला *npl* Alps
आवक्ष मूर्ति *n* bust
आवर्धक लेंस *n* magnifying glass
आवश्यक *adj* necessary
आवश्यकता *n* necessity, need
आवश्यक होना *v* must
आवाज़ *n* voice
आवारा/भिखारी *n* tramp
आवास *n* accommodation
आवासीय *adj* residential
आवासीय विद्यालय *n* boarding school
आविष्कारक *n* inventor
आवृत्ति *n* frequency
आवेदक *n* applicant
आवेदन *n* application
आवेदन करना *v* apply
आवेदन पत्र *n* application form
आवेशित करना *vt* charge
आशा *n* hope
आशा करना *v* expect, hope
आशाजनक/होनहार *adj* promising
आशान्वित *adj* hopeful
आशापूर्वक *adv* hopefully
आशावाद *n* optimism
आशावादी *n* optimist ▷ *adj* optimistic
आशीर्वाद *n* blessing
आशीर्वाद देना *vt* bless
आशुलिपि *n* shorthand
आश्चर्य *n* surprise
आश्चर्यचकित *adj* astonished
आश्चर्यजनक *adj* amazing, astonishing
आश्वस्त करने वाला *adj* reassuring
आश्वासन देना *vt* reassure
आश्रय *n* shelter
आसक्त/धुन में रत *adj* obsessed
आसक्ति/धुन *n* obsession
आस - पड़ोस *n* vicinity
आस - पास/लगभग *prep* around
आसन *n* seat
आसमान *n* sky
आसान *adj* easy
आसानी से *adv* easily
आहार *n* diet

इ

इंग्लैंड *n* England
इंगित करना *vi* point
इंजन *n* engine
इंजेक्शन *n* jab
इंटरकॉम *n* intercom
इंटरनेट *n* Internet
इंटरनेट प्रयोगकर्ता *n* Internet user
इंटरनेट सेवा प्रदाता *n* ISP
इंट्रानेट *n* intranet
इंडोनेशिया *n* Indonesia
इंडोनेशियाई *adj* Indonesian
इंडोनेशियाई नागरिक *n* Indonesian
इंतज़ार करना *vi* hang on, wait
इंद्रधनुष *n* rainbow
इंद्रियबोध *n* sense
इंसुलिन *n* insulin
इकट्ठा करना *vt* collect ▷ *v* gather
इकट्ठा होना *v* get together
इकलौता *adj* only
इकाई *n* unit
इक्का *n* ace
इक्का दुक्का *npl* ones and twos
इक्वाडोर *n* Ecuador
इक्वेटोरियल गिनी *n* Equatorial Guinea
इग्निशन *n* ignition
इच्छा *n* will, wish
इच्छाशक्ति *n* willpower
इच्छुक *adj* willing
इज़राइल *n* Israel
इज़राइली *adj* Israeli ▷ *n* Israeli
इंफाल *n* Imphal
इटली *n* Italy
इतना *adv* so
इतना अधिक *det* such
इतालवी *adj* Italian ▷ *n* Italian
इतिहास *n* history
इतिहासकार *n* historian
इत्तफ़ाक/संयोग *n* accident
इत्र *n* perfume
इथियोपिया *n* Ethiopia
इथियोपियाई *adj* Ethiopian ▷ *n* Ethiopian
इनकार *n* refusal

इनकार करना *v* refuse
इनबॉक्स *n* inbox
इमला *n* dictation
इयरफ़ोन/आकर्णक *npl* earphones
इयरप्लग *npl* earplugs
इराक *n* Iraq
इराकी *adj* Iraqi ▷ *n* Iraqi
इरादतन *adj* intentional
इरादा *n* intention
इरादा रखना *v* intend
इरिट्रिया *n* Eritrea
इलाज *n* treatment
इलास्टिक *n* elastic
इलाज करना *vt* cure
इल्ली *n* caterpillar
इलेक्ट्रॉनिक *adj* electronic
इशारा *n* gesture, hint
इशारा करना *vi* hint
इश्कबाज़ *n* flirt
इश्कबाज़ी करना *vi* flirt
इश्तिहार/पोस्टर *n* poster
इस *det* this
इसका/उसका *det* its
इसके लिए *det* that
इसी दौरान *adv* meanwhile
इसी बीच *adv* meantime
इस्तरी *n* iron
इस्तेमाल *n* use
इस्तेमाल करना *vt* use
इस्तेमाल में आसान *adj* user-friendly
इस्त्री *n* ironing
इस्त्री करना *vt* iron
इस्पात *n* steel
इस्लाम *n* Islam
इस्लामी *adj* Islamic

ईंट *n* brick
ईंधन *n* fuel
ईद *n* Muslim holiday marking the end of Ramadan
ईद उल फित्र *n* Muslim holiday marking the end of Ramadan
ईनाम *n* reward
ई-पुस्तक *n* e-book
ईमानदार/खरा *adj* sincere
ईमानदार *adj* honest

ईमानदारी *n* honesty
ईमानदारी - पूर्वक *adv* honestly
ईमारती लकड़ी *n* timber
ई-मेल *n* email
ई-मेल पता *n* email address
ईटानगर *n* Itanagar
ई.यू./यूरोपीय संघ का संक्षिप्त रूप *n* EU
ईरान *n* Iran
ईरानी *adj* Iranian ▷ *n* Iranian
ईर्ष्या *n* envy, jealousy
ईर्ष्या करना *vt* envy
ईर्ष्यालु *adj* envious, jealous
ई-वाणिज्य *n* e-commerce
ईश्वर *n* God
ईसवी *n* AD
ईसाई *adj* Christian ▷ *n* Christian
ईसाई धर्म *n* Christianity
ईसाई भजन *n* carol
ईसा पूर्व *n* BC
ईसा मसीह *n* Christ, Jesus
ईस्टर *n* Easter
ईस्टर का अंडा *n* Easter egg

उ

उगाना *vt* grow
उग्र *adj* aggressive, hostile
उघाड़ना *vt* bare
उचित *adj* (ठीक) advisable; (मुनासिब) reasonable ▷ *n* right
उचित ढंग से *adv* properly
उचित रूप से *adv* rightly
उचित सिद्ध करना *vt* justify
उच्च न्यायालय *n* High Court
उच्च माध्यमिक *n* higher secondary
उच्च शिक्षा *n* higher education
उच्चतम न्यायालय *n* Supreme Court
उच्चाधिकारी *n* mandarin
उच्चारण *n* pronunciation
उच्चारण करना/वर्तनी लिखना *vt* spell
उच्चारित करना *vt* pronounce

उछलना *v* bounce
उछालना *vt* toss
उज़बेकिस्तान *n* Uzbekistan
उठना *vi* get up
उठाना *vt* lift, raise; pick up
उठाईगिरी *n* shoplifting
उड़ जाना *vi* fly away
उड़नतश्तरी *n* UFO
उड़ना *vi* fly; take off ▷ *n* takeoff
उड़ान *n* flight
ऊतक *n* tissue
उतरना *vi* descend
उतार - चढ़ाव/दोलन *n* swing
उतारना *vt* unload
उतावला *adj* desperate
उत्कीर्ण करना *vt* engrave
उत्कृष्ट *adj* (उत्तम) classic; (सबसे अच्छा) outstanding
उत्कृष्ट उदाहरण *n* classic
उत्कृष्ट कृति *n* masterpiece
उत्तम *adj* perfect, excellent
उत्तमता *n* perfection
उत्तमता से *adv* perfectly
उत्तर *n* north
उत्तर अफ़्रीका *n* North Africa
उत्तर अफ़्रीकी *n* North African
उत्तर अमेरिका *n* North America
उत्तर अमरीकी *adj* North American
उत्तर कोरिया *n* North Korea
उत्तरकथा *n* sequel
उत्तर की ओर *adv* north
उत्तरजीविता *n* survival
उत्तरदायी ठहराना *vt* charge
उत्तरपश्चिम *n* northwest
उत्तरपूर्व *n* northeast
उत्तर प्रदेश *n* Uttar Pradesh
उत्तरमार्गी *adj* northbound
उत्तराखंड *n* Uttarakhand
उत्तराधिकारिणी *n* heiress
उत्तराधिकारी *n* heir
उत्तरी *adj* north, northern
उत्तरी आयरलैंड *n* Northern Ireland
उत्तरी ध्रुव *n* North Pole
उत्तरी सागर *n* North Sea
उत्तरोत्तर *adv* increasingly
उत्तीर्ण *n* pass
उत्तीर्ण होना *v* pass
उत्तीर्ण होना/योग्य होना *v* qualify
उत्तेजित *adj* excited
उत्तोलक *n* lever
उत्पत्ति *n* origin

उत्पन्न करना/उत्पादन करना *vt* produce
उत्परिवर्तन *n* transition
उत्पाद *n* product
उत्पादकता *n* productivity
उत्पादन *n* production
उत्पीड़न *n* harassment
उत्सव *n* celebration
उत्सव मनाना *v* celebrate
उत्साह *n* enthusiasm
उत्साह/मिजाज़ *npl* spirits
उत्साही *adj* enthusiastic
उत्सुक *adj* keen
उदार *adj* (दयालु) generous; (खुले विचारों का) understanding, broad-minded
उदारता *n* generosity
उदास *adj* depressed
उदाहरण *n* example
उद्दंड *adj* tactless
उद्देश्य *n* aim, objective
उद्देश्य रखना *v* aim
उद्धरण *n* quotation
उद्धरण चिह्न *npl* quotation marks
उद्धृत करना *vt* quote
उद्यान *n* park
उद्योग *n* industry
उधर *pron* there
उधार *n* loan
उधार देना *vt* loan
उधार लेना *vt* borrow
उड़िया *n* Oriya
उड़ीसा *n* Orissa
उन *det* those
उनका *det* their ▷ *pron* theirs
उनमें से *pron* either
उनींदा *adj* sleepy
उन्नीस *num* nineteen
उन्नीसवाँ *adj* nineteenth
उन्मूलन *n* abolition
उन्मूलन करना *vt* abolish
उन्हें *pron* them
उपकरण *n* (मिक्सी, इत्यादि) appliance; (पेंचकस, इत्यादि) tool; (प्रतीकात्मक) instrument
उपकरण कक्ष *n* utility room
उपकरण समूह *n* kit
उपग्रह *n* satellite
उपद्रवी *n* troublemaker
उपजाऊ *adj* fertile
उपनगर *n* suburb
उपनगरीय *adj* suburban
उपनाम *n* nickname, pseudonym

उपन्यास *n* novel
उपन्यासकार *n* novelist
उबाऊ/दमघोंटू *adj* stuffy
उबलते पानी में पकाया गया *adj* poached
उभरना *vt* overcome
उपभोक्ता *n* consumer
उपमार्ग/छोटी गोली *n* side street
उपयुक्त *adj* appropriate
उपयोगी *adj* useful
उपयोगी/सुविधाजनक *adj* handy
उपलब्ध *adj* available
उपलब्धता *n* availability
उपलब्धि *n* achievement
उपवास *n* Lent
उपस्थित होना *v* attend
उपस्थिति *n* appearance, attendance, presence
उपहार *n* gift, present
उपेक्षा *n* neglect
उपेक्षा करना *vt* neglect
उपेक्षित *adj* neglected
उपनिर्देशक *n* assistant director
उबलता हुआ *adj* boiling
उबलना *vi* boil
उबला *adj* boiled
उबला अण्डा *n* boiled egg
उबाऊ *vt* bore ▷ *adj* boring
उबाऊ/दमघोंटू *adj* stuffy
उबाल आना *vi* boil over
उबालना *vt* boil
उभरना *vt* get over
उम्मीदवार *n* candidate
उम्र *n* age
उम्र का *adj* aged
उरुग्वे *n* Uruguay
उरुग्वे का निवासी *n* Uruguayan
उर्फ़ *prep* alias
उर्दू *n* Urdu
उर्वरक *n* fertilizer
उलझन *n* muddle
उलझना *vi* clash
उलट देना *vt* reverse
उल्का पिंड *n* meteorite
उल्टा *adv* upside down
उल्टा फिराना *v* rewind
उल्टी करना *v* throw up, vomit
उल्टी तरफ़ से *adv* backwards
उल्लू *excl* owl
उल्लेख करना *vt* mention
उल्लेखनीय/असाधारण *adj* remarkable

उल्लेखनीय रूप से/असाधारण रूप से *adv* remarkably
उषाकाल *n* dawn
उष्णकटिबंधीय *adj* tropical
उस *pron* that
उसका (पुरुष) *pron* his
उसका (लड़के के लिए) *det* his
उसका (स्त्री) *pron* hers
उसे (पुरुष) *pron* him
उसे (स्त्री) *pron* her
उस्तरा *n* razor
उस्तरे की पत्ती *n* razor blade
उह! *excl* ugh!

ऊँचाई पर *adv* high
ऊँची एड़ी *npl* high heels
ऊँची एड़ी का *adj* high-heeled
ऊँची कुर्सी *n* highchair
ऊँची कूद *n* high jump
ऊंचा *adj* high
ऊंचा जूता *n* boot
ऊंची आवाज़ में *adv* aloud
ऊंचे स्वर में *adv* loudly
ऊंट *n* camel
ऊदबिलाव *n* beaver, otter
ऊन *n* wool
ऊनी *adj* woollen
ऊनी कपड़े *npl* woollens
ऊपर *prep* above ▷ *adv* up
ऊपर उठना *vi* rise
ऊपर का *adj* upper
ऊपर की ओर *adv* (चढ़ाई) uphill; (ऊर्ध्व) upwards
ऊपरी मंज़िल *adv* upstairs
ऊब *n* boredom
ऊबड़-खाबड़ *adj* bumpy
ऊबा हुआ *adj* bored
ऊर्जा *n* energy
ऊर्जावान *adj* energetic

ऋण *n* mortgage
ऋण देना *vt* lend
ऋणी होना *vt* owe

ए

एंग्लो-इंडियन *n* Anglo-India
एंटीहिस्टमीन - एलर्जी की दवा *n* antihistamine
एंडीज़ *npl* Andes
एक *det* a, an ▷ *pron* one
एक अरब *num* billion
एक ओर/अलग *adv* aside
एक और *det* another
एक को दूसरा समझना *vt* confuse
एक छोटा अफ़सर *n* corporal
एक छोटी चिड़िया *n* thrush
एकजुट *v* unite
एकड़ *n* acre
एकदम सही *adj* accurate, exact
एकपहिया ठेलागाड़ी *n* wheelbarrow
एक पैर से कूदना *vi* hop
एक प्रकार का कुत्ता *n* collie
एक प्रकार का दस्ताना *n* mitten
एक प्रकार का मक्खन *n* margarine
एक प्रकार की नौका *n* car ferry
एक बार *adv* once
एकबारगी *n* one-off
एक मछली *n* whiting
एकमात्र/केवल *adj* only
एक मादक पेय *n* vodka
एकल *adj* single
एकवचन *n* singular
एक विरामचिह्न *n* colon
एक वृक्ष *n* willow
एक शामक दवा *n* tranquillizer
एक समय पर होना *vi* coincide
एक समुद्री मछली *n* haddock
एक साथ जन्मे तीन बच्चे/त्रिक *npl* triplets
एक्स-रे *n* X-ray
एकांतता *n* privacy
एकाग्रता *n* concentration
एकाधिकार *n* monopoly
एच आई वी - ग्रस्त *adj* HIV-positive
एच आई वी - रहित *adj* HIV-negative
एड़ी *n* heel
एड्रियाटिक *adj* Adriatic

एड्रियाटिक सागर *n* Adriatic Sea
एड्स *n* AIDS
एम एम एस *n* MMS
एम.एस *n* MS
एनोरेक्सिक *adj* anorexic
एनोरेक्सिया *n* anorexia
एयरबैग *n* airbag
एवरेस्ट *n* Everest
एशिया *n* Asia
एशियाई *adj* Asian
एण्डोरा *n* Andorra
एस्टोनिया *n* Estonia
एस्टोनियाई *adj* Estonian ▷ *n* Estonian
एहसानमंद *adj* grateful
एहसास करना *v* realize

ऐक्य *n* communion
ऐतिहासिक *adj* historical
ऐनक *npl* spectacles
ऐसा *det* such
ऑक्टोपस *n* octopus
ऑक्सीजन *n* oxygen
ऑर्किड *n* orchid
ऑमलेट *n* omelette
ऑस्ट्रिया - मध्य यूरोप का एक गणराज्य *n* Austria
ऑस्ट्रेलिया *n* Australia
ऑस्ट्रेलेशिया *n* Australasia
ऑपरेटर/परिचालक *n* operator
ऑटो रिक्शा *n* auto rickshaw
ऑरिगानो *n* oregano
ऑस्ट्रियाई *adj* Austrian ▷ *n* Austrian
ऑस्ट्रेलियाई *adj* Australian ▷ *n* Australian

ओज़ोन *n* ozone
ओज़ोन परत *n* ozone layer
ओढ़नी *n* scarf
ओपेरा/गीतिनाट्य *n* opera
ओमान *n* Oman
ओवरकोट *n* overcoat

ओशिनिया *n* Oceania
ओणम *n* Keralan harvest festival
ओला *n* hail
ओवरहेड प्रोजेक्टर/उपरि प्रक्षेपक *n* overhead projector

औ

औंस *n* ounce
औद्योगिक *adj* industrial
औद्योगिक क्षेत्र *n* industrial estate
औपचारिक *adj* formal
औपचारिकता *n* formality
और *conj* and ▷ *prep* plus
और अधिक *adv* more ▷ *pron* more
और ख़राब *adj* worse
और ख़राब हो जाना *v* worsen
औरत *n* woman
और न *conj* nor
और भी बुरा *adv* worse
औषधालय *n* pharmacy
औषधि विक्रेता *n* pharmacist
औसत *n* average
औसतन *adj* average

कंकड़ *n* pebble
कंकरीट *n* concrete
कंकाल *n* skeleton
कंगन *n* (बांह) bracelet
कंगारू *n* kangaroo
कंघी *n* (बाल) hairbrush
कंघी करना *vt* comb
कंजूस *n* miser ▷ *adj* stingy
कंठशूल *n* angina
कंठशोथ *n* laryngitis
कंडोम *n* condom
कंद *n* bulb
कंधा *n* shoulder
कंपनी (निकाय) *n* company
कंप्यूटर/संगणक *n* computer
कंबल *n* blanket

कई *det* many ▷ *pron* many ▷ *adj* several
कक्ष साथी *n* roommate
कक्ष सेवा *n* room service
कक्षा *n* class, classroom
कक्षा सहायक *n* classroom assistant
कचरा *n* refuse
कचरा - पेटी/कूड़ादान *n* bin
कच्चा *adj* raw
कछुआ *n* tortoise, turtle
कज़ाकिस्तान *n* Kazakhstan
कटु अनुभव *n* ordeal
कटलेट *n* cutlet
कटोरा *n* bowl
कटौती *n* cutback
कटौती करना *v* cut down
कठबोली *n* slang
कठपुतली *n* puppet
कठिन *adj* hard
कठिनाई *n* difficulty
कठोर *adj* harsh
कठोर/मज़बूत *adj* tough
कड़का *adj* broke
कड़वा *adj* bitter
कड़ा *adj* hard
कड़ा *n* marriage bangle
कड़ाही *n* frying pan, pan
कढ़ाई *n* embroidery
कढ़ाई करना *vt* embroider
कण *n* grain
कतरन *n* cutting
कतरन/टुकड़ा *n* scrap
कतार *n* Qatar
कतार *n* queue
कतार में लगना *vi* queue
कत्थई *adj* maroon
कथित *adj* alleged
कद *n* height
कदम *n* (पदचिह्न) footstep; (चलना) move
कदापि *adv* ever
कद्दू *n* pumpkin
कद्दूकस करना *vt* grate
कनटोप *n* hood
कनस्तर *n* canister, tin
कनस्तर बंद *adj* tinned
कनाडा *n* Canada
कनाडावासी *n* Canadian
कनाडा से संबद्ध *adj* Canadian
कनिष्ठ *adj* junior
कन्या राशि *n* Virgo
कपड़ा *n* garment
कपड़ा *n* cloth, material
कपड़े उतारना *v* undress
कपड़े की चिमटी *n* clothes peg
कपड़े बदलना *vi* change

कपड़े बदलने का कमरा *n* changing room
कपड़े रखने की अलमारी *n* chest of drawers
कपड़ों की अलमारी *n* wardrobe
कप्तान *n* captain
कब *adv* when
कब/जब *conj* when
कबाड़ *n* junk
कबाब *n* meatball, kebab
कबीला *n* tribe
कबूतर *n* pigeon
कब्ज़ से पीड़ित *adj* constipated
कब्ज़ा *n* (दखल) occupation; (सम्पत्ति) possession
कब्र *n* grave
कब्रिस्तान *n* cemetery, graveyard
कभी - कभार *adv* rarely
कभी - कभी *adv* occasionally; sometimes
कभी - कभी का *adj* occasional
कभी नहीं *adv* never
कभी भी *adv* anytime
कम *adv* less ▷ *pron* less ▷ *adj* less
कम आँकना *vt* underestimate
कम करना *vt* minimize
कमज़ोर *adj* frail, weak
कमज़ोरी *n* weakness
कम/निम्न *adj* low
कमर *n* waist
कमरबंद *n* belt
कमरा *n* room
कम वसायुक्त *adj* low-fat
कम से कम *adv* at least ▷ *adj* minimum
कमल *n* lotus
कमाई *npl* earnings
कमाना *vt* earn
कमी *n* lack; drawback
कमी/कटौती *n* reduction
कमी महसूस करना *vt* miss
कर्म *n* (काम) work; (किस्मत) fate
कम्बोडिया *n* Cambodia
कम्बोडियाई *adj* Cambodian ▷ *n* Cambodian
कन्नड़ *n* Kannada
कर *n* tax
करंज वृक्ष *n* beech
करछुल *n* ladle
कर डालना *vt* commit
करदाता *n* taxpayer

करना *vt* make
करना चाहिए *v* ought
करना पड़ेगा *v* have to
कर रहित *n* duty-free
कर सकना *v* may
कराहना *vi* groan, moan
करोड़ *n* (पैसे) crore (ten million)
करौंदा *n* cranberry
कर्क मछली/चिंगट *n* crayfish
कर्क राशि *n* Cancer
कर्ज़ *n* debt
कर्ज़ अदायगी *n* repayment
कर्फ़्यू/निषेधाज्ञा *n* curfew
कर्मचारी *n* employee ▷ *npl* personnel
कर्मचारी दल *n* crew
कर्तव्य *n* duty
कर्नाटका *n* Karnataka
कलपुर्जा *n* mechanism
कलम *n* pen
कलमतराश *n* penknife
कलमदान *n* pencil case
कला *n* art
कलाई *n* wrist
कलाई घड़ी *n* watch
कलाकार *n* artist
कलाकृति *n* work of art
कलात्मक *adj* artistic
कलाबाज *n* acrobat
कला विद्यालय *n* art school
कला वीथि *n* art gallery
कलोंजी *n* nigella seeds
कल्पना *n* imagination
कल्पनाचित्र बनाना *vt* visualize
कर्वा चौथ *n* Hindu festival when women pray for the longevity of their husband
कवच *n* armour
कवच/आवरण *n* shell
कव्वाली *n* Muslim devotional music
कवारत्ती *n* Kavaratti
कवि *n* poet
कविता *n* poem
कष्टप्रद *adj* uncomfortable
कश्मीर *n* Kashmir
कसकर पकड़ना *vt* grip
कसना *v* tighten
कसरत *n* exercise
कसरत/जिमनास्टिक *npl* gymnastics
कसरती/जिमनास्ट *n* gymnast
कसाई *n* butcher
कसाई की दुकान *n* butcher

कसा हुआ *adj* tight
कहना *vt* say
कहना/आज्ञा देना *vt* tell
कहना/बतलाना *vt* tell
कहरुवा *n* amber
कहां *adv* where
कहानी *n* tale
कहावत *n* proverb
कहीं नहीं *adv* nowhere
कहीं भी *adv* anywhere
क़ागज़ *n* paper
क़ीमत *n* worth
का *prep* of
काँच का गिलास *n* carafe
काँटा *n* fork
काँसा *n* bronze
कांख *n* armpit
कांच *n* glass
कांटा *n* thorn
कांटेदार तार *n* barbed wire
कांपना *vi* tremble
काई *n* moss
काउंटर *n* counter
काग *n* cork
कागज़ी कार्रवाई *n* paperwork
काग-पेंच *n* corkscrew
काजू *n* cashew
काटकर निकालना *vt* cut off
काट - छांट करना *vt* trim
काटना *vt* cut (up), hack
काटने का उपकरण *npl* clippers
काट लेना (घाव लगाने के अर्थ में) *vt* cut
कान *n* ear
कान का दर्द *n* earache
कान का पर्दा *n* eardrum
कान की बाली *n* earring
कानफोड़ू *adj* deafening
कानून *n* law, legislation
कानूनी *adj* legal
काफ़िला *n* convoy
काफ़ी *adv* pretty
काबुली चना *n* chickpea
काम *n* work
काम करना *vi* work
काम करने वाली *n* maid
कामगार *n* workman
काम पर रखना *vt* hire
कामना *n* desire
कायम रहना/चलना *v* last
कायर *n* coward ▷ *adj* cowardly
कायापलट *n* makeover
कायापलट करना *vt* transform
कार किराए पर लेना *n* car hire
कार की चाभियाँ *npl* car keys

कारण *n* cause, reason
कारण होना *vt* cause
कारतूस *n* cartridge
कार बीमा *n* car insurance
कारखाना *n* factory
कारागार *n* jail
कारावकाश *n* parole
कारावास *n* prison
कारावास अधिकारी *n* prison officer
कार्बन *n* carbon
कार्ब्युरेटर *n* carburettor
कार्बोहाइड्रेट *n* carbohydrate
कार्टून फ़िल्म *n* cartoon
कार्य *n* engagement
कार्यकारी *adj* acting ▷ *n* executive
कार्यक्रम *n* programme
कार्यक्रम-स्थल *n* venue
कार्यक्षेत्र *n* workspace
कार्यदिवस *n* weekday
कार्यबल *n* workforce
कार्यभार *n* assignment
कार्यवाही *n* operation ▷ *npl* proceedings
कार्यवाही करना *vi* act
कार्यशाला *n* workshop
कार्य समय *npl* office hours
कार्यसूची *n* agenda
कार्यस्थल *n* workplace
कार्यस्थल/घटनास्थल *n* site
कार्यानुभव *n* work experience
कार्यालय *n* office
कार्रवाई *n* action
काल *n* (अवधि) period; (समय) tense
काल समंजक *n* timer
काला *adj* black
कालिख *n* soot
काली कॉफ़ी *n* black coffee
कालीन *n* carpet
काली मिर्च *n* pepper
काव्य *n* poetry
काष्ठफल *n* nut
का सहारा लेना *vt* resort to
का होना *vi* belong
कि *conj* (वस्तु) that; (यदि) whether
किंचित/कुछ भी *det* any
किंवदंती/दंतकथा *n* legend
किकियाना *vi* squeak
कितना *adv* how
किताब *n* book
किताब की अलमारी *n* bookcase, bookshelf
किताब की दुकान *n* bookshop
किनारा *n* edge, side

किफ़ायत करना *vi* economize
किफ़ायती *adj* economical
किया करता था *v* used
किया हुआ *adj* done
किरच *n* splinter
किरण *n* beam
किराए का *n* rental
किराएदार *n* lodger, tenant
किराए पर लेना *vt* rent
किराना *npl* groceries
किराया *n* rent
किर्गिज़स्तान *n* Kyrgyzstan
किला *n* fort
किलो *n* kilo
किलोमीटर *n* kilometre
किशमिश *n* raisin
किशोर *n* adolescent
किशोर/किशोरी *n* teenager
किशोरवय *npl* teens
किशोरावस्था *n* adolescence
किसका *det* whose
किसी भी तरह से *adv* anyhow
किसी को शुभकामना देते हुए शराब पीना *excl* cheers!
किस्त *n* instalment
किस्मत *n* fate
किसान *n* farmer
की अपेक्षा *prep* than
की ओर *prep* to
की ओर दौड़ना *vi* run
की ओर से *n* behalf
की ओर से/से *prep* from
कीचड़ *n* mud
कीचड़ भरा *adj* muddy
कीट *n* pest
कीटडिंभ/कोआ *n* grub
कीटनाशक *n* pesticide
कीड़ा *n* (कीट) bug, insect; (कृमी) worm
की तरफ़ *prep* towards
कीप *n* funnel
कीमत *n* price
कीमत होना *vt* cost
कीमती *adj* precious
कीमती वस्तुएं *npl* valuables
कीमा *n* mince
कीर्तन *n* musical prayer
कीर्तिमान *n* record
कील *n* nail
कुँवारा *n* bachelor
कुँवारी *n* virgin
कुंजी *n* key
कुंड *n* pool
कुंदा *n* log
कुंभ राशि *n* Aquarius
कुआं *n* well

कुकर *n* cooker
कुकुरमुत्ता *n* mushroom
कुचल देना *vt* run over
कुचलना *vt* crush
कुचलना/पैर रखना *vi* tread
कुछ *det* few
कुछ नहीं *n* nothing
कुछ भी *pron* anything
कुछ समय के लिए *adv* briefly
कुछ हद तक *adv* rather
कुटीर *n* cottage
कुतिया *n* bitch
कुपोषण *n* malnutrition
कुमारी *n* Miss
कुमुदिनी *n* lily of the valley
कुम्हलाना *vi* wilt
कुरकुरा *adj* crisp, crispy
कुरती *n* blouse
कुरान *n* Koran
कुर्ती *n* jumper
कुर्सी *n* chair
कुल *n* total
कुल आय *n* turnover
कुल मिलाकर *adv* altogether, overall
कुल्हाड़ी *n* axe
कुवैत *n* Kuwait
कुवैती नागरिक *n* Kuwaiti
कुशल *adj* well
कुशाग्र बुद्धि *adj* brainy
कुश्ती *n* wrestling
कुश्तीबाज़/पहलवान *n* wrestler
कुहनी *n* elbow
कुहरा *n* fog
कूची *n* brush
कूड़ा *n* litter, rubbish
कूड़ादान *n* litter bin
कूदना *v* jump
कृंतक/कुतरने वाले जीव *n* rodent
कृतघ्न *adj* ungrateful
कृत्य *n* act
कृत्रिम *adj* artificial
कृपया! *excl* please!
कृषि *n* agriculture
कृषि संबंधी *adj* agricultural
कृष्णकमल फल *n* passion fruit
केंद्र *n* centre
केंद्र शासित प्रदेश *n* Union Territory
केंद्रीय *adj* central
केंद्रीय तापन *n* central heating
के अतिरिक्त *prep* besides

के अनुसार *prep* according to
के अलावा *prep* apart from ▷ *adv* besides
के ऊपर *prep* over; (रखना, किताब रखना आदि) upon
के ऊपर से दिखना *vt* overlook
केकड़ा *n* crab, lobster
के कारण *prep* owing to
केतली *n* teapot
के दौर में *prep* throughout
के नीचे *prep* below, under, underneath
के परे *prep* beyond, past
के पहले *conj* before
के पीछे *prep* (समय) after; (अवस्थिति) behind
के बजाय *adv* instead
के बदले में *prep* instead of
के बारे में *prep* about, of
के बिना *prep* without
के बीच में *prep* among, between
के भीतर *prep* within
केन्या *n* Kenya
केन्याई *adj* Kenyan
केरल *n* Kerela
के रूप में *prep* as
केला *n* banana
के लिए *prep* for ▷ *part* to
के लिए पूछना *vt* ask for
के लिए प्रतीक्षा करना *vi* wait
केवल *adv* exclusively, only
के विषय में *prep* concerning
केश प्रसाधक *n* hairdresser
केशविन्यास *n* hairstyle
के समान *prep* like
के सहारे *prep* against
के सिवा *prep* excluding
कैदी *n* prisoner
कैनरी द्वीप समूह *npl* Canaries
कैमरून *n* Cameroon
कैरेबियन सागर *n* Caribbean
कैरेबियाई *adj* Caribbean
कैलोरी *n* calorie
कैसे *adv* how
कैसेट *n* cassette
काँगो *n* Congo
कॉन्टैक्ट लेंस *npl* contact lenses
कोंचना *vt* poke
कोई/कोई व्यक्ति *pron* anybody
कोई नहीं *det* no ▷ *n* nobody ▷ *pron* no one

कोई भी *pron* any ▷ *det* any
कोई भी/किसी को *pron* anyone
कोई भी नहीं *pron* none
को छोड़कर *prep* except
कोट, छाते आदि टांगने की जगह/अमानती सामानघर *n* cloakroom
कोठरी *n* cabin
कोठी *n* bungalow
कोण *n* angle
कोना *n* corner
कोमा/अचेतावस्था *n* coma
कोयल *n* cuckoo
कोयला *n* coal; (काठकोयला) charcoal
कोयले की खान *n* colliery
कोरा *adj* blank
कोरा चेक *n* blank cheque
कोरिया *n* Korea
कोरियाई *adj* Korean
कोलकाता *n* Kolkata
कोलम्बिया *n* Colombia
कोलम्बियाई *adj* Colombian
कोशिका *n* cell
कोष्ठक *npl* brackets
कोसोवो *n* Kosovo
कोस्टा रिका *n* Costa Rica
कोहरा *n* mist
कोहरे से आच्छादित *adj* misty
कोहिमा *n* Kohima
कौआ *n* crow, raven
कौन *pron* who
कौन - सा *det* which ▷ *pron* which
कौर/टुकड़ा *n* bite
कौस्तुभ/प्लेटिनम *n* platinum
क्या *det* what ▷ *pron* what
क्यूबा *n* Cuba
क्यूबा निवासी *n* Cuban
क्यों *adv* why
क्योंकि *conj* because
क्रमरहित *adj* random
क्रमानुगत/लगातार *adj* consecutive
क्रमानुसार *adv* respectively
क्रमिक *adj* gradual
क्रमिक रूप से *adv* gradually
क्रांति *n* revolution
क्रांतिकारी *adj* revolutionary
क्रिया *n* verb
क्रिया का साधारण रूप *n* infinitive
क्रियारूप संयोजन *n* conjugation

क्रिया-विशेषण *n* adverb
क्रिसमस *n* Christmas
क्रिसमस/बड़ा दिन *n* Christmas
क्रीड़ास्थल *n* pitch
क्रीम *n* cream
क्रुद्ध *adj* mad
क्रूर *adj* cruel
क्रूरता *n* cruelty
क्रॉस *n* cross
क्रॉस कंट्री *n* cross-country
क्रोएशिया *n* Croatia
क्रोएशियाई *adj* Croatian
क्रोध *n* anger, rage
क्रोधित *adj* angry
क्षण *n* moment
क्षणिक *adj* momentary
क्षतिग्रस्त करना *vt* vandalize
क्षमा करें! *excl* pardon?
क्षमादान *n* pardon
क्षमा मांगना *vi* apologize
क्षमा याचना *n* apology
क्षितिज *n* horizon
क्षुधातुर *adj* ravenous
क्षेत्र *n* (जगह) area, region, zone; (देश) territory
क्षेत्रीय *adj* regional
क्षैतिज *adj* horizontal

खंड *n* block, chunk
खंडन करना *vt* contradict
खंडित *adj* broken
खंभा *n* pole, post
खगोलशास्त्र *n* astronomy
खच्चर *n* mule
खजांची *n* cashier, treasurer
खजाना *n* treasure
खट की आवाज़ *n* click
खटखट करना *v* click
खट्टा *adj* sour
खट्टी-मीठी *adj* sweet-and-sour
खड़खड़ाहट *n* rattle
खड़ा अनाज *adj* wholemeal
खड़ाऊँ /मोजरी *n* clog
खड़िया *n* chalk
खड़ी चट्टान *n* cliff
खतरे में डालना *vt* endanger
खदान *n* quarry
खदान/खान *n* mine
खनन *n* mining
खनिक *n* miner

ख

खनिज *adj* mineral
खनिज पदार्थ *n* mineral
खपड़ा लगा हुआ *adj* tiled
खपत तिथि *n* best-before date
खपरैल/खपड़ा *n* tile
खमीर *n* yeast
खम्भा *n* pillar
खरगोश *n* rabbit
खरबूज/तरबूज *n* melon
खरहा *n* hare
खरा/असली *adj* genuine
खराब *adj* (भद्दा) awful, bad; (बुरा) nasty
खराब तरह से *adv* badly
खराब होना *v* break down
खरीददार *n* buyer
खरीदना *vt* buy
खरोंच *n* bruise
खरोंचना *vt* scratch
खर्च *n* expenditure ▷ *npl* expenses
खर्चीला *adj* extravagant
खलनायक/बदमाश *n* villain
खलिहान *n* barn
खसरा *npl* measles
ख़ाला *n* aunt (mother's sister)
ख़ेमा *n* camp
ख़ेमा डालकर रहना *vi* camp
ख़ेमे में निवास *n* camping
ख़ेमे में रहने वाला *n* camper
ख़ौफ़नाक *adj* appalling
ख़्यातिप्राप्त व्यक्ति *n* celebrity
खाँसना *vi* cough
खाँसी *n* cough
खाँसी की दवा *n* cough mixture
खाई *n* moat
खाई/खंदक *n* trench
खाका/अभिन्यास *n* layout
खाड़ी *n* bay
खाड़ी राज्य *npl* Gulf States
खाता *n* account
खाता संख्या *n* account number
खाद *n* manure
खाद्य *adj* edible
खानसामा *n* chef, cook
खाना *v* eat
खाना पकाना *n* cooking
खानाबदोश *n* gypsy
खानाबदोश/प्रवासी *n* migrant
खाने का सोडा *n* bicarbonate of soda

खारिज करना *vt* (नामंजूर) overrule; (अस्वीकृत) reject; rule out
खाली *adj* empty, bare; (सड़क) clear
खाली करना *vt* empty ▷ *v* evacuate
खासकर *adv* preferably
खास तौर पर *adv* especially
खिझाने वाला *adj* annoying
खिड़की *n* window
खिड़की का पर्दा *n* Venetian blind
खिड़की का शीशा *n* window pane
खिन्न/खेदपूर्ण *excl* sorry!
खिलखिलाना *vi* giggle
खिलाड़ी *n* (पेशेवर खिलाड़ी) athlete; (खिलाड़ी) player
खिलौना *n* toy
खींचना *vt* pull
खीझ दिलाना *vt* annoy
खीरा *n* cucumber
खुजली वाली *adj* itchy
खुजली होना *vi* itch
खुद *pron* (अपने आप) itself; (हमारा) ourselves; (उनका) themselves
खुद को *pron* yourself
खुद (पुरुष) *pron* himself
खुदरा बिक्री *n* retail
खुदरा बिक्री करना *vi* retail
खुदरा मूल्य *n* retail price
खुदरा विक्रेता *n* retailer
खुद (स्त्री) *pron* herself
खुद /हम स्वयं *pron* ourselves
खुबानी *n* apricot
खुरदरा *adj* coarse
खुरदुरा/ऊबड़खाबड़ *adj* rough
खुरपी *n* trowel
खुलना *v* open
खुलने का समय *npl* opening hours
खुला *adj* open
खुल्लम - खुल्ला *adj* blatant
खुश *adj* glad, happy
खुशदिल/प्रसन्नचित्त *adj* merry
खुशबू *n* aroma
खुशी *n* happiness
खूँटी/ काँटा *n* hook
खूँटी *n* peg
खून बहना *vi* bleed

खेना *v* row
खेमा *n* pavilion
खेमे का स्थल *n* campsite
खेल *n* game
खेल का मैदान *n* (टेनिस कोर्ट) court; (क्रीड़ा स्थल) playground
खेल का समय *n* playtime
खेलकूद *npl* athletics
खेलकूद संबंधी *adj* athletic
खेलना *vi* play
खेल प्रतियोगिता *n* tournament
खेल में होने वाली धर-पकड़ *n* tackle
खैबर पास *n* Khyber Pass
खोखला *adj* hollow
खोज *n* pursuit
खोजना *v* look up
खोज निकालना/पता चलाना *vt* track down
खोजी *n* explorer
खोट *n* vice
खो देना *vt* lose
खोना *vt* mislay
खोया हुआ *adj* missing
खोल/गिलाफ़ *n* cover
खोलना *v* open, unroll ▷ *vt* undo, untie

गंगटोक *n* Gangtok
गंगा *n* Ganges
गंजा *adj* bald
गंदगी *n* mess
गंदा *adj* foul
गांधीनगर *n* Gandhinagar
गज *n* yard
गठबंधन *n* alliance
गठिया *n* arthritis, rheumatism
गडगड़ाहट *n* thunder
गढ़ा *n* puddle
गणतंत्र *n* republic
गणना *n* calculation
गणना करना *vt* calculate
गणित *npl* mathematics
गणित के सवाल *n* sum
गणितीय *adj* mathematical
गणेश चतुर्थी *n* Indian festival honouring Ganesha, the elephant God
गण्डास्थि *n* cheekbone

गति *n* (गतिविधि) movement; (प्रगति) pace
गतिविधि *n* activity
गति वृद्धि *n* acceleration
गतिशील *n* mobile
गत्ता *n* card, cardboard
गत्ते का डिब्बा *n* carton
गद्दा *n* mattress
गद्दी *n* cushion, pad
गप मारना/अस्पष्ट बात करना *vi* waffle
गपशप/अफ़वाह *n* gossip
गपशप करना *vi* gossip
गमला *n* plant pot
गया हुआ *adj* gone
गरजनेवाला *adj* thundery
गरम करना *vt* heat ▷ *v* heat up
गरीब *adj* poor
गरीबी *n* poverty
गर्दन *n* neck
गर्भनिरोध *n* contraception
गर्भनिरोधक *n* contraceptive
गर्भपात *n* miscarriage
गर्भवती *adj* pregnant
गर्भावस्था *n* pregnancy
गर्म *adj* (अत्यंत गर्म) hot; (गुनगुना) warm
गर्म करना *v* warm up
गर्म पानी की थैली *n* hot-water bottle
गर्मी *n* summer
गर्मी/ऊष्मा *n* heat
गर्व *n* pride
गर्वित *adj* proud
गलगंड *n* mumps
गलतफ़हमी *n* misunderstanding
गलत समझना *vt* misjudge ▷ *v* misunderstand
गलत समझा हुआ *adj* mistaken
गलती *n* mistake
गलती करना *vt* mistake
गलती से *adv* mistakenly
गलतुंडिका *npl* tonsils
गला/कंठ *n* throat
गलियारा *n* aisle, corridor, passage
गलियारा/दालान *n* hallway
गली *n* lane
गलीचा *n* rug
गले का पट्टा *n* collar
गवाह *n* witness
गश्त *n* patrol
गश्ती कार *n* patrol car
गहन *adj* intensive

गहन चिकित्सा कक्ष *n* intensive care unit
गहना *n* jewellery
गहरा *n* dark
गहरा नीला *n* indigo
गहरा रंग *adj* dark
गहरा लाल *n* deep red
ग़लत *adj* wrong
ग़लत नंबर *n* wrong number
गांव *n* village
गाजर *n* carrot
गाड़ना *vt* bury
गाड़ियाँ खड़ी करने की जगह *n* car park
गाड़ी की बत्ती *npl* hazard warning lights
गाड़ी धुलवाने का स्थान *n* car wash
गाढ़ा *adj* thick
गान *n* anthem
गाय *n* cow
गायक - मंडली *n* choir
गायब होना *vi* vanish
गारा *n* mortar
गाल *n* cheek
गिद्ध *n* vulture
गिनती करना *vt* count
गिनना *vi* count
गिनी *n* Guinea
गियर *n* gear
गिरजाघर *n* church
गिरफ़्तार करना *vt* arrest
गिरफ़्तारी *n* arrest
गिरावट आना *v* go down
गिरेबान/कॉलर *n* collar
गिरोह *n* gang
गिलास *n* glass
गिल्ली डंडा *n* Indian game
गीत के बोल *npl* lyrics
गीला *adj* wet
गुंथी चोटी *n* pigtail
गुच्छा/झुण्ड *n* bunch
गुज़रना *vt* go through
गुज़रना/भोगना *vt* undergo
गुजरात *n* Gujarat
गुजराती *n* Gujarati
गुड़ *n* jaggery
गुट *n* league
गुटका *n* block
गुणन *n* multiplication
गुणवत्ता *n* quality
गुदगुदी करना *vt* tickle
गुनगुना *adj* lukewarm
गुनगुनाना *v* hum
गुप्तचरी/जासूसी *n* espionage
गुफा *n* cave
गुबरैला *n* beetle

गुब्बारा *n* balloon
गुम *adj* lost
गुमनाम *adj* anonymous
गुयाना *n* Guyana
गुर्राना *vi* growl
गुरुवार *n* Thursday
गुरू *n* (गुरु) teacher
गुरू पूरव *n* (गुरु) celebration based on life of Sikh guru
गुरू नानक जयंती *n* (गुरु) Guru Nanak's birth anniversary
गुरू हरगोविंद जयंती *n* (गुरु) Guru Hargovind's birth anniversary
गुलदस्ता *n* bouquet
गुलदाउदी *n* chrysanthemum
गुलदान *n* vase
गुलनार *n* carnation
गुलमेंहदी *n* rosemary
गुलाब *n* rose
गुलाब जामुन *n* Indian sweet
गुलाबी *adj* pink
गुलाबी शराब *n* rosé
गुलुबंद *n* headscarf, muffler
गुल्लक *n* piggybank
गुस्सा दिलाने वाला *adj* infuriating
गूंथन *n* plait
गूगल वेबसाइट पर इंटरनेट खोज करना *v* Google
गूदा *n* core
गृहकार्य *n* homework
गृह मैच अथवा अपनी ज़मीन पर खेला जाने वाला मैच *n* home match
गृह युद्ध *n* civil war
गृह सज्जाकार *n* interior designer
गृहस्वामिनी *n* housewife
गृहासक्त *adj* homesick
गेंद *n* ball
गेंदा *n* marigold
गेम्स कंसोल *n* games console
गेलिस *npl* braces
गेहूँ *n* wheat
गैबॉन *n* Gabon
गैम्बिया *n* Gambia
गैरज़िम्मेदार *adj* irresponsible
गैरदोस्ताना *adj* unfriendly
गैरभरोसेमंद *adj* unreliable
गैराज - गाड़ी की मरम्मत करने की जगह *n* garage
गैराज - गाड़ी रखने की जगह *n* garage
गोआ *n* Goa

गोंद *n* glue
गोखरू *n* bunion
गोताखोरी की पोशाक *n* wetsuit
गोद *n* lap
गोदना *n* tattoo
गोद लेना *vt* adopt ▷ *n* adoption
गोधुली *n* twilight
गोपनीय *adj* confidential
गोमांस *n* beef
गोल चक्कर रास्ता *n* roundabout
गोलरक्षक *n* goalkeeper
गोलाकार *adj* round, circular ▷ *n* round
गोली *n* (बंदूक के लिए) bullet; (गुल्ला) pellet; (औषधि) pill, tablet
गोल्फ़ *n* golf
गोल्फ़ कोर्स *n* golf course
गौण *adj* minor
गौतम बुद्ध *n* Buddha
गौरव *n* glory, honour
ग्यारह *num* eleven
ग्यारहवां *adj* eleventh
ग्रंथि *n* gland
ग्रस्त होना/होना *vt* have
ग्रह *n* planet
ग्राम *n* gram
ग्रामीण *adj* rural
ग्रामीण क्षेत्र *n* countryside
ग्राहक *n* customer
ग्रिल *n* grill
ग्रीनलैंड *n* Greenland
ग्रीस/यूनान *n* Greece
ग्रेट ब्रिटेन *n* Great Britain
ग्वाटेमाला *n* Guatemala
ग़जल *n* style of singing

घंटा *n* hour
घंटी *n* bell
घटक *n* component
घटना *v* come down ▷ *n* event, occurrence
घटना चक्र *n* cycle
घटना/दृष्टांत *n* instance
घटनापूर्ण *adj* eventful
घटाना *vt* reduce
घटाव *prep* minus
घटित होना *vi* happen, occur

घड़ियाल *n* alligator
घड़ी का पट्टा *n* watch strap
घन *n* cube ▷ *adj* cubic
घपला *n* mix-up
घबराया हुआ *adj* nervous
घमंडी *adj* arrogant, bigheaded
घर *n* home
घर का पता *n* home address
घर का बना *adj* home-made
घर के भीतर *adv* indoors
घर पर *adv* at home
घर से बाहर *adv* outside, outdoors
घरेलू कामकाज *n* housework
घाघरा *n* skirt
घाट *n* jetty, pier
घाटी *n* ravine, valley
घाना *n* Ghana
घाना का निवासी *n* Ghanaian
घायल *n* casualty ▷ *adj* hurt, injured
घायल करना *vt* injure
घाव *n* wound
घाव/चीरा *n* cut
घाव भरना *vi* heal
घास *n* grass
घास काटना *v* mow
घास का मैदान *n* lawn, meadow
घिनौना *adj* repulsive, revolting
घी *n* ghee
घुंघराला *adj* curly
घुटने तक लंबा बरसाती कोट *n* cagoule
घुड़दौड़ *n* horse racing
घुड़दौड़ का घोड़ा *n* racehorse
घुड़दौड़ का मैदान *n* racecourse
घुड़सवारी *n* horse riding
घुमक्कड़ *n* rambler
घुसपैठिया *n* intruder
घूँघट *n* veil
घूँघर/छल्ला *n* curl
घूम जाना/मुड़ना *vi* wind
घूरना *vi* gaze
घूस *vt* bribe
घूसखोरी *n* bribery
घृणा *n* hatred
घृणा करना *vt* hate, loathe
घेरना *vt* round up
घेरे हुए *adv* around
घोंसला *n* nest

घ

घोड़ा *n* horse
घोड़ा गाड़ी *n* horse carriage
घोड़ी *n* mare
घोषणा *n* announcement
घोषणा करना *vt* announce

च

चंगा *excl* expression of approval or agreement
चंगा होना *vi* recover
चंगुल *n* clutch
चंद्रमा *n* moon
चंडीगढ़ *n* Chandigarh
चंसुर *n* cress
चकराया हुआ *adj* confused
चकित *adj* amazed
चकित करना *vt* amaze, astonish
चकोतरा *n* grapefruit
चक्कर *n* vertigo
चक्की *n* mill
चक्र *n* round
चक्रवात *n* cyclone
चचेरा/ममेरा/फुफेरा/मौसेरा/ भाई या बहन *n* cousin
चटाई *n* mat
चट्टान *n* rock
चढ़ना *v* climb
चतुर *adj* clever
चतुष्टय *n* quartet
चबाना *v* chew
चमकाना *vt* polish
चमकीला *adj* bright
चमकीला/भड़कीला *adj* bright
चमगादड़ *n* bat
चमड़ा *n* leather
चमत्कार *n* miracle
चमेली *n* jasmine
चयन *n* pick
चयन/प्रकार *n* choice
चयापचय *n* metabolism
चरखी *n* reel
चरम/अत्यंत *adj* extreme
चरमपंथ *n* extremism
चरमपंथी *n* extremist
चरित्र *n* character
चरित्र/पात्र *n* character
चलचित्र *n* movie
चलन/अभ्यास *n* practice
चलना *vi* walk
चश्मा *npl* glasses

चहलकदमी *n* walking
चहलकदमी/टहल *n* walk
चहारदीवारी *n* boundary
चाचा/मामा/फूफा/मौसा *n* uncle
चाची, मामी, मौसी, बुआ *n* aunt, auntie
चाटना *vt* lick
चाबुक *n* whip
चाय *n* tea
चाय का प्याला *n* teacup
चाय का समय *n* teatime
चार *num* four
चारखानेदार *adj* checked
चारपहिया ड्राइव *n* four-wheel drive
चारों ओर *prep* around
चारों ओर देखना *v* look round
चारों तरफ़/हर ओर *prep* around
चारो ओर *prep* around
चाल *n* trick
चालक *n* chauffeur
चालबाज़ी करना/धोखा देना *vt* trick
चालीस *num* forty
चालू *adv* on
चालू करना *v* turn on
चालू खाता *n* current account
चावल *n* rice
चाहना *v* long ▷ *vt* want, wish
चाहिए *v* should
चिंकारा *n* antelope
चिंता *n* concern
चिंता करना *vi* fret, worry
चिंताजनक *adj* worrying
चिंतामुक्त *adj* relieved
चिंतित *adj* concerned, worried
चिकनाई/ग्रीस *n* grease
चिकना करना *vt* (नाखून) file
चिकित्सकीय *adj* medical
चिकित्सकीय जांच *n* medical examination
चिकित्सकीय प्रमाणपत्र *n* medical certificate
चिकित्सा *n* therapy
चिकित्सालय *n* clinic
चिटकाना *v* crack
चिटका हुआ *adj* cracked
चिट्ठा लिखना *v* blog
चिड़चिड़ा *adj* bad-tempered, irritable
चिड़चिड़ेपन व गुस्से का आवेश *n* tantrum
चिड़ियाघर *n* zoo

चिढ़ दिलाने वाला *adj* irritating
चिढ़ाना *vt* mock, tease
चिढा हुआ *adj* resentful
चित्ती *npl* freckles
चित्र *npl* graphics ▷ *n* picture
चित्रकथा *n* comic strip
चित्रकथा खंड *n* comic book
चित्रकार *n* painter
चित्रकारी *n* painting
चित्रकारी करना *v* paint
चिथड़ा *n* rag
चिनार *n* poplar
चिपकाना *vt* glue, paste
चिप्पी *n* tag
चिप्पी/सूचक पत्र *n* label
चिमटी *n* clip ▷ *npl* pliers, tweezers
चिरकालिक *adj* chronic
चिरागदान *n* candlestick
चिलमची *n* washbasin
चिली *n* Chile
चिली निवासी *n* Chilean
चिली से संबद्ध *adj* Chilean
चिल्लाना *n* cry ▷ *v* yell
चिह्नित करना *vt* mark
चींटी *n* ant
चीज़ *n* thing
चीड़ *n* pine
चीता *n* leopard
चीन *n* China
चीनी *adj* Chinese ▷ *n* Chinese
चीनी मिट्टी *n* china, porcelain
चीनी मिट्टी का *adj* ceramic
चील *n* eagle
चुंबक *n* magnet
चुंबकीय *adj* magnetic
चुकंदर (बीटरूट) *n* beetroot
चकुंदर (पारस्निप) *n* parsnip
चुकाना *vt* repay
चुटकी काटना *vt* pinch
चुड़ैल/जादूगरनी *n* witch
चुनना *v* choose
चुनरी *n* scarf
चुनाव *n* election
चुना हुआ *adj* chosen
चुन्नी *n* scarf
चुनौती *n* challenge
चुनौती देना *vt* challenge
चुनौतीपूर्ण *adj* challenging
चुप/ख़ामोश *adj* silent
चुभाना *vt* prick
चुरुट *n* cigar
चुलबुला *adj* playful

चुस्त पतलून *npl* leggings, tights
चूक जाना *v* miss
चूजा *n* chick
चूना *n* lime
चूना करना *vt* whitewash
चूना पत्थर *n* limestone
चूरा *n* crumb
चूर्ण *n* powder
चूल/कब्जा *n* hinge
चूहा (छोटा चूहा) *n* mouse
चूहा *n* rat
चेक *n* cheque
चेक आउट *v* check out
चेक इन *v* check in
चेक गणराज्य *n* Czech Republic
चेक गणराज्य से संबद्ध *adj* Czech
चेचेन्या *n* Chechnya
चेतना *n* consciousness
चेतावनी *n* warning
चेतावनी देना *vt* warn
चेन *n* zip
चेन खोलना *vt* unzip
चेन लगाना *vt* zip
चेन्नई *n* Chennai
चेरी *n* cherry
चेला *n* apprentice
चैट/वार्ता कार्यक्रम *n* chat show
चैन *n* peace
चोंच *n* beak
चोकर *n* bran
चोकीगोभी *npl* Brussels sprouts
चोट *n* injury
चोट पहुँचाना *vt* harm, hurt
चोट लगने के कारण खेल रुकने पर दिया जाने वाला अतिरिक्त समय *n* injury time
चोर *n* thief
चोरी *n* burglary, theft
चोरी करना *vt* burgle
चोली *n* bra
चौकस *adj* observant
चौकी दौड़ *n* relay
चौखटा *n* frame
चौड़ा *adj* broad, wide
चौड़ाई *n* width
चौड़ा मार्ग *n* motorway
चौड़ी - गली *n* avenue
चौथा *adj* fourth
चौथाई *n* quarter
चौदह *num* fourteen
चौदहवाँ *adj* fourteenth
चौराहा *n* crossroads

छँटनी *n* redundancy
छकड़ा गाड़ी *n* cart
छछूंदर *n* mole
छज्जा *n* balcony
छड़ *n* bar, rod
छठा *adj* sixth
छत *n* (भीतरी) ceiling; (बाहरी) roof
छत्तीसगढ़ *n* Chattisgarh
छत्रक/कुकुरमुत्ता *n* toadstool
छप्परदार *adj* thatched
छलनी *n* colander
छलांग मारना *vi* leap
छल्ला *n* finger ring
छविगृह *n* cinema
छह *num* six
छांटना/चुनना *vt* pick
छाजन - एक रोग *n* eczema
छाता *n* umbrella
छात्र *n* student
छात्र सैनिक *n* cadet
छात्रावास *n* hostel
छापना/मुद्रित करना *v* print
छापा *n* raid
छापा मारना *vt* raid
छापे की गलती *n* misprint
छायाचित्र *n* photograph
छायाचित्रण *n* photography
छायाचित्र खींचना *vt* photocopy
छिछले पानी में चलना *vi* paddle
छिद्रित *adj* pierced
छिन्न-भिन्न *adj* broken-down
छिपकली *n* lizard
छिलका *n* peel, skin
छिलका सहित भुना आलू *n* jacket potato
छिलनी *n* potato peeler
छीज/छेद *n* tear
छीलना *vt* peel
छुट्टी *n* holiday
छुपना *vi* hide
छुपा छुपी *n* hide and seek
छुपाना *vt* hide
छुरी *n* knife
छुरी-काँटा *n* cutlery
छूकर देखना *vt* feel
छूना *vt* touch

छेद *n* hole, piercing
छेनी/रुखानी *n* chisel
छोटा *adj* tiny, little; (संक्षिप्त) compact; (आयु) younger; (वहनीय) portable
छोटा गिरजा *n* chapel
छोटा बहन *n* younger sister
छोटा भाई *n* younger brother
छोटा चम्मच *n* teaspoon
छोटा तरणताल *n* paddling pool
छोटा/ नाटा *adj* short
छोटा प्याज *npl* chives
छोटा बंदरगाह *n* marina
छोटा बक्सा *n* briefcase
छोटा बच्चा *n* toddler
छोटा/बारीक *adj* minute
छोटा संतरा *n* mandarin
छोटी *n* younger girl
छोटी चिट्ठी/टिप्पणी *n* note
छोटी पुस्तिका *n* pamphlet
छोटी बस *n* minibus
छोटी माता *n* chickenpox
छोड़ना *vt* vacate; (यागना) give up; (न चुनना) leave out

जंगल *n* forest, jungle, woods
जंज़ीर *n* chain
जई *npl* oats
जई का आटा *n* oatmeal
जगह *n* room
जगह घेरना/कब्ज़ा करना *vt* occupy
जगह पर *adv* away
जगह/मक़ाम *n* place
जगा हुआ *adj* awake
जच्चा अस्पताल/प्रसूति अस्पताल *n* maternity hospital
जटिल *adj* complex, complicated
जटिलता/परेशानी *n* complication
जड़ *n* root
जड़ाऊ पिन *n* brooch
जड़ी-बूटी *npl* herbs
जत्रुक/हंसली *n* collarbone
जनगणना *n* census

जनता *n* public
जन-परिवहन *n* public transport
जनसंख्या *n* population
जन-संपर्क *npl* public relations
जनसेवक *n* civil servant
जन्म *n* birth
जन्मदिन *n* birthday
जन्मपत्री/राशिफल *n* horoscope
जन्म - प्रमाणपत्र *n* birth certificate
जन्मभूमि *n* homeland
जन्मस्थान *n* birthplace
जन्माष्टमी *n* festival to mark the birth of the Hindu God Lord Krishna
जन्नत *n* heaven
जनवरी *n* January
जबड़ा *n* jaw
जब तक *conj* till, until; (समय) while
जब तक नहीं *conj* unless
जब भी *conj* whenever
जमना *vi* freeze
जमशेद नवरोज़ *n* Parsi New Year
जमादार *n* sweeper
जमाना *vt* freeze
जमा हुआ *adj* frozen
जमाइका *n* Jamaica
जमाइका - निवासी *n* Jamaican
जमाई *n* son-in-law
जम्हाई लेना *vi* yawn
जम्मू *n* Jammu
जयचिह्न *n* trophy
जयजयकार *n* cheer
जयजयकार करना *v* cheer
जयपुर *n* Jaipur
जर्मन खसरा *n* German measles
जर्मनी *n* Germany
जर्मनी का नागरिक *n* German
जलकर खाक होना *v* burn down
जलकुंभी *n* watercress
जल - जीवशाला *n* aquarium
जलना *vi* burn
जलने का घाव *n* burn
जल पर तैरना *vi* float
जलपरी *n* mermaid
जलपान *npl* refreshments
जलपानगृह *n* cafeteria, canteen

जलरोधक *adj* waterproof
जलवायु *n* climate
जलवायु परिवर्तन *n* climate change
जलव्यवस्था *n* plumbing
जला देना *vt* burn
जलाना *vt* light
जलाना/दागना *vt* burn
जलाशय *n* reservoir
जलेबी *n* Indian sweet
जल्दबाज़ी *n* hurry
जल्दबाज़ी से *adv* hastily
जल्दी *adv* early ▷ *adj* early
जल्दी करना *vi* hurry ▷ *v* hurry up
जल्दी - जल्दी जाना *vi* rush
जल्दी/समय से पूर्व *adj* early
जवाब *n* answer, reply
जवाब देना *v* answer, reply
जस्ता *n* pewter, zinc
जहान्नुम *n* hell
जहाँ *conj* where
जापान *n* Japan
जाली/नकली *adj* fake
जासूस *n* detective
जूड़ा *n* bun (hairstyle)
ज़ख़्मी करना *vt* wound
ज़बर्दस्त *adj* tremendous
ज़बर्दस्त/शानदार *adj* terrific
ज़बर्दस्ती घुसना *v* break in
ज़ब्त करना *vt* confiscate
ज़मानत *n* bail
ज़मींदार *n* landowner
ज़मीन *n* ground
ज़मीन पर उतरना *v* land
ज़रूरत *n* requirement
ज़रूरत होना *vt* need, require
ज़रूरी *adj* essential
ज़हर *n* poison
ज़हर देना *vt* poison
ज़हरीला *adj* poisonous
ज़ाम्बिया *n* Zambia
ज़ाम्बियाई *adj* Zambian ▷ *n* Zambian
ज़ाहिर *adj* apparent, obvious
ज़ाहिर तौर पर *adv* apparently, obviously
ज़िक्र *n* reference
ज़िक्र करना *vi* refer
ज़िद्दी *adj* obstinate
ज़िद्दी/स्थायी *adj* persistent
ज़िम्बाब्वे *n* Zimbabwe
ज़िम्बाब्वे के मूलनिवासी/ज़िम्बाब्वे के नागरिक *n* Zimbabwean

ज़िम्बाब्वे - निवासी/ ज़िम्बाब्वे से संबद्ध *adj* Zimbabwean
ज़िम्मा लेना/ज़मानत देना *vt* guarantee
ज़िम्मेदार *adj* accountable, responsible
ज़िम्मेदारी *n* responsibility, accountability
ज़ुकाम *n* cold
ज़ोर देना *vt* emphasize
ज़्यादा *det* more
ज़्यादातर *pron* most
जाँघिया *npl* underpants
जाँच *n* check
जाँच करना *v* check
जाँचना *vt* examine
जांघ *n* thigh
जांघिया *npl* boxer shorts, briefs
जागना *v* wake up, awake
जातिवाद *n* racism
जातिवाद करने वाला *n* racist
जातिवादी *adj* racist
जादुई *adj* magic, magical
जादू *n* magic
जादूगर *n* conjurer, magician
जानदार/उत्साहपूर्ण *n* rave
जानना *vt* know
जाना *v* get out ▷ *vi* go
जापानी *adj* Japanese ▷ *n* Japanese
जामुन *n* jambul
जायफल *n* nutmeg
जारी करना *vt* issue
जारी रखना *v* carry on, go on
जारी रखना/करते रहना *vt* keep
जारी रहना *v* continue
जाल *n* net
जालसाज़ी *n* forgery
जाली *n* grid
जाली नकल बनाना *vt* forge
जिज्ञासु *adj* curious
जिज्ञासु/कुतुहली *adj* inquisitive
जितना जल्द हो सके *abbr* asap
जिराफ़ *n* giraffe
जिला *n* district
जिला परिषद *n* district council
जिसका *pron* whose
जिसके/जो *pron* that
जिस तरह *adv* as ... as
जिसे *pron* whom
जीजी *n* elder sister

जीत *n* victory
जीतना *v* win
जीत लेना *vt* conquer
जीना/जीवित रहना *vi* live
जीभ *n* tongue
जीरा *n* cumin
जीर्ण *adj* worn
जीव *n* organism
जीवंत *adj* (व्यक्ति) lively; (रंग, सोच) vivid
जीवन *n* life
जीवन - निर्वाह व्यय *n* cost of living
जीवन रक्षक *adj* life-saving
जीवन रक्षक गार्ड *n* lifeguard
जीवन रक्षक जैकेट *n* life jacket
जीवन रक्षक पेटी *n* lifebelt
जीवन रक्षा नौका *n* lifeboat
जीवन शैली *n* lifestyle
जीवनी *n* biography
जीव - विज्ञान *n* biology
जीवाणु *npl* bacteria
जीवित *adj* alive, live
जुआ *n* gambling
जुआखाना *n* casino
जुआ खेलना/दाँव लगाना *v* gamble
जुआरी *n* gambler
जुकाम के कारण होने वाले छाले *n* cold sore
जुड़वा *n* twin ▷ *adj* twinned
जुड़वा पलंग *npl* twin beds
जुड़ाव *n* bond
जुड़ा हुआ *adj* attached
जुर्म *n* offence
जुलाई *n* July
जुलूस *n* procession
जू *npl* lice
जूठे बर्तन धोना *n* washing-up
जूते का फीता *n* lace
जून *n* June
जेब *n* pocket
जेबकतरा *n* pickpocket
जेबखर्च *n* pocket money
जेबरा *n* zebra
जेल में डालना *vt* jail
जैतून *n* olive
जैतून का तेल *n* olive oil
जैवरसायनिकी *n* biochemistry
जैविक *adj* biological, organic
जैविक प्रतिरूप बनाना *vt* clone
जैसे ही *conj* as
जॉर्जिया *n* Georgia

जॉर्जियाई *adj* Georgian ▷ *n* Georgian
जो कुछ भी *conj* whatever
जो कोई *conj* whoever
जोखिम *n* risk
जोखिम उठाना *vt* risk
जोखिम भरा *adj* risky
जोड़ *n* joint
जोड़ देना *v* combine
जोड़ना *vt* (गणित) add (up) ▷ *v* (कड़ी जोड़ना) link, join
जोड़ा *n* pair
जोतना *vt* plough
जो भी/कोई भी *det* whichever
जोश *n* zest
जौ *n* barley
जौ से बनी शराब *n* malt whisky
जौहरी *n* jeweller
जौहरी बाज़ार *n* jeweller
ज्ञान/अक्लमंदी *n* wisdom
ज्ञापन *n* memo
ज्येष्ठ *adj* elder
ज्योतिषशास्त्र *n* astrology
ज्वार - भाटा *n* tide
ज्वालामुखी *n* volcano
जॉर्डन *n* Jordan
जॉर्डन निवासी *n* Jordanian

झगड़ा *n* quarrel, row
झगड़ा करना *vi* quarrel, row
झड़बेर *n* berry
झपकी *n* nap
झपटना *vt* grab
झमेला *n* fuss
झरना *n* cataract, waterfall
झारखंड *n* Jharkhand
झाँसा *n* bluff
झाँसा देना *v* bluff
झाड़ - झंखाड़ *n* bush
झाड़ना *vt* brush
झाड़ी *n* bush
झाड़ू *n* broom
झाड़ूदार *n* sweeper
झिरी *n* aperture
झींगा *n* prawn
झींगुर *n* cricket
झील *n* lake
झुंड *n* flock
झुकना *vi* bend; (सर झुकाना) bow

झुकना/टेक लगाना *vi* lean
झुकाना/झुकना *v* tip
झुकाना/नीचे करना *vt* lower
झुका हुआ *adj* bent
झुमके *n* earring
झुर्री *n* wrinkle
झुर्रीदार *adj* wrinkled
झूठ *n* lie
झूठा *n* liar
झूठा/पाखंडपूर्ण *adj* insincere
झूठी गवाही *n* perjury
झूलन खटोला *n* hammock
झोंका *n* gust
झोपड़ी *n* hut
झोला *n* carrier bag

ट

टंकण मशीन *n* typewriter
टंकित करना *v* type
टंकी *n* tank
टकराकर नष्ट होना *vi* crash
टकराना *vt* crash
टकसाल *n* mint
टक्कर *n* bump, collision
टक्कर/दुर्घटना *n* crash
टक्कर मारना *vt* ram
टखना *n* ankle
टटोलना *vi* grope
टट्टू *n* pony
टन *n* ton
टमाटर *n* tomato
टमाटर की चटनी *n* tomato sauce
टहनी *n* branch
टाँड़/अटारी *n* loft
टांग/पैर *n* leg
टाइपिस्ट/टंकक *n* typist
टाका *n* (बांग्लादेशी रुपय) taka
टायर के अंदर स्थित हवा भरा ट्यूब *n* inner tube
टालना *vt* put off
टिकट घर *n* box office, ticket office
टिड्डा *n* grasshopper
टिन (धातु) *n* tin
टिप्पणी *n* comment, remark

टिप्पणी करना *v* comment, remark
टीकाकरण *n* vaccination
टीका लगाना *vt* vaccinate
टीसना *vi* throb
टुकड़ा *n* piece
टुकड़े करना *vt* chop
टेनपिन बोलिंग *n* tenpin bowling
टेनिस *n* tennis
टेनिस का मैदान *n* tennis court
टेबल टेनिस *n* table tennis
टैंक *n* tank
टैंकर *n* tanker
टैंपून *n* tampon
टैक्सी *n* taxi
टैक्सी चालक *n* taxi driver
टॉनिक *n* tonic
टॉफ़ी/चीनी की मिठाई *n* toffee
टोंटी *n* tap
टोकन/रसीद *n* token
टोकना *v* interrupt
टोकरी *n* basket
टोगो *n* Togo
टोप *n* hat
टोपी *n* beret, cap
टोली *n* (समूह) party; (पक्ष, दल) team
ट्यूनिशायाई *adj* Tunisian
ट्यूनिशिया *n* Tunisia
ट्यूनिशिया का निवासी *n* Tunisian
ट्यूब *n* tube
ट्रक चालक *n* truck driver
ट्राम - एक गाड़ी *n* tram
ट्रे/तश्तरी *n* tray

ठंडा *adj* frosty
ठंडा करना *vt* chill
ठंडा/सर्द *adj* cold
ठग *n* thug
ठगना *v* rip off
ठसाठस भरा हुआ *adj* jammed
ठहरना *vi* stay
ठिठुराने वाली ठंड *adj* chilly

ठीक *adj* okay
ठीक करना *vt* fix
ठीक - ठाक *adv* all right
▷ *adj* all right
ठीक-ठीक *adv* accurately, precisely
ठीक है *excl* OK!, okay!
ठूंसना *v* cram
ठेकेदार *n* contractor
ठेठ *adj* typical
ठेला *n* trolley
ठोकर खाना/लड़खड़ाना *vi* trip
ठोड़ी *n* chin
ठोस *adj* solid

ड

डकार *n* burp
डकार लेना *vi* burp
डटे रहना *vi* persevere
डर *n* phobia
डराना *vt* frighten
डरावना *adj* frightening
डरावना *adj* hideous
डरावना चलचित्र *n* horror film
डाक *n* mail
डाक कोड *n* postcode
डाक खर्च *n* postage
डाकघर *n* post office
डाक प्रेषण सूची *n* mailing list
डाक मुहर *n* postmark
डाक में डालना *vt* post
डाक विभाग *n* post
डाक्टर *n* doctor
डाकिया *n* postman
डाकिया (महिला) *n* postwoman
डामर *n* tarmac
डिब्बा *n* compartment, container
डींग मारना *vi* boast
डूबना *vi* plunge
डोंगी *n* canoe
डोंगी चालन *n* canoeing
डोमिनिक गणराज्य *n* Dominican Republic
डोलना *v* rock
डोसा *n* Indian savoury pancake
डॉल्फिन *n* dolphin

डेनमार्क *n* Denmark
डैनिश *n* Danish
ड्राइंग पिन *n* thumbtack
ड्राइवर *n* driver

ढ

ढंकना *vt* cover
ढक्कन *n* top
ढक्कन *n* lid
ढह जाना *vi* collapse
ढहाना *vt* pull down
ढालना *vt* pour
ढालू रास्ता *n* ramp
ढीला *adj* loose
ढीला - ढाला *adj* baggy
ढूंढना *vt* look for
ढेर *n* heap, pile
ढेर सारा *n* lot
ढेला/डली *n* lump
ढोंग करना *vt* pretend
ढोलक *n* small drum
ढोना *vt* carry

तंग *adj* tight
तंगहाल *adj* hard up
तंज़ानिया *n* Tanzania
तंज़ानियाई *adj* Tanzanian
तंज़ानियाई नागरिक *n* Tanzanian
तंत्र *n* network
तंदूर/भट्टी *n* oven
तंबाकू *n* tobacco
तंबू *n* tent
तक *prep* until
तकनीक *n* technique
तकनीकी *adj* technical
तकनीशियन/तकनीकविद् *n* technician
तकिया *n* pillow
तकिया का खोल *n* pillowcase
तख़्त *n* bench
तख्ता *n* board
तटबंध *n* embankment
तटरक्षक *n* coastguard
तटस्थ *adj* neutral
तड़ित *n* lightning

ततैया *n* wasp
तत्कालीन *adj* current
तत्कालीन मुद्दे *npl* current affairs
तत्परता से *adv* readily
तत्पश्चात *adv* afterwards
तत्व *n* element
तथापि *adv* nevertheless
तथापि/फिर भी *adv* however
तदनुसार *adv* accordingly
तना *n* trunk
तनाव *n* tension
तनावग्रस्त *adj* tense, uptight
तनावपूर्ण *adj* nerve-racking
तपस्विनी *n* nun
तपेदिक *n* tuberculosis
तपेदिक/क्षय रोग *n* tuberculosis
तब *adv* then
तब तक *prep* till
तबला *n* small tambourine
तमंचा *n* revolver
तमसा *n* brace
तमिल *n* Tamil
तमिलनाडु *n* Tamil Nadu
तमाशबीन *n* onlooker
तय की गई दूरी *n* mileage
तरंगदैर्घ्य *n* wavelength
तरबूज़ *n* watermelon
तरल *n* liquid
तराशना *v* carve
तरीक़ा *n* way
तरीका *n* manner; (पद्धति) method
तरोताज़ा करना *v* freshen up
तर्क *n* argument, point
तर्क करना *vi* argue
तर्कसंगत *adj* logical, rational
तर्जनी *n* index finger
तल *n* base
तलना *vt* fry
तला/पेंदी *n* bottom
तलाश करना/खोजना *vi* hunt
तला हुआ *adj* fried
तल्लीन *adj* preoccupied
तश्तरी *n* plate
तस्मानिया *n* Tasmania
तस्वीर *n* photo; (व्यक्ति की छवि) portrait
तह *n* fold
तह करना *vt* fold
तहकीकात *n* investigation; (औपचारिक) inquest
तहखाना *n* basement, cellar
ताँबा *n* copper
ताइवान *n* Taiwan

ताइवानी *adj* Taiwanese
ताइवानी नागरिक *n* Taiwanese
ताई *n* aunt (father's older brother's wife)
ताऊ *n* uncle (father's older brother)
ताक-झांक करना *vi* pry
ताज महल *n* Taj Mahal
ताज़ा *adj* fresh
ताजिकिस्तान *n* Tajikistan
ताज्जुब करना *vt* wonder
ताड़ का पेड़ *n* palm
तात्कालिक *adj* provisional
तापक *n* (हीटर) heater
तापक पद्धति *n* heating
तापमान *n* temperature
ताबूत *n* coffin
तामचीनी *n* enamel
तानपुरा *n* stringed instrument
ताया *n* uncle (father's older brother)
तार *n* (रस्सा) cable; (बिजली) wire; (संदेश भेजना) telegram; (रस्सी) string
तारे की आकृति *n* star
ताल *n* rhythm
ताल/ध्वनि *n* beat
ताल *n* (लय) rhythm; (तालाब) pond
तालवाद्य *n* percussion
ताला *n* lock, padlock
ताला खोलना *vt* unlock
तालाब *n* pond
ताला लगाना *vt* lock
ताली बजाना *v* clap
ताश *n* card, playing card
ताहिती *n* Tahiti
तिगुना करना/तिगुना होना *v* treble
तिजोरी/छोटी आलमारी *n* locker
तितली *n* butterfly
तिथिपत्र *n* calendar
तिपहिया साइकिल *n* tricycle
तिब्बत *n* Tibet
तिब्बत का निवासी *n* Tibetan
तिब्बती *adj* Tibetan
तिब्बती भाषा *n* Tibetan
तिरपाल *n* canvas, tarpaulin
तिरस्कार *n* contempt
तिरंगा *n* flag
तिरुवनंतपुरम *n* Thiruvananthapuram
तिल *n* mole
तिलचट्टा *n* cockroach
तिहरा *adj* triple

तीखा *adj* hot, spicy
तीतर *n* partridge
तीन *num* three
तीर का चिह्न *n* arrow
तीर्थयात्री *n* pilgrim
तीव्र *adj* (प्रचंड) intense; (शोर) loud; (तेज) sharp
तीस *num* thirty
तीसरा *adj* third
तीसरा भाग *n* third
तीसरे *adv* thirdly
तुंडिका शोथ *n* tonsillitis
तुच्छ/क्षुद्र *adj* trivial
तुच्छ वस्तु *n* trifle
तुनक मिजाज़ *adj* moody
तुनकमिजाज़ *adj* grumpy
तुम *pron* you
तुम खुद *pron* yourselves
तुम्हारा *det* your ▷ *pron* yours
तुरंत *adj* instant
तुरंत/तत्क्षण *adv* instantly
तुरही *n* cornet, trombone
तुरही/तूर्य *n* trumpet
तुर्क *n* Turk
तुर्की *n* Turkey
तुर्की *adj* Turkish
तुर्की भाषा *n* Turkish
तुलना *n* comparison
तुलना करना *vt* compare
तुलसी *n* basil
तुला राशि *n* Libra
तुल्य *adj* comparable
तूफ़ान *n* hurricane
तेंदुआ *n* panther
तेजपत्ता *n* bay leaf
तेज़ करना *v* accelerate
तेज़ हवाओं वाला *adj* windy
तेज़ी का मौसम *n* high season
तेरह *num* thirteen
तेरहवां *adj* thirteenth
तेल *n* oil
तेल का कुंआ *n* oil well
तेल लगाना *vt* oil
तेलुगू *n* Telugu
तेल शोधक कारखाना *n* oil refinery
तैयार *adj* prepared, ready
तैयार करना *vt* prepare
तैयारी *n* preparation
तैराकी की पोशाक *n* bathing suit
तैलीय *adj* greasy
तोंद *n* tummy
तोड़ना *v* break (up)
तोड़ना/किनारे से तोड़ना *vt* chip

तोड़ना/चुनना *vt* pick
तोता *n* parrot
तोरी जैसी सब्ज़ी *n* courgette
तौलना *vt* weigh
तौलिया *n* bath towel, towel
त्याग देना *vt* abandon
त्यागना *vt* quit
त्यागपत्र देना *vi* resign
त्योरी चढ़ाना *vi* frown
त्रि - आयामी *adj* three-dimensional
त्रिकोण *n* triangle
त्रिनिदाद व टोबैगो *n* Trinidad and Tobago
त्रिपुरा *n* Tripura
त्रुटि *n* error
त्वरित *adj* prompt

थ

थकाऊ *adj* tiring
थका - मांदा *adj* exhausted
थका हुआ *adj* tired
थल चिह्न *n* landmark
थाइम *n* thyme
थाईलैंड *n* Thailand
थाईलैंड का निवासी *n* Thai
थाईलैंड की भाषा *n* Thai
थाईलैंड से संबद्ध *adj* Thai
थैला *n* bag
थोक *n* wholesale
थोक का *adj* wholesale
थोड़ा भी *adv* remotely
थोड़े समय *n* while

द

दंगा *n* riot
दंगा करना *vi* riot
दंड *n* penalty
दंड देना *vt* penalize
दंतखोदनी *n* toothpick
दंत चिकित्सालय *n* dentist's surgery
दक्षता से *adv* efficiently
दक्षिण *n* south
दक्षिण अफ़्रीका *n* South Africa
दक्षिण अफ़्रीकी *adj* South African

दक्षिण अमरीका *n* South America
दक्षिण अमरीकी *adj* South American
दक्षिण की ओर *adv* south
दक्षिण कोरिया *n* South Korea
दक्षिण ध्रुव *n* South Pole
दक्षिण-पूर्व *n* southeast
दक्षिणपंथी *adj* right-wing
दक्षिणावर्त *adv* clockwise
दक्षिणी *adj* south; southern
दखलअंदाज़ *adj* nosy
दत्तक *adj* adopted
दत्तक संतान *n* foster child
ददोरा/चकत्ता *n* rash
दफ़्ती/गत्ता *n* hardboard
दबाना *vt* press
दबाव *n* pressure
दबाव डालना *vt* force, pressure
दबे पांव चलना *vi* creep
दम घुटना *v* choke
दमघोंटू *adj* claustrophobic
दम निकाल देना *vt* wind
दमन *n* Daman
दमा *n* asthma
दयनीय *adj* miserable, pathetic
दयनीयता *n* misery
दया *n* mercy, pity
दया करना *vt* pity
दर *n* rate
दरजा/ओहदा *n* rank
दरबान *n* janitor, porter
दरार *n* crack
दरार/भंग *n* fracture
दरियाई घोड़ा *n* hippopotamus
दर्ज करना *vt* record
दर्ज़ी *n* tailor
दर्जा/कोटि *n* grade
दर्द *n* ache, pain
दर्द करना *vi* ache
दर्दनाक *adj* painful ▷ *n* painkiller
दर्द निवारक औषधि *n* aspirin
दर्पण *n* mirror
दर्रा *n* pass
दर्शक *n* viewer
दर्शक व श्रोता *n* audience
दर्शनशास्त्र *n* philosophy
दर्शाना/समझाना *vt* show
दलदल *n* bog, marsh
दलाल *n* broker
दलाली *n* commission
दलिया *n* porridge

द

दवा *n* medicine
दवा की दुकान *n* chemist
दवा की सूई *n* injection
दवा निर्माता/ दवा विक्रेता *n* chemist
दशमलव *adj* decimal
दशहरा *n* Indian festival
दस *num* ten
दस लाख *num* million
दसवां *adj* tenth ▷ *n* tenth
दस्त *n* diarrhoea
दस्ताना *n* glove
दहशत *n* horror
दही *n* yoghurt
दहेज *n* dowry
दामाद *n* son-in-law
दांत *n* tooth
दांत का दर्द *n* toothache
दांत निकलना *vi* teethe
दांत से काटना *v* bite
दांता *n* tooth
दाई *n* midwife
दाएँहत्था *adj* right-handed
दाखिला *n* admission
दाग़ *n* mark
दाढ़ी *n* beard
दाढ़ी वाला *adj* bearded
दादा *n* granddad, grandpa
दादा/दादी/नाना/नानी *npl* grandparents
दादा/नाना *n* grandfather
दादी *n* grandma
दादी/नानी *n* granny
दादी/नानी *n* grandmother
दायां *adj* right
दाल *npl* lentils, pulses
दालचीनी *n* cinnamon
दावत *n* party
दावत करना *vi* party
दावत देना *n* treat
दावा *n* claim
दावा करना *vt* claim
दावा छोड़ना *vt* waive
दावा प्रपत्र *n* claim form
दाहिने हाथ का *adj* right-hand
दिक करना *vt* pester
दिक्सूचक *n* compass
दिखाई देना *vt* appear ▷ *v* look
दिखाना *v* point out, show
दिग्गज *adj* veteran
दिन का समय *n* day
दिनचर्या *n* routine
दिमाग *n* brain
दिल का दौरा *n* heart attack

दिलचस्प *adj* gripping, interesting
दिलचस्पी *n* interest
दिलचस्पी पैदा करना *vt* interest
दिलचस्पी रखने वाला *adj* interested
दिल्ली *n* Delhi
दिल्ली वाले *npl* people from Delhi
दिवालिया *adj* bankrupt
दिवाली *n* Indian religious festival
दिसपुर *n* Dispur
दिसम्बर *n* December
दीपक/कंदील *n* lamp
दीपस्तंभ *n* lamppost
दीर्घ समय तक *adv* long
दीवान *n* couch
दीवार *n* wall
दीवार घड़ी *n* clock
दुआ *n* prayer
दुःखद *adj* tragic
दुःखद घटना *n* tragedy
दुःखी/खेदपूर्ण *adj* sorry
दुःस्वप्न *n* nightmare
दुनिया *n* globe, world
दुर्गा पूजा *n* Hindu festival
दुबला *adj* thin
दुभाषिया *n* interpreter
दुरुस्त करना *vt* rectify
दुर्घटना *n* accident, pile-up
दुर्घटना बीमा *n* accident insurance
दुर्घटना व आपातकक्ष *n* accident and emergency
दुर्दशा/मानसिक पीड़ा *n* wrench
दुर्भाग्य *n* misfortune
दुर्भाग्यवश *adv* unfortunately
दुर्लभ *adj* rare
दुलकी चाल से चलना *vi* canter
दुल्हन *n* bride
दुल्हन की सखी *n* bridesmaid
दुष्ट *adj* evil, wicked
दूतावास *n* consulate
दूध *n* milk
दूध दुहना *vt* milk
दूर *adv* away
दूरबीन *npl* binoculars ▷ *n* telescope
दूरभाष *n* telephone
दूरभाष निर्देशिका *n* telephone directory

दूरसंचार *npl* telecommunications
दूर हटना *vi* go away
दूल्हा *n* bridegroom
दूसरा *adv* else ▷ *adj* second
दूसरे *adv* secondly
दृश्य *adj* visible, visual
दृश्यता *n* visibility
दृष्टि *n* look; (देखने की क्षमता) eyesight
दृष्टिकोण *n* viewpoint
देखना *vi* look ▷ *v* watch
देखने में असफल/चूकना *vt* miss
देखनेवाला *n* observer
देखभाल *n* care
देखभाल करना *vi* care ▷ *vt* look after
देना *vt* give, pass
देय *adj* payable
देर गए *adv* late
देवर *n* brother-in-law (husband's younger brother)
देवरानी *n* sister-in-law (husband's younger sister)
देवदूत *n* angel
देवनागरी *n* Devanagari
देश *n* country
देशभक्त *adj* patriotic
देशांतर *n* longitude
देहरादून *n* Dehradun
देहात/गांव *n* country
दो *num* two
दोनों *det* both ▷ *pron* both
दोनों में से एक *det* either
दोनों में से कोई भी नहीं *pron* neither ▷ *adj* neither
दोपहर *n* afternoon, noon
दोपहर का भोजन *n* lunch
दो बार *adv* twice
दोबारा करना *vt* redo
दोबारा प्रयोग करना *vt* reuse
दोबारा प्राप्त करना *vt* regain
दोबारा फ़ोन करना *v* phone back, ring back
दोलन कुर्सी *n* rocking chair
दोलन घोड़ा *n* rocking horse
दो व्यक्ति या वस्तुएं *det* couple
दोष *n* blame
दोष देना *vt* blame
दोषी *n* culprit
दोषी ठहराना *vt* convict
दो सीट वाली साइकिल *n* tandem
दोस्त *n* mate
दोस्ताना *adj* friendly

दोहराना *vt* repeat
दोहराव *n* repeat
दौड़ *n* (प्रतियोगिता) race; (भागना) run
दौड़ना *vi* run
दौड़पथ *n* racetrack
दौड़ लगाना *v* race
दौरा *n* tour
दौरा करना *v* tour
द्रवित/भावविह्वल *adj* touched
द्वारा *prep* by
द्विफोकसी *npl* bifocals
द्विभाषी *adj* bilingual
द्वीप *n* island
द्वेषपूर्ण *adj* malicious

ध

धक्का देना *v* push
धड़ाका *n* crash
धन *n* money
धनवान *adj* rich, wealthy
धन वापस करना *vt* refund
धन वापसी *n* refund
धनिया *n* coriander
धनुष *n* bow
धन्यवाद! *excl* thanks!
धन्यवाद देना *vt* thank
धमकाना *vt* intimidate
धमकाने वाला *adj* threatening
धमकी/ख़तरा *n* threat
धमकी देना *vt* threaten
धमनी *n* artery
धमाका *n* bang
धर्म *n* religion
धर्मार्थ दुकान *n* charity shop
धर्मार्थ संगठन *n* charity
धागा *n* thread, yarn
धातु *n* metal
धातु का बना हुआ त्रिभुजाकार वाद्ययंत्र *n* triangle
धार *n* blade
धारा *n* current
धाराप्रवाह *adj* fluent
धार्मिक *adj* religious
धावक *n* runner, jogger
धीमी दौड़ *n* jogging
धीरे दौड़ना *vi* jog
धुँधला *adj* gloomy
धुंधला *adj* foggy

धुआँ *npl* exhaust fumes
धुआँरा *n* chimney
धुन *n* melody, tune
धुरी *n* axle
धुलाई *n* rinse
धुलाई के कपड़े *n* washing
धूप का चश्मा *npl* goggles
धूप से काला पड़ा हुआ *adj* tanned
धूप से जला हुआ *n* tan
धूमकेतु *n* comet
धूम्रपान वर्जित *adj* non-smoking
धूर्त *adj* cunning
धृष्ट *adj* cheeky
धैर्य *n* patience
धैर्यवान *adj* patient
धोखा *n* fraud
धोखा देना *vt* betray
धोखेबाज़ *n* crook
धोबी *n* washer man
धोना *vt* rinse, wash
धौंस जमाना *vt* boss around, bully
धौंस जमाने वाला *adj* bossy ▷ *n* bully
ध्यान *n* attention
ध्यान एकाग्र करना *vi* concentrate
ध्यान केंद्रित करना *v* focus
ध्यान देना *vt* notice
ध्यान में रखते हुए *prep* considering
ध्यान रखने वाला *adj* considerate
ध्यान/समाधि *n* meditation
ध्यान से सुनना *vi* listen
ध्रुव *adj* polar
ध्रुवीय भालू *n* polar bear
ध्वनिसंदेश *n* voicemail

नंगे पैर *adj* barefoot
नंगे पैर रहना *adv* barefoot
नई दिल्ली *n* New Delhi
नकद खाता *n* cash register
नकद पेटी *n* till
नकदी *n* cash
नकदी भुगतान मशीन *n* cash dispenser
नकल उतारना *vt* mimic

नकली बाल *n* wig; (पुरुषों के लिए) toupee
नकसीर *n* nosebleed
नकारात्मक *adj* negative ▷ *n* negative
नर्क *n* hell
नर्स *n* nurse
नख कटनी *npl* nail scissors
नख-प्रसाधन *n* manicure
नगर *n* city
नगर केंद्र *n* city centre, town centre
नगर भवन *n* town hall
नगर योजना *n* town planning
नग्न *adj* bare ▷ *n* nude
नज़दीक का *adj* near
नज़र डालना *vi* glance
नज़रिया *n* outlook, perspective
नतीजा *npl* repercussions
नथुना *n* nostril
नदी *n* river
नदी का किनारा *n* bank
ननद/भाभी *n* sister-in-law
नफ़ीरी - एक वाद्य *n* oboe
नब्बे *num* ninety
नम *adj* humid, moist
नमस्कार *excl* hello!
नमस्कार! *excl* hi!
नमी *n* humidity, moisture
नमूना *n* model
नमूना बनाना *vt* model
नम्र *adj* polite
नम्रता *n* politeness
नम्रतापूर्वक *adv* politely
न यह न वह *conj* neither ... nor
नया *adj* new
नरकट *n* reed
नरगिस/कुमुदिनी *n* lily
नरमी से *adv* gently
नरसंहार *n* massacre
नर्क *n* hell
नलसाज़ *n* plumber
नलिका *n* pipe
नली *n* tube
नली/पाइप *n* hose, hosepipe
नवंबर *n* November
नवजात *adj* newborn
नवप्रवर्तन/नई खोज *n* innovation
नवरात्रि *n* festival to honour the Hindu goddess Durga
नववर्ष *n* New Year

नवासा *n* grandson (daughter's son)
नवासी *n* granddaughter (daughter's daughter)
नवाँ *adj* ninth ▷ *n* ninth
नवागंतुक *n* newcomer
नवीनतम *adj* up-to-date
नवीनीकरण करना *vt* renew
नवीनीकृत करना *vt* update
नस *n* nerve
नस्ल *n* breed ▷ *adj* pedigree
नहर *n* canal
नहाना *vi* bathe
न ही *adv* either ▷ *conj* neither
नहीं *adv* no; not
नहीं तो *conj* otherwise
नांद *n* trough
नाइजर *n* Niger
नाइजीरिया *n* Nigeria
नाइजीरियाई *adj* Nigerian ▷ *n* Nigerian
नाई *n* barber
नाई की दुकान *n* hairdresser
नाउम्मीद *adj* hopeless
नाक *n* nose
नाकाम *n* flop
नाखून *n* nail
नागदौना *n* tarragon
नागफनी *n* cactus
नागरिक *n* citizen
नागरिक अधिकार *npl* civil rights
नागरिकता *n* citizenship
नागवार *adj* vile
नागालैंड *n* Nagaland
नाच गा कर धन कमाने वाला *n* busker
नाज़ुक *adj* (दुर्बल) fragile; (सूक्ष्म) tender
नाज़ुक/अत्यंत महत्वपूर्ण *adj* critical
नाटक *n* play
नाटककार *n* playwright
नाट्यगृह *n* theatre
नातिन *n* granddaughter (daughter's daughter)
नाती *n* grandson (daughter's son)
नाथ *n* (भगवान) lord; (मालिक) master; (पति) husband
नाड़ी स्पदंन *n* pulse
नान *n* naan bread
नानबाई *n* baker
नानबाई की दुकान *n* bakery

नापने का फ़ीता *n* tape measure
नाबालिग *n* minor
नाभि *n* belly button, navel
नाम *n* name
नामांकन *n* nomination
नामांकित करना *vt* nominate
नायक *n* hero
नायिका *n* heroine
नारंगी/छोटा संतरा *n* tangerine
नारंगी रंग *n* orange
नाराज़ करना/अपमान करना *vt* offend
नारियल *n* coconut
नारियल पानी *n* coconut water
नाल *n* horseshoe
नाव *n* boat
नाशपाती *n* pear
नाश्ता *n* tea
नास्तिक *n* atheist
निंदा करना *vt* condemn
निःसंदेह *adv* undoubtedly
निकटतम संबंधी *n* next of kin
निकटता *n* proximity
निकटवर्ती *adj* close by
निकट से *adv* closely
निकलना *v* pull out
निकाल देना *v* lay off
निकालना *vt* (छोड़ना) eliminate, exclude; (वापसी) withdraw
निकारागुए *n* Nicaragua
निकारागुआ का निवासी *n* Nicaraguan
निकास द्वार *n* way out
निकोटीन *n* nicotine
निगरानी *n* oversight
निग्रह/रोक *n* reservation
निचला *adj* bottom, lower
निजी *adj* private
निजी अस्पताल *n* nursing home
निजीकरण करना *vt* privatize
निजी रूप से *adv* personally
निजी शिक्षण *n* tuition
निजी संपत्ति *n* private property
निजी सहायक *n* personal assistant
नितंब *n* backside, bottom; (कूल्हा) hip
नितम्ब *npl* buttocks
निद्रामग्न *adj* asleep

निर्देशक *n* director
निधि *npl* funds
निपटना *vi* cope ▷ *vt* tackle
निबंध *n* essay
नियंत्रित करना *vt* control
नियम *n* rule
नियमित *adj* regular
नियमित रूप से *adv* regularly
नियमित सफर करने वाले *n* commuter
नियमों का कड़ाई से पालन करवाना *vt* crack down on
नियमोल्लंघन *n* foul
नियुक्त करना *vt* appoint, employ
नियुक्ति *n* appointment
नियोक्ता *n* employer
निरंतर *adj* constant, continual
निरंतर रूप से *adv* constantly, continually
निरसन *n* cancellation
निराश करना *vt* let down
निराशाजनक *adj* bleak
निराशावादी *n* pessimist ▷ *adj* pessimistic
निरीक्षक *n* (सर्वेक्षक) inspector; (परीक्षा, आदि) invigilator
निरीक्षण करना *vt* inspect
निर्गामी *adj* outgoing
निर्जन *adj* uninhabited
निर्णय *n* verdict
निर्णय करना *vt* judge
निर्णायक समिति *n* jury
निर्देश *npl* instructions
निर्देश देना *vt* instruct
निर्देश पुस्तिका *n* handbook, manual
निर्देशित दौरा *n* guided tour
निर्भर होना *vt* lean on
निर्माण *n* construction
निर्माण करना *vt* build, construct
निर्माण करना/स्थापना करना *vt* put up
निर्माता *n* manufacturer, producer
निर्माता/ब्रांड *n* make
निर्यात *n* export
निर्यात करना *v* export
निर्वाचक मंडल *n* electorate
निर्वाचन करना *vt* elect

निर्वाचन क्षेत्र *n* constituency
निर्वासन *n* exile
निर्विवाद *adj* undisputed
निवासी *n* inhabitant, resident
निवेदन *n* request
निवेदन करना *vt* request
निवेश *n* investment
निवेशक *n* investor
निवेश करना *v* invest
निशान *n* mark
निश्चिंत *adj* relaxed
निश्चित *adj* certain
निश्चित/एकदम सही *adj* precise
निश्चितता *n* certainty
निश्चित रूप से *adv* certainly
निश्चेतक *n* anaesthetic
निषिद्ध *adj* prohibited
निषिद्ध/वर्जित *adj* taboo
निषेध *n* veto
निषेध करना *vt* prohibit
निष्कर्ष *n* conclusion
निष्कर्ष निकालना *vt* conclude
निष्कासित करना *vt* expel
निष्क्रिय *adj* passive
निष्प्रभ *adj* pale
नींद न आने की बीमारी *n* insomnia
नींबू *n* (पीली नींबू) lemon; (हरी नींबू) lime
नींबू का शर्बत/शिकंजी *n* lemonade
नींव *npl* foundations
नीचा *adj* low
नीचे *adv* below, underneath
नीचे *prep* beneath
नीचे झुकना/उकड़ूँ बैठना *vi* crouch down
नीम *n* neem
नीदरलैंड *npl* Netherlands
नीदरलैंड की भाषा *n* Dutch
नीरस/उबाऊ *adj* monotonous
नीला *adj* blue
नीलामी *n* auction
नुकसान *n* loss
नुस्खा *n* formula
नुस्खा लिखना *vt* prescribe ▷ *n* prescription
नृविज्ञान *n* anthropology
नृशंस *adj* brutal
नेक *adj* good-natured
नेता *n* leader
नेतृत्व करना *vt* head

नेतृत्व करना/ले जाना *vt* lead
नेत्रहीन *adj* blind
नेमि/गोलाकार किनारा *n* rim
नेवला *n* weasel
नेपाल *n* Nepal
नेपाली *n* Nepali
नैतिक *adj* ethical, moral
नैतिक मूल्य/नैतिक शिक्षा *n* moral
नोक *n* point, tip
नौ *num* nine
नौकरशाही *n* bureaucracy
नौकरानी *n* maid
नौकरी *n* job
नौका दौड़ *n* rowing
नौसिखिया *n* beginner ▷ *adj* green
नौसिखिया चालक *n* learner driver
नौसेना *n* navy
नौसैनिक *adj* naval
नॉर्वे *n* Norway
न्याय *n* justice
न्यायाधिकरण *n* tribunal
न्यायाधीश *n* judge, magistrate
न्यायालय *n* court
न्यूमोनिया *n* pneumonia
न्यूज़ीलैंड *n* New Zealand
न्यूनतम *adj* minimal

प

पंक्ति *n* rank, row
पंख *n* wing
पंजा *n* (पक्षी) claw; (पशु) paw
पंजाब *n* Punjab
पंजाब राज्य *n* Punjab Rajya
पंजाबी *n* person from Punjab, Punjabi
पंजिका *n* register
पंजीकरण *n* registration
पंजीकरण कार्यालय *n* registry office
पंजीकृत *adj* registered
पंजीकृत करना *vi* register
पंडित *n* learned person
पंप *n* pump
पंसारी *n* grocer
पंसारी की दुकान *n* grocer
पाँच *num* five

पाँचवाँ *adj* fifth
पकड़ना *vt* catch; (कसकर पकड़ना) grasp; (थामना) hold
पकड़ना/लपक लेना *vt* catch
पकड़े रखना *v* hold on
पकाना *v* cook
पका-पकाया *adj* ready-cooked
पका हुआ *adj* ripe
पक्ष *n* side
पक्षपात *n* prejudice
पक्षपातपूर्ण *adj* biased, prejudiced
पक्ष-प्रचार करना *vi* canvass
पक्षी *n* bird
पखवाड़ा *n* fortnight
पगडंडी *n* track
पचास *num* fifty
पछतावा *n* remorse
पछतावा करना *vt* regret
पछतावा/खेद *n* regret
पटक देना *v* bang
पट्टा/ठेका *n* lease
पट्टी *n* bandage
पट्टी बाँधना *vt* bandage
पट्टे/ठेके पर देना *vt* lease
पड़ोस *n* neighbourhood
पड़ोसन *n* female neighbour
पड़ोसी *n* neighbour
पढ़ना *v* read
पतझड़ *n* autumn
पतला *adj* thin
पतलून *npl* trousers
पतले बिस्कुट *n* wafer
पतवार *n* oar
पता *n* address
पता पुस्तिका *n* address book
पता लगाना *v* explore
पति *n* husband
पत्तर/चद्दर *n* sheet
पत्तागोभी *n* cabbage
पत्ती *n* leaf
पत्ते बांटना *v* deal
पत्थर/कंकड़ *n* stone
पत्नी *n* wife
पत्र *n* letter
पत्रक/पुस्तिका *n* leaflet
पत्रकार *n* journalist
पत्रकारिता *n* journalism
पत्र पेटी *n* postbox
पत्र मित्र *n* penfriend
पत्राचार *n* correspondence
पत्रिका *n* magazine
पथ *n* course

पद *n* post
पदक *n* (प्रतियोगिता में) medal; (भूषण) medallion
पदचिह्न *n* footprint
पदयात्रा *n* tramp
पदाधिकारी *n* officer
पदावनत करना *vt* relegate
पनामा *n* Panama
पनीर *n* cottage cheese
पन्द्रह *num* fifteen
पनडुब्बी *n* submarine
पन्नी *n* foil
पणजी *n* Panaji
पटना *n* Patna
पब्लिक स्कूल *n* public school
पर *prep* onto
परंपरा *n* tradition
पर/के ऊपर *prep* on
पर/के यहां *prep* at
परखनली *n* test tube
परखना *v* try out
परखना/जांचना *vt* test
पर गुज़ारा करना *v* live on
परत *n* layer
परदादा/परनाना *n* great-grandfather
परदादी/परनानी *n* great-grandmother
पर नज़र फेरना *vi* look at
पर निर्भर होना *vt* rely on
परमाणविक *adj* atomic
परमाणु *n* atom
परमाणु बम *n* atom bomb
परमाणु भट्टी *n* reactor
परमानंद *n* bliss, ecstasy
परवाह करना *vi* care
परवाह करने वाला *adj* caring
पर से *prep* off
पराग *n* pollen
परागज ज्वर *n* hay fever
पराचिकित्सक *n* paramedic
पराजित *n* loser
पराठा *n* Indian bread
परास्नातक *n* postgraduate
परिकलक *n* calculator
परिचय कराना *vt* introduce
परिच्छेद *n* clause, paragraph
परिणाम *n* (नतीजा) consequence; outcome
परिणाम निकलना *vi* result
परिणामस्वरूप *adv* consequently
परिधान *n* clothing
परिपक्व *adj* mature
परिपथ *n* circuit

परिमाणित करना *vt* quantify
परिमित *adj* qualified
परियोजना *n* project
परिरक्षक *n* preservative
परिवर्तन *n* change
परिवर्तनशील *adj* variable
परिवर्तनीय *adj* (मौसम, मनोदशा आदि) changeable; (मुद्रा, आदि) convertible
परिवर्तित करना *v* convert
परिवहन *n* transport
परिवार *n* household
परिशुद्धता *n* accuracy
परिषद *n* council
परिषद भवन *n* council house
परिसंपत्ति *n* asset
परिसर *n* campus ▷ *npl* premises
परिस्थिति *npl* circumstances
परिहास *n* humour
परिहास/बुद्धि तीक्ष्णता *n* wit
परीक्षक *n* examiner
परीक्षण *n* check-up, test
परीक्षण अवधि *n* trial period
परीक्षा *n* exam, examination
परीक्षा/परख *n* test
परेड/अभिमुख प्रयाण *n* parade
परेशान *adj* upset
परेशान करना *vt* upset
परेशानी *n* trouble
परेशानी उठाना *v* bother
पर्दा *n* curtain
पर्यंत *prep* till
पर्यटक *n* tourist
पर्यटन *n* tourism
पर्यटन कार्यालय *n* tourist office
पर्यटन गाइड *n* tour guide
पर्यटन पुस्तिका *n* guidebook
पर्यवेक्षक *n* supervisor
पर्याप्त *det* enough ▷ *pron* enough
पर्यावरण अनुकूल *adj* environmentally friendly
पर्यावरण संबंधी *adj* environmental
पर्वत *n* mountain
पर्वतारोहण *n* mountaineering
पर्वतारोही *n* mountaineer
पर्वतीय *adj* mountainous
पलंगपोश *n* bedspread

प

पलक *n* eyelid
पलक झपकना *v* blink
पलट देना *v* capsize
पलटन *n* regiment
पल भर के लिए *adv* momentarily
पलस्तर *n* plaster
पलायन *n* escape
पवनचक्की *n* windmill
पवन वीणा *n* harp
पवित्र *adj* holy
पशु *n* animal
पशुचिकित्सक *n* vet
पश्चिम *n* west
पश्चिम की ओर *adv* west
पश्चिमी *adj* west, western
पश्चिम बंगाल *n* West Bengal
पश्चिमोन्मुख *adj* westbound
पसंद करना *vt* like; (प्यार) love
पसली *n* rib
पसीना *n* perspiration
पहचानना *vt* pick out, recognize
पहचानने योग्य *adj* recognizable
पहनकर देखना *vt* try on
पहनना *vt* wear
पहरेदार *n* watchman
पहरेदारी करना *vt* guard
पहल *n* initiative
पहला *adj* first
पहला *n* first
पहलू *n* aspect
पहले *adv* before, earlier; (भूतकाल) ago; (भूतपूर्व) formerly, previously
पहले करना *v* move forward
पहले से *adv* beforehand
पहले से रिकॉर्ड किया गया *adj* canned
पहले से ही *adv* already
पहाड़ी *n* hill
पहाड़ी प्रदेशों की सैर *n* hill-walking
पहिया *n* wheel
पहियेदार कुर्सी *n* wheelchair
पहुँचना *v* get in
पहुच *n* access
पहुचना *vi* arrive ▷ *vt* reach
पहुचने योग्य *adj* accessible
पहुच प्राप्त करना *vt* access
पहेली *n* puzzle
पांडुलिपि *n* manuscript
पाइलट लाइट *n* pilot light
पाउण्ड *n* pound
पाउण्ड स्टर्लिंग *n* pound sterling

पाक कला *n* cookery
पाक कला की पुस्तक *n* cookery book
पाकिस्तान *n* Pakistan
पाकिस्तानी *adj* Pakistani ▷ *n* Pakistani
पागल *adj* insane, mad ▷ *n* lunatic
पागलपन *n* madness
पागलों की तरह *adv* madly
पाठ *n* lesson
पाठ्य *n* text
पाठक *n* reader
पाठ संदेश *n* text message
पाठ संदेश भेजना *vt* text
पाठ्यक्रम *n* curriculum
पाठ्यपुस्तक *n* textbook
पात्र *n* pot
पान की दुकान *n* tobacconist
पाना *vt* get
पानी *n* water
पानी के रंग *n* watercolour
पाने की कोशिश करना *vt* pursue
पाबंद *adj* punctual
पाया/गोड़ा *n* leg
पारंपरिक *adj* traditional; (व्यावहारिक) conventional
पार करना *vt* cross
पार करना/गुज़रना *vt* pass
पारदर्शक कागज़ *n* tracing paper
पारदर्शी *adj* transparent
पार - पथ *n* crossing
पार पथ *n* pelican crossing
पारवहन *n* transit
पारस्परिक *adj* mutual
पारा *n* mercury
पारिस्थितिक *adj* ecological
पारिस्थितिकी *n* ecology
पार्षद *n* councillor
पार्सल/पुलिंदा *n* parcel
पार्सली *n* parsley
पालक *n* spinach
पालतू *n* pet ▷ *adj* tame
पालन करना *vt* carry out
पालन - पोषण *n* upbringing
पालन - पोषण करना *vt* foster
पालन-पोषण करना *vt* bring up
पालना *vt* breed ▷ *n* cot, cradle
पाल नौका *n* yacht
पाला/तुषार *n* frost
पाव *n* bun

पाव *n* three quarters
पावरोटी *n* bread
पास आना *v* come up
पास/पार पत्र *n* pass
पास में *adv* close, nearby
पास वाला *adj* nearby
पास/समीप *prep* near
पास से *adv* near
पिंगल फल/कर्नेल *n* hazelnut
पिंजड़ा *n* cage
पिंडली *n* calf
पिकनिक/उद्यान भोज *n* picnic
पिक्सेल/बिंदु *n* pixel
पिघलना *vi* melt
पिघलाना *vt* melt
पिछला *adj* previous; (किसी के पहले) last
पिछला हिस्सा *n* rear
पिछवाड़ा *n* back
पिछवाड़े होना *vi* back
पिता *n* daddy, father
पितृत्व अवकाश *n* paternity leave
पित्ताशय *n* gall bladder
पित्ताश्म *n* gallstone
पिन संख्या *n* PIN
पिपरमिंट *n* peppermint
पियानो वादक *n* pianist
पिल्ला *n* puppy
पिस्तौल *n* pistol
पीछा *n* chase
पीछा करना *vt* chase ▷ *v* go after
पीछे *adv* behind
पीछे का *adj* back
पीछे की ओर *adv* back, backwards ▷ *n* reverse
पीछे मुड़ना/पीछे मोड़ना *v* turn back
पीछे लौटना *vt* retrace
पीछे हटना *v* back out, move back
पीछे होना *vi* lag behind
पीटना *vt* beat
पीठ *n* back
पीठ दर्द *n* back pain
पीढ़ी *n* generation
पीतचटकी *n* canary
पीतल *n* brass
पीतल के तूर्य वाद्य *n* brass band
पीतसेवती *n* primrose
पीप/मवाद *n* pus
पीपल *n* sacred fig
पीपा *n* barrel
पीला *adj* yellow

पीलापन लिए सफेद रंग *adj* cream
पीलिया/पांडुरोग *n* jaundice
पीसना *vt* grind
पुकारना/नाम देना *vt* call
पुटक *n* cyst
पुदीना *n* mint
पुडुचेरी *n* Puducherry
पुनः *adv* again
पुनःप्रदर्शन *n* replay
पुनःप्रदर्शित करना *vt* replay
पुनरावर्तन *n* relapse
पुनरावर्ती *adj* recurring
पुनरावृत्तीय *adj* repetitive
पुनर्गठन *vt* restructure
पुनर्चक्रण *n* recycling
पुनर्जीवित करना *v* revive
पुनर्निर्माण *n* remake
पुनर्निर्मित करना *vt* rebuild
पुनर्भुगतान करना *vt* reimburse
पुनर्मिलन *n* reunion
पुनर्विचार करना *v* reconsider
पुनर्विवाह करना *vi* remarry
पुनश्चर्या पाठ्यक्रम *n* refresher course
पुत्रवधू *n* daughter-in-law
पुत्री *n* daughter
पुरस्कार *n* award, prize
पुरस्कार विजेता *n* prizewinner
पुरस्कार वितरण *n* prize-giving
पुरातत्व विज्ञान *n* archaeology
पुरातत्वविद् *n* archaeologist
पुराना *adj* old
पुराने चलन का *adj* old-fashioned
पुरालेख *n* archive
पुरुष *adj* male ▷ *n* male
पुरुष मित्र *n* boyfriend
पुरुष शौचालय *n* gents
पुर्तगाल *n* Portugal
पुर्तगाली *adj* Portuguese ▷ *n* Portuguese
पुल *n* bridge
पुलाव जैसा पकवान *n* casserole
पुलिंदा *n* package, packet
पुलिस *n* police
पुलिस अधिकारी *n* police officer
पुलिस चौकी *n* police station
पुलिसवाला *n* policeman
पुलिसवाली *n* policewoman

पुष्टि *n* confirmation
पुष्टि करना *vt* confirm
पुष्प *n* blossom
पुष्पविक्रेता *n* florist
पुष्पित होना *vi* flower
पुस्तक चिह्न *n* bookmark
पुस्तकालय *n* library
पुस्तकालयाध्यक्ष *n* librarian
पुस्तिका *n* booklet
पूछ *n* tail
पूंजी *n* capital
पूंजीवाद *n* capitalism
पूछताछ *n* enquiry, inquiry
पूछताछ करना *v* inquire ▷ *vt* interrogate
पूछताछ कार्यालय *n* inquiries office
पूछताछ मेज *n* inquiry desk
पूछना *vt* ask ▷ *v* enquire
पूजा करना *v* worship
पूरक *adj* complementary
पूरा *adj* entire
पूरा करना *vt* fulfil
पूरी तरह से *adv* wide
पूरी तरह से/अच्छी तरह से *adv* thoroughly
पूर्ण *adj* complete
पूर्ण इकाई *n* whole
पूर्णकालिक *adj* full-time
पूर्णकालिक रूप से *adv* full-time
पूर्णतया *adv* completely, fully
पूर्णविराम *n* full stop
पूर्णिमा *n* full moon
पूर्व *n* east
पूर्व एशिया *n* Orient
पूर्व एशियाई *adj* oriental
पूर्व की ओर *adv* east
पूर्वज *n* ancestor
पूर्वनिश्चित मुलाकात *n* rendezvous
पूर्व - पति *n* ex-husband
पूर्व पत्नी *n* ex-wife
पूर्ववर्ती *n* predecessor
पूर्वसंध्या *n* eve
पूर्व सूचना *n* notice
पूर्वस्नातक *n* undergraduate
पूर्वानुमेय *adj* predictable
पूर्वाभास *n* premonition
पूर्वाभिमुख *adj* eastbound
पूर्वाभ्यास *n* rehearsal
पूर्वाभ्यास करना *v* rehearse
पूर्वी *adj* east, eastern
पृथक *adj* isolated
पृथ्वी *n* earth
पृष्ठ *n* page

पृष्ठभूमि *n* background
पेंग्विन *n* penguin
पेंशन/निवृत्ति वेतन *n* pension
पेंशनभोगी *n* pensioner
पेंसिल *n* pencil
पेचीदा *adj* puzzling; (छली) tricky
पेट *n* abdomen, belly
पेट संबंधी *adj* coeliac
पेटा/पेंद *n* hull
पेटी *n* case
पेटीकोट *n* underskirt, petticoat
पेड़ *n* tree
पेनिसिलीन *n* penicillin
पेयजल *n* drinking water
पेय पीने की नली *n* straw
पेरू *n* Peru
पेरु से संबद्ध *adj* Peruvian
पेश करना *vt* offer ▷ *v* put forward
पेशगी *n* advance
पेशबंद *n* apron
पेशा *n* profession
पेशी/स्नायु *n* tendon
पेशेवर *adj* professional
पेशेवर ढंग से *adv* professionally
पेशेवर व्यक्ति *n* professional
पेस्ट करना/लगाना (कंप्यूटर के अर्थ में) *vt* paste
पैजामा *npl* pyjamas
पैदल पार पथ *n* pedestrian crossing
पैदल पारपथ *n* zebra crossing
पैदल यात्री सीमा *n* pedestrian precinct
पैदल रास्ता *n* footpath, walkway
पैदल सेना *n* infantry
पैदल सैर *n* hike, hiking
पैदाइशी *adj* born
पैबंद *n* patch
पैबंद लगा हुआ *adj* patched
पैमाना *n* gauge; scale
पैर *n* foot
पैर की अंगुलियां *n* toe
पैराग्वे *n* Paraguay
पैराग्वे से संबद्ध *adj* Paraguayan
पैराशूट/हवाई छतरी *n* parachute
पैसा एकत्र करना *v* club together
पॉप अप *n* pop-up

पोंगल *n* Tamil harvest festival
पोंछना *v* mop up, wipe up ▷ *vt* wipe
पोंछा *n* cloth, mop
पोतविहार *n* cruise
पोता/नाती *n* grandson
पोता/पोती/नाती/नातिन *n* grandchild
पोती/नातिन *n* granddaughter
पोर्ट ब्लेयर *n* Port Blair
पोल वॉल्ट *n* pole vault
पोलिनेशिया *n* Polynesia
पोलिनेशियाई *adj* Polynesian ▷ *n* Polynesian
पोलियो *n* polio
पोलिश *adj* Polish
पोलैण्ड *n* Poland
पोलैण्ड से संबद्ध *adj* Polish
पोशाक *npl* clothes ▷ *n* costume, outfit
पोषक *adj* nutritious
पोषक तत्व *n* nutrient
पोषण *n* nutrition
पोस्टकार्ड *n* postcard
पौध बिक्री केंद्र *n* garden centre
पौधा *n* plant
पौधा घर *n* greenhouse
पौधा रोपना *vt* plant
पौना किलो *n* three quarters of a kilo
पौराणिक कथाएँ *n* mythology
पौलैण्डवासी *n* Pole
प्याज़ *n* onion
प्यार करना *vt* love
प्याला *n* (छोटा) cup; (बड़ा) mug
प्यास *n* thirst
प्यासा *adj* thirsty
प्योर्टो रिको *n* Puerto Rico
प्लाज़्मा टी वी *n* plasma TV
प्रकट करना *vt* reveal
प्रकरण *n* episode
प्रकार *n* form, type
प्रकाश *n* light
प्रकाशक *n* publisher
प्रकाशन *n* publication
प्रकाशमय/उजाला *adj* light
प्रकाश व्यवस्था *n* lighting
प्रकाश स्तंभ *n* lighthouse
प्रकाशित करना *vt* publish
प्रकृति *n* nature
प्रकृतिवादी *n* naturalist
प्रकोप *n* outbreak
प्रक्रिया *n* process

प्रक्षेपक/प्रोजेक्टर *n* projector
प्रक्षेपास्त्र *n* missile
प्रक्षेपित करना *vt* launch
प्रख्यात *adj* renowned
प्रगति *n* progress
प्रगति विवरण *n* report
प्रचलन *n* trend
प्रचार *n* publicity
प्रचार करना *n* propaganda
प्रचुरता *n* plenty
प्रजाति/मूल *n* race
प्रजातीय *adj* racial
प्रजातीय या संस्कृति संबंधी *adj* ethnic
प्रणाली *n* apparatus
प्रति *n* copy ▷ *prep* per
प्रतिकूल *adj* unfavourable
प्रतिकूलता *n* contrary
प्रतिकृति *n* copy, replica
प्रतिकृति बनाना *vt* copy
प्रतिक्रिया *n* reaction, response
प्रतिक्रिया करना *vi* react
प्रतिक्रिया देना *vi* respond
प्रति घंटे की *adj* hourly
प्रतिघात करना *vi* backfire
प्रतिजैविक *n* antibiotic
प्रतिदीप्त *adj* fluorescent
प्रतिद्वन्द्विता *n* rivalry
प्रतिद्वन्द्वी *adj* rival ▷ *n* rival
प्रतिध्वनि/गूंज *n* echo
प्रतिनिधि *n* agent ▷ *adj* representative
प्रतिनिधित्व करना *vt* represent
प्रतिबंध *n* ban
प्रतिबंध लगाना *vt* ban
प्रतिबंधित *adj* banned
प्रतिबिंब *n* reflection
प्रतिबिंबित करना/दर्शाना *vt* reflect
प्रतिभा *n* talent
प्रतिभावान *adj* (प्रवीण) ingenious; (होनहार) talented
प्रतिभाशाली *adj* gifted
प्रतिभू/ज़मानत *n* guarantee
प्रतियोगिता *n* championship, contest
प्रतियोगी *n* contestant
प्रतिरक्षी *n* antibody
प्रतिरूप *n* clone
प्रतिरोध *vt* resist ▷ *n* resistance
प्रतिरोध करना *vt* resit
प्रतिलाभ *n* return

प्रति वर्ष *adv* yearly
प्रतिशत *adv* per cent
प्रतिशतता *n* percentage
प्रतिशोध *n* revenge
प्रतिष्ठा *n* (इज्जत) prestige; (नेकनामी) reputation
प्रतिष्ठापूर्ण *adj* prestigious
प्रतिष्ठित *adj* reputable
प्रतिस्थापन *n* replacement
प्रतिस्थापित करना *vt* replace
प्रतिस्पर्द्धा *n* competition
प्रतिस्पर्द्धा करना *vi* compete
प्रतिस्पर्द्धात्मक *adj* competitive
प्रतिस्पर्द्धी *n* competitor
प्रतिस्वेदक *n* antiperspirant
प्रतीक चिह्न *n* logo
प्रतीक्षालय *n* waiting room
प्रतीक्षा सूची *n* waiting list
प्रत्यय पत्र *npl* credentials
प्रत्यारोपण *n* transplant
प्रत्येक *det* each, either ▷ *pron* each ▷ *adj* every
प्रत्येक व्यक्ति *pron* everybody
प्रथम प्रदर्शन *n* premiere
प्रदर्शन *n* performance
प्रदर्शनी *n* exhibition
प्रदान करना *vt* (उपहार) present; (देना) provide
प्रदूषण *n* pollution
प्रदूषित *adj* polluted
प्रदूषित करना *vt* pollute
प्रधान कार्यालय *n* head office
प्रधान गिरजाघर *n* cathedral
प्रधानमंत्री *n* prime minister
प्रधानाचार्य *n* headteacher, principal
प्रबंध *n* arrangement
प्रबंधक *n* manager
प्रबंध करना *v* arrange
प्रबंधकर्ता *n* receiver
प्रबंधन *n* management
प्रबंधन करना *vt* manage
प्रबंध निदेशक *n* managing director
प्रभाव *n* effect, influence
प्रभावित करना *vt* affect, influence
प्रभावी *adj* effective
प्रभावी रूप से *adv* effectively
प्रभुत्व *n* control
प्रमाण *n* proof
प्रमाणपत्र *n* certificate
प्रमुख *adj* chief

प्रयत्न *n* try
प्रयाण *n* march
प्रयाण करना *v* march
प्रयास *n* attempt, effort
प्रयास करना *vt* attempt
▷ *vi* try
प्रयुक्त *adj* used
प्रयोग *n* experiment
प्रयोगकर्ता *n* user
प्रयोगशाला *n* laboratory
प्रवसन *n* migration
प्रवासगमन करना *vi* emigrate
प्रवाह/धारा *n* current
प्रविष्टि *n* entry
प्रवृत्त होना *vi* tend
प्रवृत्ति *n* tendency
प्रवेश *n* entrance
प्रवेश कक्ष *n* hall
प्रवेश करना *v* enter
प्रवेश द्वार *n* way in
प्रवेश/प्रवेश की आज्ञा *n* admittance
प्रवेश शुल्क *n* entrance fee
प्रशंसा करना *vt* compliment, praise
प्रशंसात्मक *adj* complimentary
प्रशंसोक्ति *n* compliment
प्रशांत महासागर *n* Pacific Ocean
प्रशासन *n* administration
प्रशासनिक *adj* administrative
प्रशिक्षक *n* coach, trainer
प्रशिक्षक/शिक्षक *n* instructor
प्रशिक्षण *n* training
प्रशिक्षण पाठ्यक्रम *n* training course
प्रशिक्षित *adj* trained
प्रशिक्षु *n* trainee
प्रश्न *n* query, question
प्रश्न करना *vt* query, question
प्रश्नवाचक चिह्न *n* question mark
प्रश्नावली *n* questionnaire
प्रश्नोत्तरी *n* quiz
प्रसतुतकर्ता *n* presenter
प्रसन्न *adj* pleased
प्रसन्नतापूर्वक *adv* happily
प्रसवपूर्व *adj* antenatal
प्रसाधन थैली *n* toilet bag
प्रसाधनालय *n* beauty salon
प्रसारण *n* broadcast
प्रसारण करना *v* broadcast
प्रस्ताव *n* offer, proposal

प

प्रस्तावित करना *vt* propose
प्रस्तुति *n* presentation
प्रस्थान *n* exit
प्रहसन *n* comedy
प्रहार *n* blow
प्रहार करना *vt* bash
प्रांगण *n* courtyard
प्राकृतिक गैस *n* natural gas
प्राकृतिक दृश्य *n* landscape
प्राकृतिक संसाधन *npl* natural resources
प्रागैतिहासिक *adj* prehistoric
प्राचीन *adj* ancient
प्राचीन वस्तु *n* antique
प्राणघातक *adj* (अर्बुद) malignant; (कैंसर, रोग) terminal
प्राणदंड *n* execution
प्राणदंड देना *vt* execute
प्राणि विज्ञान *n* zoology
प्राणी *n* creature
प्राथमिक *adj* primary
प्राथमिकता *n* priority
प्राथमिक पाठशाला *n* primary school
प्राधिकृत करना *vt* authorize
प्राध्यापक *n* professor
प्राप्त करना *vt* receive
प्राप्तकर्ता *n* recipient
प्रायद्वीप *n* peninsula
प्रारंभ/परिचय *n* introduction
प्रारूप *n* format
प्रार्थना *n* prayer
प्रार्थना करना *vi* pray
प्रासंगिक *adj* relevant
प्रेम *n* love; (रूमानी) romance
प्रेमिका *n* girlfriend
प्रेरणा *n* motivation
प्रेरित *adj* motivated
प्रेषित करना *vt* mail
प्रेस *n* press
प्रेसवाला *n* journalist
प्रोटीन *n* protein
प्रोत्साहक *adj* encouraging
प्रोत्साहन *n* encouragement
प्रोत्साहित करना *vt* encourage
प्रौढ़ विद्यार्थी *n* mature student
प्रौढ़ शिक्षा *n* adult education
प्रौद्योगिक/तकनीकी *adj* technological
प्रौद्योगिकी/तकनीक *n* technology
प्लास्टिक सर्जरी *n* plastic surgery

फ

फंदा/पिंजरा *n* trap
फटना *v* go off
फफूँद *n* mould
फफूंद लगा हुआ *adj* mouldy
फफोला *n* blister
फरजंज वृक्ष *n* maple
फरवरी *n* February
फल *n* fruit
फल का रस *n* fruit juice
फली *n* bean
फलों का सलाद *n* fruit salad
फसल *n* crop, harvest
फसल काटना *vt* harvest
फिल्मी गाने *n* film song
फिल्म स्टार *n* film star
फ़टकारना/झिड़कना *vt* tell off
फ़र्श *n* floor
फ़लक *n* plaque
फ़व्वारा *n* fountain
फ़ाइल में नत्थी करना *vt* file
फ़ायदा *n* advantage
फ़ारसी *adj* Persian
फ़िक्र *n* anxiety
फ़िजी *n* Fiji
फ़िरोज़ा *adj* turquoise
फ़िनलैंड *n* Finland
फ़िलिपींज *n* Phillipines
फ़िलीपिनी *adj* Filipino
फ़िलिस्तीन *n* Palestine
फ़िलिस्तीनी *adj* Palestinian ▷ *n* Palestinian
फ़ुटबॉल *n* football
फ़ुटबॉल खिलाड़ी *n* footballer
फ़ुटबॉल प्रतियोगिता *n* football match
फूफा *n* uncle (father's sister's husband)
फूफी *n* aunt (father's sister)
फ़ुर्सत *n* leisure
फ़ैशनेबल/नए चलन का *adj* trendy
फ़ॉर्मैट करना *vt* format
फ़ोन करना *v* call, ring up ▷ *vt* ring
फ़ोन की घंटी *n* ringtone
फ़ोन रखना *v* hang up
फ़ौज *adj* military
फ़्रांस *n* France

फ़्रांसीसी *adj* French ▷ *n* French
फ़्रांसीसी पुरुष *n* Frenchman
फ़्रांसीसी महिला *n* Frenchwoman
फ़्रिज *n* fridge
फ़्री किक *n* free kick
फ़्रीज़र *n* freezer
फाटक *n* gate
फाड़ना *v* rip, rip up ▷ *vt* tear
फाड़ना/चीरना *vt* take apart
फिर तरतीब देना *vt* reorganize
फिरती/छूट *n* rebate
फिर/बाद में *conj* then
फिर भी *adv* anyway
फिर से आरंभ करना *v* resume
फिर से आवेशित करना/पुनःपूरण *vt* recharge
फिर से भरना *vt* refill
फिर से सजाना *v* redecorate
फिरौती *n* ransom
फ्रिंज *n* fringe
फीका *adj* dull
फीता *n* band, ribbon
फुदकना *vi* hop
फुर्तीला *adj* quick
फुसफुसाना *v* whisper
फूंक मारना *vt* blow
फूटना *v* burst
फूल *n* flower
फूलगोभी *n* cauliflower
फूहड़ *adj* clumsy
फेंक देना *vt* throw away, throw out
फेंकना *vt* pitch, throw
फेंटी हुई मलाई *n* whipped cream
फेफड़ा *n* lung
फेरा/वापसी यात्रा *n* round trip
फैलना *vi* spread
फैलाना *vt* spread
फोड़ा *n* abscess; (नासूर) ulcer

बंगाल *n* Bengal
बंगाली *n* Bengali
बंजर प्रदेश *n* moor
बंडल *n* pack
बंद *adv* off
बंद करना *vt* close

बंद करने का समय *n* closing time
बंद-गोभी *n* cabbage
बंदर *n* monkey
बंदरगाह *n* harbour, port
बंदिश *n* concerto
बंदी *n* closure
बंदूक *n* gun
बंधक *n* hostage
बंधक रखना/गिरवी रखना *vt* mortgage
बंधा खर्च *npl* overheads
बंपर *n* bumper
बकरी *n* goat
बकरे का मांस *n* mutton
बकवास *n* nonsense
बकवास/बेकार *n* rubbish
बकसुआ *n* buckle, clasp
बकाइन का पेड़ *n* lilac
बकाया *npl* arrears
बक्सा *n* box
बख़ूबी/अच्छी तरह से *adv* well
बख़्शीश *n* tip
बख़्शीश देना *vt* tip
बगल का *adj* adjacent
बगल में *prep* beside, next to
बगल से निकलना *v* go past
बगीचा *n* garden
बगुला *n* heron
बचना *vt* avoid ▷ *v* get away
बच निकलना *vi* escape ▷ *v* get off
बचपन *n* childhood
बचाओ!/मदद करो! *excl* help!
बचाकर रखना *vt* save
बचाना *vt* rescue
बचाव *n* rescue
बचा हुआ/अधिशेष *adj* left
बच्चा *n* child
बच्चागाड़ी *n* buggy, pram
बच्चों की देखरेख *n* childcare
बच्चों की देखरेख करने वाला *n* childminder
बच्चों की बोतल *n* baby's bottle
बछड़ा *n* calf
बछड़े का मांस *n* veal
बजट *n* budget
बजरी *n* gravel, grit
बजाना *vt* play
बटन *n* button

बटमारी/लूट-खसोट *vt* hold up
बटुआ *n* (महिला का बैग) handbag; (महिला का पर्स) purse; (पुरुषों के पैसों के लिए) wallet
बटेर *n* quail
बड़बड़ाना *vi* rave
बड़ा *adj* big, large
बड़ा अक्षर *n* capital
बड़ा ईनाम *n* jackpot
बड़ा/गंभीर *adj* major
बड़ा चम्मच *n* tablespoon
बड़ा बंगला *n* villa
बड़ा बक्सा *n* chest
बड़ा होना *vi* grow up
बड़ी चूक *n* blunder
बड़ी बस *n* coach
बड़ी माप का *adj* outsize
बड़े पैमाने पर *adv* largely
बढ़ई *n* carpenter, joiner
बढ़ईगीरी *n* carpentry
बढ़त/वृद्धि *n* gain
बढ़ना *v* go up ▷ *vi* grow
बढ़ा-चढ़ा कर कहना *v* exaggerate
बढ़ावा देना *vt* boost, promote
बढ़ावा/प्रचार *n* promotion
बढ़िया/अच्छा *adj* nice
बढ़िया/शानदार *adj* great
बतख *n* duck
बतलाना *vt* tell
बताना/सूचित करना *vi* communicate
बदबू *n* odour
बदल देना/बदल जाना *v* change
बदलना *v* alter
बदलना/होना *vi* turn
बदसूरत *adj* ugly
बधाई *npl* congratulations
बधाई देना *vt* congratulate
बधाई पत्र *n* greetings card
बनना *v* become
बनाए रखना *vt* maintain
बनाना *vt* make
बनाम *prep* versus
बना रहना *v* remain
बनावटी *adj* mock
बना होना *vt* consist of
बनियान *n* vest
बम *n* bomb
बमबारी *n* bombing
बमबारी करना *vt* bomb
बमुश्किल *adv* hardly
बरगद का पेड़ *n* banyan tree

बरसात *n* monsoon
बरसाती *adj* rainy
बरसाती कोट *n* mac, raincoat
बराबर *adj* equal
बराबर करना *vt* equalize
बराबर होना *vt* equal
बरामदा *n* patio, porch
बरौनी *n* eyelash
बर्तन धोना *v* wash up
बर्तन धोने वाली *n* dishwasher woman
बर्ताव करना *vt* treat
बर्फ़ की चट्टान *n* avalanche
बर्फ़ानी तूफ़ान *n* blizzard
बर्बर *adj* barbaric ▷ *n* vandal
बर्बरता *n* vandalism
बर्बाद करना *vt* ruin, waste
बर्बादी *n* ruin, waste
बर्मी *n* burgle
बल *n* force
बलपूर्वक प्रवेश *n* break-in
बलात्कार *n* rape
बलात्कार करना *vt* rape
बलात्कारी *n* rapist
बल्ला *n* bat
बवंडर *n* tornado
बवासीर *npl* haemorrhoids
बशर्ते *conj* provided
बस *n* bus
बस अड्डा *n* bus station
बस टिकट *n* bus ticket
बस परिचालक *n* bus conductor
बस स्थानक *n* bus stop
बहकाने वाला *adj* misleading
बहरीन *n* Bahrain
बहना *vi* (हवा) blow; (पानी, नदी) flow
बहनोई *n* brother-in-law (sister's husband)
बहादुर *adj* brave
बहादुरी *n* bravery
बहामा *npl* Bahamas
बहाना *n* pretext
बहाना बनाना/सफाई देना *vt* excuse
बहाना/सफाई *n* excuse
बहाल करना/वापस लौटाना *vt* restore
बहुत *det* much ▷ *adv* very
बहुत अधिक *adv* (काफी) much; (भारी) heavily; (बुरा) awfully ▷ *n* (अनगिनत) a lot

बहुत अधिक/ज़्यादा *pron* much
बहुत खराब/भयानक *adj* terrible
बहुत ज़्यादा *adv* too
बहुत प्यार करना *vt* adore
बहुत बड़ा *adj* gigantic
बहुत बढ़िया *adj* wonderful
बहुत महत्वपूर्ण *adj* crucial
बहुत से *adj* numerous
बहुमंजिली इमारत *n* high-rise
बहुमुखी *adj* versatile
बहुमूल्य *adj* valuable
बहुराष्ट्रीय *adj* multinational
बहुराष्ट्रीय कंपनी *n* multinational
बहुलता/बड़ा हिस्सा *n* majority
बहुवचन *n* plural
बहुसृत काठिन्य *n* multiple sclerosis
बहू *n* daughter-in-law
बाबा *n* father
बाँचना/पढ़ कर सुनाना *vt* read out
बाँजफल *n* acorn
बाँटना *vt* give out
बाँसुरी *n* flute
बांगड़ा मछली *n* mackerel
बांग्लादेश *n* Bangladesh
बांग्लादेशी *adj* Bangladeshi ▷ *n* Bangladeshi
बांझ *adj* infertile
बांधना *vt* tie ▷ *v* tie up
बांस *n* bamboo
बांह *n* arm
बाइबिल *n* Bible
बाएं *adv* left
बाकला *n* broad bean
बाग *n* orchard
बागबानी *n* gardening
बाघ *n* tiger
बाज़ *n* hawk
बाज़ार *n* market, marketplace
बाज़ार संबंधी शोध *n* market research
बाज़ीगर *n* juggler
बाढ़ *n* flood
बाढ़ *n* flooding
बाढ़ आना *vt* flood
बाढ़ग्रस्त होना *vi* flood
बाण/तीर *n* arrow
बात करना *vi* talk
बातचीत *n* (अनौपचारिक) chat ▷ *n* (औपचारिक) conversation
बातचीत करना *vi* chat

बातूनी *adj* talkative
बाद *conj* after
बाद में *prep* after ▷ *adv* (अगला) next
बादाम *n* almond
बाधा *n* hurdle, obstacle
बाबू *n* Mr
बाम मछली *n* eel
बायां *adj* left-hand
बायां भाग *n* left
बार - बार *adv* repeatedly
बारबाडोस द्वीप *n* Barbados
बारह *num* twelve
बारहवां *adj* twelfth
बारहसिंगा *n* reindeer
बारिश *n* rain
बारिश होना *vi* rain
बारी-बारी से *adj* alternate
बाल *n* hair
बालगीत *n* nursery rhyme
बाल घुँघराले बनाने का उपकरण *n* curler
बालदार *adj* hairy
बाल विद्यालय *n* infant school
बालसुलभ/बचकाना *adj* childish
बालों की काट *n* haircut
बालों की मेंहदी *n* henna
बालों को मुलायम बनाने वाला पदार्थ *n* conditioner
बाल्टी *n* bucket, pail
बावला *adj* crazy
बांसुरी *n* flute
बासी *adj* stale
बास्क *n* Basque
बाहर *prep* out ▷ *adv* outdoors
बाहर आना *v* come out
बाहर की ओर *adv* outside
बाहर झांकना *v* lean out
बाहर निकलना *v* opt out
बाहर समय बिताना *v* go out
बाहरी *adj* outside, exterior
बाहरी इलाका *npl* outskirts
बाहरी भाग *n* outside
बिंदी *n* small vermillion dot on the forehead
बिक्री मशीन *n* vending machine
बिक्री विभाग *n* marketing
बिगड़ैल बच्चा *n* brat
बिगाड़ देना *v* mess up
बिच्छू - बूटी *n* nettle
बिछौना *npl* bedclothes ▷ *n* bedding, bed linen
बिजली *n* electricity

बिजली का झटका *n* electric shock
बिजली का लट्टू *n* bulb, light bulb
बिज्जू *n* badger
बिब *n* bib
बिल्कुल *adv* absolutely
बिल्कुल नया *adj* brand-new
बिल्कुल सूखा हुआ *adj* bone-dry
बिल्ला *n* badge
बिल्ली *n* cat
बिस्कुट *n* biscuit
बिस्तर *n* bed
बिस्तरबंद *n* holdall
बिहार *n* Bihar
बिहारी *n* person from Bihar
बीच में *adv* halfway
बीज *n* pip
बीजक/बिल *n* invoice
बीजक/बिल भेजना *vt* invoice
बीजिंग *n* Beijing
बीतना *v* go by
बीता हुआ कल *adv* yesterday
बीफ़बर्गर *n* beefburger
बीमा *n* insurance
बीमा करना *vt* insure
बीमाकृत *adj* insured
बीमा प्रमाणपत्र *n* insurance certificate
बीमा योजना *n* insurance policy
बीमार *adj* poorly
बिरयानी *n* biryani
बीस *num* twenty
बीसवां *adj* twentieth
बुआ *n* aunt (father's sister)
बुक करना *vt* book
बुकिंग *n* booking
बुजुर्ग *adj* elderly
बुझा हुआ *adj* out
बुढ़िया का काता *n* candyfloss
बुदबुदाना *v* mutter
बुद्धिजीवी *n* intellectual
बुद्धिमत्ता *n* intelligence
बुद्धिमान *adj* intelligent
बुधवार *n* Wednesday
बुनियादी *adj* basic
बुनियादी बातें *npl* basics
बुनियादी सुविधाएँ *n* infrastructure
बुरा *adj* bad
बुरा/ख़राब *adj* wrong
बुरा मानना *vt* resent

बुरा मानना/आपत्ति करना *vt* mind
बुरी तरह से *adv* grossly
बुलबुला *n* bubble
बुलाना *v* call
बुल्गारिया *n* Bulgaria
बुल्गारियाई *adj* Bulgarian ▷ *n* Bulgarian
बूढा *n* old man
बृहस्पतिवार *n* Thursday
बेरंग *adj* colourless
बेईमान *n* cheat
बेईमानी करना *vi* cheat
बेकार *adj* (अनुपयोगी) unhelpful; (व्यर्थ) in vain
बेघर *adj* homeless
बेचैन *adj* restless
बेड़ा *n* raft
बेढंगा *adj* awkward
बेतरतीब *adj* untidy
बेतार *adj* cordless
बेतुका *adj* absurd, ridiculous
बेदाग *adj* spotless
बेपरवाह *adj* careless
बेमेल *adj* odd
बेरोज़गार *adj* unemployed, jobless
बेरोज़गारी *n* unemployment
बेलन *n* rolling pin
बेलनाकार डिब्बा *n* cylinder
बेलारूस *n* Belarus
बेलारूसी *adj* Belarussian ▷ *n* Belarussian
बेल्जियम *n* Belgium
बेल्जियाई *adj* Belgian ▷ *n* Belgian
बेवकूफ़ *n* twit
बेवफ़ा *adj* unfaithful
बेशर्त *adj* unconditional
बेस्वाद *adj* tasteless
बेहतर *adj* better
बेहतर तरीके से *adv* better
बैंक *n* bank
बैंक अवकाश *n* bank holiday
बैंक की जमा राशि *n* bank balance
बैंक खाता *n* bank account
बैंक खाता विवरण *n* bank statement
बैंक प्रभार *npl* bank charges
बैंगन *n* aubergine
बैंगनी *adj* purple
बैंगलोर *n* Bangalore
बैटरी *n* battery
बैठक *n* assembly; (बैठक घर) living room
बैर भाव *n* grudge
बैर मोल लेना *vt* antagonize

बैरा *n* waiter
बैरा (महिला) *n* waitress
बैल *n* bull
बैल गाड़ी *n* bullock cart
बैले नर्तक *n* ballet dancer
बैले नर्तकी *n* ballerina
बैसाखी *n* crutch
बैसाखी *n* harvest festival
बॉलरूम नृत्य *n* ballroom dancing
बोझ *n* burden, load
बो टाई *n* bow tie
बोतल *n* bottle
बोत्सवाना *n* Botswana
बोनट *n* bonnet
बोरी *n* sack
बोर्ड गेम *n* board game
बोलिंग *n* bowling
बोलिंग ऐली *n* bowling alley
बोलिवियाई *adj* Bolivian ▷ *n* Bolivian
बोली *n* bid
बोली लगाना *v* bid
बोलीविया *n* Bolivia
बोल्ट *n* bolt
बोस्निया *n* Bosnia
बोस्नियाई *adj* Bosnian ▷ *n* Bosnian
बोस्निया व हर्ज़ेगोविना *n* Bosnia-Herzegovina
बौछार *n* shower
बौद्ध *adj* Buddhist ▷ *n* Buddhist
बौद्ध धर्म *n* Buddhism
बौद्ध पूर्णिमा *n* Buddhist festival to commemorate the birth of Lord Buddha
बौद्धिक *adj* intellectual
बौद्धिक स्तर *n* IQ
ब्याज *n* interest
ब्याज दर *n* interest rate
ब्रह्मांड *n* universe
ब्राह्मिन *n* Brahmin (Highest caste of the Hindu system)
ब्राज़ील *n* Brazil
ब्राज़ीलियाई *adj* Brazilian ▷ *n* Brazilian
ब्राण्ड का नाम *n* brand name
ब्राण्ड/मार्का *n* brand
ब्राण्डी *n* brandy
ब्रिटेन *n* Britain
ब्रेक *n* brake
ब्रेक की बत्ती *n* brake light
ब्रेक लगाना *v* brake
बृहस्पतिवार *n* Thursday
ब्रॉडबैण्ड *n* broadband

भ

भंग *n* break
भंग करना *v* break
भंडारगृह *n* larder
भगवान *n* God
भगा ले जाना *vt* abduct
भजन *n* devotional song
भटकटैया का पौधा *n* thistle
भटकना *vi* wander
भतीजा/भांजा *n* nephew
भतीजी/भांजी *n* niece
भद्दा *adj* vulgar
भद्र पुरुष *n* gentleman
भभक *npl* fumes
भय *n* fright
भयभीत *adj* afraid, frightened
भयभीत/आतंकित *adj* terrified
भयादोहन *n* blackmail
भयादोहन करना *vt* blackmail
भयानक *adj* (डरावना) horrendous; (बुरा) horrible
भयानक रूप से *adv* terribly
भयावह *adj* horrifying
भरण-पोषण करना *vt* provide for
भरा *adj* full
भरा हुआ *adj* crammed
भरोसा करना *vt* count on
भरोसा दिलाना *vt* assure
भर्ती *n* recruitment
भर्ती करना *vt* admit
भवन *n* building
भवन-निर्माण क्षेत्र *n* building site
भवन - निर्माता *n* builder
भविष्य *n* future
भविष्यवाणी *n* forecast
भविष्यवाणी करना *vt* predict
भविष्य सूचक शब्द/ करेगा *v* shall
भव्य *adj* grand
भाई *n* brother
भाई दूज *n* festival on last day of Diwali
भाई साहब *n* Mr
भांग *n* narcotic drink
भाग *n* module
भाग देना *vt* divide
भागना *vi* run away
भाग लेना *vi* participate
भाग्य *n* luck
भाग्यवश *adv* luckily

भाग्यशाली *adj* lucky
भांजा *n* nephew
भाड़ा/किराया *n* hire
भाभी *n* sister-in-law (brother's wife)
भारत *n* India
भारतीय *adj* Indian
भारतीय मोर *n* Indian peacock
भारतीय नागरिक *n* Indian
भारी *adj* heavy
भारी माल वाहन *n* HGV
भारी सामान उठाने की मशीन *n* crane
भारोत्तोलक *n* weightlifter
भारोत्तोलन *n* weightlifting
भाला *n* javelin
भालू *n* bear
भावना *n* emotion
भावात्मक *adj* emotional
भाषा *n* language
भाषाविद् *n* linguist
भाषा संबंधी *adj* linguistic
भिक्षु *n* monk
भिखारी *n* beggar
भिड़ जाना *vi* collide
भित्ति चित्रण/भित्ती लेख *npl* graffiti
भिनभिनाहट *vi* hum
भिन्न होना *vi* vary
भी *adv* also
भीड़ *n* crowd
भीड़-भाड़ *n* congestion
भीड़भाड़ से भरा *adj* busy
भीड़ वाला *adj* crowded
भीतर *adv* inside
भीतर जाना *v* go in
भीतरी भाग *n* inside
भुगतान *n* payment
भुगतान करना *v* pay
भुगतान किया हुआ *adj* paid
भुगतान सूची *n* bill
भुगतान स्थल *n* check-out
भुतहा *adj* haunted
भुनगा *n* maggot
भुना आलू *n* baked potato
भुना हुआ *adj* baked; grilled, roast
भुलक्कड़ *adj* absent-minded
भूकंप *n* earthquake
भूख *n* hunger, appetite
भू-खंड *n* plot
भूखा *adj* hungry
भूगर्भ शास्त्र *n* geology
भूगोल *n* geography
भूतपूर्व *adj* former
भूत/प्रेतात्मा *n* ghost
भूतल *n* ground floor

भूमध्य रेखा *n* equator
भूमध्यसागर *n* Mediterranean
भूमध्यसागरीय *adj* Mediterranean
भूमि *n* land
भूमिका *n* role
भूमिगत *adv* underground
भूमिगत स्टेशन *n* underground station
भूरा *adj* brown
भूल *n* oversight
भूलना *vt* forget
भूलभुलैया *n* maze
भुवनेश्वर *n* Bhubaneshwar
भू-संपत्ति/जागीर *n* estate
भूसा *n* hay
भूसे का ढेर *n* haystack
भू - स्खलन *n* landslide
भूटान *n* Bhutan
भेंट करना *vi* meet up ▷ *vt* see
भेक - मेंढक जैसा एक जीव *n* toad
भेड़ा *n* ram
भेड़िया *n* wolf
भेदना/छेदना *vt* pierce
भेदिया *n* mole
भैंस *n* buffalo
भैया *n* elder brother
भोंपू *n* loudspeaker
भोजन *n* food; (दावत) meal
भोजनकाल *n* mealtime
भोजनावकाश *n* lunch break
भोज वृक्ष *n* birch
भोपाल *n* Bhopal
भौंकना *vi* bark
भौंरा *n* bumblebee
भौंह *n* eyebrow
भौतिक शास्त्र *n* physics
भौतिकशास्त्री *n* physicist
भ्रम *n* confusion
भ्रमित *adj* baffled
भ्रष्ट *adj* corrupt
भ्रष्टाचार *n* corruption
भ्रामक *adj* confusing
भ्रूण *n* foetus

म

मंगलवार *n* Tuesday
मंगोलिया *n* Mongolia
मंगोलियाई *adj* Mongolian
मंगोलियाई नागरिक *n* Mongolian

मंगोलियाई भाषा *n* Mongolian
मंच *n* platform
मंज़िल/माला *n* floor
मंडल *n* board
मंत्रालय *n* ministry
मंत्री *n* minister
मंदिर *n* temple
मंदी *n* recession
मंदी का मौसम *n* low season
मंदी का समय *adj* off-season ▷ *adv* off-season
मंशा *n* motive
मई *n* May
मकड़ी *n* spider
मकड़ी का जाला *n* cobweb
मकबरा *n* tomb
मकर राशि *n* Capricorn
मकर संक्रांत *n* harvest festival
मकसद *n* cause
मकान *n* house
मकान मालकिन *n* landlady
मकान मालिक *n* landlord
मक्का *n* (भुट्टा) corn, maize; (मुसलमानों का तीरथ स्थान) Mecca
मक्की का आटा *n* cornflour
मक्खन *n* butter
मक्खी *n* fly
मखमल *n* velvet
मगरमच्छ *n* crocodile
मगर/यद्यपि *conj* though
मघ बीहू *n* harvest festival of Assam
मच्छर *n* mosquito
मजबूर करना *vt* make
मज़दूर *n* labourer
मज़दूर/कर्मी *n* worker
मज़बूत *adj* strong
मज़ा *n* fun
मज़ाक *n* (मौखिक) joke ▷ *v* (शारीरिक) trick
मज़ाक करना *vi* joke
मज़ाकिया/हास्यमय *adj* funny
मज़ेदार *adj* fun
मजीरा *npl* cymbals
मटर *npl* peas
मठ *n* monastery
मणिभ *n* crystal
मत *n* vote
मतगणना/जनमत सर्वेक्षण *n* opinion poll
मतदान *n* poll
मतदान करना *v* vote

मतभेद *n* conflict
मतलब होना *vt* mean
मतली *n* nausea
मतवाला/हल्के नशे में *adj* tipsy
मदद *n* help
मदद करना *v* help
मददगार *adj* helpful
मद्रास *n* Madras
मद्रासी *n* person from Madras (Chennai)
मर्द *n* husband, man
मद्यनिर्माणशाला *n* brewery
मद्यव्यसनी *n* alcoholic
मधुचूष *n* honeysuckle
मधुमक्खी *n* bee
मधुमास *n* honeymoon
मधुशाला *n* bar
मध्य *n* middle
मध्य अफ़्रीकी गणराज्य *n* Central African Republic
मध्य अमरीका *n* Central America
मध्यकालीन *adj* mediaeval
मध्य पूर्व *n* Middle East
मध्य प्रदेश *n* Madhya Pradesh
मध्यम *adj* medium
मध्यम आकार का *adj* medium-sized
मध्यम वर्ग *adj* middle-class
मध्य युग *npl* Middle Ages
मध्यरात्रि *n* midnight
मध्य वयस्क/प्रौढ़ *adj* middle-aged
मध्यवर्ती *adj* intermediate, mid
मध्यस्थता *n* arbitration
मध्यांतर *n* half-time, interval
मध्याह्न *n* midday
मनका *n* bead
मनबहलाव *n* pastime
मनहूस *adj* grim
मना करना *vt* forbid
मनाना *vt* persuade ▷ *v* rope in
मनोचिकित्सक *n* psychiatrist
मनोचिकित्सा *n* psychotherapy
मनोबल *n* morale
मनोरंजक *adj* entertaining
मनोरंजन उद्यान *n* theme park
मनोरंजन करना *vt* amuse ▷ *v* entertain

मनोरंजनकर्ता *n* entertainer
मनोविदालित *adj* schizophrenic
मनोविज्ञान *n* psychology
मनोविज्ञान संबंधी *adj* psychological
मनोवैज्ञानिक *n* psychologist
मनोहर/सुंदर *adj* lovely
मणिपुर *n* Manipur
ममी - सुरक्षित शव *n* mummy
मरणासन्न रूप से *adv* terminally
मरम्मत *n* repair
मरम्मत करना *vt* mend, repair
मरहम *n* ointment
मराठी *n* Marathi
मरीज़ *n* patient
मरुद्यान *n* oasis
मरुवा *n* marjoram
मरोड़ना *vt* twist, wrench
मर्तबान *n* jar
मर्द *n* man
मर्दाना *adj* masculine
मलबा *n* wreck, wreckage
मलमूत्र पात्र *n* potty
मलहम *n* lotion
मलयालम *n* Malayalam
मलेरिया *n* malaria
मलेशिया *n* Malaysia
मलेशियाई *adj* Malaysian
मलेशियाई नागरिक *n* Malaysian
मवेशी *npl* cattle
मशीन/यंत्र *n* machine
मशीनरी/यंत्र *n* machinery
मसखरा *n* clown
मस्जिद *n* mosque
मस्तिष्क *n* mind
मस्तिष्क ज्वर *n* meningitis
मस्तूल *n* mast
मस्सा *n* wart
महंगा *adj* expensive
महत्त्व *n* value
महत्वपूर्ण *adj* important
महत्वहीन *adj* unimportant
महत्व होना *vi* matter
महत्वाकांक्षा *n* ambition
महत्वाकांक्षी *adj* ambitious
महल *n* castle, palace
महँगा *adj* expensive
महाजन *n* pawnbroker
महाद्वीप *n* continent
महान/महत *adj* great
महापौर *n* mayor
महामहिम *n* majesty

महामारी *n* epidemic
महाराष्ट्र *n* Maharashtra
महाविद्यालय *n* college
महासागर *n* ocean
महासचिव *n* Secretary General
महिला *n* lady
महिला मैनेजर *n* manageress
महिला व्यवसायी *n* businesswoman
महिला सफाई कर्मचारी *n* cleaning lady
महीन/बारीक *adj* fine
महीना *n* month
महूका *n* pheasant
महोदया *n* madam
माँ *n* mother, mummy
मांग करना *vt* call for
मांग पत्र *n* order form
मांस *n* meat
मांसपेशी *n* muscle
मांसपेशीय *adj* muscular
मांसल *adj* chubby
माई *n* aunt (mother's brother's wife)
माउस *n* mouse
माचिस *n* match
मातम/विलाप *n* mourning
माता/पिता *n* parent
माताजी *n* respectful term of address to an elderly woman
मातृक *adj* maternal
मातृत्व अवकाश *n* maternity leave
मातृभाषा *n* mother tongue
मात्र *adj* mere
मात्रा *n* quantity, volume
मात्रिक *adj* metric
माथा *n* forehead
मादा भेड़ *n* ewe
मानचित्र *n* map
मानचित्र पुस्तिका *n* atlas
मानना *vt* consider ▷ *v* think
मानना/अनुमान लगाना *vt* reckon
मान लेना *vt* assume, presume
मानव *n* human being
मानव जाति *n* mankind
मानवतावादी *adj* humanitarian
मानव-निर्मित *adj* man-made
मानवशक्ति/श्रमशक्ति *n* manpower
मानवाधिकार *npl* human rights

मानवीय *adj* human
मानसिक *adj* mental, psychiatric
मानसिक चिकित्सालय *n* mental hospital
मानसिकता *n* mentality
माप *npl* measurements
मापक *n* ruler
मापदंड *n* criterion
मापना *vt* measure
मापना/आँकना *vt* gauge
माफ़ करना *n* forgive
मामला *n* (राजनीतिक) affair; (कानूनी) case
मामा *n* uncle (mother's brother)
मामू *n* uncle (mother's brother)
मायने रखना *vt* mean
मारना *vt* hit
मार्क्सवाद *n* Marxism
मार्ग अवरोध *n* roadblock
मार्ग चिह्न *n* road sign
मार्गदर्शक कुत्ता *n* guide dog
मार्गदर्शिका *n* guide
मार्च *n* March
माध्यमिक *adj* secondary
मार्मिक *adj* touching
माल *n* cargo
मालगोदाम *n* warehouse
माल भाड़ा *n* freight
मालवाहक गाड़ी *n* lorry; (सामान ले जाने के लिए) removal van
मालवाहक नौका *n* barge
माला *n* garland
मालावी *n* Malawi
मालिक *n* (स्वामी) owner; (मुखिया) master; boss
मालिक होना *vt* (स्वामित्व) own
माली *n* gardener
माल्टा *n* Malta
माल्टा का निवासी *adj* Maltese
माल्टा की भाषा *adj* Maltese
माल्टा से संबद्ध *n* Maltese
मासिक *adj* monthly
मासिक धर्म *n* menstruation
मासी *n* aunt (mother's sister)
मासूम *n* innocent
माहिर/निपुण *n* genius
मिंक *n* mink
मिक्सर *n* mixer
मिक्सी *n* liquidizer
मिजाज़ *n* mood, temper

मिजोराम *n* Mizoram
मिटाना *vt* erase
मिट्टी *n* clay
मिट्टी के बर्तन *n* pottery
मिट्टी/भूमि *n* earth
मितव्ययिता *n* austerity
मितव्ययी *adj* thrifty
मित्र *n* friend
मित्रता *n* friendship
मिथक *n* myth
मिथुन राशि *n* Gemini
मिनट *n* minute
मियादी बुखार *n* typhoid
मिर्च *n* chilli
मिलकर काम करना *vi* collaborate
मिल जाना *v* meet
मिलना *v* meet
मिलने जाना *v* go round
मिला - जुला *adj* mixed
मिलाना *vt* add ▷ *v* mix
मिलिमीटर *n* millimetre
मिश्रण *n* mix, mixture
मिश्रित शराब *n* cocktail
मिश्रित सलाद *n* mixed salad
मिष्ठान्न *n* pudding
मिस्र *n* Egypt
मिस्र वासी *n* Egyptian
मिस्र से संबद्ध *adj* Egyptian
मीटर *n* meter, metre
मीठा *adj* sweet
मीठा/ताज़ा *n* sweet, fresh
मीठे पानी की मछली *n* freshwater fish
मीन राशि *n* Pisces
मीनार *n* tower
मील *n* mile
मुंबई *n* Mumbai
मुंहफट *adj* blunt
मुंह *n* mouth
मुंह बोली बहन *adj* like a sister
मुंहासा *n* acne
मुआवज़ा *n* compensation
मुआवज़ा देना *vt* compensate
मुकुट *n* crown
मुक्का *n* punch
मुक्का मारना *vt* punch
मुक्का मारना *v* thump
मुक्केबाज़ *n* boxer
मुक्केबाज़ी *n* boxing
मुखबिर *n* grass
मुखिया *n* head
मुखौटा *n* mask
मुख्य *adj* main, principal
मुख्य कार्यकारी अधिकारी *n* CEO
मुख्य गायक *n* lead singer

मुख्यतः *adv* mainly, primarily
मुख्य भूमि *n* mainland
मुख्य भूमिका *n* lead
मुख्य भोजन *n* main course
मुख्य मार्ग *n* main road
मुख्याधिकारी *n* chief
मुख्यालय *npl* headquarters
मुझे *pron* me
मुटरी - एक पक्षी *n* magpie
मुड़ना *v* turn, turn around
मुड़ा - तुड़ा *adj* creased
मुद्दा *n* (ध्यान) focus; (विषय) point
मुद्रक *n* printer
मुद्रण *n* printing
मुद्रा *n* currency
मुद्रा विनिमय केंद्र *n* bureau de change
मुद्रा संबंधी *adj* monetary
मुद्रास्फ़ीति *n* inflation
मुफ़्त *adj* free
मुरदाघर *n* morgue
मुरमुरा *n* crisp rice
मुर्गा *n* cock, cockerel
मुर्गा/मुर्गी *n* chicken
मुर्गा/मुर्गी का मांस *n* chicken
मुर्गी *n* hen
मुलाकात *n* visit
मुलाकात करना *vt* visit
मुलाकात का समय *npl* visiting hours
मुल्ला *n* mullah
मुश्किल से *adv* barely
मुश्किल से ही/कदाचित ही *adv* hardly
मुसलमान *adj* Muslim
मुस्लिम *adj* Muslim
मुहर्रम *n* first month of Islamic calendar
मुहाँसा *n* zit
मुहांसा *n* pimple
मुहावरा *n* phrase
मूँछ *npl* whiskers
मूंगफली *n* peanut
मूंगा *n* coral
मूंछ *n* moustache
मूक अभिनय *n* pantomime
मूत्र *n* urine
मूत्राशय *n* bladder
मूत्राशय शोथ *n* cystitis
मूर्ख *n* fool
मूर्खतापूर्ण *adj* unwise
मूर्ख दिवस *n* April Fools' Day
मूर्ख बनाना *vt* fool
मूर्च्छित होना *v* pass out
मूल *adj* native

मूलतः *adv* basically
मूलभाषी *n* native speaker
मूल रूप से *adv* originally
मूली *n* radish
मूल्य सूची *n* price list
मूल्यहीन *adj* worthless
मृत्युदंड *n* capital punishment
मृत्युलेख *n* obituary
में *prep* (भीतर) in, into; (के बीच) among
में/के अंदर *prep* into
में से *prep* from
मेघ *n* cloud
मेघाछन्न *adj* cloudy
मेघालय *n* Meghalaya
मेज़ *n* table
मेज़पोश *n* tablecloth
मेज़बान *n* host
मेडागास्कर *n* Madagascar
मेढक *n* frog
मेढक का डिंभकीट *n* tadpole
मेधावी *adj* brilliant
मेमना *n* lamb
मेमरी कार्ड *n* memory card
मेरा *pron* mine
मेमसाहब *n* lady, madam
मेरुदण्ड *n* backbone
मेरुरज्जु *n* spinal cord
मेरैंग - एक मिष्ठान्न *n* meringue
मेल *n* match
मेलखाता *adj* matching
मेल खाना *v* match
मेला *n* funfair
मेष राशि *n* Aries
मेहनत से *adv* hard
मेहमान *n* guest
मेहमाननवाज़ी *n* hospitality
मेहराब *n* arch
मेंहदी *n* henna
मेंहदी लगाना *v* paint henna designs on the body
मैक्सिको *n* Mexico
मैक्सिको का नागरिक *n* Mexican
मैक्सिको से संबद्ध *adj* Mexican
मैडमजी *n* madam
मैदान *n* plain
मैराथन - लंबी दौड़ *n* marathon
मैले कपड़े/धुले कपड़े *n* laundry
मॉडल *n* model
मॉनीटर *n* monitor
मॉरिशस *n* Mauritius
मॉल्दोवा *n* Moldova

मोज़ाम्बिक *n* Mozambique
मोटरगाड़ी *n* car
मोटर चालक *n* motorist
मोटरसाइकिल चालक *n* motorcyclist
मोटा *adj* thick
मोटाई *n* thickness
मोटा धारीदार सूती कपड़ा *n* corduroy
मोड़ *n* bend, turn
मोड़ने योग्य *adj* folding
मोडेम *n* modem
मोतियाबिंद *n* cataract
मोती *n* pearl
मोपेड *n* moped
मोम *n* wax
मोमबत्ती *n* candle
मोम वाले रंग *n* crayon
मोर *n* peacock
मोरक्को *n* Morocco
मोरक्को का निवासी *n* Moroccan
मोरक्को से संबद्ध *adj* Moroccan
मोल-भाव करना *vi* haggle
मोल लगाना/मूल्यांकन करना *vt* rate
मोहक *adj* charming
मोहकता *n* charm
मौखिक *adj* oral ▷ *n* oral
मौजूद/उपस्थित होना *adj* present
मौनैको *n* Monaco
मौलिक/अभिनव *adj* innovative
मौलिक/मूलभूत *adj* original
मौसम *n* weather
मौसम संबंधी भविष्यवाणी *n* weather forecast
मौसा *n* uncle (mother's sister's husband)
मौसी *n* aunt (mother's sister)
म्यांमार *n* Myanmar

यंत्र मानव *n* robot
यकृत *n* liver
यथार्थतः *adv* exactly
यथार्थवादी *adj* realistic
यथोचित *adj* proper ▷ *adv* reasonably

यद्यपि *conj* although
यद्यपि/भले ही *conj* though
यमन *n* Yemen
यह *pron* this ▷ *det* this
यह/वह *pron* it
यह/वह/वही *det* the
यहां *adv* here
यहां तक कि *adv* even
यहूदी *n* Jew ▷ *adj* Jewish
या *conj* or
यांत्रिक *adj* mechanical
याचना करना *v* beg
याचिका *n* petition
यातना *n* torture
यातना देना *vt* torture
यातायात *n* traffic
यातायात अभिरक्षक *n* traffic warden
यातायात अवरोध *n* traffic jam
यातायात कर *n* toll
यातायात बत्ती *npl* traffic lights
यात्रा *n* (सफर) journey, trip; (भ्रमण) travel
यात्रा आयोजक कंपनी *n* travel agency
यात्रा करना *vi* travel
यात्रा बीमा *n* travel insurance
यात्रा योजना *n* itinerary
यात्री *n* passenger, traveller
याद करना *vt* memorize
यादगार/निशानी *n* memento
याद दिलाना *vt* remind
याद रखना *v* remember
याद/स्मृति *n* memory
यान *n* craft
यार *n* friend
या यह ... या वह *conj* either ... or
युक्तियां *npl* tactics
युगल *n* couple
युगांडा *n* Uganda
युद्ध *n* (लड़ाई) battle; (संग्राम) war
युद्धपोत *n* battleship
युद्धविराम *n* ceasefire, truce
युवा *adj* young
युवा क्लब *n* youth club

युवा छात्रावास *n* youth hostel
युवावस्था *n* youth
यूक्रेन *n* Ukraine
यूक्रेन से संबद्ध *adj* Ukrainian
यूक्रेनी *adj* Ukrainian
यूनानी *adj* Greek ▷ *n* Greek
यूनाइटेड किंगडम *n* United Kingdom
यूरोप *n* Europe
यूरोपीय *adj* European ▷ *n* European
यूरोपीय संघ *n* European Union
ये *det* these; this ▷ *pron* those
येलो पेजेज़ *n* Yellow Pages®
य़ोग *n* yoga
योगदान *n* contribution
योगदान देना *vi* contribute
योग्य *adj* able
योग्यता *n* (काबिलीयत) ability; (गुण) qualification
योजना *n* plan
योजना बनाना *v* plan

रंग *n* paint
रंगत *n* colouring, complexion
रंगना *v* paint
रंगाई करने की कूची *n* paintbrush
रंगीन *adj* colourful, tinted
रंगीन कागज़ के टुकड़े *npl* confetti
रंदा *n* plane
रांची *n* Ranchi
रक्त *n* blood
रक्त आधान *n* transfusion
रक्त कैंसर *n* leukaemia
रक्तचाप *n* blood pressure
रक्त परीक्षण *n* blood test
रक्त विषाक्तता *n* blood poisoning
रक्त समूह *n* blood group
रक्षा करना *vt* protect
रक्षागृह *n* conservatory
रक्षित स्थान *vt* reserve

रखना *vt* keep; (व्यवस्थित करना) lay, place, put
रख - रखाव *n* maintenance
रखवाला *n* caretaker
रगड़ना *vt* rub
रग्बी *n* rugby
रचना *n* creation
रचना करना *vt* create
रचनात्मक *adj* constructive; (सृजनात्मक) creative
रजाई *n* quilt
रजोनिवृत्ति *n* menopause
रत्ती *n* carat
रत्न *n* gem, jewel
रद्द करना *vt* call off, cancel
रद्दी की टोकरी *n* wastepaper basket
रब *n* God
रबर *n* rubber
रबर के दस्ताने *npl* rubber gloves
रबी *n* rabbi
रमज़ान *n* Ramadan
रमणीय *adj* graceful
रविवार *n* Sunday
रवैया *n* attitude
रस *n* juice
रसगुल्ले *n* Indian sweet
रसभरी *n* raspberry
रसायन *n* chemical
रसायन विज्ञान *n* chemistry
रसीद *n* receipt
रसेदार सब्ज़ी *n* curry
रस्म *n* ritual
रस्म संबंधी *adj* ritual
रस्साकशी *n* tug-of-war
रस्सी *n* rope
रहना *vi* stay, live
रहस्य *n* mystery
रहस्यमय *adj* mysterious
राक्षस *n* monster
राखदानी *n* ashtray
राग *n* tune
राज *n* (राजा) monarch; (राज्य) Raj
राजकुमार *n* prince
राजकुमारी *n* princess
राजगीर *n* bricklayer
राजदूत *n* ambassador
राजदूत आवास *n* embassy
राजधानी *n* capital
राजनीति *npl* politics
राजनेता *n* politician
राजनैतिक *adj* political
राजमार्ग संहिता *n* Highway Code

राजशाही *n* monarchy
राजस्व *n* revenue
राज हंस *n* flamingo
राज्य *n* state
राज्य सभा *n* Upper House
राजस्थान *n* Rajasthan
राज़ *n* confidence
रात *n* night
रात की पारी *n* night shift
रात्रिकालीन विद्यालय *n* night school
रानी *n* queen
राय *n* opinion, view
रायपुर *n* Raipur
राल *n* resin
राशि *n* amount
राशिचक्र *n* zodiac
राष्ट्र *n* nation
राष्ट्रगान *n* national anthem
राष्ट्रपति *n* president
राष्ट्रवाद *n* nationalism
राष्ट्रवादी *n* nationalist
राष्ट्रीय *adj* national
राष्ट्रीय उद्यान *n* national park
राष्ट्रीयकरण करना *vt* nationalize
राष्ट्रीयता *n* nationality
रास्ता *n* path
रास्ता बदलना *v* turn off
राहत *n* relief
राहत देना *vt* relieve
रिकॉर्डर *n* recorder
रिकॉर्ड करना *vt* record
रिक्शा *n* rickshaw
रिक्त *adj* vacant
रिक्तता *n* void
रिक्त पद *n* vacancy
रिक्त स्थान *n* blank
रियायत *n* concession
रिवाज़ *n* custom
रिश्तेदार *n* relative
रिसना *vi* leak
रिसाव *n* leak
रिहाई *n* release
रिहा करना *vt* release
रुई *n* cotton wool
रुई लपेटी हुई छोटी डंडी *n* cotton bud
रुखाई से *adv* roughly
रुग्ण/अपंग *n* invalid
रुग्णवाहिका *n* ambulance
रुचिरा/मक्खन फल *n* avocado
रुढ़िवादी *adj* conservative
रुपया *n* rupee
रुपरेखा *n* outline
रूखा/कड़ा *adj* rough

रूपवान *adj* handsome
रूमानी *n* romantic
रूमाल *n* (नाक) handkerchief; (मेज) serviette
रूस *n* Russia
रूसी *adj* Russian ▷ *n* Russian
रेंगना *vi* crawl, creep
रेखा *n* line
रेखांकित करना/ज़ोर देना *vt* underline
रेचक औषधि *n* laxative
रेजगारी *n* change
रेडियोधर्मी *adj* radioactive
रेडियो नियंत्रित *adj* radio-controlled
रेलगाड़ी *n* train
रेल - चौपड़ *n* level crossing
रेल मार्ग *n* railway
रेवतचीनी *n* rhubarb
रेस्तराँ/भोजनालय *n* restaurant
रैक/खूँटी *n* rack
रोआँ *n* fur
रोकड़िया *n* teller
रोकथाम *n* prevention
रोकना *v* hold up ▷ *vt* prevent
रोकना/रुकना *v* pull up
रोक/प्रतिबंध *n* curb
रोका *n* ban, restraint
रोगन *n* lacquer
रोगाणु *n* germ
रोगाणु रोधक *n* antiseptic
रोजगार *n* employment
रोज़गार केंद्र *n* job centre
रोधन *n* insulation
रोटी *n* bread
रोना *vi* cry, weep
रोम *n* Rome
रोम से संबद्ध *adj* Roman
रोमन *adj* Roman
रोमन स्थापत्यकला *adj* Romanesque
रोमांच *n* thrill
रोमांचक *adj* exciting, thrilling
रोमांचक कार्य *n* adventure
रोमांचक सामग्री *n* thriller
रोमांचित *adj* thrilled
रोमानिया *n* Romania
रोमानियाई *adj* Romanian ▷ *n* Romanian
रोशनदान *n* ventilation

लंगड़ा *adj* lame
लंगड़ाना *vi* limp
लंगर *n* anchor
लंगर डालना *v* moor
लंगोटी *n* nappy
लंदन *n* London
लंबवत *adj* vertical
लंबा *adj* (ऊंचाई) long; (कद) tall
लंबाई *n* length
लंबा और पतला *adj* lanky
लंबी कूद *n* long jump
लंबी नींद *n* lie-in
लंबोतरा *adj* oblong
लकड़ी *n* wood
लकड़ी का *adj* wooden
लकवाग्रस्त *adj* paralysed
लक्ज़मबर्ग *n* Luxembourg
लक्ष्य *n* target
लखपति *n* millionaire
लखनऊ *n* Lucknow
लगभग *adj* near, about ▷ *adv* (प्रायः) almost; (तकरीबन) nearly; approximately
लगभग/आभासी *adj* virtual
लगभग रूप से *adv* approximately
लगन *n* devotion
लगाना/बिताना *vt* put in
लगाम *npl* reins
लगाव *n* attachment
लघु *adj* miniature
लघुतम *adj* least
लघु रूप *n* miniature
लट *n* lock
लटकना *vi* hang
लटकाना *vt* hang
लड़का *n* boy, guy
लड़का/आदमी *n* chap
लड़की *n* girl
लत लगा हुआ *n* addict
लता *n* vine
लपट *n* blaze
लपसी *n* batter
लपेटना *vt* wind ▷ *v* wrap
लपेटा *n* roll
लपेटा हुआ/संवेष्टित *adj* packed
ललचाना *vt* tempt

लहर *n* wave
लहरदार *adj* wavy
लहराना *v* wave
लहसुन *n* garlic
लस्सी *n* cold drink made with yoghurt, water and sugar
लाइटर *n* lighter
लाइबेरिया *n* Liberia
लाइबेरियाई *adj* Liberian ▷ *n* Liberian
लाइसेंस/अधिकार पत्र *n* licence
लाओस *n* Laos
लाख *n* (पैसे) lakh
लागत *n* cost
लाठी *n* club
लाड़ - प्यार से बिगाड़ना *vt* spoil
लातविया *n* Latvia
लातवियाई *adj* Latvian ▷ *n* Latvian
लादना *vt* load
लाना *vt* bring
लाना - ले जाना *vt* transport
लाभ *n* profit
लाभ *n* benefit ▷ *v* benefit
लाभदायक *adj* profitable, rewarding
लाभप्रद *adj* lucrative
लालच *n* temptation
लालची *adj* greedy
लाल मांस *n* red meat
लाल सागर *n* Red Sea
लाल / सूजा हुआ *adj* inflamed
लाल हो जाना *vi* flush
लाली *n* flush
लावा *n* lava
लिंग *n* gender
लिक्टेंस्टीन *n* Liechtenstein
लिखना *v* write
लिखने का कागज़ *n* writing paper
लिखावट/लेख *n* writing
लिखित प्रतिलिपि *n* transcript
लिथुआनिया *n* Lithuania
लिथुआनियाई *adj* Lithuanian ▷ *n* Lithuanian
लिपटाना *vt* cuddle
लिफ़ाफ़ा *n* envelope
लीटर *n* litre
लीबिया *n* Libya

लीबियाई *adj* Libyan ▷ *n* Libyan
लुका-छिपी *n* hide-and-seek
लुटेरा *n* robber
लुटेरा/बदमाश *n* gangster
लुढ़कना *v* roll
लुभावना *adj* tempting
लूट *n* (व्यक्ति) mugging; (धोखा) rip-off
लूट/डकैती *n* robbery
लूटना *vt* rob
लेंस *n* lens
ले आना *vt* collect
लेकिन *conj* but
लेख *n* article
लेखक *n* author, writer
लेखा-चित्र *n* graph
लेखाचित्र *n* chart
लेखा परीक्षक *n* auditor
लेखा परीक्षण *n* audit
लेखा परीक्षण करना *vt* audit
लेखापाल *n* accountant
लेखाविधि *n* accountancy
लेज़र *n* laser
ले जाना *vt* take away
लेटना *vi* lie
लेटा हुआ *adj* reclining
लेना *vt* take
लेना/पकड़ना *vt* take
लेबनान *n* Lebanon
लेबनानी *adj* Lebanese ▷ *n* Lebanese
ले लेना/ चुरा लेना *vt* take
लेस/जालीदार गोटा *n* lace
लैटिन *n* Latin
लैटिन अमरीका *n* Latin America
लैटिन अमरीकी *adj* Latin American
लॉटरी *n* raffle
लोकतंत्र *n* democracy
लोकतंत्रात्मक *adj* democratic
लोकप्रिय *adj* popular
लोकप्रियता *n* popularity
लोकमत *n* public opinion
लोक सभा *n* Lower House
लोक संगीत *n* folk music
लोक साहित्य *n* folklore
लोग *npl* people
लोमड़ी *n* fox
लोरी *n* lullaby
लोहा *n* iron
लौकी *n* gourd
लौंग *n* clove
लौटना *vi* come back

व

वंशानुगत *adj* hereditary
वकील *n* lawyer
वक्ष *n* chest
वज़न *n* weight
वनमानुष *n* gorilla
वनमानुस *n* chimpanzee
वनस्पति *npl* flora ▷ *n* vegetation
वन्य/जंगली *adj* wild
वन्य जीवन *n* wildlife
वफ़ादारी *n* loyalty
वयस्क *n* adult
वरीयता *n* preference
वरीयता देना *vt* prefer
वर्ग *n* category
वर्ग - पहेली *n* crossword
वर्जित *adj* forbidden
वर्णलोप या संबंधकारक चिह्न *n* apostrophe
वर्णांध *adj* colour-blind
वर्णाक्षर *n* alphabet
वर्तमान *n* present
वर्तमान में *adv* currently, presently
वर्दी *n* uniform
वर्ल्ड कप *n* World Cup
वर्ष *n* year
वर्षा ऋतु *n* monsoon
वर्षा वन *n* rainforest
वसीयत *n* will
वस्तु *n* object
वस्तुतः *adv* actually, really
वस्तु/मद *n* item
वह *pron* that
वहन करना *vt* bear
वहन करने योग्य *adj* affordable, bearable
वह (पुरुष) *pron* he
वहां *adv* there
वाचन/पठन *n* reading
वाणिज्य बैंक *n* merchant bank
वातानुकूलन *n* air conditioning
वातानुकूलित *adj* air-conditioned
वातावरण *n* environment
वादक *n* player
वादक मंडली *n* orchestra
वादा *n* promise
वादा करना *vt* promise

वाद्य यंत्र *n* musical instrument
वाद्ययंत्र *n* instrument
वापस करना/लौटाना *vt* return
वापस चुकाना *vt* pay back
वापस देना *vt* give back
वापस पाना *v* get back
वापस लेना *vt* take back
वापस लौटना *vi* return
वापसी *n* (लौटना) return; (हटाना) pull-out
वापसी टिकट *n* return ticket
वाम - पंथी *adj* left-wing
वामावर्त *adv* anticlockwise
वायलिननुमा वाद्य *n* cello
वायलिन वादक *n* violinist
वायु-परिवहन नियंत्रक *n* air traffic controller
वायुमण्डल *n* atmosphere
वायु में तैरना *vi* float
वायुयान *n* aircraft
वायुयान चालक *n* pilot
वायुरोधक *adj* airtight
वायुसेना *n* air force
वारंटी *n* warranty
वार्ताकार *n* negotiator
वार्षिक *adj* annual, yearly
वार्षिक रूप से *adv* annually
वाष्पक *n* boiler
वास्कट *n* waistcoat
वास्तव में *adv* really
वास्तविक *adj* authentic, true, actual
वास्तविकता *n* reality
वास्तुकला *n* architecture
वास्तुकार *n* architect
वाह! *excl* hooray!
वाहक पट्टा *n* conveyor belt
वाहन *n* vehicle
विकल *adj* edgy
विकल्प *n* alternative, option
विकसित *adj* advanced
विकसित होना *vi* blossom
विकास *n* evolution, growth
विकिरक *n* radiator
विकिरण *n* radiation
विक्रय प्रतिनिधि *n* rep
विक्रेता *n* vendor
विक्षिप्त *n* madman
विघ्न *n* nuisance
विचार *n* idea
विचारधारा *n* ideology
विचारमग्न *adj* thoughtful
विचारशून्य/विचारहीन *adj* thoughtless

विचित्र *adj* queer; (रहस्यमय) uncanny
विजय *n* triumph
विजय हासिल करना *vi* triumph
विजयी *adj* winning
विजेता *n* champion
विज्ञापन *n* ad, commercial; (व्यापार) advertising
विज्ञापन अंतराल *n* commercial break
विज्ञापन देना *v* advertise
विज्ञान *n* science
विटामिन *n* vitamin
वितरक *n* distributor
वितरण *n* circulation
विदाई *n* parting
विदा होना/प्रस्थान करना *v* leave
विदूषक *n* comic
विदेश में *adv* abroad
विदेशी *n* foreigner ▷ *adj* foreign
विद्या *n* learning
विद्यार्थी *n* student
विद्युत आवेश *n* charge
विद्युत कटौती *n* power cut
विद्युत ग्राहक *n* aerial
विद्वेष *n* venom
विद्वेषपूर्ण *adj* vicious
विधवा *n* widow
विधि *n* method
विधि विद्यालय *n* law school
विधुर *n* widower
विधेयक *n* bill
विनष्ट कर देना *vt* wreck
विनिमय दर *n* exchange rate
विनियमन *n* regulation
विनीत *adj* modest
विनीत/नम्र *adj* humble
विनोदपूर्ण *adj* humorous, witty
विनोदी *adj* jolly
विपक्षी/विरोधी *n* opponent
विपत्ति *n* mishap
विपरीत/उल्टा *adj* opposite
विपरीतता से *adv* vice versa
विपरीत/सम्मुख *adj* opposite
विभिन्न *adj* various
विमान पट्टी *n* runway
विमान परिचारक *n* cabin crew
विमान परिचारिका *n* air hostess
विमान सेवा कंपनी *n* airline
वियतनाम *n* Vietnam

वियतनामी *adj* Vietnamese ▷ *n* Vietnamese
विरंजित *adj* bleached
विरंजित करना *n* bleach
विराम *n* pause
विराम चिह्न *n* punctuation
विरासत *n* heritage
विरासत/उत्तराधिकार *n* inheritance
विरासत में पाना *vt* inherit
विरुद्ध *prep* against
विरोध *n* objection, protest
विरोध करना *vt* oppose, object ▷ *v* protest
विरोधाभास *n* contradiction
विरोधी *n* adversary ▷ *adj* opposed, opposing
विलंब से *adv* late
विलंबित *adj* late, overdue
विलक्षण *adj* quaint
विलक्षण/विचित्र *adj* eccentric
विलय *n* merger
विलय होना/मिलना *v* merge
विलासमय *adj* luxurious
विलासिता *n* luxury
विलुप्त *adj* extinct
विवरण *n* account, report
विवरण देना *vt* report
विवरण पत्रिका *n* prospectus
विवरण-पुस्तिका *n* brochure
विवरण प्रसारक *n* commentator
विवादास्पद *adj* controversial
विवाह *n* wedding
विवाह करना *v* marry
विवाह की अंगूठी *n* wedding ring
विवाह की पोशाक *n* wedding dress
विवाह प्रमाणपत्र *n* marriage certificate
विवाहित *adj* married
विविध *adj* miscellaneous, varied
विविधता *n* variety
विवेकशील *adj* conscientious
विशाल *adj* enormous, huge
विशालकाय *adj* gigantic, massive
विशालकाय संगठन *n* giant
विशाल/वृहद *adj* mammoth
विशिष्टता *n* highlight
विशेष *adj* particular
विशेषज्ञ *n* expert
विशेषज्ञ चिकित्सक *n* consultant

विशेषण *n* adjective
विशेषता *n* characteristic
विशेष रूप से *adv* particularly
विशेषाधिकार *n* privilege
विश्राम *n* relaxation
विश्राम करना *v* rest
विश्लेषण *n* analysis
विश्लेषण करना *vt* analyse
विश्वकोश *n* encyclopaedia
विश्वविद्यालय *n* university
विश्वव्यापी *adj* global
विश्वसनीय *adj* trusted, credible, reliable
विश्वास *n* faith, trust, confidence
विश्वास करना *vt* trust ▷ *v* believe
विश्वास करने वाला *adj* trusting
विश्वास दिलाना *vt* convince
विषम *adj* odd
विषमकोणीय समचतुर्भुज *n* diamond
विषमता *n* contrast
विषय *n* topic
विषयवस्तु *n* content; (विषय) theme
विषाणु *n* virus
विषैला *adj* toxic
विस्तार *n* enlargement, extension
विस्तार/सीमा *n* range
विस्तृत *adj* extensive, widespread
विस्फोट *n* blast, explosion
विस्फोटक पदार्थ *n* explosive
विस्फोटित होना *vi* explode
विस्मयादिबोधक चिह्न *n* exclamation mark
विस्मृत *adj* forgotten
विहार मार्ग *n* promenade
वीज़ा *n* visa
वीडियो *n* video
वीडियो कैमरा *n* video camera
वीडियोफ़ोन *n* videophone
वीथिका *n* gallery
वीभत्स *adj* gruesome
वृत्त *n* circle
वृत्ताकार *adj* circular
वृद्ध *adj* old
वृद्ध पेंशनभोगी *n* old-age pensioner
वृद्ध संबंधी *adj* geriatric
वृद्धि *n* rise

वृद्धि करना/वृद्धि होना *v* multiply
वृषण *n* testicle
वृष राशि *n* Taurus
वे *pron* they; (बहुवचन) those
वेतन *n* wage, salary
वेदी *n* altar
वेधशाला *n* observatory
वेध्य/अतिसंवेदनशील *adj* vulnerable
वेनेजुएला *n* Venezuela
वेनेजुएलियाई *adj* Venezuelan ▷ *n* Venezuelan
वेब *n* Web
वेल्श *adj* Welsh
वेल्स *n* Wales
वेस्टइंडीज़ *npl* West Indies
वेस्टइंडीज़ का निवासी *n* West Indian
वेस्टर्न - काउबॉय से संबद्ध चलचित्र या पुस्तक *n* western
वैकल्पिक *adj* alternative, optional
वैद्युत *adj* electric, electrical
वैद्युत कंबल *n* electric blanket
वैयक्तिक *adj* individual
वैवाहिक स्थिति *n* marital status
वैश्वीकरण *n* globalization
वॉकी - टॉकी *n* walkie-talkie
व्यंग्य *n* irony
व्यंग्यपूर्ण *adj* ironic
व्यंजन विधि *n* recipe
व्यंजन सूची *n* menu
व्यक्ति *n* person
व्यक्तिगत *adj* personal
व्यक्तित्व *n* personality
व्यग्र *adj* frantic
व्यग्रता *n* panic
व्यग्र होना *v* panic
व्यय करना/बिताना *vt* spend
व्यर्थ *adj* useless
व्यर्थ/अर्थहीन *adj* pointless
व्यवधान *n* interruption
व्यवसाय *n* occupation
व्यवस्थित करना *vt* arrange
व्यवहार *n* behaviour
व्यवहार करना *vi* behave
व्यवहारकौशल/ चातुर्य *n* tact
व्यस्त *adj* busy
व्यस्त ध्वनि *n* engaged tone
व्यस्त/संलग्न *adj* engaged

व्यस्त समय *n* rush hour
व्याकरण *n* grammar
व्याकरण संबंधी *adj* grammatical
व्याख्या करना *vt* explain
व्याख्याता *n* lecturer
व्याख्यान *n* lecture
व्याख्यान देना *vi* lecture
व्यापक रूप से *adv* extensively
व्यापार *n* business, trade
व्यापार चिह्न *n* trademark
व्यापारिक संघ *n* trade union
व्यापारी *n* businessman
व्यायामशाला *n* gym
व्यावसायिक *adj* vocational
व्यावहारिक *adj* practical

श

शंकु *n* cone
शंकुधारी वृक्ष *n* conifer
शंबुक *n* mussel
शक्ति/अधिकार *n* power
शक्ति/ताक़त *n* power
शक्तिशाली *adj* powerful
शतरंज *n* chess
शताब्दी *n* century
शताब्दी समारोह *n* centenary
शतावर-एक सब्ज़ी *n* asparagus
शत्रु *n* enemy
शनिवार *n* Saturday
शपथ *n* oath
शफ़तालू *n* nectarine
शब्द *n* term, word
शब्दावली *n* vocabulary
शयनकक्ष *n* bedroom
शरण *n* asylum, refuge
शरणार्थी *n* asylum seeker, refugee
शरद ऋतु *n* autumn
शरमाना *vi* blush
शराब *n* wine; (मीठा और स्वादिष्ट) liqueur; (तीखी मीठी वाइन) port; (अनौपचारिक) booze; (स्कॉटलैंड से) whisky
शराब का गिलास *n* wineglass
शराब की सूची *n* wine list
शरारत *n* mischief
शरारती *adj* mischievous, naughty

शरीर *n* body
शरीर सौष्ठव *n* bodybuilding
शर्त *n* bet
शर्त लगाना *v* bet
शर्मनाक *adj* embarrassing
शर्मिंदा *adj* ashamed, embarrassed
शलगम *n* turnip
शलभ *n* moth
शल्क *n* scale
शल्य चिकित्सा *n* operation
शल्य चिकित्सा कक्ष *n* operating theatre
शल्य चिकित्सा करना *vi* operate
शव *n* corpse
शवदाहगृह/श्मशान *n* crematorium
शहद *n* honey
शहनाई *n* clarinet
शहर/कस्बा *n* town
शहीद *n* martyr
शांत *adj* calm, quiet
शांत/निश्चिंत *adj* laid-back
शांत स्वभाव का/अल्हड़ *adj* easy-going
शांत होना *v* calm down
शांति *n* peace
शांतिपूर्ण *adj* peaceful
शांति से *adv* quietly
शाकाहारी *adj* vegetarian
शाकाहारी व्यक्ति *n* vegetarian
शादी *n* marriage
शादी की सालगिरह *n* wedding anniversary
शानदार *adj* glorious, magnificent
शाप *n* curse
शाबाश! *excl* well done!
शाम *n* evening
शामिल करना *vt* involve
शामिल होना *v* join
शामिल होना/बना होना *vt* make up
शायद *adv* probably
शारीरिक *adj* physical
शारीरिक जांच *n* physical examination
शारीरिक दंड *n* corporal punishment
शावक *n* cub
शाश्वत *adj* eternal
शासक *n* ruler
शासन करना *v* rule
शास्त्रीय *adj* classical

शाहबलूत *n* oak
शाहबलूत वृक्ष *n* chestnut
शाही *adj* royal
शिकायत *n* complaint
शिकायत करना *v* complain
शिकायत/भुनभुनाहट *n* grouse
शिकार *n* (क्रिया) hunting; (पशु) prey; (व्यक्ति) victim
शिकार करना *v* hunt
शिकारी *n* hunter
शिकारी पक्षी *n* bird of prey
शिक्षक *n* teacher, tutor
शिक्षण *n* teaching
शिक्षण शुल्क *npl* tuition fees
शिक्षण सत्र *n* tutorial
शिक्षा *n* education
शिक्षा व कार्यानुभव संबंधी विवरण *n* CV
शिक्षा संस्थान *n* academy
शिक्षित *adj* educated
शिथिल/ढीला *adj* loose
शिमला *n* Shimla
शिरा *n* vein
शिला/चट्टान *n* rock
शिलांग *n* Shillong
शिल्पकार *n* craftsman
शिशु *n* baby
शिशुगृह *n* nursery
शिशुसदन *n* crèche
शिष्ट *adj* well-behaved
शिष्टाचार *npl* manners
शिष्य *n* pupil
शीघ्रता से *adv* promptly, quickly
शीत ऋतु *n* winter
शीतल *adj* cool
शीरा *n* treacle
शीर्ष अवस्था *n* peak
शीर्षक *n* title
शीर्षक पंक्ति *n* headline
शीर्षतम/सर्वोच्च *n* top
शीर्ष भाग *n* top
शीर्ष समय *npl* peak hours
शुक्रवार *n* Friday
शुतुरमुर्ग *n* ostrich
शुद्ध *adj* pure
शुरुआत *n* beginning
शुरू करना *vt* begin
शुरू होना *vi* go back
शुल्क *n* charge
शुल्क लेना *v* charge
शून्य *n* zero
शूलपर्णी *n* holly
शेयर बाज़ार *n* stock exchange
शेर *n* lion

शेरनी *n* lioness
शेष *adj* remaining
शेष भाग *n* rest
शैक्षिक *adj* academic, educational
शैक्षिक वर्ष *n* academic year
शैतान *n* Devil
शैल तोता *n* budgerigar
शोक *n* grief
शोधन संयत्र *n* refinery
शोर *n* noise
शोरगुल वाला *adj* noisy
शोरबा *n* broth; gravy
शोषण *n* exploitation
शोषण करना *vt* exploit
शौक *n* hobby
शौकीन *n* amateur
शौचालय *n* lavatory, toilet
श्यामपट्ट *n* blackboard
श्यामापक्षी *n* blackbird
श्येनक पक्षी *n* grouse
शृंगार सामग्री *n* make-up
शृंगी - एक वाद्ययंत्र *n* horn
श्रम *n* labour
श्रमजीवी *adj* working-class
श्रवण *n* hearing
श्री *n* Mr
श्रीमती *n* Mrs
श्रीनगर *n* Srinagar
श्रीलंका *n* Sri Lanka
श्रेणी *n* range
श्रोणि *n* pelvis
श्रोता *n* listener
श्वसन *n* breathing
श्वसुर *n* father-in-law
श्वासनली - शोथ *n* bronchitis

ष

षड्यंत्र *n* conspiracy, plot

स

सँकरा *adj* narrow
संकट काल *n* crisis
संकर/दोगला *n* mongrel
संकरी गली *n* alley
संकलन *n* assortment
संकल्प *n* resolution

dj closed
मानसिकता वाला adj
w-minded
n complex
n clue, sign
त करना vt indicate
ोची adj reserved
क्रमण n infection
क्रामक adj contagious,
infectious
संक्षिप्त adj brief, concise
संक्षिप्त रूप n abbreviation
संक्षेप में लिखना vt jot down
संख्या एक num one
संगठन n organization
संगणना n computing
संगमरमर n marble
संगरोधन n quarantine
संगीत n music
संगीतकार n composer
संगीत कार्यक्रम n concert
संगीत मंडली n band
संगीतमय n musical
संगीत संचालक n conductor
संगीत संबंधी adj musical
संग्रह n collection
संग्रहकर्ता n collector
संघ n club, union
संघनन n condensation
संचार n communication
संचालन करना v operate
संचालित करना vt conduct
संज्ञा n noun
संतरा n orange
संतरी/पहरेदार n guard
संतरे का रस n orange juice
संतरे जैसा फल n clementine
संतुलन n balance
संतुलित adj balanced
संतुष्ट adj content
संदर्भ n context
संदर्भ संख्या n reference number
संदूक n trunk
संदेश n message
संदेश वाहक/हरकारा n messenger
संध्या n evening
संपत्ति n (भूमि) property; (पैसे) wealth
संपर्क n contact
संपर्क करना vt contact
संपादक n editor
संपादन करना/निबाहना vt perform

संपूर्णतया *adv* entirely
संबंध *n* relation, relationship
संबंधित *adj* related
संबद्ध होना *vt* belong to
संबोधन *n* address
संभव *adj* possible
संभवतः *adv* presumably
संभालना *vt* handle
संभालने लायक *adj* manageable
संभाले रखना/जगह होना *vt* hold
संभावतः *adv* possibly
संभावना *n* chance, possibility; probability, prospect
संभावना/सामर्थ्य *n* potential
संभावना से भरे/समर्थ *adj* potential
संभावित *adj* probable
संभाव्य *adj* likely
संयत्र *n* plant
संयम *n* moderation
संयमित *adj* moderate
संयुक्त *adj* joint
संयुक्त अरब अमीरात *npl* United Arab Emirates
संयुक्त खाता *n* joint account
संयुक्त राज्य अमेरिका *n* United States
संयुक्त राष्ट्र *n* United Nation
संयोग *n* coincidence
संयोगवश *adv* accidentally
संयोगवश मिलना *vt* bump into
संयोजन *n* combination, conjunction
संरक्षक *n* caretaker, warden
संरक्षण *n* conservation, preservation
संलग्न करना *vt* attach
संवाददाता *n* correspondent, reporter
संवाददाता सम्मेलन *n* press conference
संविधान *n* constitution
संवेदनशील *adj* touchy
संवेष्टन/डिब्बाबंदी *n* packaging
संशोधन *n* revision
संशोधन *n* correction
संशोधन करना *vt* revise
संसद *n* parliament
संसाधन *n* resource
संस्करण *n* edition, version
संस्कृत *n* Sanskrit
संस्कृति *n* culture

संस्था *n* association, institution
संस्थान *n* institute
संहिता *n* code
संसार *n* world
सांभर *n* spicy lentil soup
सऊदी अरब *n* Saudi Arabia
सकना *v* can
सकारात्मक *adj* positive
सक्रिय *adj* active
सक्षम *adj* capable, competent, efficient
सक्षमता *n* capacity
सगाई की अंगूठी *n* engagement ring
सचमुच *adv* indeed
सचिव *n* Secretary (Minister)
सचेत *adj* conscious
सच्चा *adj* true, truthful
सच्चाई *n* truth
सज़ा *n* punishment
सज़ा देना *vt* punish
सड़क *n* road
सड़क कर *n* road tax
सड़क का गड्ढा *n* pothole
सड़क की मरम्मत *npl* roadworks
सड़क मानचित्र *n* road map
सड़ना/सड़ाना *v* rot
सड़ा हुआ *adj* rotten
सतरह *num* seventeen
सत्तर *num* seventy
सत्रह *num* seventeen
सत्रहवां *adj* seventeenth
सतर्क *adj* cautious
सतर्क रहना *vi* watch out
सताना *vt* persecute
सत्र *n* term
सदस्य *n* member
सदस्यता *n* membership
सदस्यता पत्र *n* membership card
सदृश होना *vt* resemble ▷ *v* take after
सनक/धुन *n* mania
सनकी/उन्मत्त *n* maniac
सनद *n* voucher
सन्नादी स्वर/व्यंजन वर्ण *n* consonant
सप्ताह *n* week
सप्ताहांत *n* weekend
सफर करना *vi* commute
सफरी पलंग *n* camp bed
सफाई *n* cleaning
सफाई कर्मचारी *n* cleaner
सफाई से *adv* neatly
सफेद *adj* white
सब *det* all ▷ *pron* all

सबकुछ *pron* everything
सबसे अच्छे से *adv* best
सबसे खराब *adj* worst
सबसे छोटा *adj* youngest
सबसे बड़ा *adj* eldest
सबसे पहले *adv* first
सबूत *n* evidence
सब्ज़ी *n* vegetable
सब्ज़ी मसाला *n* curry powder
सभा *n* assembly
सभा/जमघट *n* rally
सभापति *n* chairman
सभ्यता *n* civilization
समकामी *n* colleague
समकालीन *adj* contemporary
समकोण *n* right angle
समक्षेत्र *n* plane
समझ *n* comprehension
समझना *vt* understand
समझने योग्य *adj* understandable
समझौता *n* agreement, compromise ▷ *npl* negotiations
समझौता करना *vi* compromise ▷ *v* negotiate
समतल *adj* even
समतुल्य *n* equivalent
समय *n* time
समय पर *adj* on time
समयपूर्व *adj* premature
समय मंडल *n* time zone
समय/वक़्त *n* time
समयसारिणी *n* timetable
समर्थन देना *v* back up
समर्पण करना *vi* yield
सम संख्या *adj* even
समस्त *adj* total, whole
समस्तर *adj* level
समस्या *n* problem
समाचार *npl* news
समाचारपत्र *n* newspaper
समाचार वाचक *n* newsreader
समाधि का पत्थर *n* gravestone
समानता *n* equality
समानांतर *adj* parallel
समाप्त *adj* over
समाप्त कर देना *vi* run out
समाप्त करना *vt* use up
समाप्त होना *v* end ▷ *vi* expire
समाप्ति *n* ending
समाप्ति तिथि *n* expiry date
समायोजन *n* adjustment

समायोजन करना *v* adjust
समायोज्य *adj* adjustable
समारोह *n* ceremony
समालोचक *n* critic
समास चिह्न *n* hyphen
समिति *n* committee
समीकरण *n* equation
समीक्षा *n* review
समीप *adj* close
समीप पहुँचना *v* approach
समुदाय *n* community
समुद्रतट *n* beach, coast
समुद्र तट से ऊँचाई *n* altitude
समुद्र पार/विदेश में *adv* overseas
समुद्री *adj* maritime
समुद्री लुटेरा *n* pirate
समूह *n* group
समृद्ध *adj* well-off
समृद्धि *n* prosperity
सम्मान *n* regard
सम्मिश्रक *n* blender
सम्मुख *prep* opposite
सम्मेलन *n* conference
सम्राट *n* emperor
सरकार *n* government
सरगना *n* God
सरजी *n* Sir
सरटिका *n* newt
सरपट चाल *n* gallop
सरपट दौड़ना *vi* gallop
सरलमति/अनुभवहीन *adj* naive
सरसरी तौर पर देखना *vi* browse
सरसरी नज़र *n* glance
सरसों का पेस्ट *n* mustard
सरसों का पौधा *n* rape
सराय *n* inn
सराहना *n* admiration
सराहना करना *vt* admire, appreciate
सरीसृप *n* reptile
सर्कस *n* circus
सर्दी *n* catarrh
सर्दी *n* winter
सर्वत्र *adv* everywhere
सर्वनाम *n* pronoun
सर्वश्रेष्ठ *adj* best
सर्वसम्मत *adj* unanimous
सर्वसम्मति *n* consensus
सर्वाधिक *adv* most
सलवार कमीज *n* Indian ladies outfit
सलाद का पत्ता *n* lettuce
सलाह *n* advice, tip
सलाह देना *vt* advise

सलाह लेना *v* consult
सलीब *n* crucifix
सवा किलो *n* quarter kilo
सवार *n* rider
सवार होना/सवारी करना *v* ride
सवारी *n* (गाड़ी में, घोड़े पर) ride; (घुड़सवारी) riding
सवारी डिब्बा *n* carriage
सवेरा *n* early morning
सशर्त *adj* conditional
सशस्त्र *adj* armed
ससुर *adj* father-in-law
ससुराल पक्ष *npl* in-laws
सस्ता *adj* cheap ▷ *adv* off-peak
सस्ती शराब *n* house wine, table wine
सहकर्मी *n* colleague
सहकारिता *n* cooperation
सहज ज्ञान *n* instinct
सहज बुद्धि *n* common sense
सहपाठी *n* classmate
सहमत *adj* agreed
सहमत होना *v* agree
सहमना *adj* petrified
सहयोग *n* assistance
सहयोगी *n* associate
सहवासी *n* inmate
सह सचिव *n* joint secretary
सहसामग्री *n* accessory
सहस्राब्दि *n* millennium
सहायक *n* assistant ▷ *adj* associate
सहायता *n* aid
सहारे की छड़ी *n* walking stick
सहिष्णु *adj* tolerant
सही *adj* correct, right
सही अर्थों में/असल में *adv* truly
सही करना *vt* correct
सही का निशान *n* tick
सही का निशान लगाना *vt* tick ▷ *v* tick off
सही तरह से *adv* correctly
सही/सच्चा *adj* true
सही होना *adv* right
सहेली *n* female friend
साँचा *n* mould
साँस *n* breath
साँस खींचना *v* breathe in
साँस छोड़ना *v* breathe out
साँस लेना *v* breathe
सांयोगिक *adj* accidental
सांस्कृतिक *adj* cultural
साइकिल *n* bicycle, bike

साइकिल चलाना *vi* cycle ▷ *n* cycling
साइकिल चलाने का पथ *n* cycle path
साइकिल चलाने का मार्ग *n* cycle lane
साइकिल पंप *n* bicycle pump
साइकिल सवार *n* cyclist
साइप्रस *n* Cyprus
साइबेरिया *n* Siberia
साक्षात्कार *n* interview
साक्षात्कार करना *vt* interview
साक्षात्कारकर्ता *n* interviewer
साख/ऋण *n* credit
साठ *num* sixty
सात *num* seven
सातवां *adj* seventh
साथ *prep* with
साथ जाना *vt* accompany, escort
साथ में *adv* along
साथ - साथ *adv* together
साथी *n* (दोस्त) ally; (पति, पत्नी) partner, companion
सादा *adj* plain
सादृश्यता *n* resemblance
साधन *npl* means
साधारण *adj* ordinary
साड़ी *n* sari
साफ *adj* neat
साफ करना *v* clear up
साफ़ *adj* clean
साफ़ करना *vt* clean
साफ़ करने वाला पदार्थ *n* cleanser
साफ़/निर्मल *adj* clear
साफ़ - सुथरा *adj* tidy
साफ़ - सुथरा करना *vt* tidy
साफ़-सुथरा करना *vt* clear
साबित करना *v* prove
सामग्री *npl* contents ▷ *n* ingredient
सामग्री/पदार्थ *n* material
सामने *adv* ahead
सामने का *adj* front
सामने से खुलने वाला स्वेटर *n* cardigan
सामयिक *adj* topical
सामान *npl* belongings, goods
सामान खोलना *v* unpack
सामान बांधना *vt* pack
सामान्य *adj* general, usual, normal
सामान्य चिकित्सक *n* GP

सामान्य चेतनाहारी औषधि *n* general anaesthetic
सामान्य ज्ञान *n* general knowledge
सामान्यतया *adv* normally
सामान्यीकरण करना *vi* generalize
सामूहिक *adj* collective
सामूहिक संस्था *n* collective
साम्यवाद *n* communism
साम्यवाद संबंधी *adj* communist
साम्यवादी *n* communist
साम्राज्य *n* empire
सायं *n* p.m.
सायंकालीन कक्षा *n* evening class
सारणी *n* table
सारस *n* crane
सारंगी *n* lute
सारांश *n* summary
सार्वजनिक *adj* public
सार्वजनिक अवकाश *n* public holiday
सार्वजनिक स्नान-घर *npl* baths
सालगिरह *n* anniversary
साला/देवर/जीजा *n* brother-in-law
साली *n* sister-in-law (wife's sister)
सावधान *adj* careful
सावधान करना *vt* alert
सावधानी *n* attentiveness, precaution
सावधानीपूर्वक *adv* cautiously
सावधानी से *adv* carefully
सास *n* mother-in-law
साहब *n* (श्रीमान) Mr; (जनाब) Sir; (मालिक) boss
साहस *n* courage, nerve
साहसिक *adj* adventurous
साहसी *adj* courageous
साहित्य *n* literature
साही *n* hedgehog
सिंह राशि *n* Leo
सिंहासन *n* throne
सिक्का *n* penny
सिक्किम *n* Sikkim
सिखाना *vt* teach
सिद्धांत *n* principle, theory
सिंदूर *n* vermillion
सिंदूर *n* red dot
सितम्बर *n* September
सितार *n* sitar
सिर *n* head
सिरका *n* vinegar

सिर की चोट *n* concussion
सिरदर्द *n* headache
सिर हिलाना/सहमति प्रकट करना *vi* nod
सिलवट *n* crease
सिलवासा *n* Silvassa
सींग *n* horn
सींचना *vt* water
सीखना *v* learn
सीखने वाला *n* learner
सीट *n* berth
सीट/स्थान *n* seat
सीटी *n* whistle
सीटी बजाना *v* whistle
सीढ़ी *n* (वहनीय) portable ladder; (सोपान) step
सीढ़ीदार खेत *adj* terraced
सीधा *adv* straight
सीने की जलन *n* heartburn
सीप *n* oyster
सीमा *n* border, frontier
सीमा - शुल्क *n* tariff
सीमा शुल्क अधिकारी *n* customs officer
सीमा शुल्क विभाग *npl* customs
सीमित करना *vt* restrict
सीरिया *n* Syria
सीरियाई *n* Syrian
सीसा *n* lead
सीसा - रहित *adj* lead-free
सीसारहित *n* unleaded
सीसारहित पेट्रोल *n* unleaded petrol
सुंदर *adj* beautiful
सुदरता *n* beauty
सुदरतापूर्वक *adv* beautifully
सुदरता से *adv* prettily
सुदर/मनोहर *adj* elegant
सुदर स्थान *n* beauty spot
सुखद *adj* pleasant
सुगंध चिकित्सा *n* aromatherapy
सुदूर पूर्व *n* Far East
सुदूरवर्ती *adj* remote
सुधार *n* modification
सुधारना *vt* modify, renovate
सूडान *n* Sudan
सूडानी *adj* Sudanese
सुनना *v* hear
सुनने का यंत्र *n* hearing aid
सुनवाई *n* trial
सुनहरा भूरा *adj* blonde
सुनहला *adj* golden
सुनिश्चित करना *vt* ensure
सुन्न *adj* numb
सुबह *n* morning

सुबह का नाश्ता *n* breakfast
सुर *n* note
सुरंग *n* tunnel
सुरक्षा *n* protection
सुरक्षित भंडार *n* reserve
सुरम्य *adj* picturesque
सुरुचिपूर्ण *adj* tasteful
सुविधाएँ *npl* amenities
सुविधाजनक *adj* convenient
सुव्यवस्थित करना *v* tidy up
सुश्री *n* Ms
सुषिर काष्ठ वाद्य *adj* woodwind
सुसंगत *adj* consistent
सुसज्जित *adj* equipped, furnished
सुस्ताना/तनाव रहित होना *v* relax
सुस्पष्ट *adj* noticeable
सुहाग रात *n* wedding night
सूंड़ *n* trunk
सूअर *n* pig
सूअर का मांस *n* bacon
सूई *n* needle
सूई लगाना *vt* inject
सूक्ष्मदर्शी *n* microscope
सूखा आलूबुखारा *n* prune
सूखी मिर्च *n* dry chillies
सूखे काले अंगूर *n* currant
सूचक/संकेतक *n* indicator
सूचकांक *n* index
सूचना *n* information
सूचना कार्यालय *n* information office
सूचना देना *vt* inform
सूचना पट्ट *n* bulletin board, notice board
सूचना पत्र *n* notice
सूचनाप्रद *adj* informative
सूचना प्रौद्योगिकी *n* IT
सूचित करना *n* notify
सूचिवेध चिकित्सा *n* acupuncture
सूची *vt* catalogue ▷ *n* list
सूचीबद्ध करना *vt* list
सूजन और जलन *n* inflammation
सूती कपड़ा *n* cotton
सूत्रधार *n* compere
सूत्र/संकेत *n* cue
सूनामी (विनाशकारी समुद्री लहर) *n* tsunami
सूरज *n* sun
से *prep* from
सेंकना *vi* bake
सेंधमार चोर *n* burglar

से अलग *prep* unlike
से आना/ से संबंधित होना *vt* come from
सेकेंड/पल *n* second
सेना *n* army ▷ *npl* troops
सेनाध्यक्ष *n* general
सेनेगल *n* Senegal
सेनेगल का निवासी *n* Senegalese
सेब *n* apple
सेब से बनी शराब *n* cider
से बात करना *vt* talk to
से बाहर *prep* outside
सेम *n* runner bean
से युक्त *prep* with
सेलरी *n* celery
सेवानिवृत्त योद्धा *n* veteran
सेवामुक्त *adj* retired
सेवामुक्त होना *vi* retire
सेवामुक्ति *n* retirement
से होकर *prep* via
सैन मरीनो *n* San Marino
सैर *n* outing
सैरगाह *n* resort
सोचना *vi* think
सोच/विचार *n* thought
सोने का समय *n* bedtime
सोमवार *n* Monday
सोमालिया *n* Somalia
सोमालियाई *adj* Somali
सोलह *num* sixteen
सोलहवां *adj* sixteenth
सौ *num* hundred
सौंदर्य प्रसाधन *npl* cosmetics
सौंदर्य संबंधी शल्य चिकित्सा *n* cosmetic surgery
सौंफ *n* aniseed
सौतेला पिता *n* stepfather
सौतेला पुत्र *n* stepson
सौतेला भाई *n* stepbrother
सौतेली पुत्री *n* stepdaughter
सौतेली बहन *n* stepsister
सौतेली मां *n* stepmother
सौदा *n* transaction
सौदागर *n* dealer
सौभाग्यवश *adv* fortunately
सौम्य *adj* gentle
सौर *adj* solar
स्तंभ *n* column
स्कूटर *n* scooter
स्कैंडिनेविया *n* Scandinavia
स्कैंडिनेवियाई *adj* Scandinavian
स्कॉटलैंड *n* Scotland
स्तन *n* breast
स्तनधारी प्राणी *n* mammal

स्तनपान कराना *v* breast-feed
स्तर *n* level
स्त्री-रोग विशेषज्ञ *n* gynaecologist
स्थगित करना *vt* postpone, put back
स्थान *n* location
स्थान पर होना *v* rank
स्थानांतरण *n* transfer
स्थानीय *adj* local
स्थापन *n* placement
स्थायी *adj* permanent
स्थायी पता *n* permanent address
स्थायी रूप से *adv* permanently
स्थिति *n* (चिकित्सीय अवस्था) condition; (अवस्थिति) position
स्थूलकाय *adj* obese
स्थूल/थुलथुल *adj* plump
स्नातक *n* graduate
स्नातक उपाधि *n* graduation
स्नान-कुंड *n* bath
स्नान-घर *n* bathroom
स्नान-वस्त्र *n* bathrobe
स्नेही *adj* affectionate
स्पष्ट *adj* (परिस्थिति) clear; (लिखाई) legible
स्पष्ट करना *vt* clarify
स्पष्टतया *adv* clearly
स्पष्ट रूप से *adv* frankly
स्पष्टवादी *adj* outspoken
स्पष्टीकरण/व्याख्या *n* explanation
स्पेन *n* Spain
स्पेनवासी *n* Spaniard
स्फूर्तिदायक *adj* refreshing
स्मरण दिलाना/लौटा लाना *vt* bring back
स्मरणशक्ति/याददाश्त *n* memory
स्मारक *n* memorial, monument
स्याही *n* ink
स्याही वाली कलम *n* fountain pen
स्लेटी *adj* grey
स्लोवाकिया *n* Slovakia
स्लोवाकियाई *adj* Slovak
स्लोवेनिया *n* Slovenia
स्लोवेनियाई *adj* Slovenian
स्वर्ग *n* heaven, paradise
स्वचालित *adj* automatic
स्वचालित सीढ़ी *n* escalator
स्वच्छंद *adj* freelance

स्वच्छंद रूप से *adv* freelance
स्वच्छता *n* hygiene
स्वतंत्र/आत्मनिर्भर *adj* independent
स्वतंत्रता *n* independence
स्वतः *adv* automatically
स्वतःस्फूर्त *n* reflex
स्वत्व रखना *vt* possess
स्वयं *pron* myself
स्वयंसेवक *n* volunteer
स्वर *n* vowel
स्वरमान *n* pitch
स्वर्ग *n* heaven, paradise
स्वर्गीय *adj* late
स्वर्ण *n* gold
स्वशासन *n* autonomy
स्वस्थ *adj* healthy
स्वागत *n* welcome
स्वागत करना *vt* welcome
स्वागत है! *excl* welcome!
स्वाद *n* taste
स्वाद आना *vi* taste
स्वादिष्ट *adj* tasty
स्वाभाविक *adj* natural
स्वाभाविक रूप से *adv* naturally
स्वायत्तशासी *adj* autonomous
स्वार्थी *adj* selfish
स्वास्थ्य *n* health
स्वास्थ्यलाभ *n* recovery
स्वास्थ्यवर्द्धक *adj* healthy
स्वीकार करना *vt* accept, admit
स्विट्ज़रलैंड का निवासी *npl* Swiss
स्वीकारोक्ति *n* confession
स्वीकार्य *adj* acceptable
स्वीकृति *n* approval
स्वीकृति देना *vi* approve
स्वीडन *n* Sweden
स्वेच्छापूर्वक *adv* voluntarily
स्वेच्छा से *adv* willingly
स्वेच्छा से काम करना *v* volunteer
स्वेटर *n* pullover
स्वैच्छिक *adj* voluntary

हँसना *vi* grin
हँसमुख *adj* cheerful
हँसी *n* grin
हंगरी *n* Hungary
हंगरी से संबद्ध *adj* Hungarian

हंस *n* swan
हंसना *vi* laugh
हंसी *n* laugh, laughter
हकलाना *vi* stutter
हक्का - बक्का *adj* bewildered
हज़ार *num* thousand
हज़ारवां *adj* thousandth
हज़ारवां हिस्सा *n* thousandth
हटना/जगह बदलना *n* move
हटाना *vi* move ▷ *vt* remove; (छुपाना) put away
हटाने योग्य *adj* removable
हटाव *n* removal
हड़बड़ाहट *n* rush
हड्डी *n* bone
हड़ताल *n* strike
हताश *adj* frustrated
हत्था/मूठ *n* handle
हत्या *n* murder
हत्या करना *vt* murder
हत्यारा *n* murderer
हथकड़ी *npl* handcuffs
हथियार *n* weapon
हथेली *n* palm
हथौड़ा *n* hammer
हद *n* extent, limit
हम *pron* we
हमला *n* attack
हमला करना *v* attack
हमसफर *n* companion
हमारा *det* our ▷ *pron* ours
हमें *pron* us
हमेशा *adv* always, forever
हरकारा *n* courier
हर कोई *pron* everyone
हर घंटे पर *adv* hourly
हरा *adj* green
हराना *vt* beat
हरा - भरा *adj* lush
हरा सलाद *n* green salad
हरियाणा *n* Haryana
हरी फूलगोभी *n* broccoli
हरी मिर्च *n* green chillies
हर्निया/अंत्र वृद्धि *n* hernia
हल *n* plough
हलका/मृदु *adj* soft
हल निकालना *v* work out
हल्का *adj* light, mild
हल्की हवा *n* breeze
हल्दी *n* turmeric
हवा *n* (तत्व) air; (हवा का घुमाव) wind
हवाई अड्डा *n* airport
हवाई क्षेत्र *n* airspace
हवाई चप्पल *n* slipper

हवाई जहाज *n* plane
हवाई डाक *n* airmail
हवा भरना *vt* pump up
हवासील *n* pelican
हवेली *n* mansion
हस्तनिर्मित *adj* handmade
हस्तलेख *n* handwriting
हस्ताक्षर *n* autograph ▷ *v* sign
हाँ *excl* yes!
हाइड्रोजन - एक गैस *n* hydrogen
हाई फ़ाई *n* hi-fi
हाजिरी *n* roll call
हाथ *n* hand
हाथ का सामान *n* hand luggage
हाथ बढ़ाना *vi* reach
हाथी *n* elephant
हाथीचक-एक सब्ज़ी *n* artichoke
हाथीदांत *n* ivory
हानिकारक *adj* harmful
हानिरहित *adj* harmless
हार *n* necklace
हारना *v* lose
हार मान लेना *vi* give in
हाल का *adj* recent
हाल में *adv* lately
हाल ही में *adv* recently
हालांकि *conj* although ▷ *adv* though
हार्मोनियम *n* harmonium
हासिल करना *vt* achieve, obtain
हास्य अभिनेता *n* comedian
हास्यचित्र *n* cartoon
हिंजड़ा *n* eunuch
हिंडोला *n* merry-go-round
हिंद महासागर *n* Indian Ocean
हिंसक *adj* violent
हिंसा *n* violence
हिचक *n* inhibition
हिचकिचाना *vi* hesitate
हिचकी *npl* hiccups
हिन्द चीन *n* Indo China
हिन्दपाकिस्तान *n* Indo Pakistan
हिन्दी *n* Hindi
हिन्दुत्व/हिन्दू धर्म *n* Hinduism
हिन्दुस्तान *n* Hindustan
हिन्दुस्तानी *n* Hindustani
हिन्दू *adj* Hindu
हिन्दू धर्मानुयायी *n* Hindu
हिप्पी *n* hippy
हिमनदी *n* glacier

हिमशीतल *adj* freezing
हिमालय *n* Himalaya
हिरन का मांस *n* venison
हिलसा मछली *n* herring
हिस्सा *n* part, portion
हिस्सा/कोटा *n* quota
हिस्सेदार *n* shareholder
हीन/अवर *adj* inferior
हीन व्यक्ति *n* inferior
हीरा *n* diamond
हींग *n* asafoetida
हुल्लड़ *n* racket
हृदय *n* heart
हृदयविदारक *adj* moving
हेडमास्टर *n* headmaster
हेलमेट *n* helmet
हेलीकॉप्टर *n* helicopter
हेल्पलाइन *n* helpline
हैकर/घुसपैठिया *n* hacker
हैती *n* Haiti
हैदराबाद *n* Hyderabad
हॉकी *n* hockey
हॉथॉर्न *n* hawthorn
हॉर्मोन/अंतःस्त्राव *n* hormone
हॉलैंड *n* Holland
होंठ *n* lip
होंठलाली *n* lipstick
होगा *v* will
हो जाना *v* catch
होना *v* be; (बनना) turn out ▷ *vt* (समाविष्ट) contain
होना/रखना *v* have
होम पेज/मुख्य पृष्ठ *n* home page
होम्योपैथी *n* homeopathy
होली *n* spring festival
होश में आना *v* come round
हो सकना *v* may, might
हौज *n* sink
हौंडुरस *n* Honduras
हौसला रखना *v* bear up

ENGLISH-HINDI

अंग्रेजी – हिन्दी

a

a [eɪ] *det* एक
abandon [ə'bændən] *vt* त्याग देना
abbreviation [əˌbriːvɪ'eɪʃən] *n* संक्षिप्त रूप
abdomen ['æbdəmən] *n* *(formal)* पेट
abduct [æb'dʌkt] *vt* भगा ले जाना
ability [ə'bɪlɪtɪ] *n* योग्यता
able ['eɪbl] *adj* योग्य
abnormal [æb'nɔːməl] *adj* *(formal)* असामान्य
abolish [ə'bɒlɪʃ] *vt* उन्मूलन करना
abolition [ˌæbə'lɪʃən] *n* उन्मूलन
about [ə'baʊt] *adv* *(near to)* लगभग ▷ *prep* *(to do with)* के बारे में
above [ə'bʌv] *prep* ऊपर
abroad [ə'brɔːd] *adv* विदेश में
abrupt [ə'brʌpt] *adj* अप्रत्याशित
abruptly [ə'brʌptlɪ] *adv* अप्रत्याशित रूप से
abscess ['æbsɛs] *n* फोड़ा
absence ['æbsəns] *n* अनुपस्थिति
absent ['æbsənt] *adj* अनुपस्थित
absent-minded [ˌæbsən't'maɪndɪd] *adj* भुलक्कड़
absolutely [ˌæbsə'luːtlɪ] *adv* बिल्कुल
abstract ['æbstrækt] *adj* अमूर्त
absurd [əb'sɜːd] *adj* बेतुका
Abu Dhabi ['æbuː 'dɑːbɪ] *n* अबू धाबी - दक्षिणी-पूर्वी अरब का एक अमीरात
academic [ˌækə'dɛmɪk] *adj* शैक्षिक
academic year [ˌækə'dɛmɪk jɪə] *n* शैक्षिक वर्ष
academy [ə'kædəmɪ] *n* शिक्षा संस्थान
accelerate [æk'sɛləˌreɪt] *v* तेज़ करना
acceleration [ækˌsɛlə'reɪʃən] *n* गति वृद्धि

accelerator [æk'sɛlə,reɪtə] *n* एक्सेलरेटर- गाड़ी की गति को तेज करने वाला पैडल

accept [ək'sɛpt] *v* स्वीकार करना

acceptable [ək'sɛptəbl] *adj* स्वीकार्य

access ['æksɛs] *n* पहुंच ▷ *vt* पहुंच प्राप्त करना

accessible [ək'sɛsəbl] *adj* पहुंचने योग्य

accessory [ək'sɛsərɪ] *n* सहसामग्री

accident ['æksɪdənt] *n (mishap)* दुर्घटना; *(something unplanned)* इत्तफ़ाक/संयोग

accidental [,æksɪ'dɛntl] *adj* सांयोगिक

accidentally [,æksɪ'dɛntəlɪ] *adv* संयोगवश

accident and emergency ['æksɪdənt ənd ɪ'mɜːdʒnsɪ] *n* दुर्घटना व आपातकक्ष

accident insurance ['æksɪdənt ɪn'ʃʊərəns] *n* दुर्घटना बीमा

accommodate [ə'kɒmə,deɪt] *vt* स्थान देना/समायोजित करना

accommodation [ə,kɒmə'deɪʃən] *n* आवास

accompany [ə'kʌmpənɪ] *vt (formal)* साथ जाना

accomplice [ə'kɒmplɪs] *n* अपराध में साथी

accordingly [ə'kɔːdɪŋlɪ] *adv* तदनुसार

according to [ə'kɔːdɪŋ tə] *prep (as reported by)* के अनुसार; *(based on)* के अनुसार

accordion [ə'kɔːdɪən] *n* अकॉर्डिअन - एक तरह का बाजा

account [ə'kaʊnt] *n (report)* विवरण; *(at bank)* खाता

accountable [ə'kaʊntəbl] *adj* ज़िम्मेदार/उत्तरदायी

accountancy [ə'kaʊntənsɪ] *n* लेखाविधि

accountant [ə'kaʊntənt] *n* लेखापाल

account for [ə'kaʊnt fɔː] *v* हिसाब बताना

a

account number [ə'kaʊnt 'nʌmbə] *n* खाता संख्या

accuracy ['ækjʊrəsɪ] *n* परिशुद्धता

accurate ['ækjərɪt] *adj* एकदम सही

accurately ['ækjərɪtlɪ] *adv* ठीक-ठीक

accusation [ˌækjʊ'zeɪʃən] *n* आरोप

accuse [ə'kjuːz] *vt* आरोप लगाना

accused [ə'kjuːzd] *n* अभियुक्त

ace [eɪs] *n* इक्का

ache [eɪk] *n* दर्द ▷ *vi* दर्द करना

achieve [ə'tʃiːv] *vt* हासिल करना

achievement [ə'tʃiːvmənt] *n* उपलब्धि

acid ['æsɪd] *n* अम्ल

acid rain ['æsɪd reɪn] *n* अम्लीय वर्षा

acknowledgement [ək'nɒlɪdʒmənt] *n* अभिस्वीकृति

acne ['æknɪ] *n* मुंहासा

acorn ['eɪkɔːn] *n* बाँजफल

acoustic [ə'kuːstɪk] *adj* बिना बिजली के ध्वनि उत्पन्न करने वाला वाद्य

acre ['eɪkə] *n* एकड़

acrobat ['ækrəˌbæt] *n* कलाबाज

acronym ['ækrənɪm] *n* आदिवर्णिक शब्द

across [ə'krɒs] *prep* उस पार

act [ækt] *n* कृत्य ▷ *vi (take action)* कार्यवाही करना; *(play a part)* अभिनय करना

acting ['æktɪŋ] *adj* कार्यकारी ▷ *n* अभिनय

action ['ækʃən] *n* कार्रवाई

active ['æktɪv] *adj* सक्रिय

activity [æk'tɪvɪtɪ] *n* गतिविधि

actor ['æktə] *n* अभिनेता

actress ['æktrɪs] *n* अभिनेत्री

actual ['æktʃʊəl] *adj* वास्तविक

actually ['æktʃʊəlɪ] *adv* वस्तुतः

acupuncture ['ækjʊˌpʌŋktʃə] *n* सूचिवेध चिकित्सा

AD [eɪ diː] *abbr* ईसवी

ad [æd] *abbr (informal)* विज्ञापन
adapt [ə'dæpt] *vi* अनुकूल बनना
adaptor [ə'dæptə] *n* अडैप्टर
add [æd] *vt (put with)* मिलाना; *(numbers)* जोड़ना
addict ['ædɪkt] *n* लत लगा हुआ
addicted [ə'dɪktɪd] *adj* आदी
additional [ə'dɪʃənl] *adj* अतिरिक्त
additive ['ædɪtɪv] *n* खाद्य पदार्थों में डाली जाने वाली अतिरिक्त सामग्री
address [ə'drɛs] *n (speech)* संबोधन; *(where you live)* पता
address book [ə'drɛs bʊk] *n* पता पुस्तिका
add up [æd ʌp] *v* जोड़ना
adjacent [ə'dʒeɪsnt] *adj* बगल का
adjective ['ædʒɪktɪv] *n* विशेषण
adjust [ə'dʒʌst] *v* समायोजन करना
adjustable [ə'dʒʌstəbl] *adj* समायोज्य
adjustment [ə'dʒʌstmənt] *n* समायोजन
administration [əd,mɪnɪ'streɪʃən] *n* प्रशासन
administrative [əd'mɪnɪ,strətɪv] *adj* प्रशासनिक
admiration [,ædmə'reɪʃən] *n* सराहना
admire [əd'maɪə] *vt* सराहना करना
admission [əd'mɪʃən] *n* दाखिला
admit [əd'mɪt] *vt (allow in)* भर्ती करना ▷ *v (confess)* स्वीकार करना
admittance [əd'mɪtns] *n* प्रवेश/प्रवेश की आज्ञा
adolescence [,ædə'lɛsəns] *n* किशोरावस्था
adolescent [,ædə'lɛsnt] *n* किशोर
adopt [ə'dɒpt] *vt* गोद लेना
adopted [ə'dɒptɪd] *adj* दत्तक
adoption [ə'dɒpʃən] *n* गोद लेना
adore [ə'dɔː] *vt* बहुत प्यार करना

a

Adriatic [ˌeɪdrɪˈætɪk] *adj* एड्रियाटिक

Adriatic Sea [ˌeɪdrɪˈætɪk siː] *n* एड्रियाटिक सागर

adult [ˈædʌlt] *n* वयस्क

adult education [ˈædʌlt ˌɛdjʊˈkeɪʃən] *n* प्रौढ़ शिक्षा

advance [ədˈvɑːns] *n* पेशगी ▷ *vi* आगे बढ़ना

advanced [ədˈvɑːnst] *adj* विकसित

advantage [ədˈvɑːntɪdʒ] *n* फ़ायदा

advent [ˈædvɛnt] *n* *(formal)* आगमन

adventure [ədˈvɛntʃə] *n* रोमांचक कार्य

adventurous [ədˈvɛntʃərəs] *adj* साहसिक

adverb [ˈædˌvɜːb] *n* क्रिया-विशेषण

adversary [ˈædvəsərɪ] *n* विरोधी

advert [ˈædvɜːt] *n* विज्ञापन

advertise [ˈædvəˌtaɪz] *v* विज्ञापन देना

advertisement [ədˈvɜːtɪsmənt] *n* *(written)* विज्ञापन

advertising [ˈædvəˌtaɪzɪŋ] *n* विज्ञापन

advice [ədˈvaɪs] *n* सलाह

advisable [ədˈvaɪzəbl] *adj* *(formal)* उचित

advise [ədˈvaɪz] *vt* सलाह देना

aerial [ˈɛərɪəl] *n* विद्युत ग्राहक

aerobics [ɛəˈrəʊbɪks] *npl* एक प्रकार की कसरत

aerosol [ˈɛərəˌsɒl] *n* छिड़काव करने वाली बोतल

affair [əˈfɛə] *n* मामला

affect [əˈfɛkt] *vt* प्रभावित करना

affectionate [əˈfɛkʃənɪt] *adj* स्नेही

afford [əˈfɔːd] *vt* वहन करना

affordable [əˈfɔːdəbl] *adj* वहन करने योग्य

Afghan [ˈæfgæn] *adj* अफ़गानिस्तानी ▷ *n* अफ़गानिस्तानी

Afghanistan [æfˈgænɪˌstɑːn] *n* अफ़गानिस्तान

afraid [əˈfreɪd] *adj* भयभीत

Africa [ˈæfrɪkə] *n* अफ़्रीका

African ['æfrıkən] *adj* अफ़्रीकी ▹ *n* अफ़्रीकी

Afrikaans [ˌæfrı'kaːns] *n* अफ़्रीकान्स

Afrikaner [æfrı'kaːnə] *n* अफ़्रीकेनर - दक्षिण अफ़्रीका की श्वेत आबादी से संबद्ध ऐसा व्यक्ति, जिसके पूर्वज डच थे

after ['aːftə] *conj (later than)* बाद ▹ *prep (later than)* बाद में; *(in pursuit of)* के पीछे

afternoon [ˌaːftə'nuːn] *n* दोपहर

afters ['aːftəz] *npl (informal)* भोजन के बाद खाई जाने वाली मिठाई

aftershave ['aːftəˌʃeıv] *n* हजामत के बाद लगाया जाने वाला सुगंधित द्रव्य

afterwards ['aːftəwədz] *adv* तत्पश्चात

again [ə'gɛn] *adv* पुनः

against [ə'gɛnst] *prep (touching)* के सहारे; *(in opposition to)* विरुद्ध

age [eıdʒ] *n* उम्र

aged [eıdʒd] *adj* उम्र का

age limit [eıdʒ 'lımıt] *n* आयु सीमा

agency ['eıdʒənsı] *n* संस्था

agenda [ə'dʒɛndə] *n* कार्यसूची

agent ['eıdʒənt] *n* प्रतिनिधि

aggressive [ə'grɛsıv] *adj* उग्र

AGM [eı dʒiː ɛm] *abbr* ए. जी. एम./वार्षिक सार्वजनिक बैठक हेतु संक्षिप्त रूप

ago [ə'gəʊ] *adv* पहले

agree [ə'griː] *v* सहमत होना

agreed [ə'griːd] *adj* सहमत

agreement [ə'griːmənt] *n* समझौता

agricultural ['ægrıˌkʌltʃərəl] *adj* कृषि संबंधी

agriculture ['ægrıˌkʌltʃə] *n* कृषि

ahead [ə'hɛd] *adv* सामने

aid [eıd] *n* सहायता

AIDS [eıdz] *n* एड्स - एक यौनजनित बीमारी

aim [eım] *n* उद्देश्य ▹ *v* उद्देश्य रखना

air [ɛə] *n* हवा

airbag ['ɛəbæg] *n* एयरबैग

air-conditioned [ˌɛəkən'dıʃənd] *adj* वातानुकूलित

air conditioning [ɛə kən'dɪʃənɪŋ] *n* वातानुकूलन

aircraft ['ɛəˌkrɑːft] *n* वायुयान

air force [ɛə fɔːs] *n* वायुसेना

air hostess [ɛə 'həʊstɪs] *n (old-fashioned)* विमान परिचारिका

airline ['ɛəˌlaɪn] *n* विमान सेवा कंपनी

airmail ['ɛəˌmeɪl] *n* हवाई डाक

airport ['ɛəˌpɔːt] *n* हवाई अड्डा

airsick ['ɛəˌsɪk] *adj* हवाई यात्रा से बीमार

airspace ['ɛəˌspeɪs] *n* हवाई क्षेत्र

airtight ['ɛəˌtaɪt] *adj* वायुरोधक

air traffic controller [ɛə'træfɪk kən'trəʊlə] *n* वायु-परिवहन नियंत्रक

aisle [aɪl] *n* गलियारा

alarm [ə'lɑːm] *n* आकस्मिक भय

alarm clock [ə'lɑːm klɒk] *n* अलार्म घड़ी

alarming [ə'lɑːmɪŋ] *adj* भयानक

Albania [æl'beɪnɪə] *n* अल्बानिया

Albanian [æl'beɪnɪən] *adj* अल्बानियाई ▷ *n (person)* अल्बानियाई; *(language)* अल्बानियाई

album ['ælbəm] *n* एल्बम - संगीत-संग्रह

alcohol ['ælkəˌhɒl] *n* अल्कोहल - मादक पेय

alcohol-free ['ælkəˌhɒlfriː] *adj* अल्कोहल - रहित या मादक द्रव्य रहित

alcoholic [ˌælkə'hɒlɪk] *adj* अल्कोहलिक - मादक ▷ *n* मद्यव्यसनी

alert [ə'lɜːt] *adj* सावधान ▷ *vt* सावधान करना

Algeria [æl'dʒɪərɪə] *n* अल्जीरिया

Algerian [æl'dʒɪərɪən] *adj* अल्जीरियाई ▷ *n* अल्जीरियाई

alias ['eɪlɪəs] *prep* उर्फ़

alibi ['ælɪˌbaɪ] *n* अनुपस्थिति का कारण

alien ['eɪljən] *n (formal)* विदेशी

alive [ə'laɪv] *adj* जीवित
all [ɔːl] *det* सब ▷ *pron* सब
Allah ['ælə] *n* अल्लाह
allegation [ˌælɪ'geɪʃən] *n* आरोप
alleged [ə'lɛdʒd] *adj* *(formal)* कथित
allergic [ə'lɜːdʒɪk] *adj* अधिहृषत/एलर्जिक
allergy ['ælədʒɪ] *n* अधिहृषता/एलर्जी
alley ['ælɪ] *n* संकरी गली
alliance [ə'laɪəns] *n* गठबंधन
alligator ['ælɪˌgeɪtə] *n* घड़ियाल
allow [ə'laʊ] *vt* अनुमति देना
all right [ɔːl raɪt] *adv* *(informal)* ठीक-ठाक ▷ *adj* *(informal)* ठीक-ठाक
ally ['ælaɪ] *n* साथी
almond ['ɑːmənd] *n* बादाम
almost ['ɔːlməʊst] *adv* लगभग
alone [ə'ləʊn] *adj* अकेला
along [ə'lɒŋ] *prep* के किनारे/समानांतर ▷ *adv* साथ में
aloud [ə'laʊd] *adv* ऊंची आवाज़ में
alphabet ['ælfəˌbɛt] *n* वर्णाक्षर
Alps [ælps] *npl* आल्प्स - दक्षिण मध्य यूरोप की एक पर्वत श्रृंखला
already [ɔːl'rɛdɪ] *adv* पहले से ही
also ['ɔːlsəʊ] *adv* भी
altar ['ɔːltə] *n* वेदी
alter ['ɔːltə] *v* बदलना
alternate [ɔːl'tɜːnɪt] *adj* बारी-बारी से
alternative [ɔːl'tɜːnətɪv] *adj* वैकल्पिक ▷ *n* विकल्प
alternatively [ɔːl'tɜːnətɪvlɪ] *adv* की बजाए
although [ɔːl'ðəʊ] *conj (in contrast)* यद्यपि; *conj (even though)* हालांकि
altitude ['æltɪˌtjuːd] *n* समुद्र तट से ऊँचाई
altogether [ˌɔːltə'gɛðə] *adv* कुल मिलाकर
aluminium [ˌæljʊ'mɪnɪəm] *n* अल्युमिनियम-एक हल्की धातु
always ['ɔːlweɪz] *adv* हमेशा

Alzheimer's disease ['ælts'haɪməz dɪ'ziːz] *n* अल्ज़ाइमर रोग
a.m. [eɪ ɛm] *abbr* पूर्वाह्न के लिए संक्षिप्त रूप
amateur ['æmətə] *n* शौकीन
amaze [ə'meɪz] *vt* चकित करना
amazed [ə'meɪzd] *adj* चकित
amazing [ə'meɪzɪŋ] *adj* आश्चर्यजनक
ambassador [æm'bæsədə] *n* राजदूत
amber ['æmbə] *n* कहरुवा
ambition [æm'bɪʃən] *n* महत्वाकांक्षा
ambitious [æm'bɪʃəs] *adj* महत्वाकांक्षी
ambulance ['æmbjʊləns] *n* रुग्णवाहिका
amenities [ə'miːnɪtɪz] *npl* सुविधाएँ
America [ə'mɛrɪkə] *n* अमरीका
American [ə'mɛrɪkən] *adj* अमरीकी ▷ *n* अमरीकी
American football [ə'mɛrɪkən 'fʊt,bɔːl] *n* अमरीकी फ़ुटबॉल
among [ə'mʌŋ] *prep* *(surrounded by)* के बीच में; *(between)* में
amount [ə'maʊnt] *n* राशि
amp [æmp] *n* एम्पियर - विद्युत धारा का मात्रक
amplifier ['æmplɪ,faɪə] *n* एम्प्लिफ़ायर - एक ध्वनिवर्द्धक उपकरण
amuse [ə'mjuːz] *vt* मनोरंजन करना
amusement arcade [ə'mjuːzmənt ɑː'keɪd] *n* मशीन में पैसे डालकर खेल खेलने का स्थान
an [æn] *det* एक
anaemic [ə'niːmɪk] *adj* खून की कमी से पीड़ित
anaesthetic [,ænɪs'θɛtɪk] *n* निश्चेतक
analyse ['ænə,laɪz] *vt* विश्लेषण करना
analysis [ə'nælɪsɪs] *n* विश्लेषण
ancestor ['ænsɛstə] *n* पूर्वज
anchor ['æŋkə] *n* लंगर
anchovy ['æntʃəvɪ] *n* एक प्रकार की छोटी मछली
ancient ['eɪnʃənt] *adj* प्राचीन

and [ænd] *conj* और
Andes ['ændiːz] *npl* एंडीज़ - दक्षिण अमेरिकी पर्वत श्रृंखला
Andorra [æn'dɔːrə] *n* एण्डोरा-दक्षिणी-पश्चिमी यूरोप की एक पहाड़ी रियासत
angel ['eɪndʒəl] *n* देवदूत
anger ['æŋgə] *n* क्रोध
angina [æn'dʒaɪnə] *n* कंठशूल
angle ['æŋgl] *n* कोण
angler ['æŋglə] *n* शौकिया तौर पर बंशी से मछली पकड़ने वाला
angling ['æŋglɪŋ] *n* बंशी से मछली पकड़ना
Angola [æŋ'gəʊlə] *n* अंगोला - दक्षिणी-पश्चिमी अफ़्रीका का एक गणराज्य
Angolan [æŋ'gəʊlən] *adj* अंगोलियाई ▷ *n* अंगोलियाई
angry ['æŋgrɪ] *adj* क्रोधित
animal ['ænɪməl] *n* पशु
aniseed ['ænɪˌsiːd] *n* सौंफ
ankle ['æŋkl] *n* टखना
anniversary [ˌænɪ'vɜːsərɪ] *n* सालगिरह
announce [ə'naʊns] *vt* घोषणा करना
announcement [ə'naʊnsmənt] *n* घोषणा
annoy [ə'nɔɪ] *vt* खीझ दिलाना
annoying [ə'nɔɪɪŋ] *adj* खिझाने वाला
annual ['ænjʊəl] *adj* वार्षिक
annually ['ænjʊəlɪ] *adv* वार्षिक रूप से
anonymous [ə'nɒnɪməs] *adj* गुमनाम
anorak ['ænəˌræk] *n* टोपी वाला बरसाती जैकेट
anorexia [ˌænə'rɛksɪə] *n* एनोरेक्सिया - आहार संबंधी विकार
anorexic [ˌænə'rɛksɪk] *adj* एनोरेक्सिक - आहार संबंधी विकार से ग्रस्त
another [ə'nʌðə] *det* एक और
answer ['ɑːnsə] *n* जवाब ▷ *v* जवाब देना
answering machine ['ɑːnsərɪŋ mə'ʃiːn] *n* आंसरिंग मशीन

answerphone ['ɑːnsəfəʊn] *n* आंसरफ़ोन

ant [ænt] *n* चींटी

antagonize [æn'tægə,naɪz] *vt* बैर मोल लेना

Antarctic [ænt'ɑːktɪk] *n* अंटार्कटिक क्षेत्र

Antarctica [ænt'ɑːktɪkə] *n* अंटार्कटिका महाद्वीप

antelope ['æntɪ,ləʊp] *n* चिंकारा

antenatal [,æntɪ'neɪtl] *adj* प्रसवपूर्व

anthem ['ænθəm] *n* गान

anthropology [,ænθrə'pɒlədʒɪ] *n* नृविज्ञान

antibiotic [,æntɪbaɪ'ɒtɪk] *n* प्रतिजैविक

antibody ['æntɪ,bɒdɪ] *n* प्रतिरक्षी

anticlockwise [,æntɪ'klɒk,waɪz] *adv* वामावर्त

antidepressant [,æntɪdɪ'prɛsnt] *n* अवसादरोधी दवा

antidote ['æntɪ,dəʊt] *n* विष नाशक दवा

antifreeze ['æntɪ,friːz] *n* पानी को जमने से रोकने वाला द्रव

antihistamine [,æntɪ'hɪstə,miːn] *n* एंटीहिस्टमीन - एलर्जी की दवा

antiperspirant [,æntɪ'pɜːspərənt] *n* प्रतिस्वेदक

antique [æn'tiːk] *n* प्राचीन वस्तु

antique shop [æn'tiːk ʃɒp] *n* प्राचीन वस्तुओं की दुकान

antiseptic [,æntɪ'sɛptɪk] *n* रोगाणु रोधक

anxiety [æŋ'zaɪɪtɪ] *n* फ़िक्र

any ['ɛnɪ] *det (some)* किंचित/कुछ भी ▷ *pron* कोई भी ▷ *det (whichever)* कोई भी

anybody ['ɛnɪ,bɒdɪ] *pron* कोई/कोई व्यक्ति

anyhow ['ɛnɪ,haʊ] *adv* किसी भी तरह से

anymore [,ɛnɪ'mɔː] *adv* अब/इसके बाद

anyone ['ɛnɪ,wʌn] *pron* कोई भी/किसी को

anything ['ɛnɪˌθɪŋ] *pron* कुछ भी
anytime ['ɛnɪˌtaɪm] *adv* कभी भी
anyway ['ɛnɪˌweɪ] *adv* फिर भी
anywhere ['ɛnɪˌwɛə] *adv* कहीं भी
apart [ə'pɑːt] *adv (distant)* अलग; *(to pieces)* अलग-अलग करना
apart from [ə'pɑːt frɒm] *prep* के अलावा
apartment [ə'pɑːtmənt] *n* बड़ी ईमारत की एक आवासीय इकाई
aperitif [æˌpɛrɪ'tiːf] *n* अपेरटीफ़ - मादक पेय
aperture ['æpətʃə] *n (formal)* झिरी
apologize [ə'pɒləˌdʒaɪz] *vi* क्षमा मांगना
apology [ə'pɒlədʒɪ] *n* क्षमा याचना
apostrophe [ə'pɒstrəfɪ] *n* वर्णलोप या संबंधकारक चिह्न
appalling [ə'pɔːlɪŋ] *adj* ख़ौफ़नाक
apparatus [ˌæpə'reɪtəs] *n* प्रणाली
apparent [ə'pærənt] *adj* ज़ाहिर/स्पष्ट
apparently [ə'pærəntlɪ] *adv* ज़ाहिर तौर पर/स्पष्ट रुप से
appeal [ə'piːl] *n* आग्रह ▹ *vi* आग्रह करना
appear [ə'pɪə] *vt* दिखाई देना
appearance [ə'pɪərəns] *n* उपस्थिति
appendicitis [əˌpɛndɪ'saɪtɪs] *n* आंत का फोड़ा
appetite ['æpɪˌtaɪt] *n* भूख
applaud [ə'plɔːd] *v* प्रशंसा से ताली बजाना
applause [ə'plɔːz] *n* ताली बजा कर की गई प्रशंसा
apple ['æpl] *n* सेब
apple pie ['æpl paɪ] *n* सेब से बनी एक मिठाई
appliance [ə'plaɪəns] *n (formal)* उपकरण
applicant ['æplɪkənt] *n* आवेदक
application [ˌæplɪ'keɪʃən] *n* आवेदन

application form [ˌæplɪˈkeɪʃn fɔːm] *n* आवेदन पत्र
apply [əˈplaɪ] *v* आवेदन करना
appoint [əˈpɔɪnt] *vt* नियुक्त करना
appointment [əˈpɔɪntmənt] *n* नियुक्ति
appreciate [əˈpriːʃɪˌeɪt] *vt* सराहना करना
apprehensive [ˌæprɪˈhɛnsɪv] *adj* आंशकावान
apprentice [əˈprɛntɪs] *n* चेला
approach [əˈprəʊtʃ] *v* समीप पहुँचना
appropriate [əˈprəʊprɪɪt] *adj* उपयुक्त
approval [əˈpruːvl] *n* स्वीकृति
approve [əˈpruːv] *vi* स्वीकृति देना
approximate [əˈprɒksɪmɪt] *adj* लगभग
approximately [əˈprɒksɪmɪtlɪ] *adv* लगभग रूप से
apricot [ˈeɪprɪˌkɒt] *n* खुबानी
April [ˈeɪprəl] *n* अप्रैल
April Fools' Day [ˈeɪprəl fuːlz deɪ] *n* मूर्ख दिवस
apron [ˈeɪprən] *n* पेशबंद, पेटबंद
aquarium [əˈkwɛərɪəm] *n* जल - जीवशाला
Aquarius [əˈkwɛərɪəs] *n* कुंभ राशि
Arab [ˈærəb] *adj* अरबी ▷ *n* अरबी
Arabic [ˈærəbɪk] *n* अरबी ▷ *adj* अरबी
arbitration [ˌɑːbɪˈtreɪʃən] *n* मध्यस्थता
arch [ɑːtʃ] *n* मेहराब
archaeologist [ˌɑːkɪˈɒlədʒɪst] *n* पुरातत्वविद्
archaeology [ˌɑːkɪˈɒlədʒɪ] *n* पुरातत्व विज्ञान
architect [ˈɑːkɪˌtɛkt] *n* वास्तुकार
architecture [ˈɑːkɪˌtɛktʃə] *n* वास्तुकला
archive [ˈɑːkaɪv] *n* पुरालेख
Arctic [ˈɑːktɪk] *n* आर्कटिक क्षेत्र

Arctic Circle ['ɑːktɪk 'sɜːkl] *n* आर्कटिक वृत्त
Arctic Ocean ['ɑːktɪk 'əʊʃən] *n* आर्कटिक महासागर
area ['ɛərɪə] *n* क्षेत्र
Argentina [ˌɑːdʒən'tiːnə] *n* अर्जेंटीना - दक्षिणी अमेरिका का गणराज्य
Argentinian [ˌɑːdʒən'tɪnɪən] *adj* अर्जेंटीनियाई ▷ *n* अर्जेंटीनियाई
argue ['ɑːgjuː] *vi* तर्क करना
argument ['ɑːgjʊmənt] *n* तर्क
Aries ['ɛəriːz] *n* मेष राशि
arm [ɑːm] *n* बांह
armchair ['ɑːmˌtʃɛə] *n* हत्थेवाली कुर्सी
armed [ɑːmd] *adj* सशस्त्र
Armenia [ɑː'miːnɪə] *n* आर्मेनिया - उत्तरी-पश्चिमी एशिया का एक गणराज्य
Armenian [ɑː'miːnɪən] *adj* आर्मेनियाई ▷ *n (person)* आर्मेनियाई; *(language)* आर्मेनियाई
armour ['ɑːmə] *n* कवच
armpit ['ɑːmˌpɪt] *n* कांख
army ['ɑːmɪ] *n* सेना
aroma [ə'rəʊmə] *n* खुशबू
aromatherapy [əˌrəʊmə'θɛrəpɪ] *n* सुगंध चिकित्सा
around [ə'raʊnd] *adv* घेरे हुए ▷ *prep (surrounding)* चारों ओर; *(all over)* चारों तरफ़/हर ओर; *(near to)* आस-पास/लगभग
arrange [ə'reɪndʒ] *v (plan)* प्रबंध करना ▷ *vt (order)* व्यवस्थित करना
arrangement [ə'reɪndʒmənt] *n* प्रबंध
arrears [ə'rɪəz] *npl* बकाया
arrest [ə'rɛst] *n* गिरफ़्तारी ▷ *vt* गिरफ़्तार करना
arrival [ə'raɪvl] *n* आगमन
arrive [ə'raɪv] *vi* पहुंचना
arrogant ['ærəgənt] *adj* घमंडी
arrow ['ærəʊ] *n (weapon)* बाण/तीर; *(sign)* तीर का चिह्न
arson ['ɑːsn] *n* आगज़नी
art [ɑːt] *n* कला
artery ['ɑːtərɪ] *n* धमनी

art gallery [ɑːt 'gælərɪ] *n* कला वीथि
arthritis [ɑː'θraɪtɪs] *n* गठिया
artichoke ['ɑːtɪˌtʃəʊk] *n* हाथीचक-एक सब्ज़ी
article ['ɑːtɪkl] *n* लेख
artificial [ˌɑːtɪ'fɪʃəl] *adj* कृत्रिम
artist ['ɑːtɪst] *n* कलाकार
artistic [ɑː'tɪstɪk] *adj* कलात्मक
art school [ɑːt skuːl] *n* कला विद्यालय
as [æz; əz] *conj* जैसे ही ▷ *prep* के रूप में
asap ['eɪsæp; eɪ ɜs eɪ piː] *abbr* जितना जल्द हो सके
as ... as [æz; əz] *adv* जिस तरह
ashamed [ə'ʃeɪmd] *adj* शर्मिंदा
ashtray ['æʃˌtreɪ] *n* राखदानी
Ash Wednesday [æʃ 'wɛnzdɪ] *n* ईसाइयों के चालीस दिवसीय व्रत का पहला दिन
Asia ['eɪʃə] *n* एशिया
Asian ['eɪʃən] *adj* एशियाई ▷ *n* एशियाई
aside [ə'saɪd] *adv* एक ओर/अलग
ask [ɑːsk] *vt* पूछना
ask for [ɑːsk fɔː] *v (request)* के लिए पूछना
asleep [ə'sliːp] *adj* निद्रामग्न
asparagus [ə'spærəgəs] *n* शतावर-एक सब्ज़ी
aspect ['æspɛkt] *n* पहलू
aspirin ['æsprɪn] *n* दर्द निवारक औषधि
assembly [ə'sɛmblɪ] *n* सभा
asset ['æsɛt] *n* परिसंपत्ति
assignment [ə'saɪnmənt] *n* कार्यभार
assistance [ə'sɪstəns] *n* सहयोग
assistant [ə'sɪstənt] *n* सहायक
associate [ə'səʊʃɪɪt] *adj* सहायक ▷ [ə'səʊsɪeɪt] *n* सहयोगी
association [əˌsəʊsɪ'eɪʃən] *n* संस्था
assortment [ə'sɔːtmənt] *n* संकलन

assume [ə'sjuːm] *vt* मान लेना

assure [ə'ʃʊə] *vt* भरोसा दिलाना

asthma ['æsmə] *n* दमा

astonish [ə'stɒnɪʃ] *vt* चकित करना

astonished [ə'stɒnɪʃt] *adj* आश्चर्यचकित

astonishing [ə'stɒnɪʃɪŋ] *adj* आश्चर्यजनक

astrology [ə'strɒlədʒɪ] *n* ज्योतिषशास्त्र

astronaut ['æstrəˌnɔːt] *n* अंतरिक्षयात्री

astronomy [ə'strɒnəmɪ] *n* खगोलशास्त्र

asylum [ə'saɪləm] *n* शरण

asylum seeker [ə'saɪləm 'siːkə] *n* शरणार्थी

at [æt] *prep* पर/के यहां

atheist ['eɪθɪˌɪst] *n* नास्तिक

athlete ['æθliːt] *n* खिलाड़ी

athletic [æθ'lɛtɪk] *adj* खेलकूद संबंधी

athletics [æθ'lɛtɪks] *npl* खेलकूद

Atlantic Ocean [ət'læntɪk 'əʊʃən] *n* अटलांटिक महासागर

atlas ['ætləs] *n* मानचित्र पुस्तिका

at least [ət liːst] *adv* कम से कम

atmosphere ['ætməsˌfɪə] *n* वायुमण्डल

atom ['ætəm] *n* परमाणु

atom bomb ['ætəm bɒm] *n* परमाणु बम

atomic [ə'tɒmɪk] *adj* परमाणविक

attach [ə'tætʃ] *vt* संलग्न करना

attached [ə'tætʃt] *adj* जुड़ा हुआ

attachment [ə'tætʃmənt] *n* लगाव

attack [ə'tæk] *n* हमला ▹ *v* हमला करना

attempt [ə'tɛmpt] *n* प्रयास ▹ *vt* प्रयास करना

attend [ə'tɛnd] *v* उपस्थित होना

attendance [ə'tɛndəns] *n* उपस्थिति

attention [ə'tɛnʃən] *n* ध्यान

attic ['ætɪk] *n* अटारी
attitude ['ætɪˌtjuːd] *n* रवैया
attract [ə'trækt] *vt* आकर्षित करना
attraction [ə'trækʃən] *n* आकर्षण
attractive [ə'træktɪv] *adj* आकर्षक
aubergine ['əʊbəˌʒiːn] *n* बैंगन
auburn ['ɔːbən] *adj* लालपन लिए भूरा रंग
auction ['ɔːkʃən] *n* नीलामी
audience ['ɔːdɪəns] *n* दर्शक व श्रोता
audit ['ɔːdɪt] *n* लेखा परीक्षण ▷ *vt* लेखा परीक्षण करना
audition [ɔː'dɪʃən] *n* कलाकारों के चयन हेतु परीक्षा
auditor ['ɔːdɪtə] *n* लेखा परीक्षक
August ['ɔːgəst] *n* अगस्त
aunt [ɑːnt] *n* चाची, मामी, मौसी, बुआ
auntie ['ɑːntɪ] *n* *(informal)* चाची, मामी, मौसी, बुआ
au pair [əʊ 'pɛə] *n* एक व्यक्ति, जो विदेश में मेजबान परिवार के सदस्य के रूप में रहते हुए, उनके भाषा सीखने और घर के कामों में मदद करता है
austerity [ɒ'stɛrɪtɪ] *n* मितव्ययिता
Australasia [ˌɒstrə'leɪzɪə] *n* ऑस्ट्रेलेशिया - ऑस्ट्रेलिया, न्यूज़ीलैंड और दक्षिणी प्रशांत महासागर में स्थित द्वीपों के लिए प्रयुक्त शब्दावली
Australia [ɒ'streɪlɪə] *n* ऑस्ट्रेलिया - एक देश
Australian [ɒ'streɪlɪən] *adj* ऑस्ट्रेलियाई ▷ *n* ऑस्ट्रेलियाई
Austria ['ɒstrɪə] *n* ऑस्ट्रिया - मध्य यूरोप का एक गणराज्य
Austrian ['ɒstrɪən] *adj* ऑस्ट्रियाई ▷ *n* ऑस्ट्रियाई
authentic [ɔː'θɛntɪk] *adj* वास्तविक
author ['ɔːθə] *n* लेखक
authorize ['ɔːθəˌraɪz] *vt* प्राधिकृत करना
autobiography [ˌɔːtəʊbaɪ'ɒgrəfɪ] *n* आत्मकथा
autograph ['ɔːtəˌgrɑːf] *n* हस्ताक्षर

automatic [ˌɔːtəˈmætɪk] *adj* स्वचालित
automatically [ˌɔːtəˈmætɪklɪ] *adv* स्वतः
autonomous [ɔːˈtɒnəməs] *adj* स्वायत्तशासी
autonomy [ɔːˈtɒnəmɪ] *n* स्वशासन
autumn [ˈɔːtəm] *n* शरद ऋतु
availability [əˈveɪləbɪlɪtɪ] *n* उपलब्धता
available [əˈveɪləbl] *adj* उपलब्ध
avalanche [ˈævəˌlɑːntʃ] *n* बर्फ़ की चट्टान
avenue [ˈævɪˌnjuː] *n* चौड़ी गली
average [ˈævərɪdʒ] *adj* औसतन ▷ *n* औसत
avocado [ˌævəˈkɑːdəʊ] *n* रुचिरा/मक्खन फल
avoid [əˈvɔɪd] *vt* बचना
awake [əˈweɪk] *adj* जगा हुआ ▷ *v (literary)* जागना
award [əˈwɔːd] *n* पुरस्कार
aware [əˈwɛə] *adj* अवगत
away [əˈweɪ] *adv (in distance)* दूर; *(put)* जगह पर
away match [əˈweɪ mætʃ] *n* प्रतिद्वंदी टीम के मैदान पर खेला जाने वाला मैच
awful [ˈɔːfʊl] *adj* खराब
awfully [ˈɔːfəlɪ] *adv* बहुत अधिक
awkward [ˈɔːkwəd] *adj* बेढंगा
axe [æks] *n* कुल्हाड़ी
axle [ˈæksəl] *n* धुरी
Azerbaijan [ˌæzəbaɪˈdʒɑːn] *n* अज़रबैजान - उत्तरी-पश्चिमी एशिया का एक गणराज्य
Azerbaijani [ˌæzəbaɪˈdʒɑːnɪ] *adj* अज़रबैजानी ▷ *n* अज़रबैजानी

b

BA [biː eɪ] *abbr* कला स्नातक का संक्षिप्त रूप
baby [ˈbeɪbɪ] *n* शिशु
baby milk [ˈbeɪbɪ mɪlk] *n* बच्चों के लिए दूध

baby's bottle ['beɪbɪz bɒtl] *n* बच्चों की बोतल

babysit ['beɪbɪsɪt] *v* दूसरे के बच्चे की देखभाल करना

babysitter ['beɪbɪsɪtə] *n* आया

babysitting ['beɪbɪsɪtɪŋ] *n* दूसरे के बच्चे की देखभाल

baby wipe ['beɪbɪ waɪp] *n* बच्चों को पोंछने के लिए कागज़ के गीले तौलिए

bachelor ['bætʃələ] *n* कुँवारा

back [bæk] *adj* पीछे का ▷ *adv* पीछे की ओर ▷ *n* *(part of body)* पीठ ▷ *vi* पिछवाड़े होना ▷ *n* *(rear)* पिछवाड़ा

backache ['bæk,eɪk] *n* पीठ दर्द

backbone ['bæk,bəʊn] *n* मेरुदण्ड

backfire [,bæk'faɪə] *vi* प्रतिघात करना

background ['bæk,graʊnd] *n* पृष्ठभूमि

backing ['bækɪŋ] *n* सहायता

back out [bæk aʊt] *v* पीछे हटना

backpack ['bæk,pæk] *n* पीठ पर लटकाया जा सकने वाला थैला

backpacker ['bæk,pækə] *n* पीठ पर थैला लटकाकर यात्रा करने वाला

backpacking ['bæk,pækɪŋ] *n* पीठ पर बस एक थैला लटकाकर की जाने वाली यात्रा

back pain [bæk peɪn] *n* पीठ दर्द

backside [,bæk'saɪd] *n* *(informal)* नितंब

backslash ['bæk,slæʃ] *n* बांई ओर झुका तिर्यक चिह्न

backstroke ['bæk,strəʊk] *n* पीठ के बल तैरने का तरीका

back up [bæk ʌp] *v* समर्थन देना

backup ['bækʌp] *n* मदद

backwards ['bækwədz] *adv* *(in direction)* पीछे की ओर; *(back to front)* उल्टी तरफ़ से

bacon ['beɪkən] *n* सूअर का मांस

bacteria [bæk'tɪərɪə] *npl* जीवाणु

bad [bæd] *adj (unpleasant)* खराब; *(wicked)* बुरा
badge [bædʒ] *n* बिल्ला
badger ['bædʒə] *n* बिज्जू
badly ['bædlɪ] *adv* खराब तरह से
badminton ['bædmɪntən] *n* बैडमिंटन - एक खेल
bad-tempered [bæd'tɛmpəd] *adj* चिड़चिड़ा
baffled ['bæfld] *adj* भ्रमित
bag [bæg] *n* थैला
baggage ['bægɪdʒ] *n* यात्रा संबंधी सामान
baggy ['bægɪ] *adj* ढीला - ढाला
bagpipes ['bæg,paɪps] *npl* एक वाद्ययंत्र
Bahamas [bə'hɑːməz] *npl* बहामा द्वीप-समूह
Bahrain [bɑː'reɪn] *n* बहरीन
bail [beɪl] *n* ज़मानत
bake [beɪk] *vi* सेंकना
baked [beɪkt] *adj* भुना हुआ
baked potato [beɪkt pə'teɪtəʊ] *n* भुना आलू
baker ['beɪkə] *n* नानबाई
bakery ['beɪkərɪ] *n* नानबाई की दुकान
baking ['beɪkɪŋ] *n* सेंकने की क्रिया
baking powder ['beɪkɪŋ 'paʊdə] *n* बेकिंग पाउडर
balance ['bæləns] *n* संतुलन
balanced ['bælənst] *adj* संतुलित
balance sheet ['bæləns ʃiːt] *n* बैलेंस शीट
balcony ['bælkənɪ] *n* छज्जा
bald [bɔːld] *adj* गंजा
Balkan ['bɔːlkən] *adj* बाल्कन राज्य से संबद्ध
ball [bɔːl] *n (for playing with)* गेंद; *(dance)* बॉल/एक औपचारिक सामूहिक नृत्य
ballerina [,bælə'riːnə] *n* बैले नर्तकी
ballet ['bæleɪ] *n* बैले - एक प्रकार का नृत्य
ballet dancer ['bæleɪ 'dɑːnsə] *n* बैले नर्तक
ballet shoes ['bæleɪ ʃuːz] *npl* बैले नर्तकों द्वारा पहने जाने वाले जूते
balloon [bə'luːn] *n* गुब्बारा
ballpoint ['bɔːlpɔɪnt] *n* बॉलपेन

ballroom dancing ['bɔːlrʊm 'dɑːnsɪŋ] *n* बॉलरूम नृत्य

bamboo [bæm'buː] *n* बांस

ban [bæn] *n* प्रतिबंध ▷ *vt* प्रतिबंध लगाना

banana [bə'nɑːnə] *n* केला

band [bænd] *n (group of musicians)* संगीत मंडली; *(strip)* फीता

bandage ['bændɪdʒ] *n* पट्टी ▷ *vt* पट्टी बाँधना

bang [bæŋ] *n* धमाका ▷ *v* पटक देना

Bangladesh [ˌbɑːŋglə'dɛʃ] *n* बांग्लादेश

Bangladeshi [ˌbɑːŋglə'dɛʃɪ] *adj* बांग्लादेशी ▷ *n* बांग्लादेशी

banister ['bænɪstə] *n* रेलिंग

banjo ['bændʒəʊ] *n* गिटार जैसा एक वाद्ययंत्र

bank [bæŋk] *n (beside river)* नदी का किनारा; *(for money)* बैंक

bank account [bæŋk ə'kaʊnt] *n* बैंक खाता

bank balance [bæŋk 'bæləns] *n* बैंक की जमा राशि

bank charges [bæŋk 'tʃɑːdʒɪz] *npl* बैंक प्रभार

banker ['bæŋkə] *n* बैंक का एक उच्च अधिकारी

bank holiday [bæŋk 'hɒlɪdeɪ] *n* बैंक अवकाश

banknote ['bæŋkˌnəʊt] *n* बैंकनोट

bankrupt ['bæŋkrʌpt] *adj* दिवालिया

bank statement [bæŋk 'steɪtmənt] *n* बैंक खाता विवरण

banned [bænd] *adj* प्रतिबंधित

bar [biː eɪ] *n (metal or wooden)* छड़; *(pub)* मधुशाला

Barbados [bɑː'beɪdəʊs] *n* बारबाडोस द्वीप

barbaric [bɑː'bærɪk] *adj* बर्बर

barbecue ['bɑːbɪˌkjuː] *n* बार्बक्यू/एक प्रकार का तंदूर

barbed wire [bɑːbd 'waɪə] *n* कांटेदार तार

barber ['bɑːbə] *n* नाई

bare [bɛə] *adj (naked)* नग्न ▷ *vt* उघाड़ना ▷ *adj (empty)* खाली

barefoot ['bɛə,fʊt] *adj* नंगे पैर ▷ *adv* नंगे पैर रहना
barely ['bɛəlɪ] *adv* मुश्किल से
bargain ['bɑːgɪn] *n* अच्छा सौदा
barge [bɑːdʒ] *n* मालवाहक नौका
bark [bɑːk] *vi* भौंकना
barley ['bɑːlɪ] *n* जौ
barn [bɑːn] *n* खलिहान
barrel ['bærəl] *n* पीपा
barrier ['bærɪə] *n* अवरोध
base [beɪs] *n* तल
baseball ['beɪs,bɔːl] *n* बेसबॉल
baseball cap ['beɪs,bɔːl kæp] *n* बेसबॉल टोपी
based [beɪst] *adj* आधारित
basement ['beɪsmənt] *n* तहखाना
bash [bæʃ] *n (informal)* उत्सव ▷ *vt (informal)* प्रहार करना
basic ['beɪsɪk] *adj* बुनियादी
basically ['beɪsɪklɪ] *adv* मूलतः
basics ['beɪsɪks] *npl* बुनियादी बातें
basil ['bæzl] *n* तुलसी
basin ['beɪsn] *n* गहरा कटोरा
basis ['beɪsɪs] *n* आधार
basket ['bɑːskɪt] *n* टोकरी
basketball ['bɑːskɪt,bɔːl] *n* बास्केटबॉल
Basque [bæsk] *adj* बास्क समुदाय से संबद्ध ▷ *n (person)* बास्क समुदाय के लोग; *(language)* बास्क भाषा
bass [beɪs] *n* गंभीर व सुरीली आवाज़ वाला व्यक्ति
bass drum [beɪs drʌm] *n* बास ड्रम-एक वाद्ययंत्र
bassoon [bə'suːn] *n* अलगोज़ा
bat [bæt] *n (for games)* बल्ला; *(animal)* चमगादड़
bath [bɑːθ] *n* स्नान-कुंड
bathe [beɪð] *vi (formal)* नहाना
bathing suit ['beɪðɪŋ suːt] *n* तैराकी की पोशाक
bathrobe ['bɑːθ,rəʊb] *n* स्नान-वस्त्र
bathroom ['bɑːθ,ruːm] *n* स्नान-घर
baths [bɑːθz] *npl* सार्वजनिक स्नान-घर

bath towel [bɑːθ 'taʊəl] *n* तौलिया
bathtub ['bɑːθˌtʌb] *n* स्नान-कुंड
batter ['bætə] *n* लपसी
battery ['bætərɪ] *n* बैटरी
battle ['bætl] *n* युद्ध
battleship ['bætlˌʃɪp] *n* युद्धपोत
bay [beɪ] *n* खाड़ी
bay leaf [beɪ liːf] *n* तेजपत्ता
BC [biː siː] *abbr* ईसा पूर्व
be [biː] *v* *(person, thing)* होना; *(there)* होना
beach [biːtʃ] *n* समुद्रतट
bead [biːd] *n* मनका
beak [biːk] *n* चोंच
beam [biːm] *n* किरण
bean [biːn] *n* फली
beansprouts ['biːnspraʊts] *npl* अंकुरित फली
bear [bɛə] *n* भालू ▷ *vt* *(literary)* वहन करना
beard [bɪəd] *n* दाढ़ी
bearded ['bɪədɪd] *adj* दाढ़ी वाला
bear up [bɛə ʌp] *v* हौसला रखना
beat [biːt] *n* ताल/ध्वनि ▷ *vt* *(hit)* पीटना; *(defeat)* हराना
beautiful ['bjuːtɪfʊl] *adj* सुंदर
beautifully ['bjuːtɪflɪ] *adv* सुंदरतापूर्वक
beauty ['bjuːtɪ] *n* सुंदरता
beauty salon ['bjuːtɪ 'sælɒn] *n* प्रसाधनालय
beauty spot ['bjuːtɪ spɒt] *n* सुंदर स्थान
beaver ['biːvə] *n* ऊदबिलाव
because [bɪ'kɒz] *conj* क्योंकि
become [bɪ'kʌm] *v* बनना
bed [bɛd] *n* बिस्तर
bed and breakfast [bɛd ənd 'brɛkfəst] *n* होटल में खाना व बिस्तर मिलने की सुविधा
bedclothes ['bɛdˌkləʊðz] *npl* बिछौना
bedding ['bɛdɪŋ] *n* बिछौना
bed linen [bɛd 'lɪnɪn] *n* बिछौना
bedroom ['bɛdˌruːm] *n* शयनकक्ष
bedside lamp ['bɛdˌsaɪd læmp] *n* बिस्तर के किनारे की बत्ती

bedside table ['bɛd,saɪd 'teɪbl] *n* बिस्तर के किनारे की मेज़
bedsit ['bɛd,sɪt] *n* किराए का कमरा
bedspread ['bɛd,sprɛd] *n* पलंगपोश
bedtime ['bɛd,taɪm] *n* सोने का समय
bee [biː] *n* मधुमक्खी
beech [biːtʃ] *n* करंज वृक्ष
beef [biːf] *n* गोमांस
beefburger ['biːf,bɜːgə] *n* बीफ़बर्गर
beeper ['bliːpə] *n* *(informal)* बीपर
beer [bɪə] *n* जौ की शराब
beetle ['biːtl] *n* गुबरैला
beetroot ['biːt,ruːt] *n* चुकंदर
before [bɪ'fɔː] *adv* पहले ▹ *conj* के पहले ▹ *prep* पहले
beforehand [bɪ'fɔː,hænd] *adv* पहले से
beg [bɛg] *v* याचना करना
beggar ['bɛgə] *n* भिखारी
begin [bɪ'gɪn] *vt* शुरू करना
beginner [bɪ'gɪnə] *n* नौसिखिया
beginning [bɪ'gɪnɪŋ] *n* शुरुआत
behave [bɪ'heɪv] *vi* *(act)* व्यवहार करना ▹ *vt* *(yourself)* अच्छा आचरण करना
behaviour [bɪ'heɪvjə] *n* व्यवहार
behind [bɪ'haɪnd] *adv* पीछे ▹ *n* नितंब ▹ *prep* के पीछे
beige [beɪʒ] *adj* हल्का भूरा
Beijing ['beɪ'dʒɪŋ] *n* बीजिंग
Belarus ['bɛlə,rʌs] *n* बेलारूस/पूर्वी यूरोप का एक गणराज्य
Belarussian [,bɛləʊ'rʌʃən] *adj* बेलारूसी ▹ *n* *(person)* बेलारूसी; *(language)* बेलारूसी
Belgian ['bɛldʒən] *adj* बेल्जियाई ▹ *n* बेल्जियाई
Belgium ['bɛldʒəm] *n* बेल्जियम - उत्तरी - पश्चिमी यूरोप का एक संघीय राज्य
belief [bɪ'liːf] *n* विश्वास
believe [bɪ'liːv] *vt* *(formal)* विश्वास करना ▹ *vi* विश्वास करना
bell [bɛl] *n* घंटी

b

belly ['bɛlɪ] *n* पेट
belly button ['bɛlɪ 'bʌtn] *n* *(informal)* नाभि
belong [bɪ'lɒŋ] *vi* *(should be)* का होना; *(be a member)* संबद्ध होना
belongings [bɪ'lɒŋɪŋz] *npl* सामान
belong to *v* संबद्ध होना
below [bɪ'ləʊ] *adv* नीचे ▹ *prep* के नीचे
belt [bɛlt] *n* कमरबंद
bench [bɛntʃ] *n* तख़्त
bend [bɛnd] *n* मोड़ ▹ *vi* झुकना
bend down [bɛnd daʊn] *v* आगे झुकना
bend over [bɛnd 'əʊvə] *v* आगे झुकना
beneath [bɪ'niːθ] *prep* नीचे
benefit ['bɛnɪfɪt] *n* लाभ ▹ *v* लाभ
bent [bɛnt] *adj* *(not straight)* झुका हुआ; *(dishonest)* भ्रष्ट
beret ['bɛreɪ] *n* टोपी
berry ['bɛrɪ] *n* झड़बेर
berth [bɜːθ] *n* सीट
beside [bɪ'saɪd] *prep* बगल में
besides [bɪ'saɪdz] *adv* के अलावा ▹ *prep* के अतिरिक्त
best [bɛst] *adj* सर्वश्रेष्ठ ▹ *adv* सबसे अच्छे से
best-before date [ˌbɛstbɪ'fɔː deɪt] *n* खपत तिथि
best man [bɛst mæn] *n* दूल्हे का साथी
bestseller [ˌbɛst'sɛlə] *n* सबसे ज़्यादा बिकने वाली किताब
bet [bɛt] *n* शर्त ▹ *v* शर्त लगाना
betray [bɪ'treɪ] *vt* धोखा देना
better ['bɛtə] *adj* *(more good)* बेहतर ▹ *adv* बेहतर तरीके से ▹ *adj* *(well again)* बेहतर
between [bɪ'twiːn] *prep* के बीच में
bewildered [bɪ'wɪldəd] *adj* हक्का - बक्का
beyond [bɪ'jɒnd] *prep* के परे
biased ['baɪəst] *adj* पक्षपातपूर्ण
bib [bɪb] *n* बिब

Bible ['baɪbl] *n* बाइबिल
bicarbonate of soda [baɪ'kɑːbənət əv 'səʊdə] *n* खाने का सोडा
bicycle ['baɪsɪkl] *n* साइकिल
bicycle pump ['baɪsɪkl pʌmp] *n* साइकिल पंप
bid [bɪd] *n* बोली ▷ *v* बोली लगाना
bifocals [baɪ'fəʊklz] *npl* द्विफोकसी
big [bɪg] *adj* बड़ा
bigheaded ['bɪg,hɛdɪd] *adj* घमंडी
bike [baɪk] *n (informal)* साइकिल
bikini [bɪ'kiːnɪ] *n* महिलाओं की स्नान की पोशाक
bilingual [baɪ'lɪŋgwəl] *adj* द्विभाषी
bill [bɪl] *n (account)* भुगतान सूची; *(in parliament)* विधेयक
billiards ['bɪljədz] *npl* बिलियर्ड्स
billion ['bɪljən] *num* एक अरब
bin [bɪn] *n* कचरा - पेटी/ कूड़ादान
bingo ['bɪŋgəʊ] *n* बिंगो-एक खेल
binoculars [bɪ'nɒkjʊləz] *npl* दूरबीन
biochemistry [,baɪəʊ'kɛmɪstrɪ] *n* जैवरसायनिकी
biodegradable [,baɪəʊdɪ'greɪdəbl] *adj* प्राकृतिक रूप से सड़ने वाला
biography [baɪ'ɒgrəfɪ] *n* जीवनी
biological [,baɪə'lɒdʒɪkl] *adj* जैविक
biology [baɪ'ɒlədʒɪ] *n* जीव - विज्ञान
biometric [,baɪəʊ'mɛtrɪk] *adj* जीवमितीय
birch [bɜːtʃ] *n* भोज वृक्ष
bird [bɜːd] *n* पक्षी
bird flu [bɜːd fluː] *n* बर्ड फ़्लू
bird of prey [bɜːd əv preɪ] *n* शिकारी पक्षी
birdwatching ['bɜːd,wɒtʃɪŋ] *n* पक्षियों का निरीक्षण व अध्ययन
Biro® ['baɪrəʊ] *n* बालपेन का एक ब्रांड

birth [bɜːθ] *n* जन्म
birth certificate [bɜːθ səˈtɪfɪkɪt] *n* जन्म - प्रमाणपत्र
birthday [ˈbɜːθ,deɪ] *n* जन्मदिन
birthplace [ˈbɜːθ,pleɪs] *n* *(written)* जन्मस्थान
biscuit [ˈbɪskɪt] *n* बिस्कुट
bit [bɪt] *n* टुकड़ा
bitch [bɪtʃ] *n* कुतिया
bite [baɪt] *n* कौर/टुकड़ा ▷ *v* दांत से काटना
bitter [ˈbɪtə] *adj* कड़वा
black [blæk] *adj* काला
blackberry [ˈblækbərɪ] *n* ब्लैकबेरी - एक फल
BlackBerry® [ˈblækbərɪ] *n* मोबाइल का ब्राण्ड
blackbird [ˈblæk,bɜːd] *n* श्यामापक्षी
blackboard [ˈblæk,bɔːd] *n* श्यामपट्ट
black coffee [blæk ˈkɒfɪ] *n* काली कॉफ़ी
blackcurrant [,blækˈkʌrənt] *n* ब्लैककरंट - एक फल
black ice [blæk aɪs] *n* बर्फ़ की पारदर्शी परत
blackmail [ˈblæk,meɪl] *n* भयादोहन ▷ *vt* भयादोहन करना
blackout [ˈblækaʊt] *n* सुरक्षा कारणों से अंधेरा कर देना
bladder [ˈblædə] *n* मूत्राशय
blade [bleɪd] *n* धार
blame [bleɪm] *vt* दोष देना ▷ *n* दोष
blank [blæŋk] *adj* कोरा ▷ *n* रिक्त स्थान
blank cheque [blæŋk tʃek] *n* कोरा चेक
blanket [ˈblæŋkɪt] *n* कंबल
blast [blɑːst] *n* विस्फोट
blatant [ˈbleɪtnt] *adj* खुल्लम - खुल्ला
blaze [bleɪz] *n* लपट
blazer [ˈbleɪzə] *n* एक तरह की जैकेट
bleach [bliːtʃ] *n* विरंजित करना
bleached [bliːtʃt] *adj* विरंजित
bleak [bliːk] *adj* निराशाजनक

bleed [bliːd] *vi* खून बहना
blender ['blɛndə] *n* सम्मिश्रक
bless [blɛs] *vt* आशीर्वाद देना
blind [blaɪnd] *adj* नेत्रहीन
blindfold ['blaɪnd,fəʊld] *n* आँख पर बँधी पट्टी ▷ *vt* आँख पर पट्टी बाँधना
blink [blɪŋk] *v* पलक झपकना
bliss [blɪs] *n* परमानंद
blister ['blɪstə] *n* फफोला
blizzard ['blɪzəd] *n* बर्फ़ानी तूफ़ान
block [blɒk] *n (rectangular piece)* गुटका; *(buildings)* खंड; *(obstruction)* अवरोध ▷ *vt* अवरुद्ध करना
blockage ['blɒkɪdʒ] *n* अवरोध
blocked [blɒkt] *adj* अवरुद्ध
blog [blɒg] *v* चिट्ठा लिखना
bloke [bləʊk] *n (informal)* व्यक्ति
blonde [blɒnd] *adj* सुनहरा भूरा
blood [blʌd] *n* रक्त
blood group [blʌd gruːp] *n* रक्त समूह
blood poisoning [blʌd 'pɔɪzənɪŋ] *n* रक्त विषाक्तता
blood pressure [blʌd 'prɛʃə] *n* रक्तचाप
blood test [blʌd tɛst] *n* रक्त परीक्षण
blossom ['blɒsəm] *n* पुष्प ▷ *vi* विकसित होना
blouse [blaʊz] *n* कुरती
blow [bləʊ] *n* प्रहार ▷ *vi (wind)* बहना ▷ *vt (person)* फूंक मारना
blow-dry ['bləʊdraɪ] *n* मशीन से बाल सुखाने की क्रिया
blow up [bləʊ ʌp] *v* विस्फोट से उड़ जाना
blue [bluː] *adj* नीला
blueberry ['bluːbərɪ] *n* ब्लूबेरी
blues [bluːz] *npl* ब्लूज़/एक संगीत शैली
bluff [blʌf] *n* झाँसा ▷ *v* झाँसा देना
blunder ['blʌndə] *n* बड़ी चूक
blunt [blʌnt] *adj* मुँहफट
blush [blʌʃ] *vi* शरमाना

blusher ['blʌʃə] *n* गालों पर लगाई जाने वाली लाली

board [bɔːd] *n (directors)* मंडल; *(of wood or plastic)* तख्ता

boarder ['bɔːdə] *n* अंतेवासी

board game [bɔːd geɪm] *n* बोर्ड गेम

boarding school ['bɔːdɪŋ skuːl] *n* आवासीय विद्यालय

boast [bəʊst] *vi* डींग मारना

boat [bəʊt] *n* नाव

body ['bɒdɪ] *n* शरीर

bodybuilding ['bɒdɪˌbɪldɪŋ] *n* शरीर सौष्ठव

bodyguard ['bɒdɪˌgaːd] *n* अंगरक्षक

bog [bɒg] *n* दलदल

boil [bɔɪl] *vt (food)* उबालना ▷ *vi (water)* उबलना

boiled [bɔɪld] *adj* उबला

boiled egg [bɔɪld ɛg] *n* उबला अण्डा

boiler ['bɔɪlə] *n* वाष्पक

boiling ['bɔɪlɪŋ] *adj* उबलता हुआ

boil over [bɔɪl 'əʊvə] *v* उबाल आना

Bolivia [bə'lɪvɪə] *n* बोलीविया

Bolivian [bə'lɪvɪən] *adj* बोलिवियाई ▷ *n* बोलिवियाई

bolt [bəʊlt] *n* बोल्ट

bomb [bɒm] *n* बम ▷ *vt* बमबारी करना

bombing ['bɒmɪŋ] *n* बमबारी

bond [bɒnd] *n* जुड़ाव

bone [bəʊn] *n* हड्डी

bone dry [bəʊn draɪ] *adj* बिल्कुल सूखा हुआ

bonfire ['bɒnˌfaɪə] *n* अलाव

bonnet ['bɒnɪt] *n (car)* बोनट

bonus ['bəʊnəs] *n* अतिरिक्त भुगतान

book [bʊk] *n* किताब ▷ *vt* बुक करना

bookcase ['bʊkˌkeɪs] *n* किताब की अलमारी

booking ['bʊkɪŋ] *n* बुकिंग

booklet ['bʊklɪt] *n* पुस्तिका

bookmark ['bʊkˌmaːk] *n* पुस्तक चिह्न

bookshelf ['bʊkˌʃɛlf] *n* किताब की अलमारी

bookshop ['bʊkˌʃɒp] *n* किताब की दुकान
boost [buːst] *vt* बढ़ावा देना
boot [buːt] *n* ऊंचा जूता
booze [buːz] *n* *(informal)* शराब
border ['bɔːdə] *n* सीमा
bore [bɔː] *vt* उबाऊ
bored [bɔːd] *adj* ऊबा हुआ
boredom ['bɔːdəm] *n* ऊब
boring ['bɔːrɪŋ] *adj* उबाऊ
born [bɔːn] *adj* पैदाइशी
borrow ['bɒrəʊ] *vt* उधार लेना
Bosnia ['bɒznɪə] *n* बोस्निया
Bosnia-Herzegovina [ˌbɒznɪəhɜːtsəgəʊ'viːnə] *n* बोस्निया व हर्ज़ेगोविना
Bosnian ['bɒznɪən] *adj* बोस्नियाई ▹ *n* *(person)* बोस्नियाई
boss [bɒs] *n* मालिक
boss around [bɒs ə'raʊnd] *v* धौंस जमाना
bossy ['bɒsɪ] *adj* धौंस जमाने वाला
both [bəʊθ] *det* दोनों ▹ *pron* दोनों
bother ['bɒðə] *v* परेशानी उठाना
Botswana [bʊ'tʃwɑːnə] *n* बोत्सवाना
bottle ['bɒtl] *n* बोतल
bottle bank ['bɒtl bæŋk] *n* बोतल रखने का डिब्बा
bottle-opener ['bɒtl'əʊpənə] *n* बोतल खोलने का उपकरण
bottom ['bɒtəm] *adj* निचला ▹ *n* *(lowest part)* तला/पेंदी; *(part of body)* नितंब
bounce [baʊns] *v* उछलना
boundary ['baʊndərɪ] *n* चहारदीवारी
bouquet ['buːkeɪ] *n* गुलदस्ता
bow [bəʊ] *n* *(weapon)* धनुष; *(knot)* बो/गांठ ▹ [baʊ] *vi* झुकना
bowels ['baʊəlz] *npl* आँत
bowl [bəʊl] *n* कटोरा
bowling ['bəʊlɪŋ] *n* बोलिंग/गेंदबाजी
bowling alley ['bəʊlɪŋ 'ælɪ] *n* बोलिंग ऐली
bow tie [bəʊ taɪ] *n* बो टाई

box [bɒks] *n* बक्सा
boxer ['bɒksə] *n* मुक्केबाज़
boxer shorts ['bɒksə ʃɔːts] *npl* जांघिया
boxing ['bɒksɪŋ] *n* मुक्केबाज़ी
box office [bɒks 'ɒfɪs] *n* टिकट घर
boy [bɔɪ] *n* लड़का
boyfriend ['bɔɪˌfrɛnd] *n* पुरुष मित्र
bra [brɑː] *n* चोली
brace [breɪs] *n* तमसा
bracelet ['breɪslɪt] *n* कंगन
braces ['breɪsɪz] *npl* गेलिस
brackets ['brækɪts] *npl* कोष्ठक
brain [breɪn] *n* दिमाग
brainy ['breɪnɪ] *adj* *(informal)* कुशाग्र बुद्धि
brake [breɪk] *n* ब्रेक ▷ *v* ब्रेक लगाना
brake light [breɪk laɪt] *n* ब्रेक की बत्ती
bran [bræn] *n* चोकर
branch [brɑːntʃ] *n* टहनी
brand [brænd] *n* ब्राण्ड/मार्का
brand name [brænd neɪm] *n* ब्राण्ड का नाम
brand-new [brænd'njuː] *adj* बिल्कुल नया
brandy ['brændɪ] *n* ब्राण्डी
brass [brɑːs] *n* पीतल
brass band [brɑːs bænd] *n* पीतल के तूर्य वाद्य
brat [bræt] *n (informal)* बिगड़ैल बच्चा
brave [breɪv] *adj* बहादुर
bravery ['breɪvərɪ] *n* बहादुरी
Brazil [brə'zɪl] *n* ब्राज़ील
Brazilian [brə'zɪljən] *adj* ब्राज़ीलियाई ▷ *n* ब्राज़ीलियाई
bread [brɛd] *n* पावरोटी
bread bin [brɛd bɪn] *n* पावरोटी रखने का डिब्बा
breadcrumbs ['brɛdˌkrʌmz] *npl* सूखी पावरोटी का टुकड़ा
bread roll [brɛd rəʊl] *n* ब्रेड रोल
break [breɪk] *n* भंग ▷ *v* *(smash)* तोड़ना; *(stop working)* खराब हो जाना
break down [breɪk daʊn] *v* खराब होना

breakdown ['breɪkdaʊn] *n* भंग
breakdown truck ['breɪkˌdaʊn trʌk] *n* ब्रेकडाउन ट्रक
breakdown van ['breɪkˌdaʊn væn] *n* ब्रेकडाउन वैन
breakfast ['brɛkfəst] *n* सुबह का नाश्ता
break in [breɪk ɪn] *v* ज़बर्दस्ती घुसना
break-in ['breɪkɪn] *n* बलपूर्वक प्रवेश
break up [breɪk ʌp] *v* तोड़ना
breast [brɛst] *n* स्तन
breast-feed ['brɛstˌfiːd] *v* स्तनपान कराना
breaststroke ['brɛstˌstrəʊk] *n* पट होकर तैरने की शैली
breath [brɛθ] *n* साँस
Breathalyser® ['brɛθəˌlaɪzə] *n* शराब के सेवन की जाँच करने वाला उपकरण
breathe [briːð] *v* साँस लेना
breathe in [briːð ɪn] *v* साँस खींचना
breathe out [briːð aʊt] *v* साँस छोड़ना
breathing ['briːðɪŋ] *n* श्वसन
breed [briːd] *n* नस्ल ▷ *vt* पालना
breeze [briːz] *n* हल्की हवा
brewery ['brʊərɪ] *n* मद्यनिर्माणशाला
bribe [braɪb] *vt* घूस
bribery ['braɪbərɪ] *n* घूसखोरी
brick [brɪk] *n* ईंट
bricklayer ['brɪkˌleɪə] *n* राजगीर
bride [braɪd] *n* दुल्हन
bridegroom ['braɪdˌgruːm] *n* दूल्हा
bridesmaid ['braɪdzˌmeɪd] *n* दुल्हन की सखी
bridge [brɪdʒ] *n* पुल
brief [briːf] *adj* संक्षिप्त
briefcase ['briːfˌkeɪs] *n* छोटा बक्सा
briefing ['briːfɪŋ] *n* विवरण
briefly ['briːflɪ] *adv* कुछ समय के लिए
briefs [briːfs] *npl* जांघिया

bright [braɪt] *adj (colour)* चमकीला/भड़कीला; *(shining)* चमकीला

brilliant ['brɪljənt] *adj* मेधावी

bring [brɪŋ] *vt* लाना

bring back [brɪŋ bæk] *v* स्मरण दिलाना/लौटा लाना

bring forward [brɪŋ 'fɔːwəd] *v* आगे लाना

bring up [brɪŋ ʌp] *v* पालन-पोषण करना

Britain ['brɪtn] *n* ब्रिटेन

British ['brɪtɪʃ] *adj* आंग्लदेशीय ▷ *npl* आंग्लदेशीय

broad [brɔːd] *adj* चौड़ा

broadband ['brɔːd,bænd] *n* ब्रॉडबैण्ड

broad bean [brɔːd biːn] *n* बाकला

broadcast ['brɔːd,kɑːst] *n* प्रसारण ▷ *v* प्रसारण करना

broad-minded [brɔːd'maɪndɪd] *adj* उदार

broccoli ['brɒkəlɪ] *n* हरी फूलगोभी

brochure ['brəʊʃjʊə] *n* विवरण-पुस्तिका

broke [brəʊk] *adj (informal)* कड़का

broken ['brəʊkən] *adj* खंडित

broken down ['brəʊkən daʊn] *adj* छिन्न-भिन्न

broker ['brəʊkə] *n* दलाल

bronchitis [brɒŋ'kaɪtɪs] *n* श्वासनली - शोथ

bronze [brɒnz] *n* काँसा

brooch [brəʊtʃ] *n* जड़ाऊ पिन

broom [bruːm] *n* झाड़ू

broth [brɒθ] *n* शोरबा

brother ['brʌðə] *n* भाई

brother-in-law ['brʌðə ɪn lɔː] *n* साला/देवर/जीजा

brown [braʊn] *adj* भूरा

brown bread [braʊn brɛd] *n* बिना छने आटे की बनी पावरोटी

brown rice [braʊn raɪs] *n* बिना पॉलिश का चावल

browse [braʊz] *vi* सरसरी तौर पर देखना

browser ['braʊzə] *n* ब्राउज़र

bruise [bruːz] *n* खरोंच

brush [brʌʃ] *n* कूँची ▷ *vt* झाड़ना

Brussels sprouts ['brʌslz'sprauts] *npl* चोकीगोभी
brutal ['bruːtl] *adj* नृशंस
bubble ['bʌbl] *n* बुलबुला
bubble bath ['bʌbl bɑːθ] *n* नहाने के पानी को झागदार बनाने वाला द्रव
bubble gum ['bʌbl gʌm] *n* बबलगम
bucket ['bʌkɪt] *n* बाल्टी
buckle ['bʌkl] *n* बकसुआ
Buddha ['bʊdə] *n* गौतम बुद्ध
Buddhism ['bʊdɪzəm] *n* बौद्ध धर्म
Buddhist ['bʊdɪst] *adj* बौद्ध ▷ *n* बौद्ध
budgerigar ['bʌdʒərɪˌgɑː] *n* शैल तोता
budget ['bʌdʒɪt] *n* बजट
budgie ['bʌdʒɪ] *n* *(informal)* शैल तोता
buffalo ['bʌfəˌləʊ] *n* भैंस
buffet ['bʊfeɪ] *n* बुफ़े - एक तरह की दावत
buffet car ['bʊfeɪ kɑː] *n* बुफ़े कार
bug [bʌg] *n* *(informal)* कीड़ा
bugged ['bʌgd] *adj* छिपा कर माइक्रोफ़ोन लगाया गया
buggy ['bʌgɪ] *n* बच्चागाड़ी
build [bɪld] *vt* निर्माण करना
builder ['bɪldə] *n* भवन - निर्माता
building ['bɪldɪŋ] *n* भवन
building site ['bɪldɪŋ saɪt] *n* भवन-निर्माण क्षेत्र
bulb [bʌlb] *n* *(plant)* कंद; *(electric)* बिजली का लट्टू
Bulgaria [bʌl'gɛərɪə] *n* बुल्गारिया - दक्षिणी-पूर्वी यूरोप का एक गणराज्य
Bulgarian [bʌl'gɛərɪən] *adj* बुल्गारियाई ▷ *n* *(person)* बुल्गारियाई; *(language)* बुल्गारियाई
bulimia [bjuː'lɪmɪə] *n* ब्युलिमिआ-खाना उगलने की बीमारी
bull [bʊl] *n* बैल
bulldozer ['bʊlˌdəʊzə] *n* बुलडोज़र
bullet ['bʊlɪt] *n* गोली
bulletin board ['bʊlɪtɪn bɔːd] *n* सूचना पट्ट
bully ['bʊlɪ] *n* धौंस जमाने वाला ▷ *vt* धौंस जमाना

bum [bʌm] *n (informal)* नितंब

bum bag [bʌm bæg] *n* कमर में बाँधा जाने वाला बटुआ

bumblebee ['bʌmbl,biː] *n* भौंरा

bump [bʌmp] *n* टक्कर

bumper ['bʌmpə] *n* बंपर

bump into [bʌmp 'ɪntuː; 'ɪntə; 'ɪntʊ] *v (informal)* संयोगवश मिलना

bumpy ['bʌmpɪ] *adj* ऊबड़-खाबड़

bun [bʌn] *n* पाव

bunch [bʌntʃ] *n (informal)* गुच्छा/झुण्ड

bungalow ['bʌŋgə,ləʊ] *n* कोठी

bungee jumping ['bʌndʒɪ 'dʒʌmpɪŋ] *n* बंजी जंपिंग

bunion ['bʌnjən] *n* गोखरू

bunk [bʌŋk] *n* दीवार से जुड़ा बिस्तर

bunk beds [bʌŋk bɛdz] *npl* एक के ऊपर एक जुड़े बिस्तर

buoy [bɔɪ] *n* पानी पर तैरता चिह्न

burden ['bɜːdn] *n* बोझ

bureaucracy [bjʊə'rɒkrəsɪ] *n* नौकरशाही

bureau de change ['bjʊərəʊ də 'ʃɒnʒ] *n* मुद्रा विनिमय केंद्र

burger ['bɜːgə] *n* बर्गर

burglar ['bɜːglə] *n* सेंधमार चोर

burglar alarm ['bɜːglə ə'lɑːm] *n* चोरों से सावधान करने वाली घंटी

burglary ['bɜːglərɪ] *n* चोरी

burgle ['bɜːgl] *vt* चोरी करना

Burmese [bɜː'miːz] *n (person)* बर्मी; *(language)* बर्मी

burn [bɜːn] *n* जलने का घाव ▷ *vi (be on fire)* जलना ▷ *vt (damage with fire)* जला देना; *(yourself)* जलाना/दागना

burn down [bɜːn daʊn] *v* जलकर खाक होना

burp [bɜːp] *n* डकार ▷ *vi* डकार लेना

burst [bɜːst] *v* फूटना

bury ['bɛrɪ] *vt* गाड़ना

bus [bʌs] *n* बस

bus conductor [bʌs kən'dʌktə] *n* बस परिचालक
bush [bʊʃ] *n (cluster of shrubs)* झाड़ - झंखाड़; *(shrub)* झाड़ी
business ['bɪznɪs] *n* व्यापार
businessman ['bɪznɪsˌmæn] *n* व्यापारी
businesswoman ['bɪznɪsˌwʊmən] *n* महिला व्यवसायी
busker ['bʌskə] *n* नाच गा कर धन कमाने वाला
bus station [bʌs 'steɪʃn] *n* बस अड्डा
bus stop [bʌs stɒp] *n* बस स्थानक
bust [bʌst] *n* आवक्ष मूर्ति
bus ticket [bʌs 'tɪkɪt] *n* बस टिकट
busy ['bɪzɪ] *adj (person)* व्यस्त; *(place)* भीड़भाड़ से भरा
busy signal ['bɪzɪ 'sɪgnəl] *n* फ़ोन व्यस्त होने का संदेश
but [bʌt] *conj* लेकिन
butcher ['bʊtʃə] *n (person)* कसाई; ['bʊtʃəz] *n (shop)* कसाई की दुकान
butter ['bʌtə] *n* मक्खन
buttercup ['bʌtəˌkʌp] *n* पीले फूलों वाला एक छोटा पौधा
butterfly ['bʌtəˌflaɪ] *n* तितली
buttocks ['bʌtəkz] *npl* नितम्ब
button ['bʌtn] *n* बटन
buy [baɪ] *vt* खरीदना
buyer ['baɪə] *n* खरीददार
buyout ['baɪˌaʊt] *n* बाईआउट
by [baɪ] *prep* द्वारा
bye! [baɪ] *excl (informal)* अलविदा!
bye-bye! [ˌbaɪ'baɪ] *excl (informal)* अलविदा!
bypass ['baɪˌpɑːs] *n* हृदय संबधी शल्य चिकित्सा

C

cab [kæb] *n* टैक्सी
cabbage ['kæbɪdʒ] *n* पत्तागोभी
cabin ['kæbɪn] *n* कोठरी
cabin crew ['kæbɪn kruː] *n* विमान परिचारक

cabinet ['kæbɪnɪt] *n* अलमारी
cable ['keɪbl] *n* तार
cable car ['keɪbl kɑː] *n* तार पर सरकने वाली गाड़ी
cable television ['keɪbl 'tɛlɪ,vɪʒn] *n* केबल टीवी
cactus ['kæktəs] *n* नागफनी
cadet [kə'dɛt] *n* छात्र सैनिक
café ['kæfeɪ] *n* कॉफ़ीघर
cafeteria [,kæfɪ'tɪərɪə] *n* जलपानगृह
caffeine ['kæfiːn] *n* कैफ़ीन
cage [keɪdʒ] *n* पिंजड़ा
cagoule [kə'guːl] *n* घुटने तक लंबा बरसाती कोट
cake [keɪk] *n* केक
calcium ['kælsɪəm] *n* कैल्सियम
calculate ['kælkjʊ,leɪt] *vt* गणना करना
calculation [,kælkjʊ'leɪʃən] *n* गणना
calculator ['kælkjʊ,leɪtə] *n* परिकलक
calendar ['kælɪndə] *n* तिथिपत्र
calf [kɑːf] *n (young cow)* बछड़ा; *(leg)* पिंडली
call [kɔːl] *n* कॉल ▷ *vt (name)* पुकारना/नाम देना ▷ *v (shout)* बुलाना; *(telephone)* फ़ोन करना
call back [kɔːl bæk] *v* दोबारा फ़ोन करना
call box [kɔːl bɒks] *n* टेलीफ़ोन बूथ
call centre [kɔːl 'sɛntə] *n* कॉल सेंटर
call for [kɔːl fɔː] *v* मांग करना
call off [kɔːl ɒf] *v* रद्द करना
calm [kɑːm] *adj* शांत
calm down [kɑːm daʊn] *v* शांत होना
calorie ['kælərɪ] *n* कैलोरी
Cambodia [kæm'bəʊdɪə] *n* कम्बोडिया
Cambodian [kæm'bəʊdɪən] *adj* कम्बोडियाई ▷ *n (person)* कम्बोडियाई
camcorder ['kæm,kɔːdə] *n* छोटा वीडियो कैमरा
camel ['kæməl] *n* ऊंट
camera ['kæmərə] *n* कैमरा

cameraman ['kæmərəˌmæn] *n* कैमरामैन

camera phone ['kæmərəfəun] *n* कैमरा फ़ोन

Cameroon [ˌkæmə'ruːn] *n* कैमरून

camp [kæmp] *n* ख़ेमा ▷ *vi* ख़ेमा डालकर रहना

campaign [kæm'peɪn] *n* अभियान

camp bed [kæmp bɛd] *n* सफरी पलंग

camper ['kæmpə] *n* ख़ेमे में रहने वाला

camping ['kæmpɪŋ] *n* ख़ेमे में निवास

campsite ['kæmpˌsaɪt] *n* खेमे का स्थल

campus ['kæmpəs] *n* परिसर

can [kæn] *v* सकना ▷ *n* कनस्तर

Canada ['kænədə] *n* कनाडा

Canadian [kə'neɪdɪən] *adj* कनाडा से संबद्ध ▷ *n* कनाडावासी

canal [kə'næl] *n* नहर

Canaries [kə'nɛəriːz] *npl* कैनरी द्वीप समूह

canary [kə'nɛərɪ] *n* पीतचटकी

cancel ['kænsl] *v* रद्द करना

cancellation [ˌkænsɪ'leɪʃən] *n* निरसन

Cancer ['kænsə] *n (sign of zodiac)* कर्क राशि

cancer ['kænsə] *n (illness)* कैंसर

candidate ['kændɪˌdeɪt] *n* उम्मीदवार

candle ['kændl] *n* मोमबत्ती

candlestick ['kændlˌstɪk] *n* चिरागदान

candyfloss ['kændɪˌflɒs] *n* बुढ़िया का काता

canister ['kænɪstə] *n* कनस्तर

canned [kænd] *adj* पहले से रिकॉर्ड किया गया

canoe [kə'nuː] *n* डोंगी

canoeing [kə'nuːɪŋ] *n* डोंगी चालन

can opener [kæn 'əʊpənə] *n* कैन ओपनर

canteen [kæn'tiːn] *n* जलपानगृह

C

canter ['kæntə] *vi* दुलकी चाल से चलना
canvas ['kænvəs] *n* तिरपाल
canvass ['kænvəs] *vi* पक्ष-प्रचार करना
cap [kæp] *n* टोपी
capable ['keɪpəbl] *adj* सक्षम
capacity [kə'pæsɪtɪ] *n* सक्षमता
capital ['kæpɪtl] *n (money)* पूंजी; *(city)* राजधानी; *(letter)* बड़ा अक्षर
capitalism ['kæpɪtəˌlɪzəm] *n* पूंजीवाद
capital punishment ['kæpɪtl 'pʌnɪʃmənt] *n* मृत्युदंड
Capricorn ['kæprɪˌkɔːn] *n* मकर राशि
capsize [kæp'saɪz] *v* पलट देना
capsule ['kæpsjuːl] *n* कैप्सूल
captain ['kæptɪn] *n* कप्तान
caption ['kæpʃən] *n* अनुशीर्षक
capture ['kæptʃə] *vt* पकड़ना
car [kɑː] *n* मोटरगाड़ी
carafe [kə'ræf] *n* काँच का गिलास
caramel ['kærəməl] *n* भुनी शक्कर से बनी मिठाई
carat ['kærət] *n* रत्ती
caravan ['kærəˌvæn] *n* चलते - फिरते घर जैसी गाड़ी
carbohydrate [ˌkɑːbəʊ'haɪdreɪt] *n* कार्बोहाइड्रेट
carbon ['kɑːbn] *n* कार्बन
carbon footprint ['kɑːbən 'fʊtˌprɪnt] *n* उत्सर्जित कार्बन डाईऑक्साइड की मात्रा
carburettor [ˌkɑːbjʊ'rɛtə] *n* कार्ब्युरेटर
card [kɑːd] *n (greetings card)* बधाई पत्र; *(stiff paper)* गत्ता; *(playing card)* ताश
cardboard ['kɑːdˌbɔːd] *n* गत्ता
cardigan ['kɑːdɪgən] *n* सामने से खुलने वाला स्वेटर
cardphone ['kɑːdfəʊn] *n* कार्डफ़ोन
care [kɛə] *n* देखभाल ▷ *vi (be concerned)* परवाह करना; *(look after)* देखभाल करना

career [kə'rɪə] *n* आजीविका
careful ['kɛəfʊl] *adj* सावधान
carefully ['kɛəfʊlɪ] *adv* सावधानी से
careless ['kɛəlɪs] *adj* बेपरवाह
caretaker ['kɛəˌteɪkə] *n* संरक्षक
car ferry [kɑː 'fɛrɪ] *n* एक प्रकार की नौका
cargo ['kɑːgəʊ] *n* माल
car hire [kɑː haɪə] *n* कार किराए पर लेना
Caribbean [ˌkærɪ'biːən] *adj* कैरेबियाई ▷ *n* कैरेबियन सागर
caring ['kɛərɪŋ] *adj* परवाह करने वाला
car insurance [kɑː ɪn'ʃʊərəns] *n* कार बीमा
car keys [kɑː kiːz] *npl* कार की चाभियाँ
carnation [kɑː'neɪʃən] *n* गुलनार
carnival ['kɑːnɪvl] *n* आनंदोत्सव
carol ['kærəl] *n* ईसाई भजन
car park [kɑː pɑːk] *n* गाड़ियाँ खड़ी करने की जगह
carpenter ['kɑːpɪntə] *n* बढ़ई
carpentry ['kɑːpɪntrɪ] *n* बढ़ईगीरी
carpet ['kɑːpɪt] *n* कालीन
car rental [kɑː 'rɛntl] *n* कार किराए पर लेना
carriage ['kærɪdʒ] *n* सवारी डिब्बा
carrier bag ['kærɪə bæg] *n* झोला
carrot ['kærət] *n* गाजर
carry ['kærɪ] *vt* ढोना
carrycot ['kærɪˌkɒt] *n* पालना
carry on ['kærɪ ɒn] *v* जारी रखना
carry out ['kærɪ aʊt] *v* पालन करना
cart [kɑːt] *n* छकड़ा गाड़ी
carton ['kɑːtn] *n* गत्ते का डिब्बा
cartoon [kɑː'tuːn] *n* *(drawing)* हास्यचित्र; *(film)* कार्टून फ़िल्म
cartridge ['kɑːtrɪdʒ] *n* कारतूस

carve [kaːv] *v* तराशना
car wash [kaː wɒʃ] *n* गाड़ी धुलवाने का स्थान
case [keɪs] *n (situation)* मामला; *(container)* पेटी
cash [kæʃ] *n* नकदी
cash dispenser [kæʃ dɪ'spɛnsə] *n* नकदी भुगतान मशीन
cashew ['kæʃuː] *n* काजू
cashier [kæ'ʃɪə] *n* खजांची
cashmere ['kæʃmɪə] *n* ऊन
cash register [kæʃ 'rɛdʒɪstə] *n* नकद खाता
casino [kə'siːnəʊ] *n* जुआखाना
casserole ['kæsə,rəʊl] *n* पुलाव जैसा पकवान
cassette [kæ'sɛt] *n* कैसेट
cast [kaːst] *n* अभिनेता समूह
castle ['kaːsl] *n* महल
casual ['kæʒjʊəl] *adj* अनौपचारिक
casually ['kæʒjʊəlɪ] *adv* अनौपचारिक रूप से
casualty ['kæʒjʊəltɪ] *n* घायल
cat [kæt] *n* बिल्ली
catalogue ['kætə,lɒg] *n* सूची
catalytic converter [,kætə'lɪtɪk kən'vɜːtə] *n* कैटलिटिक कनवर्टर
cataract ['kætə,rækt] *n (waterfall)* झरना; *(in eye)* मोतियाबिंद
catarrh [kə'taː] *n* सर्दी
catastrophe [kə'tæstrəfɪ] *n* आपत्ति
catch [kætʃ] *vt (capture)* पकड़ना; *(ball)* पकड़ना/लपक लेना; *(bus, train)* पकड़ना; *(illness)* हो जाना
catching ['kætʃɪŋ] *adj* संक्रामक
catch up [kætʃ ʌp] *v* पकड़ना
category ['kætɪgərɪ] *n* वर्ग
catering ['keɪtərɪŋ] *n* भोजन प्रदाता सेवा
caterpillar ['kætə,pɪlə] *n* इल्ली
cathedral [kə'θiːdrəl] *n* प्रधान गिरजाघर
cattle ['kætl] *npl* मवेशी
Caucasus ['kɔːkəsəs] *n* काकेशस पर्वत

cauliflower ['kɒlɪˌflaʊə] *n* फूलगोभी
cause [kɔːz] *n (event)* कारण; *(aim)* मकसद ▷ *vt* कारण होना
caution ['kɔːʃən] *n* सावधानी
cautious ['kɔːʃəs] *adj* सतर्क
cautiously ['kɔːʃəslɪ] *adv* सावधानीपूर्वक
cave [keɪv] *n* गुफा
CCTV [siː siː tiː viː] *abbr* क्लोज़ सर्किट टेलीविज़न
CD [siː diː] *n* सी डी
CD burner [siː diː 'bɜːnə] *n* सी डी बर्नर
CD player [siː diː 'pleɪə] *n* सी डी प्लेयर
CD-ROM [siː diː 'rɒm] *n* सी डी रोम
ceasefire ['siːsˌfaɪə] *n* युद्धविराम
ceiling ['siːlɪŋ] *n* छत
celebrate ['sɛlɪˌbreɪt] *v* उत्सव मनाना
celebration ['sɛlɪˌbreɪʃən] *n* उत्सव
celebrity [sɪ'lɛbrɪtɪ] *n* ख़्यातिप्राप्त व्यक्ति
celery ['sɛlərɪ] *n* सेलरी
cell [sɛl] *n* कोशिका
cellar ['sɛlə] *n* तहखाना
cello ['tʃɛləʊ] *n* वायलिननुमा वाद्य
cement [sɪ'mɛnt] *n* सीमेंट
cemetery ['sɛmɪtrɪ] *n* कब्रिस्तान
census ['sɛnsəs] *n* जनगणना
cent [sɛnt] *n* सेंट
centenary [sɛn'tiːnərɪ] *n* शताब्दी समारोह
centimetre ['sɛntɪˌmiːtə] *n* सेंटीमीटर
central ['sɛntrəl] *adj* केंद्रीय
Central African Republic ['sɛntrəl 'æfrɪkən rɪ'pʌblɪk] *n* मध्य अफ़्रीकी गणराज्य
Central America ['sɛntrəl ə'mɛrɪkə] *n* मध्य अमेरिका
central heating ['sɛntrəl 'hiːtɪŋ] *n* केंद्रीय तापन
centre ['sɛntə] *n* केंद्र
century ['sɛntʃərɪ] *n* शताब्दी
CEO [siː iː əʊ] *abbr* मुख्य कार्यकारी अधिकारी
ceramic [sɪ'ræmɪk] *adj* चीनी मिट्टी का

cereal ['sɪərɪəl] *n (breakfast food)* अनाज; *(plants)* अन्न/धान्य

ceremony ['sɛrɪmənɪ] *n* समारोह

certain ['sɜːtn] *adj* निश्चित

certainly ['sɜːtnlɪ] *adv* निश्चित रूप से

certainty ['sɜːtntɪ] *n* निश्चितता

certificate [sə'tɪfɪkɪt] *n* प्रमाणपत्र

Chad [tʃæd] *n* चाड

chain [tʃeɪn] *n* ज़ंजीर

chair [tʃɛə] *n (seat)* कुर्सी

chairlift ['tʃɛə,lɪft] *n* चेयरलिफ़्ट

chairman ['tʃɛəmən] *n* सभापति

chalk [tʃɔːk] *n* खड़िया

challenge ['tʃælɪndʒ] *n* चुनौती ▷ *vt* चुनौती देना

challenging ['tʃælɪndʒɪŋ] *adj* चुनौतीपूर्ण

chambermaid ['tʃeɪmbə,meɪd] *n* शयनकक्ष साफ करने वाली नौकरानी

champagne [ʃæm'peɪn] *n* शैंपेन

champion ['tʃæmpɪən] *n* विजेता

championship ['tʃæmpɪən,ʃɪp] *n* प्रतियोगिता

chance [tʃɑːns] *n* संभावना

change [tʃeɪndʒ] *n (alteration)* परिवर्तन ▷ *vi (put on different clothes)* कपड़े बदलना ▷ *v (become different)* बदल देना/बदल जाना ▷ *n (money)* रेजगारी

changeable ['tʃeɪndʒəbl] *adj* परिवर्तनीय

changing room ['tʃeɪndʒɪŋ rʊm] *n* कपड़े बदलने का कमरा

channel ['tʃænl] *n* चैनल

chaos ['keɪɒs] *n* अव्यवस्था

chaotic ['keɪ'ɒtɪk] *adj* अस्तव्यस्त

chap [tʃæp] *n (informal)* लड़का/आदमी

chapel ['tʃæpl] *n* छोटा गिरजा

chapter ['tʃæptə] *n* अध्याय

character ['kærɪktə] *n (personality)* चरित्र; *(in story or film)* चरित्र/पात्र

characteristic [ˌkærɪktəˈrɪstɪk] *n* विशेषता
charcoal [ˈtʃɑːˌkəʊl] *n* कोयला
charge [tʃɑːdʒ] *n (price)* शुल्क; *(crime)* आरोप; *(electrical)* विद्युत आवेश ▹ *v (ask to pay)* शुल्क लेना ▹ *vt (police)* उत्तरदायी ठहराना; *(battery)* आवेशित करना
charger [ˈtʃɑːdʒə] *n* चार्जर
charity [ˈtʃærɪtɪ] *n* धर्मार्थ संगठन
charity shop [ˈtʃærɪtɪ ʃɒp] *n* धर्मार्थ दुकान
charm [tʃɑːm] *n* मोहकता
charming [ˈtʃɑːmɪŋ] *adj* मोहक
chart [tʃɑːt] *n* लेखाचित्र
chase [tʃeɪs] *n* पीछा ▹ *vt* पीछा करना
chat [tʃæt] *n* बातचीत ▹ *vi* बातचीत करना
chatroom [ˈtʃætˌruːm] *n* चैट रूम
chat show [tʃæt ʃəʊ] *n* चैट/वार्ता कार्यक्रम
chauffeur [ˈʃəʊfə] *n* चालक
chauvinist [ˈʃəʊvɪˌnɪst] *n* अपने लिंग को श्रेष्ठ मानने वाला व्यक्ति
cheap [tʃiːp] *adj* सस्ता
cheat [tʃiːt] *n* बेईमान ▹ *vi* बेईमानी करना
Chechnya [ˈtʃɛtʃnjə] *n* चेचेन्या
check [tʃɛk] *n* जाँच ▹ *v* जाँच करना
checked [tʃɛkt] *adj* चारखानेदार
check in [tʃɛk ɪn] *v* चेक इन
check out [tʃɛk aʊt] *v* चेक आउट
checkout [ˈtʃɛkaʊt] *n* भुगतान स्थल
check-up [ˈtʃɛkʌp] *n* परीक्षण
cheek [tʃiːk] *n* गाल
cheekbone [ˈtʃiːkˌbəʊn] *n* गण्डास्थि
cheeky [ˈtʃiːkɪ] *adj* धृष्ट
cheer [tʃɪə] *n* जयजयकार ▹ *v* जयजयकार करना
cheerful [ˈtʃɪəfʊl] *adj* हँसमुख

cheerio! ['tʃɪərɪ'əʊ] *excl (informal)* अलविदा!
cheers! [tʃɪəz] *excl* चीयर्स
cheese [tʃiːz] *n* चीज़
chef [ʃɛf] *n* खानसामा
chemical ['kɛmɪkl] *n* रसायन
chemist ['kɛmɪst] *n (person)* दवा निर्माता/ दवा विक्रेता; *(shop)* दवा की दुकान
chemistry ['kɛmɪstrɪ] *n* रसायन विज्ञान
cheque [tʃɛk] *n* चेक
chequebook ['tʃɛk,bʊk] *n* चेकबुक
cherry ['tʃɛrɪ] *n* चेरी
chess [tʃɛs] *n* शतरंज
chest [tʃɛst] *n (part of body)* वक्ष; *(box)* बड़ा बक्सा
chestnut ['tʃɛs,nʌt] *n* शाहबलूत वृक्ष
chest of drawers [tʃɛst əv drɔːz] *n* कपड़े रखने की अलमारी
chew [tʃuː] *v* चबाना
chewing gum ['tʃuːɪŋ gʌm] *n* च्यूइंग गम
chick [tʃɪk] *n* चूजा
chicken ['tʃɪkɪn] *n (bird)* मुर्गा/मुर्गी; *(meat)* मुर्गा/मुर्गी का मांस
chickenpox ['tʃɪkɪn,pɒks] *n* छोटी माता
chickpea ['tʃɪk,piː] *n* काबुली चना
chief [tʃiːf] *adj* प्रमुख ▷ *n* मुख्याधिकारी
child [tʃaɪld] *n* बच्चा
childcare ['tʃaɪld,kɛə] *n* बच्चों की देखरेख
childhood ['tʃaɪldhʊd] *n* बचपन
childish ['tʃaɪldɪʃ] *adj* बालसुलभ/बचकाना
childminder ['tʃaɪld,maɪndə] *n* बच्चों की देखरेख करने वाला
Chile ['tʃɪlɪ] *n* चिली
Chilean ['tʃɪlɪən] *adj* चिली से संबद्ध ▷ *n* चिली निवासी
chill [tʃɪl] *v* ठंडा करना
chilli ['tʃɪlɪ] *n* मिर्च
chilly ['tʃɪlɪ] *adj* ठिठुराने वाली ठंड
chimney ['tʃɪmnɪ] *n* धुआँरा
chimpanzee [,tʃɪmpæn'ziː] *n* वनमानुस

chin [tʃɪn] *n* ठोड़ी
China ['tʃaɪnə] *n* चीन
china ['tʃaɪnə] *n* चीनी मिट्टी
Chinese [tʃaɪ'niːz] *adj* चीनी ▷ *n (person)* चीनी; *(language)* चीनी
chip [tʃɪp] *n (small piece)* टुकड़ा; *(electronic)* चिप ▷ *vt* तोड़ना/किनारे से तोड़ना
chips [tʃɪps] *npl (potatoes)* चिप्स
chiropodist [kɪ'rɒpədɪst] *n* किरोपॉडिस्ट - पैरों की देखभाल व चिकित्सा करने वाला
chisel ['tʃɪzl] *n* छेनी/रुखानी
chives *npl* छोटा प्याज
chlorine ['klɔːriːn] *n* क्लोरीन
chocolate ['tʃɒkəlɪt] *n* चॉकलेट
choice [tʃɔɪs] *n* चयन/प्रकार
choir [kwaɪə] *n* गायक - मंडली
choke [tʃəʊk] *v* दम घुटना
cholesterol [kə'lɛstəˌrɒl] *n* कोलेस्ट्रॉल
choose [tʃuːz] *v* चुनना
chop [tʃɒp] *n* टुकड़ा ▷ *vt* टुकड़े करना
chopsticks ['tʃɒpstɪks] *npl* चॉपस्टिक
chosen ['tʃəʊzn] *adj* चुना हुआ
Christ [kraɪst] *n* ईसा मसीह
Christian ['krɪstʃən] *adj* ईसाई ▷ *n* ईसाई
Christianity [ˌkrɪstɪ'ænɪtɪ] *n* ईसाई धर्म
Christmas ['krɪsməs] *n* क्रिसमस/बड़ा दिन
Christmas card ['krɪsməs kɑːd] *n* क्रिसमस कार्ड
Christmas Eve ['krɪsməs iːv] *n* क्रिसमस के पहले की शाम
Christmas tree ['krɪsməs triː] *n* क्रिसमस ट्री
chrome [krəʊm] *n* क्रोम-एक धातु
chronic ['krɒnɪk] *adj* चिरकालिक
chrysanthemum [krɪ'sænθəməm] *n* गुलदाउदी
chubby ['tʃʌbɪ] *adj* मांसल
chunk [tʃʌŋk] *n* खंड

church [tʃɜːtʃ] *n* गिरजाघर
cider ['saɪdə] *n* सेब से बनी शराब
cigar [sɪ'gɑː] *n* चुरुट
cigarette [ˌsɪgə'rɛt] *n* सिगरेट
cigarette lighter [ˌsɪgə'rɛt 'laɪtə] *n* सिगरेट लाइटर
cinema ['sɪnɪmə] *n* छविगृह
cinnamon ['sɪnəmən] *n* दालचीनी
circle ['sɜːkl] *n* वृत्त
circuit ['sɜːkɪt] *n* परिपथ
circular ['sɜːkjʊlə] *adj* वृत्ताकार
circulation [ˌsɜːkjʊ'leɪʃən] *n* वितरण
circumstances ['sɜːkəmstənsɪz] *npl* परिस्थिति
circus ['sɜːkəs] *n* सर्कस
citizen ['sɪtɪzn] *n* नागरिक
citizenship ['sɪtɪzənˌʃɪp] *n* नागरिकता
city ['sɪtɪ] *n* नगर
city centre ['sɪtɪ 'sɛntə] *n* नगर केंद्र
civilian [sɪ'vɪljən] *adj* असैनिक ▷ *n* असैनिक
civilization [ˌsɪvɪlaɪ'zeɪʃən] *n* सभ्यता
civil rights ['sɪvl raɪts] *npl* नागरिक अधिकार
civil servant ['sɪvl 'sɜːvnt] *n* जनसेवक
civil war ['sɪvl wɔː] *n* गृह युद्ध
claim [kleɪm] *n* दावा ▷ *vt* दावा करना
claim form [kleɪm fɔːm] *n* दावा प्रपत्र
clap [klæp] *v* ताली बजाना
clarify ['klærɪˌfaɪ] *vt* *(formal)* स्पष्ट करना
clarinet [ˌklærɪ'nɛt] *n* शहनाई
clash [klæʃ] *vi* उलझना
clasp [klɑːsp] *n* बकसुआ
class [klɑːs] *n* कक्षा
classic ['klæsɪk] *adj* उत्कृष्ट ▷ *n* उत्कृष्ट उदाहरण
classical ['klæsɪkl] *adj* शास्त्रीय
classmate ['klɑːsˌmeɪt] *n* सहपाठी
classroom ['klɑːsˌruːm] *n* कक्षा

classroom assistant ['klɑːsrʊm ə'sɪstənt] *n* कक्षा सहायक
clause [klɔːz] *n* परिच्छेद
claustrophobic [ˌklɔːstrə'fəʊbɪk] *adj* दमघोंटू
claw [klɔː] *n* पंजा
clay [kleɪ] *n* मिट्टी
clean [kliːn] *adj* साफ़ ▷ *vt* साफ़ करना
cleaner ['kliːnə] *n* सफाई कर्मचारी
cleaning ['kliːnɪŋ] *n* सफाई
cleaning lady ['kliːnɪŋ 'leɪdɪ] *n* महिला सफाई कर्मचारी
cleanser ['klɛnzə] *n* साफ़ करने वाला पदार्थ
cleansing lotion ['klɛnzɪŋ 'ləʊʃən] *n* साफ करने वाला लोशन
clear [klɪə] *adj* *(easily seen or understood)* स्पष्ट; *(see-through)* साफ़/निर्मल; *(unobstructed)* खाली ▷ *vt* साफ़-सुथरा करना
clearly ['klɪəlɪ] *adv* स्पष्टतया
clear off [klɪə ɒf] *v* *(informal)* भागना
clear up [klɪə ʌp] *v* साफ करना
clementine ['klɛmənˌtiːn] *n* संतरे जैसा फल
clever ['klɛvə] *adj* चतुर
click [klɪk] *n* खट की आवाज़ ▷ *v* खटखट करना
client ['klaɪənt] *n* असामी
cliff [klɪf] *n* खड़ी चट्टान
climate ['klaɪmɪt] *n* जलवायु
climate change ['klaɪmɪt tʃeɪndʒ] *n* जलवायु परिवर्तन
climb [klaɪm] *v* चढ़ना
climber ['klaɪmə] *n* आरोही
climbing ['klaɪmɪŋ] *n* आरोहण
clinic ['klɪnɪk] *n* चिकित्सालय
clip [klɪp] *n* चिमटी
clippers ['klɪpəz] *npl* काटने का उपकरण
cloakroom ['kləʊkˌruːm] *n* कोट, छाते आदि टांगने की जगह/अमानती सामानघर
clock [klɒk] *n* दीवार घड़ी
clockwise ['klɒkˌwaɪz] *adv* दक्षिणावर्त

clog [klɒg] *n* खड़ाऊँ /मोजरी
clone [kləʊn] *n* प्रतिरूप ▷ *vt* जैविक प्रतिरूप बनाना
close [kləʊs] *adj* समीप ▷ *adv* पास में ▷ [kləʊz] *vt* बंद करना
close by [kləʊs baɪ] *adj* निकटवर्ती
closed [kləʊzd] *adj* संकीर्ण
closely [kləʊslɪ] *adv* निकट से
closing time ['kləʊzɪŋ taɪm] *n* बंद करने का समय
closure ['kləʊʒə] *n* बंदी
cloth [klɒθ] *n* *(material)* कपड़ा; *(for cleaning)* पोंछा
clothes [kləʊðz] *npl* पोशाक
clothes line [kləʊðz laɪn] *n* अलगनी
clothes peg [kləʊðz pɛg] *n* कपड़े की चिमटी
clothing ['kləʊðɪŋ] *n* परिधान
cloud [klaʊd] *n* मेघ
cloudy ['klaʊdɪ] *adj* मेघाछन्न
clove [kləʊv] *n* लौंग
clown [klaʊn] *n* मसखरा
club [klʌb] *n* *(organization)* संघ; *(stick)* लाठी
club together [klʌb tə'gɛðə] *v* पैसा एकत्र करना
clue [kluː] *n* संकेत
clumsy ['klʌmzɪ] *adj* फूहड़
clutch [klʌtʃ] *n* चंगुल
clutter ['klʌtə] *n* अव्यवस्था
coach [kəʊtʃ] *n* *(trainer)* प्रशिक्षक; *(bus)* बड़ी बस
coal [kəʊl] *n* कोयला
coarse [kɔːs] *adj* खुरदरा
coast [kəʊst] *n* समुद्रतट
coastguard ['kəʊst,gɑːd] *n* तटरक्षक
coat [kəʊt] *n* कोट
coathanger ['kəʊt,hæŋə] *n* कोट टांगने का हैंगर
cobweb ['kɒb,wɛb] *n* मकड़ी का जाला
cock [kɒk] *n* मुर्गा
cockerel ['kɒkərəl] *n* मुर्गा
cockpit ['kɒk,pɪt] *n* कॉकपिट
cockroach ['kɒk,rəʊtʃ] *n* तिलचट्टा
cocktail ['kɒk,teɪl] *n* मिश्रित शराब
cocoa ['kəʊkəʊ] *n* कोको
coconut ['kəʊkə,nʌt] *n* नारियल

cod [kɒd] *n* एक प्रकार की मछली
code [kəʊd] *n* संहिता
coeliac ['siːlɪ,æk] *adj* पेट संबंधी
coffee ['kɒfɪ] *n* कॉफ़ी
coffee bean ['kɒfɪ biːn] *n* कॉफी के बीज
coffeepot ['kɒfɪ,pɒt] *n* कॉफ़ीदान
coffee table ['kɒfɪ 'teɪbl] *n* छोटी मेज़
coffin ['kɒfɪn] *n* ताबूत
coin [kɔɪn] *n* सिक्का
coincide [,kəʊɪn'saɪd] *vi* एक समय पर होना
coincidence [kəʊ'ɪnsɪdəns] *n* संयोग
Coke® [kəʊk] *n* कोक
colander ['kɒləndə] *n* छलनी
cold [kəʊld] *adj (weather)* ठंडा/सर्द ▷ *n* ज़ुकाम ▷ *adj (person)* ठंडा/सर्द
cold sore [kəʊld sɔː] *n* जुकाम के कारण होने वाले छाले
coleslaw ['kəʊl,slɔː] *n* सलाद
collaborate [kə'læbə,reɪt] *vi* मिलकर काम करना
collapse [kə'læps] *vi* ढह जाना
collar ['kɒlə] *n (garment)* गिरेबान/कॉलर; *(pet)* गले का पट्टा
collarbone ['kɒlə,bəʊn] *n* जत्रुक/हंसली
colleague ['kɒliːg] *n* सहकर्मी
collect [kə'lɛkt] *vt (gather)* इकट्ठा करना; *(person)* ले आना
collection [kə'lɛkʃən] *n* संग्रह
collective [kə'lɛktɪv] *adj* सामूहिक ▷ *n* सामूहिक संस्था
collector [kə'lɛktə] *n* संग्रहकर्ता
college ['kɒlɪdʒ] *n* महाविद्यालय
collide [kə'laɪd] *vi* भिड़ जाना
collie ['kɒlɪ] *n* एक प्रकार का कुत्ता
colliery ['kɒljərɪ] *n* कोयले की खान
collision [kə'lɪʒən] *n* टक्कर
Colombia [kə'lɒmbɪə] *n* कोलम्बिया

Colombian [kə'lɒmbɪən] *adj* कोलम्बियाई ▷ *n* कोलम्बियाई
colon ['kəʊlən] *n* एक विरामचिह्न
colonel ['kɜːnl] *n* कर्नल
colour ['kʌlə] *n* रंग
colour-blind ['kʌlə'blaɪnd] *adj* वर्णांध
colourful ['kʌləfʊl] *adj* रंगीन
colouring ['kʌlərɪŋ] *n* रंगत
column ['kɒləm] *n* स्तंभ
coma ['kəʊmə] *n* कोमा/ अचेतावस्था
comb [kəʊm] *n* कंघी ▷ *vt* कंघी करना
combination [,kɒmbɪ'neɪʃən] *n* संयोजन
combine [kəm'baɪn] *v* जोड़ देना
come [kʌm] *vi* आना
come back [kʌm bæk] *v* लौटना
comedian [kə'miːdɪən] *n* हास्य अभिनेता
come down [kʌm daʊn] *v* घटना
comedy ['kɒmɪdɪ] *n* प्रहसन
come from [kʌm frəm] *v* से आना/ से संबंधित होना
come in [kʌm ɪn] *v* आना
come out [kʌm aʊt] *v* बाहर आना
come round [kʌm raʊnd] *v* होश में आना
comet ['kɒmɪt] *n* धूमकेतु
come up [kʌm ʌp] *v* पास आना
comfortable ['kʌmftəbl] *adj* आरामदेह
comic ['kɒmɪk] *n* विदूषक
comic book ['kɒmɪk bʊk] *n* चित्रकथा खंड
comic strip ['kɒmɪk strɪp] *n* चित्रकथा
coming ['kʌmɪŋ] *adj* आगामी
comma ['kɒmə] *n* अल्पविराम
command [kə'mɑːnd] *n* *(written)* आदेश
comment ['kɒmɛnt] *n* टिप्पणी ▷ *v* टिप्पणी करना
commentary ['kɒməntərɪ] *n* आंखों देखा विवरण
commentator ['kɒmən,teɪtə] *n* विवरण प्रसारक

C

commercial [kəˈmɜːʃəl] *n* विज्ञापन
commercial break [kəˈmɜːʃəl breɪk] *n* विज्ञापन अंतराल
commission [kəˈmɪʃən] *n* दलाली
commit [kəˈmɪt] *vt* कर डालना
committee [kəˈmɪtɪ] *n* समिति
common [ˈkɒmən] *adj* सामान्य
common sense [ˈkɒmən sɛns] *n* सहज बुद्धि
communicate [kəˈmjuːnɪˌkeɪt] *vi* बताना/सूचित करना
communication [kəˌmjuːnɪˈkeɪʃən] *n* संचार
communion [kəˈmjuːnjən] *n* ऐक्य
communism [ˈkɒmjʊˌnɪzəm] *n* साम्यवाद
communist [ˈkɒmjʊnɪst] *adj* साम्यवाद संबंधी ▷ *n* साम्यवादी
community [kəˈmjuːnɪtɪ] *n* समुदाय
commute [kəˈmjuːt] *vi* सफर करना
commuter [kəˈmjuːtə] *n* नियमित सफर करने वाले
compact [ˌkəmˈpækt] *adj* छोटा
compact disc [ˈkɒmpækt dɪsk] *n* कॉम्पैक्ट डिस्क
companion [kəmˈpænjən] *n* साथी
company [ˈkʌmpənɪ] *n* कंपनी (निकाय)
company car [ˈkʌmpənɪ kɑː] *n* कंपनी कार
comparable [ˈkɒmpərəbl] *adj* तुल्य
comparatively [kəmˈpærətɪvlɪ] *adv* अपेक्षाकृत
compare [kəmˈpɛə] *vt* तुलना करना
comparison [kəmˈpærɪsn] *n* तुलना
compartment [kəmˈpɑːtmənt] *n* डिब्बा
compass [ˈkʌmpəs] *n* दिक्सूचक
compatible [kəmˈpætəbl] *adj* अनुरूप/मुआफ़िक

compensate ['kɒmpɛn,seɪt] *vt* मुआवज़ा देना
compensation [,kɒmpɛn'seɪʃən] *n* मुआवज़ा
compere ['kɒmpɛə] *n* सूत्रधार
compete [kəm'piːt] *vi* प्रतिस्पर्द्धा करना
competent ['kɒmpɪtənt] *adj* सक्षम
competition [,kɒmpɪ'tɪʃən] *n* प्रतिस्पर्द्धा
competitive [kəm'pɛtɪtɪv] *adj* प्रतिस्पर्द्धात्मक
competitor [kəm'pɛtɪtə] *n* प्रतिस्पर्द्धी
complain [kəm'pleɪn] *v* शिकायत करना
complaint [kəm'pleɪnt] *n* शिकायत
complementary [,kɒmplɪ'mɛntərɪ] *adj* *(formal)* पूरक
complete [kəm'pliːt] *adj* पूर्ण
completely [kəm'pliːtlɪ] *adv* पूर्णतया
complex ['kɒmplɛks] *adj* जटिल ▷ *n* संकुल
complexion [kəm'plɛkʃən] *n* रंगत
complicated ['kɒmplɪ,keɪtɪd] *adj* जटिल
complication [,kɒmplɪ'keɪʃən] *n* जटिलता/परेशानी
compliment ['kɒmplɪ,mɛnt] *n* प्रशंसोक्ति ▷ ['kɒmplɪment] *vt* प्रशंसा करना
complimentary [,kɒmplɪ'mɛntərɪ] *adj* प्रशंसात्मक
component [kəm'pəʊnənt] *n* घटक
composer [kəm'pəʊzə] *n* संगीतकार
composition [,kɒmpə'zɪʃən] *n* संयोजन
comprehension [,kɒmprɪ'hɛnʃən] *n* *(formal)* समझ
comprehensive [,kɒmprɪ'hɛnsɪv] *adj* विस्तृत
compromise ['kɒmprə,maɪz] *n* समझौता ▷ *vi* समझौता करना

compulsory [kəm'pʌlsərɪ] *adj* अनिवार्य

computer [kəm'pjuːtə] *n* कंप्यूटर/संगणक

computer game [kəm'pjuːtə geɪm] *n* कंप्यूटर गेम

computer science [kəm'pjuːtə 'saɪəns] *n* कंप्यूटर विज्ञान

computing [kəm'pjuːtɪŋ] *n* संगणना

concentrate ['kɒnsən,treɪt] *vi* ध्यान एकाग्र करना

concentration [,kɒnsən'treɪʃən] *n* एकाग्रता

concern [kən'sɜːn] *n* चिंता

concerned [kən'sɜːnd] *adj* चिंतित

concerning [kən'sɜːnɪŋ] *prep (formal)* के विषय में

concert ['kɒnsət] *n* संगीत कार्यक्रम

concerto [kən'tʃɛətəʊ] *n* बंदिश

concession [kən'sɛʃən] *n* रियायत

concise [kən'saɪs] *adj* संक्षिप्त

conclude [kən'kluːd] *vt* निष्कर्ष निकालना

conclusion [kən'kluːʒən] *n* निष्कर्ष

concrete ['kɒnkriːt] *n* कंकरीट

concussion [kən'kʌʃən] *n* सिर की चोट

condemn [kən'dɛm] *vt* निंदा करना

condensation [,kɒndɛn'seɪʃən] *n* संघनन

condition [kən'dɪʃən] *n* स्थिति

conditional [kən'dɪʃənl] *adj* सशर्त

conditioner [kən'dɪʃənə] *n* बालों को मुलायम बनाने वाला पदार्थ

condom ['kɒndɒm] *n* कंडोम

conduct [kən'dʌkt] *vt* संचालित करना

conductor [kən'dʌktə] *n* संगीत संचालक

cone [kəʊn] *n* शंकु

conference ['kɒnfərəns] *n* सम्मेलन

confess [kən'fɛs] *v* स्वीकार करना

confession [kən'fɛʃən] *n* स्वीकारोक्ति
confetti [kən'fɛtɪ] *npl* रंगीन कागज़ के टुकड़े
confidence ['kɒnfɪdəns] *n (mainly trust)* विश्वास; *(self-assurance)* आत्मविश्वास; *(secret)* राज़
confident ['kɒnfɪdənt] *adj* आत्मविश्वासी
confidential [ˌkɒnfɪ'dɛnʃəl] *adj* गोपनीय
confirm [kən'fɜːm] *vt* पुष्टि करना
confirmation [ˌkɒnfə'meɪʃən] *n* पुष्टि
confiscate ['kɒnfɪˌskeɪt] *vt* ज़ब्त करना
conflict ['kɒnflɪkt] *n* मतभेद
confuse [kən'fjuːz] *vt* एक को दूसरा समझना
confused [kən'fjuːzd] *adj* चकराया हुआ
confusing [kən'fjuːzɪŋ] *adj* भ्रामक
confusion [kən'fjuːʒən] *n* भ्रम
congestion [kən'dʒɛstʃən] *n* भीड़-भाड़
Congo ['kɒŋgəʊ] *n* काँगो
congratulate [kən'grætjʊˌleɪt] *vt* बधाई देना
congratulations [kənˌgrætjʊ'leɪʃənz] *npl* बधाई
conifer ['kəʊnɪfə] *n* शंकुधारी वृक्ष
conjugation [ˌkɒndʒʊ'geɪʃən] *n* क्रियारूप संयोजन
conjunction [kən'dʒʌŋkʃən] *n (formal)* संयोजन
conjurer ['kʌndʒərə] *n* जादूगर
connection [kə'nɛkʃən] *n* संबंध
conquer ['kɒŋkə] *vt* जीत लेना
conscience ['kɒnʃəns] *n* अंतःकरण
conscientious [ˌkɒnʃɪ'ɛnʃəs] *adj* विवेकशील
conscious ['kɒnʃəs] *adj* सचेत
consciousness ['kɒnʃəsnɪs] *n* चेतना

consecutive [kən'sɛkjʊtɪv] *adj* क्रमानुगत/लगातार
consensus [kən'sɛnsəs] *n* सर्वसम्मति
consequence ['kɒnsɪkwəns] *n* परिणाम
consequently ['kɒnsɪkwəntlɪ] *adv (formal)* परिणामस्वरूप
conservation [ˌkɒnsə'veɪʃən] *n* संरक्षण
conservative [kən'sɜːvətɪv] *adj* रुढ़िवादी
conservatory [kən'sɜːvətrɪ] *n* रक्षागृह
consider [kən'sɪdə] *vt* मानना
considerate [kən'sɪdərɪt] *adj* ध्यान रखने वाला
considering [kən'sɪdərɪŋ] *prep* ध्यान में रखते हुए
consistent [kən'sɪstənt] *adj* सुसंगत
consist of [kən'sɪst ɒv; əv] *v* बना होना
consonant ['kɒnsənənt] *n* सन्नादी स्वर/व्यंजन वर्ण
conspiracy [kən'spɪrəsɪ] *n* षड्यंत्र
constant ['kɒnstənt] *adj* निरंतर
constantly ['kɒnstəntlɪ] *adv* निरंतर रूप से
constipated ['kɒnstɪˌpeɪtɪd] *adj* कब्ज़ से पीड़ित
constituency [kən'stɪtjʊənsɪ] *n* निर्वाचन क्षेत्र
constitution [ˌkɒnstɪ'tjuːʃən] *n* संविधान
construct [kən'strʌkt] *vt* निर्माण करना
construction [kən'strʌkʃən] *n* निर्माण
constructive [kən'strʌktɪv] *adj* रचनात्मक
consul ['kɒnsl] *n* राजदूत
consulate ['kɒnsjʊlɪt] *n* दूतावास
consult [kən'sʌlt] *v* सलाह लेना
consultant [kən'sʌltnt] *n* विशेषज्ञ चिकित्सक
consumer [kən'sjuːmə] *n* उपभोक्ता
contact ['kɒntækt] *n* संपर्क ▷ *vt* संपर्क करना

C

contact lenses ['kɒntækt 'lɛnzɪz] *npl* कॉन्टैक्ट लेंस
contagious [kən'teɪdʒəs] *adj* संक्रामक
contain [kən'teɪn] *vt* होना
container [kən'teɪnə] *n* डिब्बा
contemporary [kən'tɛmprərɪ] *adj* समकालीन
contempt [kən'tɛmpt] *n* तिरस्कार
content ['kɒntɛnt] *n* विषयवस्तु ▷ [kən'tent] *adj* संतुष्ट
contents ['kɒntɛnts] *npl* सामग्री
contest ['kɒntɛst] *n* प्रतियोगिता
contestant [kən'tɛstənt] *n* प्रतियोगी
context ['kɒntɛkst] *n* संदर्भ
continent ['kɒntɪnənt] *n* महाद्वीप
continual [kən'tɪnjʊəl] *adj* निरंतर
continually [kən'tɪnjʊəlɪ] *adv* निरंतर रूप से
continue [kən'tɪnjuː] *vt* जारी रहना ▷ *vi* जारी रहना
continuous [kən'tɪnjʊəs] *adj* निरंतर
contraception [ˌkɒntrə'sɛpʃən] *n* गर्भनिरोध
contraceptive [ˌkɒntrə'sɛptɪv] *n* गर्भनिरोधक
contract ['kɒntrækt] *n* अनुबंध
contractor ['kɒntræktə] *n* ठेकेदार
contradict [ˌkɒntrə'dɪkt] *vt* खंडन करना
contradiction [ˌkɒntrə'dɪkʃən] *n* विरोधाभास
contrary ['kɒntrərɪ] *n* प्रतिकूलता
contrast ['kɒntrɑːst] *n* विषमता
contribute [kən'trɪbjuːt] *vi* योगदान देना
contribution [ˌkɒntrɪ'bjuːʃən] *n* योगदान
control [kən'trəʊl] *n* प्रभुत्व ▷ *vt* नियंत्रित करना

controversial [ˌkɒntrəˈvɜːʃəl] *adj* विवादास्पद
convenient [kənˈviːnɪənt] *adj* सुविधाजनक
conventional [kənˈvɛnʃənl] *adj* पारंपरिक
conversation [ˌkɒnvəˈseɪʃən] *n* बातचीत
convert [kənˈvɜːt] *v* परिवर्तित करना
convertible [kənˈvɜːtəbl] *adj* परिवर्तनीय ▹ *n* कन्वर्टिबल कार
conveyor belt [kənˈveɪə bɛlt] *n* वाहक पट्टा
convict [kənˈvɪkt] *vt* दोषी ठहराना
convince [kənˈvɪns] *vt* विश्वास दिलाना
convincing [kənˈvɪnsɪŋ] *adj* विश्वसनीय
convoy [ˈkɒnvɔɪ] *n* काफ़िला
cook [kʊk] *n* खानसामा ▹ *v* पकाना
cookbook [ˈkʊkˌbʊk] *n* पाक कला की पुस्तक
cooker [ˈkʊkə] *n* कुकर
cookery [ˈkʊkərɪ] *n* पाक कला
cookery book [ˈkʊkərɪ bʊk] *n* पाक कला की पुस्तक
cooking [ˈkʊkɪŋ] *n* खाना पकाना
cool [kuːl] *adj (slightly cold)* शीतल; *(informal) (stylish)* आकर्षक व सजीला
cooperation [kəʊˌɒpəˈreɪʃən] *n* सहकारिता
cop [kɒp] *n (informal)* पुलिस अधिकारी
cope [kəʊp] *vi* निपटना
copper [ˈkɒpə] *n* ताँबा
copy [ˈkɒpɪ] *n (duplicate)* प्रतिकृति; *(publication)* प्रति ▹ *vt* प्रतिकृति बनाना
copyright [ˈkɒpɪˌraɪt] *n* मुद्राधिकार
coral [ˈkɒrəl] *n* मूंगा
cordless [ˈkɔːdlɪs] *adj* बेतार
corduroy [ˈkɔːdəˌrɔɪ] *n* मोटा धारीदार सूती कपड़ा
core [kɔː] *n* गूदा
coriander [ˌkɒrɪˈændə] *n* धनिया
cork [kɔːk] *n* काग

corkscrew ['kɔːkˌskruː] *n* काग-पेंच
corn [kɔːn] *n* मक्का
corner ['kɔːnə] *n* कोना
cornet ['kɔːnɪt] *n* तुरही
cornflakes ['kɔːnˌfleɪks] *npl* कॉर्नफ़्लेक्स
cornflour ['kɔːnˌflaʊə] *n* मक्की का आटा
corporal ['kɔːpərəl] *n* एक छोटा अफ़सर
corporal punishment ['kɔːprəl 'pʌnɪʃmənt] *n* शारीरिक दंड
corpse [kɔːps] *n* शव
correct [kə'rɛkt] *adj (formal)* सही ▷ *vt* सही करना
correction [kə'rɛkʃən] *n* संशोधन
correctly [kə'rɛktlɪ] *adv* सही तरह से
correspondence [ˌkɒrɪ'spɒndəns] *n* पत्राचार
correspondent [ˌkɒrɪ'spɒndənt] *n* संवाददाता
corridor ['kɒrɪˌdɔː] *n* गलियारा
corrupt [kə'rʌpt] *adj* भ्रष्ट
corruption [kə'rʌpʃən] *n* भ्रष्टाचार
cosmetics [kɒz'mɛtɪks] *npl* सौंदर्य प्रसाधन
cosmetic surgery [kɒz'mɛtɪk 'sɜːdʒərɪ] *n* सौंदर्य संबंधी शल्य चिकित्सा
cost [kɒst] *n* लागत ▷ *vt* कीमत होना
Costa Rica ['kɒstə 'riːkə] *n* कोस्टा रिका
cost of living [kɒst əv 'lɪvɪŋ] *n* जीवन - निर्वाह व्यय
costume ['kɒstjuːm] *n* पोशाक
cosy ['kəʊzɪ] *adj* आरामदायक
cot [kɒt] *n* पालना
cottage ['kɒtɪdʒ] *n* कुटीर
cottage cheese ['kɒtɪdʒ tʃiːz] *n* पनीर
cotton ['kɒtn] *n (cloth)* सूती कपड़ा; *(thread)* धागा
cotton bud ['kɒtən bʌd] *n* रुई लपेटी हुई छोटी डंडी
cotton wool ['kɒtən wʊl] *n* रुई

couch [kaʊtʃ] *n* दीवान
couchette [kuː'ʃɛt] *n* ट्रेन आदि की फ़ोल्डिंग सीट
cough [kɒf] *n* खाँसी ▷ *vi* खाँसना
cough mixture [kɒf 'mɪkstʃə] *n* खाँसी की दवा
could [kʊd] *v* सकना
council ['kaʊnsəl] *n* परिषद
council house ['kaʊnsəl haʊs] *n* परिषद भवन
councillor ['kaʊnsələ] *n* पार्षद
count [kaʊnt] *vi* *(say numbers in order)* गिनना ▷ *vt* *(add up)* गिनती करना
counter ['kaʊntə] *n* काउंटर
count on [kaʊnt ɒn] *v* भरोसा करना
country ['kʌntrɪ] *n* *(nation)* देश; *(countryside)* देहात/गांव
countryside ['kʌntrɪˌsaɪd] *n* ग्रामीण क्षेत्र
couple ['kʌpl] *n* युगल ▷ *det* दो व्यक्ति या वस्तुएं
courage ['kʌrɪdʒ] *n* साहस
courageous [kə'reɪdʒəs] *adj* साहसी
courgette [kʊə'ʒɛt] *n* तोरी जैसी सब्ज़ी
courier ['kʊərɪə] *n* हरकारा
course [kɔːs] *n* पथ
court [kɔːt] *n* *(law)* न्यायालय; *(tennis)* खेल का मैदान
courtyard ['kɔːtˌjɑːd] *n* प्रांगण
cousin ['kʌzn] *n* चचेरा/ममेरा/फुफेरा/मौसेरा/ भाई या बहन
cover ['kʌvə] *n* खोल/गिलाफ़ ▷ *vt* ढंकना
cover charge ['kʌvə tʃɑːdʒ] *n* खाने-पीने के अलावा चुकाई जाने वाली कीमत
cow [kaʊ] *n* गाय
coward ['kaʊəd] *n* कायर
cowardly ['kaʊədlɪ] *adj* कायर
cowboy ['kaʊˌbɔɪ] *n* काउब्वाय
crab [kræb] *n* केकड़ा
crack [kræk] *n* *(gap)* दरार; *(line)* दरार ▷ *v* चिटकाना
crack down on [kræk daʊn ɒn] *v* नियमों का कड़ाई से पालन करवाना

cracked [krækt] *adj* चिटका हुआ
cracker ['krækə] *n* पतले बिस्कुट
cradle ['kreɪdl] *n* पालना
craft [krɑːft] *n* यान
craftsman ['krɑːftsmən] *n* शिल्पकार
cram [kræm] *v* ठूंसना
crammed [kræmd] *adj* भरा हुआ
cranberry ['krænbərɪ] *n* करौंदा
crane [kreɪn] *n (bird)* सारस; *(machine)* भारी सामान उठाने की मशीन
crash [kræʃ] *n (accident)* टक्कर/दुर्घटना ▷ *vt* टकराना ▷ *vi* टकराकर नष्ट होना ▷ *n (noise)* धड़ाका
crawl [krɔːl] *vi* रेंगना
crayfish ['kreɪˌfɪʃ] *n* कर्क मछली/चिंगट
crayon ['kreɪən] *n* मोम वाले रंग
crazy ['kreɪzɪ] *adj (informal)* बावला
cream [kriːm] *adj* पीलापन लिए सफेद रंग ▷ *n* क्रीम
crease [kriːs] *n* सिलवट
creased [kriːst] *adj* मुड़ा - तुड़ा
create [kriːˈeɪt] *vt* रचना करना
creation [kriːˈeɪʃən] *n* रचना
creative [kriːˈeɪtɪv] *adj* रचनात्मक
creature ['kriːtʃə] *n* प्राणी
crèche [krɛʃ] *n* शिशुसदन
credentials [krɪˈdɛnʃəlz] *npl* प्रत्यय पत्र
credible ['krɛdɪbl] *adj* विश्वसनीय
credit ['krɛdɪt] *n* साख/ऋण
credit card ['krɛdɪt kɑːd] *n* क्रेडिट कार्ड
creep [kriːp] *vi (person)* दबे पांव चलना; *(animal)* रेंगना
crematorium [ˌkrɛməˈtɔːrɪəm] *n* शवदाहगृह/श्मशान
cress [krɛs] *n* चंसुर
crew [kruː] *n* कर्मचारी दल
crew cut [kruː kʌt] *n* क्रू कट - बाल की एक स्टाइल
cricket ['krɪkɪt] *n (game)* क्रिकेट; *(insect)* झींगुर

crime [kraɪm] *n* अपराध
criminal ['krɪmɪnl] *adj* आपराधिक ▷ *n* अपराधी
crisis ['kraɪsɪs] *n* संकट काल
crisp [krɪsp] *adj* कुरकुरा
crisps [krɪsps] *npl* आलू के चिप्स
crispy ['krɪspɪ] *adj* कुरकुरा
criterion [kraɪ'tɪərɪən] *n* मापदंड
critic ['krɪtɪk] *n* समालोचक
critical ['krɪtɪkl] *adj* नाज़ुक/अत्यंत महत्वपूर्ण
criticism ['krɪtɪˌsɪzəm] *n* आलोचना
criticize ['krɪtɪˌsaɪz] *vt* आलोचना करना
Croatia [krəʊ'eɪʃə] *n* क्रोएशिया
Croatian [krəʊ'eɪʃən] *adj* क्रोएशियाई ▷ *n* *(person)* क्रोएशियाई; *(language)* क्रोएशियाई
crochet ['krəʊʃeɪ] *v* क्रोशिया चलाना
crocodile ['krɒkəˌdaɪl] *n* मगरमच्छ
crocus ['krəʊkəs] *n* क्रोकस - एक फूल
crook [krʊk] *n* *(informal)* धोखेबाज़
crop [krɒp] *n* फसल
crore [krɔː] *n* *(ten million)* करोड़
cross [krɒs] *adj* अप्रसन्न ▷ *n* क्रॉस ▷ *vt* पार करना
cross-country ['krɒs'kʌntrɪ] *n* क्रॉस कंट्री
crossing ['krɒsɪŋ] *n* पार - पथ
cross out [krɒs aʊt] *v* गलत का निशान लगाकर काटना
crossroads ['krɒsˌrəʊdz] *n* चौराहा
crossword ['krɒsˌwɜːd] *n* वर्ग - पहेली
crouch down [kraʊtʃ daʊn] *v* नीचे झुकना/ठंकड़ू बैठना
crow [krəʊ] *n* कौआ
crowd [kraʊd] *n* भीड़
crowded [kraʊdɪd] *adj* भीड़ वाला
crown [kraʊn] *n* मुकुट
crucial ['kruːʃəl] *adj* बहुत महत्वपूर्ण
crucifix ['kruːsɪfɪks] *n* सलीब
crude [kruːd] *adj* अपरिष्कृत
cruel ['kruːəl] *adj* क्रूर
cruelty ['kruːəltɪ] *n* क्रूरता

cruise [kruːz] *n* पोतविहार
crumb [krʌm] *n* चूरा
crush [krʌʃ] *vt* कुचलना
crutch [krʌtʃ] *n* बैसाखी
cry [kraɪ] *n* चिल्लाना ▷ *vi* रोना
crystal ['krɪstl] *n* मणिभ
cub [kʌb] *n* शावक
Cuba ['kjuːbə] *n* क्यूबा
Cuban ['kjuːbən] *adj* क्यूबा से संबद्ध ▷ *n* क्यूबा निवासी
cube [kjuːb] *n* घन
cubic ['kjuːbɪk] *adj* घन
cuckoo ['kʊkuː] *n* कोयल
cucumber ['kjuːˌkʌmbə] *n* खीरा
cuddle ['kʌdl] *n* आलिंगन ▷ *vt* लिपटाना
cue [kjuː] *n* सूत्र/संकेत
cufflinks ['kʌflɪŋks] *npl* कफ़लिंक
culprit ['kʌlprɪt] *n* दोषी
cultural ['kʌltʃərəl] *adj* सांस्कृतिक
culture ['kʌltʃə] *n* संस्कृति
cumin ['kʌmɪn] *n* जीरा
cunning ['kʌnɪŋ] *adj* धूर्त
cup [kʌp] *n* प्याला
cupboard ['kʌbəd] *n* अलमारी
curb [kɜːb] *n* रोक/प्रतिबंध
cure [kjʊə] *n* इलाज ▷ *vt* इलाज करना
curfew ['kɜːfjuː] *n* कर्फ़्यू/निषेधाज्ञा
curious ['kjʊərɪəs] *adj* जिज्ञासु
curl [kɜːl] *n* घूँघर/छल्ला
curler ['kɜːlə] *n* बाल घुँघराले बनाने का उपकरण
curly ['kɜːlɪ] *adj* घुंघराला
currant ['kʌrənt] *n* सूखे काले अंगूर
currency ['kʌrənsɪ] *n* मुद्रा
current ['kʌrənt] *adj* तत्कालीन ▷ *n (flow)* प्रवाह/धारा; *(electric)* धारा
current account ['kʌrənt ə'kaʊnt] *n* चालू खाता
current affairs ['kʌrənt ə'fɛəz] *npl* तत्कालीन मुद्दे
currently ['kʌrəntlɪ] *adv* वर्तमान में
curriculum [kə'rɪkjʊləm] *n* पाठ्यक्रम
curriculum vitae [kə'rɪkjʊləm 'viːtaɪ] *n* शिक्षा व कार्यानुभव संबंधी विवरण

curry ['kʌrɪ] *n* रसेदार सब्ज़ी
curry powder ['kʌrɪ 'paʊdə] *n* सब्ज़ी मसाला
curse [kɜːs] *n (written)* शाप
cursor ['kɜːsə] *n* कर्सर
curtain ['kɜːtn] *n* पर्दा
cushion ['kʊʃən] *n* गद्दी
custard ['kʌstəd] *n* कस्टर्ड
custody ['kʌstədɪ] *n* संरक्षण
custom ['kʌstəm] *n* रिवाज़
customer ['kʌstəmə] *n* ग्राहक
customized ['kʌstəˌmaɪzd] *adj* अनुकूलित
customs ['kʌstəmz] *npl* सीमा शुल्क विभाग
customs officer ['kʌstəmz 'ɒfɪsə] *n* सीमा शुल्क अधिकारी
cut [kʌt] *n* घाव/चीरा ▹ *v (chop or slice)* काटना ▹ *vt (yourself)* काट लेना (घाव लगाने के अर्थ में)
cutback ['kʌtˌbæk] *n* कटौती
cut down [kʌt daʊn] *v* कटौती करना
cute [kjuːt] *adj (informal)* आकर्षक
cutlery ['kʌtlərɪ] *n* छुरी-काँटा
cutlet ['kʌtlɪt] *n* कटलेट
cut off [kʌt ɒf] *v* काटकर निकालना
cutting ['kʌtɪŋ] *n* कतरन
cut up [kʌt ʌp] *v* काटना
CV [siː viː] *abbr* शिक्षा व कार्यानुभव संबंधी विवरण
cybercafé ['saɪbəˌkæfeɪ] *n* साइबर कैफ़े
cybercrime ['saɪbəˌkraɪm] *n* साइबर अपराध
cycle ['saɪkl] *n (bicycle)* साइकिल; *(series of events)* घटना चक्र ▹ *vi* साइकिल चलाना
cycle lane ['saɪkl leɪn] *n* साइकिल चलाने का मार्ग
cycle path ['saɪkl pɑːθ] *n* साइकिल चलाने का पथ
cycling ['saɪklɪŋ] *n* साइकिल चलाना
cyclist ['saɪklɪst] *n* साइकिल सवार
cyclone ['saɪkləʊn] *n* चक्रवात
cylinder ['sɪlɪndə] *n* बेलनाकार डिब्बा
cymbals ['sɪmblz] *npl* मजीरा

Cypriot ['sɪprɪət] *adj* साइप्रस से संबद्ध ▹ *n* साइप्रस का निवासी
Cyprus ['saɪprəs] *n* साइप्रस
cyst [sɪst] *n* पुटक
cystitis [sɪ'staɪtɪs] *n* मूत्राशय शोथ
Czech [tʃɛk] *adj* चेक गणराज्य से संबद्ध ▹ *n* *(person)* चेक गणराज्य का निवासी; *(language)* चेक गणराज्य की भाषा
Czech Republic [tʃɛk rɪ'pʌblɪk] *n* चेक गणराज्य

d

dad [dæd] *n* *(informal)* पिता
daddy ['dædɪ] *n* *(informal)* पिता
daffodil ['dæfədɪl] *n* डैफ़ोडिल
daft [dɑːft] *adj* बेवकूफ़ाना
daily ['deɪlɪ] *adj* दैनिक ▹ *adv* प्रतिदिन
dairy ['dɛərɪ] *n* दुग्धशाला
dairy produce ['dɛərɪ 'prɒdjuːs] *n* दुग्ध उत्पाद
dairy products ['dɛərɪ 'prɒdʌkts] *npl* दुग्ध उत्पाद
daisy ['deɪzɪ] *n* गुलबहार
dam [dæm] *n* बांध
damage ['dæmɪdʒ] *n* क्षति ▹ *vt* क्षति पहुँचाना
damp [dæmp] *adj* नम
dance [dɑːns] *n* नृत्य ▹ *vi* नाचना
dancer ['dɑːnsə] *n* नर्तक
dancing ['dɑːnsɪŋ] *n* नृत्य
dandelion ['dændɪˌlaɪən] *n* सिंहपर्णी
dandruff ['dændrəf] *n* रूसी
Dane [deɪn] *n* डेनमार्क वासी
danger ['deɪndʒə] *n* खतरा
dangerous ['deɪndʒərəs] *adj* खतरनाक
Danish ['deɪnɪʃ] *adj* डेनमार्क से संबद्ध ▹ *n* *(language)* डैनिश/डेनमार्क की भाषा
dare [dɛə] *vt* हिम्मत करना
daring ['dɛərɪŋ] *adj* हिम्मती
dark [dɑːk] *adj* *(not light)* अंधेरा ▹ *n* अंधकार ▹ *adj* *(not pale)* गहरा रंग

darkness ['dɑːknɪs] *n* अंधकार
darling ['dɑːlɪŋ] *n* प्रिय
dart [dɑːt] *n* छोटा नुकीला शंकु
darts [dɑːts] *npl* डार्ट - निशाना लगाने का खेल
dash [dæʃ] *vi* तेज़ी से घुसना
dashboard ['dæʃˌbɔːd] *n* डैशबोर्ड
data ['deɪtə] *npl* आंकड़ा
database ['deɪtəˌbeɪs] *n* डेटाबेस
date [deɪt] *n* दिनांक
daughter ['dɔːtə] *n* पुत्री
daughter-in-law ['dɔːtə ɪn lɔː] *n* पुत्रवधू
dawn [dɔːn] *n* भोर
day [deɪ] *n (period of 24 hours)* दिन; *(daytime)* दिन का समय
day return [deɪ rɪ'tɜːn] *n* वापसी टिकट
daytime ['deɪˌtaɪm] *n* दिन
dead [dɛd] *adj* मृत ▷ *adv* सर्वथा/बिल्कुल
dead end [dɛd ɛnd] *n* बंद गली
deadline ['dɛdˌlaɪn] *n* अंतिम तिथि
deaf [dɛf] *adj* बहरा
deafening ['dɛfnɪŋ] *adj* कानफोड़ू
deal [diːl] *n* समझौता/सौदा ▷ *v* पत्ते बांटना
dealer ['diːlə] *n* सौदागर
deal with [diːl wɪð] *v* निपटना
dear [dɪə] *adj (friend)* प्रिय; *(informal) (expensive)* महँगा
death [dɛθ] *n* मृत्यु
debate [dɪ'beɪt] *n* वादविवाद ▷ *vt* वादविवाद करना
debit ['dɛbɪt] *n* विकलन ▷ *vt* विकलित करना
debit card ['dɛbɪt kɑːd] *n* डेबिट कार्ड
debt [dɛt] *n* कर्ज़
decade ['dɛkeɪd] *n* दशक
decaffeinated coffee [diː'kæfɪneɪtɪd 'kɒfɪ] *n* कैफ़ीन रहित कॉफ़ी
decay [dɪ'keɪ] *vi* क्षय होना
deceive [dɪ'siːv] *vt* धोखा देना
December [dɪ'sɛmbə] *n* दिसंबर
decent ['diːsnt] *adj* समुचित
decide [dɪ'saɪd] *vt* निश्चय करना

decimal ['dɛsɪməl] *adj* दशमलव
decision [dɪ'sɪʒən] *n* निर्णय
decisive [dɪ'saɪsɪv] *adj* निर्णयात्मक
deck [dɛk] *n* डेक/जहाज या बस का निचला या ऊपरी हिस्सा
deckchair ['dɛk,tʃɛə] *n* डेकचेयर
declare [dɪ'klɛə] *vt* *(written)* घोषणा करना
decorate ['dɛkə,reɪt] *vt* सजाना
decorator ['dɛkə,reɪtə] *n* सज्जाकार
decrease ['diːkriːs] *n* कमी ▷ [dɪ'kriːs] *v* कम होना
dedicated ['dɛdɪ,keɪtɪd] *adj* समर्पित
dedication [,dɛdɪ'keɪʃən] *n* समर्पण
deduct [dɪ'dʌkt] *vt* घटाना
deep [diːp] *adj* गहरा
deep-fry ['diːpfraɪ] *vt* तेल में डुबा के तलना
deeply ['diːplɪ] *adv* गहराई से/बेहद
deer [dɪə] *n* हिरन
defeat [dɪ'fiːt] *n* हार ▷ *vt* हराना
defect ['diːfɛkt] *n* दोष
defence [dɪ'fɛns] *n* रक्षा
defend [dɪ'fɛnd] *vt* रक्षा करना
defendant [dɪ'fɛndənt] *n* प्रतिवादी
defender [dɪ'fɛndə] *n* समर्थक
deficit ['dɛfɪsɪt] *n* घाटा/कमी
define [dɪ'faɪn] *vt* परिभाषित करना
definite ['dɛfɪnɪt] *adj* निश्चित
definitely ['dɛfɪnɪtlɪ] *adv* निश्चित रूप से
definition [,dɛfɪ'nɪʃən] *n* परिभाषा
degree [dɪ'griː] *n* दरजा
degree Celsius [dɪ'griː 'sɛlsɪəs] *n* डिग्री सेल्सियस
degree centigrade [dɪ'griː 'sɛntɪ,greɪd] *n* डिग्री सेंटिग्रेड
degree Fahrenheit [dɪ'griː 'færən,haɪt] *n* डिग्री फ़ॉरेनहाइट
dehydrated [diːhaɪ'dreɪtɪd] *adj* निर्जलित

d

delay [dɪ'leɪ] *n* विलंब ▹ *vt* विलंब करना
delayed [dɪ'leɪd] *adj* विलंबित
delegate ['dɛlɪgət] *n* प्रतिनिधि ▹ ['dɛlɪˌgeɪt] *vt* सौंपना
delete [dɪ'liːt] *vt* मिटाना/हटाना
deliberate [dɪ'lɪbərɪt] *adj* सुविचारित
deliberately [dɪ'lɪbərətlɪ] *adv* जानबूझ कर
delicate ['dɛlɪkɪt] *adj* नाज़ुक
delicatessen [ˌdɛlɪkə'tɛsn] *n* दुर्लभ वस्तुओं की दुकान
delicious [dɪ'lɪʃəs] *adj* स्वादिष्ट
delight [dɪ'laɪt] *n* आनंद
delighted [dɪ'laɪtɪd] *adj* आनंदित
delightful [dɪ'laɪtfʊl] *adj* आनंददायक
deliver [dɪ'lɪvə] *vt* पहुँचाना
delivery [dɪ'lɪvərɪ] *n* सुपुर्दगी
demand [dɪ'mɑːnd] *n* माँग ▹ *vt* मांग करना
demanding [dɪ'mɑːndɪŋ] *adj* बहुत मेहनत की अपेक्षा वाला
demo ['dɛməʊ] *n (informal)* प्रदर्शन
democracy [dɪ'mɒkrəsɪ] *n* लोकतंत्र
democratic [ˌdɛmə'krætɪk] *adj* लोकतंत्रात्मक
demolish [dɪ'mɒlɪʃ] *vt* ढहाना
demonstrate ['dɛmənˌstreɪt] *vt* निरूपित करना/प्रदर्शित करना
demonstration [ˌdɛmən'streɪʃən] *n* प्रदर्शन
demonstrator ['dɛmənˌstreɪtə] *n* प्रदर्शनकारी
denim ['dɛnɪm] *n* डेनिम - मोटा सूती कपड़ा
denims ['dɛnɪmz] *npl* डेनिम से बना पैंट
Denmark ['dɛnmɑːk] *n* डेनमार्क
dense [dɛns] *adj* घना
density ['dɛnsɪtɪ] *n* घनत्व/सघनता
dent [dɛnt] *n* गाड़ियों या वस्तुओं का पिचका हुआ भाग ▹ *vt* पिचका देना

dental ['dɛntl] *adj* दंत संबंधी
dental floss ['dɛntl flɒs] *n* दाँत के बीच की जगह साफ करने का धागा
dentist ['dɛntɪst] *n* दंत चिकित्सक
dentures ['dɛntʃəz] *npl* नकली दाँत
deny [dɪ'naɪ] *vt* नकारना
deodorant [diː'əʊdərənt] *n* डीओडरन्ट
depart [dɪ'pɑːt] *vi* प्रस्थान करना
department [dɪ'pɑːtmənt] *n* विभाग
department store [dɪ'pɑːtmənt stɔː] *n* बड़ी दुकान
departure [dɪ'pɑːtʃə] *n* प्रस्थान
departure lounge [dɪ'pɑːtʃə laʊndʒ] *n* प्रस्थान प्रतीक्षालय
depend [dɪ'pɛnd] *vi* निर्भर होना
deport [dɪ'pɔːt] *vt* देश निकाला देना
deposit [dɪ'pɒzɪt] *n* जमा/गिरवी
depressed [dɪ'prɛst] *adj* उदास
depressing [dɪ'prɛsɪŋ] *adj* अवसादकारी
depression [dɪ'prɛʃən] *n* अवसाद
depth [dɛpθ] *n* गहराई
deputy head ['dɛpjʊtɪ hɛd] *n* उपाध्यक्ष
descend [dɪ'sɛnd] *v* *(formal)* उतरना
describe [dɪ'skraɪb] *vt* वर्णन करना
description [dɪ'skrɪpʃən] *n* विवरण
desert ['dɛzət] *n* रेगिस्तान
desert island ['dɛzət 'aɪlənd] *n* निर्जन द्वीप
deserve [dɪ'zɜːv] *vt* लायक होना
design [dɪ'zaɪn] *n* खाका ▷ *vt* खाका तैयार करना
designer [dɪ'zaɪnə] *n* अभिकल्पकार
desire [dɪ'zaɪə] *n* कामना ▷ *vt* कामना करना
desk [dɛsk] *n* मेज़
despair [dɪ'spɛə] *n* मायूसी

desperate ['dɛspərɪt] *adj* उतावला
desperately ['dɛspərɪtlɪ] *adv* उतावलेपन में
despise [dɪ'spaɪz] *vt* घृणा करना
despite [dɪ'spaɪt] *prep* होने पर भी
dessert [dɪ'zɜːt] *n* मिठाई
dessert spoon [dɪ'zɜːt spuːn] *n* मिठाई खाने का चम्मच
destination [ˌdɛstɪ'neɪʃən] *n* गंतव्य
destiny ['dɛstɪnɪ] *n* भाग्य
destroy [dɪ'strɔɪ] *vt* नष्ट करना
destruction [dɪ'strʌkʃən] *n* नाश
detached house [dɪ'tætʃt haʊs] *n* अलग मकान
detail ['diːteɪl] *n* ब्यौरा
detailed ['diːteɪld] *adj* ब्यौरेवार
detective [dɪ'tɛktɪv] *n* जासूस
detention [dɪ'tɛnʃən] *n* कारावास
detergent [dɪ'tɜːdʒənt] *n* प्रक्षालक
deteriorate [dɪ'tɪərɪəˌreɪt] *vi* बिगड़ना
determined [dɪ'tɜːmɪnd] *adj* दृढ़ संकल्प
detour ['diːtʊə] *n* लंबा मार्ग
devaluation [diːˌvæljuː'eɪʃən] *n* अवमूल्यन
devastated ['dɛvəˌsteɪtɪd] *adj* सदमाग्रस्त
devastating ['dɛvəˌsteɪtɪŋ] *adj* विध्वंसकारी/सदमा देने वाला
develop [dɪ'vɛləp] *vt* विकसित करना ▷ *vi* विकसित होना
developing country [dɪ'vɛləpɪŋ 'kʌntrɪ] *n* विकासशील देश
development [dɪ'vɛləpmənt] *n* विकास
device [dɪ'vaɪs] *n* उपकरण
Devil ['dɛvl] *n* शैतान
devise [dɪ'vaɪz] *vt* उपाय निकालना
devoted [dɪ'vəʊtɪd] *adj* समर्पित
diabetes [ˌdaɪə'biːtɪs] *n* मधुमेह

diabetic [ˌdaɪəˈbɛtɪk] *adj* मधुमेह संबंधी/मधुमेह पीड़ित ▷ *n* मधुमेह पीड़ित
diagnosis [ˌdaɪəgˈnəʊsɪs] *n* निदान
diagonal [daɪˈægənl] *adj* तिरछा
diagram [ˈdaɪəˌgræm] *n* चित्र
dial [ˈdaɪəl] *v* टेलीफ़ोन नंबर लगाना
dialect [ˈdaɪəˌlɛkt] *n* बोली
dialling code [ˈdaɪəlɪŋ kəʊd] *n* डायलिंग कोड
dialling tone [ˈdaɪəlɪŋ təʊn] *n* डायलिंग टोन
dialogue [ˈdaɪəˌlɒg] *n* संवाद
diameter [daɪˈæmɪtə] *n* व्यास
diamond [ˈdaɪəmənd] *n (jewel)* हीरा; *(shape)* विषमकोणीय समचतुर्भुज
diarrhoea [ˌdaɪəˈrɪə] *n* दस्त
diary [ˈdaɪərɪ] *n* दैनंदिनी
dice [daɪs] *npl* पासा
dictation [dɪkˈteɪʃən] *n* इमला
dictator [dɪkˈteɪtə] *n* तानाशाह
dictionary [ˈdɪkʃənərɪ] *n* शब्दकोश
die [daɪ] *vi* मरना
diet [ˈdaɪət] *n* आहार ▷ *vi* संतुलित आहार लेना
difference [ˈdɪfərəns] *n* अंतर
different [ˈdɪfərənt] *adj* अलग
difficult [ˈdɪfɪklt] *adj* कठिन
difficulty [ˈdɪfɪkltɪ] *n* कठिनाई
dig [dɪg] *v* खोदना
digest [dɪˈdʒɛst] *v* पचाना
digestion [dɪˈdʒɛstʃən] *n* पाचन
digger [ˈdɪgə] *n* खुदाई करने की मशीन
digital [ˈdɪdʒɪtl] *adj* डिजिटल
digital camera [ˈdɪdʒɪtl ˈkæmərə] *n* डिजिटल कैमरा
digital radio [ˈdɪdʒɪtl ˈreɪdɪəʊ] *n* डिजिटल रेडियो
digital television [ˈdɪdʒɪtl ˌtɛlɪˈvɪʒn] *n* डिजिटल टेलीविज़न
digital watch [ˈdɪdʒɪtl wɒtʃ] *n* डिजिटल वॉच

d

dignity ['dɪgnɪtɪ] *n* शालीनता
dilemma [dɪ'lɛmə] *n* दुविधा
dilute [daɪ'luːt] *v* पतला करना ▹ [daɪ'luːtɪd] *adj* पतला
dim [dɪm] *adj* मद्धम
dimension [dɪ'mɛnʃən] *n* आयाम
diminish [dɪ'mɪnɪʃ] *v* क्षीण होना
din [dɪn] *n* शोर
diner ['daɪnə] *n (US)* ढाबा
dinghy ['dɪŋɪ] *n* डोंगी
dining car ['daɪnɪŋ kɑː] *n* डाइनिंग कार
dining room ['daɪnɪŋ rʊm] *n* भोजन कक्ष
dinner ['dɪnə] *n* रात का भोजन
dinner jacket ['dɪnə 'dʒækɪt] *n* डिनर जैकेट
dinner party ['dɪnə 'pɑːtɪ] *n* रात के भोजन की दावत
dinner time ['dɪnə taɪm] *n* रात के भोजन का समय
dinosaur ['daɪnəˌsɔː] *n* डायनासोर
dip [dɪp] *n* एक प्रकार की चटनी ▹ *vt* डुबकी लगाना
diploma [dɪ'pləʊmə] *n* डिप्लोमा
diplomat ['dɪpləˌmæt] *n* राजदूत
diplomatic [ˌdɪplə'mætɪk] *adj* राजनयिक
dipstick ['dɪpˌstɪk] *n* द्रव की मात्रा मापने का पैमाना
direct [dɪ'rɛkt] *adj* सीधा ▹ *vt* लक्ष करना
direct debit [dɪ'rɛkt 'dɛbɪt] *n* प्रत्यक्ष विकलन
direction [dɪ'rɛkʃən] *n (way)* दिशा/ओर
directions [dɪ'rɛkʃənz] *npl (instructions)* निर्देश
directly [dɪ'rɛktlɪ] *adv* सीधे
director [dɪ'rɛktə] *n* निदेशक/निर्देशक
directory [dɪ'rɛktərɪ] *n* निदेशिका
directory enquiries [dɪ'rɛktərɪ ɪn'kwaɪərɪz] *npl* फ़ोन नंबर संबंधी पूछताछ सुविधा
dirt [dɜːt] *n* गंदगी
dirty ['dɜːtɪ] *adj* गंदा
disability [ˌdɪsə'bɪlɪtɪ] *n* विकलांगता

disabled [dɪ'seɪbld] *adj* विकलांग
disadvantage [ˌdɪsəd'vɑːntɪdʒ] *n* नुकसान
disagree [ˌdɪsə'griː] *vi* असहमत होना
disagreement [ˌdɪsə'griːmənt] *n* असहमति
disappear [ˌdɪsə'pɪə] *vi* गायब होना
disappearance [ˌdɪsə'pɪərəns] *n* लोप
disappoint [ˌdɪsə'pɔɪnt] *vt* निराश करना
disappointed [ˌdɪsə'pɔɪntɪd] *adj* निराश
disappointing [ˌdɪsə'pɔɪntɪŋ] *adj* निराशाजनक
disappointment [ˌdɪsə'pɔɪntmənt] *n* निराशा
disaster [dɪ'zɑːstə] *n* तबाही
disastrous [dɪ'zɑːstrəs] *adj* विनाशकारी
disc [dɪsk] *n* डिस्क
discipline ['dɪsɪplɪn] *n* अनुशासन
disc jockey [dɪsk 'dʒɒkɪ] *n* डिस्क जॉकी-संगीत बजाने वाला
disclose [dɪs'kləʊz] *vt* ज़ाहिर करना
disco ['dɪskəʊ] *n* डिस्को/नाचने का स्थान
disconnect [ˌdɪskə'nɛkt] *vt* प्लग निकालना/अलग करना
discount ['dɪskaʊnt] *n* छूट
discourage [dɪs'kʌrɪdʒ] *vt* हताश करना
discover [dɪ'skʌvə] *vt* पता लगाना
discretion [dɪ'skrɛʃən] *n* *(formal)* समझदारी
discrimination [dɪˌskrɪmɪ'neɪʃən] *n* भेदभाव
discuss [dɪ'skʌs] *vt* चर्चा करना
discussion [dɪ'skʌʃən] *n* चर्चा
disease [dɪ'ziːz] *n* बीमारी
disgraceful [dɪs'greɪsfʊl] *adj* शर्मनाक
disguise *vt* भेष बदलना
disgusted [dɪs'gʌstɪd] *adj* चिढ़ा हुआ
disgusting [dɪs'gʌstɪŋ] *adj* घृणित
dish [dɪʃ] *n* थाली

dishcloth [ˈdɪʃˌklɒθ] *n* बर्तन सुखाने का कपड़ा
dishonest [dɪsˈɒnɪst] *adj* बेईमान
dish towel [dɪʃ ˈtaʊəl] *n* बर्तन सुखाने का कपड़ा
dishwasher [ˈdɪʃˌwɒʃə] *n* बर्तन धोने की मशीन
disinfectant [ˌdɪsɪnˈfɛktənt] *n* कीटाणुनाशक
disk [dɪsk] *n* डिस्क
disk drive [dɪsk draɪv] *n* डिस्क ड्राइव
diskette [dɪsˈkɛt] *n* डिस्केट
dislike [dɪsˈlaɪk] *vt* नापसंद करना
dismal [ˈdɪzməl] *adj* दारुण
dismiss [dɪsˈmɪs] *vt* खारिज करना
disobedient [ˌdɪsəˈbiːdɪənt] *adj* अवज्ञाकारी
disobey [ˌdɪsəˈbeɪ] *v* अवज्ञा करना
dispenser [dɪˈspɛnsə] *n* डिस्पेंसर - एक मशीन
display [dɪˈspleɪ] *n* प्रदर्शन ▷ *vt* प्रदर्शित करना
disposable [dɪˈspəʊzəbl] *adj* उपयोग के बाद फेंकने योग्य
disqualify [dɪsˈkwɒlɪˌfaɪ] *vt* अयोग्य ठहराना
disrupt [dɪsˈrʌpt] *vt* तितर - बितर करना
dissatisfied [dɪsˈsætɪsˌfaɪd] *adj* असंतुष्ट
dissolve [dɪˈzɒlv] *v* घुलना
distance [ˈdɪstəns] *n* दूरी
distant [ˈdɪstənt] *adj* दूर
distillery [dɪˈstɪlərɪ] *n* शराब बनाने का स्थान
distinction [dɪˈstɪŋkʃən] *n* अंतर
distinctive [dɪˈstɪŋktɪv] *adj* विशिष्ट
distinguish [dɪˈstɪŋgwɪʃ] *v* फ़र्क बताना
distract *vt* ध्यान भंग करना
distribute [dɪˈstrɪbjuːt] *vt* वितरित करना
distributor [dɪˈstrɪbjʊtə] *n* वितरक
district [ˈdɪstrɪkt] *n* जिला
disturb [dɪˈstɜːb] *vt* परेशान करना
ditch [dɪtʃ] *n* नाली ▷ *vt* छोड़ देना
dive [daɪv] *n* गोता ▷ *vi* गोता लगाना

diver ['daɪvə] *n* गोताखोर
diversion [daɪ'vɜːʃən] *n* पथातंरण
divide [dɪ'vaɪd] *vt (object)* विभाजित करना; *(number)* भाग देना
diving ['daɪvɪŋ] *n* गोताखोरी
diving board ['daɪvɪŋ bɔːd] *n* गोता लगाने का पटरा
division [dɪ'vɪʒən] *n* विभाजन
divorce [dɪ'vɔːs] *n* तलाक
divorced [dɪ'vɔːst] *adj* तलाकशुदा
DIY [diː aɪ waɪ] *abbr* खुद करें' का संक्षिप्त रूप
dizzy ['dɪzɪ] *adj* चक्कर से ग्रस्त
DJ [diː dʒeɪ] *abbr* डी जे/संगीत बजाने वाला
DNA [diː ɛn eɪ] *n* डी एन ए
do [dʊ] *vt* करना
dock [dɒk] *n* बंदरगाह/गोदी
doctor ['dɒktə] *n* चिकित्सक
document ['dɒkjʊmənt] *n* दस्तावेज़
documentary [ˌdɒkjʊ'mɛntərɪ] *n* वृत्तचित्र
documentation [ˌdɒkjʊmɛn'teɪʃən] *n* दस्तावेज़ीकरण
documents ['dɒkjʊmənts] *npl* दस्तावेज़
dodge [dɒdʒ] *vi* कतराना/चकमा देकर हट जाना
dog [dɒg] *n* कुत्ता
dole [dəʊl] *n* खैरात
doll [dɒl] *n* गुड़िया
dollar ['dɒlə] *n* डॉलर
dolphin ['dɒlfɪn] *n* डॉल्फ़िन
domestic [də'mɛstɪk] *adj* घरेलू/देशीय
Dominican Republic [də'mɪnɪkən rɪ'pʌblɪk] *n* डोमिनिक गणराज्य
domino ['dɒmɪˌnəʊ] *n* पासे का एक खेल
dominoes ['dɒmɪˌnəʊz] *npl* पासे का एक खेल
donate [dəʊ'neɪt] *vt* दान देना
done [dʌn] *adj* किया हुआ
donkey ['dɒŋkɪ] *n* खच्चर
donor ['dəʊnə] *n* दाता
door [dɔː] *n* दरवाज़ा
doorbell ['dɔːˌbɛl] *n* दरवाज़े की घंटी

door handle [dɔː 'hændl] *n* दरवाज़े की घुंडी
doorman ['dɔːˌmæn] *n* दरबान
doorstep ['dɔːˌstɛp] *n* दहलीज़
dormitory ['dɔːmɪtərɪ] *n* बड़ा शयनकक्ष
dose [dəʊs] *n* खुराक
dot [dɒt] *n* बिंदु
double ['dʌbl] *adj* दोगुना ▹ *v* दोगुना होना
double bass ['dʌbl beɪs] *n* डबल बास-एक वाद्य
double glazing ['dʌbl 'gleɪzɪŋ] *n* दोहरा कांच लगाने की पद्धति
doubt [daʊt] *n* संदेह ▹ *vt* संदेह करना
doubtful ['daʊtfʊl] *adj* संदेहजनक
dough [dəʊ] *n* गूंथा हुआ आटा
doughnut ['dəʊnʌt] *n* डोनट
do up [dʊ ʌp] *v* बांधना
dove [dʌv] *n* फ़ाख्ता
do without [dʊ wɪ'ðaʊt] *v* के बिना काम चलाना
down [daʊn] *adv* नीचे की ओर
download ['daʊnˌləʊd] *vt* डाउनलोड करना
downpour ['daʊnˌpɔː] *n* मूसलाधार बारिश
Down's syndrome [daʊnz 'sɪndrəʊm] *n* डाउंज सिंड्रोम - एक विकार
downstairs ['daʊn'stɛəz] *adj* नीचे ▹ *adv* निचली मंज़िल पर
doze [dəʊz] *vi* ऊँघना
dozen ['dʌzn] *num* दर्जन
doze off [dəʊz ɒf] *v* आँख लगना
drab [dræb] *adj* नीरस
draft [drɑːft] *n* प्रारूप
drag [dræg] *vt* घसीटना
dragon ['drægən] *n* ड्रैगन - एक काल्पनिक प्राणी
dragonfly ['drægənˌflaɪ] *n* व्याध पतंग
drain [dreɪn] *n* नाली ▹ *v* बहाना
draining board ['dreɪnɪŋ bɔːd] *n* धोकर बर्तन सुखाने का स्थान

drainpipe ['dreɪn,paɪp] *n* परनाला
drama ['drɑːmə] *n* नाटक
dramatic [drə'mætɪk] *adj* नाटकीय
drastic ['dræstɪk] *adj* प्रबल
draught [drɑːft] *n* हवा का झोंका
draughts [drɑːfts] *npl* ड्राट्स - बोर्ड पर खेला जाने वाला खेल
draw [drɔː] *v (picture)* अंकित करना ▷ *vi (in game)* बराबरी पर खत्म होना ▷ *v (move)* खींचना
drawback ['drɔː,bæk] *n* कमी
drawer ['drɔːə] *n* दराज
drawing ['drɔːɪŋ] *n* रेखाचित्र
drawing pin ['drɔːɪŋ pɪn] *n* ड्राइंग पिन
dreadful ['drɛdfʊl] *adj* बेकार
dream [driːm] *n* सपना ▷ *v* सपना देखना
drench [drɛntʃ] *vt* भिगोना
dress [drɛs] *n* पोशाक ▷ *vi* कपड़े पहनना
dressed [drɛst] *adj* कपड़े पहना हुआ
dresser ['drɛsə] *n* शीशा लगी दराज वाली मेज़
dressing gown ['drɛsɪŋ gaʊn] *n* ड्रेसिंग गाउन
dressing table ['drɛsɪŋ 'teɪbl] *n* प्रसाधन मेज़
dress up [drɛs ʌp] *v* अच्छे कपड़े पहनना
dried [draɪd] *adj* शुष्क
drift [drɪft] *n* बहाव ▷ *vi* बहना
drill [drɪl] *n* छेद करने की मशीन ▷ *v* छेद करना
drink [drɪŋk] *n* पेयपदार्थ ▷ *v* पीना
drink-driving ['drɪŋk'draɪvɪŋ] *n* शराब पीकर गाड़ी चलाने का अपराध
drinking water ['drɪŋkɪŋ 'wɔːtə] *n* पेयजल
drip [drɪp] *n* बूंद ▷ *vi* टपकना
drive [draɪv] *n* गाड़ी में सैर ▷ *v* गाड़ी चलाना
driver ['draɪvə] *n* चालक
driveway ['draɪv,weɪ] *n* वाहनमार्ग
driving instructor ['draɪvɪŋ ɪn'strʌktə] *n* गाड़ी चलाना सिखाने वाला

d

driving lesson ['draɪvɪŋ 'lɛsn] *n* गाड़ी चलाने का प्रशिक्षण
driving licence ['draɪvɪŋ 'laɪsəns] *n* गाड़ी चलाने का लाइसेंस
driving test ['draɪvɪŋ tɛst] *n* गाड़ी चलाने का योग्यता परीक्षण
drizzle ['drɪzl] *n* हल्की बारिश
drop [drɒp] *n* गिरावट ▷ *v* गिरना
drought [draʊt] *n* अनावृष्टि/सूखा
drown [draʊn] *v* डूबना
drowsy ['draʊzɪ] *adj* ऊँघता हुआ
drug [drʌg] *n* दवा
drum [drʌm] *n* ढोल
drummer ['drʌmə] *n* ढोलकिया
drunk [drʌŋk] *adj* मत्त ▷ *n* पियक्कड़
dry [draɪ] *adj* सूखा ▷ *v* सूखना/सुखाना
dry cleaner [draɪ 'kliːnə] *n* बिना जल के धुलाई करने वाला
dry-cleaning ['draɪ'kliːnɪŋ] *n* निर्जल धुलाई
dryer ['draɪə] *n* सुखाने की मशीन
dual carriageway ['djuːəl 'kærɪdʒˌweɪ] *n* दोहरा वाहन मार्ग
dubbed [dʌbt] *adj* डब किया हुआ
dubious ['djuːbɪəs] *adj* संदेहास्पद
duck [dʌk] *n* बत्तख
due [djuː] *adj* बकाया
due to [djuː tʊ] *prep* की वजह से
dull [dʌl] *adj (boring)* नीरस; *(colour)* फीका
dumb [dʌm] *adj* गूंगा
dummy ['dʌmɪ] *n* पुतला
dump [dʌmp] *n* कूड़ा फेंकने की जगह/घूरा ▷ *vt (informal)* फेंकना
dumpling ['dʌmplɪŋ] *n* डंपलिंग - आटे से बना पकवान
dungarees [ˌdʌŋgə'riːz] *npl* डंगरीज़ - एक प्रकार की पतलून
dungeon ['dʌndʒən] *n* तहखाना

duration [djʊ'reɪʃən] *n* अवधि

during ['djʊərɪŋ] *prep* दौरान

dusk [dʌsk] *n* गोधूलि वेला

dust [dʌst] *n* धूल ▷ *v* धूल झाड़ना

dustbin ['dʌstˌbɪn] *n* कूड़ेदान

dustman ['dʌstmən] *n* सफ़ाईकर्मी

dustpan ['dʌstˌpæn] *n* कूड़े का तसला

dusty ['dʌstɪ] *adj* धूलधूसरित

Dutch [dʌtʃ] *adj* नीदरलैंड से संबंधित ▷ *n* नीदरलैंड की भाषा

Dutchman ['dʌtʃmən] *n* नीदरलैंड का निवासी पुरुष

Dutchwoman ['dʌtʃwʊmən] *n* नीदरलैंड की निवासी महिला

duty ['djuːtɪ] *n* कर्तव्य

duty-free ['djuːtɪˌfriː] *adj* कर रहित ▷ *n* कर रहित

duvet ['duːveɪ] *n* पंख भरी रजाई

DVD [diː viː diː] *n* डी वी डी

DVD burner [diːviːdiː 'bɜːnə] *n* डी वी डी बर्नर

DVD player [diːviːdiː 'pleɪə] *n* डी वी डी प्लेयर

dwarf [dwɔːf] *n* बौना

dye [daɪ] *n* रंग ▷ *vt* रंगना

dynamic [daɪ'næmɪk] *adj* सक्रिय

dyslexia [dɪs'lɛksɪə] *n* पढ़ने - लिखने संबंधी मानसिक विकार

dyslexic [dɪs'lɛksɪk] *adj* पढ़ने - लिखने संबंधी विकार से ग्रस्त

e

each [iːtʃ] *det* प्रत्येक ▷ *pron* प्रत्येक

eagle ['iːgl] *n* चील

ear [ɪə] *n* कान

earache ['ɪərˌeɪk] *n* कान का दर्द

eardrum ['ɪəˌdrʌm] *n* कान का पर्दा

earlier ['ɜːlɪə] *adv* पहले

early ['ɜːlɪ] *adj (ahead of time)* जल्दी/समय से पूर्व ▷ *adv* जल्दी ▷ *adj (near the beginning)* जल्दी
earn [ɜːn] *vt* कमाना
earnings ['ɜːnɪŋz] *npl* कमाई
earphones ['ɪəˌfəʊnz] *npl* इयरफ़ोन/आकर्णक
earplugs ['ɪəˌplʌgz] *npl* इयरप्लग
earring ['ɪəˌrɪŋ] *n* कान की बाली
earth [ɜːθ] *n (planet)* पृथ्वी; *(soil)* मिट्टी/भूमि
earthquake ['ɜːθˌkweɪk] *n* भूकंप
easily ['iːzɪlɪ] *adv* आसानी से
east [iːst] *adj* पूर्वी ▷ *adv* पूर्व की ओर ▷ *n* पूर्व
eastbound ['iːstˌbaʊnd] *adj (formal)* पूर्वाभिमुख
Easter ['iːstə] *n* ईस्टर
Easter egg ['iːstə ɛg] *n* ईस्टर का अंडा
eastern ['iːstən] *adj* पूर्वी
easy ['iːzɪ] *adj* आसान
easy chair ['iːzɪ tʃɛə] *n* आरामकुर्सी
easy-going ['iːzɪ'gəʊɪŋ] *adj* शांत स्वभाव का/अल्हड़
eat [iːt] *v* खाना
e-book ['iːˌbʊk] *n* ई - पुस्तक
eccentric [ɪk'sɛntrɪk] *adj* विलक्षण/विचित्र
echo ['ɛkəʊ] *n* प्रतिध्वनि/गूंज
ecofriendly ['iːkəʊˌfrɛndlɪ] *adj* पर्यावरण अनुकूल
ecological [ˌiːkə'lɒdʒɪkl] *adj* पारिस्थितिक
ecology [ɪ'kɒlədʒɪ] *n* पारिस्थितिकी
e-commerce [ˌiː'kɒmɜːs] *n* ई-वाणिज्य
economic [ˌiːkə'nɒmɪk] *adj* आर्थिक
economical [ˌiːkə'nɒmɪkl] *adj* किफ़ायती
economics [ˌiːkə'nɒmɪks] *npl* अर्थशास्त्र
economist [ɪ'kɒnəmɪst] *n* अर्थशास्त्री
economize [ɪ'kɒnəˌmaɪz] *vi* किफ़ायत करना
economy [ɪ'kɒnəmɪ] *n* अर्थव्यवस्था
economy class [ɪ'kɒnəmɪ klɑːs] *n* इकॉनॉमी क्लास/सस्ती श्रेणी
ecstasy ['ɛkstəsɪ] *n* परमानंद

Ecuador ['ɛkwəˌdɔː] *n* इक्वाडोर
eczema ['ɛksɪmə] *n* छाजन - एक रोग
edge [ɛdʒ] *n* किनारा
edgy ['ɛdʒɪ] *adj (informal)* विकल
edible ['ɛdɪbl] *adj* खाद्य
edition [ɪ'dɪʃən] *n* संस्करण
editor ['ɛdɪtə] *n* संपादक
educated ['ɛdjʊˌkeɪtɪd] *adj* शिक्षित
education [ˌɛdjʊ'keɪʃən] *n* शिक्षा
educational [ˌɛdjʊ'keɪʃənl] *adj* शैक्षिक
eel [iːl] *n* बाम मछली
effect [ɪ'fɛkt] *n* प्रभाव
effective [ɪ'fɛktɪv] *adj* प्रभावी
effectively [ɪ'fɛktɪvlɪ] *adv* प्रभावी रूप से
efficient [ɪ'fɪʃənt] *adj* सक्षम
efficiently [ɪ'fɪʃəntlɪ] *adv* दक्षता से
effort ['ɛfət] *n* प्रयास
e.g. [iː dʒiː] *abbr* उदाहरण स्वरूप का संक्षिप्त रूप
egg [ɛg] *n* अंडा
eggcup ['ɛgˌkʌp] *n* अंडा रखने का प्याला
egg white [ɛg waɪt] *n* अंडे की सफेदी
egg yolk [ɛg jəʊk] *n* अंडे की जर्दी
Egypt ['iːdʒɪpt] *n* मिस्र
Egyptian [ɪ'dʒɪpʃən] *adj* मिस्र से संबद्ध ▷ *n* मिस्र वासी
eight [eɪt] *num* आठ
eighteen ['eɪ'tiːn] *num* अठारह
eighteenth ['eɪ'tiːnθ] *adj* अठारहवां
eighth [eɪtθ] *adj* आठवां ▷ *n* आठवां
eighty ['eɪtɪ] *num* अस्सी
Eire ['ɛərə] *n* आयरलैंड
either ['aɪðə; 'iːðə] *adv* न ही ▷ *det (each)* प्रत्येक ▷ *pron* उनमें से ▷ *det (one of two things)* दोनों में से एक
either ... or ['aɪðə; 'iːðə ɔː] *conj* या यह... या वह
elastic [ɪ'læstɪk] *n* इलास्टिक
elastic band [ɪ'læstɪk bænd] *n* रबर बैंड
Elastoplast® [ɪ'læstəˌplɑːst] *n* इलास्टोप्लास्ट
elbow ['ɛlbəʊ] *n* कुहनी
elder ['ɛldə] *adj* ज्येष्ठ
elderly ['ɛldəlɪ] *adj* बुजुर्ग

e

eldest ['ɛldɪst] *adj* सबसे बड़ा
elect [ɪ'lɛkt] *vt* निर्वाचन करना
election [ɪ'lɛkʃən] *n* चुनाव
electorate [ɪ'lɛktərɪt] *n* निर्वाचक मंडल
electric [ɪ'lɛktrɪk] *adj* वैद्युत
electrical [ɪ'lɛktrɪkl] *adj* वैद्युत
electric blanket [ɪ'lɛktrɪk 'blæŋkɪt] *n* वैद्युत कंबल
electrician [ɪlɛk'trɪʃən] *n* बिजली का काम करने वाला
electricity [ɪlɛk'trɪsɪtɪ] *n* बिजली
electric shock [ɪ'lɛktrɪk ʃɒk] *n* बिजली का झटका
electronic [ɪlɛk'trɒnɪk] *adj* इलेक्ट्रॉनिक
electronics [ɪlɛk'trɒnɪks] *npl* इलेक्ट्रॉनिक्स
elegant ['ɛlɪgənt] *adj* सुंदर/मनोहर
element ['ɛlɪmənt] *n* तत्व
elephant ['ɛlɪfənt] *n* हाथी
eleven [ɪ'lɛvn] *num* ग्यारह
eleventh [ɪ'lɛvnθ] *adj* ग्यारहवां
eliminate [ɪ'lɪmɪˌneɪt] *vt* *(formal)* निकालना
elm [ɛlm] *n* एक बड़ा पेड़
else [ɛls] *adv* दूसरा
elsewhere [ˌɛls'wɛə] *adv* अन्यत्र
email ['iːmeɪl] *n* ई-मेल ▷ *v* ई-मेल करना
email address ['iːmeɪl ə'drɛs] *n* ई-मेल पता
embankment [ɪm'bæŋkmənt] *n* तटबंध
embarrassed [ˌɪm'bærəst] *adj* शर्मिंदा
embarrassing [ɪm'bærəsɪŋ] *adj* शर्मनाक
embassy ['ɛmbəsɪ] *n* राजदूत
embroider [ɪm'brɔɪdə] *vt* कढ़ाई करना
embroidery [ɪm'brɔɪdərɪ] *n* कढ़ाई
emergency [ɪ'mɜːdʒənsɪ] *n* आपातकाल
emergency exit [ɪ'mɜːdʒensɪ 'ɛksɪt] *n* आपातकालीन निकास
emergency landing [ɪ'mɜːdʒensɪ 'lændɪŋ] *n* अपातकालीन अवतरण

emigrate ['ɛmɪˌgreɪt] *vi* प्रवासगमन करना
emotion [ɪ'məʊʃən] *n* भावना
emotional [ɪ'məʊʃənl] *adj* भावात्मक
emperor ['ɛmpərə] *n* सम्राट
emphasize ['ɛmfəˌsaɪz] *vt* ज़ोर देना
empire ['ɛmpaɪə] *n* साम्राज्य
employ [ɪm'plɔɪ] *vt* नियुक्त करना
employee [ɛm'plɔɪiː] *n* कर्मचारी
employer [ɪm'plɔɪə] *n* नियोक्ता
employment [ɪm'plɔɪmənt] *n* रोजगार
empty ['ɛmptɪ] *adj* खाली ▷ *vt* खाली करना
enamel [ɪ'næməl] *n* तामचीनी
encourage [ɪn'kʌrɪdʒ] *vt* प्रोत्साहित करना
encouragement [ɪn'kʌrɪdʒmənt] *n* प्रोत्साहन
encouraging [ɪn'kʌrɪdʒɪŋ] *adj* प्रोत्साहक
encyclopaedia [ɛnˌsaɪkləʊ'piːdɪə] *n* विश्वकोश
end [ɛnd] *n* अंत ▷ *v* समाप्त होना
endanger [ɪn'deɪndʒə] *vt* खतरे में डालना
ending ['ɛndɪŋ] *n* समाप्ति
endless ['ɛndlɪs] *adj* अनंत
enemy ['ɛnəmɪ] *n* शत्रु
energetic [ˌɛnə'dʒɛtɪk] *adj* ऊर्जावान
energy ['ɛnədʒɪ] *n* *(strength)* ऊर्जा; *(power)* ऊर्जा
engaged [ɪn'geɪdʒd] *adj* *(formal)* व्यस्त/संलग्न
engaged tone [ɪn'geɪdʒd təʊn] *n* व्यस्त ध्वनि
engagement [ɪn'geɪdʒmənt] *n* कार्य
engagement ring [ɪn'geɪdʒmənt rɪŋ] *n* सगाई की अंगूठी
engine ['ɛndʒɪn] *n* *(machine)* इंजन; *(train)* इंजन
engineer [ˌɛndʒɪ'nɪə] *n* अभियंता
engineering [ˌɛndʒɪ'nɪərɪŋ] *n* अभियांत्रिकी

e

England ['ɪŋglənd] *n* इंग्लैंड

English ['ɪŋglɪʃ] *adj* अंग्रेज़ी ▷ *n* अंग्रेज़ी

Englishman ['ɪŋglɪʃmən] *n* अंग्रेज़ पुरुष

Englishwoman ['ɪŋglɪʃˌwʊmən] *n* अंग्रेज़ महिला

engrave [ɪn'greɪv] *vt* उत्कीर्ण करना

enjoy [ɪn'dʒɔɪ] *vt* आनंद उठाना

enjoyable [ɪn'dʒɔɪəbl] *adj* आनंददायक

enlargement [ɪn'lɑːdʒmənt] *n* विस्तार

enormous [ɪ'nɔːməs] *adj* विशाल

enough [ɪ'nʌf] *det* पर्याप्त ▷ *pron* पर्याप्त

enquire [ɪn'kwaɪə] *v* *(formal)* पूछना

enquiry [ɪn'kwaɪərɪ] *n* पूछताछ

ensure [ɛn'ʃʊə] *vt* *(formal)* सुनिश्चित करना

enter ['ɛntə] *v* *(formal)* प्रवेश करना

entertain [ˌɛntə'teɪn] *v* मनोरंजन करना

entertainer [ˌɛntə'teɪnə] *n* मनोरंजनकर्ता

entertaining [ˌɛntə'teɪnɪŋ] *adj* मनोरंजक

enthusiasm [ɪn'θjuːzɪˌæzəm] *n* उत्साह

enthusiastic [ɪnˌθjuːzɪ'æstɪk] *adj* उत्साही

entire [ɪn'taɪə] *adj* पूरा

entirely [ɪn'taɪəlɪ] *adv* संपूर्णतया

entrance ['ɛntrəns] *n* प्रवेश

entrance fee ['ɛntrəns fiː] *n* प्रवेश शुल्क

entry ['ɛntrɪ] *n* प्रविष्टि

entry phone ['ɛntrɪ fəʊn] *n* प्रवेश द्वार के पास लगा फ़ोन

envelope ['ɛnvəˌləʊp] *n* लिफ़ाफ़ा

envious ['ɛnvɪəs] *adj* ईर्ष्यालु

environment [ɪn'vaɪrənmənt] *n* वातावरण

environmental [ɪnˌvaɪrən'mɛntəl] *adj* पर्यावरण संबंधी

environmentally friendly [ɪnˌvaɪərən'mɛntəlɪ 'frɛndlɪ] *adj* पर्यावरण अनुकूल
envy ['ɛnvɪ] *n* ईर्ष्या ▷ *vt* ईर्ष्या करना
epidemic [ˌɛpɪ'dɛmɪk] *n* महामारी
episode ['ɛpɪˌsəʊd] *n* प्रकरण
equal ['iːkwəl] *adj* बराबर ▷ *vt* बराबर होना
equality [ɪ'kwɒlɪtɪ] *n* समानता
equalize ['iːkwəˌlaɪz] *vt* बराबर करना
equation [ɪ'kweɪʒən] *n* समीकरण
equator [ɪ'kweɪtə] *n* भूमध्य रेखा
Equatorial Guinea [ˌɛkwə'tɔːrɪəl 'gɪnɪ] *n* इक्वेटोरियल गिनी
equipment [ɪ'kwɪpmənt] *n* उपकरण
equipped [ɪ'kwɪpt] *adj* सुसज्जित
equivalent [ɪ'kwɪvələnt] *n* समतुल्य
erase [ɪ'reɪz] *vt* मिटाना
Eritrea [ˌɛrɪ'treɪə] *n* इरिट्रिया
error ['ɛrə] *n* त्रुटि
escalator ['ɛskəˌleɪtə] *n* स्वचालित सीढ़ी
escape [ɪ'skeɪp] *n* पलायन ▷ *vi* बच निकलना
escort [ɪs'kɔːt] *vt* साथ जाना
especially [ɪ'spɛʃəlɪ] *adv* खास तौर पर
espionage ['ɛspɪəˌnɑːʒ; ˌɛspɪə'nɑːʒ] *n* *(formal)* गुप्तचरी/जासूसी
essay ['ɛseɪ] *n* निबंध
essential [ɪ'sɛnʃəl] *adj* ज़रूरी
estate [ɪ'steɪt] *n* भू-संपत्ति/जागीर
estate agent [ɪ'steɪt 'eɪdʒənt] *n* भू-संपत्ति का दलाल
estate car [ɪ'steɪt kɑː] *n* लंबी कार
estimate ['ɛstɪˌmeɪt] *n* आकलन ▷ ['ɛstɪmət] *vt* आकलन करना
Estonia [ɛ'stəʊnɪə] *n* एस्टोनिया

e

Estonian [ɛ'stəʊnɪən] *adj* एस्टोनियाई ▷ *n (person)* एस्टोनियाई; *(language)* एस्टोनियाई

etc [ɪt'sɛtrə] *abbr* आदि का संक्षिप्त रूप

eternal [ɪ'tɜːnl] *adj* शाश्वत

eternity [ɪ'tɜːnɪtɪ] *n* अनंत काल/अमरत्व

ethical ['ɛθɪkl] *adj* नैतिक

Ethiopia [ˌiːθɪ'əʊpɪə] *n* इथियोपिया

Ethiopian [ˌiːθɪ'əʊpɪən] *adj* इथियोपियाई ▷ *n* इथियोपियाई

ethnic ['ɛθnɪk] *adj* प्रजातीय या संस्कृति संबंधी

EU [iː juː] *abbr* ई.यू./ यूरोपीय संघ का संक्षिप्त रूप

euro ['jʊərəʊ] *n* यूरो

Europe ['jʊərəp] *n* यूरोप

European [ˌjʊərə'pɪən] *adj* यूरोपीय ▷ *n* यूरोपीय

European Union [ˌjʊərə'piːən 'juːnjən] *n* यूरोपीय संघ

evacuate [ɪ'vækjʊˌeɪt] *v* खाली करना

eve [iːv] *n* पूर्वसंध्या

even ['iːvn] *adj (flat and smooth)* समतल ▷ *adv* यहां तक कि ▷ *adj (number)* सम संख्या

evening ['iːvnɪŋ] *n* शाम

evening class ['iːvnɪŋ klɑːs] *n* सायंकालीन कक्षा

evening dress ['iːvnɪŋ drɛs] *n* शाम के समय पहनी जाने वाली पोशाक

event [ɪ'vɛnt] *n* घटना

eventful [ɪ'vɛntfʊl] *adj* घटनापूर्ण

eventually [ɪ'vɛntʃʊəlɪ] *adv* आखिरकार

ever ['ɛvə] *adv* कदापि

every ['ɛvrɪ] *adj* प्रत्येक

everybody ['ɛvrɪˌbɒdɪ] *pron* प्रत्येक व्यक्ति

everyone ['ɛvrɪˌwʌn] *pron* हर कोई

everything ['ɛvrɪθɪŋ] *pron* सबकुछ

everywhere ['ɛvrɪˌwɛə] *adv* सर्वत्र

evidence ['ɛvɪdəns] *n* सबूत

evil ['iːvl] *adj* दुष्ट

evolution [ˌiːvə'luːʃən] *n* विकास

ewe [juː] *n* मादा भेड़
exact [ɪɡ'zækt] *adj* एकदम सही
exactly [ɪɡ'zæktlɪ] *adv* यथार्थतः
exaggerate [ɪɡ'zædʒə,reɪt] *v* बढ़ा-चढ़ा कर कहना
exaggeration [ɪɡ'zædʒə,reɪʃən] *n* अतिशयोक्ति
exam [ɪɡ'zæm] *n* परीक्षा
examination [ɪɡ,zæmɪ'neɪʃən] *n* *(formal)* परीक्षा
examine [ɪɡ'zæmɪn] *vt* जाँचना
examiner [ɪɡ'zæmɪnə] *n* परीक्षक
example [ɪɡ'zɑːmpl] *n* उदाहरण
excellent ['ɛksələnt] *adj* उत्तम
except [ɪk'sɛpt] *prep* को छोड़कर
exception [ɪk'sɛpʃən] *n* अपवाद
exceptional [ɪk'sɛpʃənl] *adj* असाधारण
excess baggage ['ɛksɛs 'bæɡɪdʒ] *n* अतिरिक्त सामान
excessive [ɪk'sɛsɪv] *adj* अत्यधिक
exchange [ɪks'tʃeɪndʒ] *vt* आदान - प्रदान करना
exchange rate [ɪks'tʃeɪndʒ reɪt] *n* विनिमय दर
excited [ɪk'saɪtɪd] *adj* उत्तेजित
exciting [ɪk'saɪtɪŋ] *adj* रोमांचक
exclamation mark [,ɛksklə'meɪʃən mɑːk] *n* विस्मयादिबोधक चिह्न
exclude [ɪk'skluːd] *vt* निकालना
excluding [ɪk'skluːdɪŋ] *prep* के सिवा
exclusively [ɪk'skluːsɪvlɪ] *adv* केवल
excuse [ɪk'skjuːs] *n* बहाना/सफाई ▷ [ɪk'skjuːz] *vt* बहाना बनाना/सफाई देना
execute ['ɛksɪ,kjuːt] *vt* प्राणदंड देना
execution [,ɛksɪ'kjuːʃən] *n* प्राणदंड
executive [ɪɡ'zɛkjʊtɪv] *n* कार्यकारी

e

exercise ['ɛksəˌsaɪz] *n* *(formal, physical)* कसरत; *(school work)* अभ्यास

exhaust [ɪg'zɔːst] *n* धुआँ निकालने का पाइप

exhausted [ɪg'zɔːstɪd] *adj* थका - मांदा

exhaust fumes [ɪg'zɔːst fjuːmz] *npl* धुआँ

exhibition [ˌɛksɪ'bɪʃən] *n* प्रदर्शनी

ex-husband [ɛks'hʌzbənd] *n* पूर्व - पति

exile ['ɛgzaɪl] *n* निर्वासन

exist [ɪg'zɪst] *vi* अस्तित्व होना

exit ['ɛgzɪt] *n* प्रस्थान

exotic [ɪg'zɒtɪk] *adj* अनोखा

expect [ɪk'spɛkt] *vt* आशा करना

expedition [ˌɛkspɪ'dɪʃən] *n* अभियान

expel [ɪk'spɛl] *vt* निष्कासित करना

expenditure [ɪk'spɛndɪtʃə] *n* *(formal)* खर्च

expenses [ɪk'spɛnsɪz] *npl* खर्च

expensive [ɪk'spɛnsɪv] *adj* महंगा

experience [ɪk'spɪərɪəns] *n* अनुभव

experienced [ɪk'spɪərɪənst] *adj* अनुभवी

experiment [ɪk'spɛrɪmənt] *n* प्रयोग

expert ['ɛkspɜːt] *n* विशेषज्ञ

expire [ɪk'spaɪə] *vi* समाप्त होना

expiry date [ɪk'spaɪərɪ deɪt] *n* समाप्ति तिथि

explain [ɪk'spleɪn] *vt* व्याख्या करना

explanation [ˌɛksplə'neɪʃən] *n* स्पष्टीकरण/व्याख्या

explode [ɪk'spləʊd] *vi* विस्फोटित होना

exploit [ɪk'splɔɪt] *vt* शोषण करना

exploitation [ˌɛksplɔɪ'teɪʃən] *n* शोषण

explore [ɪk'splɔː] *v* पता लगाना

explorer [ɪk'splɔːrə] *n* खोजी

explosion [ɪk'spləʊʒən] *n* विस्फोट

explosive [ɪk'spləʊsɪv] *n* विस्फोटक पदार्थ

export ['ɛkspɔːt] *n* निर्यात ▷ [ɪk'spɔːt] *v* निर्यात करना

express [ɪk'sprɛs] *vt* अभिव्यक्त करना
expression [ɪk'sprɛʃən] *n* अभिव्यक्ति
extension [ɪk'stɛnʃən] *n* विस्तार
extension cable [ɪk'stɛnʃən 'keɪbl] *n* एक्सटेंशन केबल
extensive [ɪk'stɛnsɪv] *adj* विस्तृत
extensively [ɪk'stɛnsɪvlɪ] *adv* व्यापक रूप से
extent [ɪk'stɛnt] *n* हद
exterior [ɪk'stɪərɪə] *adj* बाहरी
external [ɪk'stɜːnl] *adj* बाहरी
extinct [ɪk'stɪŋkt] *adj* विलुप्त
extinguisher [ɪk'stɪŋgwɪʃə] *n* अग्निशामक
extortionate [ɪk'stɔːʃənɪt] *adj* अतिशय
extra ['ɛkstrə] *adj* अतिरिक्त ▷ *adv* अतिरिक्त रूप से
extraordinary [ɪk'strɔːdnrɪ] *adj* असाधारण
extravagant [ɪk'strævɪgənt] *adj* खर्चीला
extreme [ɪk'striːm] *adj* चरम/अत्यंत
extremely [ɪk'striːmlɪ] *adv* अत्यधिक
extremism [ɪk'striːmɪzəm] *n* चरमपंथ
extremist [ɪk'striːmɪst] *n* चरमपंथी
ex-wife [ɛks'waɪf] *n* पूर्व पत्नी
eye [aɪ] *n* आँख
eyebrow ['aɪˌbraʊ] *n* भौंह
eye drops [aɪ drɒps] *npl* आँख में डालने की दवा
eyelash ['aɪˌlæʃ] *n* बरौनी
eyelid ['aɪˌlɪd] *n* पलक
eyeliner ['aɪˌlaɪnə] *n* पलकों पर लगाने का काजल
eye shadow [aɪ 'ʃædəʊ] *n* पलकों पर लगाने का रंग
eyesight ['aɪˌsaɪt] *n* दृष्टि

f

fabric ['fæbrɪk] *n* कपड़ा
fabulous ['fæbjʊləs] *adj* *(informal)* शानदार
face [feɪs] *n* चेहरा ▷ *vt* अभिमुख होना/सामने होना

face cloth [feɪs klɒθ] *n* चेहरा पोंछने का कपड़ा
facial ['feɪʃəl] *adj* चेहरे का ▷ *n* चेहरे की मालिश
facilities [fə'sɪlɪtɪz] *npl* सुविधाएँ
fact [fækt] *n* तथ्य
factory ['fæktərɪ] *n* कारखाना
fade [feɪd] *v* धुँधला पड़ जाना
fail [feɪl] *v* असफल होना
failure ['feɪljə] *n* असफलता
faint [feɪnt] *adj* हल्का/धीमा ▷ *vi* बेहोश होना
fair [fɛə] *adj (just)* उचित; *(blond)* हल्का पीला/गोरा ▷ *n* मेला
fairground ['fɛə,graʊnd] *n* मेले का मैदान
fairly ['fɛəlɪ] *adv* काफ़ी हद तक
fairness ['fɛənɪs] *n* निष्पक्षता
fairy ['fɛərɪ] *n* परी
fairy tale ['fɛərɪ teɪl] *n* परीकथा
faith [feɪθ] *n* निष्ठा
faithful ['feɪθfʊl] *adj* निष्ठावान
faithfully ['feɪθfʊlɪ] *adv* निष्ठापूर्वक
fake [feɪk] *adj* जाली/नकली ▷ *n* नकली वस्तु/जाली वस्तु
fall [fɔːl] *n* गिरावट ▷ *vi* गिरना
fall down [fɔːl daʊn] *v* नीचे गिरना
fall for [fɔːl fɔː] *v* प्रेम में पड़ना
fall out [fɔːl aʊt] *v* झड़ना
false [fɔːls] *adj* गलत
false alarm [fɔːls ə'lɑːm] *n* झूठी चेतावनी
fame [feɪm] *n* यश
familiar [fə'mɪlɪə] *adj* परिचित
family ['fæmɪlɪ] *n* परिवार
famine ['fæmɪn] *n* अकाल
famous ['feɪməs] *adj* प्रसिद्ध
fan [fæn] *n* प्रशंसक
fanatic [fə'nætɪk] *n* कट्टरपंथी
fan belt [fæn bɛlt] *n* फ़ैन बेल्ट
fancy ['fænsɪ] *vt (informal)* पसंद करना ▷ *adj* अलबेला/बढ़िया
fancy dress ['fænsɪ drɛs] *n* किसी का रूप धारण करने के लिए पहनी जाने वाली पोशाक

fantastic [fæn'tæstɪk] *adj (informal)* शानदार
FAQ [ɛf eɪ kjuː] *abbr* आम सवाल हेतु संक्षिप्त रूप
far [fɑː] *adj* दूर ▹ *adv* दूर
fare [fɛə] *n* किराया
Far East [fɑː iːst] *n* सुदूर पूर्व
farewell! [fɛə'wel] *excl* विदाई!
farm [fɑːm] *n* खेत
farmer ['fɑːmə] *n* किसान
farmhouse ['fɑːm,haʊs] *n* फ़ार्म हाउस
farming ['fɑːmɪŋ] *n* खेती
Faroe Islands ['fɛərəʊ 'aɪləndz] *npl* फ़रो आइलैंड्स
fascinating ['fæsɪ,neɪtɪŋ] *adj* मोहक/दिलचस्प
fashion ['fæʃən] *n* वेश-भूषा
fashionable ['fæʃənəbl] *adj* प्रचलित
fast [fɑːst] *adj* तेज ▹ *adv* शीघ्र
fat [fæt] *adj* मोटा ▹ *n* वसा
fatal ['feɪtl] *adj* घातक
fate [feɪt] *n* किस्मत
father ['fɑːðə] *n* पिता
father-in-law ['fɑːðə ɪn lɔː] *n* श्वसुर
fault [fɔːlt] *n* गलती
faulty ['fɔːltɪ] *adj* त्रुटिपूर्ण
fauna ['fɔːnə] *npl* पशुवर्ग
favour ['feɪvə] *n* पक्ष
favourite ['feɪvərɪt] *adj* मनभावन ▹ *n* पसंदीदा
fax [fæks] *n* फ़ैक्स ▹ *vt* फ़ैक्स
fear [fɪə] *n* भय ▹ *vt* डरना
feasible ['fiːzəbl] *adj* संभव
feather ['fɛðə] *n* पंख
feature ['fiːtʃə] *n* विशेषता
February ['fɛbrʊərɪ] *n* फरवरी
fed up [fɛd ʌp] *adj (informal)* ऊबा हुआ
fee [fiː] *n* शुल्क
feed [fiːd] *vt* खिलाना
feedback ['fiːd,bæk] *n* प्रतिपुष्टि
feel [fiːl] *v (have a particular feeling)* महसूस करना ▹ *vt (touch)* छूकर देखना
feeling ['fiːlɪŋ] *n* भावना
feet [fiːt] *npl* पैर
felt [fɛlt] *n* नमदा
felt-tip ['fɛlt,tɪp] *n* स्केच पेन
female ['fiːmeɪl] *adj* जनाना ▹ *n* महिला

feminine ['fɛmɪnɪn] *adj* स्त्रियोचित
feminist ['fɛmɪnɪst] *n* नारीवादी
fence [fɛns] *n* बाड़ा
fennel ['fɛnl] *n* सौंफ़
fern [fɜːn] *n* फ़र्न
ferret ['fɛrɪt] *n* नेवले की जाति का एक पशु
ferry ['fɛrɪ] *n* नौका
fertile ['fɜːtaɪl] *adj* उपजाऊ
fertilizer ['fɜːtɪˌlaɪzə] *n* उर्वरक
festival ['fɛstɪvl] *n* त्यौहार
fetch [fɛtʃ] *vt* ले आना
fever ['fiːvə] *n* बुखार
few [fjuː] *det* कुछ ▹ *pron* कुछ
fewer [fjuːə] *adj* से कम
fiancé [fɪ'ɒnseɪ] *n* मंगेतर (पुरुष)
fiancée [fɪ'ɒnseɪ] *n* मंगेतर (महिला)
fibre ['faɪbə] *n* रेशा
fibreglass ['faɪbəˌglɑːs] *n* फ़ाइबरग्लास
fiction ['fɪkʃən] *n* कल्पित कथा
field [fiːld] *n* खेत
fierce [fɪəs] *adj* आगबबूला/क्रुद्ध
fifteen ['fɪf'tiːn] *num* पंद्रह
fifteenth ['fɪf'tiːnθ] *adj* पंद्रहवाँ
fifth [fɪfθ] *adj* पाँचवाँ
fifty ['fɪftɪ] *num* पचास
fifty-fifty ['fɪftɪˌfɪftɪ] *adj (informal)* आधा-आधा ▹ *adv (informal)* बराबर रूप से
fig [fɪg] *n* अंजीर
fight [faɪt] *n* संघर्ष ▹ *v* संघर्ष करना
fighting [faɪtɪŋ] *n* लड़ाई
figure ['fɪgə] *n* आँकड़ा
figure out ['fɪgə aʊt] *v (informal)* समझना/हल करना
Fiji ['fiːdʒiː] *n* फ़िजी
file [faɪl] *n (for documents)* फ़ाइल; *(tool)* रंदा/रेती ▹ *vt (document)* फ़ाइल में नत्थी करना; *(object)* चिकना करना
Filipino [ˌfɪlɪ'piːnəʊ] *adj* फ़िलीपिनी ▹ *n* फ़िलीपिनी
fill [fɪl] *v* भरना
fillet ['fɪlɪt] *n* हड्डी रहित मांस ▹ *vt* हड्डी निकालना
fill in [fɪl ɪn] *v* भरना
fill up [fɪl ʌp] *v* पूरा भरना

film [fɪlm] *n* चलचित्र
film star [fɪlm stɑː] *n* चलचित्र के कलाकार
filter ['fɪltə] *n* छन्ना ▷ *vt* छानना
filthy ['fɪlθɪ] *adj* गंदा
final ['faɪnl] *adj* अंतिम ▷ *n* अंतिम दौर का खेल
finalize ['faɪnə,laɪz] *vt* अंतिम रूप देना
finally ['faɪnəlɪ] *adv* अंततः
finance [fɪ'næns] *n* पूँजी ▷ *vt* पूँजी देना
financial [fɪ'nænʃəl] *adj* वित्तीय
financial year [fɪ'nænʃəl jɪə] *n* वित्तीय वर्ष
find [faɪnd] *vt* पाना
find out [faɪnd aʊt] *v* पता लगाना
fine [faɪn] *adj* *(sunny)* सुहावना; *(well or happy)* अच्छा ▷ *n* जुर्माना ▷ *adj* *(thin)* महीन/बारीक
finger ['fɪŋgə] *n* अँगुली
fingernail ['fɪŋgə,neɪl] *n* नाखून
fingerprint ['fɪŋgə,prɪnt] *n* अँगुली का निशान
finish ['fɪnɪʃ] *n* समाप्ति ▷ *vt* समाप्त करना
finished ['fɪnɪʃt] *adj* समाप्त
Finland ['fɪnlənd] *n* फ़िनलैंड
Finn [fɪn] *n* फ़िनलैंड का निवासी
Finnish ['fɪnɪʃ] *adj* फ़िनलैंड से संबद्ध ▷ *n* फ़िनलैंड की भाषा
fire [faɪə] *n* आग
fire alarm [faɪə ə'lɑːm] *n* आग की चेतावनी की घंटी
fire brigade ['faɪə brɪ'geɪd] *n* दमकल
fire escape ['faɪə ɪ'skeɪp] *n* आग लगने पर भागने का रास्ता
fire extinguisher ['faɪə ɪk'stɪŋgwɪʃə] *n* अग्निशामक यंत्र
fireman ['faɪəmən] *n* दमकल का कर्मचारी
fireplace ['faɪə,pleɪs] *n* कमरे में स्थित भट्टी
firewall ['faɪə,wɔːl] *n* फ़ायरवाल
fireworks ['faɪə,wɜːks] *npl* पटाखे

firm [fɜːm] *adj* दृढ़ ▹ *n* व्यापारिक निकाय
first [fɜːst] *adj* पहला ▹ *adv* सबसे पहले ▹ *n* पहला
first aid [fɜːst eɪd] *n* प्राथमिक चिकित्सा
first-aid kit [ˌfɜːst'eɪd kɪt] *n* प्राथमिक चिकित्सा किट
first-class ['fɜːst'klɑːs] *adj* प्रथम श्रेणी/उत्कृष्ट
firstly ['fɜːstlɪ] *adv* सबसे पहला
first name [fɜːst neɪm] *n* प्रथम नाम
fir tree [fɜː triː] *n* फ़र का पेड़/देवदार
fiscal ['fɪskl] *adj* राजकोषीय/वित्तीय
fiscal year ['fɪskl jɪə] *n* वित्तीय वर्ष
fish [fɪʃ] *n* मछली ▹ *vi* मछली मारना
fisherman ['fɪʃəmən] *n* मछुआरा
fishing ['fɪʃɪŋ] *n* मछली पकड़ना
fishing boat ['fɪʃɪŋ bəʊt] *n* मछली पकड़ने की नाव
fishing rod ['fɪʃɪŋ rɒd] *n* बंसी
fishing tackle ['fɪʃɪŋ 'tækl] *n* मछली पकड़ने का सामान
fishmonger ['fɪʃˌmʌŋgə] *n* मछली बेचने वाला
fist [fɪst] *n* मुट्ठी
fit [fɪt] *adj* योग्य ▹ *n* नाप का ▹ *v* माप का/उपयुक्त
fit in [fɪt ɪn] *v* समय निकालना
fitted carpet ['fɪtɪd 'kɑːpɪt] *n* पूरे कमरे को घेरने वाला कालीन
fitted kitchen ['fɪtɪd 'kɪtʃɪn] *n* दीवार में अलमारियों वाला रसोईघर
fitted sheet ['fɪtɪd ʃiːt] *n* फ़िटेड शीट
fitting room ['fɪtɪŋ rʊm] *n* कपड़े पहनकर देखने का कमरा
five [faɪv] *num* पाँच
fix [fɪks] *vt (attach)* लगाना; *(mend)* ठीक करना
fixed [fɪkst] *adj* नियत
fizzy ['fɪzɪ] *adj* फेनिल
flabby ['flæbɪ] *adj* थुलथुल
flag [flæg] *n* झंडा
flame [fleɪm] *n* ज्वाला

flamingo [flə'mɪŋgəʊ] *n* मराल
flammable ['flæməbl] *adj* ज्वलनशील
flan [flæn] *n* एक प्रकार का केक
flannel ['flænl] *n* फ़लालेन
flap [flæp] *v* फड़फड़ाना
flash [flæʃ] *n* चमक ▹ *v* चमकना
flask [flɑːsk] *n* थर्मस
flat [flæt] *adj* चिपटा/सपाट ▹ *n* फ़्लैट
flat-screen ['flæt,skriːn] *adj* सपाट स्क्रीन
flatter ['flætə] *vt* चापलूसी करना
flattered ['flætəd] *adj* खुश
flavour ['fleɪvə] *n* स्वाद
flavouring ['fleɪvərɪŋ] *n* स्वादवर्द्धक पदार्थ
flaw [flɔː] *n* दोष
flea [fliː] *n* पिस्सू
flea market [fliː 'mɑːkɪt] *n* कबाड़ी बाज़ार
flee [fliː] *v (written)* फ़रार होना
fleece [fliːs] *n* ऊनी कपड़ा
fleet [fliːt] *n* बेड़ा
flex [flɛks] *n* बिजली का तार
flexible ['flɛksɪbl] *adj* लचीला
flexitime ['flɛksɪ,taɪm] *n* काम करने का समय बदलने की सुविधा
flight [flaɪt] *n* उड़ान
flight attendant [flaɪt ə'tɛndənt] *n* विमान परिचारक
fling [flɪŋ] *vt* फेंकना
flip-flops ['flɪp,flɒpz] *npl* एक प्रकार का जूता
flippers ['flɪpəz] *npl* तरणक पाद
flirt [flɜːt] *n* इश्कबाज़ ▹ *vi* इश्कबाज़ी करना
float [fləʊt] *n* डोंगी ▹ *vi (on water)* जल पर तैरना; *(in the air)* वायु में तैरना
flock [flɒk] *n* झुंड
flood [flʌd] *n* बाढ़ ▹ *vt* बाढ़ आना ▹ *vi* बाढ़ग्रस्त होना
flooding ['flʌdɪŋ] *n* बाढ़
floodlight ['flʌd,laɪt] *n* तेज़ रोशनी वाली बत्ती
floor [flɔː] *n (room)* फ़र्श; *(storey)* मंज़िल/माला
flop [flɒp] *n* नाकाम

floppy disk ['flɒpɪ dɪsk] *n* फ़्लॉपी डिस्क
flora ['flɔːrə] *npl (formal)* वनस्पति
florist ['flɒrɪst] *n* पुष्पविक्रेता
flour ['flaʊə] *n* आटा
flow [fləʊ] *vi* बहना
flower ['flaʊə] *n* फूल ▹ *vi* पुष्पित होना
flu [fluː] *n* फ़्लू
fluent ['fluːənt] *adj* धाराप्रवाह
fluorescent [ˌflʊə'rɛsnt] *adj* प्रतिदीप्त
flush [flʌʃ] *n* लाली ▹ *vi* लाल हो जाना
flute [fluːt] *n* बाँसुरी
fly [flaɪ] *n* मक्खी ▹ *vi* उड़ना
fly away [flaɪ ə'weɪ] *v* उड़ जाना
foal [fəʊl] *n* घोड़े का बच्चा
focus ['fəʊkəs] *n* मुद्दा ▹ *v* ध्यान केंद्रित करना
foetus ['fiːtəs] *n* भ्रूण
fog [fɒg] *n* कुहरा
foggy ['fɒgɪ] *adj* धुंधला
fog light [fɒg laɪt] *n* गाड़ी के आगे या पीछे लगी तेज़ रोशनी
foil [fɔɪl] *n* पन्नी
fold [fəʊld] *n* तह ▹ *vt* तह करना
folder ['fəʊldə] *n* फ़ोल्डर
folding ['fəʊldɪŋ] *adj* मोड़ने योग्य
folklore ['fəʊkˌlɔː] *n* लोक साहित्य
folk music [fəʊk 'mjuːzɪk] *n* लोक संगीत
follow ['fɒləʊ] *v* अनुसरण करना
following ['fɒləʊɪŋ] *adj* अगला
food [fuːd] *n* भोजन
food poisoning [fuːd 'pɔɪzənɪŋ] *n* खराब भोजन खाने से हुई बीमारी
food processor [fuːd 'prəʊsɛsə] *n* फ़ूड प्रोसेसर
fool [fuːl] *n* मूर्ख ▹ *vt* मूर्ख बनाना
foot [fʊt] *n* पैर
football ['fʊtˌbɔːl] *n (game)* फ़ुटबॉल का खेल; *(ball)* फ़ुटबॉल
footballer ['fʊtˌbɔːlə] *n* फ़ुटबॉल खिलाड़ी
football match ['fʊtˌbɔːl mætʃ] *n* फ़ुटबॉल प्रतियोगिता

football player ['fʊtˌbɔːl 'pleɪə] *n* फुटबॉल खिलाड़ी
footpath ['fʊtˌpɑːθ] *n* पैदल रास्ता
footprint ['fʊtˌprɪnt] *n* पदचिह्न
footstep ['fʊtˌstɛp] *n* कदम
for [fɔː] *prep (intended for)* के लिए; *(denoting purpose)* के लिए; *(to help someone)* के लिए
forbid [fə'bɪd] *vt* मना करना
forbidden [fə'bɪdn] *adj* वर्जित
force [fɔːs] *n* बल ▷ *vt* दबाव डालना
forecast ['fɔːˌkɑːst] *n* भविष्यवाणी
foreground ['fɔːˌgraʊnd] *n* अग्रभाग
forehead ['fɒrɪd] *n* माथा
foreign ['fɒrɪn] *adj* विदेशी
foreigner ['fɒrɪnə] *n* विदेशी
foresee [fɔː'siː] *vt* अंदाज़ लगाना
forest ['fɒrɪst] *n* जंगल
forever [fɔː'rɛvə] *adv* हमेशा
forge [fɔːdʒ] *vt* जाली नकल बनाना
forgery ['fɔːdʒərɪ] *n* जालसाज़ी
forget [fə'gɛt] *vt* भूलना
forgive [fə'gɪv] *vt* माफ़ करना
forgotten [fə'gɒtn] *adj* विस्मृत
fork [fɔːk] *n* काँटा
form [fɔːm] *n* प्रकार
formal ['fɔːməl] *adj* औपचारिक
formality [fɔː'mælɪtɪ] *n* औपचारिकता
format ['fɔːmæt] *n* प्रारूप ▷ *vt* फ़ॉर्मैट करना
former ['fɔːmə] *adj* भूतपूर्व
formerly ['fɔːməlɪ] *adv* पहले
formula ['fɔːmjʊlə] *n* नुस्खा
fort [fɔːt] *n* किला
fortnight ['fɔːtˌnaɪt] *n* पखवाड़ा
fortunate ['fɔːtʃənɪt] *adj* भाग्यशाली
fortunately ['fɔːtʃənɪtlɪ] *adv* सौभाग्यवश
fortune ['fɔːtʃən] *n* संपत्ति
forty ['fɔːtɪ] *num* चालीस
forward ['fɔːwəd] *adv* आगे ▷ *vt* अग्रसारित करना

forward slash ['fɔːwəd slæʃ] *n* आगे की ओर झुका तिर्यक निशान
foster ['fɒstə] *vt* पालन - पोषण करना
foster child ['fɒstə tʃaɪld] *n* दत्तक संतान
foul [faʊl] *adj* गंदा ▷ *n* नियमोल्लंघन
foundations [faʊn'deɪʃənz] *npl* नींव
fountain ['faʊntɪn] *n* फ़व्वारा
fountain pen ['faʊntɪn pɛn] *n* स्याही वाली कलम
four [fɔː] *num* चार
fourteen ['fɔː'tiːn] *num* चौदह
fourteenth ['fɔː'tiːnθ] *adj* चौदहवाँ
fourth [fɔːθ] *adj* चौथा
four-wheel drive ['fɔːˌwiːl draɪv] *n* चारपहिया ड्राइव
fox [fɒks] *n* लोमड़ी
fracture ['fræktʃə] *n* दरार/भंग
fragile ['frædʒaɪl] *adj* नाज़ुक
frail [freɪl] *adj* कमज़ोर
frame [freɪm] *n* चौखटा
France [frɑːns] *n* फ़्रांस
frankly ['fræŋklɪ] *adv* स्पष्ट रूप से
frantic ['fræntɪk] *adj* व्यग्र
fraud [frɔːd] *n* धोखा
freckles ['frɛklz] *npl* चित्ती
free [friː] *adj (at liberty)* आज़ाद; *(at no cost)* मुफ़्त ▷ *vt* आज़ाद करना
freedom ['friːdəm] *n* आज़ादी
free kick [friː kɪk] *n* फ़्री किक
freelance ['friːˌlɑːns] *adj* स्वच्छंद ▷ *adv* स्वच्छंद रूप से
freeze [friːz] *vi (water)* जमना ▷ *vt (food)* जमाना
freezer ['friːzə] *n* फ़्रीज़र
freezing ['friːzɪŋ] *adj* हिमशीतल
freight [freɪt] *n* माल भाड़ा
French [frɛntʃ] *adj* फ़्रांसीसी ▷ *n* फ़्रांसीसी
French beans [frɛntʃ biːnz] *npl* फ़्रेंच बीन
French horn [frɛntʃ hɔːn] *n* फ़्रेंच हॉर्न - एक वाद्य
Frenchman ['frɛntʃmən] *n* फ़्रांसीसी पुरुष
Frenchwoman ['frɛntʃwʊmən] *n* फ़्रांसीसी महिला

frequency ['friːkwənsɪ] *n* आवृत्ति

frequent ['friːkwənt] *adj* अक्सर

fresh [frɛʃ] *adj (replacing something)* ताज़ा; *(food)* ताज़ा; *(water)* मीठा/ताज़ा; *(air)* ताज़ा

freshen up ['frɛʃən ʌp] *v* तरोताज़ा करना

freshwater fish ['frɛʃˌwɔːtə fɪʃ] *n* मीठे पानी की मछली

fret [frɛt] *vi* चिंता करना

Friday ['fraɪdɪ] *n* शुक्रवार

fridge [frɪdʒ] *n* फ़्रिज

fried [fraɪd] *adj* तला हुआ

friend [frɛnd] *n* मित्र

friendly ['frɛndlɪ] *adj* दोस्ताना

friendship ['frɛndʃɪp] *n* मित्रता

fright [fraɪt] *n* भय

frighten ['fraɪtn] *vt* डराना

frightened ['fraɪtənd] *adj* भयभीत

frightening ['fraɪtnɪŋ] *adj* डरावना

fringe [frɪndʒ] *n* लट

frog [frɒg] *n* मेढक

from [frɒm] *prep (given or sent by)* की ओर से/से; *(out of)* में से; *(denoting ingredients)* से

front [frʌnt] *adj* सामने का ▷ *n* अग्र भाग

frontier ['frʌntɪə] *n* सीमा

frost [frɒst] *n* पाला/तुषार

frosty ['frɒstɪ] *adj* ठंडा

frown [fraʊn] *vi* त्योरी चढ़ाना

frozen ['frəʊzn] *adj* जमा हुआ

fruit [fruːt] *n* फल

fruit juice [fruːt dʒuːs] *n* फल का रस

fruit salad [fruːt 'sæləd] *n* फलों का सलाद

frustrated [frʌ'streɪtɪd] *adj* हताश

fry [fraɪ] *vt* तलना

frying pan ['fraɪɪŋ pæn] *n* कड़ाही

fuel [fjʊəl] *n* ईंधन

fulfil [fʊl'fɪl] *vt* पूरा करना

full [fʊl] *adj* भरा

full moon [fʊl muːn] *n* पूर्णिमा

full stop [fʊl stɒp] *n* पूर्णविराम

full-time ['fʊl,taɪm] *adj* पूर्णकालिक ▹ *adv* पूर्णकालिक रूप से
fully ['fʊlɪ] *adv* पूर्णतया
fumes [fjuːmz] *npl* भभक
fun [fʌn] *adj* मज़ेदार ▹ *n* मज़ा
funds [fʌndz] *npl* निधि
funeral ['fjuːnərəl] *n* अंत्येष्टि
funeral parlour ['fjuːnərəl 'pɑːlə] *n* अंत्येष्टि गृह
funfair ['fʌn,fɛə] *n* मेला
funnel ['fʌnl] *n* कीप
funny ['fʌnɪ] *adj* *(amusing)* मज़ाकिया/हास्यमय; *(strange)* अजीब
fur [fɜː] *n* रोआँ
fur coat [fɜː kəʊt] *n* रोएँ से बना कोट
furious ['fjʊərɪəs] *adj* आगबबूला
furnished ['fɜːnɪʃt] *adj* सुसज्जित
furniture ['fɜːnɪtʃə] *n* फ़र्नीचर
further ['fɜːðə] *adj* आगे का ▹ *adv* अधिक
further education ['fɜːðə ,ɛdʒʊ'keɪʃən] *n* आगे की शिक्षा
fuse [fjuːz] *n* फ़्यूज़
fuse box [fjuːz bɒks] *n* फ़्यूज़ बॉक्स
fuss [fʌs] *n* झमेला
fussy ['fʌsɪ] *adj* मीन - मेख निकालने वाला
future ['fjuːtʃə] *adj* आगामी ▹ *n* भविष्य

g

Gabon [gə'bɒn] *n* गैबॉन
gain [geɪn] *n* बढ़त/वृद्धि ▹ *vt* अर्जित करना
gale [geɪl] *n* आँधी
gall bladder [gɔːl 'blædə] *n* पित्ताशय
gallery ['gælərɪ] *n* वीथिका
gallop ['gæləp] *n* सरपट चाल ▹ *vi* सरपट दौड़ना
gallstone ['gɔːl,stəʊn] *n* पित्ताश्म

Gambia ['gæmbɪə] *n* गैम्बिया
gamble ['gæmbl] *v* जुआ खेलना/दाँव लगाना
gambler ['gæmblə] *n* जुआरी
gambling ['gæmblɪŋ] *n* जुआ
game [geɪm] *n (with rules)* खेल; *(imaginative)* खेल
games console [geɪmz 'kɒnsəʊl] *n* गेम्स कंसोल
gang [gæŋ] *n* गिरोह
gangster ['gæŋstə] *n* लुटेरा/बदमाश
gap [gæp] *n* अंतराल/अंतर
garage ['gærɑːʒ] *n (shelter for car)* गैराज - गाड़ी रखने की जगह; *(for repairs)* गैराज - गाड़ी की मरम्मत करने की जगह
garden ['gɑːdn] *n* बगीचा
garden centre ['gɑːdn 'sɛntə] *n* पौध बिक्री केंद्र
gardener ['gɑːdnə] *n* माली
gardening ['gɑːdnɪŋ] *n* बागबानी
garlic ['gɑːlɪk] *n* लहसुन
garment ['gɑːmənt] *n* कपड़ा
gas [gæs] *n* गैस
gas cooker [gæs 'kʊkə] *n* गैस कुकर
gasket ['gæskɪt] *n* गैस्केट
gate [geɪt] *n* फाटक
gateau ['gætəʊ] *n* बहुत सजा हुआ केक
gather ['gæðə] *v* इकट्ठा करना
gauge [geɪdʒ] *n* पैमाना ▷ *vt* मापना/आँकना
gaze [geɪz] *vi* घूरना
gear [gɪə] *n (in car or on bicycle)* गियर; *(clothes and equipment)* उपकरण
gearbox ['gɪəbɒks] *n* गियर बॉक्स
gear lever [gɪə 'liːvə] *n* गियर लीवर
gel [dʒɛl] *n* जेल - एक गाढ़ा, चिकना पदार्थ
gem [dʒɛm] *n* रत्न
Gemini ['dʒɛmɪˌnaɪ] *n* मिथुन राशि
gender ['dʒɛndə] *n* लिंग
gene [dʒiːn] *n* जीन
general ['dʒɛnərəl] *adj* सामान्य ▷ *n* सेनाध्यक्ष
general anaesthetic ['dʒɛnərəl ˌænɪs'θɛtɪk] *n* सामान्य चेतनाहारी औषधि

g

general election ['dʒɛnərəl ɪ'lɛkʃən] *n* आम चुनाव

generalize ['dʒɛnrə,laɪz] *v* सामान्यीकरण करना

general knowledge ['dʒɛnərəl 'nɒlɪdʒ] *n* सामान्य ज्ञान

generally ['dʒɛnrəlɪ] *adv* आम तौर पर

generation [,dʒɛnə'reɪʃən] *n* पीढ़ी

generator ['dʒɛnə,reɪtə] *n* जेनरेटर

generosity [,dʒɛnə'rɒsɪtɪ] *n* उदारता

generous ['dʒɛnərəs] *adj* उदार

genetic [dʒɪ'nɛtɪk] *adj* आनुवंशिक

genetically-modified [dʒɪ'nɛtɪklɪ'mɒdɪ,faɪd] *adj* आनुवंशिक रूप से संशोधित

genetics [dʒɪ'nɛtɪks] *n* आनुवंशिकी

genius ['dʒiːnɪəs] *n* माहिर/निपुण

gentle ['dʒɛntl] *adj* सौम्य

gentleman ['dʒɛntlmən] *n* भद्र पुरुष

gently ['dʒɛntlɪ] *adv* नरमी से

gents [dʒɛnts] *n* पुरुष शौचालय

genuine ['dʒɛnjʊɪn] *adj* खरा/असली

geography [dʒɪ'ɒgrəfɪ] *n* भूगोल

geology [dʒɪ'ɒlədʒɪ] *n* भूगर्भ शास्त्र

Georgia ['dʒɔːdʒjə] *n (US state)* जॉर्जिया; *(country)* जॉर्जिया

Georgian ['dʒɔːdʒjən] *adj (from Georgia)* जॉर्जियाई ▷ *n (person)* जॉर्जियाई

geranium [dʒɪ'reɪnɪəm] *n* अधिरक्तापीत

gerbil ['dʒɜːbɪl] *n* चूहे जैसा जानवर

geriatric [,dʒɛrɪ'ætrɪk] *adj* वृद्ध संबंधी

germ [dʒɜːm] *n* रोगाणु

German ['dʒɜːmən] *adj* जर्मनी से संबद्ध ▷ *n (person)* जर्मनी का नागरिक; *(language)* जर्मनी की भाषा

German measles ['dʒɜːmən 'miːzəlz] *n* जर्मन खसरा
Germany ['dʒɜːmənɪ] *n* जर्मनी
gesture ['dʒɛstʃə] *n* इशारा
get [gɛt] *v (become)* होना ▷ *vi (arrive)* पहुंचना ▷ *vt (be given)* पाना; *(fetch)* लाना
get away [gɛt ə'weɪ] *v* बचना
get back [gɛt bæk] *v* वापस पाना
get in [gɛt ɪn] *v* पहुँचना
get into [gɛt 'ɪntə] *v* शामिल होना
get off [gɛt ɒf] *v* बच निकलना
get on [gɛt ɒn] *v* अच्छी निभना
get out [gɛt aʊt] *v* जाना
get over [gɛt 'əʊvə] *v* उभरना
get together [gɛt tə'gɛðə] *v* इकट्ठा होना
get up [gɛt ʌp] *v* उठना
Ghana ['gɑːnə] *n* घाना
Ghanaian [gɑː'neɪən] *adj* घाना से संबद्ध ▷ *n* घाना का निवासी
ghost [gəʊst] *n* भूत/प्रेतात्मा
giant ['dʒaɪənt] *adj* बहुत बड़ा ▷ *n* विशालकाय संगठन
gift [gɪft] *n* उपहार
gifted ['gɪftɪd] *adj* प्रतिभाशाली
gift voucher [gɪft 'vaʊtʃə] *n* उपहार की रसीद
gigantic [dʒaɪ'gæntɪk] *adj* विशालकाय
giggle ['gɪgl] *vi* खिलखिलाना
gin [dʒɪn] *n* एक प्रकार की शराब
ginger ['dʒɪndʒə] *adj* नारंगीपन लिए भूरा रंग ▷ *n* अदरक
giraffe [dʒɪ'rɑːf] *n* जिराफ़
girl [gɜːl] *n* लड़की
girlfriend ['gɜːlˌfrɛnd] *n* प्रेमिका
give [gɪv] *vt* देना
give back [gɪv bæk] *v* वापस देना
give in [gɪv ɪn] *v* हार मान लेना
give out [gɪv aʊt] *v* बाँटना
give up [gɪv ʌp] *v* छोड़ना

glacier ['glæsɪə] *n* हिमनदी
glad [glæd] *adj* खुश
glamorous ['glæmərəs] *adj* आकर्षक
glance [glɑːns] *n* सरसरी नज़र ▹ *vi* नज़र डालना
gland [glænd] *n* ग्रंथि
glare [glɛə] *vi* आँखें तरेरना
glaring ['glɛərɪŋ] *adj* स्पष्ट
glass [glɑːs] *n (material)* कांच; *(tumbler)* गिलास
glasses ['glɑːsɪz] *npl* चश्मा
glider ['glaɪdə] *n* ग्लाइडर - हवा से उड़ना वाला बिना इंजन का वायुयान
gliding ['glaɪdɪŋ] *n* ग्लाइडिंग - एक प्रकार का खेल
global ['gləʊbl] *adj* विश्वव्यापी
globalization [ˌgləʊblaɪ'zeɪʃən] *n* वैश्वीकरण
global warming ['gləʊbl 'wɔːmɪŋ] *n* भूमण्डलीय ताप का बढ़ना
globe [gləʊb] *n* दुनिया
gloomy ['gluːmɪ] *adj* धुँधला
glorious ['glɔːrɪəs] *adj* शानदार
glory ['glɔːrɪ] *n* गौरव
glove [glʌv] *n* दस्ताना
glove compartment [glʌv kəm'pɑːtmənt] *n* गाड़ी के सामने वाले शीशे के नीचे की आलमारी
glucose ['gluːkəʊz] *n* ग्लूकोज़ - एक प्रकार की शर्करा
glue [gluː] *n* गोंद ▹ *vt* चिपकाना
gluten ['gluːtn] *n* गेहूं जैसे अनाज में पाया जाने वाला लासा
GM [dʒiː ɛm] *abbr* आनुवंशिक रूप से संशोधित
go [gəʊ] *vi (move)* जाना ▹ *v (denoting future action)* होना
go after [gəʊ 'ɑːftə] *v* पीछा करना
go ahead [gəʊ ə'hɛd] *v* आगे बढ़ना
goal [gəʊl] *n* गोल - वह स्थान जिसमें खिलाड़ी गेंद को डालने की कोशिश करते हैं
goalkeeper ['gəʊlˌkiːpə] *n* गोलरक्षक
goat [gəʊt] *n* बकरी
go away [gəʊ ə'weɪ] *v* दूर हटना

go back [gəʊ bæk] *v* शुरू होना
go by [gəʊ baɪ] *v* बीतना
God [gɒd] *n* ईश्वर
godfather ['gɒd,fɑːðə] *n* सरगना
go down [gəʊ daʊn] *v* गिरावट आना
goggles ['gɒglz] *npl* धूप का चश्मा
go in [gəʊ ɪn] *v* भीतर जाना
gold [gəʊld] *n* स्वर्ण
golden ['gəʊldən] *adj* सुनहला
goldfish ['gəʊld,fɪʃ] *n* गोल्डफ़िश - एक प्रकार की छोटी मछली
gold-plated ['gəʊld,pleɪtɪd] *adj* सोने का पत्तर चढ़ा
golf [gɒlf] *n* गोल्फ़ - एक प्रकार का खेल
golf club [gɒlf klʌb] *n* *(stick)* गोल्फ़ खेलने की छड़ी; *(organization)* गोल्फ़ क्लब - अपने सदस्यों को गोल्फ़ से जुड़ी सामग्री उपलब्ध कराने वाला संगठन
golf course [gɒlf kɔːs] *n* गोल्फ़ कोर्स - गोल्फ़ खेलने का मैदान
gone [gɒn] *adj* गया हुआ
good [gʊd] *adj* *(enjoyable)* अच्छा; *(well-behaved)* अच्छा; *(talented)* अच्छा
goodbye! ['gʊd'baɪ] *excl* अलविदा
good-looking ['gʊd'lʊkɪŋ] *adj* सुंदर
good-natured ['gʊd'neɪtʃəd] *adj* नेक
goods [gʊdz] *npl* सामान
go off [gəʊ ɒf] *v* फटना
google ['guːgl] *v* गूगल वेबसाइट पर इंटरनेट खोज करना
go on [gəʊ ɒn] *v* जारी रखना
goose [guːs] *n* बत्तख जैसा पक्षी
gooseberry ['gʊzbərɪ] *n* एक फल
goose pimples [guːs 'pɪmplz] *npl* सिहरन के कारण रोमछिद्रों में आया उभार
go out [gəʊ aʊt] *v* बाहर समय बिताना
go past [gəʊ pɑːst] *v* बगल से निकलना

g

gorgeous ['gɔːdʒəs] *adj (informal)* भव्य

gorilla [gə'rɪlə] *n* वनमानुष

go round [gəʊ raʊnd] *v* मिलने जाना

gossip ['gɒsɪp] *n* गपशप/अफ़वाह ▷ *vi* गपशप करना

go through [gəʊ θruː] *v* गुज़रना

go up [gəʊ ʌp] *v* बढ़ना

government ['gʌvənmənt] *n* सरकार

GP [dʒiː piː] *abbr* सामान्य चिकित्सक

GPS [dʒiː piː ɛs] *abbr* ग्लोबल पोज़िशनिंग प्रणाली हेतु संक्षिप्त रूप

grab [græb] *vt* झपटना

graceful ['greɪsfʊl] *adj* रमणीय

grade [greɪd] *n* दर्जा/कोटि

gradual ['grædjʊəl] *adj* क्रमिक

gradually ['grædjʊəlɪ] *adv* क्रमिक रूप से

graduate ['grædjʊɪt] *n* स्नातक

graduation [ˌgrædjʊ'eɪʃən] *n* स्नातक उपाधि

graffiti [græ'fiːtiː] *npl* भित्ति चित्रण/भित्ती लेख

grain [greɪn] *n (seed of cereal plant)* अनाज; *(tiny piece)* कण

gram [græm] *n* ग्राम

grammar ['græmə] *n* व्याकरण

grammatical [grə'mætɪkl] *adj* व्याकरण संबंधी

grand [grænd] *adj* भव्य

grandchild ['grænˌtʃaɪld] *n* पोता/पोती/नाती/नातिन

granddad ['grænˌdæd] *n (informal)* दादा

granddaughter ['grænˌdɔːtə] *n* पोती/नातिन

grandfather ['grænˌfɑːðə] *n* दादा/नाना

grandma ['grænˌmɑː] *n (informal)* दादी

grandmother ['grænˌmʌðə] *n* दादी/नानी

grandpa ['grænˌpɑː] *n (informal)* दादा

grandparents ['grænˌpɛərəntz] *npl* दादा/दादी/नाना/नानी

grandson ['grænsʌn] *n* पोता/नाती
granite ['grænɪt] *n* ग्रेनाइट
granny ['grænɪ] *n* *(informal)* दादी/नानी
grant [grɑːnt] *n* अनुदान
grape [greɪp] *n* अंगूर
grapefruit ['greɪpˌfruːt] *n* चकोतरा
graph [grɑːf] *n* लेखा-चित्र
graphics ['græfɪks] *npl* चित्र
grasp [grɑːsp] *vt* पकड़ना
grass [grɑːs] *n* *(plant)* घास; *(informal, informer)* मुखबिर
grasshopper ['grɑːsˌhɒpə] *n* टिड्डा
grate [greɪt] *vt* कद्दूकस करना
grateful ['greɪtfʊl] *adj* एहसानमंद
grave [greɪv] *n* कब्र
gravel ['grævl] *n* बजरी
gravestone ['greɪvˌstəʊn] *n* समाधि का पत्थर
graveyard ['greɪvˌjɑːd] *n* कब्रिस्तान
gravy ['greɪvɪ] *n* शोरबा
grease [griːs] *n* चिकनाई/ग्रीस
greasy ['griːzɪ] *adj* तैलीय
great [greɪt] *adj* *(very large)* विशाल; *(very important)* महान/महत; *(excellent)* बढ़िया/शानदार
Great Britain ['greɪt 'brɪtn] *n* ग्रेट ब्रिटेन
great-grandfather ['greɪt'grænˌfɑːðə] *n* परदादा/परनाना
great-grandmother ['greɪt'grænˌmʌðə] *n* परदादी/परनानी
Greece [griːs] *n* ग्रीस/यूनान
greedy ['griːdɪ] *adj* लालची
Greek [griːk] *adj* यूनानी ▷ *n* *(person)* यूनानी; *(language)* यूनानी
green [griːn] *adj* *(in colour)* हरा; *(inexperienced)* नौसिखिया
Green [griːn] *n* ग्रीन राजनैतिक आंदोलन के सदस्य
greengrocer ['griːnˌgrəʊsə] *n* सब्ज़ी और फल की दुकान
greenhouse ['griːnˌhaʊs] *n* पौधा घर
Greenland ['griːnlənd] *n* ग्रीनलैंड

g

green salad [griːn 'sæləd] *n* हरा सलाद
greet [griːt] *vt* अभिवादन करना
greeting ['griːtɪŋ] *n* अभिवादन
greetings card ['griːtɪŋz kaːd] *n* बधाई पत्र
grey [greɪ] *adj* स्लेटी
grey-haired [ˌgreɪ'hɛəd] *adj* स्लेटी रंग के बालों वाला व्यक्ति
grid [grɪd] *n* जाली
grief [griːf] *n* शोक
grill [grɪl] *n* ग्रिल ▷ *vt* भूनना
grilled [grɪld] *adj* भुना हुआ
grim [grɪm] *adj* मनहूस
grin [grɪn] *n* हँसी ▷ *vi* हँसना
grind [graɪnd] *vt* पीसना
grip [grɪp] *vt* कसकर पकड़ना
gripping ['grɪpɪŋ] *adj* दिलचस्प
grit [grɪt] *n* बजरी
groan [grəʊn] *vi* कराहना
grocer ['grəʊsə] *n (person)* पंसारी; ['grəʊsəz] *n (shop)* पंसारी की दुकान
groceries ['grəʊsərɪz] *npl* किराना
groom [gruːm] *n* दूल्हा
grope [grəʊp] *vi* टटोलना
gross [grəʊs] *adj* अशिष्ट/घटिया
grossly ['grəʊslɪ] *adv* बुरी तरह से
ground [graʊnd] *n* ज़मीन ▷ *vt* आधारित होना
ground floor [graʊnd flɔː] *n* भूतल
group [gruːp] *n* समूह
grouse [graʊs] *n (complaint)* शिकायत/भुनभुनाहट; *(bird)* श्येनक पक्षी
grow [grəʊ] *vt* उगाना ▷ *vi* बढ़ना
growl [graʊl] *vi* गुर्राना
grown-up ['grəʊnʌp] *n* वयस्क
growth [grəʊθ] *n* विकास
grow up [grəʊ ʌp] *v* बड़ा होना
grub [grʌb] *n* कीटडिंभ/कोआ
grudge [grʌdʒ] *n* बैर भाव
gruesome ['gruːsəm] *adj* वीभत्स
grumpy ['grʌmpɪ] *adj* तुनकमिजाज़

guarantee [ˌgærən'tiː] *n* प्रतिभू/ज़मानत ▷ *vt* ज़िम्मा लेना/ज़मानत देना
guard [gɑːd] *n* संतरी/पहरेदार ▷ *vt* पहरेदारी करना
Guatemala [ˌgwɑːtə'mɑːlə] *n* ग्वाटेमाला
guess [gɛs] *n* अनुमान ▷ *v* अनुमान लगाना
guest [gɛst] *n* मेहमान
guesthouse ['gɛstˌhaʊs] *n* अतिथिगृह
guide [gaɪd] *n* मार्गदर्शिका
guidebook ['gaɪdˌbʊk] *n* पर्यटन पुस्तिका
guide dog [gaɪd dɒg] *n* मार्गदर्शक कुत्ता
guided tour ['gaɪdɪd tʊə] *n* निर्देशित दौरा
guilt [gɪlt] *n* अपराध
guilty ['gɪltɪ] *adj* अपराधी
Guinea ['gɪnɪ] *n* गिनी
guinea pig ['gɪnɪ pɪg] *n* *(person)* प्रयोग कार्य के लिए इस्तेमाल होने वाला; *(animal)* चूहे की तरह का जानवर
guitar [gɪ'tɑː] *n* गिटार
Gulf States [gʌlf steɪts] *npl* खाड़ी राज्य
gum [gʌm] *n* च्युइंगम
gun [gʌn] *n* बंदूक
gust [gʌst] *n* झोंका
gut [gʌt] *n* अँतड़ी
guy [gaɪ] *n* *(informal)* लड़का
Guyana [gaɪ'ænə] *n* गुयाना
gym [dʒɪm] *n* व्यायामशाला
gymnast ['dʒɪmnæst] *n* कसरती/जिमनास्ट
gymnastics [dʒɪm'næstɪks] *npl* कसरत/जिमनास्टिक
gynaecologist [ˌgaɪnɪ'kɒlədʒɪst] *n* स्त्री-रोग विशेषज्ञ
gypsy ['dʒɪpsɪ] *n* खानाबदोश

h

habit ['hæbɪt] *n* आदत
hack [hæk] *v* काटना
hacker ['hækə] *n* हैकर/घुसपैठिया
haddock ['hædək] *n* एक समुद्री मछली

haemorrhoids ['hɛmə,rɔɪdz] *npl* बवासीर
haggle ['hægl] *vi* मोल-भाव करना
hail [heɪl] *n* ओला ▹ *vt* सराहना करना
hair [hɛə] *n* बाल
hairband ['hɛə,bænd] *n* हेयरबैंड
hairbrush ['hɛə,brʌʃ] *n* कंघी
haircut ['hɛə,kʌt] *n* बालों की काट
hairdo ['hɛə,duː] *n* *(informal)* केशविन्यास
hairdresser ['hɛə,drɛsə] *n (person)* केश प्रसाधक; *(salon)* नाई की दुकान
hairdryer ['hɛə,draɪə] *n* हेयर ड्रायर
hair gel [hɛə dʒɛl] *n* बालों में लगाने का जेल
hairgrip ['hɛəgrɪp] *n* बालों की चिमटी
hair spray ['hɛəspreɪ] *n* बालों में लगाने का स्प्रे
hairstyle ['hɛəstaɪl] *n* केशविन्यास
hairy ['hɛərɪ] *adj* बालदार
Haiti ['heɪtɪ] *n* हैती
half [hɑːf] *adj* आधा ▹ *adv* अंशतः ▹ *n* आधा
half board [hɑːf bɔːd] *n* हाफ़बोर्ड
half-hour ['hɑːf,aʊə] *n* आधा घंटा
half-price ['hɑːf,praɪs] *adj* आधी कीमत ▹ *adv* आधी कीमत पर
half-term ['hɑːf,tɜːm] *n* अर्द्धसत्रीय अवकाश
half-time ['hɑːf,taɪm] *n* मध्यांतर
halfway [,hɑːf'weɪ] *adv* बीच में
hall [hɔːl] *n* प्रवेश कक्ष
hallway ['hɔːl,weɪ] *n* गलियारा/दालान
halt [hɔːlt] *n* विराम
hamburger ['hæm,bɜːgə] *n* हैमबर्गर
hammer ['hæmə] *n* हथौड़ा
hammock ['hæmək] *n* झूलन खटोला
hamster ['hæmstə] *n* चूहे जैसा एक पशु
hand [hænd] *n* हाथ ▹ *vt* देना

handbag ['hænd,bæg] *n* बटुआ
handball ['hænd,bɔːl] *n* हैंडबॉल
handbook ['hænd,bʊk] *n* निर्देश पुस्तिका
handbrake ['hænd,breɪk] *n* हैंडब्रेक
handcuffs ['hænd,kʌfs] *npl* हथकड़ी
handkerchief ['hæŋkətʃɪf] *n* रूमाल
handle ['hændl] *n (tool, bag)* हत्था/मूठ ▷ *vt* संभालना ▷ *n (knob)* हत्था/मूठ
handlebars ['hændl,bɑːz] *npl* साइकल का हैंडल
hand luggage [hænd 'lʌgɪdʒ] *n* हाथ का सामान
handmade [,hænd'meɪd] *adj* हस्तनिर्मित
hands-free ['hændz,friː] *adj* हैंड्स फ़्री
hands-free kit [,hændz'friː kɪt] *n* हैंड्स फ़्री किट
handsome ['hændsəm] *adj* रूपवान
handwriting ['hænd,raɪtɪŋ] *n* हस्तलेख
handy ['hændɪ] *adj* उपयोगी/सुविधाजनक
hang [hæŋ] *vt (attach)* लटकाना ▷ *vi (be attached)* लटकना
hanger ['hæŋə] *n* हैंगर
hang-gliding ['hæŋ'glaɪdɪŋ] *n* हैंग ग्लाइडिंग
hang on [hæŋ ɒn] *v (informal)* इंतज़ार करना
hangover ['hæŋ,əʊvə] *n* खुमार/ शराब पीने के बाद शरीर को होने वाला कष्ट
hang up [hæŋ ʌp] *v* फ़ोन रखना
hankie ['hæŋkɪ] *n (informal)* रूमाल
happen ['hæpn] *vi* घटित होना
happily ['hæpɪlɪ] *adv* प्रसन्नतापूर्वक
happiness ['hæpɪnɪs] *n* खुशी
happy ['hæpɪ] *adj* खुश
harassment ['hærəsmənt] *n* उत्पीड़न
harbour ['hɑːbə] *n* बंदरगाह
hard [hɑːd] *adj (difficult)* कठिन; *(solid)* कड़ा ▷ *adv* मेहनत से

h

hardboard ['hɑːd,bɔːd] *n* दफ़्ती/गत्ता
hard disk [hɑːd dɪsk] *n* हार्ड डिस्क
hardly ['hɑːdlɪ] *adv (only just)* बमुश्किल; *(almost never)* मुश्किल से ही/कदाचित ही
hard shoulder [hɑːd 'ʃəʊldə] *n* आपातकाल में वाहनों के रुकने का स्थान
hard up [hɑːd ʌp] *adj (informal)* तंगहाल
hardware ['hɑːd,wɛə] *n* हार्डवेयर
hare [hɛə] *n* खरहा
harm [hɑːm] *vt* चोट पहुँचाना
harmful ['hɑːmfʊl] *adj* हानिकारक
harmless ['hɑːmlɪs] *adj* हानिरहित
harp [hɑːp] *n* पवन वीणा
harsh [hɑːʃ] *adj* कठोर
harvest ['hɑːvɪst] *n* फसल ▷ *vt* फसल काटना
hastily ['heɪstɪlɪ] *adv* जल्दबाज़ी से
hat [hæt] *n* टोप
hatchback ['hætʃ,bæk] *n* पीछे के दरवाज़े वाली कार
hate [heɪt] *vt* घृणा करना
hatred ['heɪtrɪd] *n* घृणा
haunted ['hɔːntɪd] *adj* भुतहा
have [hæv] *v (denoting present perfect tense)* होना/रखना; *(experience)* ग्रस्त होना/होना
have to [hæv tʊ] *v* करना पड़ेगा
hawthorn ['hɔː,θɔːn] *n* हॉथॉर्न
hay [heɪ] *n* भूसा
hay fever [heɪ 'fiːvə] *n* परागज ज्वर
haystack ['heɪ,stæk] *n* भूसे का ढेर
hazard warning lights ['hæzəd 'wɔːnɪŋ laɪts] *npl* गाड़ी की बत्ती
hazelnut ['heɪzl,nʌt] *n* पिंगल फल/कर्नेल
he [hiː] *pron* वह (पुरुष)
head [hɛd] *n (leader)* मुखिया; *(part of the body)* सिर ▷ *vt* नेतृत्व करना
headache ['hɛd,eɪk] *n* सिरदर्द

headlight ['hɛd,laɪt] *n* गाड़ी के सामने की बत्ती
headline ['hɛd,laɪn] *n* शीर्षक पंक्ति
head office [hɛd 'ɒfɪs] *n* प्रधान कार्यालय
headphones ['hɛd,fəʊnz] *npl* हेडफ़ोन
headquarters [,hɛd'kwɔːtəz] *npl* मुख्यालय
headroom ['hɛd,rʊm] *n* छत के नीचे की जगह
headscarf ['hɛd,skaːf] *n* गुलुबंद
headteacher ['hɛd,tiːtʃə] *n* प्रधानाचार्य
heal [hiːl] *vi* घाव भरना
health [hɛlθ] *n* स्वास्थ्य
healthy ['hɛlθɪ] *adj (in good health)* स्वस्थ; *(health-giving)* स्वास्थ्यवर्द्धक
heap [hiːp] *n* ढेर
hear [hɪə] *v* सुनना
hearing ['hɪərɪŋ] *n* श्रवण
hearing aid ['hɪərɪŋ eɪd] *n* सुनने का यंत्र
heart [haːt] *n* हृदय
heart attack [haːt ə'tæk] *n* दिल का दौरा
heartbroken ['haːt,brəʊkən] *adj* अत्यंत दुःखी
heartburn ['haːt,bɜːn] *n* सीने की जलन
heat [hiːt] *n* गर्मी/ऊष्मा ▷ *vt* गरम करना
heater ['hiːtə] *n* तापक
heather ['hɛðə] *n* फूलों की झाड़ी
heating ['hiːtɪŋ] *n* तापक
heat up [hiːt ʌp] *v* गरम करना
heaven ['hɛvn] *n* स्वर्ग
heavily ['hɛvɪlɪ] *adv* बहुत अधिक
heavy ['hɛvɪ] *adj* भारी
hedge [hɛdʒ] *n* झाड़ी से बनी बाड़
hedgehog ['hɛdʒ,hɒg] *n* साही
heel [hiːl] *n* एड़ी
height [haɪt] *n* कद
heir [ɛə] *n* उत्तराधिकारी
heiress ['ɛərɪs] *n* उत्तराधिकारिणी
helicopter ['hɛlɪ,kɒptə] *n* हेलीकॉप्टर
hell [hɛl] *n* नर्क

hello! [hʌ'ləʊ] *excl* नमस्कार
helmet ['hɛlmɪt] *n* हेलमेट
help! [help] *excl* बचाओ!/ मदद करो!
help [help] *n* मदद ▹ *v* मदद करना
helpful ['hɛlpfʊl] *adj* मददगार
helpline ['hɛlp,laɪn] *n* हेल्पलाइन
hen [hɛn] *n* मुर्गी
hen night [hɛn naɪt] *n* किसी लड़की की शादी से पूर्व होने वाली महिलाओं की पार्टी
hepatitis [,hɛpə'taɪtɪs] *n* हैपेटाइटिस
her [hɜː] *det* अपना (स्त्री) ▹ *pron* उसे (स्त्री)
herbal tea ['hɜːbl tiː] *n* जड़ी-बूटी युक्त चाय
herbs [hɜːbz] *npl* जड़ी-बूटी
here [hɪə] *adv* यहां
hereditary [hɪ'rɛdɪtərɪ] *adj* वंशानुगत
heritage ['hɛrɪtɪdʒ] *n* विरासत
hernia ['hɜːnɪə] *n* हर्निया/ अंत्र वृद्धि
hero ['hɪərəʊ] *n* नायक
heroine ['hɛrəʊɪn] *n* नायिका
heron ['hɛrən] *n* बगुला
herring ['hɛrɪŋ] *n* हिलसा मछली
hers [hɜːz] *pron* उसका (स्त्री)
herself [hə'sɛlf] *pron* खुद (स्त्री)
hesitate ['hɛzɪ,teɪt] *vi* हिचकिचाना
HGV [eɪtʃ dʒiː viː] *abbr* भारी माल वाहन
hi! [haɪ] *excl* नमस्कार!
hiccups ['hɪkʌps] *npl* हिचकी
hidden ['hɪdn] *adj* अदृश्य/ प्रच्छन्न
hide [haɪd] *vt (object)* छुपाना ▹ *vi (conceal yourself)* छुपना ▹ *vt (feelings)* छुपाना
hide-and-seek [,haɪdænd'siːk] *n* लुका-छिपी
hideous ['hɪdɪəs] *adj* डरावना
hifi ['haɪ'faɪ] *n* हाई फ़ाई
high [haɪ] *adj (tall)* ऊंचा ▹ *adv* ऊँचाई पर ▹ *adj (price)* अधिक; *(sound)* ऊंचा

highchair ['haɪˌtʃɛə] *n* ऊँची कुर्सी

higher education ['haɪə ˌɛdʒʊ'keɪʃən] *n* उच्च शिक्षा

high-heeled ['haɪˌhiːld] *adj* ऊँची एड़ी का

high heels [haɪ hiːlz] *npl* ऊँची एड़ी

high jump [haɪ dʒʌmp] *n* ऊँची कूद

highlight ['haɪˌlaɪt] *n* विशिष्टता ▷ *vt* विशिष्ट रूप से दर्शाना

highlighter ['haɪˌlaɪtə] *n* हाइलाइटर

high-rise ['haɪˌraɪz] *n* बहुमंजिली इमारत

high season [haɪ 'siːzn] *n* तेज़ी का मौसम

Highway Code ['haɪˌweɪ kəʊd] *n* राजमार्ग संहिता

hijack ['haɪˌdʒæk] *vt* अपहरण करना

hijacker ['haɪˌdʒækə] *n* अपहरणकर्ता

hike [haɪk] *n* पैदल सैर

hiking ['haɪkɪŋ] *n* पैदल सैर

hilarious [hɪ'lɛərɪəs] *adj* अत्यधिक हास्यप्रद

hill [hɪl] *n* पहाड़ी

hill-walking ['hɪlˌwɔːkɪŋ] *n* पहाड़ी प्रदेशों की सैर

him [hɪm] *pron* उसे (पुरुष)

himself [hɪm'sɛlf] *pron* खुद (पुरुष)

Hindu ['hɪnduː] *adj* हिन्दू ▷ *n* हिन्दू धर्मानुयायी

Hinduism ['hɪndʊˌɪzəm] *n* हिन्दुत्व/हिन्दू धर्म

hinge [hɪndʒ] *n* चूल/कब्जा

hint [hɪnt] *n* इशारा ▷ *vi* इशारा करना

hip [hɪp] *n* नितंब

hippie ['hɪpɪ] *n* हिप्पी

hippo ['hɪpəʊ] *n (informal)* दरियाई घोड़ा

hippopotamus [ˌhɪpə'pɒtəməs] *n* दरियाई घोड़ा

hire ['haɪə] *n* भाड़ा/किराया ▷ *vt* काम पर रखना

his [hɪz] *det* उसका (लड़के के लिए) ▷ *pron* उसका (पुरुष)

historian [hɪ'stɔːrɪən] *n* इतिहासकार

historical [hɪ'stɒrɪkl] *adj* ऐतिहासिक

history ['hɪstərɪ] *n* इतिहास
hit [hɪt] *n* टक्कर ▷ *vt* मारना
hitch [hɪtʃ] *n* अड़चन
hitchhike ['hɪtʃ,haɪk] *vi* दूसरे की गाड़ी में मुफ़्त सैर करना
hitchhiker ['hɪtʃ,haɪkə] *n* दूसरे की गाड़ी में मुफ़्त सैर करने वाला
hitchhiking ['hɪtʃ,haɪkɪŋ] *n* दूसरे की गाड़ी में मुफ़्त सैर
HIV-negative [eɪtʃ aɪ viː 'nɛgətɪv] *adj* एच आई वी - रहित
HIV-positive [eɪtʃ aɪ viː 'pɒzɪtɪv] *adj* एच आई वी - ग्रस्त
hobby ['hɒbɪ] *n* शौक
hockey ['hɒkɪ] *n* हॉकी
hold [həʊld] *vt* *(in hands or arms)* पकड़ना; *(accommodate)* संभाले रखना/जगह होना
holdall ['həʊld,ɔːl] *n* बिस्तरबंद
hold on [həʊld ɒn] *v* पकड़े रखना
hold up [həʊld ʌp] *v* रोकना
hold-up [həʊldʌp] *n* बटमारी/लूट-खसोट
hole [həʊl] *n* छेद
holiday ['hɒlɪ,deɪ] *n* छुट्टी
Holland ['hɒlənd] *n* हॉलैंड
hollow ['hɒləʊ] *adj* खोखला
holly ['hɒlɪ] *n* शूलपर्णी
holy ['həʊlɪ] *adj* पवित्र
home [həʊm] *adv* घर पर ▷ *n* घर
home address [həʊm ə'drɛs] *n* घर का पता
homeland ['həʊm,lænd] *n* *(written)* जन्मभूमि
homeless ['həʊmlɪs] *adj* बेघर
home-made ['həʊm'meɪd] *adj* घर का बना
home match [həʊm mætʃ] *n* गृह मैच अथवा अपनी ज़मीन पर खेला जाने वाला मैच
homeopathic [,həʊmɪəʊ'pæθɪk] *adj* होम्योपैथिक
homeopathy [,həʊmɪ'ɒpəθɪ] *n* होम्योपैथी
home page [həʊm peɪdʒ] *n* होम पेज/मुख्य पृष्ठ
homesick ['həʊm,sɪk] *adj* गृहासक्त

homework ['həʊm,wɜːk] *n* गृहकार्य
Honduras [hɒn'djʊərəs] *n* हौंडुरस
honest ['ɒnɪst] *adj* ईमानदार
honestly ['ɒnɪstlɪ] *adv* ईमानदारी - पूर्वक
honesty ['ɒnɪstɪ] *n* ईमानदारी
honey ['hʌnɪ] *n* शहद
honeymoon ['hʌnɪ,muːn] *n* मधुमास
honeysuckle ['hʌnɪ,sʌkl] *n* मधुचूष
honour ['ɒnə] *n* गौरव
hood [hʊd] *n* कनटोप
hook [hʊk] *n* खूँटी/ काँटा
hooray! [hʊ'reɪ] *excl* वाह!
Hoover® ['huːvə] *n* हूवर
hoover ['huːvə] *v* वैक्यूम क्लीनर से साफ करना
hop [hɒp] *vi (person)* एक पैर से कूदना; *(mainly bird, animal)* फुदकना
hope [həʊp] *n* आशा ▷ *v* आशा करना
hopeful ['həʊpfʊl] *adj* आशान्वित
hopefully ['həʊpfʊlɪ] *adv* आशापूर्वक
hopeless ['həʊplɪs] *adj* नाउम्मीद
horizon [hə'raɪzn] *n* क्षितिज
horizontal [,hɒrɪ'zɒntl] *adj* क्षैतिज
hormone ['hɔːməʊn] *n* हॉर्मोन/अंतःस्त्राव
horn [hɔːn] *n (car)* गाड़ी का भोंपू; *(animal)* सींग; *(musical instrument)* श्रृंगी - एक वाद्ययंत्र
horoscope ['hɒrə,skəʊp] *n* जन्मपत्री/राशिफल
horrendous [hɒ'rɛndəs] *adj* भयानक
horrible ['hɒrəbl] *adj (informal)* भयानक
horrifying ['hɒrɪ,faɪɪŋ] *adj* भयावह
horror ['hɒrə] *n* दहशत
horror film ['hɒrə fɪlm] *n* डरावना चलचित्र
horse [hɔːs] *n* घोड़ा
horse racing [hɔːs 'reɪsɪŋ] *n* घुड़दौड़
horseradish ['hɔːs,rædɪʃ] *n* एक तरह की मूली

horse riding [hɔːs 'raɪdɪŋ] *n* घुड़सवारी
horseshoe ['hɔːs,ʃuː] *n* नाल
hose [həʊz] *n* नली/पाइप
hosepipe ['həʊz,paɪp] *n* नली/पाइप
hospital ['hɒspɪtl] *n* अस्पताल
hospitality [,hɒspɪ'tælɪtɪ] *n* मेहमाननवाज़ी
host [həʊst] *n* *(party)* मेज़बान; *(large number)* समूह
hostage ['hɒstɪdʒ] *n* बंधक
hostel ['hɒstl] *n* छात्रावास
hostile ['hɒstaɪl] *adj* उग्र
hot [hɒt] *adj* गर्म
hot dog [hɒt dɒg] *n* हॉट डॉग
hotel [həʊ'tɛl] *n* सराय
hot-water bottle [,hɒt'wɔːtə 'bɒtl] *n* गर्म पानी की थैली
hour [aʊə] *n* घंटा
hourly ['aʊəlɪ] *adj* प्रति घंटे की ▷ *adv* हर घंटे पर
house [haʊs] *n* मकान
household ['haʊs,həʊld] *n* परिवार
housewife ['haʊs,waɪf] *n* गृहस्वामिनी
house wine [haʊs waɪn] *n* सस्ती शराब
housework ['haʊs,wɜːk] *n* घरेलू कामकाज
hovercraft ['hɒvə,krɑːft] *n* होवरक्राफ्ट-ज़मीन और पानी पर चलने वाला एक वाहन
how [haʊ] *adv* *(in what way)* कैसे; *(asking about number or amount)* कितना
however [haʊ'ɛvə] *adv* तथापि/फिर भी
howl [haʊl] *vi* कुत्ते या भेड़िए की चिल्लाहट
HQ [eɪtʃ kjuː] *abbr* मुख्यालय हेतु संक्षिप्त रूप
hubcap ['hʌb,kæp] *n* हबकैप
hug [hʌg] *n* आलिंगन ▷ *vt* आलिंगन करना
huge [hjuːdʒ] *adj* विशाल
hull [hʌl] *n* पेटा/पेंद
hum [hʌm] *vi* भिनभिनाहट
human ['hjuːmən] *adj* मानवीय
human being ['hjuːmən 'biːɪŋ] *n* मानव
humanitarian [hjuː,mænɪ'tɛərɪən] *adj* मानवतावादी

human rights ['hjuːmən raɪts] *npl* मानवाधिकार
humble ['hʌmbl] *adj* विनीत/नम्र
humid ['hjuːmɪd] *adj* नम
humidity [hjuː'mɪdɪtɪ] *n* नमी
humorous ['hjuːmərəs] *adj* विनोदपूर्ण
humour ['hjuːmə] *n* परिहास
hundred ['hʌndrəd] *num* सौ
Hungarian [hʌŋ'gɛərɪən] *adj* हंगरी से संबद्ध ▹ *n* हंगरी का निवासी
Hungary ['hʌŋgərɪ] *n* हंगरी
hunger ['hʌŋgə] *n* भूख
hungry ['hʌŋgrɪ] *adj* भूखा
hunt [hʌnt] *vi (search)* तलाश करना/खोजना ▹ *v (animal)* शिकार करना
hunter ['hʌntə] *n* शिकारी
hunting ['hʌntɪŋ] *n* शिकार
hurdle ['hɜːdl] *n* बाधा
hurricane ['hʌrɪkn] *n* तूफ़ान
hurry ['hʌrɪ] *n* जल्दबाज़ी ▹ *vi* जल्दी करना
hurry up ['hʌrɪ ʌp] *v* जल्दी करना
hurt [hɜːt] *adj* घायल ▹ *vt* चोट पहुँचाना
husband ['hʌzbənd] *n* पति
hut [hʌt] *n* झोपड़ी
hyacinth ['haɪəsɪnθ] *n* गुलाबी तुरसावा - फूल का एक पौधा
hydrogen ['haɪdrɪdʒən] *n* हाइड्रोजन - एक गैस
hygiene ['haɪdʒiːn] *n* स्वच्छता
hypermarket ['haɪpəˌmɑːkɪt] *n* बड़ा सुपर बाज़ार
hyphen ['haɪfn] *n* समास चिह्न

i

I [aɪ] *pron* मैं
ice [aɪs] *n* बर्फ़
iceberg ['aɪsbɜːg] *n* हिमशैल
icebox ['aɪsˌbɒks] *n (old-fashioned)* प्रशीतक/आइस बॉक्स

ice cream ['aɪs 'kriːm] *n* आइसक्रीम
ice cube [aɪs kjuːb] *n* बर्फ़ का टुकड़ा
ice hockey [aɪs 'hɒkɪ] *n* आइस हॉकी
Iceland ['aɪslənd] *n* आइसलैंड
Icelandic [aɪs'lændɪk] *adj* आइसलैंड से संबद्ध ▷ *n* आइसलैंड की भाषा
ice lolly [aɪs 'lɒlɪ] *n* बर्फ़ का गोला
ice rink [aɪs rɪŋk] *n* बर्फ़ का मैदान
ice-skating ['aɪsˌskeɪtɪŋ] *n* बर्फ़ पर स्केटिंग
icing ['aɪsɪŋ] *n* केक सजाने हेतु चीनी का बना मिश्रण
icing sugar ['aɪsɪŋ 'ʃʊgə] *n* महीन चीनी
icon ['aɪkɒn] *n* चिह्न
icy ['aɪsɪ] *adj* सर्द
ID card [ˌaɪ'diː kɑːd] *abbr* पहचान पत्र
idea [aɪ'dɪə] *n* विचार
ideal [aɪ'dɪəl] *adj* आदर्श
ideally [aɪ'dɪəlɪ] *adv* आदर्शतः
identical [aɪ'dɛntɪkl] *adj* एक समान/अभिन्न
identification [aɪˌdɛntɪfɪ'keɪʃən] *n* पहचान
identify [aɪ'dɛntɪˌfaɪ] *vt* पहचान करना
identity [aɪ'dɛntɪtɪ] *n* पहचान
identity card [aɪ'dɛntɪtɪ kɑːd] *n* पहचान पत्र
identity theft [aɪ'dɛntɪtɪ θɛft] *n* निजी जानकारी की चोरी
ideology [ˌaɪdɪ'ɒlədʒɪ] *n* विचारधारा
idiot ['ɪdɪət] *n* बेवकूफ़
idiotic [ˌɪdɪ'ɒtɪk] *adj* बेवकूफ़ाना
idle ['aɪdl] *adj* सुस्त
i.e. [aɪ iː] *abbr* अर्थात्
if [ɪf] *conj* यदि
ignition [ɪg'nɪʃən] *n* इग्निशन
ignorance ['ɪgnərəns] *n* अज्ञानता
ignorant ['ɪgnərənt] *adj* अज्ञानी
ignore [ɪg'nɔː] *vt* उपेक्षा करना

ill [ɪl] *adj* बीमार
illegal [ɪ'liːgl] *adj* गैरकानूनी
illegible [ɪ'lɛdʒɪbl] *adj* अस्पष्ट/गिचपिच
illiterate [ɪ'lɪtərɪt] *adj* अनपढ़
illness ['ɪlnɪs] *n* बीमारी
ill-treat [ɪl'triːt] *vt* दुर्व्यवहार करना
illusion [ɪ'luːʒən] *n* भ्रम
illustration [ˌɪlə'streɪʃən] *n* मिसाल
image ['ɪmɪdʒ] *n* चित्र/छवि
imaginary [ɪ'mædʒɪnərɪ] *adj* काल्पनिक
imagination [ɪˌmædʒɪ'neɪʃən] *n* कल्पना
imagine [ɪ'mædʒɪn] *vt* कल्पना करना
imitate ['ɪmɪˌteɪt] *vt* नकल करना
imitation [ˌɪmɪ'teɪʃən] *n* नकल
immature [ˌɪmə'tjʊə] *adj* अपरिपक्व
immediate [ɪ'miːdɪət] *adj* तुरंत
immediately [ɪ'miːdɪətlɪ] *adv* तत्काल
immigrant ['ɪmɪgrənt] *n* अप्रवासी
immigration [ˌɪmɪ'greɪʃən] *n* अप्रवासन
immoral [ɪ'mɒrəl] *adj* अनैतिक
immune system [ɪ'mjuːn 'sɪstəm] *n* प्रतिरक्षा प्रणाली
impact ['ɪmpækt] *n* प्रभाव
impartial [ɪm'pɑːʃəl] *adj* निष्पक्ष
impatience [ɪm'peɪʃəns] *n* अधैर्य
impatient [ɪm'peɪʃənt] *adj* अधीर
impatiently [ɪm'peɪʃəntlɪ] *adv* अधीरता से
impersonal [ɪm'pɜːsənl] *adj* अवैयक्तिक
import ['ɪmpɔːt] *n* आयात ▷ [ɪm'pɔːt] *vt* आयात करना
importance [ɪm'pɔːtns] *n* महत्ता
important [ɪm'pɔːtnt] *adj* *(matter)* महत्त्वपूर्ण; *(person)* महत्त्वपूर्ण
impossible [ɪm'pɒsəbl] *adj* असंभव

impractical [ɪm'præktɪkl] *adj* अव्यावहारिक

impress [ɪm'prɛs] *v* प्रभावित करना

impressed [ɪm'prɛst] *adj* प्रभावित

impression [ɪm'prɛʃən] *n* प्रभाव

impressive [ɪm'prɛsɪv] *adj* प्रभावशाली

improve [ɪm'pruːv] *v* सुधरना

improvement [ɪm'pruːvmənt] *n* सुधार

in [ɪn] *prep (denoting place)* में/ के अंदर; *(denoting time)* में

inaccurate [ɪn'ækjʊrɪt] *adj* अशुद्ध

inadequate [ɪn'ædɪkwɪt] *adj* अपर्याप्त

inadvertently [ˌɪnəd'vɜːtntlɪ] *adv* अनजाने में

inbox ['ɪnbɒks] *n* इनबॉक्स

incentive [ɪn'sɛntɪv] *n* प्रोत्साहन

inch [ɪntʃ] *n* इंच

incident ['ɪnsɪdənt] *n (formal)* घटना

include [ɪn'kluːd] *vt* शामिल करना/समावेश करना

included [ɪn'kluːdɪd] *adj* शामिल

including [ɪn'kluːdɪŋ] *prep* सहित

inclusive [ɪn'kluːsɪv] *adj* सम्मिलित

income ['ɪnkʌm] *n* आय

income tax ['ɪnkəm tæks] *n* आयकर

incompetent [ɪn'kɒmpɪtənt] *adj* अक्षम

incomplete [ˌɪnkəm'pliːt] *adj* अपूर्ण

inconsistent [ˌɪnkən'sɪstənt] *adj* असंगत

inconvenience [ˌɪnkən'viːnjəns] *n* असुविधा

inconvenient [ˌɪnkən'viːnjənt] *adj* असुविधाजनक

incorrect [ˌɪnkə'rɛkt] *adj* गलत

increase ['ɪnkriːs] *n* बढ़ोत्तरी ▷ [ɪn'kriːs] *v* बढ़ाना/बढ़ना

increasingly [ɪn'kriːsɪŋlɪ] *adv* उत्तरोत्तर

incredible [ɪn'krɛdəbl] *adj* असाधारण

indecisive [ˌɪndɪ'saɪsɪv] *adj* अस्थिरमति/ढुलमुल

indeed [ɪn'diːd] *adv* वास्तव में

independence [ˌɪndɪ'pɛndəns] *n* स्वतंत्रता

independent [ˌɪndɪ'pɛndənt] *adj* स्वतंत्र/आत्मनिर्भर

index ['ɪndɛks] *n (in book)* सूची; *(numerical scale)* सूचकांक

index finger ['ɪndɛks 'fɪŋgə] *n* तर्जनी

India ['ɪndɪə] *n* भारत

Indian ['ɪndɪən] *adj* भारतीय ▷ *n* भारतीय नागरिक

Indian Ocean ['ɪndɪən 'əʊʃən] *n* हिंद महासागर

indicate ['ɪndɪˌkeɪt] *vt* संकेत करना

indicator ['ɪndɪˌkeɪtə] *n* सूचक/संकेतक

indigestion [ˌɪndɪ'dʒɛstʃən] *n* अपच

indirect [ˌɪndɪ'rɛkt] *adj* अप्रत्यक्ष

indispensable [ˌɪndɪ'spɛnsəbl] *adj* अनिवार्य

individual [ˌɪndɪ'vɪdjʊəl] *adj* वैयक्तिक

Indonesia [ˌɪndəʊ'niːzɪə] *n* इंडोनेशिया

Indonesian [ˌɪndəʊ'niːzɪən] *adj* इंडोनेशियाई ▷ *n* इंडोनेशियाई नागरिक

indoor ['ɪnˌdɔː] *adj* अंदर का

indoors [ˌɪn'dɔːz] *adv* घर के भीतर

industrial [ɪn'dʌstrɪəl] *adj* औद्योगिक

industrial estate [ɪn'dʌstrɪəl ɪ'steɪt] *n* औद्योगिक क्षेत्र

industry ['ɪndəstrɪ] *n* उद्योग

inefficient [ˌɪnɪ'fɪʃənt] *adj* अक्षम

inevitable [ɪn'ɛvɪtəbl] *adj* अपरिहार्य

inexpensive [ˌɪnɪk'spɛnsɪv] *adj* सस्ता

inexperienced [ˌɪnɪk'spɪərɪənst] *adj* अनुभवहीन

infantry ['ɪnfəntrɪ] *n* पैदल सेना
infant school ['ɪnfənt skuːl] *n* बाल विद्यालय
infection [ɪn'fɛkʃən] *n* संक्रमण
infectious [ɪn'fɛkʃəs] *adj* संक्रामक
inferior [ɪn'fɪərɪə] *adj* हीन/अवर ▷ *n* हीन व्यक्ति
infertile [ɪn'fɜːtaɪl] *adj* बांझ
infinitive [ɪn'fɪnɪtɪv] *n* क्रिया का साधारण रूप
infirmary [ɪn'fɜːmərɪ] *n* अस्पताल
inflamed [ɪn'fleɪmd] *adj* लाल / सूजा हुआ
inflammation [ˌɪnflə'meɪʃən] *n (formal)* सूजन और जलन
inflatable [ɪn'fleɪtəbl] *adj* हवा भरी जाने वाली वस्तु
inflation [ɪn'fleɪʃən] *n* मुद्रास्फ़ीति
inflexible [ɪn'flɛksəbl] *adj* अनम्य/अड़ियल
influence ['ɪnflʊəns] *n* प्रभाव ▷ *vt* प्रभावित करना
influenza [ˌɪnflʊ'ɛnzə] *n (formal)* एक प्रकार का बुखार
inform [ɪn'fɔːm] *vt* सूचना देना
informal [ɪn'fɔːməl] *adj* अनौपचारिक
information [ˌɪnfə'meɪʃən] *n* सूचना
information office [ˌɪnfə'meɪʃən 'ɒfɪs] *n* सूचना कार्यालय
informative [ɪn'fɔːmətɪv] *adj* सूचनाप्रद
infrastructure ['ɪnfrəˌstrʌktʃə] *n* बुनियादी सुविधाएँ
infuriating [ɪn'fjʊərɪeɪtɪŋ] *adj* गुस्सा दिलाने वाला
ingenious [ɪn'dʒiːnjəs] *adj* प्रतिभावान
ingredient [ɪn'griːdɪənt] *n* सामग्री
inhabitant [ɪn'hæbɪtənt] *n* निवासी
inhaler [ɪn'heɪlə] *n* सांस द्वारा अंदर खींची जाने वाली औषधि
inherit [ɪn'hɛrɪt] *vt* विरासत में पाना

inheritance [ɪn'hɛrɪtəns] *n* विरासत/उत्तराधिकार
inhibition [ˌɪnɪ'bɪʃən] *n* हिचक
initial [ɪ'nɪʃəl] *adj* आरंभिक ▷ *vt* आद्यक्षर लिखना/नाम का पहला अक्षर लिखना
initially [ɪ'nɪʃəlɪ] *adv* आरंभ में
initials [ɪ'nɪʃəlz] *npl* आद्याक्षर
initiative [ɪ'nɪʃɪətɪv] *n* पहल
inject [ɪn'dʒɛkt] *vt* सूई लगाना
injection [ɪn'dʒɛkʃən] *n* दवा की सूई
injure ['ɪndʒə] *vt* घायल करना
injured ['ɪndʒəd] *adj* घायल
injury ['ɪndʒərɪ] *n* चोट
injury time ['ɪndʒərɪ taɪm] *n* चोट लगने के कारण खेल रुकने पर दिया जाने वाला अतिरिक्त समय
injustice [ɪn'dʒʌstɪs] *n* अन्याय
ink [ɪŋk] *n* स्याही
in-laws ['ɪnlɔːz] *npl* ससुराल पक्ष
inmate ['ɪnˌmeɪt] *n* सहवासी
inn [ɪn] *n (old-fashioned)* सराय
inner ['ɪnə] *adj* आंतरिक
inner tube ['ɪnə tjuːb] *n* टायर के अंदर स्थित हवा भरा ट्यूब
innocent ['ɪnəsənt] *adj* मासूम
innovation [ˌɪnə'veɪʃən] *n* नवप्रवर्तन/नई खोज
innovative ['ɪnəˌveɪtɪv] *adj* मौलिक/अभिनव
inquest ['ɪnˌkwɛst] *n* तहकीकात
inquire [ɪn'kwaɪə] *v (formal)* पूछताछ करना
inquiries office [ɪn'kwaɪərɪz-] *n* पूछताछ कार्यालय
inquiry [ɪn'kwaɪərɪ] *n* पूछताछ
inquiry desk [ɪn'kwaɪərɪ dɛsk] *n* पूछताछ मेज
inquisitive [ɪn'kwɪzɪtɪv] *adj* जिज्ञासु/कुतुहली
insane [ɪn'seɪn] *adj* पागल
inscription [ɪn'skrɪpʃən] *n* अभिलेख

i

insect ['ɪnsɛkt] *n* कीड़ा
insecure [ˌɪnsɪ'kjʊə] *adj* असुरक्षित
insensitive [ɪn'sɛnsɪtɪv] *adj* असंवेदनशील
inside ['ɪn'saɪd] *adv* भीतर ▹ *n* भीतरी भाग ▹ *prep* अंदर
insincere [ˌɪnsɪn'sɪə] *adj* झूठा/पाखंडपूर्ण
insist [ɪn'sɪst] *v* आग्रह करना/ज़ोर डालना
insomnia [ɪn'sɒmnɪə] *n* नींद न आने की बीमारी
inspect [ɪn'spɛkt] *vt* निरीक्षण करना
inspector [ɪn'spɛktə] *n* निरीक्षक
instability [ˌɪnstə'bɪlɪtɪ] *n* अस्थिरता
instalment [ɪn'stɔːlmənt] *n* किस्त
instance ['ɪnstəns] *n* घटना/दृष्टांत
instant ['ɪnstənt] *adj* तुरंत
instantly ['ɪnstəntlɪ] *adv* तुरंत/तत्क्षण
instead [ɪn'stɛd] *adv* के बजाय
instead of [ɪn'stɛd ɒv; əv] *prep* के बदले में
instinct ['ɪnstɪŋkt] *n* सहज ज्ञान
institute ['ɪnstɪˌtjuːt] *n* संस्थान
institution [ˌɪnstɪ'tjuːʃən] *n* संस्था
instruct [ɪn'strʌkt] *vt* *(formal)* निर्देश देना
instructions [ɪn'strʌkʃənz] *npl* निर्देश
instructor [ɪn'strʌktə] *n* प्रशिक्षक/शिक्षक
instrument ['ɪnstrəmənt] *n (tool)* उपकरण; *(musical)* वाद्ययंत्र
insufficient [ˌɪnsə'fɪʃənt] *adj (formal)* अपर्याप्त
insulation [ˌɪnsjʊ'leɪʃən] *n* रोधन
insulin ['ɪnsjʊlɪn] *n* इंसुलिन
insult ['ɪnsʌlt] *n* अपमान ▹ [ɪn'sʌlt] *vt* अपमान करना
insurance ['θɜːd'pɑːtɪ ɪn'ʃʊərəns; -'ʃɔː-] *n* बीमा
insurance certificate [ɪn'ʃʊərəns sə'tɪfɪkət] *n* बीमा प्रमाणपत्र

insurance policy [ɪn'ʃʊərəns 'pɒlɪsɪ] *n* बीमा योजना

insure [ɪn'ʃʊə] *v* बीमा करना

insured [ɪn'ʃʊəd] *adj* बीमाकृत

intact [ɪn'tækt] *adj* अक्षत/अक्षुण्ण

intellectual [ˌɪntɪ'lɛktʃʊəl] *adj* बौद्धिक ▷ *n* बुद्धिजीवी

intelligence [ɪn'tɛlɪdʒəns] *n* बुद्धिमत्ता

intelligent [ɪn'tɛlɪdʒənt] *adj* बुद्धिमान

intend [ɪn'tɛnd] *v* इरादा रखना

intense [ɪn'tɛns] *adj* तीव्र

intensive [ɪn'tɛnsɪv] *adj* गहन

intensive care unit [ɪn'tɛnsɪv kɛə 'juːnɪt] *n* गहन चिकित्सा कक्ष

intention [ɪn'tɛnʃən] *n* इरादा

intentional [ɪn'tɛnʃənl] *adj* इरादतन

intercom ['ɪntəˌkɒm] *n* इंटरकॉम

interest ['ɪntrɪst] *n (curiosity)* दिलचस्पी; *(money)* ब्याज ▷ *vt* दिलचस्पी पैदा करना

interested ['ɪntrɪstɪd] *adj* दिलचस्पी रखने वाला

interesting ['ɪntrɪstɪŋ] *adj* दिलचस्प

interest rate ['ɪntrəst reɪt] *n* ब्याज दर

interior [ɪn'tɪərɪə] *n* आंतरिक भाग

interior designer [ɪn'tɪərɪə dɪ'zaɪnə] *n* गृह सज्जाकार

intermediate [ˌɪntə'miːdɪɪt] *adj* मध्यवर्ती

internal [ɪn'tɜːnl] *adj* आंतरिक

international [ˌɪntə'næʃənl] *adj* अंतर्राष्ट्रीय

Internet ['ɪntəˌnɛt] *n* इंटरनेट

Internet café ['ɪntəˌnɛt 'kæfeɪ] *n* इंटरनेट कैफ़े

Internet user ['ɪntəˌnɛt 'juːzə] *n* इंटरनेट प्रयोगकर्ता

interpret [ɪn'tɜːprɪt] *vt* अर्थ लगाना/विवेचन करना

interpreter [ɪn'tɜːprɪtə] *n* दुभाषिया

interrogate [ɪn'tɛrə,geɪt] *vt* पूछताछ करना
interrupt [,ɪntə'rʌpt] *v* टोकना
interruption [,ɪntə'rʌpʃən] *n* व्यवधान
interval ['ɪntəvəl] *n* मध्यांतर
interview ['ɪntə,vjuː] *n* साक्षात्कार ▷ *vt* साक्षात्कार करना
interviewer ['ɪntə,vjuːə] *n* साक्षात्कारकर्ता
intimate ['ɪntɪmɪt] *adj* अंतरंग
intimidate [ɪn'tɪmɪ,deɪt] *vt* धमकाना
into ['ɪntuː] *prep (put)* में; *(go)* में/के अंदर
intolerant [ɪn'tɒlərənt] *adj* असहिष्णु
intranet ['ɪntrə,nɛt] *n* इंट्रानेट
introduce [,ɪntrə'djuːs] *vt* परिचय कराना
introduction [,ɪntrə'dʌkʃən] *n* प्रारंभ/परिचय
intruder [ɪn'truːdə] *n* घुसपैठिया
intuition [,ɪntjʊ'ɪʃən] *n* अंतर्ज्ञान
invade [ɪn'veɪd] *v* आक्रमण करना
invalid ['ɪnvə,lɪd] *n* रुग्ण/अपंग
invent [ɪn'vɛnt] *vt* अविष्कार करना
invention [ɪn'vɛnʃən] *n* अविष्कार
inventor [ɪn'vɛntə] *n* आविष्कारक
inventory ['ɪnvəntərɪ] *n* सूची
inverted commas [ɪn'vɜːtɪd 'kɒməz] *npl* उद्धरण चिह्न
invest [ɪn'vɛst] *v* निवेश करना
investigation [ɪn,vɛstɪ'geɪʃən] *n* तहकीकात
investment [ɪn'vɛstmənt] *n* निवेश
investor [ɪn'vɛstə] *n* निवेशक
invigilator [ɪn'vɪdʒɪ,leɪtə] *n* निरीक्षक
invisible [ɪn'vɪzəbl] *adj* अदृश्य
invitation [,ɪnvɪ'teɪʃən] *n* आमंत्रण

invite [ɪn'vaɪt] *vt* आमंत्रित करना

invoice ['ɪnvɔɪs] *n* बीजक/बिल ▷ *vt* बीजक/बिल भेजना

involve [ɪn'vɒlv] *vt* शामिल करना

iPod® ['aɪˌpɒd] *n* आई पॉड

IQ [aɪ kjuː] *abbr* बौद्धिक स्तर

Iran [ɪ'rɑːn] *n* ईरान

Iranian [ɪ'reɪnɪən] *adj* ईरानी ▷ *n (person)* ईरानी

Iraq [ɪ'rɑːk] *n* इराक

Iraqi [ɪ'rɑːkɪ] *adj* इराकी ▷ *n* इराकी

Ireland ['aɪələnd] *n* आयरलैंड

iris ['aɪrɪs] *n* आंख की पुतली

Irish ['aɪrɪʃ] *adj* आयरलैंड से संबद्ध ▷ *n* आयरलैंड की भाषा

Irishman ['aɪrɪʃmən] *n* आयरलैंड का पुरुष

Irishwoman ['aɪrɪʃwʊmən] *n* आयरलैंड की महिला

iron ['aɪən] *n (metal)* लोहा ▷ *v* इस्त्री करना ▷ *n (for pressing clothes)* इस्तरी

ironic [aɪ'rɒnɪk] *adj* व्यंग्यपूर्ण

ironing ['aɪənɪŋ] *n* इस्त्री

ironing board ['aɪənɪŋ bɔːd] *n* इस्त्री करने की मेज़

ironmonger ['aɪənˌmʌŋgə] *n* लोहे की वस्तुओं की दुकान

irony ['aɪrənɪ] *n* व्यंग्य

irregular [ɪ'rɛgjʊlə] *adj* अनियमित

irrelevant [ɪ'rɛləvənt] *adj* असंबद्ध

irresponsible [ˌɪrɪ'spɒnsəbl] *adj* गैरज़िम्मेदार

irritable ['ɪrɪtəbl] *adj* चिड़चिड़ा

irritating ['ɪrɪˌteɪtɪŋ] *adj* चिढ़ दिलाने वाला

Islam ['ɪzlɑːm] *n* इस्लाम

Islamic [ɪz'lɑːmɪk] *adj* इस्लामी

island ['aɪlənd] *n* द्वीप

isolated ['aɪsəˌleɪtɪd] *adj* पृथक

ISP [aɪ ɛs piː] *abbr* इंटरनेट सेवा प्रदाता

Israel ['ɪzreɪəl] *n* इज़राइल

Israeli [ɪz'reɪlɪ] *adj* इज़राइली ▷ *n* इज़राइली

issue ['ɪʃjuː] *n* मुद्दा ▷ *vt* जारी करना

IT [aɪ tiː] *abbr* सूचना प्रौद्योगिकी

it [ɪt] *pron* यह/वह
Italian [ɪ'tæljən] *adj* इतालवी ▷ *n (person)* इतालवी; *(language)* इतालवी
Italy ['ɪtəlɪ] *n* इटली
itch [ɪtʃ] *vi* खुजली होना
itchy ['ɪtʃɪ] *adj (informal)* खुजली वाली
item ['aɪtəm] *n* वस्तु/मद
itinerary [aɪ'tɪnərərɪ] *n* यात्रा योजना
its [ɪts] *det* इसका/उसका
itself [ɪt'sɛlf] *pron* खुद
ivory ['aɪvərɪ] *n* हाथीदांत
ivy ['aɪvɪ] *n* एक प्रकार की लता

j

jab [dʒæb] *n* इंजेक्शन
jack [dʒæk] *n* भारी बोझ उठाने का यंत्र
jacket ['dʒækɪt] *n* जैकेट
jacket potato ['dʒækɪt pə'teɪtəʊ] *n* छिलका सहित भुना आलू
jackpot ['dʒæk,pɒt] *n* बड़ा ईनाम
jail [dʒeɪl] *n* कारागार ▷ *vt* जेल में डालना
jam [dʒæm] *n* जैम
Jamaican [dʒə'meɪkən] *adj* जमाइका से संबद्ध ▷ *n* जमाइका - निवासी
jam jar [dʒæm dʒɑː] *n* जैम का मर्तबान
jammed [dʒæmd] *adj* ठसाठस भरा हुआ
janitor ['dʒænɪtə] *n* दरबान
January ['dʒænjʊərɪ] *n* जनवरी
Japan [dʒə'pæn] *n* जापान
Japanese [,dʒæpə'niːz] *adj* जापानी ▷ *n (people)* जापानी; *(language)* जापानी
jar [dʒɑː] *n* मर्तबान
jaundice ['dʒɔːndɪs] *n* पीलिया/पांडुरोग
javelin ['dʒævlɪn] *n* भाला
jaw [dʒɔː] *n* जबड़ा
jazz [dʒæz] *n* जैज़ - एक संगीत शैली
jealous ['dʒɛləs] *adj* ईर्ष्यालु
jeans [dʒiːnz] *npl* जीन्स

Jehovah's Witness [dʒɪ'həʊvəz 'wɪtnəs] *n* एक धार्मिक संस्था के सदस्य
jelly ['dʒɛlɪ] *n* जेली
jellyfish ['dʒɛlɪˌfɪʃ] *n* जेलीफ़िश
jersey ['dʒɜːzɪ] *n (old-fashioned)* जर्सी
Jesus ['dʒiːzəs] *n* ईसा मसीह
jet [dʒɛt] *n* जेट जहाज
jetlag ['dʒɛtlæg] *n* हवाई यात्रा के बाद होने वाली थकान
jetty ['dʒɛtɪ] *n* घाट
Jew [dʒuː] *n* यहूदी
jewel ['dʒuːəl] *n (precious stone)* रत्न; *(item of jewellery)* आभूषण/गहना
jeweller ['dʒuːələ] *n (person)* जौहरी; ['dʒuːələz] *n (shop)* जौहरी बाज़ार
jewellery ['dʒuːəlrɪ] *n* गहना
Jewish ['dʒuːɪʃ] *adj* यहूदी
jigsaw ['dʒɪgˌsɔː] *n* जिग्सॉ पहेली
job [dʒɒb] *n* नौकरी
job centre [dʒɒb 'sɛntə] *n* रोज़गार केंद्र
jobless ['dʒɒblɪs] *adj* बेरोज़गार
jockey ['dʒɒkɪ] *n* घुड़दौड़ का घुड़सवार
jog [dʒɒg] *vi* धीरे दौड़ना
jogging ['dʒɒgɪŋ] *n* कसरत के लिए धीमी दौड़
join [dʒɔɪn] *v (link)* जोड़ना; *(become a member of)* शामिल होना
joiner ['dʒɔɪnə] *n* बढ़ई
joint [dʒɔɪnt] *adj* संयुक्त ▷ *n (join)* जोड़; *(meat)* मांस का बड़ा टुकड़ा
joint account [dʒɔɪnt ə'kaʊnt] *n* संयुक्त खाता
joke [dʒəʊk] *n* मज़ाक ▷ *vi* मज़ाक करना
jolly ['dʒɒlɪ] *adj* विनोदी
Jordan ['dʒɔːdn] *n* जॉर्डन
Jordanian [dʒɔː'deɪnɪən] *adj* जॉर्डन से संबद्ध ▷ *n* जॉर्डन निवासी
jot down [dʒɒt daʊn] *v* संक्षेप में लिखना
jotter ['dʒɒtə] *n* छोटी कापी

journalism ['dʒɜːnˌlɪzəm] *n* पत्रकारिता
journalist ['dʒɜːnlɪst] *n* पत्रकार
journey ['dʒɜːnɪ] *n* यात्रा
joy [dʒɔɪ] *n* आनंद
joystick ['dʒɔɪˌstɪk] *n* जॉयस्टिक
judge [dʒʌdʒ] *n* न्यायाधीश ▷ *vt* निर्णय करना
judo ['dʒuːdəʊ] *n* जूडो
jug [dʒʌg] *n* जग
juggler ['dʒʌglə] *n* बाज़ीगर
juice [dʒuːs] *n* रस
July [dʒuː'laɪ] *n* जुलाई
jumbo jet ['dʒʌmbəʊ dʒɛt] *n* बड़ा जेट हवाईजहाज
jump [dʒʌmp] *v* कूदना
jumper ['dʒʌmpə] *n* कुर्ती
jump leads [dʒʌmp liːdz] *npl* जंप लीड्स
junction ['dʒʌŋkʃən] *n* जंक्शन
June [dʒuːn] *n* जून
jungle ['dʒʌŋgl] *n* जंगल
junior ['dʒuːnjə] *adj* कनिष्ठ
junk [dʒʌŋk] *n* कबाड़
junk mail [dʒʌŋk meɪl] *n* जंक मेल
jury ['dʒʊərɪ] *n* निर्णायक समिति
just [dʒəst] *adv* अभी-अभी
justice ['dʒʌstɪs] *n* न्याय
justify ['dʒʌstɪˌfaɪ] *vt* उचित सिद्ध करना

k

kangaroo [ˌkæŋgə'ruː] *n* कंगारू
karaoke [ˌkaːrə'əʊkɪ] *n* संगीत की धुन के साथ गाना
karate [kə'raːtɪ] *n* कराटे
Kazakhstan [ˌkaːzaːk'stæn] *n* कज़ाकिस्तान
kebab [kə'bæb] *n* कबाब
keen [kiːn] *adj* उत्सुक
keep [kiːp] *v* *(stay in a particular condition)* बनाए रखना ▷ *vi* *(stay in a particular position)* रहना ▷ *vt* *(continue)* जारी रखना/करते रहना; *(store)* रखना
keep-fit ['kiːpˌfɪt] *n* व्यायाम

keep out [kiːp aʊt] *v* बचना
keep up [kiːp ʌp] *v* बराबरी पर रहना
kennel ['kɛnl] *n* कुत्ता घर
Kenya ['kɛnjə] *n* केन्या
Kenyan ['kɛnjən] *adj* केन्याई ▷ *n* केन्याई
kerb [kɜːb] *n* सड़क और फुटपाथ को अलग करने वाली पटरी
kerosene ['kɛrəˌsiːn] *n* *(US)* मिट्टी का तेल
ketchup ['kɛtʃəp] *n* चटनी
kettle ['kɛtl] *n* केतली
key [kiː] *n* *(computer, instrument)* कुंजी; *(for lock)* चाबी
keyboard ['kiːˌbɔːd] *n* कीबोर्ड
keyring ['kiːˌrɪŋ] *n* चाबी का छल्ला
kick [kɪk] *n* लात/ पद प्रहार ▷ *v* लात मारना
kick off [kɪk ɒf] *v* आरंभ करना
kick-off ['kɪkɒf] *n* आरंभ
kid [kɪd] *n* *(informal)* बच्चा ▷ *vi* *(informal)* मज़ाक करना
kidnap ['kɪdnæp] *vt* अपहरण करना
kidney ['kɪdnɪ] *n* गुर्दा
kill [kɪl] *v* मार डालना
killer ['kɪlə] *n* हत्यारा
kilo ['kiːləʊ] *n* किलो
kilometre [kɪ'lɒmɪtə] *n* किलोमीटर
kilt [kɪlt] *n* स्कर्ट
kind [kaɪnd] *adj* दयालु ▷ *n* प्रकार
kindly ['kaɪndlɪ] *adv* दयापूर्वक
kindness ['kaɪndnɪs] *n* दयालुता
king [kɪŋ] *n* राजा
kingdom ['kɪŋdəm] *n* राज्य
kingfisher ['kɪŋˌfɪʃə] *n* रामचिरैया
kiosk ['kiːɒsk] *n* छोटी दुकान
kipper ['kɪpə] *n* सुखाई गई मछली
kiss [kɪs] *n* चुंबन ▷ *v* चूमना
kit [kɪt] *n* उपकरण समूह
kitchen ['kɪtʃɪn] *n* रसोईघर
kite [kaɪt] *n* पतंग
kitten ['kɪtn] *n* बिलौटा
kiwi ['kiːwiː] *n* कीवी फ़्रूट - एक फल
km/h *abbr* किलोमीटर प्रति घंटा

knee [niː] *n* घुटना
kneecap ['niːˌkæp] *n* घुटने के ऊपर की हड्डी
kneel [niːl] *vi* घुटने टेकना
kneel down [niːl daʊn] *v* घुटने टेकना
knickers ['nɪkəz] *npl* चड्ढी
knife [naɪf] *n* चाकू
knit [nɪt] *v* बुनना
knitting ['nɪtɪŋ] *n* बुनाई
knitting needle ['nɪtɪŋ 'niːdl] *n* बुनने की सलाई
knob [nɒb] *n* घुंडी
knock [nɒk] *n* दस्तक ▷ *vi* दस्तक देना
knock down [nɒk daʊn] *v* ढहा देना
knock out [nɒk aʊt] *v* बेहोश कर देना
knot [nɒt] *n* गांठ
know [nəʊ] *vt (fact)* जानना; *(person)* जानना
know-all ['nəʊɔːl] *n (informal)* सर्वज्ञ
know-how ['nəʊˌhaʊ] *n (informal)* तकनीक की जानकारी
knowledge ['nɒlɪdʒ] *n* ज्ञान
knowledgeable ['nɒlɪdʒəbl] *adj* ज्ञानवान
known [nəʊn] *adj* ज्ञात
Koran [kɔː'rɑːn] *n* कुरान
Korea [kə'riːə] *n* कोरिया
Korean [kə'riːən] *adj* कोरियाई ▷ *n (person)* कोरियाई; *(language)* कोरियाई
kosher ['kəʊʃə] *adj* यहूदी धर्म के अनुसार विधिसम्मत
Kosovo ['kɒsəvəʊ] *n* कोसोवो
Kuwait [kʊ'weɪt] *n* कुवैत
Kuwaiti [kʊ'weɪtɪ] *adj* कुवैत से संबद्ध ▷ *n* कुवैती नागरिक
Kyrgyzstan ['kɪəgɪzˌstɑːn] *n* किर्गिज़स्तान

l

lab [læb] *n* प्रयोगशाला
label ['leɪbl] *n* चिप्पी/सूचक पत्र
laboratory [lə'bɒrətərɪ] *n* प्रयोगशाला

labour ['leɪbə] *n* श्रम
labourer ['leɪbərə] *n* मज़दूर
lace [leɪs] *n (cloth)* लेस/जालीदार गोटा; *(shoelace)* जूते का फीता
lack [læk] *n* कमी
lacquer ['lækə] *n* रोग़न
lad [læd] *n (informal)* लड़का
ladder ['lædə] *n* सीढ़ी
ladies ['leɪdɪz] *n* शौचालय
ladle ['leɪdl] *n* करछुल
lady ['leɪdɪ] *n* महिला
ladybird ['leɪdɪˌbɜːd] *n* एक प्रकार का गुबरैला
lag behind [læg bɪ'haɪnd] *vi* पीछे होना
lager ['lɑːgə] *n* एक प्रकार की मदिरा
lagoon [lə'guːn] *n* अनूप झील
laid-back ['leɪdbæk] *adj (informal)* शांत/निश्चिंत
lake [leɪk] *n* झील
lakh [lɑːk] *n (100,000)* लाख
lamb [læm] *n* मेमना
lame [leɪm] *adj* लंगड़ा
lamp [læmp] *n* दीपक/कंदील
lamppost ['læmpˌpəʊst] *n* दीपस्तंभ
lampshade ['læmpˌʃeɪd] *n* लैंपशेड
land [lænd] *n* भूमि ▷ *v* ज़मीन पर उतरना
landing ['lændɪŋ] *n* सीढ़ी का ऊपरी हिस्सा
landlady ['lændˌleɪdɪ] *n* मकान मालकिन
landlord ['lændˌlɔːd] *n* मकान मालिक
landmark ['lændˌmɑːk] *n* थल चिह्न
landowner ['lændˌəʊnə] *n* ज़मींदार
landscape ['lændˌskeɪp] *n* प्राकृतिक दृश्य
landslide ['lændˌslaɪd] *n* भू - स्खलन
lane [leɪn] *n* गली
language ['læŋgwɪdʒ] *n* भाषा
language laboratory ['læŋgwɪdʒ lə'bɒrətərɪ] *n* भाषाएं सीखने की कक्षा
language school ['læŋgwɪdʒ skuːl] *n* विदेशी भाषा सिखाने वाला विद्यालय
lanky ['læŋkɪ] *adj* लंबा और पतला

Laos [laʊz] *n* लाओस
lap [læp] *n* गोद
laptop ['læp,tɒp] *n* लैपटॉप
larder ['lɑːdə] *n* भंडारगृह
large [lɑːdʒ] *adj* बड़ा
largely ['lɑːdʒlɪ] *adv* बड़े पैमाने पर
laryngitis [,lærɪn'dʒaɪtɪs] *n* कंठशोथ
laser ['leɪzə] *n* लेज़र
lass [læs] *n* लड़की
last [lɑːst] *adj (previous)* पिछला ▹ *adv* आखिर में ▹ *v* कायम रहना/चलना ▹ *adj (coming after all others)* अंतिम
lastly ['lɑːstlɪ] *adv* आखिरकार
late [leɪt] *adj (after the proper time)* विलंबित; *(dead)* स्वर्गीय ▹ *adv* विलंब से; *(near the end)* देर गए
lately ['leɪtlɪ] *adv* हाल में
later ['leɪtə] *adv* बाद में
Latin ['lætɪn] *n* लैटिन
Latin America ['lætɪn ə'mɛrɪkə] *n* लैटिन अमरीका
Latin American ['lætɪn ə'mɛrɪkən] *adj* लैटिन अमरीकी
latitude ['lætɪ,tjuːd] *n* अक्षांश
Latvia ['lætvɪə] *n* लातविया
Latvian ['lætvɪən] *adj* लातवियाई ▹ *n (person)* लातवियाई; *(language)* लातवियाई
laugh [lɑːf] *n* हंसी ▹ *vi* हंसना
laughter ['lɑːftə] *n* हंसी
launch [lɔːntʃ] *vt* प्रक्षेपित करना
Launderette® [,lɔːndə'rɛt] *n* पैसे देकर मशीन से खुद कपड़े धोने की जगह
laundry ['lɔːndrɪ] *n* मैले कपड़े/धुले कपड़े
lava ['lɑːvə] *n* लावा
lavatory ['lævətərɪ] *n* शौचालय
lavender ['lævəndə] *n* लैवेंडर - फूल का पौधा
law [lɔː] *n* कानून
lawn [lɔːn] *n* घास का मैदान
lawnmower ['lɔːn,məʊə] *n* घास काटने की मशीन
law school [lɔː skuːl] *n* विधि विद्यालय
lawyer ['lɔːjə] *n* वकील

laxative ['læksətɪv] *n* रेचक औषधि

lay [leɪ] *vt (put down)* रखना; *(egg)* अंडे देना

layby ['leɪ,baɪ] *n* सड़क के किनारे गाड़ियों के रुकने की जगह

layer ['leɪə] *n* परत

lay off [leɪ ɒf] *v* निकाल देना

layout ['leɪ,aʊt] *n* खाका/अभिन्यास

lazy ['leɪzɪ] *adj* आलसी

lead [lɛd] *n (metal)* सीसा; [liːd] *n (in a play or film)* मुख्य भूमिका; *(in a race or competition)* आगे होना ▷ *vt* नेतृत्व करना/ले जाना

leader ['liːdə] *n* नेता

lead-free [,lɛd'friː] *adj* सीसा - रहित

lead singer [liːd 'sɪŋə] *n* मुख्य गायक

leaf [liːf] *n* पत्ती

leaflet ['liːflɪt] *n* पत्रक/पुस्तिका

league [liːg] *n* गुट

leak [liːk] *n* रिसाव ▷ *vi* रिसना

lean [liːn] *vi* झुकना/टेक लगाना

lean forward [liːn 'fɔːwəd] *v* आगे झुकना

lean on [liːn ɒn] *v* निर्भर होना

lean out [liːn aʊt] *v* बाहर झांकना

leap [liːp] *vi* छलांग मारना

leap year [liːp jɪə] *n* अधिवर्ष

learn [lɜːn] *v* सीखना

learner ['lɜːnə] *n* सीखने वाला

learner driver ['lɜːnə 'draɪvə] *n* नौसिखिया चालक

lease [liːs] *n* पट्टा/ठेका ▷ *vt* पट्टे/ठेके पर देना

least [liːst] *adj* लघुतम

leather ['lɛðə] *n* चमड़ा

leave [liːv] *n* अवकाश ▷ *v (place)* विदा होना/प्रस्थान करना ▷ *vt (let remain somewhere)* छोड़ना

leave out [liːv aʊt] *v* छोड़ना

Lebanese [,lɛbə'niːz] *adj* लेबनानी ▷ *n* लेबनानी

Lebanon ['lɛbənən] *n* लेबनान

lecture ['lɛktʃə] *n* व्याख्यान ▷ *vi* व्याख्यान देना
lecturer ['lɛktʃərə] *n* व्याख्याता
leek [liːk] *n* प्याज जैसी एक सब्ज़ी
left [lɛft] *adj* बचा हुआ/ अधिशेष ▷ *adv* बाएं ▷ *n* बायां भाग
left-hand [ˌlɛft'hænd] *adj* बायां
left-hand drive ['lɛftˌhænd draɪv] *n* बाईं तरफ़ के स्टीअरिंग व्हील वाली गाड़ी
left-handed [ˌlɛft'hændɪd] *adj* बांए हत्था/बांए हाथ से काम करने वाला
left luggage [lɛft 'lʌgɪdʒ] *n* रखा गया सामान
left-luggage office [ˌlɛft'lʌgɪdʒ 'ɒfɪs] *n* सामान रखने का कार्यालय
leftovers ['lɛftˌəʊvəz] *npl* अवशिष्ट भोजन
left-wing ['lɛftˌwɪŋ] *adj* वाम - पंथी
leg [lɛg] *n (person, animal)* टांग/पैर; *(table, chair)* पाया/ गोड़ा
legal ['liːgl] *adj* कानूनी
legend ['lɛdʒənd] *n* किंवदंती/दंतकथा
leggings ['lɛgɪŋz] *npl* चुस्त पतलून
legible ['lɛdʒəbl] *adj* स्पष्ट
legislation [ˌlɛdʒɪs'leɪʃən] *n (formal)* कानून
leisure ['lɛʒə] *n* फ़ुर्सत
leisure centre ['lɛʒə 'sɛntə] *n* अवकाश केंद्र
lemon ['lɛmən] *n* नींबू
lemonade [ˌlɛmə'neɪd] *n* नींबू का शर्बत/शिकंजी
lend [lɛnd] *vt* ऋण देना
length [lɛŋkθ] *n* लंबाई
lens [lɛnz] *n* लेंस
Lent [lɛnt] *n* उपवास
lentils ['lɛntɪlz] *npl* दाल
Leo ['liːəʊ] *n* सिंह राशि
leopard ['lɛpəd] *n* तेंदुआ
leotard ['lɪəˌtaːd] *n* एक प्रकार का चुस्त वस्त्र
less [lɛs] *adv* कम ▷ *pron* कम ▷ *adj* कम
lesson ['lɛsn] *n* पाठ
let [lɛt] *vt* अनुमति देना
let down [lɛt daʊn] *v* निराश करना

let in [lɛt ɪn] *v* आने देना
letter ['lɛtə] *n* *(alphabet)* अक्षर; *(message)* पत्र
letterbox ['lɛtəˌbɒks] *n* चिठ्ठी डालने का बक्सा
lettuce ['lɛtɪs] *n* सलाद का पत्ता
leukaemia [luːˈkiːmɪə] *n* रक्त कैंसर
level ['lɛvl] *adj* समस्तर ▷ *n* स्तर
level crossing ['lɛvl 'krɒsɪŋ] *n* रेल - चौपड़
lever ['liːvə] *n* उत्तोलक
liar ['laɪə] *n* झूठा
liberal ['lɪbərəl] *adj* उदार
liberation [ˌlɪbə'reɪʃən] *n* आज़ादी
Liberia [laɪ'bɪərɪə] *n* लाइबेरिया
Liberian [laɪ'bɪərɪən] *adj* लाइबेरियाई ▷ *n* लाइबेरियाई
Libra ['liːbrə] *n* तुला राशि
librarian [laɪ'brɛərɪən] *n* पुस्तकालयाध्यक्ष
library ['laɪbrərɪ] *n* पुस्तकालय
Libya ['lɪbɪə] *n* लीबिया
Libyan ['lɪbɪən] *adj* लीबियाई ▷ *n* लीबियाई
lice [laɪs] *npl* जूं
licence ['laɪsəns] *n* लाइसेंस/अधिकार पत्र
lick [lɪk] *vt* चाटना
lid [lɪd] *n* ढक्कन
lie [laɪ] *n* झूठ ▷ *vi* लेटना
Liechtenstein ['lɪktənˌstaɪn] *n* लिक्टेंस्टीन
lie-in ['laɪɪn] *n* *(informal)* लंबी नींद
lieutenant [lɛf'tɛnənt] *n* लेफ़्टिनेंट
life [laɪf] *n* जीवन
lifebelt ['laɪfˌbɛlt] *n* जीवन रक्षक पेटी
lifeboat ['laɪfˌbəʊt] *n* जीवन रक्षा नौका
lifeguard ['laɪfˌgɑːd] *n* जीवन रक्षक गार्ड
life jacket [laɪf 'dʒækɪt] *n* जीवन रक्षक जैकैट
life-saving ['laɪfˌseɪvɪŋ] *adj* जीवन रक्षक
lifestyle ['laɪfˌstaɪl] *n* जीवन शैली

lift [lɪft] *n (in car)* मुफ़्त सवारी देना; *(in a tall building)* लिफ़्ट ▷ *vt* उठाना
light [laɪt] *adj (weighing little)* हल्का; *(bright)* प्रकाशमय/उजाला ▷ *n (sun)* प्रकाश ▷ *vt* जलाना ▷ *n (lamp)* प्रकाश ▷ *adj (pale)* हल्का
light bulb [laɪt bʌlb] *n* बिजली का लट्टू
lighter ['laɪtə] *n* लाइटर
lighthouse ['laɪt,haʊs] *n* प्रकाश स्तंभ
lighting ['laɪtɪŋ] *n* प्रकाश व्यवस्था
lightning ['laɪtnɪŋ] *n* तड़ित
like [laɪk] *prep* के समान ▷ *vt (enjoy)* पसंद करना ▷ *v (be)* सदृश/जैसा
likely ['laɪklɪ] *adj* संभाव्य
lilac ['laɪlək] *adj* हल्के बैंगनी-गुलाबी रंग का ▷ *n* बकाइन का पेड़
lily ['lɪlɪ] *n* नरगिस/कुमुदिनी
lily of the valley ['lɪlɪ əv ðə 'vælɪ] *n* कुमुदिनी
lime [laɪm] *n (fruit)* नींबू; *(substance)* चूना
limestone ['laɪm,stəʊn] *n* चूना पत्थर
limit ['lɪmɪt] *n* हद
limousine ['lɪmə,ziːn] *n* लिमोज़ीन - एक कार
limp [lɪmp] *vi* लंगड़ाना
line [laɪn] *n* रेखा
linen ['lɪnɪn] *n* अलसी के रेशों से बना कपड़ा
liner ['laɪnə] *n* बड़ा यात्री जलयान
linguist ['lɪŋgwɪst] *n* भाषाविद्
linguistic [lɪŋ'gwɪstɪk] *adj* भाषा संबंधी
lining ['laɪnɪŋ] *n* अस्तर
link [lɪŋk] *n* संबंध ▷ *vt* जोड़ना
lino ['laɪnəʊ] *n* फ़र्श पर बिछाने का आच्छादन
lion ['laɪən] *n* शेर
lioness ['laɪənɪs] *n* शेरनी
lip [lɪp] *n* होंठ
lip-read ['lɪp,riːd] *vi* होंठों के गति से बात समझने की कला
lip salve [lɪp sælv] *n* होंठ पर लगाने की क्रीम
lipstick ['lɪp,stɪk] *n* होंठलाली

liqueur [lɪ'kjʊə] *n* शराब
liquid ['lɪkwɪd] *n* तरल
liquidizer ['lɪkwɪˌdaɪzə] *n* मिक्सी
list [lɪst] *n* सूची ▷ *vt* सूचीबद्ध करना
listen ['lɪsn] *vi (pay attention)* ध्यान से सुनना; *(take heed)* ध्यान से सुनना
listener ['lɪsnə] *n* श्रोता
literally ['lɪtərəlɪ] *adv* वस्तुतः
literature ['lɪtərɪtʃə] *n* साहित्य
Lithuania [ˌlɪθjʊ'eɪnɪə] *n* लिथुआनिया
Lithuanian [ˌlɪθjʊ'eɪnɪən] *adj* लिथुआनियाई ▷ *n (person)* लिथुआनियाई; *(language)* लिथुआनियाई
litre ['liːtə] *n* लीटर
litter ['lɪtə] *n (rubbish)* कूड़ा; *(animals)* पशुओं के एक साथ पैदा हुए बच्चे
litter bin ['lɪtə bɪn] *n* कूड़ादान
little ['lɪtl] *adj* छोटा
live [laɪv] *adj* जीवित ▷ [lɪv] *vi (dwell)* रहना; *(be alive)* जीना/जीवित रहना
lively ['laɪvlɪ] *adj* जीवंत
live on [lɪv ɒn] *v* पर गुज़ारा करना
liver ['lɪvə] *n* यकृत
living ['lɪvɪŋ] *n* आजीविका
living room ['lɪvɪŋ rʊm] *n* बैठक
lizard ['lɪzəd] *n* छिपकली
load [ləʊd] *n* बोझ ▷ *vt* लादना
loaf [ləʊf] *n* पावरोटी
loan [ləʊn] *n* उधार ▷ *vt* उधार देना
loathe [ləʊð] *vt* घृणा करना
lobster ['lɒbstə] *n* केकड़ा
local ['ləʊkl] *adj* स्थानीय
local anaesthetic ['ləʊkl ˌænɪs'θɛtɪk] *n* शरीर के कुछ हिस्से को चेतनाशून्य करने वाली औषधि
location [ləʊ'keɪʃən] *n* स्थान
lock [lɒk] *n (on door)* ताला; *(hair)* लट ▷ *vt* ताला लगाना
locker ['lɒkə] *n* तिजोरी/छोटी आलमारी
locket ['lɒkɪt] *n* लॉकेट
lock out [lɒk aʊt] *v* ताला लगाकर बाहर कर देना

locksmith ['lɒk,smɪθ] *n* ताला बनाने वाला
lodger ['lɒdʒə] *n* किराएदार
loft [lɒft] *n* टाँड़/अटारी
log [lɒg] *n* कुंदा
logical ['lɒdʒɪkl] *adj* तर्कसंगत
log in [lɒg ɪn] *v* लॉग - इन
logo ['ləʊgəʊ] *n* प्रतीक चिह्न
log out [lɒg aʊt] *v* लॉग - आउट
lollipop ['lɒlɪ,pɒp] *n* लॉलीपॉप
lolly ['lɒlɪ] *n* लॉलीपॉप
London ['lʌndən] *n* लंदन
loneliness ['ləʊnlɪnɪs] *n* अकेलापन
lonely ['ləʊnlɪ] *adj* अकेला
lonesome ['ləʊnsəm] *adj* अकेला
long [lɒŋ] *adj (in time)* लंबा ▹ *adv* दीर्घ समय तक ▹ *v* चाहना ▹ *adj (in distance)* लंबा
longer ['lɒŋgə] *adv* अधिक समय के लिए
longitude ['lɒndʒɪ,tjuːd] *n* देशांतर
long jump [lɒŋ dʒʌmp] *n* लंबी कूद
loo [luː] *n (informal)* शौचालय
look [lʊk] *n* दृष्टि ▹ *vi (regard)* देखना ▹ *v (appear)* दिखाई देना
look after [lʊk 'ɑːftə] *v* देखभाल करना
look at [lʊk æt] *vi* पर नज़र फेरना
look for [lʊk fɔː] *v* ढूंढना
look round [lʊk raʊnd] *v* चारों ओर देखना
look up [lʊk ʌp] *v* खोजना
loose [luːs] *adj (not fixed)* शिथिल/ढीला; *(baggy)* ढीला
lorry ['lɒrɪ] *n* मालवाहक गाड़ी
lorry driver ['lɒrɪ 'draɪvə] *n* मालवाहक गाड़ी का चालक
lose [luːz] *v* हारना ▹ *vt (misplace)* खो देना
loser ['luːzə] *n* पराजित
loss [lɒs] *n* नुकसान
lost [lɒst] *adj* गुम
lot [lɒt] *n* ढेर सारा
lotion ['ləʊʃən] *n* मलहम
lottery ['lɒtərɪ] *n* लॉटरी
loud [laʊd] *adj* तीव्र

loudly ['laʊdlɪ] *adv* ऊंचे स्वर में

loudspeaker [ˌlaʊd'spiːkə] *n* भोंपू

lounge [laʊndʒ] *n* बैठक

lousy ['laʊzɪ] *adj (informal)* खराब

love [lʌv] *n* प्रेम ▷ *vt (care about)* प्यार करना; *(enjoy)* पसंद करना

lovely ['lʌvlɪ] *adj* मनोहर/सुंदर

low [ləʊ] *adj (in height)* नीचा ▷ *adv* नीचे ▷ *adj (number)* कम/निम्न

low-alcohol ['ləʊˌælkəhɒl] *adj* हल्का मादक द्रव्य

lower ['ləʊə] *adj* निचला ▷ *vt* झुकाना/नीचे करना

low-fat ['ləʊˌfæt] *adj* कम वसायुक्त

low season [ləʊ 'siːzn] *n* मंदी का मौसम

loyalty ['lɔɪəltɪ] *n* वफ़ादारी

luck [lʌk] *n* भाग्य

luckily ['lʌkɪlɪ] *adv* भाग्यवश

lucky ['lʌkɪ] *adj* भाग्यशाली

lucrative ['luːkrətɪv] *adj* लाभप्रद

luggage ['lʌgɪdʒ] *n* असबाब/सामान

luggage rack ['lʌgɪdʒ ræk] *n* गाड़ी में सामान रखने की जगह

lukewarm [ˌluːk'wɔːm] *adj* गुनगुना

lullaby ['lʌləˌbaɪ] *n* लोरी

lump [lʌmp] *n* ढेला/डली

lunatic ['luːnətɪk] *n (informal)* पागल

lunch [lʌntʃ] *n* दोपहर का भोजन

lunch break [lʌntʃ breɪk] *n* भोजनावकाश

lunchtime ['lʌntʃˌtaɪm] *n* दोपहर के भोजन का समय

lung [lʌŋ] *n* फेफड़ा

lush [lʌʃ] *adj* हरा - भरा

Luxembourg ['lʌksəmˌbɜːg] *n* लक्ज़मबर्ग

luxurious [lʌg'zjʊərɪəs] *adj* विलासमय

luxury ['lʌkʃərɪ] *n* विलासिता

lyrics ['lɪrɪks] *npl* गीत के बोल

mac [mæk] *n* बरसाती कोट

macaroni [ˌmækəˈrəʊnɪ] *npl* मैकरोनी - एक प्रकार का पास्ता

machine [məˈʃiːn] *n* मशीन/यंत्र

machine gun [məˈʃiːn ɡʌn] *n* मशीनगन

machinery [məˈʃiːnərɪ] *n* मशीनरी/यंत्र

machine washable [məˈʃiːn ˈwɒʃəbl] *adj* वॉशिंग मशीन में धोने लायक कपड़े

mackerel [ˈmækrəl] *n* बांगड़ा मछली

mad [mæd] *adj* *(mentally ill)* पागल; *(informal, angry)* क्रुद्ध

Madagascar [ˌmædəˈɡæskə] *n* मेडागास्कर

madam [ˈmædəm] *n* महोदया

madly [ˈmædlɪ] *adv* पागलों की तरह

madman [ˈmædmən] *n* विक्षिप्त

madness [ˈmædnɪs] *n* पागलपन

magazine [ˌmæɡəˈziːn] *n* *(publication)* पत्रिका; *(gun)* मैगज़ीन - पिस्तौल का एक भाग

maggot [ˈmæɡət] *n* भुनगा

magic [ˈmædʒɪk] *adj* जादुई ▷ *n* जादू

magical [ˈmædʒɪkəl] *adj* जादुई

magician [məˈdʒɪʃən] *n* जादूगर

magistrate [ˈmædʒɪˌstreɪt] *n* न्यायाधीश

magnet [ˈmæɡnɪt] *n* चुंबक

magnetic [mæɡˈnɛtɪk] *adj* चुंबकीय

magnificent [mæɡˈnɪfɪsnt] *adj* शानदार

magnifying glass [ˈmæɡnɪfaɪɪŋ ɡlɑːs] *n* आवर्धक लेंस

magpie [ˈmæɡˌpaɪ] *n* मुटरी - एक पक्षी

mahogany [mə'hɒgənɪ] *n* महोगनी - एक प्रकार का लकड़ी
maid [meɪd] *n* नौकरानी
maiden name ['meɪdn neɪm] *n* लड़की का विवाहपूर्व का नाम
mail [meɪl] *n* डाक ▷ *vt* प्रेषित करना
mailing list ['meɪlɪŋ lɪst] *n* डाक प्रेषण सूची
main [meɪn] *adj* मुख्य
main course [meɪn kɔːs] *n* मुख्य भोजन
mainland ['meɪnlənd] *n* मुख्य भूमि
mainly ['meɪnlɪ] *adv* मुख्यतः
main road [meɪn rəʊd] *n* मुख्य मार्ग
maintain [meɪn'teɪn] *vt* बनाए रखना
maintenance ['meɪntɪnəns] *n* रख - रखाव
maize [meɪz] *n* मक्का
majesty ['mædʒɪstɪ] *n* महामहिम
major ['meɪdʒə] *adj* बड़ा/गंभीर
majority [mə'dʒɒrɪtɪ] *n* बहुलता/बड़ा हिस्सा
make [meɪk] *n* निर्माता/ब्रांड ▷ *vt (carry out)* करना; *(create)* बनाना; *(force)* मजबूर करना
makeover ['meɪk,əʊvə] *n* कायापलट
maker ['meɪkə] *n* निर्माता
make up [meɪk ʌp] *v* शामिल होना/बना होना
make-up ['meɪkʌp] *n* श्रृंगार सामग्री
malaria [mə'lɛərɪə] *n* मलेरिया
Malawi [mə'lɑːwɪ] *n* मालावी
Malaysia [mə'leɪzɪə] *n* मलेशिया
Malaysian [mə'leɪzɪən] *adj* मलेशियाई ▷ *n* मलेशियाई नागरिक
male [meɪl] *adj* पुरुष ▷ *n* पुरुष
malicious [mə'lɪʃəs] *adj* द्वेषपूर्ण
malignant [mə'lɪgnənt] *adj* प्राणघातक
malnutrition [,mælnjuː'trɪʃən] *n* कुपोषण

Malta ['mɔːltə] *n* माल्टा
Maltese [mɔːl'tiːz] *adj* माल्टा से संबद्ध ▷ *n (person)* माल्टा का निवासी; *(language)* माल्टा की भाषा
malt whisky [mɔːlt 'wɪskɪ] *n* जौ से बनी शराब
mammal ['mæməl] *n* स्तनधारी प्राणी
mammoth ['mæməθ] *adj* विशाल/वृहद ▷ *n* मैमथ-विशालकाय प्रागैतिहासिक हाथी
man [mæn] *n* मर्द
manage ['mænɪdʒ] *vt* प्रबंधन करना
manageable ['mænɪdʒəbl] *adj* संभालने लायक
management ['mænɪdʒmənt] *n* प्रबंधन
manager ['mænɪdʒə] *n* प्रबंधक
manageress [ˌmænɪdʒə'rɛs] *n* महिला मैनेजर
managing director ['mænɪdʒɪŋ dɪ'rɛktə] *n* प्रबंध निदेशक
mandarin ['mændərɪn] *n (person in influential job)* उच्चाधिकारी; *(fruit)* छोटा संतरा
mangetout [ˌmɑ̃ʒ'tuː] *n* एक तरह का मटर
mango ['mæŋgəʊ] *n* आम
mania ['meɪnɪə] *n* सनक/धुन
maniac ['meɪnɪˌæk] *n* सनकी/उन्मत्त
manicure ['mænɪˌkjʊə] *n* नख-प्रसाधन ▷ *vt* नख प्रसाधन करना
manipulate [mə'nɪpjʊˌleɪt] *vt* चालाकी से काम निकालना
mankind [ˌmæn'kaɪnd] *n* मानव जाति
man-made ['mænˌmeɪd] *adj* मानव-निर्मित
manner ['mænə] *n* तरीका
manners ['mænəz] *npl* शिष्टाचार
manpower ['mænˌpaʊə] *n* मानवशक्ति/श्रमशक्ति
mansion ['mænʃən] *n* हवेली
mantelpiece ['mæntlˌpiːs] *n* अग्निकोष्ठ के ऊपर की ताक

manual ['mænjʊəl] *n* निर्देश पुस्तिका

manufacture [ˌmænjʊ'fæktʃə] *vt* निर्माण करना

manufacturer [ˌmænjʊ'fæktʃərə] *n* निर्माता

manure [mə'njʊə] *n* खाद

manuscript ['mænjʊˌskrɪpt] *n* पांडुलिपि

many ['mɛnɪ] *det* कई ▷ *pron* कई

Maori ['maʊrɪ] *adj* माओरी - न्यूज़ीलैंड के मूल निवासियों से संबद्ध ▷ *n* *(person)* माओरी - न्यूज़ीलैंड के मूल निवासी; *(language)* माओरी - न्यूज़ीलैंड के मूल निवासियों की भाषा

map [mæp] *n* मानचित्र

maple ['meɪpl] *n* फरजंज वृक्ष

marathon ['mærəθən] *n* मैराथन - लंबी दौड़

marble ['mɑːbl] *n* संगमरमर

march [mɑːtʃ] *n* प्रयाण ▷ *v* प्रयाण करना

March [mɑːtʃ] *n* मार्च

mare [mɛə] *n* घोड़ी

margarine [ˌmɑːdʒə'riːn] *n* एक प्रकार का मक्खन

margin ['mɑːdʒɪn] *n* अंतर

marigold ['mærɪˌgəʊld] *n* गेंदा

marina [mə'riːnə] *n* छोटा बंदरगाह

marinade [ˌmærɪ'neɪd] *n* मैरिनेड - एक प्रकार का स्वादवर्द्धक मिश्रण ▷ ['mærɪneɪd] *v* स्वादवर्द्धक मिश्रण में मिलाना

marital status ['mærɪtl 'steɪtəs] *n* *(formal)* वैवाहिक स्थिति

maritime ['mærɪˌtaɪm] *adj* समुद्री

marjoram ['mɑːdʒərəm] *n* मरुवा

mark [mɑːk] *n* *(dirty)* दाग़ ▷ *vt* *(write something on)* चिह्नित करना; *(grade)* अंक देना ▷ *n* *(written or drawn shape)* निशान

market ['mɑːkɪt] *n* बाज़ार

marketing ['mɑːkɪtɪŋ] *n* बिक्री विभाग

m

marketplace ['mɑːkɪtˌpleɪs] *n* बाज़ार
market research ['mɑːkɪt rɪ'sɜːtʃ] *n* बाज़ार संबंधी शोध
marmalade ['mɑːməˌleɪd] *n* एक तरह का मुरब्बा
maroon [mə'ruːn] *adj* कत्थई
marriage ['mærɪdʒ] *n* शादी
marriage certificate ['mærɪdʒ sə'tɪfɪkət] *n* विवाह प्रमाणपत्र
married ['mærɪd] *adj* विवाहित
marrow ['mærəʊ] *n* एक तरह का कुम्हड़ा
marry ['mærɪ] *v* विवाह करना
marsh [mɑːʃ] *n* दलदल
martyr ['mɑːtə] *n* शहीद
marvellous ['mɑːvləs] *adj* शानदार
Marxism ['mɑːksɪzəm] *n* मार्क्सवाद
marzipan ['mɑːzɪˌpæn] *n* बादाम की मिठाई
mascara [mæ'skɑːrə] *n* पलकों पर लगाया जाने वाला काजल
masculine ['mæskjʊlɪn] *adj* मर्दाना
mashed potatoes [mæʃt pə'teɪtəʊz] *npl* आलू का भरता
mask [mɑːsk] *n* मुखौटा
masked [mɑːskt] *adj* मुखौटा लगा हुआ
mass [mæs] *n* ढेर
Mass [mæs] *n* ईसाइयों की प्रार्थना सभा
massacre ['mæsəkə] *n* नरसंहार
massive ['mæsɪv] *adj* विशालकाय
mast [mɑːst] *n* मस्तूल
master ['mɑːstə] *n* मालिक ▷ *vt* निपुणता हासिल करना
masterpiece ['mɑːstəˌpiːs] *n* उत्कृष्ट कृति
mat [mæt] *n* चटाई
match [mætʃ] *n (game)* खेल प्रतियोगिता; *(good)* मेल ▷ *v* मेल खाना ▷ *n (matchstick)* माचिस
matching ['mætʃɪŋ] *adj* मेलखाता
mate [meɪt] *n (informal)* दोस्त

material [mə'tɪərɪəl] *n* *(what something is made of)* सामग्री/पदार्थ; *(cloth)* कपड़ा
maternal [mə'tɜːnl] *adj* मातृक
maternity hospital [mə'tɜːnɪtɪ 'hɒspɪtəl] *n* जच्चा अस्पताल/प्रसूति अस्पताल
maternity leave [mə'tɜːnɪtɪ liːv] *n* मातृत्व अवकाश
mathematical [ˌmæθə'mætɪkl] *adj* गणितीय
mathematics [ˌmæθə'mætɪks] *npl* गणित
maths [mæθs] *npl* गणित
matter ['mætə] *n* मामला ▹ *v* महत्व होना
mattress ['mætrɪs] *n* गद्दा
mature [mə'tjʊə] *adj* परिपक्व
mature student [mə'tjʊə 'stjuːdnt] *n* प्रौढ़ विद्यार्थी
Mauritania [ˌmɒrɪ'teɪnɪə] *n* मॉरिटानिया
Mauritius [mə'rɪʃəs] *n* मॉरिशस
mauve [məʊv] *adj* हल्का बैंगनी रंग
maximum ['mæksɪməm] *adj* अधिकतम ▹ *n* अधिकतम राशि या संख्या
May [meɪ] *n* मई
may [meɪ] *v* *(possibly)* हो सकना; *(be allowed to)* कर सकना
maybe ['meɪˌbiː] *adv* शायद
mayonnaise [ˌmeɪə'neɪz] *n* मेयोनीज - तेल व अंडे की ज़र्दी का मिश्रण
mayor [mɛə] *n* महापौर
maze [meɪz] *n* भूलभुलैया
me [miː] *pron* मुझे
meadow ['mɛdəʊ] *n* घास का मैदान
meal [miːl] *n* भोजन
mealtime ['miːlˌtaɪm] *n* भोजनकाल
mean [miːn] *adj* अनुदार/घटिया ▹ *vt* *(signify)* मतलब होना; *(be serious about)* मायने रखना; *(intend)* अभिप्राय रखना/इरादा रखना
meaning ['miːnɪŋ] *n* अर्थ
means [miːnz] *npl* साधन

meantime ['miːnˌtaɪm] *adv* इसी बीच
meanwhile ['miːnˌwaɪl] *adv* इसी दौरान
measles ['miːzəlz] *npl* खसरा
measure ['mɛʒə] *vt* मापना
measurements ['mɛʒəmənts] *npl* माप
meat [miːt] *n* मांस
meatball ['miːtˌbɔːl] *n* कबाब
Mecca ['mɛkə] *n* मक्का
mechanic [mɪ'kænɪk] *n* मशीनों का मिस्त्री
mechanical [mɪ'kænɪkl] *adj* यांत्रिक
mechanism ['mɛkəˌnɪzəm] *n* कलपुर्जा
medal ['mɛdl] *n* पदक
medallion [mɪ'dæljən] *n* पदक
media ['miːdɪə] *npl* संचार माध्यम/मीडिया
mediaeval [ˌmɛdɪ'iːvl] *adj* मध्यकालीन
medical ['mɛdɪkl] *adj* चिकित्सकीय ▷ *n* चिकित्सकीय जांच
medical certificate ['mɛdɪkl sə'tɪfɪkət] *n* चिकित्सकीय प्रमाणपत्र
medicine ['mɛdɪsɪn] *n* दवा
meditation [ˌmɛdɪ'teɪʃən] *n* ध्यान/समाधि
Mediterranean [ˌmɛdɪtə'reɪnɪən] *adj* भूमध्यसागरीय ▷ *n* भूमध्यसागर
medium ['miːdɪəm] *adj* मध्यम
medium-sized ['miːdɪəmˌsaɪzd] *adj* मध्यम आकार का
meet [miːt] *vt* मिलना ▷ *vi* मिल जाना
meeting ['miːtɪŋ] *n* बैठक
meet up [miːt ʌp] *v* भेंट करना
mega ['mɛgə] *adj* *(informal)* बहुत बड़ा
melody ['mɛlədɪ] *n* *(formal)* धुन
melon ['mɛlən] *n* खरबूज/तरबूज
melt [mɛlt] *vt* पिघलाना ▷ *vi* पिघलना
member ['mɛmbə] *n* सदस्य

membership ['mɛmbə,ʃɪp] *n* सदस्यता

membership card ['mɛmbəʃɪp kaːd] *n* सदस्यता पत्र

memento [mɪ'mɛntəʊ] *n* यादगार/निशानी

memo ['mɛməʊ] *n* ज्ञापन

memorial [mɪ'mɔːrɪəl] *n* स्मारक

memorize ['mɛmə,raɪz] *vt* याद करना

memory ['mɛmərɪ] *n* *(ability to remember)* स्मरणशक्ति/याददाश्त; *(reminiscence)* याद/स्मृति

memory card ['mɛmərɪ kaːd] *n* मेमरी कार्ड

mend [mɛnd] *vt* मरम्मत करना

meningitis [,mɛnɪn'dʒaɪtɪs] *n* मस्तिष्क ज्वर

menopause ['mɛnəʊ,pɔːz] *n* रजोनिवृत्ति

menstruation [,mɛnstrʊ'eɪʃən] *n* मासिक धर्म

mental ['mɛntl] *adj* मानसिक

mental hospital ['mɛntl 'hɒspɪtl] *n* मानसिक चिकित्सालय

mentality [mɛn'tælɪtɪ] *n* मानसिकता

mention ['mɛnʃən] *vt* उल्लेख करना

menu ['mɛnjuː] *n* व्यंजन सूची

merchant bank ['mɜːtʃənt bæŋk] *n* वाणिज्य बैंक

mercury ['mɜːkjʊrɪ] *n* पारा

mercy ['mɜːsɪ] *n* दया

mere [mɪə] *adj* मात्र

merge [mɜːdʒ] *v* विलय होना/मिलना

merger ['mɜːdʒə] *n* विलय

meringue [mə'ræŋ] *n* मेरैंग - एक मिष्ठान्न

mermaid ['mɜː,meɪd] *n* जलपरी

merry ['mɛrɪ] *adj (old-fashioned)* खुशदिल/प्रसन्नचित्त

merry-go-round ['mɛrɪgəʊ'raʊnd] *n* हिंडोला

mess [mɛs] *n* गंदगी

mess about [mɛs ə'baʊt] *v* इधर-उधर में समय बिताना

m

message ['mɛsɪdʒ] *n* संदेश
messenger ['mɛsɪndʒə] *n* संदेश वाहक/हरकारा
mess up [mɛs ʌp] *v* *(informal)* बिगाड़ देना
messy ['mɛsɪ] *adj* अस्तव्यस्त
metabolism [mɪ'tæbəˌlɪzəm] *n* चयापचय
metal ['mɛtl] *n* धातु
meteorite ['miːtɪəˌraɪt] *n* उल्का पिंड
meter ['miːtə] *n* मीटर
method ['mɛθəd] *n* विधि
metre ['miːtə] *n* मीटर
metric ['mɛtrɪk] *adj* मात्रिक
Mexican ['mɛksɪkən] *adj* मैक्सिको से संबद्ध ▷ *n* मैक्सिको का नागरिक
Mexico ['mɛksɪˌkəʊ] *n* मैक्सिको
microchip ['maɪkrəʊˌtʃɪp] *n* माइक्रोचिप
microphone ['maɪkrəˌfəʊn] *n* माइक्रोफ़ोन
microscope ['maɪkrəˌskəʊp] *n* सूक्ष्मदर्शी
microwave ['maɪkrəʊˌweɪv] *n* माइक्रोवेव ओवन
mid [mɪd] *adj* मध्यवर्ती
midday ['mɪd'deɪ] *n* मध्याह्न
middle ['mɪdl] *n* मध्य
middle-aged ['mɪdlˌeɪdʒd] *adj* मध्य वयस्क/प्रौढ़
Middle Ages ['mɪdl 'eɪdʒɪz] *npl* मध्य युग
middle-class ['mɪdlˌklɑːs] *adj* मध्यम वर्ग
Middle East ['mɪdl iːst] *n* मध्य पूर्व
midge [mɪdʒ] *n* एक प्रकार का छोटा मच्छर
midnight ['mɪdˌnaɪt] *n* मध्यरात्रि
midwife ['mɪdˌwaɪf] *n* दाई
might [maɪt] *v* हो सकना
migraine ['miːgreɪn] *n* अर्द्धकपारी/अर्ध-कपाली
migrant ['maɪgrənt] *n* खानाबदोश/प्रवासी
migration [maɪ'greɪʃən] *n* प्रवसन
mild [maɪld] *adj* हल्का
mile [maɪl] *n* मीन

mileage ['maɪlɪdʒ] *n* तय की गई दूरी
mileometer [maɪ'lɒmɪtə] *n* माइलोमीटर
military ['mɪlɪtərɪ] *adj* फ़ौज
milk [mɪlk] *n* दूध ▷ *vt* दूध दुहना
milk chocolate [mɪlk 'tʃɒklət] *n* दूध से बना चॉकलेट
milkshake ['mɪlk,ʃeɪk] *n* दूध और फलों से बना पेय
mill [mɪl] *n* चक्की
millennium [mɪ'lɛnɪəm] *n* *(formal)* सहस्राब्दि
millimetre ['mɪlɪ,miːtə] *n* मिलिमीटर
million ['mɪljən] *num* दस लाख
millionaire [,mɪljə'nɛə] *n* लखपति
mimic ['mɪmɪk] *vt* नकल उतारना
mince [mɪns] *n* कीमा
mind [maɪnd] *n* मस्तिष्क ▷ *vt* बुरा मानना/आपत्ति करना
mine [maɪn] *n* खदान/खान ▷ *pron* मेरा
miner ['maɪnə] *n* खनिक
mineral ['mɪnərəl] *adj* *(of minerals)* खनिज ▷ *n* खनिज पदार्थ
mineral water ['mɪnrəl 'wɔːtə] *n* खनिज पदार्थ युक्त पानी
miniature ['mɪnɪtʃə] *adj* लघु ▷ *n* लघु रूप
minibus ['mɪnɪ,bʌs] *n* छोटी बस
minicab ['mɪnɪ,kæb] *n* पहले से तय की गई किराए की टैक्सी
minimal ['mɪnɪməl] *adj* न्यूनतम
minimize ['mɪnɪ,maɪz] *vt* कम करना
minimum ['mɪnɪməm] *adj* कम से कम ▷ *n* कम से कम परिमाण
mining ['maɪnɪŋ] *n* खनन
minister ['mɪnɪstə] *n* *(government)* मंत्री
ministry ['mɪnɪstrɪ] *n* *(government department)* मंत्रालय
mink [mɪŋk] *n* मिंक

minor ['maɪnə] *adj* गौण ▹ *n* नाबालिग
minority [maɪ'nɒrɪtɪ] *n* अल्पसंख्यक
mint [mɪnt] *n (place where coins are made)* टकसाल; *(herb)* पुदीना
minus ['maɪnəs] *prep* घटाव
minute [maɪ'njuːt] *adj* छोटा/बारीक ▹ ['mɪnɪt] *n* मिनट
miracle ['mɪrəkl] *n* चमत्कार
mirror ['mɪrə] *n* दर्पण
misbehave [ˌmɪsbɪ'heɪv] *vi* अभद्र व्यवहार करना
miscarriage [mɪs'kærɪdʒ] *n* गर्भपात
miscellaneous [ˌmɪsə'leɪnɪəs] *adj* विविध
mischief ['mɪstʃɪf] *n* शरारत
mischievous ['mɪstʃɪvəs] *adj* शरारती
miser ['maɪzə] *n* कंजूस
miserable ['mɪzərəbl] *adj* दयनीय
misery ['mɪzərɪ] *n* दयनीयता
misfortune [mɪs'fɔːtʃən] *n* दुर्भाग्य
mishap ['mɪshæp] *n* विपत्ति
misjudge [ˌmɪs'dʒʌdʒ] *vt* गलत समझना
mislay [mɪs'leɪ] *vt* खोना
misleading [mɪs'liːdɪŋ] *adj* बहकाने वाला
misprint ['mɪsˌprɪnt] *n* छापे की गलती
miss [mɪs] *v (fail to catch or to hit)* चूक जाना ▹ *vt (fail to notice)* देखने में असफल/चूकना; *(someone who is absent)* कमी महसूस करना
Miss [mɪs] *n* कुमारी
missile ['mɪsaɪl] *n* प्रक्षेपास्त्र
missing ['mɪsɪŋ] *adj* खोया हुआ
mist [mɪst] *n* कोहरा
mistake [mɪ'steɪk] *n* गलती ▹ *vt* गलती करना
mistaken [mɪ'steɪkən] *adj* गलत समझा हुआ
mistakenly [mɪ'steɪkənlɪ] *adv* गलती से
mistletoe ['mɪslˌtəʊ] *n* अमर बेल
misty ['mɪstɪ] *adj* कोहरे से आच्छादित

misunderstand [ˌmɪsʌndəˈstænd] *v* गलत समझना
misunderstanding [ˌmɪsʌndəˈstændɪŋ] *n* गलतफ़हमी
mitten [ˈmɪtn] *n* एक प्रकार का दस्ताना
mix [mɪks] *n* मिश्रण ▷ *v* मिलाना
mixed [mɪkst] *adj* मिला - जुला
mixed salad [mɪkst ˈsæləd] *n* मिश्रित सलाद
mixer [ˈmɪksə] *n* मिक्सर
mixture [ˈmɪkstʃə] *n* मिश्रण
mix up [mɪks ʌp] *v* पहचानने में गड़बड़ करना
mix-up [ˈmɪksʌp] *n* *(informal)* घपला
MMS [ɛm ɛm ɛs] *abbr* एम एम एस
moan [məʊn] *vi* कराहना
moat [məʊt] *n* खाई
mobile [ˈməʊbaɪl] *n* गतिशील
mobile home [ˈməʊbaɪl həʊm] *n* कारवां/कैरावैन/एक सर्वसुविधासंपन्न गाड़ी
mobile number [ˈməʊbaɪl ˈnʌmbə] *n* मोबाइल नंबर
mobile phone [ˈməʊbaɪl fəʊn] *n* मोबाइल फ़ोन
mock [mɒk] *adj* बनावटी ▷ *vt* चिढ़ाना
mod cons [mɒd kɒnz] *npl* *(informal)* आधुनिक सुविधाएँ
model [ˈmɒdl] *adj* आदर्श ▷ *n* *(replica)* नमूना ▷ *vt* नमूना बनाना ▷ *n* *(mannequin)* मॉडल
modem [ˈməʊdɛm] *n* मोडेम
moderate [ˈmɒdərɪt] *adj* संयमित
moderation [ˌmɒdəˈreɪʃən] *n* संयम
modern [ˈmɒdən] *adj* आधुनिक
modernize [ˈmɒdəˌnaɪz] *vt* आधुनिकीकरण
modern languages [ˈmɒdən ˈlæŋgwɪdʒɪz] *npl* आधुनिक भाषाएँ
modest [ˈmɒdɪst] *adj* विनीत
modification [ˌmɒdɪfɪˈkeɪʃən] *n* सुधार

modify ['mɒdɪˌfaɪ] *vt* सुधारना
module ['mɒdjuːl] *n* भाग
moist [mɔɪst] *adj* नम
moisture ['mɔɪstʃə] *n* नमी
moisturizer ['mɔɪstʃəˌraɪzə] *n* मॉइस्चराइजर
Moldova [mɒl'dəʊvə] *n* मॉल्दोवा
Moldovan [mɒl'dəʊvən] *adj* मॉल्दोवा से संबद्ध ▹ *n* मॉल्दोवा - निवासी
mole [məʊl] *n* *(animal)* छछूंदर; *(person)* भेदिया; *(dark spot)* तिल
molecule ['mɒlɪˌkjuːl] *n* अणु
moment ['məʊmənt] *n* क्षण
momentarily ['məʊməntərəlɪ] *adv* *(written)* पल भर के लिए
momentary ['məʊməntərɪ] *adj* क्षणिक
momentous [məʊ'mɛntəs] *adj* महत्वपूर्ण
Monaco ['mɒnəˌkəʊ; mə'nɑːkəʊ] *n* मौनैको
monarch ['mɒnək] *n* राज
monarchy ['mɒnəkɪ] *n* राजशाही
monastery ['mɒnəstərɪ] *n* मठ
Monday ['mʌndɪ] *n* सोमवार
monetary ['mʌnɪtərɪ] *adj* मुद्रा संबंधी
money ['mʌnɪ] *n* धन
Mongolia [mɒŋ'gəʊlɪə] *n* मंगोलिया
Mongolian [mɒŋ'gəʊlɪən] *adj* मंगोलियाई ▹ *n* *(person)* मंगोलियाई नागरिक; *(language)* मंगोलियाई भाषा
mongrel ['mʌŋgrəl] *n* संकर/दोगला
monitor ['mɒnɪtə] *n* मॉनीटर
monk [mʌŋk] *n* भिक्षु
monkey ['mʌŋkɪ] *n* बंदर
monopoly [mə'nɒpəlɪ] *n* एकाधिकार
monotonous [mə'nɒtənəs] *adj* नीरस/उबाऊ
monsoon [mɒn'suːn] *n* वर्षा ऋतु
monster ['mɒnstə] *n* राक्षस

month [mʌnθ] *n* महीना
monthly ['mʌnθlɪ] *adj* मासिक
monument ['mɒnjʊmənt] *n* स्मारक
mood [muːd] *n* मिजाज़
moody ['muːdɪ] *adj* तुनक मिजाज़
moon [muːn] *n* चंद्रमा
moor [mʊə] *n* बंजर प्रदेश ▷ *v* लंगर डालना
mop [mɒp] *n* पोंछा
moped ['məʊpɛd] *n* मोपेड
mop up [mɒp ʌp] *v* पोंछना
moral ['mɒrəl] *adj* नैतिक ▷ *n* नैतिक मूल्य/नैतिक शिक्षा
morale [mɒ'rɑːl] *n* मनोबल
more [mɔː] *det* ज़्यादा ▷ *adv* और अधिक ▷ *pron* और अधिक
morgue [mɔːg] *n* मुरदाघर
morning ['mɔːnɪŋ] *n* सुबह
morning sickness ['mɔːnɪŋ 'sɪknəs] *n* गर्भावस्था में सुबह के समय आने वाली मिचली
Moroccan [mə'rɒkən] *adj* मोरक्को से संबद्ध ▷ *n* मोरक्को का निवासी
Morocco [mə'rɒkəʊ] *n* मोरक्को
morphine ['mɔːfiːn] *n* अफ़ीम का सत्व-एक दर्दनाशक औषधि
morse code [mɔːs kəʊd] *n* मॉर्स कोड- संदेश प्रेषित करने हेतु कोड
mortar ['mɔːtə] *n (cannon)* मोर्टार- गोले बरसाने वाला एक हथियार; *(for building)* गारा
mortgage ['mɔːgɪdʒ] *n* ऋण ▷ *vt* बंधक रखना/गिरवी रखना
mosaic [mə'zeɪɪk] *n* मोज़ैक-रंगीन काँच के टुकड़ों से बनी डिज़ाइन
Muslim ['mɒzləm] *adj* मुस्लिम ▷ *n* मुस्लिम
mosque [mɒsk] *n* मस्जिद
mosquito [mə'skiːtəʊ] *n* मच्छर
moss [mɒs] *n* काई
most [məʊst] *adj* अधिकतम ▷ *adv* सर्वाधिक ▷ *pron* ज़्यादातर
mostly ['məʊstlɪ] *adv* अधिकतर

m

MOT [ɛm əʊ tiː] *abbr* गाड़ियों की सुरक्षा जाँच हेतु संक्षिप्त रूप
motel [məʊ'tɛl] *n* सराय
moth [mɒθ] *n* शलभ
mother ['mʌðə] *n* माँ
mother-in-law ['mʌðə ɪn lɔː] *n* सास
mother tongue ['mʌðə tʌŋ] *n* मातृभाषा
motionless ['məʊʃənlɪs] *adj* अचल
motivated ['məʊtɪˌveɪtɪd] *adj* प्रेरित
motivation [ˌməʊtɪ'veɪʃən] *n* प्रेरणा
motive ['məʊtɪv] *n* मंशा
motor ['məʊtə] *n* मोटर
motorbike ['məʊtəˌbaɪk] *n* मोटरसाइकिल
motorboat ['məʊtəˌbəʊt] *n* मोटरबोट
motorcycle ['məʊtəˌsaɪkl] *n* मोटरसाइकिल
motorcyclist ['məʊtəˌsaɪklɪst] *n* मोटरसाइकिल चालक
motorist ['məʊtərɪst] *n* मोटर चालक
motor mechanic ['məʊtə mə'kænɪk] *n* मोटर ठीक करने वाला कारीगर
motor racing ['məʊtə 'reɪsɪŋ] *n* मोटर रेस
motorway ['məʊtəˌweɪ] *n* चौड़ा मार्ग
mould [məʊld] *n (shape)* साँचा; *(substance)* फफूँद
mouldy ['məʊldɪ] *adj* फफूँद लगा हुआ
mount [maʊnt] *vt* आयोजित करना
mountain ['maʊntɪn] *n* पर्वत
mountain bike ['maʊntɪn baɪk] *n* मोटे पहियों की साइकिल
mountaineer [ˌmaʊntɪ'nɪə] *n* पर्वतारोही
mountaineering [ˌmaʊntɪ'nɪərɪŋ] *n* पर्वतारोहण
mountainous ['maʊntɪnəs] *adj* पर्वतीय
mount up [maʊnt ʌp] *v* बढ़ना
mourning ['mɔːnɪŋ] *n* मातम/विलाप

mouse [maʊs] *n (animal)* चूहा; *(computer)* माउस
mouse mat [maus mæt] *n* माउस पैड
mousse [muːs] *n* अंडे और मलाई से बना मिष्ठान्न
moustache [mə'stɑːʃ] *n* मूंछ
mouth [maʊθ] *n* मुंह
mouth organ [maʊθ 'ɔːɡən] *n* माउथ ऑर्गन-एक वाद्य
mouthwash ['maʊθ,wɒʃ] *n* माउथ वॉश
move [muːv] *n* कदम ▷ *vt (reposition)* हटाना ▷ *vi (relocate)* हटना/जगह बदलना
move back [muːv bæk] *v* पीछे हटना
move forward [muːv 'fɔːwəd] *v* पहले करना
move in [muːv ɪn] *v* मकान में आकर रहने लगना
movement ['muːvmənt] *n* गति
movie ['muːvɪ] *n (informal)* चलचित्र
moving ['muːvɪŋ] *adj* हृदयविदारक
mow [məʊ] *v* घास काटना
mower ['məʊə] *n* घास काटने की मशीन
Mozambique [,məʊzəm'biːk] *n* मोज़ाम्बिक
MP3 player [,ɛmpiː'θriː 'pleɪə] *n* एम पी थ्री प्लेयर
MP4 player [,ɛmpiː'fɔː 'pleɪə] *n* एम पी फ़ोर प्लेयर
mph [maɪlz pə aʊə] *abbr* मील प्रति घंटा हेतु संक्षिप्त रूप
Mr ['mɪstə] *n* श्री
Mrs ['mɪsɪz] *n* श्रीमती
MS [ɛm ɛs] *abbr* एम.एस
Ms [mɪz] *n* सुश्री
much [mʌtʃ] *det* बहुत ▷ *adv* बहुत अधिक ▷ *pron* बहुत अधिक/ज़्यादा
mud [mʌd] *n* कीचड़
muddle ['mʌdl] *n* उलझन
muddy ['mʌdɪ] *adj* कीचड़ भरा
mudguard ['mʌd,ɡɑːd] *n* मडगार्ड
muesli ['mjuːzlɪ] *n* म्युएसली - अन्न और फलों का मिश्रण

m

muffler [ˈmʌflə] *n (old-fashioned)* गुलुबंद
mug [mʌg] *n* प्याला ▷ *vt* लूटना
mugger [ˈmʌgə] *n* लुटेरा
mugging [ˈmʌgɪŋ] *n* लूट
mule [mjuːl] *n* खच्चर
multinational [ˌmʌltɪˈnæʃənl] *adj* बहुराष्ट्रीय ▷ *n* बहुराष्ट्रीय कंपनी
multiple sclerosis [ˌmʌltɪpəl skləˈrəʊsɪs] *n* बहुसृत काठिन्य
multiplication [ˌmʌltɪplɪˈkeɪʃən] *n* गुणन
multiply [ˈmʌltɪˌplaɪ] *v* वृद्धि करना/वृद्धि होना
mum [mʌm] *n (informal)* माँ
mummy [ˈmʌmɪ] *n (informal) (mother)* माँ; *(preserved dead body)* ममी - सुरक्षित शव
mumps [mʌmps] *n* गलगंड
murder [ˈmɜːdə] *n* हत्या ▷ *vt* हत्या करना
murderer [ˈmɜːdərə] *n* हत्यारा
muscle [ˈmʌsl] *n* मांसपेशी
muscular [ˈmʌskjʊlə] *adj* मांसपेशीय
museum [mjuːˈzɪəm] *n* अजायबघर
mushroom [ˈmʌʃruːm] *n* कुकुरमुत्ता
music [ˈmjuːzɪk] *n* संगीत
musical [ˈmjuːzɪkl] *adj* संगीत संबंधी ▷ *n* संगीतमय
musical instrument [ˈmjuːzɪkl ˈɪnstrəmənt] *n* वाद्य यंत्र
musician [mjuːˈzɪʃən] *n* संगीतकार
Muslim [ˈmʊzlɪm] *adj* मुस्लिम ▷ *n* मुस्लिम
mussel [ˈmʌsl] *n* शंबुक
must [mʌst] *v* आवश्यक होना
mustard [ˈmʌstəd] *n* सरसों का पेस्ट
mutter [ˈmʌtə] *v* बुदबुदाना
mutton [ˈmʌtn] *n* बकरे का मांस
mutual [ˈmjuːtʃʊəl] *adj* पारस्परिक
my [maɪ] *det* अपना/मेरा
Myanmar [ˈmaɪænmɑː] *n* म्यांमार
myself [maɪˈsɛlf] *pron* स्वयं

mysterious [mɪ'stɪərɪəs] *adj* रहस्यमय
mystery ['mɪstərɪ] *n* रहस्य
myth [mɪθ] *n* मिथक
mythology [mɪ'θɒlədʒɪ] *n* पौराणिक कथाएँ

n

naff [næf] *adj (informal)* अपरिष्कृत
nag [næg] *v* किसी काम के लिए पीछे पड़ना
nail [neɪl] *n (metal)* कील; *(finger, toe)* नाखून
nailbrush ['neɪlˌbrʌʃ] *n* नाखून साफ करने का ब्रश
nailfile ['neɪlˌfaɪl] *n* नाखून तराशने का उपकरण
nail polish [neɪl 'pɒlɪʃ] *n* नाखून पॉलिश
nail-polish remover ['neɪlpɒlɪʃ rɪ'muːvə] *n* नाखून पॉलिश छुड़ाने का पदार्थ
nail scissors [neɪl 'sɪzəz] *npl* नख कटनी
naive [naɪ'iːv] *adj* सरलमति/अनुभवहीन
naked ['neɪkɪd] *adj* नग्न
name [neɪm] *n* नाम
nanny ['nænɪ] *n* आया
nap [næp] *n* झपकी
napkin ['næpkɪn] *n* रूमाल
nappy ['næpɪ] *n* लंगोटी
narrow ['nærəʊ] *adj* सँकरा
narrow-minded ['nærəʊ'maɪndɪd] *adj* संकीर्ण मानसिकता वाला
nasty ['nɑːstɪ] *adj* खराब
nation ['neɪʃən] *n* राष्ट्र
national ['næʃənəl] *adj* राष्ट्रीय
national anthem ['næʃənl 'ænθəm] *n* राष्ट्रगान
nationalism ['næʃənəˌlɪzəm] *n* राष्ट्रवाद
nationalist ['næʃənəlɪst] *n* राष्ट्रवादी
nationality [ˌnæʃə'nælɪtɪ] *n* राष्ट्रीयता
nationalize ['næʃənəˌlaɪz] *vt* राष्ट्रीयकरण करना
national park ['næʃənl pɑːk] *n* राष्ट्रीय उद्यान
native ['neɪtɪv] *adj* मूल

n

native speaker ['neɪtɪv 'spiːkə] *n* मूलभाषी
NATO ['neɪtəʊ] *abbr* नाटो - एक संगठन
natural ['nætʃrəl] *adj* स्वाभाविक
natural gas ['nætʃrəl gæs] *n* प्राकृतिक गैस
naturalist ['nætʃrəlɪst] *n* प्रकृतिवादी
naturally ['nætʃrəlɪ] *adv* स्वाभाविक रूप से
natural resources ['nætʃrəl rɪ'zɔːsɪz] *npl* प्राकृतिक संसाधन
nature ['neɪtʃə] *n* प्रकृति
naughty ['nɔːtɪ] *adj* शरारती
nausea ['nɔːzɪə] *n* मतली
naval ['neɪvl] *adj* नौसैनिक
navel ['neɪvl] *n* नाभि
navy ['neɪvɪ] *n* नौसेना ▹ ['neɪvɪ'bluː] *adj* गाढ़ा नीला रंग
NB [ɛn biː] *abbr* ध्यान दीजिए - संक्षिप्त रूप
near [nɪə] *adj* नज़दीक का ▹ *adv* पास से ▹ *prep* पास/समीप
nearby [ˌnɪə'baɪ] *adj* पास वाला ▹ ['nɪəbaɪ] *adv* पास में
nearly ['nɪəlɪ] *adv* लगभग
near-sighted [ˌnɪə'saɪtɪd] *adj (US)* निकट दृष्टि दोष से पीड़ित
neat [niːt] *adj* साफ
neatly ['niːtlɪ] *adv* सफाई से
necessarily ['nɛsɪsərɪlɪ] *adv* अनिवार्य रूप से
necessary ['nɛsɪsərɪ] *adj* आवश्यक
necessity [nɪ'sɛsɪtɪ] *n* आवश्यकता
neck [nɛk] *n* गर्दन
necklace ['nɛklɪs] *n* हार
nectarine ['nɛktərɪn] *n* शफ़तालू
need [niːd] *n* आवश्यकता ▹ *vt* ज़रूरत होना
needle ['niːdl] *n* सूई
negative ['nɛgətɪv] *adj* नकारात्मक ▹ *n* नकारात्मक
neglect [nɪ'glɛkt] *n* उपेक्षा ▹ *vt* उपेक्षा करना
neglected [nɪ'glɛktɪd] *adj* उपेक्षित

negotiate [nɪ'gəʊʃɪˌeɪt] *v* समझौता करना
negotiations [nɪˌgəʊʃɪ'eɪʃənz] *npl* समझौता
negotiator [nɪ'gəʊʃɪˌeɪtə] *n* वार्ताकार
neighbour ['neɪbə] *n* पड़ोसी
neighbourhood ['neɪbəˌhʊd] *n* पड़ोस
neither ['naɪðə; 'niːðə] *conj* न ही ▹ *pron* दोनों में से कोई भी नहीं ▹ *adj* दोनों में से कोई भी नहीं
neither ... nor ['naɪðə; 'niːðə nɔː; nə] *conj* न यह न वह
neon ['niːɒn] *n* निऑन-एक गैस
Nepal [nɪ'pɔːl] *n* नेपाल
nephew ['nɛvjuː] *n* भतीजा/भांजा
nerve [nɜːv] *n (in body)* नस; *(courage)* साहस
nerve-racking ['nɜːv'rækɪŋ] *adj* तनावपूर्ण
nervous ['nɜːvəs] *adj* घबराया हुआ
nest [nɛst] *n* घोंसला
net [nɛt] *n* जाल
netball ['nɛtˌbɔːl] *n* नेटबॉल
Netherlands ['nɛðələndz] *npl* नीदरलैंड
nettle ['nɛtl] *n* बिच्छू - बूटी
network ['nɛtˌwɜːk] *n* तंत्र
neurotic [njʊ'rɒtɪk] *adj* न्यूरोटिक - विक्षिप्त व्यक्ति
neutral ['njuːtrəl] *adj* तटस्थ ▹ *n* न्यूट्रल
never ['nɛvə] *adv* कभी नहीं
nevertheless [ˌnɛvəðə'lɛs] *adv (formal)* तथापि
new [njuː] *adj (that did not exist before)* नया; *(not used before)* नया; *(different)* नया
newborn ['njuːˌbɔːn] *adj* नवजात
newcomer ['njuːˌkʌmə] *n* नवागंतुक
news [njuːz] *npl* समाचार
newsagent ['njuːzˌeɪdʒənt] *n* अखबारवाला
newspaper ['njuːzˌpeɪpə] *n* समाचारपत्र
newsreader ['njuːzˌriːdə] *n* समाचार वाचक
newt [njuːt] *n* सरटिका

New Year [njuː jɪə] *n* नववर्ष
New Zealand [njuː 'ziːlənd] *n* न्यूज़ीलैंड
New Zealander [njuː 'ziːləndə] *n* न्यूज़ीलैंड का निवासी
next [nɛkst] *adj* अगला ▹ *adv* बाद में
next of kin [nɛkst əv kɪn] *n (formal)* निकटतम संबंधी
next to [nɛkst tə] *prep* बगल में
Nicaragua [ˌnɪkə'rægjʊə] *n* निकारागुआ
Nicaraguan [ˌnɪkə'rægjʊən] *adj* निकारागुआ से संबद्ध ▹ *n* निकारागुआ का निवासी
nice [naɪs] *adj* बढ़िया/अच्छा
nickname ['nɪkˌneɪm] *n* उपनाम
nicotine ['nɪkəˌtiːn] *n* निकोटीन
niece [niːs] *n* भतीजी/भांजी
Niger [niː'ʒɛə] *n* नाइजर
Nigeria [naɪ'dʒɪərɪə] *n* नाइजीरिया
Nigerian [naɪ'dʒɪərɪən] *adj* नाइजीरियाई ▹ *n* नाइजीरियाई
night [naɪt] *n* रात
nightclub ['naɪtˌklʌb] *n* रात्रि क्लब
nightdress ['naɪtˌdrɛs] *n* नाइट ड्रेस/रात्रिकालीन पोशाक
nightlife ['naɪtˌlaɪf] *n* रात्रिकालीन जन-जीवन
nightmare ['naɪtˌmɛə] *n* दुःस्वप्न
night school [naɪt skuːl] *n* रात्रिकालीन विद्यालय
night shift [naɪt ʃɪft] *n* रात की पारी
nil [nɪl] *n* शून्य
nine [naɪn] *num* नौ
nineteen [ˌnaɪn'tiːn] *num* उन्नीस
nineteenth [ˌnaɪn'tiːnθ] *adj* उन्नीसवाँ
ninety ['naɪntɪ] *num* नब्बे
ninth [naɪnθ] *adj* नवाँ ▹ *n* नवाँ
nitrogen ['naɪtrədʒən] *n* नाइट्रोजन
no [nəʊ] *det* कोई नहीं ▹ *adv* नहीं ▹ *excl* नहीं

nobody ['nəʊbədɪ] *n* कोई नहीं
nod [nɒd] *vi* सिर हिलाना/सहमति प्रकट करना
noise [nɔɪz] *n* शोर
noisy ['nɔɪzɪ] *adj* शोरगुल वाला
nominate ['nɒmɪˌneɪt] *vt* नामांकित करना
nomination [ˌnɒmɪ'neɪʃən] *n* नामांकन
none [nʌn] *pron* कोई भी नहीं
nonsense ['nɒnsəns] *n* बकवास
non-smoker [nɒn'sməʊkə] *n* धूम्रपान न करने वाला
non-smoking [nɒn'sməʊkɪŋ] *adj* धूम्रपान वर्जित
non-stop ['nɒn'stɒp] *adv* अविराम
noodles ['nuːdlz] *npl* नूडल
noon [nuːn] *n* दोपहर
no one ['nəʊwʌn] *pron* कोई नहीं
nor [nɔː] *conj* और न
normal ['nɔːml] *adj* सामान्य
normally ['nɔːməlɪ] *adv* सामान्यतया
north [nɔːθ] *adj* उत्तरी ▷ *adv* उत्तर की ओर ▷ *n* उत्तर
North Africa [nɔːθ 'æfrɪkə] *n* उत्तर अफ़्रीका
North African [nɔːθ 'æfrɪkən] *adj* उत्तर अफ़्रीकी ▷ *n* उत्तर अफ़्रीकी
North America [nɔːθ ə'mɛrɪkə] *n* उत्तर अमेरिका
North American [nɔːθ ə'mɛrɪkən] *adj* उत्तर अमेरिकी ▷ *n* उत्तर अमेरिकी
northbound ['nɔːθˌbaʊnd] *adj* उत्तरमार्गी
northeast [ˌnɔːθ'iːst] *n* उत्तरपूर्व
northern ['nɔːðən] *adj* उत्तरी
Northern Ireland ['nɔːðən 'aɪələnd] *n* उत्तरी आयरलैंड
North Korea [nɔːθ kə'rɪə] *n* उत्तर कोरिया
North Pole [nɔːθ pəʊl] *n* उत्तरी ध्रुव
North Sea [nɔːθ siː] *n* उत्तरी सागर

northwest [ˌnɔːθ'wɛst] *n* उत्तरपश्चिम

Norway ['nɔːˌweɪ] *n* नॉर्वे

Norwegian [nɔː'wiːdʒən] *adj* नॉर्वे से संबद्ध ▹ *n* *(person)* नॉर्वे का निवासी; *(language)* नॉर्वे की भाषा

nose [nəʊz] *n* नाक

nosebleed ['nəʊzˌbliːd] *n* नकसीर

nostril ['nɒstrɪl] *n* नथुना

nosy ['nəʊzɪ] *adj* *(informal)* दखलअंदाज़

not [nɒt] *adv* नहीं

note [nəʊt] *n* *(musical)* सुर; *(banknote)* नोट; *(message)* छोटी चिट्ठी/टिप्पणी

notebook ['nəʊtˌbʊk] *n* कापी

note down [nəʊt daʊn] *v* लिखना

notepad ['nəʊtˌpæd] *n* नोटपैड

notepaper ['nəʊtˌpeɪpə] *n* नोटपेपर

nothing ['nʌθɪŋ] *n* कुछ नहीं

notice ['nəʊtɪs] *n* *(sign)* सूचना पत्र; *(warning)* पूर्व सूचना ▹ *vt* ध्यान देना

noticeable ['nəʊtɪsəbl] *adj* सुस्पष्ट

notice board ['nəutɪsbɔːd] *n* सूचना पट्ट

notify ['nəʊtɪˌfaɪ] *vt* *(formal)* सूचित करना

nought [nɔːt] *n* शून्य

noun [naʊn] *n* संज्ञा

novel ['nɒvl] *n* उपन्यास

novelist ['nɒvəlɪst] *n* उपन्यासकार

November [nəʊ'vɛmbə] *n* नवंबर

now [naʊ] *adv* अब

nowadays ['naʊəˌdeɪz] *adv* आजकल

nowhere ['nəʊˌwɛə] *adv* कहीं नहीं

nuclear ['njuːklɪə] *adj* आणविक

nude [njuːd] *adj* नग्न ▹ *n* नग्न

nuisance ['njuːsəns] *n* विघ्न

numb [nʌm] *adj* सुन्न

number ['nʌmbə] *n* अंक

number plate ['nʌmbə pleɪt] *n* नंबर प्लेट

numerous ['nju:mərəs] *adj* बहुत से
nun [nʌn] *n* तपस्विनी
nurse [nɜ:s] *n* नर्स
nursery ['nɜ:sərɪ] *n* शिशुगृह
nursery rhyme ['nɜ:sərɪ raɪm] *n* बालगीत
nursery school ['nɜ:sərɪ sku:l] *n* नर्सरी स्कूल
nursing home ['nɜ:sɪŋ həʊm] *n* निजी अस्पताल
nut [nʌt] *n (metal)* नट; *(edible)* काष्ठफल
nut allergy [nʌt 'ælədʒɪ] *n* काष्ठफल से होने वाली एलर्जी
nutmeg ['nʌtmɛg] *n* जायफल
nutrient ['nju:trɪənt] *n* पोषक तत्व
nutrition [nju:'trɪʃən] *n* पोषण
nutritious [nju:'trɪʃəs] *adj* पोषक
nutter ['nʌtə] *n (informal)* पागल
nylon ['naɪlɒn] *n* नायलॉन - एक प्रकार का कपड़ा

O

oak [əʊk] *n* शाहबलूत
oar [ɔ:] *n* पतवार
oasis [əʊ'eɪsɪs] *n* मरुद्यान
oath [əʊθ] *n* शपथ
oatmeal ['əʊt,mi:l] *n* जई का आटा
oats [əʊts] *npl* जई
obedient [ə'bi:dɪənt] *adj* आज्ञाकारी
obese [əʊ'bi:s] *adj* स्थूलकाय
obey [ə'beɪ] *v* आज्ञा पालन
obituary [ə'bɪtjʊərɪ] *n* मृत्युलेख
object ['ɒbdʒɪkt] *n* वस्तु
objection [əb'dʒɛkʃən] *n* आपत्ति
objective [əb'dʒɛktɪv] *n* उद्देश्य
oblong ['ɒb,lɒŋ] *adj* लंबोतरा
obnoxious [əb'nɒkʃəs] *adj* अप्रिय
oboe ['əʊbəʊ] *n* नफ़ीरी - एक वाद्य

observant [əb'zɜːvənt] *adj* चौकस

observatory [əb'zɜːvətərɪ] *n* वेधशाला

observe [əb'zɜːv] *vt* अवलोकन करना

observer [əb'zɜːvə] *n* देखनेवाला

obsessed [əb'sɛst] *adj* आसक्त/धुन में रत

obsession [əb'sɛʃən] *n* आसक्ति/धुन

obsolete ['ɒbsəˌliːt] *adj* अप्रचलित

obstacle ['ɒbstəkl] *n* बाधा

obstinate ['ɒbstɪnɪt] *adj* ज़िद्दी

obstruct [əb'strʌkt] *vt* अवरुद्ध करना

obtain [əb'teɪn] *vt (formal)* हासिल करना

obvious ['ɒbvɪəs] *adj* ज़ाहिर

obviously ['ɒbvɪəslɪ] *adv* ज़ाहिर तौर पर

occasion [ə'keɪʒən] *n* अवसर

occasional [ə'keɪʒənl] *adj* कभी - कभी का

occasionally [ə'keɪʒənəlɪ] *adv* कभी - कभी

occupation [ˌɒkjʊ'peɪʃən] *n (job)* व्यवसाय; *(country)* कब्ज़ा

occupy ['ɒkjʊˌpaɪ] *vt* जगह घेरना/कब्ज़ा करना

occur [ə'kɜː] *vi* घटित होना

occurrence [ə'kʌrəns] *n (formal)* घटना

ocean ['əʊʃən] *n* महासागर

Oceania [ˌəʊʃɪ'ɑːnɪə] *n* ओशिनिया

October [ɒk'təʊbə] *n* अक्टूबर

octopus ['ɒktəpəs] *n* ऑक्टोपस

odd [ɒd] *adj (strange)* अजीब; *(nonmatching)* बेमेल; *(number)* विषम

odour ['əʊdə] *n* बदबू

of [ɒv] *prep (belonging to)* का; *(used to talk about amounts)* का; *(about)* के बारे में

off [ɒf] *adv* बंद ▷ *prep* पर से

offence [ə'fɛns] *n* जुर्म

offend [ə'fɛnd] *vt* नाराज़ करना/अपमान करना
offensive [ə'fɛnsɪv] *adj* अपमानजनक
offer ['ɒfə] *n* प्रस्ताव ▷ *vt* पेश करना
office ['ɒfɪs] *n* कार्यालय
office hours ['ɒfɪs aʊəz] *npl* कार्य समय
officer ['ɒfɪsə] *n* पदाधिकारी
official [ə'fɪʃəl] *adj* आधिकारिक
off-peak ['ɒf,piːk] *adv* सस्ता
off-season ['ɒf,siːzn] *adj* मंदी का समय ▷ *adv* मंदी का समय
offside ['ɒf'saɪd] *adj* ऑफ़साइड
often ['ɒfn] *adv* अक्सर
oil [ɔɪl] *n* तेल ▷ *vt* तेल लगाना
oil refinery [ɔɪl rɪ'faɪnərɪ] *n* तेल शोधक कारखाना
oil rig [ɔɪl rɪg] *n* तेल निकालने का प्लेटफ़ॉर्म
oil slick [ɔɪl slɪk] *n* पानी पर तैरता हुआ तेल
oil well [ɔɪl wɛl] *n* तेल का कुंआ
ointment ['ɔɪntmənt] *n* मरहम
OK! [,əʊ'keɪ] *excl* ठीक है
okay [,əʊ'keɪ] *adj (informal)* ठीक ▷ *excl* ठीक है
old [əʊld] *adj (aged)* वृद्ध; *(made a long time ago)* पुराना
old-age pensioner [əʊld'eɪdʒ 'pɛnʃənə] *n* वृद्ध पेंशनभोगी
old-fashioned ['əʊld'fæʃənd] *adj* पुराने चलन का
olive ['ɒlɪv] *n (fruit)* जैतून; *(tree)* जैतून का पेड़
olive oil ['ɒlɪv ɔɪl] *n* जैतून का तेल
Oman [əʊ'mɑːn] *n* ओमान
omelette ['ɒmlɪt] *n* ऑमलेट
on [ɒn] *adv* चालू ▷ *prep* पर/के ऊपर
on behalf of [ɒn bɪ'hɑːf ɒv; əv] *n* की ओर से
once [wʌns] *adv* एक बार
one [wʌn] *num* संख्या एक ▷ *pron* एक
one-off ['wʌnɒf] *n* एकबारगी

one's [wʌnz] *det* अपनी
oneself [wʌn'self] *pron* अपने लिए/खुद
onion ['ʌnjən] *n* प्याज़
online ['ɒn,laɪn] *adj* ऑनलाइन ▹ *adv* ऑनलाइन होकर
onlooker ['ɒn,lʊkə] *n* तमाशबीन
only ['əʊnlɪ] *adj (sole)* एकमात्र/केवल ▹ *adv* केवल ▹ *adj (child)* इकलौता
on time [ɒn taɪm] *adj* समय पर
onto ['ɒntʊ] *prep (on top of)* पर; *(bus, train, plane)* में
open ['əʊpn] *adj* खुला ▹ *v (make or be no longer closed)* खोलना; *(shop, office)* खुलना
opening hours ['əʊpənɪŋ aʊəz] *npl* खुलने का समय
opera ['ɒpərə] *n* ओपेरा/गीतिनाट्य
operate ['ɒpə,reɪt] *v (business, organization)* संचालन करना ▹ *vi (surgeon)* शल्य चिकित्सा करना
operating theatre ['ɒpə,reɪtɪŋ 'θɪətə] *n* शल्य चिकित्सा कक्ष
operation [,ɒpə'reɪʃən] *n (organized activity)* कार्यवाही; *(surgical)* शल्य चिकित्सा
operator ['ɒpə,reɪtə] *n* ऑपरेटर/परिचालक
opinion [ə'pɪnjən] *n* राय
opinion poll [ə'pɪnjən pəʊl] *n* मतगणना/जनमत सर्वेक्षण
opponent [ə'pəʊnənt] *n* विपक्षी/विरोधी
opportunity [,ɒpə'tjuːnɪtɪ] *n* अवसर
oppose [ə'pəʊz] *vt* विरोध करना
opposed [ə'pəʊzd] *adj* विरोधी
opposing [ə'pəʊzɪŋ] *adj* विरोधी
opposite ['ɒpəzɪt] *adj (far)* विपरीत/सम्मुख ▹ *adv* आमने-सामने ▹ *prep* सम्मुख ▹ *adj (completely different)* विपरीत/उल्टा
opposition [,ɒpə'zɪʃən] *n* विरोध

optician [ɒp'tɪʃən] *n* चश्मा बनाने वाला

optimism ['ɒptɪˌmɪzəm] *n* आशावाद

optimist ['ɒptɪˌmɪst] *n* आशावादी

optimistic [ɒptɪ'mɪstɪk] *adj* आशावादी

option ['ɒpʃən] *n* विकल्प

optional ['ɒpʃənl] *adj* वैकल्पिक

opt out [ɒpt aʊt] *v* बाहर निकलना

or [ɔː] *conj* या

oral ['ɔːrəl] *adj* मौखिक ▹ *n* मौखिक

orange ['ɒrɪndʒ] *n (colour)* नारंगी रंग; *(fruit)* संतरा

orange juice ['ɒrɪndʒ dʒuːs] *n* संतरे का रस

orchard ['ɔːtʃəd] *n* बाग

orchestra ['ɔːkɪstrə] *n* वादक मंडली

orchid ['ɔːkɪd] *n* ऑर्किड

ordeal [ɔː'diːl] *n* कटु अनुभव

order ['ɔːdə] *n* आज्ञा ▹ *vt* आज्ञा देना

order form ['ɔːdə fɔːm] *n* मांग पत्र

ordinary ['ɔːdnrɪ] *adj* साधारण

oregano [ˌɒrɪ'gɑːnəʊ] *n* अजवाइन

organ ['ɔːgən] *n (musical instrument)* ऑर्गन - एक वाद्य यंत्र; *(part of the body)* अंग

organic [ɔː'gænɪk] *adj* जैविक

organism ['ɔːgəˌnɪzəm] *n* जीव

organization [ˌɔːgənaɪ'zeɪʃən] *n* संगठन

organize ['ɔːgəˌnaɪz] *vt* आयोजित करना

Orient ['ɔːrɪənt] *n (literary, old-fashioned)* पूर्व एशिया

oriental [ˌɔːrɪ'ɛntl] *adj* पूर्व एशियाई

origin ['ɒrɪdʒɪn] *n* उत्पत्ति

original [ə'rɪdʒɪnl] *adj* मौलिक/मूलभूत

originally [ə'rɪdʒɪnəlɪ] *adv* मूल रूप से

ornament ['ɔːnəmənt] *n* आभूषण

orphan ['ɔːfən] *n* अनाथ
ostrich ['ɒstrɪtʃ] *n* शुतुरमुर्ग
other ['ʌðə] *adj* अन्य
otherwise ['ʌðə,waɪz] *adv* अन्यथा ▷ *conj* नहीं तो ▷ *adv (in other circumstances)* अन्यथा
otter ['ɒtə] *n* ऊदबिलाव
ought [ɔːt] *vt* करना चाहिए
ounce [aʊns] *n* औंस
our [aʊə] *det* हमारा
ours [aʊəz] *pron* हमारा
ourselves [aʊə'sɛlvz] *pron* खुद; *pron* खुद /हम स्वयं
out [aʊt] *adj* बुझा हुआ ▷ *adv* घर से बाहर ▷ *prep* बाहर
outbreak ['aʊt,breɪk] *n* प्रकोप
outcome ['aʊt,kʌm] *n* परिणाम
outdoor ['aʊt'dɔː] *adj* बाहरी
outdoors [,aʊt'dɔːz] *adv* बाहर
outfit ['aʊt,fɪt] *n* पोशाक
outgoing ['aʊt,gəʊɪŋ] *adj* निर्गामी
outing ['aʊtɪŋ] *n* सैर
outline ['aʊt,laɪn] *n* रूपरेखा
outlook ['aʊt,lʊk] *n* नज़रिया
out of date [aʊt ɒv deɪt] *adj* अप्रचलित
out-of-doors ['aʊtɒv'dɔːz] *adv* घर से बाहर
outrageous [aʊt'reɪdʒəs] *adj* असंयमित
outset ['aʊt,sɛt] *n* आरंभ
outside ['aʊt'saɪd] *adj* बाहरी ▷ *adv* बाहर की ओर ▷ *n* बाहरी भाग ▷ *prep* से बाहर
outsize ['aʊt,saɪz] *adj* बड़ी माप का
outskirts ['aʊt,skɜːts] *npl* बाहरी इलाका
outspoken [,aʊt'spəʊkən] *adj* स्पष्टवादी
outstanding [,aʊt'stændɪŋ] *adj* उत्कृष्ट
oval ['əʊvl] *adj* अंडाकार
ovary ['əʊvərɪ] *n* अंडाशय
oven ['ʌvn] *n* तंदूर/भट्टी
oven glove ['ʌvən glʌv] *n* तंदूर में खाना बनाते समय पहने जाने वाले दस्ताने
ovenproof ['ʌvn,pruːf] *adj* तंदूर में खाना पकाने हेतु सुरक्षित
over ['əʊvə] *adj* समाप्त ▷ *prep* के ऊपर

overall [ˌəʊvər'ɔːl] *adv* कुल मिलाकर
overalls ['əʊvərɔːlz] *npl* ओवरऑल - एक प्रकार का वस्त्र
overcast ['əʊvəˌkaːst] *adj* आच्छादित/घटाटोप
overcharge [ˌəʊvə'tʃaːdʒ] *vt* अधिक दाम लेना
overcoat ['əʊvəˌkəʊt] *n* ओवरकोट
overcome [ˌəʊvə'kʌm] *vt* उबरना
overdone [ˌəʊvə'dʌn] *adj* ज़्यादा पका हुआ
overdraft ['əʊvəˌdraːft] *n* जमा रुपए से अधिक रुपया निकालना
overdrawn [ˌəʊvə'drɔːn] *adj* जमा रुपए से अधिक रुपए निकाला हुआ
overdue [ˌəʊvə'djuː] *adj* विलंबित
overestimate [ˌəʊvər'ɛstɪˌmeɪt] *vt* अधिक आँकना
overhead projector ['əʊvəˌhɛd prə'dʒɛktə] *n* ओवरहेड प्रोजेक्टर/ऊपरि प्रक्षेपक
overheads ['əʊvəˌhɛdz] *npl* बंधा खर्च
overlook [ˌəʊvə'lʊk] *vt* के ऊपर से दिखना
overrule [ˌəʊvə'ruːl] *vt* खारिज करना
overseas [ˌəʊvə'siːz] *adv* समुद्र पार/विदेश में
oversight ['əʊvəˌsaɪt] *n (overseeing)* निगरानी; *(mistake)* भूल
oversleep [ˌəʊvə'sliːp] *vi* अधिक देर तक सोना
overtake [ˌəʊvə'teɪk] *v* से आगे बढ़ना
overtime ['əʊvəˌtaɪm] *n* अतिरिक्त समय
overweight [ˌəʊvə'weɪt] *adj* ज़रूरत से ज़्यादा वजनदार
owe [əʊ] *vt* ऋणी होना
owing to ['əʊɪŋ tuː] *prep* के कारण
owl [aʊl] *n* उल्लू
own [əʊn] *adj* अपना/खुद का ▷ *vt* मालिक होना
owner ['əʊnə] *n* मालिक

O

own up [əʊn ʌp] *v* अपराध मानना
oxygen ['ɒksɪdʒən] *n* ऑक्सीजन
oyster ['ɔɪstə] *n* सीप
ozone ['əʊzəʊn] *n* ओज़ोन
ozone layer ['əʊzəʊn 'leɪə] *n* ओज़ोन परत

p

PA [piː eɪ] *abbr* निजी सहायक हेतु संक्षिप्त रूप
pace [peɪs] *n* गति
pacemaker ['peɪsˌmeɪkə] *n* पेसमेकर
Pacific Ocean [pə'sɪfɪk 'əʊʃən] *n* प्रशांत महासागर
pack [pæk] *n* बंडल ▷ *vt* सामान बांधना
package ['pækɪdʒ] *n* पुलिंदा
packaging ['pækɪdʒɪŋ] *n* संवेष्टन/डिब्बाबंदी
packed [pækt] *adj* लपेटा हुआ/संवेष्टित
packed lunch [pækt lʌntʃ] *n* टिफ़िन में रखा भोजन
packet ['pækɪt] *n* पुलिंदा
pad [pæd] *n* गद्दी
paddle ['pædl] *n* डांड/पतवार ▷ *vt* *(boat)* नाव खेना/डांड चलाना ▷ *vi* *(wade)* छिछले पानी में चलना
paddling pool ['pædəlɪŋ puːl] *n* छोटा तरणताल
padlock ['pædˌlɒk] *n* ताला
page [peɪdʒ] *n* पृष्ठ ▷ *v* लाउडस्पीकर पर घोषणा करके नाम बुलाना
pager ['peɪdʒə] *n* पेजर
paid [peɪd] *adj* भुगतान किया हुआ
pail [peɪl] *n* *(old-fashioned)* बाल्टी
pain [peɪn] *n* दर्द
painful ['peɪnfʊl] *adj* दर्दनाक
painkiller ['peɪnˌkɪlə] *n* दर्दनाक
paint [peɪnt] *n* रंग ▷ *v* *(wall, door)* रंगना; *(make a picture of)* चित्रकारी करना

paintbrush ['peɪnt,brʌʃ] *n* रंगाई करने की कूची
painter ['peɪntə] *n* चित्रकार
painting ['peɪntɪŋ] *n* चित्रकारी
pair [pɛə] *n* जोड़ा
Pakistan [,pɑːkɪ'stɑːn] *n* पाकिस्तान
Pakistani [,pɑːkɪ'stɑːnɪ] *adj* पाकिस्तानी ▷ *n* पाकिस्तानी
pal [pæl] *n (informal, old-fashioned)* मित्र
palace ['pælɪs] *n* महल
pale [peɪl] *adj* निष्प्रभ
Palestine ['pælɪ,staɪn] *n* फ़िलिस्तीन
Palestinian [,pælɪ'stɪnɪən] *adj* फ़िलिस्तीनी ▷ *n* फ़िलिस्तीनी
palm [pɑːm] *n (hand)* हथेली; *(tree)* ताड़ का पेड़
pamphlet ['pæmflɪt] *n* छोटी पुस्तिका
pan [pæn] *n* कड़ाही
Panama [,pænə'mɑː] *n* पनामा
pancake ['pæn,keɪk] *n* पैनकेक
panda ['pændə] *n* पांडा
panic ['pænɪk] *n* व्यग्रता ▷ *v* व्यग्र होना
panther ['pænθə] *n* तेंदुआ
pantomime ['pæntə,maɪm] *n* मूक अभिनय
pants [pænts] *npl* जांघिया
paper ['peɪpə] *n (material)* क़ागज़; *(newspaper)* अख़बार
paperback ['peɪpə,bæk] *n* जिल्द चढ़ी किताब
paperclip ['peɪpə,klɪp] *n* पेपर क्लिप
paper round ['peɪpə raʊnd] *n* अखबार वितरण सेवा
paperweight ['peɪpə,weɪt] *n* पेपरवेट
paperwork ['peɪpə,wɜːk] *n* कागज़ी कार्रवाई
paprika ['pæprɪkə] *n* लाल मिर्च का चूर्ण
parachute ['pærə,ʃuːt] *n* पैराशूट/हवाई छतरी
parade [pə'reɪd] *n* परेड/अभिमुख प्रयाण
paradise ['pærə,daɪs] *n* स्वर्ग

paraffin ['pærəfɪn] *n* पैराफ़िन
paragraph ['pærəˌgrɑːf] *n* परिच्छेद
Paraguay ['pærəˌgwaɪ] *n* पैराग्वे
Paraguayan [ˌpærə'gwaɪən] *adj* पैराग्वे से संबद्ध ▷ *n* पैराग्वे का निवासी
parallel ['pærəˌlɛl] *adj* समानांतर
paralysed ['pærəˌlaɪzd] *adj* लकवाग्रस्त
paramedic [ˌpærə'medɪk] *n* पराचिकित्सक
parcel ['pɑːsl] *n* पार्सल/पुलिंदा
pardon ['pɑːdn] *excl* क्षमा करें! ▷ *n* क्षमादान
parent ['pɛərənt] *n* माता/पिता
park [pɑːk] *n* उद्यान ▷ *v* निश्चित स्थान पर गाड़ी खड़ी करना
parking ['pɑːkɪŋ] *n* पार्किंग
parking meter ['pɑːkɪŋ 'miːtə] *n* पार्किंग मीटर
parking ticket ['pɑːkɪŋ 'tɪkɪt] *n* पार्किंग टिकट
parliament ['pɑːləmənt] *n* संसद
parole [pə'rəʊl] *n* कारावकाश
parrot ['pærət] *n* तोता
parsley ['pɑːslɪ] *n* अजमोद
parsnip ['pɑːsnɪp] *n* चुकंदर
part [pɑːt] *n* हिस्सा
partial ['pɑːʃəl] *adj* आंशिक
participate [pɑː'tɪsɪˌpeɪt] *vi* भाग लेना
particular [pə'tɪkjʊlə] *adj* विशेष
particularly [pə'tɪkjʊləlɪ] *adv* विशेष रूप से
parting ['pɑːtɪŋ] *n* विदाई
partly ['pɑːtlɪ] *adv* आंशिक रूप से
partner ['pɑːtnə] *n* साथी
partridge ['pɑːtrɪdʒ] *n* तीतर
part-time ['pɑːtˌtaɪm] *adj* अंशकालिक ▷ *adv* अंशकालिक रूप से
part with [pɑːt wɪð] *v* अलग होना
party ['pɑːtɪ] *n (social event)* दावत; *(group)* टोली ▷ *vi* दावत करना

pass [pɑːs] *n (document)* पास/पार पत्र; *(mountain)* दर्रा; *(in an examination or test)* उत्तीर्ण ▷ *vt (hand)* देना; *(go past)* पार करना/गुज़रना ▷ *v (test)* उत्तीर्ण होना

passage ['pæsɪdʒ] *n (corridor)* गलियारा; *(excerpt)* अवतरण

passenger ['pæsɪndʒə] *n* यात्री

passion fruit ['pæʃən fruːt] *n* कृष्णकमल फल

passive ['pæsɪv] *adj* निष्क्रिय

pass out [pɑːs aʊt] *v* मूर्च्छित होना

Passover ['pɑːsˌəʊvə] *n* यहूदियों का एक त्यौहार

passport ['pɑːspɔːt] *n* पासपोर्ट

password ['pɑːsˌwɜːd] *n* पासवर्ड

past [pɑːst] *adj* अतीतकालीन ▷ *n* अतीत ▷ *prep (after)* अनंतर/के बाद; *(farther than)* के परे

pasta ['pæstə] *n* पास्ता

paste [peɪst] *n* गाढ़ा, चिपचिपा मिश्रण ▷ *vt (glue)* चिपकाना; *(on computer)* पेस्ट करना/लगाना (कंप्यूटर के अर्थ में)

pasteurized ['pæstəˌraɪzd] *adj* गर्म करके कीटाणु रहित किया गया

pastime ['pɑːsˌtaɪm] *n* मनबहलाव

pastry ['peɪstrɪ] *n* पेस्ट्री

patch [pætʃ] *n* पैबंद

patched [pætʃt] *adj* पैबंद लगा हुआ

paternity leave [pə'tɜːnɪtɪ liːv] *n* पितृत्व अवकाश

path [pɑːθ] *n* रास्ता

pathetic [pə'θɛtɪk] *adj* दयनीय

patience ['peɪʃəns] *n* धैर्य

patient ['peɪʃənt] *adj* धैर्यवान ▷ *n* मरीज़

patio ['pætɪˌəʊ] *n* बरामदा

patriotic ['pætrɪ'ɒtɪk] *adj* देशभक्त

patrol [pə'trəʊl] *n* गश्त

patrol car [pə'trəʊl kɑː] *n* गश्ती कार

pattern ['pætn] *n* तरीका

pause [pɔːz] *n* विराम
pavement ['peɪvmənt] *n* सड़क का पक्का किनारा
pavilion [pə'vɪljən] *n* खेमा
paw [pɔː] *n* पंजा
pawnbroker ['pɔːnˌbrəʊkə] *n* महाजन
pay [peɪ] *n* वेतन ▷ *v* भुगतान करना
payable ['peɪəbl] *adj* देय
pay back [peɪ bæk] *v* वापस चुकाना
payment ['peɪmənt] *n* भुगतान
payphone ['peɪˌfəʊn] *n* पैसे डालकर इस्तेमाल किया जाने वाला फ़ोन
PC [piː siː] *n* कम्प्यूटर
PDF [piː diː ɛf] *n* पी डी एफ़
peace [piːz] *n* शांति
peaceful ['piːsfʊl] *adj* शांतिपूर्ण
peach [piːtʃ] *n* आड़ू
peacock ['piːˌkɒk] *n* मोर
peak [piːk] *n* शीर्ष अवस्था
peak hours [piːk aʊəz] *npl* शीर्ष समय
peanut ['piːˌnʌt] *n* मूंगफली
peanut allergy ['piːˌnʌt 'ælədʒɪ] *n* मूंगफली से होने वाली एलर्जी
peanut butter ['piːˌnʌt 'bʌtə] *n* मूंगफली से बना मक्खन
pear [pɛə] *n* नाशपाती
pearl [pɜːl] *n* मोती
peas [piːz] *npl* मटर
peat [piːt] *n* वनस्पतियों के आंशिक अपघटन से बना ईंधन/पांस
pebble ['pɛbl] *n* कंकड़
peculiar [pɪ'kjuːlɪə] *adj* विचित्र
pedal ['pɛdl] *n* पेडल
pedestrian [pɪ'dɛstrɪən] *n* पैदल चलने वाले
pedestrian crossing [pə'dɛstrɪən 'krɒsɪŋ] *n* पैदल पार पथ
pedestrianized [pɪ'dɛstrɪəˌnaɪzd] *adj* केवल पैदल यात्रियों हेतु
pedestrian precinct [pə'dɛstrɪən 'priːsɪŋkt] *n* पैदल यात्री सीमा
pedigree ['pɛdɪˌgriː] *adj* नस्ल

peel [piːl] *n* छिलका ▷ *vt* छीलना

peg [pɛg] *n* खूंटी

Pekinese [ˌpiːkəˈniːz] *n* कुत्ते की एक नस्ल

pelican [ˈpɛlɪkən] *n* हवासील

pelican crossing [ˈpɛlɪkən ˈkrɒsɪŋ] *n* पार पथ

pellet [ˈpɛlɪt] *n* गोली

pelvis [ˈpɛlvɪs] *n* श्रोणि

pen [pɛn] *n* कलम

penalize [ˈpiːnəˌlaɪz] *vt* दंड देना

penalty [ˈpɛnltɪ] *n* दंड

pencil [ˈpɛnsəl] *n* पेंसिल

pencil case [ˈpɛnsəl keɪs] *n* कलमदान

pencil sharpener [ˈpɛnsəl ˈʃɑːpənə] *n* पेंसिल छीलने का उपकरण

pendant [ˈpɛndənt] *n* लॉकेट/लटकन

penfriend [ˈpɛnˌfrɛnd] *n* पत्र मित्र

penguin [ˈpɛŋgwɪn] *n* पेंग्विन

penicillin [ˌpɛnɪˈsɪlɪn] *n* पेनिसिलीन

peninsula [pɪˈnɪnsjʊlə] *n* प्रायद्वीप

penknife [ˈpɛnˌnaɪf] *n* कलमतराश

penny [ˈpɛnɪ] *n* सिक्का

pension [ˈpɛnʃən] *n* पैंशन/निवृत्ति वेतन

pensioner [ˈpɛnʃənə] *n* पैंशनभोगी

pentathlon [pɛnˈtæθlən] *n* एक खेल प्रतियोगिता

penultimate [pɪˈnʌltɪmɪt] *adj (formal)* आखिरी से पहले

people [ˈpiːpl] *npl* लोग

pepper [ˈpɛpə] *n (spice)* काली मिर्च; *(vegetable)* काली मिर्च

peppermill [ˈpɛpəˌmɪl] *n* काली मिर्च पीसने का उपकरण

peppermint [ˈpɛpəˌmɪnt] *n* पिपरमिंट

per [pɜː] *prep* प्रति

per cent [pɜː sɛnt] *adv* प्रतिशत

percentage [pəˈsɛntɪdʒ] *n* प्रतिशतता

percussion [pəˈkʌʃən] *n* तालवाद्य

P

perfect ['pɜːfɪkt] *adj* उत्तम
perfection [pə'fɛkʃən] *n* उत्तमता
perfectly ['pɜːfɪktlɪ] *adv* उत्तमता से
perform [pə'fɔːm] *vt* संपादन करना/निबाहना
performance [pə'fɔːməns] *n* प्रदर्शन
perfume ['pɜːfjuːm] *n* इत्र
perhaps [pə'hæps] *adv* शायद
period ['pɪərɪəd] *n* काल
perjury ['pɜːdʒərɪ] *n* झूठी गवाही
perm [pɜːm] *n* बालों को घुंघराला बनाने की क्रिया
permanent ['pɜːmənənt] *adj* स्थायी
permanently ['pɜːmənəntlɪ] *adv* स्थायी रूप से
permission [pə'mɪʃən] *n* अनुमति
permit ['pɜːmɪt] *n* अनुज्ञा पत्र/परवाना
persecute ['pɜːsɪˌkjuːt] *vt* सताना
persevere [ˌpɜːsɪ'vɪə] *vi* डटे रहना
Persian ['pɜːʃən] *adj* फ़ारसी
persistent [pə'sɪstənt] *adj* ज़िद्दी/स्थायी
person ['pɜːsn] *n* व्यक्ति
personal ['pɜːsənəl] *adj* व्यक्तिगत
personal assistant ['pɜːsənəl ə'sɪstənt] *n* निजी सहायक
personality [ˌpɜːsə'nælɪtɪ] *n* व्यक्तित्व
personally ['pɜːsənəlɪ] *adv* निजी रूप से
personal organizer ['pɜːsənəl 'ɔːgənaɪzə] *n* निजी विवरण पुस्तिका
personal stereo ['pɜːsənəl 'stɛrɪəʊ] *n* पर्सनल स्टीरियो
personnel [ˌpɜːsə'nɛl] *npl* कर्मचारी
perspective [pə'spɛktɪv] *n* नज़रिया
perspiration [ˌpɜːspə'reɪʃən] *n (formal)* पसीना
persuade [pə'sweɪd] *vt* मनाना

persuasive [pə'sweɪsɪv] *adj* समझाने - बुझाने वाला
Peru [pə'ruː] *n* पेरू
Peruvian [pə'ruːvɪən] *adj* पेरु से संबद्ध ▷ *n* पेरू का निवासी
pessimist ['pɛsɪˌmɪst] *n* निराशावादी
pessimistic ['pɛsɪˌmɪstɪk] *adj* निराशावादी
pest [pɛst] *n* कीट
pester ['pɛstə] *vt* दिक करना
pesticide ['pɛstɪˌsaɪd] *n* कीटनाशक
pet [pɛt] *n* पालतू
petition [pɪ'tɪʃən] *n* याचिका
petrified ['pɛtrɪˌfaɪd] *adj* सहमना
petrol ['pɛtrəl] *n* पेट्रोल
petrol station ['pɛtrəl 'steɪʃən] *n* पेट्रोल स्टेशन
petrol tank ['pɛtrəl tæŋk] *n* पेट्रोल टैंक
pewter ['pjuːtə] *n* जस्ता
pharmacist ['fɑːməsɪst] *n* औषधि विक्रेता
pharmacy ['fɑːməsɪ] *n* औषधालय
PhD [piː eɪtʃ diː] *n* डॉक्टरेट की उपाधि
pheasant ['fɛznt] *n* महूका
philosophy [fɪ'lɒsəfɪ] *n* दर्शनशास्त्र
phobia ['fəʊbɪə] *n* डर
phone [fəʊn] *n* फ़ोन ▷ *v* फ़ोन करना
phone back [fəʊn bæk] *v* दोबारा फ़ोन करना
phone bill [fəʊn bɪl] *n* फ़ोन का बिल
phonebook ['fəʊnˌbʊk] *n* दूरभाष संख्या पुस्तिका
phonebox ['fəʊnˌbɒks] *n* फ़ोनबॉक्स
phone call [fəʊn kɔːl] *n* फ़ोन कॉल
phonecard ['fəʊnˌkɑːd] *n* फ़ोन कार्ड
phone number [fəʊn 'nʌmbə] *n* दूरभाष संख्या
photo ['fəʊtəʊ] *n* तस्वीर
photo album ['fəʊtəʊ 'ælbəm] *n* फ़ोटो अल्बम/छायाचित्र संग्रहिका

photocopier ['fəʊtəʊˌkɒpɪə] *n* फ़ोटोकॉपी मशीन

photocopy ['fəʊtəʊˌkɒpɪ] *n* फ़ोटोकॉपी ▷ *vt* फ़ोटोकॉपी बनाना

photograph ['fəʊtəˌgrɑːf] *n* छायाचित्र ▷ *vt* छायाचित्र खींचना

photographer [fə'tɒgrəfə] *n* छायाचित्र खींचने वाला

photography [fə'tɒgrəfɪ] *n* छायाचित्रण

phrase [freɪz] *n* मुहावरा

phrasebook ['freɪzˌbʊk] *n* शब्द प्रयोग पद्धति शब्दकोश

physical ['fɪzɪkl] *adj* शारीरिक ▷ *n* शारीरिक जांच

physicist ['fɪzɪsɪst] *n* भौतिकशास्त्री

physics ['fɪzɪks] *n* भौतिक शास्त्र

physiotherapist [ˌfɪzɪəʊ'θɛrəpɪst] *n* व्यायाम द्वारा मांसपेशियों को सक्रिय बनाने वाला

physiotherapy [ˌfɪzɪəʊ'θɛrəpɪ] *n* व्यायाम द्वारा मांसपेशियों को सक्रिया बनाने वाली चिकित्सा

pianist ['pɪənɪst] *n* पियानो वादक

piano [pɪ'ænəʊ] *n* पियानो

pick [pɪk] *n* चयन ▷ *vt* *(choose)* छांटना/चुनना; *(pluck)* तोड़ना/चुनना

pick on [pɪk ɒn] *v* *(informal)* आरोप लगाना

pick out [pɪk aʊt] *v* पहचानना

pickpocket ['pɪkˌpɒkɪt] *n* जेबकतरा

pick up [pɪk ʌp] *v* उठाना

picnic ['pɪknɪk] *n* पिकनिक/उद्यान भोज

picture ['pɪktʃə] *n* चित्र

picture frame ['pɪktʃə freɪm] *n* चित्र का चौखटा

picturesque [ˌpɪktʃə'rɛsk] *adj* सुरम्य

pie [paɪ] *n* समोसे जैसा पकवान

piece [piːz] *n* टुकड़ा

pie chart [paɪ tʃɑːt] *n* पाई आरेख

pier [pɪə] *n* घाट

pierce [pɪəs] *vt* भेदना/छेदना

pierced [pɪəst] *adj* छिद्रित

piercing ['pɪəsɪŋ] *n* छेद

pig [pɪg] *n* सूअर
pigeon ['pɪdʒɪn] *n* कबूतर
piggybank ['pɪgɪˌbæŋk] *n* गुल्लक
pigtail ['pɪgˌteɪl] *n* गुंथी चोटी
pile [paɪl] *n* ढेर
piles [paɪlz] *npl* बवासीर
pile-up ['paɪlʌp] *n* दुर्घटना
pilgrim ['pɪlgrɪm] *n* तीर्थयात्री
pilgrimage ['pɪlgrɪmɪdʒ] *n* तीर्थयात्री
pill [pɪl] *n* गोली
pillar ['pɪlə] *n* खम्भा
pillow ['pɪləʊ] *n* तकिया
pillowcase ['pɪləʊˌkeɪs] *n* तकिया का खोल
pilot ['paɪlət] *n* वायुयान चालक
pilot light ['paɪlət laɪt] *n* पाइलट लाइट
pimple ['pɪmpl] *n* मुहांसा
PIN [pɪn] *n* पिन संख्या
pin [pɪn] *n* पिन
pinafore ['pɪnəˌfɔː] *n* बिना बांहों की एक पोशाक
pinch [pɪntʃ] *vt* चुटकी काटना
pine [paɪn] *n* चीड़
pineapple ['paɪnˌæpl] *n* अन्नानास
pink [pɪŋk] *adj* गुलाबी
pint [paɪnt] *n* पिंट - द्रव की एक माप
pip [pɪp] *n* बीज
pipe [paɪp] *n* नलिका
pipeline ['paɪpˌlaɪn] *n* पाइपलाइन
pirate ['paɪrɪt] *n* समुद्री लुटेरा
Pisces ['paɪsiːz] *n* मीन राशि
pistol ['pɪstl] *n* पिस्तौल
piston ['pɪstən] *n* पिस्टन
pitch [pɪtʃ] *n (sports ground)* क्रीड़ास्थल; *(sound)* स्वरमान ▹ *vt* फेंकना
pity ['pɪtɪ] *n* दया ▹ *vt* दया करना
pixel ['pɪksl] *n* पिक्सेल/बिंदु
pizza ['piːtsə] *n* पिज़्ज़ा
place [pleɪs] *n (location)* स्थान ▹ *vt* रखना ▹ *n (proper position)* जगह/मक़ाम
placement ['pleɪsmənt] *n* स्थापन

P

place of birth [pleɪs ɒv; əv bɜːθ] *n* जन्मस्थान

plain [pleɪn] *adj* सादा ▷ *n* मैदान

plain chocolate [pleɪn 'tʃɒklət] *n* अपेक्षाकृत कड़वी चॉकलेट

plait [plæt] *n* गूंथन

plan [plæn] *n* योजना ▷ *v* योजना बनाना

plane [pleɪn] *n (aeroplane)* हवाई जहाज; *(flat surface)* समक्षेत्र; *(tool)* रंदा

planet ['plænɪt] *n* ग्रह

planning ['plænɪŋ] *n* योजना

plant [plɑːnt] *n (factory)* संयत्र; *(something that grows in the earth)* पौधा ▷ *vt* पौधा रोपना

plant pot [plɑːnt pɒt] *n* गमला

plaque [plæk] *n* फ़लक

plasma screen ['plæzmə skriːn] *n* प्लाज़्मा स्क्रीन

plasma TV ['plæzmə tiː viː] *n* प्लाज़्मा टी वी

plaster *n* पलस्तर; ['plɑːstə] *n (sticking plaster)* चिपकने वाली पट्टी

plastic ['plæstɪk] *n* प्लास्टिक

plastic bag ['plæstɪk bæg] *n* प्लास्टिक की थैली

plastic surgery ['plæstɪk 'sɜːdʒərɪ] *n* प्लास्टिक सर्जरी

plate [pleɪt] *n* तश्तरी

platform ['plætfɔːm] *n* मंच

platinum ['plætɪnəm] *n* कौस्तुभ/प्लेटिनम

play [pleɪ] *n* नाटक ▷ *vi (children)* खेलना ▷ *vt (musical instrument)* बजाना

player ['pleɪə] *n (of sport)* खिलाड़ी; *(of musical instrument)* वादक

playful ['pleɪfʊl] *adj* चुलबुला

playground ['pleɪˌgraʊnd] *n* खेल का मैदान

playgroup ['pleɪˌgruːp] *n* छोटे बच्चों का विद्यालय

playing card ['pleɪɪŋ kɑːd] *n* ताश

playing field ['pleɪɪŋ fiːld] *n* खेल का मैदान

PlayStation® ['pleɪˌsteɪʃən] *n* प्ले स्टेशन

playtime ['pleɪ,taɪm] *n* खेल का समय
play truant [pleɪ 'truənt] *v* बिना अनुमति विद्यालय से अनुपस्थित रहना
playwright ['pleɪ,raɪt] *n* नाटककार
pleasant ['plɛznt] *adj* सुखद
please! [pliːz] *excl* कृपया!
pleased [pliːzd] *adj* प्रसन्न
pleasure ['plɛʒə] *n* आनंद
plenty ['plɛntɪ] *n* प्रचुरता
pliers ['plaɪəz] *npl* चिमटी
plot [plɒt] *n (piece of land)* भू-खंड; *(plan)* षड्यंत्र
plough [plaʊ] *n* हल ▷ *vt* जोतना
plug [plʌg] *n* प्लग
plughole ['plʌg,həʊl] *n* डाट लगाने का छेद
plug in [plʌg ɪn] *v* प्लग लगाना
plum [plʌm] *n* आलूबुखारा
plumber ['plʌmə] *n* नलसाज़
plumbing ['plʌmɪŋ] *n* जलव्यवस्था
plump [plʌmp] *adj* स्थूल/थुलथुल
plunge [plʌndʒ] *vi* डूबना
plural ['plʊərəl] *n* बहुवचन
plus [plʌs] *prep* और
plywood ['plaɪ,wʊd] *n* परतदार लकड़ी
p.m. [piː ɛm] *abbr* सायं
pneumatic drill [njʊ'mætɪk drɪl] *n* न्यूमेटिक ड्रिल/हवा के दबाव से खुदाई करने वाला उपकरण
pneumonia [njuː'məʊnɪə] *n* न्यूमोनिया
poached [pəʊtʃt] *adj (fish, animal, bird)* घुसपैठ करके शिकार करना; *(eggs, fish)* उबलते पानी में पकाया गया
pocket ['pɒkɪt] *n* जेब
pocket calculator ['pɒkɪt 'kælkjʊ,leɪtə] *n* छोटा कैलक्युलेटर
pocket money ['pɒkɪt 'mʌnɪ] *n* जेबखर्च
podcast ['pɒd,kɑːst] *n* पॉडकास्ट
poem ['pəʊɪm] *n* कविता
poet ['pəʊɪt] *n* कवि
poetry ['pəʊɪtrɪ] *n* काव्य

point [pɔɪnt] *n (something stated)* तर्क ▷ *vi* इंगित करना ▷ *n (needle, pin, knife)* नोक; *(in a game or sport)* अंक
pointless ['pɔɪntlɪs] *adj* व्यर्थ/अर्थहीन
point out [pɔɪnt aʊt] *v* दिखाना
poison ['pɔɪzn] *n* ज़हर ▷ *vt* ज़हर देना
poisonous ['pɔɪzənəs] *adj* ज़हरीला
poke [pəʊk] *vt* कोंचना
poker ['pəʊkə] *n* ताश का खेल
Poland ['pəʊlənd] *n* पोलैण्ड
polar ['pəʊlə] *adj* ध्रुव
polar bear ['pəʊlə bɛə] *n* ध्रुवीय भालू
Pole [pəʊl] *n* पौलैण्डवासी
pole [pəʊl] *n* खंभा
pole vault [pəʊl vɔːlt] *n* पोल वॉल्ट
police [pə'liːs] *n* पुलिस
policeman [pə'liːsmən] *n* पुलिसवाला
police officer [pə'liːs 'ɒfɪsə] *n* पुलिस अधिकारी
police station [pə'liːs 'steɪʃən] *n* पुलिस चौकी
policewoman [pə'liːswʊmən] *n* पुलिसवाली
polio ['pəʊlɪəʊ] *n* पोलियो
Polish ['pəʊlɪʃ] *adj* पोलैण्ड से संबद्ध ▷ *n* पोलैण्ड की भाषा
polish ['pɒlɪʃ] *n* पॉलिश ▷ ['pəʊlɪʃ] *vt* चमकाना
polite [pə'laɪt] *adj* नम्र
politely [pə'laɪtlɪ] *adv* नम्रतापूर्वक
politeness [pə'laɪtnɪs] *n* नम्रता
political [pə'lɪtɪkl] *adj* राजनैतिक
politician [ˌpɒlɪ'tɪʃən] *n* राजनेता
politics ['pɒlɪtɪks] *npl* राजनीति
poll [pəʊl] *n* मतदान
pollen ['pɒlən] *n* पराग
pollute [pə'luːt] *vt* प्रदूषित करना
polluted [pə'luːtɪd] *adj* प्रदूषित
pollution [pə'luːʃən] *n* प्रदूषण

polo-necked sweater ['pəʊləʊnɛkt 'swɛtə] *n* बंद गले का स्वेटर
polo shirt ['pəʊləʊ ʃɜːt] *n* पोलो शर्ट
Polynesia [ˌpɒlɪ'niːʒə] *n* पोलिनेशिया
Polynesian [ˌpɒlɪ'niːʒən] *adj* पोलिनेशियाई ▷ *n (person)* पोलिनेशियाई; *(language)* पोलिनेशियाई
polythene bag ['pɒlɪˌθiːn bæg] *n* पन्नी की थैली
pomegranate ['pɒmɪˌgrænɪt] *n* अनार
pond [pɒnd] *n* तालाब
pony ['pəʊnɪ] *n* टट्टू
ponytail ['pəʊnɪˌteɪl] *n* पोनीटेल
pony trekking ['pəʊnɪ 'trɛkɪŋ] *n* टट्टू पर सैर
poodle ['puːdl] *n* एक छोटा कुत्ता
pool [puːl] *n (resources)* संसाधन; *(water)* कुंड
poor [pʊə] *adj* गरीब
poorly ['pʊəlɪ] *adj* बीमार
popcorn ['pɒpˌkɔːn] *n* मक्के का लावा
pope [pəʊp] *n* पोप
poplar ['pɒplə] *n* चिनार
poppy ['pɒpɪ] *n* अफ़ीम
popular ['pɒpjʊlə] *adj* लोकप्रिय
popularity ['pɒpjʊlærɪtɪ] *n* लोकप्रियता
population [ˌpɒpjʊ'leɪʃən] *n* जनसंख्या
pop-up ['pɒpʌp] *n* पॉप अप
porch [pɔːtʃ] *n* बरामदा
porridge ['pɒrɪdʒ] *n* दलिया
port [pɔːt] *n (drink)* शराब; *(for ships)* बंदरगाह
portable ['pɔːtəbl] *adj* छोटा
porter ['pɔːtə] *n* दरबान
portfolio [pɔːt'fəʊlɪəʊ] *n* पोर्टफ़ोलियो
portion ['pɔːʃən] *n* हिस्सा
portrait ['pɔːtrɪt] *n* तस्वीर
Portugal ['pɔːtjʊgl] *n* पुर्तगाल
Portuguese [ˌpɔːtjʊ'giːz] *adj* पुर्तगाली ▷ *n (people)* पुर्तगाली; *(language)* पुर्तगाली
position [pə'zɪʃən] *n* स्थिति
positive ['pɒzɪtɪv] *adj* सकारात्मक

possess [pəˈzɛs] *vt* स्वत्व रखना

possession [pəˈzɛʃən] *n* *(formal)* कब्ज़ा

possibility [ˌpɒsɪˈbɪlɪtɪ] *n* संभावना

possible [ˈpɒsɪbl] *adj* संभव

possibly [ˈpɒsɪblɪ] *adv* संभावतः

post [pəʊst] *n* *(stake)* खंभा; *(position)* पद; *(mail)* डाक विभाग ▹ *vt* डाक में डालना

postage [ˈpəʊstɪdʒ] *n* डाक खर्च

postal order [ˈpəʊstəl ˈɔːdə] *n* पोस्टल ऑर्डर

postbox [ˈpəʊstˌbɒks] *n* पत्र पेटी

postcard [ˈpəʊstˌkɑːd] *n* पोस्टकार्ड

postcode [ˈpəʊstˌkəʊd] *n* डाक कोड

poster [ˈpəʊstə] *n* इश्तिहार/पोस्टर

postgraduate [pəʊstˈgrædjʊɪt] *n* परास्नातक

postman [ˈpəʊstmən] *n* डाकिया

postmark [ˈpəʊstˌmɑːk] *n* डाक मुहर

post office [pəʊst ˈɒfɪs] *n* डाकघर

postpone [pəʊstˈpəʊn] *vt* स्थगित करना

postwoman [ˈpəʊstwʊmən] *n* डाकिया (महिला)

pot [pɒt] *n* पात्र

potato [pəˈteɪtəʊ] *n* आलू

potato peeler [pəˈteɪtəʊ ˈpiːlə] *n* छिलनी

potential [pəˈtɛnʃəl] *adj* संभावना से भरे/समर्थ ▹ *n* संभावना/सामर्थ्य

pothole [ˈpɒtˌhəʊl] *n* सड़क का गड्ढा

pot plant [pɒt plɑːnt] *n* गमले में उगने वाला पौधा

pottery [ˈpɒtərɪ] *n* मिट्टी के बर्तन

potty [ˈpɒtɪ] *n* मलमूत्र पात्र

pound [paʊnd] *n* पाउण्ड

pound sterling [paʊnd ˈstɜːlɪŋ] *n* पाउण्ड स्टर्लिंग

pour [pɔː] *vt* ढालना

poverty [ˈpɒvətɪ] *n* गरीबी

powder [ˈpaʊdə] *n* चूर्ण

power ['paʊə] *n (control)* शक्ति/अधिकार; *(strength)* शक्ति/ताक़त

power cut ['paʊə kʌt] *n* विद्युत कटौती

powerful ['paʊəfʊl] *adj* शक्तिशाली

practical ['præktɪkl] *adj* व्यावहारिक

practically ['præktɪkəlɪ] *adv* लगभग

practice ['præktɪs] *n* चलन/अभ्यास

practise ['præktɪs] *vt* अभ्यास करना

praise [preɪz] *vt* प्रशंसा करना

pram [præm] *n* बच्चागाड़ी

prank [præŋk] *n (old-fashioned)* मज़ाक

prawn [prɔːn] *n* झींगा

pray [preɪ] *v* प्रार्थना करना

prayer [prɛə] *n* प्रार्थना

precaution [prɪ'kɔːʃən] *n* सावधानी

preceding [prɪ'siːdɪŋ] *adj* पिछला

precinct ['priːsɪŋkt] *n* वाहनों हेतु निषिद्ध क्षेत्र

precious ['prɛʃəs] *adj* कीमती

precise [prɪ'saɪs] *adj* निश्चित/एकदम सही

precisely [prɪ'saɪslɪ] *adv* ठीक-ठीक

predecessor ['priːdɪˌsɛsə] *n* पूर्ववर्ती

predict [prɪ'dɪkt] *vt* भविष्यवाणी करना

predictable [prɪ'dɪktəbl] *adj* पूर्वानुमेय

prefect ['priːfɛkt] *n* शिक्षक का सहायक छात्र

prefer [prɪ'fɜː] *vt* वरीयता देना

preferably ['prɛfərəblɪ] *adv* खासकर

preference ['prɛfərəns] *n* वरीयता

pregnancy ['prɛgnənsɪ] *n* गर्भावस्था

pregnant ['prɛgnənt] *adj* गर्भवती

prehistoric [ˌpriːhɪ'stɒrɪk] *adj* प्रागैतिहासिक

prejudice ['prɛdʒʊdɪs] *n* पक्षपात

prejudiced ['prɛdʒʊdɪst] *adj* पक्षपातपूर्ण

premature [ˌprɛmə'tjʊə] *adj* समयपूर्व
premiere ['prɛmɪˌɛə] *n* प्रथम प्रदर्शन
premises ['prɛmɪsɪz] *npl* परिसर
premonition [ˌprɛmə'nɪʃən] *n* पूर्वाभास
preoccupied [priː'ɒkjʊˌpaɪd] *adj* तल्लीन
prepaid [priː'peɪd] *adj* पहले से भुगतान किया हुआ
preparation [ˌprɛpə'reɪʃən] *n* तैयारी
prepare [prɪ'pɛə] *vt* तैयार करना
prepared [prɪ'pɛəd] *adj* तैयार
prescribe [prɪ'skraɪb] *vt* नुस्खा लिखना
prescription [prɪ'skrɪpʃən] *n* नुस्खा लिखना
presence ['prɛzəns] *n* उपस्थिति
present ['prɛzənt] *adj* मौजूद/उपस्थित होना ▷ *n* *(gift)* उपहार; *(current time)* वर्तमान ▷ [prɪ'zɛnt] *vt* प्रदान करना
presentation [ˌprɛzən'teɪʃən] *n* प्रस्तुति
presenter [prɪ'zɛntə] *n* प्रस्तुतकर्ता
presently ['prɛzəntlɪ] *adv* वर्तमान में
preservative [prɪ'zɜːvətɪv] *n* परिरक्षक
president ['prɛzɪdənt] *n* राष्ट्रपति
press [prɛs] *n* प्रेस ▷ *vt* दबाना
press conference [prɛs 'kɒnfrəns] *n* संवाददाता सम्मेलन
press-up ['prɛsʌp] *n* एक प्रकार की कसरत
pressure ['prɛʃə] *n* दबाव ▷ *vt* दबाव डालना
prestige [prɛ'stiːʒ] *n* प्रतिष्ठा
prestigious [prɛ'stɪdʒəs] *adj* प्रतिष्ठापूर्ण
presumably [prɪ'zjuːməblɪ] *adv* संभवतः
presume [prɪ'zjuːm] *vt* मान लेना
pretend [prɪ'tɛnd] *vt* ढोंग करना

pretext ['priːtɛkst] *n* बहाना
prettily ['prɪtɪlɪ] *adv* सुंदरता से
pretty ['prɪtɪ] *adj* सुंदर ▷ *adv* काफ़ी
prevent [prɪ'vɛnt] *vt* रोकना
prevention [prɪ'vɛnʃən] *n* रोकथाम
previous ['priːvɪəs] *adj* पिछला
previously ['priːvɪəslɪ] *adv* पहले
prey [preɪ] *n* शिकार
price [praɪs] *n* कीमत
price list [praɪs lɪst] *n* मूल्य सूची
prick [prɪk] *vt* चुभाना
pride [praɪd] *n* गर्व
primarily ['praɪmərəlɪ] *adv* मुख्यतः
primary ['praɪmərɪ] *adj* *(formal)* प्राथमिक
primary school ['praɪmərɪ skuːl] *n* प्राथमिक पाठशाला
prime minister [praɪm 'mɪnɪstə] *n* प्रधानमंत्री
primitive ['prɪmɪtɪv] *adj* आदिम
primrose ['prɪm,rəʊz] *n* पीतसेवती
prince [prɪns] *n* राजकुमार
princess [prɪn'sɛs] *n* राजकुमारी
principal ['prɪnsɪpl] *adj* मुख्य ▷ *n* प्रधानाचार्य
principle ['prɪnsɪpl] *n* सिद्धांत
print [prɪnt] *n* मुद्रण ▷ *v* *(with machine)* छापना/मुद्रित करना; *(when writing)* छापना/मुद्रित करना
printer ['prɪntə] *n* *(person)* मुद्रक; *(machine)* प्रिंटर
printout ['prɪntaʊt] *n* प्रिंटआउट
priority [praɪ'ɒrɪtɪ] *n* प्राथमिकता
prison ['prɪzn] *n* कारावास
prisoner ['prɪzənə] *n* कैदी
prison officer ['prɪzən 'ɒfɪsə] *n* कारावास अधिकारी
privacy ['praɪvəsɪ] *n* एकांतता
private ['praɪvɪt] *adj* निजी
private property ['praɪvət 'prɒpətɪ] *n* निजी संपत्ति

privatize ['praɪvɪˌtaɪz] *vt* निजीकरण करना
privilege ['prɪvɪlɪdʒ] *n* विशेषाधिकार
prize [praɪz] *n* पुरस्कार
prize-giving ['praɪzˌgɪvɪŋ] *n* पुरस्कार वितरण
prizewinner ['praɪzˌwɪnə] *n* पुरस्कार विजेता
probability [ˌprɒbə'bɪlɪtɪ] *n* संभावना
probable ['prɒbəbl] *adj* संभावित
probably ['prɒbəblɪ] *adv* शायद
problem ['prɒbləm] *n* समस्या
proceedings [prə'siːdɪŋz] *npl (formal)* कार्यवाही
proceeds ['prəʊsiːdz] *npl* आमदनी
process ['prəʊsɛs] *n* प्रक्रिया
procession [prə'sɛʃən] *n* जुलूस
produce [prə'djuːs] *vt* उत्पन्न करना/उत्पादन करना
producer [prə'djuːsə] *n* निर्माता
product ['prɒdʌkt] *n* उत्पाद
production [prə'dʌkʃən] *n* उत्पादन
productivity [ˌprɒdʌk'tɪvɪtɪ] *n* उत्पादकता
profession [prə'fɛʃən] *n* पेशा
professional [prə'fɛʃənl] *adj* पेशेवर ▷ *n* पेशेवर व्यक्ति
professionally [prə'fɛʃənəlɪ] *adv* पेशेवर ढंग से
professor [prə'fɛsə] *n* प्राध्यापक
profit ['prɒfɪt] *n* लाभ
profitable ['prɒfɪtəbl] *adj* लाभदायक
program ['prəʊgræm] *n* प्रोग्राम ▷ *vt* प्रोग्राम करना
programme ['prəʊgræm] *n* कार्यक्रम
programmer ['prəʊgræmə] *n* प्रोग्रामर
programming ['prəʊgræmɪŋ] *n* प्रोग्रामिंग
progress ['prəʊgrɛs] *n* प्रगति

prohibit [prə'hɪbɪt] *vt* *(formal)* निषेध करना
prohibited [prə'hɪbɪtɪd] *adj* निषिद्ध
project ['prɒdʒɛkt] *n* परियोजना
projector [prə'dʒɛktə] *n* प्रक्षेपक/प्रोजेक्टर
promenade [ˌprɒmə'nɑːd] *n* विहार मार्ग
promise ['prɒmɪs] *n* वादा ▷ *vt* वादा करना
promising ['prɒmɪsɪŋ] *adj* आशाजनक/होनहार
promote [prə'məʊt] *vt* बढ़ावा देना
promotion [prə'məʊʃən] *n* बढ़ावा/प्रचार
prompt [prɒmpt] *adj* त्वरित
promptly ['prɒmptlɪ] *adv* शीघ्रता से
pronoun ['prəʊˌnaʊn] *n* सर्वनाम
pronounce [prə'naʊns] *vt* उच्चारित करना
pronunciation [prəˌnʌnsɪ'eɪʃən] *n* उच्चारण
proof [pruːf] *n* *(evidence)* प्रमाण; *(printed)* प्रूफ़-जांच हेतु प्रथम मुद्रित प्रति
propaganda [ˌprɒpə'gændə] *n* प्रचार करना
proper ['prɒpə] *adj* यथोचित
properly ['prɒpəlɪ] *adv* उचित ढंग से
property ['prɒpətɪ] *n* *(formal)* संपत्ति
proportion [prə'pɔːʃən] *n* *(formal)* अनुपात
proportional [prə'pɔːʃənl] *adj* *(formal)* आनुपातिक
proposal [prə'pəʊzl] *n* प्रस्ताव
propose [prə'pəʊz] *vt* प्रस्तावित करना
prosecute ['prɒsɪˌkjuːt] *v* अभियोग लगाना
prospect ['prɒspɛkt] *n* संभावना
prospectus [prə'spɛktəs] *n* विवरण पत्रिका
prosperity [prɒ'spɛrɪtɪ] *n* समृद्धि

P

protect [prə'tɛkt] *vt* रक्षा करना

protection [prə'tɛkʃən] *n* सुरक्षा

protein ['prəʊtiːn] *n* प्रोटीन

protest ['prəʊtɛst] *n* विरोध ▷ [prə'tɛst] *v* विरोध करना

proud [praʊd] *adj* गर्वित

prove [pruːv] *v* साबित करना

proverb ['prɒvɜːb] *n* कहावत

provide [prə'vaɪd] *vt* प्रदान करना

provided [prə'vaɪdɪd] *conj* बशर्ते

provide for [prə'vaɪd fɔː; fə] *v* भरण-पोषण करना

provisional [prə'vɪʒənl] *adj* तात्कालिक

proximity [prɒk'sɪmɪtɪ] *n (formal)* निकटता

prune [pruːn] *n* सूखा आलूबुखारा

pry [praɪ] *vi* ताक-झांक करना

pseudonym ['sjuːdə,nɪm] *n* उपनाम

psychiatric [,saɪkɪ'ætrɪk] *adj* मानसिक

psychiatrist [saɪ'kaɪətrɪst] *n* मनोचिकित्सक

psychological [,saɪkə'lɒdʒɪkl] *adj* मनोविज्ञान संबंधी

psychologist [saɪ'kɒlədʒɪst] *n* मनोवैज्ञानिक

psychology [saɪ'kɒlədʒɪ] *n* मनोविज्ञान

psychotherapy [,saɪkəʊ'θɛrəpɪ] *n* मनोचिकित्सा

PTO [piː tiː əʊ] *abbr* कृपया पलटें हेतु संक्षिप्त रूप

public ['pʌblɪk] *adj* सार्वजनिक ▷ *n* जनता

publication [,pʌblɪ'keɪʃən] *n* प्रकाशन

public holiday ['pʌblɪk 'hɒlɪdeɪ] *n* सार्वजनिक अवकाश

publicity [pʌ'blɪsɪtɪ] *n* प्रचार

public opinion ['pʌblɪk ə'pɪnjən] *n* लोकमत

public relations ['pʌblɪk rɪ'leɪʃənz] *npl* जन-संपर्क

public school ['pʌblɪk skuːl] *n* पब्लिक स्कूल

public transport ['pʌblɪk 'træns,pɔːt] *n* जन-परिवहन

publish ['pʌblɪʃ] *vt* प्रकाशित करना
publisher ['pʌblɪʃə] *n* प्रकाशक
pudding ['pʊdɪŋ] *n* मिष्ठान्न
puddle ['pʌdl] *n* गढ़ा
Puerto Rico ['pwɜːtəʊ 'riːkəʊ] *n* प्योर्टो रिको
puff pastry [pʌf 'peɪstrɪ] *n* पफ़ पेस्ट्री
pull [pʊl] *vt* खींचना
pull down [pʊl daʊn] *v* ढहाना
pull out [pʊl aʊt] *v* निकलना
pullover ['pʊl,əʊvə] *n* स्वेटर
pull up [pʊl ʌp] *v* रोकना/रुकना
pulse [pʌls] *n* नाड़ी स्पदंन
pulses ['pʌlsɪz] *npl* दाल
pump [pʌmp] *n* पंप ▷ *vt* पंप करना
pumpkin ['pʌmpkɪn] *n* कद्दू
pump up [pʌmp ʌp] *v* हवा भरना
punch [pʌntʃ] *n* *(blow)* मुक्का; *(drink)* एक प्रकार का मादक शरबत ▷ *vt* मुक्का मारना
punctual ['pʌŋktjʊəl] *adj* पाबंद
punctuation [,pʌŋktjʊ'eɪʃən] *n* विराम चिह्न
puncture ['pʌŋktʃə] *n* पंक्चर
punish ['pʌnɪʃ] *vt* सज़ा देना
punishment ['pʌnɪʃmənt] *n* सज़ा
punk [pʌŋk] *n* एक प्रकार का संगीत
pupil ['pjuːpl] *n* *(schoolchild)* शिष्य; *(eye)* आंख की पुतली
puppet ['pʌpɪt] *n* कठपुतली
puppy ['pʌpɪ] *n* पिल्ला
purchase ['pɜːtʃɪs] *vt* *(formal)* खरीदना
pure [pjʊə] *adj* शुद्ध
purple ['pɜːpl] *adj* बैंगनी
purpose ['pɜːpəs] *n* उद्देश्य
purr [pɜː] *vi* बिल्ली की घुरघुराहट
purse [pɜːs] *n* बटुआ
pursue [pə'sjuː] *vt* *(formal)* पाने की कोशिश करना
pursuit [pə'sjuːt] *n* खोज
pus [pʌs] *n* पीप/मवाद

P

push [pʊʃ] *v* धक्का देना
pushchair ['pʊʃˌtʃɛə] *n* बच्चागाड़ी
push-up ['pʊʃʌp] *n (US)* एक प्रकार की कसरत
put [pʊt] *vt* रखना
put aside [pʊt ə'saɪd] *v* अलग रखना
put away [pʊt ə'weɪ] *v* हटाना
put back [pʊt bæk] *v* स्थगित करना
put forward [pʊt 'fɔːwəd] *v* पेश करना
put in [pʊt ɪn] *v* लगाना/बिताना
put off [pʊt ɒf] *v* टालना
put up [pʊt ʌp] *v* निर्माण करना/स्थापना करना
puzzle ['pʌzl] *n* पहेली
puzzled ['pʌzld] *adj* भ्रम में पड़ा हुआ
puzzling ['pʌzlɪŋ] *adj* पेचीदा
pyjamas [pə'dʒɑːməz] *npl* पैजामा
pylon ['paɪlən] *n* बिजली का बड़ा खंभा
pyramid ['pɪrəmɪd] *n* पिरामिड

q

Qatar [kæ'tɑː] *n* कतर
quail [kweɪl] *n* बटेर
quaint [kweɪnt] *adj* विलक्षण
qualification [ˌkwɒlɪfɪ'keɪʃən] *n* योग्यता
qualified ['kwɒlɪˌfaɪd] *adj* परिमित
qualify ['kwɒlɪˌfaɪ] *v* उत्तीर्ण होना/योग्य होना
quality ['kwɒlɪtɪ] *n* गुणवत्ता
quantify ['kwɒntɪˌfaɪ] *v* परिमाणित करना
quantity ['kwɒntɪtɪ] *n* मात्रा
quarantine ['kwɒrənˌtiːn] *n* संगरोधन
quarrel ['kwɒrəl] *n* झगड़ा ▷ *vi* झगड़ा करना
quarry ['kwɒrɪ] *n* खदान
quarter ['kwɔːtə] *n* चौथाई
quarter final ['kwɔːtə 'faɪnl] *n* क्वार्टर फ़ाइनल

quartet [kwɔːˈtɛt] *n* चतुष्टय

quay [kiː] *n* घाट

queen [kwiːn] *n* रानी

query [ˈkwɪərɪ] *n* प्रश्न ▷ *vt* प्रश्न करना

question [ˈkwɛstʃən] *n* प्रश्न ▷ *vt* प्रश्न करना

question mark [ˈkwɛstʃən mɑːk] *n* प्रश्नवाचक चिह्न

questionnaire [ˌkwɛstʃəˈnɛə] *n* प्रश्नावली

queue [kjuː] *n* कतार ▷ *vi* कतार में लगना

quick [kwɪk] *adj* फुर्तीला

quickly [ˈkwɪklɪ] *adv* शीघ्रता से

quiet [ˈkwaɪət] *adj* शांत

quietly [ˈkwaɪətlɪ] *adv* शांति से

quilt [kwɪlt] *n* रजाई

quit [kwɪt] *vt (informal)* त्यागना

quite [kwaɪt] *adv* अत्यंत

quiz [kwɪz] *n* प्रश्नोत्तरी

quota [ˈkwəʊtə] *n* हिस्सा/कोटा

quotation [kwəʊˈteɪʃən] *n* उद्धरण

quotation marks [kwəʊˈteɪʃən mɑːks] *npl* उद्धरण चिह्न

quote [kwəʊt] *n* उद्धरण ▷ *vt* उद्धृत करना

r

rabbit [ˈræbɪt] *n* खरगोश

rabies [ˈreɪbiːz] *n* रेबीज़

race [reɪs] *n (speed contest)* दौड़; *(group of human beings)* प्रजाति/मूल ▷ *v* दौड़ लगाना

racecourse [ˈreɪsˌkɔːs] *n* घुड़दौड़ का मैदान

racehorse [ˈreɪsˌhɔːs] *n* घुड़दौड़ का घोड़ा

racer [ˈreɪsə] *n* धावक

racetrack [ˈreɪsˌtræk] *n (US)* दौड़पथ

racial [ˈreɪʃəl] *adj* प्रजातीय

racing car [ˈreɪsɪŋ kɑː] *n* रेसिंग कार

racing driver [ˈreɪsɪŋ ˈdraɪvə] *n* कार रेस में भाग लेने वाला चालक

racism ['reɪsɪzəm] *n* जातिवाद
racist ['reɪsɪst] *adj* जातिवादी ▹ *n* जातिवाद करने वाला
rack [ræk] *n* रैक/खूँटी
racket ['rækɪt] *n (noise)* हुल्लड़; *(for tennis, squash, or badminton)* रैकेट
racoon [rə'kuːn] *n* रकून- एक पशु
radar ['reɪdɑː] *n* रडार
radiation [ˌreɪdɪ'eɪʃən] *n* विकिरण
radiator ['reɪdɪˌeɪtə] *n* विकिरक
radio ['reɪdɪəʊ] *n* रेडियो
radioactive [ˌreɪdɪəʊ'æktɪv] *adj* रेडियोधर्मी
radio-controlled ['reɪdɪəʊ'kən'trəʊld] *adj* रेडियो नियंत्रित
radio station ['reɪdɪəʊ 'steɪʃən] *n* रेडियो स्टेशन
radish ['rædɪʃ] *n* मूली
raffle ['ræfl] *n* लॉटरी
raft [rɑːft] *n* बेड़ा
rag [ræg] *n* चिथड़ा
rage [reɪdʒ] *n* क्रोध
raid [reɪd] *n* छापा ▹ *vt* छापा मारना
rail [reɪl] *n* छड़ से बना बाड़ा
railcard ['reɪlˌkɑːd] *n* रेलकार्ड
railings ['reɪlɪŋz] *npl* छड़ से बना बाड़ा
railway ['reɪlˌweɪ] *n* रेल मार्ग
railway station ['reɪlweɪ 'steɪʃən] *n* रेलवे स्टेशन
rain [reɪn] *n* बारिश ▹ *vi* बारिश होना
rainbow ['reɪnˌbəʊ] *n* इंद्रधनुष
raincoat ['reɪnˌkəʊt] *n* बरसाती कोट
rainforest ['reɪnˌfɒrɪst] *n* वर्षा वन
rainy ['reɪnɪ] *adj* बरसाती
raise [reɪz] *vt* उठाना
raisin ['reɪzn] *n* किशमिश
rake [reɪk] *n* दाँतेदार फावड़ा
rally ['rælɪ] *n* सभा/जमघट
ram [ræm] *n* भेड़ा ▹ *vt* टक्कर मारना
Ramadan [ˌræmə'dɑːn] *n* रमज़ान

rambler ['ræmblə] *n* घुमक्कड़

ramp [ræmp] *n* ढालू रास्ता

random ['rændəm] *adj* क्रमरहित

range [reɪndʒ] *n (area covered)* विस्तार/सीमा; *(mountains)* श्रेणी ▷ *vi* सीमाओं के बीच होना

rank [ræŋk] *n (status)* दरजा/ओहदा; *(row)* पंक्ति ▷ *v* स्थान पर होना

ransom ['rænsəm] *n* फिरौती

rape [reɪp] *n (sexual attack)* बलात्कार; *(US) (plant)* सरसों का पौधा ▷ *vt* बलात्कार करना

rapids ['ræpɪdz] *npl* नदी का वह भाग, जहाँ उसका प्रवाह तीव्रतम हो

rapist ['reɪpɪst] *n* बलात्कारी

rare [rɛə] *adj (uncommon)* दुर्लभ; *(lightly cooked)* अधपका

rarely ['rɛəlɪ] *adv* कभी - कभार

rash [ræʃ] *n* ददोरा/चकत्ता

raspberry ['rɑːzbərɪ] *n* रसभरी

rat [ræt] *n* चूहा

rate [reɪt] *n* दर ▷ *vt* मोल लगाना/मूल्यांकन करना

rate of exchange [reɪt ɒv; əv ɪks'tʃeɪndʒ] *n* विनिमय दर

rather ['rɑːðə] *adv* कुछ हद तक

ratio ['reɪʃɪˌəʊ] *n* अनुपात

rational ['ræʃənl] *adj* तर्कसंगत

rattle ['rætl] *n* खड़खड़ाहट

rattlesnake ['rætlˌsneɪk] *n* एक प्रकार का सांप

rave [reɪv] *n* जानदार/उत्साहपूर्ण ▷ *v* बड़बड़ाना

raven ['reɪvn] *n* कौआ

ravenous ['rævənəs] *adj* क्षुधातुर

ravine [rə'viːn] *n* घाटी

raw [rɔː] *adj* कच्चा

razor ['reɪzə] *n* उस्तरा

razor blade ['reɪzə bleɪd] *n* उस्तरे की पत्ती

reach [riːtʃ] *vt (arrive at)* पहुंचना ▷ *vi (stretch)* हाथ बढ़ाना

r

react [rɪ'ækt] *vi* प्रतिक्रिया करना

reaction [rɪ'ækʃən] *n* प्रतिक्रिया

reactor [rɪ'æktə] *n* परमाणु भट्टी

read [riːd aʊt] *v* पढ़ना

reader ['riːdə] *n* पाठक

readily ['rɛdɪlɪ] *adv* तत्परता से

reading ['riːdɪŋ] *n* वाचन/पठन

read out [riːd aʊt] *v* बाँचना/पढ़ कर सुनाना

ready ['rɛdɪ] *adj* तैयार

ready-cooked ['rɛdɪ'kʊkt] *adj* पका-पकाया

real ['rɪəl] *adj (factual)* वास्तविक; *(authentic)* असली

realistic [ˌrɪə'lɪstɪk] *adj* यथार्थवादी

reality [rɪ'ælɪtɪ] *n* वास्तविकता

reality TV [riː'ælɪtɪ tiː'viː] *n* रिएलिटी टी वी

realize ['rɪəˌlaɪz] *v* एहसास करना

really ['rɪəlɪ] *adv (spoken, sincerely)* सचमुच; *(actually)* वास्तव में

rear [rɪə] *adj* पिछला ▷ *n* पिछला हिस्सा

rear-view mirror ['rɪəvjuː 'mɪrə] *n* पीछे का यातायात दिखाने वाले शीशे

reason ['riːzn] *n* कारण

reasonable ['riːzənəbl] *adj* उचित

reasonably ['riːzənəblɪ] *adv* यथोचित

reassure [ˌriːə'ʃʊə] *vt* आश्वासन देना

reassuring [ˌriːə'ʃʊəɪŋ] *adj* आश्वस्त करने वाला

rebate ['riːbeɪt] *n* फिरती/छूट

rebellious [rɪ'bɛljəs] *adj* अवज्ञाकारी

rebuild [riː'bɪld] *vt* पुनर्निर्मित करना

receipt [rɪ'siːt] *n* रसीद

receive [rɪ'siːv] *vt* प्राप्त करना

receiver [rɪ'siːvə] *n (telephone)* रिसीवर; *(person)* प्रबंधकर्ता

recent ['riːsnt] *adj* हाल का

recently ['riːsəntlɪ] *adv* हाल ही में

reception [rɪ'sɛpʃən] *n* रिसेप्शन/स्वागत मेज़

receptionist [rɪ'sɛpʃənɪst] *n* अभ्यर्थक

recession [rɪ'sɛʃən] *n* मंदी

recharge [riː'tʃɑːdʒ] *vt* फिर से आवेशित करना/पुनःपूरण

recipe ['rɛsɪpɪ] *n* व्यंजन विधि

recipient [rɪ'sɪpɪənt] *n (formal)* प्रापकर्ता

reckon ['rɛkən] *vt (informal)* मानना/अनुमान लगाना

reclining [rɪ'klaɪnɪŋ] *adj* लेटा हुआ

recognizable ['rɛkəg,naɪzəbl] *adj* पहचानने योग्य

recognize ['rɛkəg,naɪz] *vt* पहचानना

recommend [,rɛkə'mɛnd] *vt* अनुशंसा करना

recommendation [,rɛkəmɛn'deɪʃən] *n* अनुशंसा

reconsider [,riːkən'sɪdə] *v* पुनर्विचार करना

record ['rɛkɔːd] *n (written account)* अभिलेख/सुरक्षित विवरण; *(best result ever)* कीर्तिमान ▷ [rɪ'kɔːd] *vt (write down)* दर्ज करना; *(TV programme)* रिकॉर्ड करना

recorded delivery [rɪ'kɔːdɪd dɪ'lɪvərɪ] *n* दर्ज की गई सुपुर्दगी

recorder [rɪ'kɔːdə] *n (musical instrument)* रिकॉर्डर; *(machine)* रिकॉर्डर

recording [rɪ'kɔːdɪŋ] *n* रिकॉर्डिंग

recover [rɪ'kʌvə] *vi* चंगा होना

recovery [rɪ'kʌvərɪ] *n* स्वास्थ्यलाभ

recruitment [rɪ'kruːtmənt] *n* भर्ती

rectangle ['rɛk,tæŋgl] *n* आयत

rectangular [rɛk'tæŋgjʊlə] *adj* आयताकार

rectify ['rɛktɪ,faɪ] *vt* दुरुस्त करना

recurring [rɪ'kɜːrɪŋ] *adj* पुनरावर्ती
recycle [riː'saɪkl] *vt* प्रयुक्त वस्तु का दोबारा प्रयोग
recycling [riː'saɪklɪŋ] *n* पुनर्चक्रण
red [rɛd] *adj* लाल
Red Cross [rɛd krɒs] *n* रेड क्रॉस
redcurrant ['rɛd'kʌrənt] *n* रेडकरेंट - एक फल
redecorate [riː'dɛkəˌreɪt] *v* फिर से सजाना
red-haired ['rɛdˌhɛəd] *adj* लाल बाल वाला
redhead ['rɛdˌhɛd] *n* लाल बाल वाला
red meat [rɛd miːt] *n* लाल मांस
redo [riː'duː] *vt* दोबारा करना
Red Sea [rɛd siː] *n* लाल सागर
reduce [rɪ'djuːs] *vt* घटाना
reduction [rɪ'dʌkʃən] *n* कमी/कटौती
redundancy [rɪ'dʌndənsɪ] *n* छँटनी
redundant [rɪ'dʌndənt] *adj* छँटनी किया गया
red wine [rɛd waɪn] *n* लाल रंग की शराब
reed [riːd aʊt] *n* नरकट
reel [riːl] *n* चरखी
refer [rɪ'fɜː] *vi* ज़िक्र करना
referee [ˌrɛfə'riː] *n* रेफ़री
reference ['rɛfərəns] *n* ज़िक्र
reference number ['rɛfərəns 'nʌmbə] *n* संदर्भ संख्या
refill [riː'fɪl] *vt* फिर से भरना
refinery [rɪ'faɪnərɪ] *n* शोधन संयंत्र
reflect [rɪ'flɛkt] *vt* प्रतिबिंबित करना/दर्शाना
reflection [rɪ'flɛkʃən] *n* प्रतिबिंब
reflex ['riːflɛks] *n* स्वतःस्फूर्त
refresher course [rɪ'frɛʃə kɔːs] *n* पुनश्चर्या पाठ्यक्रम
refreshing [rɪ'frɛʃɪŋ] *adj* स्फूर्तिदायक
refreshments [rɪ'frɛʃmənts] *npl* जलपान

refrigerator [rɪˈfrɪdʒəˌreɪtə] *n* फ़्रिज
refuel [riːˈfjuːəl] *v* दोबारा ईंधन डालना
refuge [ˈrɛfjuːdʒ] *n* शरण
refugee [ˌrɛfjʊˈdʒiː] *n* शरणार्थी
refund [rɪˈfʌnd] *vt* धन वापसी ▹ [ˈriːfʌnd] *n* धन वापस करना
refusal [rɪˈfjuːzl] *n* इनकार
refuse [ˈrɛfjuːs] *n* कचरा ▹ [rɪˈfjuːz] *v* इनकार करना
regain [rɪˈgeɪn] *vt* दोबारा प्राप्त करना
regard [rɪˈgɑːd] *n* सम्मान ▹ *vt* समझना
regarding [rɪˈgɑːdɪŋ] *prep* के बारे में
regiment [ˈrɛdʒɪmənt] *n* पलटन
region [ˈriːdʒən] *n* क्षेत्र
regional [ˈriːdʒənl] *adj* क्षेत्रीय
register [ˈrɛdʒɪstə] *n* पंजिका ▹ *vi* पंजीकृत करना
registered [ˈrɛdʒɪstəd] *adj* पंजीकृत
registration [ˌrɛdʒɪˈstreɪʃən] *n* पंजीकरण
registry office [ˈrɛdʒɪstrɪ ˈɒfɪs] *n* पंजीकरण कार्यालय
regret [rɪˈgrɛt] *n* पछतावा/खेद ▹ *vt* पछतावा करना
regular [ˈrɛgjʊlə] *adj* नियमित
regularly [ˈrɛgjʊləlɪ] *adv* नियमित रूप से
regulation [ˌrɛgjʊˈleɪʃən] *n* विनियमन
rehearsal [rɪˈhɜːsl] *n* पूर्वाभ्यास
rehearse [rɪˈhɜːs] *v* पूर्वाभ्यास करना
reimburse [ˌriːɪmˈbɜːs] *vt* *(formal)* पुनर्भुगतान करना
reindeer [ˈreɪnˌdɪə] *n* बारहसिंगा
reins [reɪnz] *npl* लगाम
reject [rɪˈdʒɛkt] *vt* खारिज करना
relapse [ˈriːˌlæps] *n* पुनरावर्तन
related [rɪˈleɪtɪd] *adj* संबंधित
relation [rɪˈleɪʃən] *n* संबंध

relationship [rɪˈleɪʃənʃɪp] *n* संबंध
relative [ˈrɛlətɪv] *n* रिश्तेदार
relatively [ˈrɛlətɪvlɪ] *adv* अपेक्षाकृत
relax [rɪˈlæks] *v* सुस्ताना/तनाव रहित होना
relaxation [ˌriːlækˈseɪʃən] *n* विश्राम
relaxed [rɪˈlækst] *adj* निश्चिंत
relaxing [rɪˈlæksɪŋ] *adj* आरामदेह
relay [ˈriːleɪ] *n* चौकी दौड़
release [rɪˈliːs] *n* रिहाई ▷ *vt* रिहा करना
relegate [ˈrɛlɪˌgeɪt] *vt* पदावनत करना
relevant [ˈrɛlɪvənt] *adj* प्रासंगिक
reliable [rɪˈlaɪəbl] *adj* विश्वसनीय
relief [rɪˈliːf] *n* राहत
relieve [rɪˈliːv] *vt* राहत देना
relieved [rɪˈliːvd] *adj* चिंतामुक्त
religion [rɪˈlɪdʒən] *n* धर्म
religious [rɪˈlɪdʒəs] *adj* धार्मिक
reluctant [rɪˈlʌktənt] *adj* अनिच्छुक
reluctantly [rɪˈlʌktəntlɪ] *adv* अनिच्छापूर्वक
rely on [rɪˈlaɪ ɒn] *v* पर निर्भर होना
remain [rɪˈmeɪn] *v* बना रहना
remaining [rɪˈmeɪnɪŋ] *adj* शेष
remains [rɪˈmeɪnz] *npl* अवशेष
remake [ˈriːˌmeɪk] *n* पुनर्निर्माण
remark [rɪˈmɑːk] *n* टिप्पणी
remarkable [rɪˈmɑːkəbl] *adj* उल्लेखनीय/असाधारण
remarkably [rɪˈmɑːkəblɪ] *adv* उल्लेखनीय रूप से/असाधारण रूप से
remarry [riːˈmærɪ] *vi* पुनर्विवाह करना
remedy [ˈrɛmɪdɪ] *n* इलाज
remember [rɪˈmɛmbə] *v* याद रखना
remind [rɪˈmaɪnd] *vt* याद दिलाना

reminder [rɪˈmaɪndə] *n* *(written)* अनुस्मारक
remorse [rɪˈmɔːs] *n* पछतावा
remote [rɪˈməʊt] *adj* सुदूरवर्ती
remote control [rɪˈməʊt kənˈtrəʊl] *n* रिमोट कंट्रोल
remotely [rɪˈməʊtlɪ] *adv* थोड़ा भी
removable [rɪˈmuːvəbl] *adj* हटाने योग्य
removal [rɪˈmuːvl] *n* हटाव
removal van [rɪˈmuːvəl væn] *n* मालवाहक गाड़ी
remove [rɪˈmuːv] *vt* *(written)* हटाना
rendezvous [ˈrɒndɪˌvuː] *n* पूर्वनिश्चित मुलाकात
renew [rɪˈnjuː] *vt* नवीनीकरण करना
renewable [rɪˈnjuːəbl] *adj* अक्षय/नवीकरणीय
renovate [ˈrɛnəˌveɪt] *vt* सुधारना
renowned [rɪˈnaʊnd] *adj* प्रख्यात
rent [rɛnt] *n* किराया ▷ *vt* किराए पर लेना
rental [ˈrɛntl] *n* किराए का
reorganize [riːˈɔːgəˌnaɪz] *vt* फिर तरतीब देना
rep [rɛp] *n* विक्रय प्रतिनिधि
repair [rɪˈpɛə] *n* मरम्मत ▷ *vt* मरम्मत करना
repair kit [rɪˈpɛə kɪt] *n* मरम्मत का सामान
repay [rɪˈpeɪ] *vt* चुकाना
repayment [rɪˈpeɪmənt] *n* कर्ज़ अदायगी
repeat [rɪˈpiːt] *n* दोहराव ▷ *vt* दोहराना
repeatedly [rɪˈpiːtɪdlɪ] *adv* बार - बार
repellent [rɪˈpɛlənt] *adj* *(formal)* घिनौना
repercussions [ˌriːpəˈkʌʃənz] *npl* *(formal)* नतीजा
repetitive [rɪˈpɛtɪtɪv] *adj* पुनरावृत्तीय
replace [rɪˈpleɪs] *vt* प्रतिस्थापित करना
replacement [rɪˈpleɪsmənt] *n* प्रतिस्थापन
replay [ˈriːˌpleɪ] *n* पुनःप्रदर्शन ▷ [ˌriːˈpleɪ] *vt* पुनःप्रदर्शित करना

replica ['rɛplɪkə] *n* प्रतिकृति
reply [rɪ'plaɪ] *n* जवाब ▷ *vi* जवाब देना
report [rɪ'pɔːt] *n (news)* विवरण ▷ *vt* विवरण देना ▷ *n (school)* प्रगति विवरण
reporter [rɪ'pɔːtə] *n* संवाददाता
represent [ˌrɛprɪ'zɛnt] *vt* प्रतिनिधित्व करना
representative [ˌrɛprɪ'zɛntətɪv] *adj* प्रतिनिधि
reproduction [ˌriːprə'dʌkʃən] *n* प्रतिकृति
reptile ['rɛptaɪl] *n* सरीसृप
republic [rɪ'pʌblɪk] *n* गणतंत्र
repulsive [rɪ'pʌlsɪv] *adj* घिनौना
reputable ['rɛpjʊtəbl] *adj* प्रतिष्ठित
reputation [ˌrɛpjʊ'teɪʃən] *n* प्रतिष्ठा
request [rɪ'kwɛst] *n (formal)* निवेदन ▷ *vt (formal)* निवेदन करना
require [rɪ'kwaɪə] *vt (formal)* ज़रूरत होना
requirement [rɪ'kwaɪəmənt] *n* ज़रूरत
rescue ['rɛskjuː] *n* बचाव ▷ *vt* बचाना
research [rɪ'sɜːtʃ] *n* अनुसंधान
resemblance [rɪ'zɛmbləns] *n* सादृश्यता
resemble [rɪ'zɛmbl] *vt* सदृश होना
resent [rɪ'zɛnt] *vt* बुरा मानना
resentful [rɪ'zɛntfʊl] *adj* चिढ़ा हुआ
reservation [ˌrɛzə'veɪʃən] *n* निग्रह/रोक
reserve [rɪ'zɜːv] *n (supply)* सुरक्षित भंडार; *(nature)* रक्षित स्थान ▷ *vt* आरक्षित करना
reserved [rɪ'zɜːvd] *adj* संकोची
reservoir ['rɛzəˌvwɑː] *n* जलाशय
resident ['rɛzɪdənt] *n* निवासी
residential [ˌrɛzɪ'dɛnʃəl] *adj* आवासीय

resign [rɪ'zaɪn] *vi* त्यागपत्र देना
resin ['rɛzɪn] *n* राल
resist [rɪ'zɪst] *vt* प्रतिरोध
resistance [rɪ'zɪstəns] *n* प्रतिरोध
resit [riː'sɪt] *v* प्रतिरोध करना
resolution [ˌrɛzə'luːʃən] *n* संकल्प
resort [rɪ'zɔːt] *n* सैरगाह
resort to [rɪ'zɔːt tuː; tʊ; tə] *v* का सहारा लेना
resource [rɪ'zɔːs] *n* संसाधन
respect [rɪ'spɛkt] *n* आदर ▷ *vt* आदर करना
respectable [rɪ'spɛktəbl] *adj* आदरणीय
respectively [rɪ'spɛktɪvlɪ] *adv* क्रमानुसार
respond [rɪ'spɒnd] *vi* प्रतिक्रिया देना
response [rɪ'spɒns] *n* प्रतिक्रिया
responsibility [rɪˌspɒnsə'bɪlɪtɪ] *n* ज़िम्मेदारी
responsible [rɪ'spɒnsəbl] *adj* ज़िम्मेदार
rest [rɛst] *n* शेष भाग ▷ *v* विश्राम करना
restaurant ['rɛstəˌrɒŋ] *n* रेस्तराँ/भोजनालय
restful ['rɛstfʊl] *adj* आरामदायक
restless ['rɛstlɪs] *adj* बेचैन
restore [rɪ'stɔː] *vt* बहाल करना/वापस लौटाना
restrict [rɪ'strɪkt] *vt* सीमित करना
restructure [riː'strʌktʃə] *vt* पुनर्गठन
result [rɪ'zʌlt] *n* परिणाम ▷ *vi* परिणाम निकलना
resume [rɪ'zjuːm] *v* *(formal)* फिर से आरंभ करना
retail ['riːteɪl] *n* खुदरा बिक्री ▷ *vi* खुदरा बिक्री करना
retailer ['riːteɪlə] *n* खुदरा विक्रेता
retail price ['riːteɪl praɪs] *n* खुदरा मूल्य
retire [rɪ'taɪə] *vi* सेवामुक्त होना
retired [rɪ'taɪəd] *adj* सेवामुक्त
retirement [rɪ'taɪəmənt] *n* सेवामुक्ति

retrace [rɪ'treɪs] *vt* पीछे लौटना

return [rɪ'tɜːn] *n* *(coming back)* वापसी; *(on an investment)* प्रतिलाभ ▷ *vt* *(give back)* वापस करना/लौटाना ▷ *vi* *(go back)* वापस लौटना ▷ *n* *(ticket)* वापसी टिकट

reunion [riː'juːnjən] *n* पुनर्मिलन

reuse [riː'juːz] *vt* दोबारा प्रयोग करना

reveal [rɪ'viːl] *vt* प्रकट करना

revenge [rɪ'vɛndʒ] *n* प्रतिशोध

revenue ['rɛvɪˌnjuː] *n* राजस्व

reverse [rɪ'vɜːs] *n* पीछे की ओर ▷ *vt* उलट देना

review [rɪ'vjuː] *n* समीक्षा

revise [rɪ'vaɪz] *vt* संशोधन करना

revision [rɪ'vɪʒən] *n* संशोधन

revive [rɪ'vaɪv] *v* पुनर्जीवित करना

revolting [rɪ'vəʊltɪŋ] *adj* घिनौना

revolution [ˌrɛvə'luːʃən] *n* क्रांति

revolutionary [ˌrɛvə'luːʃənərɪ] *adj* क्रांतिकारी

revolver [rɪ'vɒlvə] *n* तमंचा

reward [rɪ'wɔːd] *n* ईनाम

rewarding [rɪ'wɔːdɪŋ] *adj* लाभदायक

rewind [riː'waɪnd] *v* उल्टा फिराना

rheumatism ['ruːməˌtɪzəm] *n* गठिया

rhubarb ['ruːbɑːb] *n* रेवतचीनी

rhythm ['rɪðəm] *n* ताल

rib [rɪb] *n* पसली

ribbon ['rɪbn] *n* फीता

rice [raɪs] *n* चावल

rich [rɪtʃ] *adj* धनवान

ride [raɪd] *n* सवारी ▷ *v* सवार होना/सवारी करना

rider ['raɪdə] *n* सवार

ridiculous [rɪ'dɪkjʊləs] *adj* बेतुका

riding ['raɪdɪŋ] *n* सवारी

rifle ['raɪfl] *n* एक बंदूक

rig [rɪg] *n* ज़मीन से तेल निकालने का उपकरण

right [raɪt] *adj (correct)* सही; *(opposite of left)* दायां ▷ *adv* सही होना ▷ *n* उचित
right angle [raɪt 'æŋgl] *n* समकोण
right-hand ['raɪt,hænd] *adj* दाहिने हाथ का
right-hand drive ['raɪt,hænd draɪv] *n* दाईं ओर से गाड़ी चलाने की व्यवस्था
right-handed ['raɪt,hændɪd] *adj* दाएँहत्था
rightly ['raɪtlɪ] *adv* उचित रूप से
right of way [raɪt əv weɪ] *n* अधिकृत रास्ता/निजी रास्ता
right-wing ['raɪt,wɪŋ] *adj* दक्षिणपंथी
rim [rɪm] *n* नेमि/गोलाकार किनारा
ring [rɪŋ] *n* अंगूठी ▷ *vt (telephone)* फ़ोन करना ▷ *v (bell)* घंटी बजना
ring back [rɪŋ bæk] *v* दोबारा फ़ोन करना
ring binder [rɪŋ 'baɪndə] *n* एक प्रकार की फ़ाइल
ring road [rɪŋ rəʊd] *n* गोलाकार उपमार्ग
ringtone ['rɪŋ,təʊn] *n* फ़ोन की घंटी
ring up [rɪŋ ʌp] *v* फ़ोन करना
rink [rɪŋk] *n* स्केटिंग करने का मैदान
rinse [rɪns] *n* धुलाई ▷ *vt* धोना
riot ['raɪət] *n* दंगा ▷ *vi* दंगा करना
rip [rɪp] *v* फाड़ना
ripe [raɪp] *adj* पका हुआ
rip off [rɪp ɒf] *v (informal)* ठगना
rip-off ['rɪpɒf] *n (informal)* लूट
rip up [rɪp ʌp] *v* फाड़ना
rise [raɪz] *n* वृद्धि ▷ *vi* ऊपर उठना
risk [rɪsk] *n* जोखिम ▷ *vt* जोखिम उठाना
risky ['rɪskɪ] *adj* जोखिम भरा
ritual ['rɪtjʊəl] *adj* रस्म संबंधी ▷ *n* रस्म
rival ['raɪvl] *adj* प्रतिद्वन्द्वी ▷ *n* प्रतिद्वन्द्वी

rivalry ['raɪvəlrɪ] *n* प्रतिद्वन्द्विता
river ['rɪvə] *n* नदी
road [rəʊd] *n* सड़क
roadblock ['rəʊd,blɒk] *n* मार्ग अवरोध
road map [rəʊd mæp] *n* सड़क मानचित्र
road rage [rəʊd reɪdʒ] *n* सड़क पर होने वाली लड़ाई
road sign [rəʊd saɪn] *n* मार्ग चिह्न
road tax [rəʊd tæks] *n* सड़क कर
roadworks ['rəʊd,wɜːks] *npl* सड़क की मरम्मत
roast [rəʊst] *adj* भुना हुआ
rob [rɒb] *vt* लूटना
robber ['rɒbə] *n* लुटेरा
robbery ['rɒbərɪ] *n* लूट/डकैती
robin ['rɒbɪn] *n* रॉबिन - एक पक्षी
robot ['rəʊbɒt] *n* यंत्र मानव
rock [rɒk] *n (material)* चट्टान ▷ *v* डोलना ▷ *n (piece of rock)* शिला/चट्टान
rock climbing [rɒk 'klaɪmɪŋ] *n* चट्टानों पर चढ़ाई
rocket ['rɒkɪt] *n* रॉकेट
rocking chair ['rɒkɪŋ tʃɛə] *n* दोलन कुर्सी
rocking horse ['rɒkɪŋ hɔːs] *n* दोलन घोड़ा
rod [rɒd] *n* छड़
rodent ['rəʊdnt] *n* कृंतक/कुतरने वाले जीव
role [rəʊl] *n* भूमिका
roll [rəʊl] *n* लपेटा ▷ *v* लुढ़कना
roll call [rəʊl kɔːl] *n* हाजिरी
roller ['rəʊlə] *n* रोलर
rollercoaster ['rəʊlə,kəʊstə] *n* रोलरकोस्टर - एक झूला
rollerskates ['rəʊlə,skeɪts] *npl* रोलरस्केट - पहिएदार जूता
rollerskating ['rəʊlə,skeɪtɪŋ] *n* रोलरस्केटिंग
rolling pin ['rəʊlɪŋ pɪn] *n* बेलन
Roman ['rəʊmən] *adj* रोम से संबद्ध

romance [rə'mæns] *n* प्रेम
Romanesque [ˌrəʊmə'nɛsk] *adj* रोमन स्थापत्यकला
Romania [rəʊ'meɪnɪə] *n* रोमानिया
Romanian [rəʊ'meɪnɪən] *adj* रोमानियाई ▷ *n (person)* रोमानियाई; *(language)* रोमानियाई
romantic [rəʊ'mæntɪk] *adj* रूमानी
roof [ruːf] *n* छत
room [ruːm] *n (section of a building)* कमरा; *(space)* जगह
roommate ['ruːmˌmeɪt] *n* कक्ष साथी
room service [ruːm; rʊm 'sɜːvɪs] *n* कक्ष सेवा
root [ruːt] *n* जड़
rope [rəʊp] *n* रस्सी
rope in [rəʊp ɪn] *v (informal)* मनाना
rose [rəʊz] *n* गुलाब
rosé ['rəʊzeɪ] *n* गुलाबी शराब
rosemary ['rəʊzmərɪ] *n* गुलमेंहदी
rot [rɒt] *v* सड़ना/सड़ाना
rotten ['rɒtn] *adj* सड़ा हुआ
rough [rʌf] *adj (not smooth)* खुरदुरा/ऊबड़खाबड़; *(not gentle)* रूखा/कड़ा
roughly ['rʌflɪ] *adv* रुखाई से
roulette [ruː'lɛt] *n* जुए का एक खेल
round [raʊnd] *adj* गोलाकार ▷ *n (series)* चक्र; *(circle)* गोलाकार ▷ *prep* चारो ओर
roundabout ['raʊndəˌbaʊt] *n* गोल चक्कर रास्ता
round trip [raʊnd trɪp] *n* फेरा/वापसी यात्रा
round up [raʊnd ʌp] *v* घेरना
route [ruːt] *n* रास्ता
routine [ruː'tiːn] *n* दिनचर्या
row [rəʊ] *n (line)* पंक्ति; [raʊ] *n (argument)* झगड़ा ▷ [rəʊ] *v (in boat)* खेना ▷ [raʊ] *vi (argue)* झगड़ा करना
rowing ['rəʊɪŋ] *n* नौका दौड़
rowing boat ['rəʊɪŋ bəʊt] *n* पतवार वाली छोटी नाव
royal ['rɔɪəl] *adj* शाही

r

rub [rʌb] *vt* रगड़ना
rubber ['rʌbə] *n* *(material)* रबर; *(eraser)* रबर
rubber band ['rʌbə bænd] *n* रबर बैंड
rubber gloves ['rʌbə glʌvz] *npl* रबर के दस्ताने
rubbish ['rʌbɪʃ] *adj* *(informal)* बकवास/बेकार ▷ *n* कूड़ा
rubbish dump ['rʌbɪʃ dʌmp] *n* कूड़ादान
rucksack ['rʌk,sæk] *n* पीठ पर टांगने वाला थैला
rude [ruːd] *adj* अशिष्ट
rug [rʌg] *n* गलीचा
rugby ['rʌgbɪ] *n* रग्बी
ruin ['ruːɪn] *n* बर्बादी ▷ *vt* बर्बाद करना
rule [ruːl] *n* नियम ▷ *v* शासन करना
rule out [ruːl aʊt] *v* खारिज करना
ruler ['ruːlə] *n* *(leader)* शासक; *(for measuring)* मापक
rum [rʌm] *n* शराब
rumour ['ruːmə] *n* अफ़वाह
run [rʌn] *n* दौड़ ▷ *vi* *(follow a particular course)* की ओर दौड़ना; *(move quickly)* दौड़ना
run away [rʌn ə'weɪ] *v* भागना
runner ['rʌnə] *n* धावक
runner bean ['rʌnə biːn] *n* सेम
runner-up ['rʌnəʌp] *n* प्रतियोगिता का द्वितीय विजेता
running ['rʌnɪŋ] *n* दौड़
run out [rʌn aʊt] *v* समाप्त कर देना
run over [rʌn 'əʊvə] *v* कुचल देना
runway ['rʌn,weɪ] *n* विमान पट्टी
rupee [ruː'piː] *n* रुपया
rural ['rʊərəl] *adj* ग्रामीण
rush [rʌʃ] *n* हड़बड़ाहट ▷ *vi* जल्दी - जल्दी जाना
rush hour [rʌʃ aʊə] *n* व्यस्त समय
rusk [rʌsk] *n* एक तरह का बिस्कुट
Russia ['rʌʃə] *n* रूस

Russian ['rʌʃən] *adj* रूसी ▷ *n (person)* रूसी; *(language)* रूसी

rust [rʌst] *n* जंग

rusty ['rʌstɪ] *adj* जंग लगा हुआ

ruthless ['ruːθlɪs] *adj* निर्मम

rye [raɪ] *n* एक तरह का अनाज

S

sabotage ['sæbə,tɑːʒ] *n* तोड़ - फ़ोड़ ▷ *vt* तोड़ - फोड़ करना

sachet ['sæʃeɪ] *n* छोटा पैकेट

sack [sæk] *n (bag)* बोरी; *(dismissal)* बर्खास्तगी ▷ *vt* बर्खास्त करना

sacred ['seɪkrɪd] *adj* पवित्र

sacrifice ['sækrɪ,faɪs] *n* बलि

sad [sæd] *adj* दुःखी

saddle ['sædl] *n* घोड़े की जीन

saddlebag ['sædl,bæg] *n* फीतेदार झोला, जिसे वाहन पर बांधा जा सकता हो

sadly ['sædlɪ] *adv* दुःखपूर्वक

safari [sə'fɑːrɪ] *n* वन्य जीवन दर्शन यात्रा

safe [seɪf] *adj* सुरक्षित ▷ *n* तिजोरी

safety ['seɪftɪ] *n* सुरक्षा

safety belt ['seɪftɪ bɛlt] *n* सुरक्षा पट्टा

safety pin ['seɪftɪ pɪn] *n* आलपिन

saffron ['sæfrən] *n* केसर

Sagittarius [,sædʒɪ'tɛərɪəs] *n* धनु राशि

Sahara [sə'hɑːrə] *n* सहारा मरुस्थल

sail [seɪl] *n* पाल ▷ *v* खेना

sailing ['seɪlɪŋ] *n* नौकायन/समुद्र यात्रा

sailing boat ['seɪlɪŋ bəʊt] *n* पाल नौका

sailor ['seɪlə] *n* नाविक

saint [seɪnt] *n* संत

salad ['sæləd] *n* सलाद

salad dressing ['sæləd 'dresɪŋ] *n* सलाद में डालने की सामग्री

salami [sə'lɑːmɪ] *n* सलामी - मसालेदार गोश्त
salary ['sælərɪ] *n* तनख़्वाह
sale [seɪl] *n* बिक्री
sales assistant [seɪlz ə'sɪstənt] *n* बिक्री सहायक
salesman ['seɪlzmən] *n* विक्रेता
salesperson ['seɪlzpɜːsn] *n* विक्रेता
sales rep [seɪlz rɛp] *n* बिक्री प्रतिनिधि
saleswoman ['seɪlzwʊmən] *n* महिला विक्रेता
saliva [sə'laɪvə] *n* लार
salmon ['sæmən] *n* सामन - एक मछली
saloon [sə'luːn] *n* एक प्रकार की कार
saloon car [sə'luːn kɑː] *n* एक प्रकार की कार
salt [sɔːlt] *n* नमक
saltwater ['sɔːltˌwɔːtə] *adj* खारे पानी का
salty ['sɔːltɪ] *adj* खारा
salute [sə'luːt] *v* सलामी देना
same [seɪm] *adj* एक जैसा
sample ['sɑːmpl] *n* नमूना
sand [sænd] *n* रेत
sandal ['sændl] *n* सैंडल
sandcastle ['sændkɑːsl] *n* रेत का महल
sand dune [sænd djuːn] *n* रेत का टीला
sandpaper ['sændˌpeɪpə] *n* बालू कागज
sandpit ['sændˌpɪt] *n* बालू का गढ्ढा
sandstone ['sændˌstəʊn] *n* बलुआ पत्थर
sandwich ['sænwɪdʒ] *n* सैंडविच
sanitary towel ['sænɪtərɪ 'taʊəl] *n* सैनिटरी नैपकिन
San Marino [ˌsæn mə'riːnəʊ] *n* सैन मरीनो
sapphire ['sæfaɪə] *n* नीलम
sarcastic [sɑː'kæstɪk] *adj* व्यंग्यात्मक
sardine [sɑː'diːn] *n* पेडवे मछली
satchel ['sætʃəl] *n* बस्ता
satellite ['sætəlaɪt] *n* उपग्रह
satellite dish ['sætəlaɪt dɪʃ] *n* सैटेलाइट डिश

satisfaction [ˌsætɪsˈfækʃən] *n* संतोष

satisfactory [ˌsætɪsˈfæktərɪ] *adj* संतोषजनक

satisfied [ˈsætɪsˌfaɪd] *adj* संतुष्ट

sat nav [ˈsætnæv] *n* सैटेलाइट नैविगेशन

Saturday [ˈsætədɪ] *n* शनिवार

sauce [sɔːs] *n* चटनी

saucepan [ˈsɔːspən] *n* पकाने का हत्थेदार बर्तन

saucer [ˈsɔːsə] *n* तश्तरी

Saudi [ˈsɔːdɪ əˈreɪbɪə] *adj* सउदी अरब से संबद्ध ▷ *n* सउदी अरब का निवासी

Saudi Arabia [ˈsɔːdɪ əˈreɪbɪə] *n* सउदी अरब

Saudi Arabian [ˈsɔːdɪ əˈreɪbɪən] *adj* सउदी अरब से संबद्ध ▷ *n* सउदी अरब का निवासी

sauna [ˈsɔːnə] *n* वाष्प स्नान

sausage [ˈsɒsɪdʒ] *n* सॉसेज

save [seɪv] *vt (rescue)* बचाना; *(money)* बचाकर रखना

save up [seɪv ʌp] *v* बचत करना

savings [ˈseɪvɪŋz] *npl* बचत

savoury [ˈseɪvərɪ] *adj* चटपटा

saw [sɔː] *n* आरी

sawdust [ˈsɔːˌdʌst] *n* बुरादा

saxophone [ˈsæksəˌfəʊn] *n* सैक्सोफ़ोन - एक वाद्य

say [seɪ] *vt* कहना

saying [ˈseɪɪŋ] *n* लोकोक्ति

scaffolding [ˈskæfəldɪŋ] *n* मचान

scale [skeɪl] *n (for measuring)* पैमाना; *(fish, reptile)* शल्क

scales [skeɪlz] *npl* पैमाना

scallop [ˈskɒləp] *n* सीप वाली मछली

scam [skæm] *n (informal)* घोटाला

scampi [ˈskæmpɪ] *npl* बड़ा झींगा

scan [skæn] *n* स्कैन ▷ *vt* बारीकी से देखना

scandal [ˈskændl] *n* घोटाला

Scandinavia [ˌskændɪˈneɪvɪə] *n* स्कैंडिनेविया

Scandinavian [ˌskændɪˈneɪvɪən] *adj* स्कैंडिनेवियाई
scanner [ˈskænə] *n* स्कैनर
scar [skɑː] *n* घाव का निशान
scarce [skɛəs] *adj* अपर्याप्त
scarcely [ˈskɛəslɪ] *adv* मुश्किल से
scare [skɛə] *n* भय ▹ *vt* डराना
scarecrow [ˈskɛəˌkrəʊ] *n* बिजूका
scared [skɛəd] *adj* भयभीत
scarf [skɑːf] *n* गुलुबंद
scarlet [ˈskɑːlɪt] *adj* गाढ़ा लाल
scary [ˈskɛərɪ] *adj* डरावना
scene [siːn] *n* दृश्य
scenery [ˈsiːnərɪ] *n* प्राकृतिक दृश्य
scent [sɛnt] *n* खुशबू
sceptical [ˈskɛptɪkl] *adj* संशयात्मक
schedule [ˈʃɛdjuːl] *n* समय - सारणी
scheme [skiːm] *n* योजना
schizophrenic [ˌskɪtsəʊˈfrɛnɪk] *adj* मनोविदालित
scholarship [ˈskɒləʃɪp] *n* छात्रवृत्ति
school [skuːl] *n* विद्यालय
schoolbag [ˈskuːlˌbæg] *n* बस्ता
schoolbook [ˈskuːlˌbʊk] *n* पाठ्यपुस्तक
schoolboy [ˈskuːlˌbɔɪ] *n* छात्र
schoolchildren [ˈskuːlˌtʃɪldrən] *npl* स्कूली बच्चे
schoolgirl [ˈskuːlˌgɜːl] *n* छात्रा
schoolteacher [ˈskuːlˌtiːtʃə] *n* शिक्षक
school uniform [skuːl ˈjuːnɪfɔːm] *n* विद्यालय की वर्दी
science [ˈsaɪəns] *n* विज्ञान
science fiction [ˈsaɪəns ˈfɪkʃən] *n* विज्ञान कथा
scientific [ˌsaɪənˈtɪfɪk] *adj* वैज्ञानिक
scientist [ˈsaɪəntɪst] *n* वैज्ञानिक
sci-fi [ˈsaɪˌfaɪ] *n (informal)* विज्ञान कथा हेतु संक्षिप्त रूप
scissors [ˈsɪzəz] *npl* कैंची

scoff [skɒf] *vi* मज़ाक उड़ाना

scold [skəʊld] *vt (formal)* फटकारना

scooter ['skuːtə] *n* स्कूटर

score [skɔː] *n (in a game)* अंक; *(music)* स्वर लिपि ▷ *v* अंक प्राप्त करना

Scorpio ['skɔːpɪˌəʊ] *n* वृश्चिक राशि

scorpion ['skɔːpɪən] *n* बिच्छू

Scot [skɒt] *n* स्कॉटलैंड का निवासी

Scotland ['skɒtlənd] *n* स्कॉटलैंड

Scots [skɒts] *adj* स्कॉटलैंड से संबद्ध

Scotsman ['skɒtsmən] *n* स्कॉटलैंड का पुरुष

Scotswoman ['skɒtsˌwʊmən] *n* स्कॉटलैंड की महिला

Scottish ['skɒtɪʃ] *adj* स्कॉटलैंड से संबद्ध

scout [skaʊt] *n* गुप्तचर

scrambled eggs ['skræmbld ɛgz] *npl* अंडे की भुर्जी

scrap [skræp] *n (small piece)* कतरन/टुकड़ा; *(fight)* झगड़ा ▷ *vt* फेंकना

scrapbook ['skræpˌbʊk] *n* स्क्रैप बुक

scrap paper [skræp 'peɪpə] *n* कागज का टुकड़ा

scratch [skrætʃ] *n* खरोंच ▷ *v (with nails)* खुजाना/खरोंचना ▷ *vt (something sharp)* खरोंचना

scream [skriːm] *n* चीख ▷ *vi* चीखना

screen [skriːn] *n* परदा ▷ *vt* दिखाया जाना

screensaver ['skriːnseɪvə] *n* स्क्रीनसेवर

screw [skruː] *n* पेंच

screwdriver ['skruːˌdraɪvə] *n* पेंचकस

scribble ['skrɪbl] *v* घसीट कर लिखना

scrub [skrʌb] *vt* रगड़ना

scuba diving ['skuːbə 'daɪvɪŋ] *n* गोताखोरी

sculptor ['skʌlptə] *n* मूर्तिकार

sculpture ['skʌlptʃə] *n* मूर्ति

sea [siː] *n* समुद्र
seafood ['siːˌfuːd] *n* समुद्री भोजन
seagull ['siːˌgʌl] *n* समुद्री पक्षी
seal [siːl] *n (animal)* सील; *(on a document)* मुहर ▷ *vt* मुहरबंद करना/बंद करना
sea level [siː 'lɛvl] *n* समुद्र - स्तर
seam [siːm] *n* सिलाई
seaman ['siːmən] *n* नाविक
search [sɜːtʃ] *n* खोज ▷ *v* खोज करना
search engine [sɜːtʃ 'ɛndʒɪn] *n* सर्च इंजन
search party [sɜːtʃ 'pɑːtɪ] *n* खोजी दस्ता
seashore ['siːˌʃɔː] *n* समुद्र तट
seasick ['siːˌsɪk] *adj* समुद्री यात्रा के कारण बीमार
seaside ['siːˌsaɪd] *n* समुद्रतटीय क्षेत्र
season ['siːzn] *n* मौसम
seasonal ['siːzənl] *adj* मौसमी
seasoning ['siːzənɪŋ] *n* मसाला
season ticket ['siːzn 'tɪkɪt] *n* मियादी टिकट
seat [siːt] *n (for sitting on)* आसन; *(in election)* सीट/स्थान
seatbelt ['siːtˌbɛlt] *n* सीटबेल्ट
sea water [siː 'wɔːtə] *n* समुद्री जल
seaweed ['siːˌwiːd] *n* समुद्री शैवाल
second ['sɛkənd] *adj* दूसरा ▷ *n* सेकेंड/पल
secondary school ['sɛkəndərɪ skuːl] *n* माध्यमिक विद्यालय
second class ['sɛkənd klɑːs] *n* दूसरा दर्जा
second-class ['sɛkəndˌklɑːs] *adj* द्वितीय श्रेणी
secondhand ['sɛkəndˌhænd] *adj* पुराना/इस्तेमाल किया हुआ
secondly ['sɛkəndlɪ] *adv* दूसरे
second-rate ['sɛkəndˌreɪt] *adj* दूसरे दर्जे का

secret ['siːkrɪt] *adj* गोपनीय ▷ *n* रहस्य
secretary ['sɛkrətrɪ] *n* सचिव
secretly ['siːkrɪtlɪ] *adv* गुप्त रूप से
secret service ['siːkrɪt 'sɜːvɪs] *n* गुप्तचर विभाग
sect [sɛkt] *n* पंथ/संप्रदाय
section ['sɛkʃən] *n* अनुभाग
sector ['sɛktə] *n* क्षेत्र
secure [sɪ'kjʊə] *adj* सुरक्षित
security [sɪ'kjʊərɪtɪ] *n* सुरक्षा
security guard [sɪ'kjʊərɪtɪ gɑːd] *n* सुरक्षा गार्ड
sedative ['sɛdətɪv] *n* शामक औषधि
see [siː] *v* *(with eyes)* देखना ▷ *vt* *(meet)* भेंट करना
seed [siːd] *n* बीज
seek [siːk] *vt* *(formal)* खोजना
seem [siːm] *v* प्रतीत होना
seesaw ['siːˌsɔː] *n* सी - सॉ/ढेंकुली जैसा झूला
see-through ['siːˌθruː] *adj* पारदर्शी
seize [siːz] *vt* पकड़ना
seizure ['siːʒə] *n* दौरा
seldom ['sɛldəm] *adv* कभी - कभी
select [sɪ'lɛkt] *vt* चयन करना
selection [sɪ'lɛkʃən] *n* चयन
self-assured ['sɛlfə'ʃʊəd] *adj* आत्मविश्वासी
self-catering ['sɛlf'keɪtərɪŋ] *n* ऐसा अतिथिगृह जहां अपने खान-पान का इंतज़ाम खुद करना होता है
self-centred ['sɛlf'sɛntəd] *adj* आत्म - केंद्रित
self-conscious ['sɛlf'kɒnʃəs] *adj* संकोची
self-contained ['sɛlfˌkən'teɪnd] *adj* आत्मनिर्भर
self-control ['sɛlfˌkən'trəʊl] *n* आत्म - नियंत्रण
self-defence ['sɛlfˌdɪ'fɛns] *n* आत्म - रक्षा
self-discipline ['sɛlf'dɪsɪplɪn] *n* स्व - अनुशासन

self-employed ['sɛlfɪm'plɔɪd] *adj* स्वनियोजित
selfish ['sɛlfɪʃ] *adj* स्वार्थी
self-service ['sɛlf'sɜːvɪs] *adj* स्वयंसेवा
sell [sɛl] *vt* बेचना
sell-by date ['sɛlbaɪ deɪt] *n* उत्पाद के उपयोग की अंतिम तिथि
selling price ['sɛlɪŋ praɪs] *n* बिक्री मूल्य
sell off [sɛl ɒf] *v* औने - पौने दाम पर बेचना
Sellotape® ['sɛlə,teɪp] *n* सेलोटेप
sell out [sɛl aʊt] *v* बेच देना
semester [sɪ'mɛstə] *n* सत्र
semicircle ['sɛmɪ,sɜːkl] *n* अर्द्धवृत्त
semi-colon [,sɛmɪ'kəʊlən] *n* अर्द्धविराम
semi-detached house [sɛmɪdɪ'tætʃt haʊs] *n* अर्द्धसंलग्न मकान
semifinal [,sɛmɪ'faɪnl] *n* सेमीफ़ाइनल
semi-skimmed milk ['sɛmɪskɪmd mɪlk] *n* आंशिक रूप से मलाई निकला दूध
send [sɛnd] *vt* भेजना
send back [sɛnd bæk] *v* वापस भेजना
sender ['sɛndə] *n* प्रेषक
send off [sɛnd ɒf] *v* प्रेषित करना
send out [sɛnd aʊt] *v* भेजना
Senegal [,sɛnɪ'gɔːl] *n* सेनेगल
Senegalese [,sɛnɪgə'liːz] *adj* सेनेगल से संबद्ध ▷ *n* सेनेगल का निवासी
senior ['siːnjə] *adj* वरिष्ठ
senior citizen ['siːnɪə 'sɪtɪzn] *n* वरिष्ठ नागरिक
sensational [sɛn'seɪʃənl] *adj* सनसनीख़ेज
sense [sɛns] *n* इंद्रियबोध
senseless ['sɛnslɪs] *adj* बेमतलब
sense of humour [sɛns ɒv 'hjuːmə] *n* हंसोड़पन/विनोदप्रियता
sensible ['sɛnsɪbl] *adj* समझदार

sensitive ['sɛnsɪtɪv] *adj* संवेदनशील

sensuous ['sɛnsjʊəs] *adj* इंद्रिय विषयक/सुखकर

sentence ['sɛntəns] *n (statement)* वाक्य; *(punishment)* दंड ▷ *vt* दंड देना

sentimental [ˌsɛntɪ'mɛntl] *adj* भावुक

separate ['seprɪt] *adj* अलग ▷ ['sɛpəˌreɪt] *v* अलग करना

separately ['sɛpərətlɪ] *adv* अलग से

separation [ˌsɛpə'reɪʃən] *n* अलगाव

September [sɛp'tɛmbə] *n* सितंबर

septic tank ['sɛptɪk tæŋk] *n* सेप्टिक टैंक

sequel ['siːkwəl] *n* उत्तरकथा

sequence ['siːkwəns] *n* सिलसिला

Serbia ['sɜːbɪə] *n* सर्बिया

Serbian ['sɜːbɪən] *adj* सर्बियाई ▷ *n (person)* सर्बियाई; *(language)* सर्बियाई

sergeant ['sɑːdʒənt] *n* एक सैनिक पदाधिकारी

serial ['sɪərɪəl] *n* धारावाहिक

series ['sɪəriːz] *n* क्रम

serious ['sɪərɪəs] *adj* गंभीर

seriously ['sɪərɪəslɪ] *adv* गंभीर रूप से

servant ['sɜːvnt] *n* नौकर

serve [sɜːv] *n* सर्व - गेंद को बैडमिंटन से मारने की क्रिया ▷ *vt* सेवा करना

server ['sɜːvə] *n (of a computer network)* सर्वर; *(tennis player)* सर्वर - गेंद को बैडमिंटन से मारकर खेल शुरु करने वाला खिलाड़ी

service ['sɜːvɪs] *n* सेवा ▷ *vt* गाड़ी की साफ - सफाई करवाना

service area ['sɜːvɪs 'ɛərɪə] *n* सेवा क्षेत्र

service charge ['sɜːvɪs tʃɑːdʒ] *n* सेवा शुल्क

serviceman ['sɜːvɪsˌmæn] *n* सैनिक

service station ['sɜːvɪs 'steɪʃən] *n* सर्विस स्टेशन

servicewoman ['sɜːvɪsˌwʊmən] *n* महिला सैनिक
serviette [ˌsɜːvɪ'ɛt] *n* रूमाल
session ['sɛʃən] *n* सत्र
set [sɛt] *n* समुच्चय ▷ *vt* व्यवस्थित करना
setback ['sɛtbæk] *n* रुकावट
set off [sɛt ɒf] *v* प्रस्थान करना
set out [sɛt aʊt] *v* रवाना होना
settee [sɛ'tiː] *n* छोटा सोफ़ा
settle ['sɛtl] *vt* निपटाना
settle down ['sɛtl daʊn] *v* बसना
seven ['sɛvn] *num* सात
seventeen ['sɛvn'tiːn] *num* सत्रह
seventeenth ['sɛvn'tiːnθ] *adj* सत्रहवां
seventh ['sɛvnθ] *adj* सातवां ▷ *n* सातवां
seventy ['sɛvntɪ] *num* सत्तर
several ['sɛvrəl] *det* कई ▷ *pron* कई ▷ *adj* कई
sew [səʊ] *v* सीना/सिलाई करना
sewer ['suːə] *n* भूमिगत नाली
sewing ['səʊɪŋ] *n* सिलाई
sewing machine ['səʊɪŋ mə'ʃiːn] *n* सिलाई मशीन
sew up [səʊ ʌp] *v* सीना/ सिलाई करना
sex [sɛks] *n* लिंग
sexism ['sɛksɪzəm] *n* लिंगभेद
sexist ['sɛksɪst] *adj* लिंगवादी
shabby ['ʃæbɪ] *adj* फटेहाल/जर्जर
shade [ʃeɪd] *n* छाया
shadow ['ʃædəʊ] *n* परछाई
shake [ʃeɪk] *vt (move up and down)* हिलाना ▷ *v (tremble)* हिलना
shaken ['ʃeɪkən] *adj* विचलित
shaky ['ʃeɪkɪ] *adj* अस्थिर/ कंपित
shall [ʃæl] *v* भविष्य सूचक शब्द/ करेगा
shallow ['ʃæləʊ] *adj* छिछला
shambles ['ʃæmblz] *npl* बेतरतीब स्थान

shame [ʃeɪm] *n* शर्म
shampoo [ʃæm'puː] *n* शैंपू
shape [ʃeɪp] *n* आकार
share [ʃɛə] *n* हिस्सा ▷ *vt* साझा करना
shareholder ['ʃɛə,həʊldə] *n* हिस्सेदार
share out [ʃɛə aʊt] *v* हिस्सा देना
shark [ʃɑːk] *n* शार्क
sharp [ʃɑːp] *adj (point)* धारदार/पैना; *(pain)* तीव्र
shave [ʃeɪv] *v* हजामत करना
shaver ['ʃeɪvə] *n* उस्तरा
shaving cream ['ʃeɪvɪŋ kriːm] *n* हजामत करने की क्रीम
shaving foam ['ʃeɪvɪŋ fəʊm] *n* हजामत करने की क्रीम
shawl [ʃɔːl] *n* दुशाला
she [ʃiː] *pron* वह (लड़की के लिए)
shed [ʃɛd] *n* छप्पर
sheep [ʃiːp] *n* भेड़
sheepdog ['ʃiːp,dɒg] *n* एक प्रकार का कुत्ता
sheepskin ['ʃiːp,skɪn] *n* भेड़ का चमड़ा
sheer [ʃɪə] *adj* निरा/कोरा
sheet [ʃiːt] *n (for bed)* चादर; *(paper)* पत्तर/चद्दर
shelf [ʃɛlf] *n* ताखा
shell [ʃɛl] *n (egg, nut)* कवच/कड़ा छिलका; *(animal)* कवच/आवरण
shellfish ['ʃɛl,fɪʃ] *n* घोंघा
shell suit [ʃɛl suːt] *n* शेल सूट - एक प्रकार का वस्त्र
shelter ['ʃɛltə] *n* आश्रय
shepherd ['ʃɛpəd] *n* गड़ेरिया
sherry ['ʃɛrɪ] *n* शराब
shield [ʃiːld] *n* कवच
shift [ʃɪft] *n* बदलाव ▷ *v* खिसकाना/खिसकना
shifty ['ʃɪftɪ] *adj (informal)* कुटिल
shin [ʃɪn] *n* पिंडली
shine [ʃaɪn] *vi* चमकना
shiny ['ʃaɪnɪ] *adj* चमकीला
ship [ʃɪp] *n* जहाज
shipbuilding ['ʃɪp,bɪldɪŋ] *n* पोत निर्माण
shipment ['ʃɪpmənt] *n* पोत में लदी वस्तु

S

shipwreck ['ʃɪp,rɛk] *n* जहाज की तबाही
shipwrecked ['ʃɪp,rɛkt] *adj* टूटा हुआ जहाज
shipyard ['ʃɪp,jɑːd] *n* पोत कारखाना/डाक
shirt [ʃɜːt] *n* कमीज
shiver ['ʃɪvə] *vi* कांपना
shock [ʃɒk] *n* सदमा ▷ *vt* सदमा पहुंचाना/भौंचक्का करना
shocking ['ʃɒkɪŋ] *adj* *(informal)* दिल दहलाने वाली
shoe [ʃuː] *n* जूता
shoelace ['ʃuː,leɪs] *n* जूते का फीता
shoe polish [ʃuː 'pɒlɪʃ] *n* जूते की पॉलिश
shoe shop [ʃuː ʃɒp] *n* जूते की दुकान
shoot [ʃuːt] *vt* गोली मारना
shooting ['ʃuːtɪŋ] *n* गोलीबारी
shop [ʃɒp] *n* दुकान
shop assistant [ʃɒp ə'sɪstənt] *n* सहायक विक्रेता
shopkeeper ['ʃɒp,kiːpə] *n* दुकानदार
shoplifting ['ʃɒp,lɪftɪŋ] *n* उठाईगिरी
shopping ['ʃɒpɪŋ] *n* खरीददारी
shopping bag ['ʃɒpɪŋ bæg] *n* खरीदारी का झोला
shopping centre ['ʃɒpɪŋ 'sɛntə] *n* बिक्री केंद्र
shopping trolley ['ʃɒpɪŋ 'trɒlɪ] *n* खरीदारी करने की ट्रॉली
shop window [ʃɒp 'wɪndəʊ] *n* दुकान की खिड़की
shore [ʃɔː] *n* किनारा
short [ʃɔːt] *adj* *(in time)* छोटा/संक्षिप्त; *(in length or distance)* छोटा/ नाटा
shortage ['ʃɔːtɪdʒ] *n* कमी
shortcoming ['ʃɔːt,kʌmɪŋ] *n* कमी
shortcrust pastry ['ʃɔːtkrʌst 'peɪstrɪ] *n* कुरकुरी पेस्ट्री
shortcut ['ʃɔːt,kʌt] *n* छोटा रास्ता
shortfall ['ʃɔːt,fɔːl] *n* कमी
shorthand ['ʃɔːt,hænd] *n* आशुलिपि

shortlist [ˈʃɔːtˌlɪst] *n* चयनित सूची
shortly [ˈʃɔːtlɪ] *adv* थोड़ी देर
shorts [ʃɔːts] *npl* छोटी पतलून
short-sighted [ˈʃɔːtˈsaɪtɪd] *adj* निकट दृष्टिदोष से पीड़ित
short-sleeved [ˈʃɔːtˌsliːvd] *adj* छोटी बांह वाला
short story [ʃɔːt ˈstɔːrɪ] *n* लघु कथा
shot [ʃɒt] *n* निशाना
shotgun [ˈʃɒtˌɡʌn] *n* बंदूक/मशीनगन
should [ʃʊd] *v* चाहिए
shoulder [ˈʃəʊldə] *n* कंधा
shoulder blade [ˈʃəʊldə bleɪd] *n* स्कंधास्थि
shout [ʃaʊt] *n* चिल्लाहट ▷ *v* चिल्लाना
shovel [ˈʃʌvl] *n* बेलचा
show [ʃəʊ] *n* प्रदर्शन ▷ *vt (prove)* प्रदर्शित करना ▷ *v (let see)* दिखाना ▷ *vt (teach)* दर्शाना/समझाना
show business [ʃəʊ ˈbɪznɪs] *n* मनोरंजन व्यवसाय
shower [ˈʃaʊə] *n (type of bath)* फुहारा; *(rain)* बौछार
shower cap [ˈʃaʊə kæp] *n* फुहारे में नहाते समय लगाई जाने वाली टोपी
shower gel [ˈʃaʊə dʒɛl] *n* नहाने का तरल साबुन
showerproof [ˈʃaʊəˌpruːf] *adj* बरसाती वस्त्र
showing [ˈʃəʊɪŋ] *n* प्रदर्शन
show jumping [ʃəʊ ˈdʒʌmpɪŋ] *n* घुड़सवारी प्रतियोगिता
show off [ʃəʊ ɒf] *v* दिखावा करना
show-off [ˈʃəʊɒf] *n (informal)* दिखावा करना
show up [ʃəʊ ʌp] *v* आना
shriek [ʃriːk] *vi* चीखना
shrimp [ʃrɪmp] *n* झींगा
shrine [ʃraɪn] *n* पुण्यस्थली
shrink [ʃrɪŋk] *v* सिकुड़ना
shrub [ʃrʌb] *n* झाड़ी
shrug [ʃrʌɡ] *vi* कंधे उचकाना
shrunken [ˈʃrʌŋkən] *adj* संकुचित
shudder [ˈʃʌdə] *vi* थरथराना

shuffle ['ʃʌfl] *vi* घसीट कर चलना

shut [ʃʌt] *v* बंद करना

shut down [ʃʌt daʊn] *v* हमेशा के लिए बंद होना

shutters ['ʃʌtəz] *npl* चिक

shuttle ['ʃʌtl] *n* शटल- एक अंतरिक्ष यान

shuttlecock ['ʃʌtl,kɒk] *n* बैडमिंटन की चिड़िया

shut up [ʃʌt ʌp] *v* चुप होना

shy [ʃaɪ] *adj* शर्मीला

Siberia [saɪ'bɪərɪə] *n* साइबेरिया

siblings ['sɪblɪŋz] *npl* *(formal)* सहोदर

sick [sɪk] *adj* बीमार/तंग आया हुआ

sickening ['sɪkənɪŋ] *adj* अरुचिकर

sick leave [sɪk liːv] *n* रुग्णतावकाश

sickness ['sɪknɪs] *n* बीमारी

sick note [sɪk nəʊt] *n* अस्वस्थता प्रमाण पत्र

sick pay [sɪk peɪ] *n* अस्वस्थता भुगतान

side [saɪd] *n* *(right or left part)* पहलू; *(edge)* किनारा; *(team)* पक्ष

sideboard ['saɪd,bɔːd] *n* अलमारी

side effect [saɪd ɪ'fɛkt] *n* अतिरिक्त प्रभाव

sidelight ['saɪd,laɪt] *n* गाड़ी के सामने की बत्ती

side street [saɪd striːt] *n* उपमार्ग/छोटी गोली

sideways ['saɪd,weɪz] *adv* तरफ़ से

sieve [sɪv] *n* छलनी

sigh [saɪ] *n* निःश्वास ▷ *vi* निःश्वास छोड़ना

sight [saɪt] *n* दृष्टि

sightseeing ['saɪt,siːɪŋ] *n* दृश्यावलोकन

sign [saɪn] *n* *(symbol)* चिह्न ▷ *v* हस्ताक्षर ▷ *n* *(gesture)* संकेत

signal ['sɪgnl] *n* संकेत ▷ *v* संकेत करना

signature ['sɪgnɪtʃə] *n* हस्ताक्षर

significance [sɪg'nɪfɪkəns] *n* महत्ता

significant [sɪg'nɪfɪkənt] *adj* महत्वपूर्ण
sign language [saɪn 'læŋgwɪdʒ] *n* सांकेतिक भाषा
sign on [saɪn ɒn] *v* दर्ज कराना
signpost ['saɪn,pəʊst] *n* दिशासूचक पट्ट
Sikh [siːk] *adj* सिक्ख ▷ *n* सिक्ख
silence ['saɪləns] *n* चुप्पी
silencer ['saɪlənsə] *n* साइलेंसर
silent ['saɪlənt] *adj (with no sound)* शांत/ निःशब्द; *(not talking)* चुप/ख़ामोश
silicon chip ['sɪlɪkən tʃɪp] *n* सिलिकॉन चिप
silk [sɪlk] *n* रेशमी कपड़ा
silly ['sɪlɪ] *adj* बेवकूफ़ाना
silver ['sɪlvə] *n* चांदी
similar ['sɪmɪlə] *adj* समान
similarity ['sɪmɪ'lærɪtɪ] *n* समानता
simmer ['sɪmə] *v* धीमी आंच पर पकाना
simple ['sɪmpl] *adj* सरल
simplify ['sɪmplɪ,faɪ] *vt* सरलीकृत करना
simply ['sɪmplɪ] *adv* सरलता से
simultaneous [,sɪməl'teɪnɪəs] *adj* समकालिक
simultaneously [,sɪməl'teɪnɪəslɪ] *adv* एक साथ
since [sɪns] *adv* तब से ▷ *conj* जब से ▷ *prep* से
sincere [sɪn'sɪə] *adj* ईमानदार/खरा
sincerely [sɪn'sɪəlɪ] *adv* ईमानदारी से
sing [sɪŋ] *v* गाना
singer ['sɪŋə] *n* गायक
singing ['sɪŋɪŋ] *n* गायन
single ['sɪŋgl] *adj* एकल
single parent ['sɪŋgl 'pɛərənt] *n* एकल अभिभावक
singles *npl* सिंगल्स - एक के मुकाबले एक का खेल
single ticket ['sɪŋgl 'tɪkɪt] *n* एक तरफ का टिकट
singular ['sɪŋgjʊlə] *n* एकवचन

sinister ['sɪnɪstə] *adj* अशुभ/मनहूस
sink [sɪŋk] *n* हौज ▷ *v* डूबना
sinus ['saɪnəs] *n* साइनस
sir [sɜː] *n* महाशय
siren ['saɪərən] *n* भोंपू
sister ['sɪstə] *n* बहन
sister-in-law ['sɪstə ɪn lɔː] *n* ननद/भाभी
sit [sɪt] *vi* बैठना
sitcom ['sɪt,kɒm] *n* परिस्थितिजन्य हास्य
sit down [sɪt daʊn] *v* बैठ जाना
site [saɪt] *n* कार्यस्थल/घटनास्थल
sitting room ['sɪtɪŋ rʊm] *n* बैठकखाना
situated ['sɪtjʊ,eɪtɪd] *adj* स्थित
situation [,sɪtjʊ'eɪʃən] *n* परिस्थिति
six [sɪks] *num* छह
sixteen ['sɪks'tiːn] *num* सोलह
sixteenth ['sɪks'tiːnθ] *adj* सोलहवां
sixth [sɪksθ] *adj* छठा
sixty ['sɪkstɪ] *num* साठ
size [saɪz] *n* आकार/माप
skate [skeɪt] *vi* स्केटिंग करना
skateboard ['skeɪt,bɔːd] *n* स्केटबोर्ड
skateboarding ['skeɪt,bɔːdɪŋ] *n* स्केटिंग का खेल
skates [skeɪts] *npl* स्केट्स
skating ['skeɪtɪŋ] *n* स्केटिंग
skating rink ['skeɪtɪŋ rɪŋk] *n* स्केटिंग करने का क्षेत्र
skeleton ['skɛlɪtən] *n* कंकाल
sketch [skɛtʃ] *n* रेखाचित्र ▷ *v* रेखाचित्र बनाना
skewer ['skjʊə] *n* कबाब की सीख
ski [skiː] *n* स्की ▷ *vi* स्कीइंग करना
skid [skɪd] *vi* फिसलना
skier ['skiːə] *n* स्की करने वाला
skiing ['skiːɪŋ] *n* स्कीइंग का खेल
skilful ['skɪlfʊl] *adj* कुशल
ski lift [skiː lɪft] *n* स्की लिफ़्ट
skill [skɪl] *n* कौशल

skilled [skɪld] *adj* कुशल
skimmed milk [skɪmd mɪlk] *n* मलाई निकला दूध
skimpy ['skɪmpɪ] *adj* बहुत छोटा
skin [skɪn] *n (person)* त्वचा; *(fruit, vegetable)* छिलका
skinhead ['skɪn,hɛd] *n* छोटे बालों वाला बदमाश लड़का
skinny ['skɪnɪ] *adj (informal)* दुबला-पतला
skin-tight ['skɪn'taɪt] *adj* बहुत चुस्त/बहुत तंग
skip [skɪp] *vi (with feet)* कूदना ▷ *vt (not have)* छोड़ना
skirt [skɜːt] *n* घाघरा
skirting board ['skɜːtɪŋ bɔːd] *n* दीवार के किनारे लगी लकड़ी की पट्टी
skive [skaɪv] *v (informal)* कामचोरी करना
skull [skʌl] *n* खोपड़ी
sky [skaɪ] *n* आसमान
skyscraper ['skaɪ,skreɪpə] *n* गगनचुंबी इमारत
slack [slæk] *adj* ढीला
slag off [slæg ɒf] *v (informal)* आलोचना करना
slam [slæm] *v* ज़ोर से बंद करना
slang [slæŋ] *n* कठबोली
slap [slæp] *vt* थप्पड़ करना
slate [sleɪt] *n* स्लेट - एक पत्थर
slave [sleɪv] *n* गुलाम ▷ *vi* गुलामी करना
sledge [slɛdʒ] *n* स्लेज - बर्फ़ पर चलने वाली गाड़ी
sledging ['slɛdʒɪŋ] *n* स्लेज पर सवारी करना
sleep [sliːp] *n* नींद ▷ *vi* सोना
sleep in [sliːp ɪn] *v* देर तक सोना
sleeping bag ['sliːpɪŋ bæg] *n* स्लीपिंग बैग
sleeping car ['sliːpɪŋ kɑː] *n* शयनयान
sleeping pill ['sliːpɪŋ pɪl] *n* नींद की गोली
sleepwalk ['sliːp,wɔːk] *vi* नींद में चलना
sleepy ['sliːpɪ] *adj* उनींदा
sleet [sliːt] *n* ओलों वाली वर्षा ▷ *v* ओलों वाली वर्षा होना
sleeve [sliːv] *n* बांह

sleeveless ['sliːvlɪs] *adj* बिना बांह का
slender ['slɛndə] *adj* *(written)* छरहरा
slice [slaɪs] *n* फांक/कतला ▷ *vt* फांक काटना
slide [slaɪd] *n* फिसलपट्टी ▷ *v* फिसलना
slight [slaɪt] *adj* थोड़ा
slightly ['slaɪtlɪ] *adv* किंचित/थोड़ा सा
slim [slɪm] *adj* छरहरा
sling [slɪŋ] *n* झलुआ/लटकन
slip [slɪp] *n* *(mistake)* चूक; *(paper)* पर्ची; *(petticoat)* समीज ▷ *vi* फिसलना
slipped disc [slɪpt dɪsk] *n* रीढ़ की खिसकी हड्डी
slipper ['slɪpə] *n* हवाई चप्पल
slippery ['slɪpərɪ] *adj* फिसलन भरा/रपटीला
slip road [slɪp rəʊd] *n* सड़क
slip up [slɪp ʌp] *v* गलती करना
slip-up ['slɪpʌp] *n* *(informal)* चूक
slope [sləʊp] *n* ढाल
sloppy ['slɒpɪ] *adj* लापरवाह
slot [slɒt] *n* सिक्के डालने हेतु दरार
slot machine [slɒt mə'ʃiːn] *n* सिक्के डालने की मशीन
Slovak ['sləʊvæk] *adj* स्लोवाकियाई ▷ *n* *(language)* स्लोवाकियाई; *(person)* स्लोवाकियाई
Slovakia [sləʊ'vækɪə] *n* स्लोवाकिया
Slovenia [sləʊ'viːnɪə] *n* स्लोवेनिया
Slovenian [sləʊ'viːnɪən] *adj* स्लोवेनियाई ▷ *n* *(person)* स्लोवेनियाई; *(language)* स्लोवेनियाई
slow [sləʊ] *adj* धीमा
slow down [sləʊ daʊn] *v* धीमा होना/धीमा करना
slowly ['sləʊlɪ] *adv* धीमे से
slug [slʌg] *n* बिना आवरण का घोंघा
slum [slʌm] *n* झोपड़पट्टी
slush [slʌʃ] *n* पिघलती बर्फ़
sly [slaɪ] *adj* शातिर/कुटिल
smack [smæk] *vt* चांटा मारना
small [smɔːl] *adj* छोटा

small ads [smɔːl ædz] *npl* संक्षिप्त विज्ञापन
smart [smɑːt] *adj* बांका
smart phone [smɑːt fəʊn] *n* स्मार्ट फ़ोन
smash [smæʃ] *v* टकराना/टुकड़े - टुकड़े करना
smashing ['smæʃɪŋ] *adj* *(informal)* ज़बर्दस्त/बहुत बढ़िया
smear [smɪə] *n* स्मियर परीक्षण - कैंसर का एक परीक्षण
smell [smɛl] *n* गंध ▷ *vt* सूंघना ▷ *vi* महकना
smelly ['smɛlɪ] *adj* बदबूदार
smile [smaɪl] *n* मुस्कुराहट ▷ *vi* मुस्कुराना
smiley ['smaɪlɪ] *n* *(informal)* हंसते चेहरे का चिह्न
smoke [sməʊk] *n* धुंआ ▷ *vi* धुंआ देना
smoke alarm [sməʊk ə'lɑːm] *n* धुंए की चेतावनी घंटी
smoked ['sməʊkt] *adj* काला शीशा
smoker ['sməʊkə] *n* धूम्रपान करने वाला
smoking ['sməʊkɪŋ] *n* धूम्रपान
smooth [smuːð] *adj* चिकना
SMS [ɛs ɛm ɛs] *n* एस एम एस
smudge [smʌdʒ] *n* धब्बा
smug [smʌg] *adj* आत्मसंतुष्ट
smuggle ['smʌgl] *vt* तस्करी करना
smuggler ['smʌglə] *n* तस्कर
smuggling ['smʌglɪŋ] *n* तस्करी
snack [snæk] *n* जलपान
snack bar [snæk bɑː] *n* जलपान गृह
snail [sneɪl] *n* घोंघा
snake [sneɪk] *n* सांप
snap [snæp] *v* चिटकाना\चिटकना
snapshot ['snæpˌʃɒt] *n* छायाचित्र
snarl [snɑːl] *vi* गुर्राना
snatch [snætʃ] *v* झपटना/छीनना
sneeze [sniːz] *vi* छींक मारना

sniff [snɪf] *v* नाक सुड़कना
snigger ['snɪgə] *vi* मुंह दबाकर हंसना
snob [snɒb] *n* दंभी
snooker ['snuːkə] *n* स्नूकर - एक खेल
snooze [snuːz] *n (informal)* झपकी ▷ *vi (informal)* झपकी लेना
snore [snɔː] *vi* खर्राटा लेना
snorkel ['snɔːkl] *n* श्वास नली
snow [snəʊ] *n* बर्फ़ ▷ *vi* बर्फ़ गिरना
snowball ['snəʊˌbɔːl] *n* बर्फ़ का गोला
snowflake ['snəʊˌfleɪk] *n* हिमकण
snowman ['snəʊˌmæn] *n* बर्फ़ का पुतला
snowplough ['snəʊˌplaʊ] *n* बर्फ़ हटाने का वाहन
snowstorm ['snəʊˌstɔːm] *n* बर्फ़ानी तूफ़ान
so [səʊ] *adv (referring to something already mentioned)* ऐसा ▷ *conj* ताकि ▷ *adv (very)* इतना
soak [səʊk] *v* भिगोना
soaked [səʊkt] *adj* तरबतर/भीगा हुआ
soap [səʊp] *n* साबुन
soap dish [səʊp dɪʃ] *n* साबुनदानी
soap opera [səʊp 'ɒpərə] *n* धारावाहिक
soap powder [səʊp 'paʊdə] *n* चूरा साबुन
sob [sɒb] *vi* सिसकना
sober ['səʊbə] *adj* बिना नशे में
sociable ['səʊʃəbl] *adj* मिलनसार
social ['səʊʃəl] *adj* सामाजिक
socialism ['səʊʃəˌlɪzəm] *n* समाजवाद
socialist ['səʊʃəlɪst] *adj* समाजवादी ▷ *n* समाजवादी
social security ['səʊʃəl sɪ'kjuərɪtɪ] *n* सामाजिक सुरक्षा
social services ['səʊʃəl 'sɜːvɪsɪs] *npl* समाज सेवा
social worker ['səʊʃəl 'wɜːkə] *n* समाज सेवक
society [sə'saɪətɪ] *n* समाज

sociology [ˌsəʊsɪˈɒlədʒɪ] *n* समाजशास्त्र
sock [sɒk] *n* मोज़ा
socket [ˈsɒkɪt] *n* सॉकेट - प्लग लगाने का छेद
sofa [ˈsəʊfə] *n* सोफ़ा
sofa bed [ˈsəʊfə bɛd] *n* सोफा, जिसे खोलकर बिस्तर बनाया जा सके
soft [sɒft] *adj (to touch)* मुलायम; *(gentle)* हलका/मृदु
soft drink [sɒft drɪŋk] *n* मद्यरहित शीतल पेय
software [ˈsɒftˌwɛə] *n* साफ़्टवेयर
soggy [ˈsɒgɪ] *adj* लथपथ हुआ/ भीग कर नर्म हुआ
soil [sɔɪl] *n* मिट्टी
solar [ˈsəʊlə] *adj* सौर
solar power [ˈsəʊlə ˈpaʊə] *n* सौर ऊर्जा
solar system [ˈsəʊlə ˈsɪstəm] *n* सौर मंडल
soldier [ˈsəʊldʒə] *n* योद्धा
sold out [səʊld aʊt] *adj* बिक चुका
solicitor [səˈlɪsɪtə] *n* वकील
solid [ˈsɒlɪd] *adj (not liquid or gas)* ठोस; *(not hollow)* ठोस
solo [ˈsəʊləʊ] *n* एकल
soloist [ˈsəʊləʊɪst] *n* एकल कलाकार
soluble [ˈsɒljʊbl] *adj* घुलनशील
solution [səˈluːʃən] *n* समाधान
solve [sɒlv] *vt* हल करना
solvent [ˈsɒlvənt] *n* विलायक
Somali [səʊˈmɑːlɪ] *adj* सोमालियाई ▷ *n (language)* सोमालियाई; *(person)* सोमालियाई
Somalia [səʊˈmɑːlɪə] *n* सोमालिया
some [sʌm] *det* कुछ ▷ *pron* कुछ
somebody [ˈsʌmbədɪ] *pron* कोई
somehow [ˈsʌmˌhaʊ] *adv* पता नहीं कैसे/किसी तरह से
someone [ˈsʌmˌwʌn] *pron* कोई
someplace [ˈsʌmˌpleɪs] *adv* किसी जगह

something ['sʌmθɪŋ] *pron* कुछ/कोई चीज़
sometime ['sʌm,taɪm] *adv* कभी
sometimes ['sʌm,taɪmz] *adv* कभी - कभी
somewhere ['sʌm,wɛə] *adv* कहीं
son [sʌn] *n* बेटा
song [sɒŋ] *n* गाना
son-in-law [sʌn ɪn lɔː] *n* दामाद
soon [suːn] *adv* जल्दी ही
soot [sʊt] *n* कालिख
sophisticated [sə'fɪstɪ,keɪtɪd] *adj* अभिजात्य
soppy ['sɒpɪ] *adj* बहुत भावुक
soprano [sə'prɑːnəʊ] *n* उच्चतम सुर वाला गायक
sorbet ['sɔːbeɪ] *n* शरबत
sorcerer ['sɔːsərə] *n* जादूगर
sore [sɔː] *adj* पीड़ादायक ▷ *n* घाव
sorry ['sɒrɪ] *excl* क्षमा करें ▷ *adj (regretful)* खिन्न/खेदपूर्ण; *(sympathetic)* दुःखी/खेदपूर्ण
sort [sɔːt] *n* प्रकार
sort out [sɔːt aʊt] *v* सुलझाना
SOS [ɛs əʊ ɛs] *n* संकट संकेत
so-so ['səʊ'səʊ] *adv (informal)* ठीक - ठाक/कामचलाऊ
soul [səʊl] *n* आत्मा
sound [saʊnd] *adj* चंगा ▷ *n* ध्वनि
soundtrack ['saʊnd,træk] *n* ध्वनि
soup [suːp] *n* झोल
sour ['saʊə] *adj* खट्टा
south [saʊθ] *adj* दक्षिणी ▷ *adv* दक्षिण की ओर ▷ *n* दक्षिण
South Africa [saʊθ 'æfrɪkə] *n* दक्षिण अफ़्रीका
South African [saʊθ 'æfrɪkən] *adj* दक्षिण अफ़्रीकी ▷ *n* दक्षिण अफ़्रीकी
South America [saʊθ ə'mɛrɪkə] *n* दक्षिण अमरीका
South American [saʊθ ə'merɪkən] *adj* दक्षिण अमरीकी ▷ *n* दक्षिण अमरीका

southbound ['saʊθ,baʊnd] *adj* दक्षिण की ओर जाने वाला
southeast [ˌsaʊθ'iːst] *n* दक्षिण-पूर्व
southern ['sʌðən] *adj* दक्षिणी
South Korea [saʊθ kə'riːə] *n* दक्षिण कोरिया
South Pole [saʊθ pəʊl] *n* दक्षिण ध्रुव
southwest [ˌsaʊθ'wɛst] *n* दक्षिण - पश्चिम
souvenir [ˌsuːvə'nɪə] *n* स्मृति चिह्न/यादगार
soya ['sɔɪə] *n* सोया
soy sauce [sɔɪ sɔːs] *n* सोया की चटनी
spa [spɑː] *n* खनिज जल स्त्रोत
space [speɪs] *n* *(empty area)* जगह/; *(where the planets are)* अंतरिक्ष
spacecraft ['speɪsˌkrɑːft] *n* अंतरिक्ष यान
spade [speɪd] *n* कुदाल
spaghetti [spə'gɛtɪ] *n* एक तरह का पास्ता
Spain [speɪn] *n* स्पेन
spam [spæm] *n* अवांछनीय ई-मेल
Spaniard ['spænjəd] *n* स्पेनवासी
spaniel ['spænjəl] *n* एक प्रकार का कुत्ता
Spanish ['spænɪʃ] *adj* स्पेन से संबद्ध ▷ *n* स्पेन की भाषा
spank [spæŋk] *vt* नितंबों पर चांटे मारना
spanner ['spænə] *n* पाना
spare [spɛə] *adj* अतिरिक्त ▷ *vi* बिताना/खर्च करना
spare part [spɛə pɑːt] *n* अतिरिक्त पुर्जा
spare room [spɛə ruːm; rʊm] *n* अतिरिक्त कक्ष
spare time [spɛə taɪm] *n* खाली समय
spare tyre [spɛə 'taɪə] *n* अतिरिक्त टायर
spare wheel [spɛə wiːl] *n* अतिरिक्त टायर
spark [spɑːk] *n* चिंगारी
sparkling water ['spɑːklɪŋ 'wɔːtə] *n* झागदार पानी
spark plug [spɑːk plʌg] *n* स्पार्क प्लग
sparrow ['spærəʊ] *n* गौरैया

spasm ['spæzəm] *n* अकड़न

spatula ['spætjʊlə] *n* पौना/कड़छी

speak [spiːk] *v* बोलना

speaker ['spiːkə] *n* वक्ता

speak up [spiːk ʌp] *v* ज़ोर से बोलना

special ['spɛʃəl] *adj* ख़ास

specialist ['spɛʃəlɪst] *n* विशेषज्ञ

speciality [ˌspɛʃɪ'ælɪtɪ] *n* विशेषता

specialize ['spɛʃəˌlaɪz] *vi* विशेषज्ञता प्राप्त करना

specially ['spɛʃəlɪ] *adv* ख़ास कर

special offer ['spɛʃəl 'ɒfə] *n* विशेष प्रस्ताव

species ['spiːʃiːz] *n* प्रजातियां

specific [spɪ'sɪfɪk] *adj* विशिष्ट

specifically [spɪ'sɪfɪklɪ] *adv* विशिष्ट रूप से

specify ['spɛsɪˌfaɪ] *vt* निर्दिष्ट करना

spectacles ['spɛktəklz] *npl (formal)* ऐनक

spectacular [spɛk'tækjʊlə] *adj* शानदार/भव्य

spectator [spɛk'teɪtə] *n* दर्शक

speculate ['spɛkjʊˌleɪt] *v* अंदाज़ लगाना

speech [spiːtʃ] *n* वाणी

speechless ['spiːtʃlɪs] *adj* अवाक

speed [spiːd] *n* गति

speedboat ['spiːdˌbəʊt] *n* इंजन वाली नाव

speeding ['spiːdɪŋ] *n* तेज़ गति

speed limit [spiːd 'lɪmɪt] *n* गति सीमा

speedometer [spɪ'dɒmɪtə] *n* गति मापक यंत्र

speed up [spiːd ʌp] *v* गति बढ़ाना

spell [spɛl] *n (period)* दौर; *(magic)* जादू - टोना ▹ *vt* उच्चारण करना/वर्तनी लिखना

spellchecker ['spɛlˌtʃɛkə] *n* स्पेलचेकर

spelling ['spɛlɪŋ] *n* वर्तनी

spend [spɛnd] *vt (money)* खर्च करना; *(time)* व्यय करना/बिताना
sperm [spɜːm] *n* शुक्राणु
spice [spaɪs] *n* मसाला
spicy ['spaɪsɪ] *adj* मसालेदार
spider ['spaɪdə] *n* मकड़ी
spill [spɪl] *v* छलकना/छलकाना
spinach ['spɪnɪdʒ] *n* पालक
spinal cord ['spaɪnəl kɔːd] *n* मेरुरज्जु
spin drier [spɪn 'draɪə] *n* निचोड़ कर कपड़े सुखाने की मशीन
spine [spaɪn] *n* मेरुदंड
spinster ['spɪnstə] *n (old-fashioned)* अविवाहिता
spire [spaɪə] *n* मीनार/शिखर
spirit ['spɪrɪt] *n* आत्मा
spirits ['spɪrɪts] *npl* उत्साह/मिजाज़
spiritual ['spɪrɪtjʊəl] *adj* आध्यात्मिक
spit [spɪt] *n* थूक ▷ *v* थूकना
spite [spaɪt] *n* द्वेष ▷ *vt* तंग करना
spiteful ['spaɪtfʊl] *adj* द्वेषी
splash [splæʃ] *vi* छपछपाना
splendid ['splɛndɪd] *adj* शानदार
splint [splɪnt] *n* कमठी/खपच्ची
splinter ['splɪntə] *n* किरच
split [splɪt] *v* टूटना/तोड़ना
split up [splɪt ʌp] *v* संबंध विच्छेद करना
spoil [spɔɪl] *vt (ruin)* बिगाड़ देना; *(child)* लाड़ - प्यार से बिगाड़ना
spoilsport ['spɔɪlˌspɔːt] *n (informal)* मज़ा खराब करने वाला
spoilt [spɔɪlt] *adj* बिगड़ा हुआ
spoke [spəʊk] *n* तीली
spokesman ['spəʊksmən] *n* प्रवक्ता (पुरुष)
spokesperson ['spəʊksˌpɜːsən] *n* प्रवक्ता
spokeswoman ['spəʊksˌwʊmən] *n* प्रवक्ता (महिला)
sponge [spʌndʒ] *n (for washing)* स्पंज; *(cake)* एक प्रकार का केक
sponge bag [spʌndʒ bæg] *n* प्रसाधन थैली

S

sponsor ['spɒnsə] *n* प्रायोजक ▷ *vt* प्रायोजित करना
sponsorship ['spɒnsəʃɪp] *n* प्रायोजन
spontaneous [spɒn'teɪnɪəs] *adj* स्वतः स्फूर्त
spooky ['spuːkɪ] *adj* *(informal)* ख़ौफ़नाक
spoon [spuːn] *n* चम्मच
spoonful ['spuːnˌfʊl] *n* चम्मच भर
sport [spɔːt] *n* खेल-कूद
sportsman ['spɔːtsmən] *n* खिलाड़ी
sportswear ['spɔːtsˌwɛə] *n* खेल की पोशाक
sportswoman ['spɔːtsˌwʊmən] *n* महिला खिलाड़ी
sporty ['spɔːtɪ] *adj* खेल - कूद में रुचि रखने वाला
spot [spɒt] *n* *(round mark)* धब्बा/दाग; *(place)* स्थल ▷ *vt* देखना
spotless ['spɒtlɪs] *adj* बेदाग
spotlight ['spɒtˌlaɪt] *n* स्पॉट लाइट
spotty ['spɒtɪ] *adj* धब्बेदार/चितकबरा
spouse [spaʊs] *n* पति/पत्नी
sprain [spreɪn] *n* मोच ▷ *vt* मुड़काना
spray [spreɪ] *n* फुहार ▷ *v* फुहार डालना
spread [sprɛd] *n* स्प्रेड - ब्रेड पर लगाया जाने वाला पदार्थ ▷ *vt* *(open out)* फैलाना; *(butter, jam)* फैलाना ▷ *vi* *(reach a larger area)* फैलना
spread out [sprɛd aʊt] *v* तितर - बितर होना/फैलना
spreadsheet ['sprɛdˌʃiːt] *n* स्प्रेडशीट
spring [sprɪŋ] *n* *(season)* बसंत; *(coil)* स्प्रिंग
spring-cleaning ['sprɪŋˌkliːnɪŋ] *n* पूरे तौर पर साफ़ - सफ़ाई
spring onion [sprɪŋ 'ʌnjən] *n* हरा प्याज़
springtime ['sprɪŋˌtaɪm] *n* वसंत काल
sprinkler ['sprɪŋklə] *n* छिड़काव उपकरण/फव्वारा

sprint [sprɪnt] *n* लघु दौड़ ▷ *vi* थोड़ी दूरी तक पूरे वेग से भागना
sprinter ['sprɪntə] *n* धावक
sprouts [spraʊts] *npl* छोटी पत्तागोभी
spy [spaɪ] *n* जासूस ▷ *vi* जासूसी करना
spying ['spaɪɪŋ] *n* जासूसी
squabble ['skwɒbl] *vi* तकरार करना
squander ['skwɒndə] *vt* अपव्यय करना
square [skwɛə] *adj* वर्गाकार ▷ *n* वर्ग
squash [skwɒʃ] *n* स्क्वाश ▷ *vt* कुचलना/दबाना
squeak [skwiːk] *vi* किकियाना
squeeze [skwiːz] *vt* भींचना
squeeze in [skwiːz ɪn] *v* ठूंसना
squid [skwɪd] *n* विद्रूप-एक समुद्री जीव
squint [skwɪnt] *vi* कनखियों से देखना
squirrel ['skwɪrəl] *n* गिलहरी
Sri Lanka [ˌsriː 'læŋkə] *n* श्रीलंका
stab [stæb] *vt* भोंकना
stability [stə'bɪlɪtɪ] *n* स्थिरता
stable ['steɪbl] *adj* स्थिर ▷ *n* घुड़साल
stack [stæk] *n* व्यवस्थित ढेर
stadium ['steɪdɪəm] *n* क्रीड़ांगन
staff [stɑːf] *npl (personnel)* कर्मचारी ▷ *n (stick)* बल्लम
staffroom ['stɑːfˌruːm] *n* कर्मचारी कक्ष
stage [steɪdʒ] *n* अवस्था/चरण
stagger ['stægə] *vi* लड़खड़ाना
stag night [stæg naɪt] *n* विवाह पूर्व पुरुषों की पार्टी
stain [steɪn] *n* दाग ▷ *vt* दाग लगाना
stained glass [steɪnd glɑːs] *n* रंगीन कांच
stainless steel ['steɪnlɪs stiːl] *n* स्टेनलेस स्टील

stain remover [steɪn rɪ'muːvə] *n* दाग निकालने वाला

staircase ['stɛəˌkeɪs] *n* सीढ़ी

stairs [stɛəz] *npl* सीढियां

stale [steɪl] *adj* बासी

stalemate ['steɪlˌmeɪt] *n* गतिरोध

stall [stɔːl] *n* छोटी दुकान

stamina ['stæmɪnə] *n* सहनशक्ति/ताकत

stammer ['stæmə] *v* हकलाना

stamp [stæmp] *n* डाकटिकट ▹ *vt* मुहर लगाना

stand [stænd] *vi* खड़े रहना ▹ ['stændz] *n* स्टैंड

standard ['stændəd] *adj* मानक ▹ *n* मानदंड

standard of living ['stændəd ɒv; əv 'lɪvɪŋ] *n* जीवन - स्तर

stand for [stænd fɔː] *v* का प्रतीक होना/का अर्थ होना

standing order ['stændɪŋ 'ɔːdə] *n* स्थायी

stand out [stænd aʊt] *v* अलग से दिखना

standpoint ['stændˌpɔɪnt] *n* दृष्टिकोण

stand up [stænd ʌp] *v* खड़े होना

staple ['steɪpl] *n* *(piece of bent wire)* स्टेपल - मुड़ी हुई पिन; *(basic food)* बुनियादी ▹ *vt* पिन द्वारा नत्थी करना

stapler ['steɪplə] *n* स्टेपलर

star [stɑː] *n* *(in the sky)* तारा; *(celebrity)* ख्यातिप्राप्त व्यक्ति ▹ *v* मुख्य या प्रसिद्ध चलचित्र कलाकार ▹ *n* *(shape)* तारे की आकृति

starch [stɑːtʃ] *n* मंड

stare [stɛə] *vi* घूरना

stark [stɑːk] *adj* कठोर/नितांत

start [stɑːt] *n* आरंभ ▹ *vt* *(to do something)* आरंभ करना ▹ *v* *(activity, event)* आरंभ होना

starter ['stɑːtə] *n* मुख्य भोजन से पहले खाया जाने वाला खाद्य

startle ['stɑːtl] *vt* चौंकाना

start off [stɑːt ɒf] *v* शुरु करना

starve [stɑːv] *vi* भूखा मरना

state [steɪt] *n* राज्य ▷ *vt* कहना/बताना
stately home ['steɪtlɪ həʊm] *n* आलीशान घर
statement ['steɪtmənt] *n* वक्तव्य
station ['steɪʃən] *n* स्टेशन/अड्डा
stationer ['steɪʃənə] *n* लेखन सामग्री की दुकान
stationery ['steɪʃənərɪ] *n* लेखन सामग्री
statistics [stə'tɪstɪks] *npl* आंकड़े
statue ['stætjuː] *n* मूर्ति
status quo ['steɪtəs kwəʊ] *n* वर्तमान स्थिति/यथापूर्व स्थिति
stay [steɪ] *n* ठहराव ▷ *vi* *(remain)* बना रहना; *(live for a short time)* ठहरना
stay in [steɪ ɪn] *v* घर में रहना
stay up [steɪ ʌp] *v* जगा रहना
steady ['stɛdɪ] *adj* नियमित/स्थायी
steak [steɪk] *n* गोमांस
steal [stiːl] *v* चुराना
steam [stiːm] *n* भाप
steel [stiːl] *n* इस्पात
steep [stiːp] *adj* खड़ा
steeple ['stiːpl] *n* मीनार
steering ['stɪərɪŋ] *n* स्टीअरिंग
steering wheel ['stɪərɪŋ wiːl] *n* स्टीअरिंग ह्वील
step [stɛp] *n* *(pace)* कदम; *(stair)* सीढ़ी
stepbrother ['stɛp,brʌðə] *n* सौतेला भाई
stepdaughter ['stɛp,dɔːtə] *n* सौतेली पुत्री
stepfather ['stɛp,fɑːðə] *n* सौतेला पिता
stepladder ['stɛp,lædə] *n* सीढ़ी
stepmother ['stɛp,mʌðə] *n* सौतेली मां
stepsister ['stɛp,sɪstə] *n* सौतेली बहन
stepson ['stɛp,sʌn] *n* सौतेला पुत्र
stereo ['stɛrɪəʊ] *n* स्टीरियो
stereotype ['stɛrɪə,taɪp] *n* मान्यतावाद/प्रतिमान
sterile ['stɛraɪl] *adj* रोगाणु रहित

sterilize ['stɛrɪˌlaɪz] *vt* रोगाणु रहित करना
sterling ['stɜːlɪŋ] *n* स्टर्लिंग - ग्रेट ब्रिटेन की मुद्रा
steroid ['stɪərɔɪd] *n* स्टेरॉयड - एक रासायनिक पदार्थ
stew [stjuː] *n* स्ट्यू - एक तरह की रसेदार सब्ज़ी
steward ['stjʊəd] *n* विमान, पोत या रेल परिचारक
stick [stɪk] *n* छड़ी ▷ *vt* चिपकाना
sticker ['stɪkə] *n* चिप्पी/स्टिकर
stick insect [stɪk'ɪnsɛkt] *n* टहनीनुमा एक कीड़ा
stick out [stɪk aʊt] *v* निकला हुआ होना
sticky ['stɪkɪ] *adj* चिपचिपा
stiff [stɪf] *adj* कड़ा
stifling ['staɪflɪŋ] *adj* दमघोंटू
still [stɪl] *adj* अचल/स्थिर ▷ *adv* अभी तक
sting [stɪŋ] *n* डंक ▷ *v* डंक मारना
stingy ['stɪndʒɪ] *adj* *(informal)* कंजूस
stink [stɪŋk] *n* बदबू ▷ *vi* बदबू मारना
stir [stɜː] *vt* मिलाना
stitch [stɪtʃ] *n* टांका ▷ *vt* सिलाई करना
stock [stɒk] *n* स्टॉक/मूलधन ▷ *vt* रखना
stockbroker ['stɒkˌbrəʊkə] *n* शेयर दलाल
stock cube [stɒk kjuːb] *n* स्टॉक क्यूब - एक खाद्य सामग्री
stock exchange [stɒk ɪks'tʃeɪndʒ] *n* शेयर बाज़ार
stock market [stɒk 'mɑːkɪt] *n* शेयर बाज़ार
stock up [stɒk ʌp] *v* संचित करना
stomach ['stʌmək] *n* आमाशय
stomachache ['stʌməkˌeɪk] *n* पेट दर्द
stone [stəʊn] *n* *(material)* पत्थर; *(piece of rock)* पत्थर/कंकड़
stool [stuːl] *n* तिपाई
stop [stɒp] *n* विराम ▷ *v* *(doing something)* रोकना ▷ *vi* *(not continue)* रुक जाना

stopover ['stɒp,əʊvə] *n* पड़ाव
stopwatch ['stɒp,wɒtʃ] *n* विराम घड़ी
storage ['stɔːrɪdʒ] *n* भंडारण
store [stɔː] *n* दुकान ▷ *vt* संचित करना
storm [stɔːm] *n* तूफ़ान
stormy ['stɔːmɪ] *adj* तूफ़ानी
story ['stɔːrɪ] *n* कहानी
stove [stəʊv] *n* चूल्हा
straight [streɪt] *adj* सीधा
straighteners ['streɪtnəz] *npl* बालों को सीधा करने का उपकरण
straightforward [,streɪt'fɔːwəd] *adj* स्पष्ट
straight on [streɪt ɒn] *adv* सीधे
strain [streɪn] *n* तनाव/दबाव ▷ *vt* दबाव डालना
strained [streɪnd] *adj* तनावग्रस्त
stranded ['strændɪd] *adj* फंसा हुआ
strange [streɪndʒ] *adj* विचित्र
stranger ['streɪndʒə] *n* अजनबी
strangle ['stræŋgl] *vt* गला घोंटना
strap [stræp] *n* पट्टा/फीता
strategic [strə'tiːdʒɪk] *adj* कूटनीतिक/रणनीतिक
strategy ['strætɪdʒɪ] *n* रणनीति
straw [strɔː] *n* *(dried stalks of crops)* भूसा; *(for drinking through)* पेय पीने की नली
strawberry ['strɔːbərɪ] *n* स्ट्रॉबेरी
stray [streɪ] *n* भटका हुआ पशु
stream [striːm] *n* धारा/छोटी नदी
street [striːt] *n* गली
streetlamp ['striːt,læmp] *n* सड़क के किनारे की बत्ती
street map [striːt mæp] *n* नगर का मानचित्र
streetwise ['striːt,waɪz] *adj* *(informal)* बड़े शहर की कठिनाइयों से परिचित
strength [strɛŋθ] *n* ताक़त
strengthen ['strɛŋθən] *vt* दृढ़ करना
stress [strɛs] *n* ज़ोर ▷ *vt* ज़ोर देना

S

stressed [strɛst] *adj* तनावग्रस्त
stressful ['strɛsfʊl] *adj* तनावपूर्ण
stretch [strɛtʃ] *vi (extend)* फैलना; *(with your body)* अंगड़ाई लेना
stretcher ['strɛtʃə] *n* स्ट्रेचर
stretchy ['strɛtʃɪ] *adj* लचीला
strict [strɪkt] *adj* सख़्त
strictly ['strɪktlɪ] *adv* सख़्ती से
strike [straɪk] *n* हड़ताल ▹ *vt* मारना ▹ *vi* हड़ताल करना ▹ *v (hit)* प्रहार करना
striker ['straɪkə] *n* हड़ताली
striking ['straɪkɪŋ] *adj* असाधारण/ध्यानाकर्षक
string [strɪŋ] *n (for parcel)* रस्सी; *(musical instrument)* तार
strip [strɪp] *n* पट्टी ▹ *v* नग्न करना/उघाड़ना
stripe [straɪp] *n* धारी
striped [straɪpt] *adj* धारीदार
stripy ['straɪpɪ] *adj (informal)* धारीदार
stroke [strəʊk] *n* पक्षाघात ▹ *vt* थपथपाना
stroll [strəʊl] *n* चहलकदमी
strong [strɒŋ] *adj (person)* शक्तिशाली; *(object)* मज़बूत
strongly ['strɒŋlɪ] *adv* दृढ़तापूर्वक
structure ['strʌktʃə] *n* ढांचा/स्वरूप
struggle ['strʌgl] *n* संघर्ष ▹ *v* संघर्ष करना
stub [stʌb] *n* ठूंठ
stubborn ['stʌbn] *adj* अड़ियल
stub out [stʌb aʊt] *v* मसलकर बुझाना
stuck [stʌk] *adj (unable to move)* अटका हुआ; *(stumped)* अटका हुआ
stuck-up ['stʌk'ʌp] *adj (informal)* घमंडी
stud [stʌd] *n* धातु के जड़े हुए छोटे टुकड़े
student ['stjuːdnt] *n* छात्र
student discount ['stjuːdnt 'dɪskaʊnt] *n* छात्रों को दी जाने वाली छूट
studio ['stjuːdɪˌəʊ] *n* शिल्पशाला

studio flat ['stjuːdɪəʊ flæt] *n* छोटा फ़्लैट
study ['stʌdɪ] *v* अध्ययन करना
stuff [stʌf] *n (informal)* सामान
stuffy ['stʌfɪ] *adj* उबाऊ/दमघोंटू
stumble ['stʌmbl] *vi* लड़खड़ाना
stunned [stʌnd] *adj* भौंचक्का
stunning ['stʌnɪŋ] *adj* गजब का/बेहद सुंदर
stunt [stʌnt] *n* तमाशा
stuntman ['stʌntmən] *n* खतरनाक करतब करने वाला
stupid ['stjuːpɪd] *adj* बेवकूफ
stutter ['stʌtə] *vi* हकलाना
style [staɪl] *n* शैली
stylist ['staɪlɪst] *n* शैलीकार
subject ['sʌbdʒɪkt] *n* विषय
submarine ['sʌbməˌriːn] *n* पनडुब्बी
subscription [səb'skrɪpʃən] *n* ग्राहक सदस्यता शुल्क/चंदा
subsidiary [səb'sɪdɪərɪ] *n* सहायक
subsidize ['sʌbsɪˌdaɪz] *vt* अनुदान देना
subsidy ['sʌbsɪdɪ] *n* अनुदान
substance ['sʌbstəns] *n* तत्व
substitute ['sʌbstɪˌtjuːt] *n* विकल्प ▷ *v* स्थानापन्न करना
subtitled ['sʌbˌtaɪtld] *adj* लिखित भाषांतर किया हुआ
subtitles ['sʌbˌtaɪtlz] *npl* लिखित भाषांतर
subtle ['sʌtl] *adj* सूक्ष्म/हल्का
subtract [səb'trækt] *vt* घटाना
suburb ['sʌbɜːb] *n* उपनगर
suburban [sə'bɜːbn] *adj* उपनगरीय
subway ['sʌbˌweɪ] *n* तलमार्ग
succeed [sək'siːd] *vi* सफल होना
success [sək'sɛs] *n* सफलता
successful [sək'sɛsfʊl] *adj* सफल

successfully [sək'sɛsfʊlɪ] *adv* सफलतापूर्वक

successive [sək'sɛsɪv] *adj* क्रमिक

successor [sək'sɛsə] *n* उत्तराधिकारी

such [sʌtʃ] *det (like the one previously mentioned)* ऐसा; *det (intensifying an adjective)* इतना; *det (like that)* ऐसा; *det (followed by `a' or `an')* इतना अधिक

suck [sʌk] *v* चूसना

Sudan [suː'dɑːn] *n* सूडान

Sudanese [ˌsuːd'niːz] *adj* सूडानी ▷ *npl* सूडानी

sudden ['sʌdn] *adj* अचानक

suddenly ['sʌdnlɪ] *adv* अचानक से

sue [sjuː] *v* नालिश करना

suede [sweɪd] *n* एक प्रकार का चमड़ा

suffer ['sʌfə] *v* भुगतना/कष्ट उठाना

suffocate ['sʌfəˌkeɪt] *vi* दम घुटना

sugar ['ʃʊgə] *n* चीनी

sugar-free ['ʃʊgəfriː] *adj* शर्करा रहित

suggest [sə'dʒɛst] *vt* सुझाव देना

suggestion [sə'dʒɛstʃən] *n* सुझाव

suicide ['suːɪˌsaɪd] *n* आत्महत्या

suicide bomber ['suɪsaɪd 'bɔmə] *n* आत्मघाती हमलावर

suit [suːt] *n* सूट ▷ *vt* फबना/जंचना

suitable ['suːtəbl] *adj* सुयोग्य

suitcase ['suːtˌkeɪs] *n* अटैची

suite [swiːt] *n* कमरों का सेट

sulk [sʌlk] *vi* रूठना

sulky ['sʌlkɪ] *adj* रुष्ट

sultana [sʌl'tɑːnə] *n* किशमिश

sum [sʌm] *n (amount)* राशि; *(in maths)* गणित के सवाल

summarize ['sʌməˌraɪz] *v* सारांश प्रस्तुत करना

summary ['sʌmərɪ] *n* सारांश

summer ['sʌmə] *n* ग्रीष्म ऋतु

summer holidays ['sʌmə 'hɒlədeɪz] *npl* गर्मी की छुट्टियां
summertime ['sʌmə,taɪm] *n* गर्मी का मौसम
summit ['sʌmɪt] *n* शिखर सम्मेलन
sum up [sʌm ʌp] *v* सार प्रस्तुत करना
sun [sʌn] *n* सूर्य
sunbathe ['sʌn,beɪð] *vi* धूप सेंकना
sunbed ['sʌn,bɛd] *n* पराबैंगनी किरणें उत्सर्जित करने वाला बिस्तर
sunblock ['sʌn,blɒk] *n* धूप से बचाने वाली क्रीम
sunburn ['sʌn,bɜːn] *n* धूप से त्वचा पर आई कालिमा
sunburnt ['sʌn,bɜːnt] *adj* धूप से झुलसा हुआ
suncream ['sʌn,kriːm] *n* धूप से बचाने वाली क्रीम
Sunday ['sʌndɪ] *n* रविवार
sunflower ['sʌn,flaʊə] *n* सूरजमुखी
sunglasses ['sʌn,glɑːsɪz] *npl* धूप का चश्मा
sunlight ['sʌnlaɪt] *n* धूप
sunny ['sʌnɪ] *adj* धूप से भरा
sunrise ['sʌn,raɪz] *n* सूर्योदय
sunroof ['sʌn,ruːf] *n* कार की छत का खुलने वाला हिस्सा
sunscreen ['sʌn,skriːn] *n* धूप से बचाने वाली क्रीम
sunset ['sʌn,sɛt] *n* सूर्यास्त
sunshine ['sʌn,ʃaɪn] *n* धूप
sunstroke ['sʌn,strəʊk] *n* लू
suntan ['sʌn,tæn] *n* धूप से त्वचा पर आई कालिमा
suntan lotion ['sʌntæn 'ləʊʃən] *n* धूप से बचाने वाली क्रीम
suntan oil ['sʌntæn ɔɪl] *n* धूप से बचाने वाला तेल
super ['suːpə] *adj (informal, old-fashioned)* बहुत बढ़िया
superb [sʊ'pɜːb] *adj* शानदार
superficial [,suːpə'fɪʃəl] *adj* सतही/छिछला
superior [suː'pɪərɪə] *adj* श्रेष्ठतर ▷ *n* वरिष्ठ अधिकारी

S

supermarket ['suːpəˌmɑːkɪt] *n* सुपर बाज़ार
supernatural [ˌsuːpə'nætʃrəl] *adj* अलौकिक
superstitious [ˌsuːpə'stɪʃəs] *adj* अंधविश्वासी
supervise ['suːpəˌvaɪz] *vt* पर्यवेक्षण करना
supervisor ['suːpəˌvaɪzə] *n* पर्यवेक्षक
supper ['sʌpə] *n* रात का भोजन
supplement ['sʌplɪmənt] *n* अनुपूरक
supplier [sə'plaɪə] *n* आपूर्तिकर्ता
supplies [sə'plaɪz] *npl* आपूर्ति
supply [sə'plaɪ] *n* आपूर्ति ▹ *vt* आपूर्ति करना
supply teacher [sə'plaɪ 'tiːtʃə] *n* अस्थायी शिक्षक/वैकल्पिक शिक्षक
support [sə'pɔːt] *n* समर्थन ▹ *vt* समर्थन करना
supporter [sə'pɔːtə] *n* समर्थक
suppose [sə'pəʊz] *vt* मानना
supposedly [sə'pəʊzɪdlɪ] *adv* कथित रूप से/समझी जाने वाली
supposing [sə'pəʊzɪŋ] *conj* अगर
surcharge ['sɜːˌtʃɑːdʒ] *n* अधिभार
sure [ʃʊə] *adj* सुनिश्चित
surely ['ʃʊəlɪ] *adv* सुनिश्चित रूप से
surf [sɜːf] *n* फ़ेन ▹ *vi* समुद्री लहरों पर नाव चलाने का खेल
surface ['sɜːfɪs] *n* सतह
surfboard ['sɜːfˌbɔːd] *n* एक पतली नाव
surfer ['sɜːfə] *n* समुद्री लहरों पर नाव चलाने वाला
surfing ['sɜːfɪŋ] *n* समुद्री लहरों पर नाव चलाना
surge [sɜːdʒ] *n* चढ़ाव/हिलोर
surgeon ['sɜːdʒən] *n* शल्य चिकित्सक

surgery ['sɜːdʒərɪ] *n* *(medical treatment)* शल्य चिकित्सा; *(place)* शल्य चिकित्सा कक्ष
surname ['sɜːˌneɪm] *n* कुलनाम
surplus ['sɜːpləs] *adj* अधिशेष/अतिरिक्त ▷ *n* अधिकता
surprise [sə'praɪz] *n* आश्चर्य
surprised [sə'praɪzd] *adj* आश्चर्यचकित
surprising [sə'praɪzɪŋ] *adj* आश्चर्यजनक
surprisingly [sə'praɪzɪŋlɪ] *adv* आश्चर्यजनक रूप से
surrender [sə'rɛndə] *vi* आत्मसमर्पण करना
surrogate mother ['sʌrəgɪt 'mʌðə] *n* दूसरे का बच्चा अपनी कोख में पालने वाली मां
surround [sə'raʊnd] *vt* घिरा होना
surroundings [sə'raʊndɪŋz] *npl* माहौल
survey ['sɜːveɪ] *n* सर्वेक्षण
surveyor [sɜː'veɪə] *n* सर्वेक्षक
survival [sə'vaɪvl] *n* उत्तरजीविता
survive [sə'vaɪv] *v* बचा रहना
survivor [sə'vaɪvə] *n* जीवित बचा हुआ व्यक्ति
suspect ['sʌspekt] *n* संदिग्ध व्यक्ति ▷ [sə'spɛkt] *vt* संदेह करना
suspend [sə'spɛnd] *vt* निलंबित करना/स्थगित करना
suspense [sə'spɛns] *n* रहस्य
suspension [sə'spɛnʃən] *n* निलम्बन/स्थगन
suspension bridge [səs'pɛnʃən brɪdʒ] *n* झूला पुल
suspicious [sə'spɪʃəs] *adj* संदेहग्रस्त
swallow ['swɒləʊ] *n* घूंट ▷ *vt* निगलना ▷ *vi* निगलना
swamp [swɒmp] *n* दलदल
swan [swɒn] *n* हंस
swap [swɒp] *v* अदला - बदली करना
swat [swɒt] *vt* फ़टाक कर के मार देना

S

sway [sweɪ] *vi* डोलना/झूमना
Swaziland ['swɑːzɪˌlænd] *n* स्वाज़ीलैंड
swear [swɛə] *vi* दुर्वचन कहना
swearword ['swɛəˌwɜːd] *n* दुर्वचन
sweat [swɛt] *n* पसीना ▷ *vi* पसीना बहना
sweater ['swɛtə] *n* स्वेटर
sweatshirt ['swɛtˌʃɜːt] *n* स्वेटशर्ट
sweaty ['swɛtɪ] *adj* पसीने से भीगा
Swede [swiːd] *n* स्वीडन का निवासी
swede [swiːd] *n* शलगम
Sweden ['swiːdn] *n* स्वीडन
Swedish ['swiːdɪʃ] *adj* स्वीडन से संबद्ध ▷ *n* स्वीडन की भाषा
sweep [swiːp] *vt* झाड़ू लगाना
sweet [swiːt] *adj (food, drink)* मीठा; *(enjoyable)* प्यारा ▷ *n* मिठाई
sweetcorn ['swiːtˌkɔːn] *n* मीठी मकई
sweetener ['swiːtnə] *n* मिठास लाने वाला पदार्थ
sweets ['swiːtz] *npl* मिठाई
sweltering ['swɛltərɪŋ] *adj* तप्त
swerve [swɜːv] *v* झटके से मुड़ना
swim [swɪm] *vi* तैरना
swimmer ['swɪmə] *n* तैराक
swimming ['swɪmɪŋ] *n* तैराकी
swimming costume ['swɪmɪŋ 'kɒstjuːm] *n* तैराकी की पोशाक
swimming pool ['swɪmɪŋ puːl] *n* तरणताल
swimming trunks ['swɪmɪŋ trʌŋks] *npl* तैराकी जांघिया
swimsuit ['swɪmˌsuːt] *n* तैराकी की पोशाक
swing [swɪŋ] *n* उतार - चढ़ाव/दोलन ▷ *v* झूलना
Swiss [swɪs] *adj* स्विट्ज़रलैंड से संबद्ध ▷ *npl* स्विट्ज़रलैंड का निवासी
switch [swɪtʃ] *n* बिजली का बटन ▷ *vi* बदलना

switchboard ['swɪtʃˌbɔːd] *n* स्विचबोर्ड
switch off [swɪtʃ ɒf] *v* बंद करना
switch on [swɪtʃ ɒn] *v* चालू करना
Switzerland ['swɪtsələnd] *n* स्विट्ज़रलैंड
swollen ['swəʊlən] *adj* सूजा हुआ
sword [sɔːd] *n* तलवार
swordfish ['sɔːdˌfɪʃ] *n* तलवार के आकार की एक मछली
swot [swɒt] *vi (informal)* मेहनत से पढ़ना
syllable ['sɪləbl] *n* शब्दांश
syllabus ['sɪləbəs] *n* पाठ्यक्रम
symbol ['sɪmbl] *n* प्रतीक
symmetrical [sɪ'mɛtrɪkl] *adj* सममित
sympathetic [ˌsɪmpə'θɛtɪk] *adj* सहानुभूतिपूर्ण
sympathize ['sɪmpəˌθaɪz] *vi* सहानुभूति दिखाना
sympathy ['sɪmpəθɪ] *n* सहानुभूति
symphony ['sɪmfənɪ] *n* सिंफ़नी - संगीत रचना
symptom ['sɪmptəm] *n* लक्षण
synagogue ['sɪnəˌgɒg] *n* यहूदियों का उपासनागृह
Syria ['sɪrɪə] *n* सीरिया
Syrian ['sɪrɪən] *adj* सीरियाई ▷ *n* सीरियाई
syringe ['sɪrɪndʒ] *n* सुई
syrup ['sɪrəp] *n* चाशनी
system ['sɪstəm] *n* व्यवस्था
systematic [ˌsɪstɪ'mætɪk] *adj* व्यवस्थित
systems analyst ['sɪstəms 'ænəlɪst] *n* सिस्टम विश्लेषक

t

table ['teɪbl] *n (piece of furniture)* मेज़; *(chart)* सारणी
tablecloth ['teɪblˌklɒθ] *n* मेज़पोश
tablespoon ['teɪblˌspuːn] *n* बड़ा चम्मच

tablet ['tæblɪt] *n* गोली
table tennis ['teɪbl 'tɛnɪs] *n* टेबल टेनिस
table wine ['teɪbl waɪn] *n* सस्ती शराब
taboo [tə'buː] *adj* निषिद्ध/वर्जित ▷ *n* निषेध/वर्जना
tackle ['tækl] *n* खेल में होने वाली धर-पकड़ ▷ *vt* निपटना
tact [tækt] *n* व्यवहारकौशल/चातुर्य
tactful ['tæktfʊl] *adj* व्यवहारकुशलता
tactics ['tæktɪks] *npl* युक्तियां
tactless ['tæktlɪs] *adj* उद्दंड
tadpole ['tæd,pəʊl] *n* मेढक का डिंभकीट
tag [tæg] *n* चिप्पी
Tahiti [tə'hiːtɪ] *n* ताहिती
tail [teɪl] *n* पूंछ
tailor ['teɪlə] *n* दर्ज़ी
Taiwan ['taɪ'wɑːn] *n* ताइवान
Taiwanese [,taɪwɑː'niːz] *adj* ताइवानी ▷ *n* ताइवानी नागरिक
Tajikistan [tɑː,dʒɪkɪ'stɑːn] *n* ताजिकिस्तान
taka ['tɑːkɑː] *n* टाका
take [teɪk] *vt* *(travel in)* लेना/पकड़ना; *(carry)* लेना; *(steal)* ले लेना/ चुरा लेना
take after [teɪk 'ɑːftə] *v* सदृश होना
take apart [teɪk ə'pɑːt] *v* फाड़ना/चीरना
take away [teɪk ə'weɪ] *v* ले जाना
takeaway ['teɪkə,weɪ] *n* खाना बांध कर देने वाला भोजनालय/बंधवाकर लाया गया भोजन
take back [teɪk bæk] *v* वापस लेना
take off [teɪk ɒf] *v* उड़ना
takeoff ['teɪk,ɒf] *n* उड़ना
take over [teɪk 'əʊvə] *v* अधिग्रहण करना
takeover ['teɪk,əʊvə] *n* अधिग्रहण
takings ['teɪkɪŋz] *npl* आय
talcum powder ['tælkəm 'paʊdə] *n* टैल्कम पाउडर
tale [teɪl] *n* कहानी
talent ['tælənt] *n* प्रतिभा
talented ['tæləntɪd] *adj* प्रतिभावान

talk [tɔːk] *n* बातचीत ▷ *vi* बात करना
talkative ['tɔːkətɪv] *adj* बातूनी
talk to [tɔːk tʊ; tuː; tə] *v* से बात करना
tall [tɔːl] *adj* लंबा
tame [teɪm] *adj* पालतू
tampon ['tæmpɒn] *n* टैंपून
tan [tæn] *n* धूप से जला हुआ
tandem ['tændəm] *n* दो सीट वाली साइकिल
tangerine [ˌtændʒə'riːn] *n* नारंगी/छोटा संतरा
tank [tæŋk] *n (container)* टंकी; *(vehicle)* टैंक
tanker ['tæŋkə] *n* टैंकर
tanned [tænd] *adj* धूप से काला पड़ा हुआ
tantrum ['tæntrəm] *n* चिड़चिड़ेपन व गुस्से का आवेश
Tanzania [ˌtænzə'nɪə] *n* तंज़ानिया
Tanzanian [ˌtænzə'nɪən] *adj* तंज़ानियाई ▷ *n* तंज़ानियाई नागरिक
tap [tæp] *n* टोंटी
tap-dancing ['tæpˌdɑːnsɪŋ] *n* टैप डांसिंग - जूते की आवाज़ के साथ किया जाने वाला एक नृत्य
tape [teɪp] *n* टेप ▷ *vt* रिकॉर्ड करना/अभिलेखित करना
tape measure [teɪp 'mɛʒə] *n* नापने का फ़ीता
tape recorder [teɪp rɪ'kɔːdə] *n* टेप रिकॉर्डर
target ['tɑːgɪt] *n* लक्ष्य
tariff ['tærɪf] *n* सीमा - शुल्क
tarmac ['tɑːmæk] *n* डामर
tarpaulin [tɑː'pɔːlɪn] *n* तिरपाल
tarragon ['tærəgən] *n* नागदौना
tart [tɑːt] *n* पेस्ट्री का निचला हिस्सा
tartan ['tɑːtn] *adj* चारखानेदार कपड़ा
task [tɑːsk] *n* काम
Tasmania [tæz'meɪnɪə] *n* तस्मानिया
taste [teɪst] *n* स्वाद ▷ *vi* स्वाद आना

tasteful ['teɪstfʊl] *adj* सुरुचिपूर्ण
tasteless ['teɪstlɪs] *adj* बेस्वाद
tasty ['teɪstɪ] *adj* स्वादिष्ट
tattoo [tæ'tuː] *n* गोदना
Taurus ['tɔːrəs] *n* वृष राशि
tax [tæks] *n* कर
taxi ['tæksɪ] *n* टैक्सी
taxi driver ['tæksɪ 'draɪvə] *n* टैक्सी चालक
taxpayer ['tæks,peɪə] *n* करदाता
tax return [tæks rɪ'tɜːn] *n* आयकर विवरणी
TB [tiː biː] *n* तपेदिक
tea [tiː] *n (drink)* चाय; *(meal)* नाश्ता
tea bag [tiː bæg] *n* चाय की पत्ती के छोटे थैले
teach [tiːtʃ] *vt* सिखाना
teacher ['tiːtʃə] *n* शिक्षक
teaching ['tiːtʃɪŋ] *n* शिक्षण
teacup ['tiː,kʌp] *n* चाय का प्याला
team [tiːm] *n* टोली
teapot ['tiː,pɒt] *n* केतली
tear [tɪə] *n (from eye)* आंसू; [tɛə] *n (rip)* छीज/छेद ▷ *vt* फाड़ना
tear gas [tɪə gæs] *n* आंसू गैस
tear up [tɛə ʌp] *v* फाड़कर चिंदी - चिंदी करना
tease [tiːz] *vt* चिढ़ाना
teaspoon ['tiː,spuːn] *n* छोटा चम्मच
teatime ['tiː,taɪm] *n* चाय का समय
tea towel [tiː 'taʊəl] *n* बर्तन पोंछने का कपड़ा
technical ['tɛknɪkl] *adj* तकनीकी
technician [tɛk'nɪʃən] *n* तकनीशियन/तकनीकविद्
technique [tɛk'niːk] *n* तकनीक
techno ['tɛknəʊ] *n* आधुनिक संगीत का एक प्रकार
technological [tɛknə'lɒdʒɪkl] *adj* प्रौद्योगिक/तकनीकी
technology [tɛk'nɒlədʒɪ] *n* प्रौद्योगिकी/तकनीक

teddy bear ['tɛdɪ bɛə] *n* खिलौना भालू
tee [tiː] *n* टी-गोल्फ़ की गेंद को रखने का आधार
teenager ['tiːn,eɪdʒə] *n* किशोर/किशोरी
teens [tiːnz] *npl* किशोरवय
tee-shirt ['tiː,ʃɜːt] *n* टी - शर्ट
teethe [tiːð] *vi* दांत निकलना
teetotal [tiː'təʊtl] *adj* शराब न पीने वाला
telecommunications [,tɛlɪkə,mjuːnɪ'keɪʃənz] *npl* दूरसंचार
telegram ['tɛlɪ,græm] *n* तार
telephone ['tɛlɪ,fəʊn] *n* दूरभाष
telephone directory ['tɛlɪfəʊn dɪ'rɛktərɪ; -trɪ; daɪ-] *n* दूरभाष निर्देशिका
telesales ['tɛlɪ,seɪlz] *n* फ़ोन पर सामान बेचने की पद्धति
telescope ['tɛlɪ,skəʊp] *n* दूरबीन
television ['tɛlɪ,vɪʒən] *n* टेलीविज़न
tell [tɛl] *vt (inform)* बतलाना; *(order)* कहना/आज्ञा देना; *(sense)* कहना/बतलाना
teller ['tɛlə] *n* रोकड़िया
tell off [tɛl ɒf] *v* फ़टकारना/झिड़कना
telly ['tɛlɪ] *n (informal)* टेलीविज़न
temp [tɛmp] *n* अस्थायी कर्मचारी
temper ['tɛmpə] *n* मिजाज़
temperature ['tɛmprɪtʃə] *n* तापमान
temple ['tɛmpl] *n* मंदिर
temporary ['tɛmpərərɪ] *adj* अस्थायी
tempt [tɛmpt] *v* ललचाना
temptation [tɛmp'teɪʃən] *n* लालच
tempting ['tɛmptɪŋ] *adj* लुभावना
ten [tɛn] *num* दस
tenant ['tɛnənt] *n* किराएदार
tend [tɛnd] *vi* प्रवृत्त होना
tendency ['tɛndənsɪ] *n* प्रवृत्ति
tender ['tɛndə] *adj* नाज़ुक

t

tendon ['tɛndən] *n* पेशी/स्नायु
tennis ['tɛnɪs] *n* टेनिस
tennis court ['tɛnɪs kɔːt] *n* टेनिस का मैदान
tennis player ['tɛnɪs 'pleɪə] *n* टेनिस का खिलाड़ी
tennis racket ['tɛnɪs 'rækɪt] *n* टेनिस रैकैट
tenor ['tɛnə] *n* ऊंचे सुर में गाने वाला गायक
tenpin bowling ['tɛnpɪn 'bəʊlɪŋ] *n* बोलिंग - एक प्रकार का खेल
tense [tɛns] *adj* तनावग्रस्त ▷ *n* काल
tension ['tɛnʃən] *n* तनाव
tent [tɛnt] *n* तंबू
tenth [tɛnθ] *adj* दसवां ▷ *n* दसवां
term [tɜːm] *n (expression)* शब्द; *(school, college, university)* सत्र
terminal ['tɜːmɪnl] *adj* प्राणघातक ▷ *n* टर्मिनल
terminally ['tɜːmɪnlɪ] *adv* मरणासन्न रूप से
terrace ['tɛrəs] *n* परस्पर जुड़े एक जैसे घरों की पंक्ति
terraced ['tɛrəst] *adj* सीढ़ीदार खेत
terrible ['tɛrəbl] *adj* बहुत खराब/भयानक
terribly ['tɛrəblɪ] *adv* भयानक रूप से
terrier ['tɛrɪə] *n* एक प्रकार का छोटा कुत्ता
terrific [tə'rɪfɪk] *adj (informal)* ज़बर्दस्त/शानदार
terrified ['tɛrɪˌfaɪd] *adj* भयभीत/आतंकित
terrify ['tɛrɪˌfaɪ] *vt* आतंकित करना
territory ['tɛrɪtərɪ] *n* क्षेत्र
terrorism ['tɛrəˌrɪzəm] *n* आतंकवाद
terrorist ['tɛrərɪst] *n* आतंकवादी
terrorist attack ['tɛrərɪst ə'tæk] *n* आतंकवादी हमला
test [tɛst] *n (experiment)* परीक्षण ▷ *vt* परखना/जांचना ▷ *n (person, knowledge)* परीक्षा/परख
testicle ['tɛstɪkl] *n* वृषण
test tube [tɛst tjuːb] *n* परखनली

tetanus ['tɛtənəs] *n* टिटेनस - एक बैक्टिरिया जनित रोग

text [tɛkst] *n* पाठ ▷ *vt* पाठ संदेश भेजना

textbook ['tɛkst,bʊk] *n* पाठ्यपुस्तक

textile ['tɛkstaɪl] *n* बुना हुआ कपड़ा

text message [tɛkst 'mɛsɪdʒ] *n* पाठ संदेश

Thai [taɪ] *adj* थाईलैंड से संबद्ध ▷ *n (person)* थाईलैंड का निवासी; *(language)* थाईलैंड की भाषा

Thailand ['taɪ,lænd] *n* थाईलैंड

than [ðæn] *prep* की अपेक्षा

thank [θæŋk] *vt* धन्यवाद देना

thanks! ['θæŋks] *excl* धन्यवाद!

that [ðæt] *det (denoting something previously mentioned)* इसके लिए ▷ *conj (joining clauses)* कि ▷ *pron (denoting something previously mentioned)* वह ▷ *det (referring to a person or thing a distance away)* उस ▷ *pron (referring to a person or thing a distance away)* उस; *pron (who or which)* जिसके/जो

thatched [θætʃt] *adj* छप्परदार

the [ðə] *det (referring to a specific person or thing)* एक निश्चयवाचक उपपद; *det (with singular noun referring to things of that type generally)* यह/वह/वही

theatre ['θɪətə] *n* नाट्यगृह

theft [θɛft] *n* चोरी

their [ðɛə] *det* उनका

theirs [ðɛəz] *pron* उनका

them [ðɛm] *pron* उन्हें

theme [θiːm] *n* विषयवस्तु

theme park [θiːm pɑːk] *n* मनोरंजन उद्यान

themselves [ðəm'sɛlvz] *pron* खुद

then [ðɛn] *adv* तब ▷ *conj (informal)* फिर/बाद में

theology [θɪ'ɒlədʒɪ] *n* अध्यात्मविद्या

theory ['θɪərɪ] *n* सिद्धांत

therapy ['θɛrəpɪ] *n* चिकित्सा

there [ðɛə] *adv* वहां ▹ *pron* उधर

therefore ['ðɛəˌfɔː] *adv* अतएव

thermometer [θə'mɒmɪtə] *n* थर्मामीटर

Thermos® ['θɜːməs] *n* थर्मस

thermostat ['θɜːməˌstæt] *n* थर्मोस्टेट - ताप नियत रखने का उपकरण

these [ðiːz] *det (referring to people or things previously mentioned)* ये ▹ *pron* ये ▹ *det* ये; *det (referring to people or things you are going to talk about)* ये

they [ðeɪ] *pron* वे

thick [θɪk] *adj (measuring a lot from one side to the other)* मोटा; *(liquid)* गाढ़ा

thickness ['θɪknɪs] *n* मोटाई

thief [θiːf] *n* चोर

thigh [θaɪ] *n* जांघ

thin [θɪn] *adj (not measuring much from one side to the other)* पतला; *(slim)* दुबला

thing [θɪŋ] *n* चीज़

think [θɪŋk] *v (believe)* मानना ▹ *vi (use your mind)* सोचना

third [θɜːd] *adj* तीसरा ▹ *n* तीसरा भाग

thirdly ['θɜːdlɪ] *adv* तीसरे

third-party insurance ['θɜːd'pɑːtɪ ɪn'ʃʊərəns; -'ʃɔː-] *n* तीसरे पक्ष की क्षतिपूर्ति का बीमा

thirst [θɜːst] *n* प्यास

thirsty ['θɜːstɪ] *adj* प्यासा

thirteen ['θɜː'tiːn] *num* तेरह

thirteenth ['θɜː'tiːnθ] *adj* तेरहवां

thirty ['θɜːtɪ] *num* तीस

this [ðɪs] *det (referring to a person or thing previously mentioned)* इस ▹ *pron (person or thing near you)* यह ▹ *det (referring to a person or thing near you)* यह ▹ *pron (referring to a person or thing you are going to talk about)* यह

thistle ['θɪsl] *n* भटकटैया का पौधा

thorn [θɔːn] *n* कांटा

thorough ['θʌrə] *adj* आद्योपांत/संपूर्ण
thoroughly ['θʌrəlɪ] *adv* पूरी तरह से/अच्छी तरह से
those [ðəʊz] *det (referring to people or things previously mentioned)* उन ▷ *pron* वे ▷ *det* वे
though [ðəʊ] *adv* हालांकि ▷ *conj (even although)* मगर/यद्यपि; *conj (in contrast)* यद्यपि/भले ही
thought [θɔːt] *n* सोच/विचार
thoughtful ['θɔːtfʊl] *adj* विचारमग्न
thoughtless ['θɔːtlɪs] *adj* विचारशून्य/विचारहीन
thousand ['θaʊzənd] *num* हज़ार
thousandth ['θaʊzənθ] *adj* हज़ारवां ▷ *n* हज़ारवां हिस्सा
thread [θrɛd] *n* धागा
threat [θrɛt] *n* धमकी/ख़तरा
threaten ['θrɛtn] *vt* धमकी देना
threatening ['θrɛtnɪŋ] *adj* धमकाने वाला
three [θriː] *num* तीन
three-dimensional [ˌθriːdɪ'mɛnʃənl] *adj* त्रि - आयामी
thrifty ['θrɪftɪ] *adj* मितव्ययी
thrill [θrɪl] *n* रोमांच
thrilled [θrɪld] *adj* रोमांचित
thriller ['θrɪlə] *n* रोमांचक सामग्री
thrilling ['θrɪlɪŋ] *adj* रोमांचक
throat [θrəʊt] *n (back of mouth)* गला/कंठ; *(front of neck)* गला/कंठ
throb [θrɒb] *vi* टीसना
throne [θrəʊn] *n* सिंहासन
through [θruː] *prep (from one side to the other of)* आरपार
throughout [θruː'aʊt] *prep* के दौर में
throw [θrəʊ] *vt* फेंकना
throw away [θrəʊ ə'weɪ] *v* फेंक देना
throw out [θrəʊ aʊt] *v* फेंक देना
throw up [θrəʊ ʌp] *v (informal)* उल्टी करना

thrush [θrʌʃ] *n* एक छोटी चिड़िया
thug [θʌg] *n* ठग
thumb [θʌm] *n* अंगूठा
thumbtack ['θʌm,tæk] *n (US)* ड्राइंग पिन
thump [θʌmp] *v* मुक्का मारना
thunder ['θʌndə] *n* गड़गड़ाहट
thunderstorm ['θʌndə,stɔːm] *n* बारिश, बिजली और गड़गड़ाहट के साथ तूफ़ान
thundery ['θʌndərɪ] *adj* गरजनेवाला
Thursday ['θɜːzdɪ] *n* बृहस्पतिवार
thyme [taɪm] *n* अजवायन
Tibet [tɪ'bɛt] *n* तिब्बत
Tibetan [tɪ'bɛtn] *adj* तिब्बती ▷ *n (person)* तिब्बत का निवासी; *(language)* तिब्बती भाषा
tick [tɪk] *n* सही का निशान ▷ *vt* सही का निशान लगाना
ticket ['tɪkɪt] *n* टिकट
ticket machine ['tɪkɪt mə'ʃiːn] *n* टिकट निकालने की मशीन
ticket office ['tɪkɪt 'ɒfɪs] *n* टिकट घर
tickle ['tɪkl] *vt* गुदगुदी करना
ticklish ['tɪklɪʃ] *adj* पेचीदा
tick off [tɪk ɒf] *v* सही का निशान लगाना
tide [taɪd] *n* ज्वार - भाटा
tidy ['taɪdɪ] *adj* साफ़ - सुथरा ▷ *vt* साफ़ - सुथरा करना
tidy up ['taɪdɪ ʌp] *v* सुव्यवस्थित करना
tie [taɪ] *n (necktie)* टाई ▷ *vt* बांधना
tie up [taɪ ʌp] *v* बांधना
tiger ['taɪgə] *n* बाघ
tight [taɪt] *adj (clothes)* तंग; *(knot)* कसा हुआ
tighten ['taɪtn] *v* कसना
tights [taɪts] *npl* चुस्त पतलून
tile [taɪl] *n* खपरैल/खपड़ा
tiled ['taɪld] *adj* खपड़ा लगा हुआ

till [tɪl] *conj (informal)* जब तक ▹ *n* नकद पेटी ▹ *prep (informal, until but not later than)* पर्यंत; *(informal, before)* तब तक

timber ['tɪmbə] *n* ईमारती लकड़ी

time [taɪm] *n (how long something takes to happen)* समय/वक़्त; *(current)* समय

time bomb [taɪm bɒm] *n* टाइम बम

time off [taɪm ɒf] *n* अवकाश

timer ['taɪmə] *n* काल समंजक

timetable ['taɪm,teɪbl] *n* समयसारिणी

time zone [taɪm zəʊn] *n* समय मंडल

tin [tɪn] *n (metal)* टिन (धातु); *(can)* कनस्तर

tinfoil ['tɪn,fɔɪl] *n* खाना लपेटने की चमकीली पन्नी

tinned [tɪnd] *adj* कनस्तर बंद

tin opener [tɪn 'əʊpnə] *n* कनस्तर खोलने का उपकरण

tinsel ['tɪnsəl] *n* सजाने की चमकीली झालर

tinted ['tɪntɪd] *adj* रंगीन

tiny ['taɪnɪ] *adj* छोटा

tip [tɪp] *n (end)* नोक; *(gratuity)* बख़्शीश; *(hint)* सलाह ▹ *v (incline)* झुकाना/झुकना ▹ *vt (give money to)* बख़्शीश देना

tipsy ['tɪpsɪ] *adj* मतवाला/हल्के नशे में

tired ['taɪəd] *adj* थका हुआ

tiring ['taɪərɪŋ] *adj* थकाऊ

tissue ['tɪsjuː] *n* ऊतक

title ['taɪtl] *n* शीर्षक

to [tuː] *prep* की ओर ▹ *part* के लिए

toad [təʊd] *n* भेक - मेंढक जैसा एक जीव

toadstool ['təʊd,stuːl] *n* छत्रक/कुकुरमुत्ता

toast [təʊst] *n (bread)* सेंकी हुई पावरोटी; *(drink)* किसी को शुभकामना देते हुए शराब पीना

toaster ['təʊstə] *n* टोस्टर - पावरोटी सेंकने का उपकरण

tobacco [tə'bækəʊ] *n* तंबाकू

tobacconist [tə'bækənɪst] *n* पान की दुकान

toboggan [tə'bɒgən] *n* बर्फ़ पर फिसलने का पटरा

tobogganing [tə'bɒgənɪŋ] *n* पटरे पर बैठकर बर्फ़ पर फिसलना

today [tə'deɪ] *adv* आज

toddler ['tɒdlə] *n* छोटा बच्चा

toe [təʊ] *n* पैर की अंगुलियां

toffee ['tɒfɪ] *n* टॉफ़ी/चीनी की मिठाई

together [tə'gɛðə] *adv* साथ - साथ

Togo ['təʊgəʊ] *n* टोगो

toilet ['tɔɪlɪt] *n* शौचालय

toilet bag ['tɔɪlɪt bæg] *n* प्रसाधन थैली

toilet paper ['tɔɪlɪt 'peɪpə] *n* टॉयलेट पेपर

toiletries ['tɔɪlɪtriːz] *npl* नित्यकर्म हेतु इस्तेमाल होने वाली प्रसाधन सामग्री

toilet roll ['tɔɪlɪt rəʊl] *n* टॉयलेट रोल

token ['təʊkən] *n* टोकन/रसीद

tolerant ['tɒlərənt] *adj* सहिष्णु

toll [təʊl] *n* यातायात कर

tomato [tə'mɑːtəʊ] *n* टमाटर

tomato sauce [tə'mɑːtəʊ sɔːs] *n* टमाटर की चटनी

tomb [tuːm] *n* मकबरा

tomboy ['tɒm,bɔɪ] *n* लड़कों जैसी चाल-ढाल वाली लड़की

tomorrow [tə'mɒrəʊ] *adv* आने वाला कल

ton [tʌn] *n* टन

tongue [tʌŋ] *n* जीभ

tonic ['tɒnɪk] *n* टॉनिक

tonight [tə'naɪt] *adv* आज रात को

tonsillitis [,tɒnsɪ'laɪtɪs] *n* तुंडिका शोथ

tonsils ['tɒnsəlz] *npl* गलतुंडिका

too [tuː] *adv (also)* भी; *(excessively)* बहुत ज़्यादा

tool [tuːl] *n* उपकरण

tooth [tuːθ] *n (in your mouth)* दांत; *(comb, zip, saw)* दांता

toothache ['tuːθ,eɪk] *n* दांत का दर्द

toothbrush ['tuːθ,brʌʃ] *n* दांत साफ करने का ब्रश
toothpaste ['tuːθ,peɪst] *n* टूथपेस्ट
toothpick ['tuːθ,pɪk] *n* दंतखोदनी
top [tɒp] *n* शीर्षतम/सर्वोच्च; *(highest part)* शीर्ष भाग; *(lid)* ढक्कन
topic ['tɒpɪk] *n* विषय
topical ['tɒpɪkl] *adj* सामयिक
top-secret ['tɒp'siːkrɪt] *adj* अति गोपनीय
top-up card ['tɒpʌp kɑːd] *n* टॉप - अप कार्ड
torch [tɔːtʃ] *n* टॉर्च
tornado [tɔː'neɪdəʊ] *n* बवंडर
tortoise ['tɔːtəs] *n* कछुआ
torture ['tɔːtʃə] *n* यातना ▹ *vt* यातना देना
toss [tɒs] *vt* उछालना
total ['təʊtl] *adj* समस्त ▹ *n* कुल
totally ['təʊtlɪ] *adv* पूर्णतया
touch [tʌtʃ] *vt (with your fingers)* छूना ▹ *v (come into contact with)* स्पर्श करना
touchdown ['tʌtʃ,daʊn] *n* अवतरण
touched [tʌtʃt] *adj* द्रवित/भावविह्वल
touching ['tʌtʃɪŋ] *adj* मार्मिक
touchline ['tʌtʃ,laɪn] *n* टच लाइन - खेल के मैदान की सीमा रेखा
touch pad [tʌtʃ pæd] *n* टच पैड
touchy ['tʌtʃɪ] *adj* संवेदनशील
tough [tʌf] *adj* कठोर/मज़बूत
toupee ['tuːpeɪ] *n* नकली बाल
tour [tʊə] *n* दौरा ▹ *v* दौरा करना
tour guide [tʊə gaɪd] *n* पर्यटन गाइड
tourism ['tʊərɪzəm] *n* पर्यटन
tourist ['tʊərɪst] *n* पर्यटक
tourist office ['tʊərɪst 'ɒfɪs] *n* पर्यटन कार्यालय
tournament ['tʊənəmənt] *n* खेल प्रतियोगिता

towards [tə'wɔːdz] *prep* की तरफ़

tow away [təʊ ə'weɪ] *v* एक गाड़ी द्वारा दूसरी गाड़ी को खींचकर ले जाया जाना

towel ['taʊəl] *n* तौलिया

tower ['taʊə] *n* मीनार

town [taʊn] *n* शहर/कस्बा

town centre [taʊn 'sɛntə] *n* नगर केंद्र

town hall [taʊn hɔːl] *n* नगर भवन

town planning [taʊn 'plænɪŋ] *n* नगर योजना

toxic ['tɒksɪk] *adj* विषैला

toy [tɔɪ] *n* खिलौना

trace [treɪs] *n* अवशेष

tracing paper ['treɪsɪŋ 'peɪpə] *n* पारदर्शक कागज़

track [træk] *n* पगडंडी

track down [træk daʊn] *v* खोज निकालना/पता चलाना

tracksuit ['træk,suːt] *n* ट्रैक सूट

tractor ['træktə] *n* ट्रैक्टर

trade [treɪd] *n* व्यापार

trademark ['treɪd,mɑːk] *n* व्यापार चिह्न

trade union [treɪd 'juːnjən] *n* व्यापारिक संघ

trade unionist [treɪd 'juːnjənɪst] *n* श्रमिक संघ का सदस्य

tradition [trə'dɪʃən] *n* परंपरा

traditional [trə'dɪʃənl] *adj* पारंपरिक

traffic ['træfɪk] *n* यातायात

traffic jam ['træfɪk dʒæm] *n* यातायात अवरोध

traffic lights ['træfɪk laɪts] *npl* यातायात बत्ती

traffic warden ['træfɪk 'wɔːdn] *n* यातायात अभिरक्षक

tragedy ['trædʒɪdɪ] *n* दुःखद घटना

tragic ['trædʒɪk] *adj* दुःखद

trailer ['treɪlə] *n* खींची जाने वाली बिना इंजन की गाड़ी

train [treɪn] *n* रेलगाड़ी ▷ *vt* प्रशिक्षित करना/प्रशिक्षित होना

trained [treɪnd] *adj* प्रशिक्षित

trainee [treɪ'niː] *n* प्रशिक्षु

trainer ['treɪnə] *n* प्रशिक्षक

trainers ['treɪnəz] *npl* दौड़ते या खेलते समय पहने जाने वाले जूते

training ['treɪnɪŋ] *n* प्रशिक्षण

training course ['treɪnɪŋ kɔːs] *n* प्रशिक्षण पाठ्यक्रम

tram [træm] *n* ट्राम - एक गाड़ी

tramp [træmp] *n* *(vagabond)* आवारा/भिखारी; *(walk)* पदयात्रा

trampoline ['træmpəlɪn] *n* ट्रैंपलीन - तना हुआ कपड़ा, जिस पर उछला जाता है

tranquillizer ['træŋkwɪˌlaɪzə] *n* एक शामक दवा

transaction [træn'zækʃən] *n (formal)* सौदा

transcript ['trænskrɪpt] *n* लिखित प्रतिलिपि

transfer ['trænsfɜː] *n* स्थानांतरण

transform [træns'fɔːm] *vt* कायापलट करना

transfusion [træns'fjuːʒən] *n* रक्त आधान

transistor [træn'zɪstə] *n* ट्रांजिस्टर

transit ['trænsɪt] *n* पारवहन

transition [træn'zɪʃən] *n* उत्परिवर्तन

translate [træns'leɪt] *vt* अनुवाद करना

translation [træns'leɪʃən] *n* अनुवाद

translator [træns'leɪtə; trænz-] *n* अनुवादक

transparent [træns'pærənt] *adj* पारदर्शी

transplant ['trænsˌplɑːnt] *n* प्रत्यारोपण

transport ['trænspɔːt] *n* परिवहन ▹ [træns'pɔːt] *vt* लाना - ले जाना

transvestite [trænz'vɛstaɪt] *n* विपरीत लिंग के कपड़े पहनने वाला व्यक्ति

trap [træp] *n* फंदा/पिंजरा

traumatic [trɔː'mætɪk] *adj* मानसिक आघात देने वाला

travel ['trævl] *n* यात्रा ▹ *vi* यात्रा करना

t

travel agency ['trævl 'eɪdʒənsɪ] *n* यात्रा आयोजक कंपनी
travel agent ['trævl 'eɪdʒənt] *n (person)* यात्रा आयोजक कंपनी
travel insurance ['trævl ɪn'ʃʊərəns; -'ʃɔː-] *n* यात्रा बीमा
traveller ['trævələ] *n* यात्री
traveller's cheque ['trævləz tʃɛk] *n* ट्रैवेलर चेक - विदेशी मुद्रा से बदले जा सकने वाले चेक
travelling ['trævlɪŋ] *n* यात्रा
tray [treɪ] *n* ट्रे/तश्तरी
treacle ['triːkl] *n* शीरा
tread [trɛd] *vi* कुचलना/पैर रखना
treasure ['trɛʒə] *n (literary)* खजाना
treasurer ['trɛʒərə] *n* खजांची
treat [triːt] *n* दावत देना ▷ *vt* बर्ताव करना
treatment ['triːtmənt] *n* इलाज
treaty ['triːtɪ] *n* अनुबंध/संधि
treble ['trɛbl] *v* तिगुना करना/तिगुना होना
tree [triː] *n* पेड़
trek [trɛk] *n* कठिन पैदल यात्रा ▷ *vi* कठिन पैदल यात्रा करना
tremble ['trɛmbl] *vi* कांपना
tremendous [trɪ'mɛndəs] *adj* ज़बर्दस्त
trench [trɛntʃ] *n* खाई/खंदक
trend [trɛnd] *n* प्रचलन
trendy ['trɛndɪ] *adj (informal)* फ़ैशनेबल/नए चलन का
trial ['traɪəl] *n* सुनवाई
trial period ['traɪəl 'pɪərɪəd] *n* परीक्षण अवधि
triangle ['traɪˌæŋgl] *n (shape)* त्रिकोण; *(musical instrument)* धातु का बना हुआ त्रिभुजाकार वाद्ययंत्र
tribe [traɪb] *n* कबीला
tribunal [traɪ'bjuːnl] *n* न्यायाधिकरण
trick [trɪk] *n* चाल ▷ *vt* चालबाज़ी करना/धोखा देना
tricky ['trɪkɪ] *adj* पेचीदा

tricycle ['traɪsɪkl] *n* तिपहिया साइकिल
trifle ['traɪfl] *n* तुच्छ वस्तु
trim [trɪm] *vt* काट - छांट करना
Trinidad and Tobago ['trɪnɪˌdæd ænd tə'beɪgəʊ] *n* त्रिनिदाद व टोबैगो
trip [trɪp] *n* यात्रा ▷ *vi* ठोकर खाना/लड़खड़ाना
triple ['trɪpl] *adj* तिहरा
triplets ['trɪplɪts] *npl* एक साथ जन्मे तीन बच्चे/त्रिक
triumph ['traɪəmf] *n* विजय ▷ *vi* विजय हासिल करना
trivial ['trɪvɪəl] *adj* तुच्छ/क्षुद्र
trolley ['trɒlɪ] *n* ठेला
trombone [trɒm'bəʊn] *n* तुरही
troops ['tru:ps] *npl* सेना
trophy ['trəʊfɪ] *n* जयचिह्न
tropical ['trɒpɪkl] *adj* उष्णकटिबंधीय
trot [trɒt] *vi* तेज़ चाल से चलना
trouble ['trʌbl] *n* परेशानी
troublemaker ['trʌblˌmeɪkə] *n* उपद्रवी
trough [trɒf] *n* नांद
trousers ['traʊzəz] *npl* पतलून
trout [traʊt] *n* ट्राउट - एक प्रकार की मछली
trowel ['traʊəl] *n* खुरपी
truce [tru:s] *n* युद्धविराम
truck [trʌk] *n (US)* ट्रक
truck driver [trʌk 'draɪvə] *n (US)* ट्रक चालक
true [tru:] *adj (factual)* सच्चा; *(correct)* सही/सच्चा
truly ['tru:lɪ] *adv* सही अर्थों में/असल में
trumpet ['trʌmpɪt] *n* तुरही/तूर्य
trunk [trʌŋk] *n (tree)* तना; *(elephant)* सूंड़; *(box)* संदूक
trunks [trʌŋks] *npl* तैराकी के समय पहनी जाने वाली पुरुषों की निकर
trust [trʌst] *n* विश्वास ▷ *vt* विश्वास करना
trusting ['trʌstɪŋ] *adj* विश्वास करने वाला
truth [tru:θ] *n* सच्चाई
truthful ['tru:θfʊl] *adj* सच्चा

t

try [traɪ] *n* प्रयत्न ▷ *vi* *(attempt)* प्रयास करना ▷ *vt* *(test)* आज़माना

try on [traɪ ɒn] *v* पहनकर देखना

try out [traɪ aʊt] *v* परखना

T-shirt ['tiːˌʃɜːt] *n* टी - शर्ट

tsunami [tsʊ'næmɪ] *n* सूनामी - विशालकाय लहर

tube [tjuːb] *n* *(long hollow object)* नली; *(container)* ट्यूब

tuberculosis [tjʊˌbɜːkjʊ'ləʊsɪs] *n* तपेदिक/क्षय रोग

Tuesday ['tjuːzdɪ] *n* मंगलवार

tug-of-war ['tʌgɒv'wɔː] *n* रस्साकशी

tuition [tjuː'ɪʃən] *n* निजी शिक्षण

tuition fees [tjuː'ɪʃən fiːz] *npl* शिक्षण शुल्क

tulip ['tjuːlɪp] *n* ट्यूलिप - वसंत ऋतु में खिलने वाले फूल

tumble dryer ['tʌmbl 'draɪə] *n* टंबल ड्रायर - कपड़े सुखाने की मशीन

tummy ['tʌmɪ] *n* तोंद

tumour ['tjuːmə] *n* अर्बुद

tuna ['tjuːnə] *n* ट्यूना - एक प्रकार की मछली

tune [tjuːn] *n* धुन

Tunisia [tjuː'nɪzɪə] *n* ट्यूनिशिया

Tunisian [tjuː'nɪzɪən] *adj* ट्यूनिशायाई ▷ *n* ट्यूनिशिया का निवासी

tunnel ['tʌnl] *n* सुरंग

turbulence ['tɜːbjʊləns] *n* अशांति

Turk [tɜːk] *n* तुर्क

Turkey ['tɜːkɪ] *n* तुर्की

turkey ['tɜːkɪ] *n* टर्की - एक पक्षी

Turkish ['tɜːkɪʃ] *adj* तुर्की से संबद्ध ▷ *n* तुर्की भाषा

turn [tɜːn] *n* मोड़ ▷ *v* *(move in a different direction)* मुड़ना; *(move round in a circle)* मुड़ना ▷ *vi* *(change)* बदलना/होना

turn around [tɜːn ə'raʊnd] *v* मुड़ना

turn back [tɜːn bæk] *v* पीछे मुड़ना/पीछे मोड़ना

turn down [tɜːn daʊn] *v* अस्वीकृत करना

turning ['tɜːnɪŋ] *n* मोड़
turnip ['tɜːnɪp] *n* शलगम
turn off [tɜːn ɒf] *v* रास्ता बदलना
turn on [tɜːn ɒn] *v* चालू करना
turn out [tɜːn aʊt] *v* होना
turnover ['tɜːnˌəʊvə] *n* कुल आय
turn up [tɜːn ʌp] *v* आना
turquoise ['tɜːkwɔɪz] *adj* फ़िरोज़ा
turtle ['tɜːtl] *n* कछुआ
tutor ['tjuːtə] *n* शिक्षक
tutorial [tjuː'tɔːrɪəl] *n* शिक्षण सत्र
tuxedo [tʌk'siːdəʊ] *n* औपचारिक अवसरों पर पहना जाने वाला कोट
TV [tiː viː] *n* टी वी
tweezers ['twiːzəz] *npl* चिमटी
twelfth [twɛlfθ] *adj* बारहवां
twelve [twɛlv] *num* बारह
twentieth ['twɛntɪɪθ] *adj* बीसवां
twenty ['twɛntɪ] *num* बीस
twice [twaɪs] *adv* दो बार
twin [twɪn] *n* जुड़वा
twin beds [twɪn bɛdz] *npl* जुड़वा पलंग
twinned [twɪnd] *adj* जुड़वा
twist [twɪst] *vt* मरोड़ना
twit [twɪt] *n (informal)* बेवकूफ़
two [tuː] *num* दो
type [taɪp] *n* प्रकार ▷ *v* टंकित करना
typewriter ['taɪpˌraɪtə] *n* टंकण मशीन
typhoid ['taɪfɔɪd] *n* मियादी बुखार
typical ['tɪpɪkl] *adj* ठेठ
typist ['taɪpɪst] *n* टाइपिस्ट/टंकक
tyre ['taɪə] *n* टायर

U

UFO ['juːfəʊ] *abbr* उड़नतश्तरी
Uganda [juː'gændə] *n* युगांडा
Ugandan [juː'gændən] *adj* युगांडा से संबद्ध ▷ *n* युगांडा का निवासी

ugh! [ʌh] *excl* उह!
ugly ['ʌglɪ] *adj* बदसूरत
UHT milk [juː eɪtʃ tiː mɪlk] *n* उच्च तापमान पर उबालकर रखा गया दूध
UK [juː keɪ] *n* यूनाइटेड किंगडम
Ukraine [juː'kreɪn] *n* यूक्रेन
Ukrainian [juː'kreɪnɪən] *adj* यूक्रेन से संबद्ध ▷ *n (person)* यूक्रेन का निवासी; *(language)* यूक्रेनी भाषा
ulcer ['ʌlsə] *n* फोड़ा
Ulster ['ʌlstə] *n* अल्स्टर
ultimate ['ʌltɪmɪt] *adj* अंतिम
ultimately ['ʌltɪmɪtlɪ] *adv* अंततोगत्वा
ultimatum [ˌʌltɪ'meɪtəm] *n* अंतिम चेतावनी
ultrasound ['ʌltrəˌsaʊnd] *n* अल्ट्रासाउंड
umbrella [ʌm'brɛlə] *n* छाता
umpire ['ʌmpaɪə] *n* अंपायर
UN [juː ɛn] *abbr* यू. एन./संयुक्त राष्ट्र का संक्षिप्त नाम
unable [ʌn'eɪbl] *adj* असमर्थ
unacceptable [ˌʌnək'sɛptəbl] *adj* अस्वीकार्य
unanimous [juː'nænɪməs] *adj* सर्वसम्मत
unattended [ˌʌnə'tɛndɪd] *adj* अरक्षित
unavoidable [ˌʌnə'vɔɪdəbl] *adj* अपरिहार्य
unbearable [ʌn'bɛərəbl] *adj* असहनीय
unbeatable [ʌn'biːtəbl] *adj* अद्वितीय
unbelievable [ˌʌnbɪ'liːvəbl] *adj* अविश्वसनीय
unbreakable [ʌn'breɪkəbl] *adj* अटूट
uncanny [ʌn'kænɪ] *adj* विचित्र
uncertain [ʌn'sɜːtn] *adj* अनिश्चित
uncertainty [ʌn'sɜːtntɪ] *n* अनिश्चय
unchanged [ʌn'tʃeɪndʒd] *adj* अपरिवर्तित
uncivilized [ʌn'sɪvɪˌlaɪzd] *adj* असभ्य
uncle ['ʌŋkl] *n* चाचा/मामा/फूफा/मौसा

unclear [ʌn'klɪə] *adj* अस्पष्ट
uncomfortable [ʌn'kʌmftəbl] *adj* कष्टप्रद
unconditional [ˌʌnkən'dɪʃənl] *adj* बेशर्त
unconscious [ʌn'kɒnʃəs] *adj* अचेत
uncontrollable [ˌʌnkən'trəʊləbl] *adj* अनियंत्रित
unconventional [ˌʌnkən'vɛnʃənl] *adj* अपरंपरागत
undecided [ˌʌndɪ'saɪdɪd] *adj* अनिर्णीत
undeniable [ˌʌndɪ'naɪəbl] *adj* अविवादित
under ['ʌndə] *prep* के नीचे
underage [ˌʌndər'eɪdʒ] *adj* अवयस्क
underestimate [ˌʌndər'ɛstɪmeɪt] *vt* कम आँकना
undergo [ˌʌndə'gəʊ] *vt* गुज़रना/भोगना
undergraduate [ˌʌndə'grædjʊɪt] *n* पूर्वस्नातक
underground [ˌʌndə'graʊnd] *adv* भूमिगत ▷ ['ʌndəgraʊnd] *n* भूमिगत रेलवे स्टेशन
underground station ['ʌndəgraʊnd 'steɪʃən] *n* भूमिगत स्टेशन
underline [ˌʌndə'laɪn] *vt* रेखांकित करना/ज़ोर देना
underneath [ˌʌndə'niːθ] *adv* नीचे ▷ *prep* के नीचे
underpaid [ˌʌndə'peɪd] *adj* जिन्हें काम से कम वेतन मिलता है
underpants ['ʌndəˌpænts] *npl* जाँघिया
underpass ['ʌndəˌpɑːs] *n* अंडरपास
underskirt ['ʌndəˌskɜːt] *n* पेटीकोट
understand [ˌʌndə'stænd] *vt* समझना
understandable [ˌʌndə'stændəbl] *adj* समझने योग्य
understanding [ˌʌndə'stændɪŋ] *adj* उदार
undertaker ['ʌndəˌteɪkə] *n* मृतसंस्कार करने वाला

underwater ['ʌndə'wɔːtə] *adv* अंतर्जलीय
underwear ['ʌndə,wɛə] *n* अंतःवस्त्र
undisputed [,ʌndɪ'spjuːtɪd] *adj* निर्विवाद
undo [ʌn'duː] *vt* खोलना
undoubtedly [ʌn'daʊtɪdlɪ] *adv* निःसंदेह
undress [ʌn'drɛs] *v* कपड़े उतारना
unemployed [,ʌnɪm'plɔɪd] *adj* बेरोज़गार
unemployment [,ʌnɪm'plɔɪmənt] *n* बेरोज़गारी
unexpected [,ʌnɪk'spɛktɪd] *adj* अनपेक्षित
unexpectedly [,ʌnɪk'spɛktɪdlɪ] *adv* अनपेक्षित रूप से
unfair [ʌn'fɛə] *adj* अनुचित
unfaithful [ʌn'feɪθfʊl] *adj* बेवफ़ा
unfamiliar [,ʌnfə'mɪljə] *adj* अपरिचित
unfashionable [ʌn'fæʃənəbl] *adj* अप्रचलित
unfavourable [ʌn'feɪvərəbl] *adj* प्रतिकूल
unfit [ʌn'fɪt] *adj* अस्वस्थ
unforgettable [,ʌnfə'gɛtəbl] *adj* अविस्मरणीय
unfortunately [ʌn'fɔːtʃənɪtlɪ] *adv* दुर्भाग्यवश
unfriendly [ʌn'frɛndlɪ] *adj* गैरदोस्ताना
ungrateful [ʌn'greɪtfʊl] *adj* कृतघ्न
unhappy [ʌn'hæpɪ] *adj* अप्रसन्न
unhealthy [ʌn'hɛlθɪ] *adj* अस्वास्थ्यकर
unhelpful [ʌn'hɛlpfʊl] *adj* बेकार
uni ['juːnɪ] *n (informal)* विश्वविद्यालय
unidentified [,ʌnaɪ'dɛntɪ,faɪd] *adj* अज्ञात
uniform ['juːnɪ,fɔːm] *n* वर्दी

unimportant [ˌʌnɪm'pɔːtnt] *adj* महत्वहीन
uninhabited [ˌʌnɪn'hæbɪtɪd] *adj* निर्जन
unintentional [ˌʌnɪn'tɛnʃənl] *adj* अनजाने में हुआ
union ['juːnjən] *n* संघ
unique [juː'niːk] *adj* अनूठा
unit ['juːnɪt] *n* इकाई
unite [juː'naɪt] *v* एकजुट
United Arab Emirates [juː'naɪtɪd 'ærəb e'mɪərɪts] *npl* संयुक्त अरब अमीरात
United Kingdom [juː'naɪtɪd 'kɪŋdəm] *n* यूनाइटेड किंगडम
United Nations [juː'naɪtɪd 'neɪʃənz] *n* संयुक्त राष्ट्र
United States of America [juː'naɪtɪd steɪts ɒv ə'mɛrɪkə] *n* संयुक्त राज्य अमेरिका
universe ['juːnɪˌvɜːs] *n* ब्रह्मांड
university [ˌjuːnɪ'vɜːsɪtɪ] *n* विश्वविद्यालय
unknown [ʌn'nəʊn] *adj* अविदित
unleaded [ʌn'lɛdɪd] *n* सीसारहित
unleaded petrol [ʌn'lɛdɪd 'pɛtrəl] *n* सीसारहित पेट्रोल
unless [ʌn'lɛs] *conj* जब तक नहीं
unlike [ʌn'laɪk] *prep* से अलग
unlikely [ʌn'laɪklɪ] *adj* असम्भाव्य
unlisted [ʌn'lɪstɪd] *adj* असूचीबद्ध
unload [ʌn'ləʊd] *vt* उतारना
unlock [ʌn'lɒk] *vt* ताला खोलना
unlucky [ʌn'lʌkɪ] *adj* अभागा
unmarried [ʌn'mærɪd] *adj* अविवाहित
unnecessary [ʌn'nɛsɪsərɪ] *adj* अनावश्यक
unofficial [ˌʌnə'fɪʃəl] *adj* अनौपचारिक
unpack [ʌn'pæk] *v* सामान खोलना
unpaid [ʌn'peɪd] *adj* अवैतनिक

unpleasant [ʌn'plɛznt] *adj* अप्रिय
unplug [ʌn'plʌg] *vt* प्लग निकालना
unpopular [ʌn'pɒpjʊlə] *adj* अलोकप्रिय
unprecedented [ʌn'prɛsɪˌdɛntɪd] *adj* अभूतपूर्व
unpredictable [ˌʌnprɪ'dɪktəbl] *adj* अपूर्वानुमेय
unreal [ʌn'rɪəl] *adj* अवास्तविक
unrealistic [ˌʌnrɪə'lɪstɪk] *adj* अयथार्थवादी
unreasonable [ʌn'riːznəbl] *adj* अतर्कसंगत
unreliable [ˌʌnrɪ'laɪəbl] *adj* गैरभरोसेमंद
unroll [ʌn'rəʊl] *v* खोलना
unsatisfactory [ˌʌnsætɪs'fæktərɪ] *adj* असंतोषजनक
unscrew [ʌn'skruː] *v* खोलना
unshaven [ʌn'ʃeɪvn] *adj* बगैर हजामत का
unskilled [ʌn'skɪld] *adj* अकुशल
unstable [ʌn'steɪbl] *adj* असंतुलित
unsteady [ʌn'stɛdɪ] *adj* अस्थिर
unsuccessful [ˌʌnsək'sɛsfʊl] *adj* असफल
unsuitable [ʌn'suːtəbl] *adj* अनुपयुक्त
unsure [ʌn'ʃʊə] *adj* अनिश्चित
untidy [ʌn'taɪdɪ] *adj* बेतरतीब
untie [ʌn'taɪ] *vt* खोलना
until [ʌn'tɪl] *conj* जब तक ▷ *prep* तक
unusual [ʌn'juːʒʊəl] *adj* असामान्य
unwell [ʌn'wɛl] *adj* अस्वस्थ
unwind [ʌn'waɪnd] *vi* आराम करना
unwise [ʌn'waɪz] *adj* मूर्खतापूर्ण
unwrap [ʌn'ræp] *vt* खोलना
unzip [ʌn'zɪp] *vt* चेन खोलना
up [ʌp] *adv* ऊपर

upbringing ['ʌpˌbrɪŋɪŋ] *n* पालन - पोषण
update [ʌp'deɪt] *vt* नवीनीकृत करना
uphill ['ʌp'hɪl] *adv* ऊपर की ओर
upon [ə'pɒn] *prep* के ऊपर
upper ['ʌpə] *adj* ऊपर का
upright ['ʌpˌraɪt] *adv* सीधा
upset [ʌp'sɛt] *adj* परेशान ▷ [ʌp'set] *vt* परेशान करना
upside down ['ʌpˌsaɪd daʊn] *adv* उल्टा ▷ *adj* उल्टा
upstairs ['ʌp'stɛəz] *adv* ऊपरी मंज़िल
uptight [ʌp'taɪt] *adj* *(informal)* तनावग्रस्त
up-to-date [ˌʌptʊ'deɪt] *adj* नवीनतम
upwards ['ʌpwədz] *adv* ऊपर की ओर
uranium [jʊ'reɪnɪəm] *n* यूरेनियम
urgency ['ɜːdʒənsɪ] *n* अत्यावश्यकता
urgent ['ɜːdʒənt] *adj* अत्यावश्यक
urine ['jʊərɪn] *n* मूत्र
URL [juː ɑː ɛl] *n* यू आर एल
Uruguay ['jʊərəˌgwaɪ] *n* उरुग्वे
Uruguayan [ˌjʊərə'gwaɪən] *adj* उरुग्वे से संबद्ध ▷ *n* उरुग्वे का निवासी
US [juː ɛs] *n* यू. एस./ संयुक्त राज्य अमेरिका हेतु संक्षिप्ताक्षर
us [ʌs] *pron* हमें
USA [juː ɛs eɪ] *n* यू. एस. ए./संयुक्त राज्य अमेरिका हेतु संक्षिप्ताक्षर
use [juːs] *n* इस्तेमाल ▷ [juːz] *vt* इस्तेमाल करना
used [juːzd] *adj* प्रयुक्त ▷ *v* किया करता था
useful ['juːsfʊl] *adj* उपयोगी
useless ['juːslɪs] *adj* व्यर्थ
user ['juːzə] *n* प्रयोगकर्ता
user-friendly ['juːzəˌfrɛndlɪ] *adj* इस्तेमाल में आसान
use up [juːz ʌp] *v* समाप्त करना
usual ['juːʒʊəl] *adj* आम
usually ['juːʒʊəlɪ] *adv* आमतौर पर

utility room [juː'tɪlɪtɪ rʊm] *n* उपकरण कक्ष
U-turn ['juːˌtɜːn] *n* यू आकार का मोड़
Uzbekistan [ˌʌzbɛkɪ'stɑːn] *n* उज़बेकिस्तान

V

vacancy ['veɪkənsɪ] *n* रिक्त पद
vacant ['veɪkənt] *adj* रिक्त
vacate [və'keɪt] *vt (formal)* छोड़ना
vaccinate ['væksɪˌneɪt] *vt* टीका लगाना
vaccination [ˌvæksɪ'neɪʃən] *n* टीकाकरण
vacuum ['vækjʊəm] *v* वैक्यूम क्लीनर से साफ करना
vacuum cleaner ['vækjʊəm 'kliːnə] *n* वैक्यूम क्लीनर
vague [veɪg] *adj* अस्पष्ट
vain [veɪn] *adj* बेकार
Valentine's Day ['væləntaɪnz deɪ] *n* वेलेन्टाइन दिवस
valid ['vælɪd] *adj* सही
valley ['vælɪ] *n* घाटी
valuable ['væljʊəbl] *adj* बहुमूल्य
valuables ['væljʊəblz] *npl* कीमती वस्तुएं
value ['væljuː] *n* महत्त्व
vampire ['væmpaɪə] *n* खून पीने वाला काल्पनिक भूत
van [væn] *n* वैन
vandal ['vændl] *n* बर्बर
vandalism ['vændəˌlɪzəm] *n* बर्बरता
vandalize ['vændəˌlaɪz] *v* क्षतिग्रस्त करना
vanilla [və'nɪlə] *n* वनीला - एक स्वादवर्द्धक पदार्थ
vanish ['vænɪʃ] *vi* गायब होना
variable ['vɛərɪəbl] *adj* परिवर्तनशील
varied ['vɛərɪd] *adj* विविध
variety [və'raɪɪtɪ] *n* विविधता
various ['vɛərɪəs] *adj* विभिन्न

varnish ['vɑːnɪʃ] *n* वार्निश ▷ *vt* वार्निश लगाना
vary ['vɛərɪ] *vi* भिन्न होना
vase [vɑːz] *n* गुलदान
VAT [væt] *abbr* एक प्रकार का कर
Vatican ['vætɪkən] *n* वेटिकन
veal [viːl] *n* बछड़े का मांस
vegan ['viːgən] *n* किसी भी तरह के पशु उत्पादों का प्रयोग न करने वाले
vegetable ['vɛdʒtəbl] *n* सब्ज़ी
vegetarian [ˌvɛdʒɪ'tɛərɪən] *adj* शाकाहारी ▷ *n* शाकाहारी व्यक्ति
vegetation [ˌvɛdʒɪ'teɪʃən] *n (formal)* वनस्पति
vehicle ['viːɪkl] *n* वाहन
veil [veɪl] *n* घूँघट
vein [veɪn] *n* शिरा
Velcro® ['vɛlkrəʊ] *n* वेलक्रो - चिपकाकर बंद करने वाली पट्टी
velvet ['vɛlvɪt] *n* मखमल
vending machine ['vɛndɪŋ məˈʃiːn] *n* बिक्री मशीन
vendor ['vɛndɔː] *n* विक्रेता
Venetian blind [vɪ'niːʃən blaɪnd] *n* खिड़की का पर्दा
Venezuela [ˌvɛnɪ'zweɪlə] *n* वेनेजुएला
Venezuelan [ˌvɛnɪ'zweɪlən] *adj* वेनेजुएलियाई ▷ *n* वेनेजुएलियाई
venison ['vɛnɪzn] *n* हिरन का मांस
venom ['vɛnəm] *n* विद्वेष
ventilation [ˌvɛntɪ'leɪʃən] *n* रोशनदान
venue ['vɛnjuː] *n* कार्यक्रम - स्थल
verb [vɜːb] *n* क्रिया
verdict ['vɜːdɪkt] *n* निर्णय
versatile ['vɜːsəˌtaɪl] *adj* बहुमुखी
version ['vɜːʃən] *n* संस्करण
versus ['vɜːsəs] *prep* बनाम
vertical ['vɜːtɪkl] *adj* लंबवत
vertigo ['vɜːtɪˌgəʊ] *n* चक्कर
very ['vɛrɪ] *adv* बहुत
vest [vɛst] *n* बनियान
vet [vɛt] *n* पशुचिकित्सक
veteran ['vɛtərən] *adj* दिग्गज ▷ *n* सेवानिवृत्त योद्धा

veto ['vi:təʊ] *n* निषेध
via ['vaɪə] *prep* से होकर
vice [vaɪs] *n* खोट
vice versa ['vaɪsɪ 'vɜ:sə] *adv* विपरीतता से
vicinity [vɪ'sɪnɪtɪ] *n* *(formal)* आस - पड़ोस
vicious ['vɪʃəs] *adj* विद्वेषपूर्ण
victim ['vɪktɪm] *n* शिकार
victory ['vɪktərɪ] *n* जीत
video ['vɪdɪˌəʊ] *n* वीडियो
video camera ['vɪdɪəʊ 'kæmərə; 'kæmrə] *n* वीडियो कैमरा
videophone ['vɪdɪəʊˌfəʊn] *n* वीडियोफ़ोन
Vietnam [ˌvjɛt'næm] *n* वियतनाम
Vietnamese [ˌvjɛtnə'mi:z] *adj* वियतनामी ▷ *n (person)* वियतनामी; *(language)* वियतनामी
view [vju:] *n* राय
viewer ['vju:ə] *n* दर्शक
viewpoint ['vju:ˌpɔɪnt] *n* दृष्टिकोण
vile [vaɪl] *adj* नागवार
villa ['vɪlə] *n* बड़ा बंगला
village ['vɪlɪdʒ] *n* गांव
villain ['vɪlən] *n* खलनायक/बदमाश
vinaigrette [ˌvɪnɪ'grɛt] *n* सलाद को सजाने वाला एक मिश्रण
vine [vaɪn] *n* लता
vinegar ['vɪnɪgə] *n* सिरका
vineyard ['vɪnjəd] *n* अंगूर का बगीचा
viola [vɪ'əʊlə] *n* वायलिन के जैसा वाद्ययंत्र
violence ['vaɪələns] *n* हिंसा
violent ['vaɪələnt] *adj* हिंसक
violin [ˌvaɪə'lɪn] *n* वायलिन
violinist [ˌvaɪə'lɪnɪst] *n* वायलिन वादक
virgin ['vɜ:dʒɪn] *n* कुँवारी
Virgo ['vɜ:gəʊ] *n* कन्या राशि
virtual ['vɜ:tʃʊəl] *adj* लगभग/आभासी
virtual reality ['vɜ:tjʊəl ri:'ælɪtɪ] *n* आभासी वास्तविकता
virus ['vaɪrəs] *n* विषाणु
visa ['vi:zə] *n* वीज़ा

visibility [ˌvɪzɪˈbɪlɪtɪ] *n* दृश्यता

visible [ˈvɪzɪbl] *adj* दृश्य

visit [ˈvɪzɪt] *n* मुलाकात ▷ *vt* मुलाकात करना

visiting hours [ˈvɪzɪtɪŋ aʊəz] *npl* मुलाकात का समय

visitor [ˈvɪzɪtə] *n* आगंतुक

visitor centre [ˈvɪzɪtə ˈsɛntə] *n* आगंतुक सूचना केंद्र

visual [ˈvɪʒʊəl] *adj* दृश्य

visualize [ˈvɪʒʊəˌlaɪz] *vt* कल्पनाचित्र बनाना

vital [ˈvaɪtl] *adj* अत्यावश्यक

vitamin [ˈvɪtəmɪn] *n* विटामिन

vivid [ˈvɪvɪd] *adj* जीवंत

vocabulary [vəˈkæbjʊlərɪ] *n* शब्दावली

vocational [vəʊˈkeɪʃənl] *adj* व्यावसायिक

vodka [ˈvɒdkə] *n* एक मादक पेय

voice [vɔɪs] *n* आवाज़

voicemail [ˈvɔɪsˌmeɪl] *n* ध्वनिसंदेश

void [vɔɪd] *adj* अमान्य ▷ *n* रिक्तता

volcano [vɒlˈkeɪnəʊ] *n* ज्वालामुखी

volleyball [ˈvɒlɪˌbɔːl] *n* वॉलीबाल

volt [vəʊlt] *n* वोल्ट - विद्युत धारा का मापक

voltage [ˈvəʊltɪdʒ] *n* वोल्टेज - विद्युत धारा की शक्ति

volume [ˈvɒljuːm] *n* मात्रा

voluntarily [ˈvɒləntrəlɪ] *adv* स्वेच्छापूर्वक

voluntary [ˈvɒləntərɪ] *adj* स्वैच्छिक

volunteer [ˌvɒlənˈtɪə] *n* स्वयंसेवक ▷ *v* स्वेच्छा से काम करना

vomit [ˈvɒmɪt] *vi* उल्टी करना

vote [vəʊt] *n* मत ▷ *v* मतदान करना

voucher [ˈvaʊtʃə] *n* सनद

vowel [ˈvaʊəl] *n* स्वर

vulgar [ˈvʌlgə] *adj* भद्दा

vulnerable [ˈvʌlnərəbl] *adj* वेध्य/अतिसंवेदनशील

vulture [ˈvʌltʃə] *n* गिद्ध

W

wafer ['weɪfə] *n* पतले बिस्कुट
waffle ['wɒfl] *n (informal)* अस्पष्ट बात/गप ▷ *vi (informal)* गप मारना/अस्पष्ट बात करना
wage [weɪdʒ] *n* वेतन
waist [weɪst] *n* कमर
waistcoat ['weɪsˌkəʊt] *n* वास्कट
wait [weɪt] *vi (be delayed)* के लिए प्रतीक्षा करना
waiter ['weɪtə] *n* बैरा
waiting list ['weɪtɪŋ lɪst] *n* प्रतीक्षा सूची
waiting room ['weɪtɪŋ rʊm] *n* प्रतीक्षालय
waitress ['weɪtrɪs] *n* बैरा (महिला)
wait up [weɪt ʌp] *v* प्रतीक्षा करते हुए जागना
waive [weɪv] *vt* दावा छोड़ना
wake up [weɪk ʌp] *v* जागना
Wales [weɪlz] *n* वेल्स
walk [wɔːk] *n* चहलकदमी/टहल ▷ *vi* चलना
walkie-talkie [ˌwɔːkɪ'tɔːkɪ] *n* वॉकी - टॉकी
walking ['wɔːkɪŋ] *n* चहलकदमी
walking stick ['wɔːkɪŋ stɪk] *n* सहारे की छड़ी
walkway ['wɔːkˌweɪ] *n* पैदल रास्ता
wall [wɔːl] *n* दीवार
wallet ['wɒlɪt] *n* बटुआ
wallpaper ['wɔːlˌpeɪpə] *n* दीवार पर लगाने वाला कागज़
walnut ['wɔːlˌnʌt] *n* अखरोट
walrus ['wɔːlrəs] *n* वॉलरस
waltz [wɔːls] *n* एक प्रकार का नृत्य संगीत ▷ *vi* एक प्रकार के संगीत पर नाचना
wander ['wɒndə] *vi* भटकना
want [wɒnt] *vt* चाहना
war [wɔː] *n* युद्ध
ward [wɔːd] *n (hospital room)* अस्पताल का कमरा; *(district)* क्षेत्र
warden ['wɔːdn] *n* संरक्षक
wardrobe ['wɔːdrəʊb] *n* कपड़ों की अलमारी

warehouse ['wɛəˌhaʊs] *n* मालगोदाम
warm [wɔːm] *adj* गर्म
warm up [wɔːm ʌp] *v* गर्म करना
warn [wɔːn] *v* चेतावनी देना
warning ['wɔːnɪŋ] *n* चेतावनी
warranty ['wɒrəntɪ] *n* वारंटी
wart [wɔːt] *n* मस्सा
wash [wɒʃ] *vt* धोना
washbasin ['wɒʃˌbeɪsn] *n* चिलमची
washing ['wɒʃɪŋ] *n* धुलाई के कपड़े
washing line ['wɒʃɪŋ laɪn] *n* अलगनी
washing machine ['wɒʃɪŋ məˈʃiːn] *n* कपड़े धोने की मशीन
washing powder ['wɒʃɪŋ 'paʊdə] *n* कपड़े धोने का चूरा पाउडर
washing-up ['wɒʃɪŋʌp] *n* जूठे बर्तन धोना
washing-up liquid ['wɒʃɪŋ ʌp 'lɪkwɪd] *n* बर्तन धोने का तरल साबुन
wash up [wɒʃ ʌp] *v* बर्तन धोना
wasp [wɒsp] *n* ततैया
waste [weɪst] *n* बर्बादी ▷ *vt* बर्बाद करना
wastepaper basket [ˌweɪst'peɪpə 'bɑːskɪt] *n* रद्दी की टोकरी
watch [wɒtʃ] *n* कलाई घड़ी ▷ *v* देखना
watch out [wɒtʃ aʊt] *v* सतर्क रहना
watch strap [wɒtʃ stræp] *n* घड़ी का पट्टा
water ['wɔːtə] *n* पानी ▷ *vt* सींचना
watercolour ['wɔːtəˌkʌlə] *n* पानी के रंग
watercress ['wɔːtəˌkrɛs] *n* जलकुंभी
waterfall ['wɔːtəˌfɔːl] *n* झरना
watering can ['wɔːtərɪŋ kæn] *n* सिंचाई करने का बर्तन
watermelon ['wɔːtəˌmelən] *n* तरबूज़
waterproof ['wɔːtəˌpruːf] *adj* जलरोधक

water-skiing ['wɔːtəˌskiːɪŋ] *n* वॉटर - स्कीइंग
wave [weɪv] *n (greeting)* लहर ▷ *v (gesture)* लहराना ▷ *n (of the sea)* लहर
wavelength ['weɪvˌlɛŋθ] *n* तरंगदैर्ध्य
wavy ['weɪvɪ] *adj* लहरदार
wax [wæks] *n* मोम
way [weɪ] *n (manner)* तरीका; *(route)* रास्ता
way in [weɪ ɪn] *n* प्रवेश द्वार
way out [weɪ aʊt] *n* निकास द्वार
we [wiː] *pron* हम
weak [wiːk] *adj* कमज़ोर
weakness ['wiːknɪs] *n* कमज़ोरी
wealth [wɛlθ] *n* संपत्ति
wealthy ['wɛlθɪ] *adj* धनवान
weapon ['wɛpən] *n* हथियार
wear [wɛə] *vt* पहनना
weasel ['wiːzl] *n* नेवला
weather ['wɛðə] *n* मौसम
weather forecast ['wɛðə 'fɔːkaːst] *n* मौसम संबंधी भविष्यवाणी
web [web] *n* मकड़ी का जाला
Web [web] *n* वेब
Web 2.0 [web tuːpɔɪnt 'zɪərəʊ] *n* वेब 2.0
web address [wɛb ə'drɛs] *n* वेब एड्रेस
web browser [wɛb 'braʊzə] *n* वेब ब्राउज़र
webcam ['wɛbˌkæm] *n* वेबकैम
webmaster ['wɛbˌmaːstə] *n* वेबमास्टर
website ['wɛbˌsaɪt] *n* वेबसाइट
webzine ['wɛbˌziːn] *n* वेबज़ीन
wedding ['wɛdɪŋ] *n* विवाह
wedding anniversary ['wɛdɪŋ ˌænɪ'vɜːsərɪ] *n* शादी की सालगिरह
wedding dress ['wɛdɪŋ drɛs] *n* विवाह की पोशाक
wedding ring ['wɛdɪŋ rɪŋ] *n* विवाह की अंगूठी
Wednesday ['wɛnzdɪ] *n* बुधवार
weed [wiːd] *n* अपतृण/जंगली घास

weedkiller ['wiːdˌkɪlə] *n* जंगली घास को नष्ट करने वाला पदार्थ
week [wiːk] *n* सप्ताह
weekday ['wiːkˌdeɪ] *n* कार्यदिवस
weekend [ˌwiːk'ɛnd] *n* सप्ताहांत
weep [wiːp] *v (literary)* रोना
weigh [weɪ] *vt* तौलना
weight [weɪt] *n* वज़न
weightlifter ['weɪtˌlɪftə] *n* भारोत्तोलक
weightlifting ['weɪtˌlɪftɪŋ] *n* भारोत्तोलन
weird [wɪəd] *adj (informal)* अजीब
welcome ['welkəm] *excl* स्वागत है! ▹ *n* स्वागत ▹ *vt* स्वागत करना
well [wɛl] *adj* कुशल ▹ *adv* बख़ूबी/अच्छी तरह से ▹ *n* कुआं
well-behaved ['wɛl'bɪ'heɪvd] *adj* शिष्ट
well done! [wɛl dʌn] *excl* शाबाश!
wellingtons ['wɛlɪŋtənz] *npl* वेलिंगटन जूते
well-known ['wɛl'nəʊn] *adj* जाना - माना/मशहूर
well-off ['wɛl'ɒf] *adj (informal)* समृद्ध
well-paid ['wɛl'peɪd] *adj* अच्छी तनख्वाह पाना
Welsh [wɛlʃ] *adj* वेल्स से संबद्ध ▹ *n* वेल्स की भाषा
west [wɛst] *adj* पश्चिमी ▹ *adv* पश्चिम की ओर ▹ *n* पश्चिम
westbound ['wɛstˌbaʊnd] *adj* पश्चिमोन्मुख
western ['wɛstən] *adj* पश्चिमी ▹ *n* वेस्टर्न - काउबॉय से संबद्ध चलचित्र या पुस्तक
West Indian [wɛst 'ɪndɪən] *adj* वेस्टइंडीज़ से संबद्ध ▹ *n* वेस्टइंडीज़ का निवासी
West Indies [wɛst 'ɪndɪz] *npl* वेस्टइंडीज़
wet [wɛt] *adj* गीला
wetsuit ['wɛtˌsuːt] *n* गोताखोरी की पोशाक
whale [weɪl] *n* व्हेल
what [wɒt] *det* क्या ▹ *pron* क्या

whatever [wɒt'ɛvə] *conj* जो कुछ भी

wheat [wiːt] *n* गेहूँ

wheat intolerance [wiːt ɪn'tɒlərəns] *n* गेहूं से होने वाली एलर्जी

wheel [wiːl] *n* पहिया

wheelbarrow ['wiːl,bærəʊ] *n* एकपहिया ठेलागाड़ी

wheelchair ['wiːl,tʃɛə] *n* पहियेदार कुर्सी

when [wɛn] *adv* कब ▹ *conj* कब/जब

whenever [wɛn'ɛvə] *conj* जब भी

where [wɛə] *adv* कहां ▹ *conj* जहाँ

whether ['wɛðə] *conj* कि

which [wɪtʃ] *det* कौन - सा ▹ *pron* कौन - सा

whichever [wɪtʃ'ɛvə] *det* जो भी/कोई भी

while [waɪl] *conj* जब तक ▹ *n* थोड़े समय

whip [wɪp] *n* चाबुक

whipped cream [wɪpt kriːm] *n* फेंटी हुई मलाई

whisk [wɪsk] *n* अंडे फेंटने का उपकरण

whiskers ['wɪskəz] *npl* मूँछ

whisky ['wɪskɪ] *n* शराब

whisper ['wɪspə] *v* फुसफुसाना

whistle ['wɪsl] *n* सीटी ▹ *v* सीटी बजाना

white [waɪt] *adj* सफेद

whiteboard ['waɪt,bɔːd] *n* लिखने का सफेद बोर्ड

whitewash ['waɪt,wɒʃ] *v* चूना करना

whiting ['waɪtɪŋ] *n* एक मछली

who [huː] *pron* कौन

whoever [huː'ɛvə] *conj* जो कोई

whole *adj* समस्त ▹ [həʊl] *n* पूर्ण इकाई

wholefoods ['həʊl,fuːdz] *npl* प्राकृतिक और जैविक उत्पाद

wholemeal ['həʊl,miːl] *adj* खड़ा अनाज

wholesale ['həʊl,seɪl] *adj* थोक का ▹ *n* थोक

whom [huːm] *pron (formal)* जिसे

whose [huːz] *det* किसका ▹ *pron* जिसका

why [waɪ] *adv* क्यों
wicked ['wɪkɪd] *adj* दुष्ट
wide [waɪd] *adj* चौड़ा ▷ *adv* पूरी तरह से
widespread ['waɪdˌsprɛd] *adj* विस्तृत
widow ['wɪdəʊ] *n* विधवा
widower ['wɪdəʊə] *n* विधुर
width [wɪdθ] *n* चौड़ाई
wife [waɪf] *n* पत्नी
Wi-Fi ['waɪfaɪ] *n* वाई - फ़ाई
wig [wɪg] *n* नकली बाल
wild [waɪld] *adj* वन्य/जंगली
wildlife ['waɪldˌlaɪf] *n* वन्य जीवन
will [wɪl] *n* *(determination)* इच्छा; *(document)* वसीयत ▷ *v* होगा
willing ['wɪlɪŋ] *adj* इच्छुक
willingly ['wɪlɪŋlɪ] *adv* स्वेच्छा से
willow ['wɪləʊ] *n* एक वृक्ष
willpower ['wɪlˌpaʊə] *n* इच्छाशक्ति
wilt [wɪlt] *vi* कुम्हलाना
win [wɪn] *v* जीतना
wind [wɪnd] *n* हवा ▷ *vt* *(cause to have difficulty breathing)* दम निकाल देना ▷ [waɪnd] *vi* *(road, river)* घूम जाना/मुड़ना ▷ *vt* *(wrap)* लपेटना
windmill ['wɪndˌmɪl] *n* पवनचक्की
window ['wɪndəʊ] *n* खिड़की
window pane ['wɪndəʊ peɪn] *n* खिड़की का शीशा
window seat ['wɪndəʊ siːt] *n* खिड़की के पास की सीट
windowsill ['wɪndəʊˌsɪl] *n* खिड़की के नीचे की आलमारी
windscreen ['wɪndˌskriːn] *n* गाड़ी के सामने का शीशा
windscreen wiper ['wɪndskriːn 'waɪpə] *n* विंडस्क्रीन वाइपर
windsurfing ['wɪndˌsɜːfɪŋ] *n* विंडसर्फ़िंग
windy ['wɪndɪ] *adj* तेज़ हवाओं वाला
wine [waɪn] *n* शराब
wineglass ['waɪnˌglɑːs] *n* शराब का गिलास
wine list [waɪn lɪst] *n* शराब की सूची
wing [wɪŋ] *n* पंख

W

wing mirror [wɪŋ 'mɪrə] *n* गाड़ी के किनारे लगा शीशा
wink [wɪŋk] *vi* आंख मारना
winner ['wɪnə] *n* विजेता
winning ['wɪnɪŋ] *adj* विजयी
winter ['wɪntə] *n* शीत ऋतु
winter sports ['wɪntə spɔːts] *npl* बर्फ़ पर खेले जाने वाले खेल
wipe [waɪp] *vt* पोंछना
wipe up [waɪp ʌp] *v* पोंछना
wire [waɪə] *n* तार
wisdom ['wɪzdəm] *n* ज्ञान/अक्लमंदी
wisdom tooth ['wɪzdəm tuːθ] *n* अकल दाढ़
wise [waɪz] *adj* बुद्धिमान
wish [wɪʃ] *n* इच्छा ▷ *vt* चाहना
wit [wɪt] *n* परिहास/बुद्धि तीक्ष्णता
witch [wɪtʃ] *n* चुड़ैल/जादूगरनी
with [wɪð] *prep* *(accompanied by)* साथ; *(having)* से युक्त
withdraw [wɪð'drɔː] *vt* *(formal)* निकालना
withdrawal [wɪð'drɔːəl] *n* *(formal)* वापसी
within [wɪ'ðɪn] *prep* *(formal)* के भीतर
without [wɪ'ðaʊt] *prep* के बिना
witness ['wɪtnɪs] *n* गवाह
witty ['wɪtɪ] *adj* विनोदपूर्ण
wolf [wʊlf] *n* भेड़िया
woman ['wʊmən] *n* औरत
wonder ['wʌndə] *vt* ताज्जुब करना
wonderful ['wʌndəfʊl] *adj* बहुत बढ़िया
wood [wʊd] *n* *(material)* लकड़ी; *(forest)* जंगल
wooden ['wʊdn] *adj* लकड़ी का
woodwind ['wʊd,wɪnd] *adj* सुषिर काष्ठ वाद्य
woodwork ['wʊd,wɜːk] *n* लकड़ी से बनी चीज़ें
wool [wʊl] *n* ऊन
woollen ['wʊlən] *adj* ऊनी
woollens ['wʊlənz] *npl* ऊनी कपड़े
word [wɜːd] *n* शब्द

work [wɜːk] *n* काम ▷ *vi* *(toil)* काम करना; *(machine)* काम करना
worker ['wɜːkə] *n* मज़दूर/कर्मी
work experience [wɜːk ɪk'spɪərɪəns] *n* कार्यानुभव
workforce ['wɜːkˌfɔːs] *n* कार्यबल
working-class ['wɜːkɪŋklɑːs] *adj* श्रमजीवी
workman ['wɜːkmən] *n* कामगार
work of art [wɜːk ɒv; əv ɑːt] *n* कलाकृति
work out [wɜːk aʊt] *v* हल निकालना
work permit [wɜːk 'pɜːmit] *n* काम करने का आज्ञापत्र
workplace ['wɜːkˌpleɪs] *n* कार्यस्थल
workshop ['wɜːkˌʃɒp] *n* कार्यशाला
workspace ['wɜːkˌspeɪs] *n* कार्यक्षेत्र
workstation ['wɜːkˌsteɪʃən] *n* कंप्यूटर
world [wɜːld] *n* दुनिया
World Cup [wɜːld kʌp] *n* वर्ल्ड कप
worm [wɜːm] *n* कीड़ा
worn [wɔːn] *adj* जीर्ण
worried ['wʌrɪd] *adj* चिंतित
worry *vi* चिंता करना
worrying ['wʌrɪɪŋ] *adj* चिंताजनक
worse [wɜːs] *adj* और ख़राब ▷ *adv* और भी बुरा
worsen ['wɜːsn] *v* और ख़राब हो जाना
worship ['wɜːʃɪp] *v* पूजा करना
worst [wɜːst] *adj* सबसे खराब
worth [wɜːθ] *n* क़ीमत
worthless ['wɜːθlɪs] *adj* मूल्यहीन
would [wʊd] *v* होगा
wound [wuːnd] *n* घाव ▷ *vt* ज़ख्मी करना
wrap [ræp] *vt* लपेटना
wrapping paper ['ræpɪŋ 'peɪpə] *n* सामान लपेटने का कागज
wrap up [ræp ʌp] *v* लपेटना
wreck [rɛk] *n* मलबा ▷ *vt* विनष्ट कर देना

wreckage ['rɛkɪdʒ] *n* मलबा
wren [rɛn] *n* एक छोटी चिड़िया
wrench [rɛntʃ] *n* दुर्दशा/मानसिक पीड़ा ▷ *vt* मरोड़ना
wrestler ['rɛslə] *n* कुश्तीबाज़/पहलवान
wrestling ['rɛslɪŋ] *n* कुश्ती
wrinkle ['rɪŋkl] *n* झुर्री
wrinkled ['rɪŋkld] *adj* झुर्रीदार
wrist [rɪst] *n* कलाई
write [raɪt] *v* लिखना
write down [raɪt daʊn] *v* लिखना
writer ['raɪtə] *n* लेखक
writing ['raɪtɪŋ] *n* लिखावट/लेख
writing paper ['raɪtɪŋ 'peɪpə] *n* लिखने का कागज़
wrong [rɒŋ] *adj (amiss)* ग़लत; *(incorrect)* ग़लत; *(morally)* बुरा/ख़राब
wrong number [rɒŋ 'nʌmbə] *n* ग़लत नंबर

X

Xmas ['ɛksməs] *n (informal)* क्रिसमस
X-ray ['ɛksreɪ] *n* एक्स - रे ▷ *vt* एक्स - रे करना
xylophone ['zaɪlə,fəʊn] *n* लकड़ी से बना एक बाजा

y

yacht [jɒt] *n* पाल नौका
yard [jɑːd] *n (unit of length)* गज; *(courtyard)* अहाता
yawn [jɔːn] *vi* जम्हाई लेना
year [jɪə] *n* वर्ष
yearly ['jɪəlɪ] *adj* वार्षिक ▷ *adv* प्रति वर्ष
yeast [jiːst] *n* खमीर
yell [jɛl] *v* चिल्लाना
yellow ['jɛləʊ] *adj* पीला

Yellow Pages® ['jɛləʊ 'peɪdʒɪz] *n* येलो पेजेज़
Yemen ['jɛmən] *n* यमन
yes! [jɛs] *excl* हाँ
yesterday ['jɛstədɪ] *adv* बीता हुआ कल
yet [jɛt] *adv* अभी तक
yew [juː] *n* एक सदाबहार पेड़
yield [jiːld] *vi (formal)* समर्पण करना
yoga ['jəʊgə] *n* योग
yoghurt ['jəʊgət] *n* दही
yolk [jəʊk] *n* अण्डे की ज़रदी
you [juː] *pron* तुम
young [jʌŋ] *adj* युवा
younger ['jʌŋgə] *adj* छोटा
youngest ['jʌŋgɪst] *adj* सबसे छोटा
your [jɔː] *det* तुम्हारा
yours [jɔːz] *pron* तुम्हारा
yourself [jɔː'sɛlf] *pron* खुद को
yourselves [jɔː'sɛlvz] *pron* तुम खुद
youth [juːθ] *n* युवावस्था
youth club [juːθ klʌb] *n* युवा क्लब
youth hostel [juːθ 'hɒstl] *n* युवा छात्रावास

Z

Zambia ['zæmbɪə] *n* ज़ाम्बिया-दक्षिणी अफ़्रीका का एक गणराज्य
Zambian ['zæmbɪən] *adj* ज़ाम्बियाई ▷ *n* ज़ाम्बियाई
zebra ['ziːbrə] *n* जेबरा
zebra crossing ['ziːbrə 'krɒsɪŋ] *n* पैदल पारपथ
zero ['zɪərəʊ] *n* शून्य
zest [zɛst] *n (vitality)* जोश; *(rind)* नींबू या संतरे का छिलका
Zimbabwe [zɪm'bɑːbwɪ] *n* ज़िम्बाब्वे - दक्षिणी-पूर्वी अफ़्रीका का एक देश

Zimbabwean [zɪm'bɑːbwɪən] *adj* ज़िम्बाब्वे - निवासी/ ज़िम्बाब्वे से संबद्ध ▷ *n* ज़िम्बाब्वे के मूलनिवासी/ ज़िम्बाब्वे के नागरिक

Zimmer® frame ['zɪmə freɪm] *n* विकलांग या बूढे लोगों हेतु पकड़कर चलने का एक उपकरण

zinc [zɪŋk] *n* जस्ता

zip [zɪp] *n* चेन ▷ *vt* चेन लगाना

zit [zɪt] *n (informal)* मुहाँसा

zodiac ['zəʊdɪˌæk] *n* राशिचक्र

zone [zəʊn] *n* क्षेत्र

zoo [zuː] *n* चिड़ियाघर

zoology [zəʊ'ɒlədʒɪ] *n* प्राणि विज्ञान

zoom lens [zuːm lɛnz] *n* वस्तु को बड़ा-छोटा करके दिखाने वाला काँच

Milton Keynes UK
Ingram Content Group UK Ltd.
UKHW040858240724
446055UK00004B/128